FIFTH EDITION

Check-In Check-Out

Gary K. Vallen
Northern Arizona University

Jerome J. Vallen
University of Nevada, Las Vegas
Australian International Hotel School

IRWIN

Chicago • Bogotá • Boston • Buenos Aires • Caracas
London • Madrid • Mexico City • Sydney • Toronto

Irwin Book Team

Executive editor: *Kurt L. Strand*
Associate marketing manager: *Heather L. Woods*
Project editor: *Beth Cigler*
Production supervisor: *Dina L. Treadaway*
Designer: *Matthew Baldwin*
Cover photo: *Hedrich Blessing, Chicago, Illinois*
Manager, graphics and desktop services: *Kim Meriwether*
Compositor: *Wm. C. Brown Publishers*
Typeface: *10/12 Times Roman*
Printer: *R. R. Donnelley & Sons Company*

Times Mirror
Higher Education Group

Library of Congress Cataloging-In-Publication Data

Vallen, Gary K.
    Check-in check-out/Gary K. Vallen, Jerome J. Vallen--5th ed.
      p. cm.
    Includes bibliographical references and index
    ISBN 0-256-17212-9
    1. Hotel management.   2. Motel management.   I. Vallen, Gary K.
  II. Title.
  TX911.3.M27V352   1996
  647.94′068—dc20   95–11079

Printed in the United States of America
1 2 3 4 5 6 7 8 9 0 DO 2 1 0 9 8 7 6 5

To fathers and sons who work together

Preface

Hotelkeeping is a resilient business. Three thousand years of survival and growth testify to its adaptability and to its capacity to accommodate an ever-changing marketplace. The interplay between the hotel industry and its environment is ongoing. Many events, as diverse as ecotourism and the collapse of the real estate market, have had an impact on the hotel business since the last edition of the text. In those brief four years, the front office has undergone amazing technological changes and traumatic organizational restructuring. *Check-In, Check-Out* has kept pace with five major revisions in 21 years!

Not Just a Front-Office Book

In this edition, as in previous ones, the authors give special attention to innkeeping's interdependence with other industries. There is information about franchising, sections about credit cards, and part of a chapter dealing with telecommunication. Legal issues, safety and security, employee scheduling, and more are discussed where appropriate throughout the book.

The text presents this material at an undergraduate level, even as it serves as a reference book on the shelves of many hotel managers. *Check-In, Check-Out* has been the leader in rooms management education for over two decades. It has also been a tool for on-the-job training. It has been used at both two-year and four-year institutions as a front-office book, an introductory book, a source book, and an enrichment for hotel accounting courses. Such flexibility is possible because each edition is current, complete, and thorough.

Changes in the Fifth Edition

Good front-office management blends an understanding of operational tasks with an awareness of concepts and theory. Recognizing this, each edition of the text has treated both the how-to (completing a reg card, for example) and the wherefore (yield management, for example). Edition five continues this tradition by updating the front office's mechanical elements (computerized folios, for example) and developing its management rationale (quality assurance, for example).

In keeping with the high standard of past revisions, an extensive rewrite has been carried out. Some highlights of the new edition are listed for the user's review.

- NCR posting machines, billing, and related information have been deleted from the text, paralleling their disappearance from the industry.

- Quality assurance has grown to a full chapter from its previous appearance in Chapter 3 because the concept, presaged by earlier editions, has been widely adopted.

- Figures and photographs have been added, updated, and improved.

- Chapters have been reorganized within a new framework in a continuing effort to better synchronize the chapter flow with the guests' record flow.

- Only brief references to racks (room racks, reservation racks, and information racks) have been retained because racks have been replaced almost entirely with property management systems.

- Guest billing and accounting chapters have been restructured to accommodate the nonaccountant without diminishing the importance of accounting to a better managed property.

- Rather than positioning statistics in one chapter, this edition places the elements at strategic points within the other chapters, adding immediate relevancy to the discussion.

- Numerous changes that previous editions foreshadowed have been tracked and updated, including self-registration consoles, the use of television/computers in operations, and integrated reservation systems worldwide.

- The credit chapter has been enlarged to include master accounts, travel agencies, frequent-travel programs, and coupon payments as well as the general management of credit.

- Some discussion of the manual (hand) night audit remains as a basis for understanding the audit, but detailed, numerical, pencil procedures have been replaced with property management systems and their computerized audits.

Supplemental Materials

As past users of *Check-In, Check-Out* know, an *Instructor's Manual* adds to the convenience of using the text. In this supporting manual, the faculty member will find guidelines to the use of the book, including alternative academic calendars, and a summary of each chapter's contents. Questions for each chapter and for each unit are provided for those who need ideas for building examinations. A complete final examination is included. It contains objective-style questions, short-answer problems, and brief essays.

Each chapter of the text is followed by questions. These can be used as homework assignments, additions to examinations, or as classroom discussions. The *Instructor's Manual* includes suggested answers to the text questions, although some are designed merely to encourage classroom discussion.

Although the glossary, bibliography, and detailed, cross-referenced index are not truly supplemental (they are included in the text), they do represent an immense amount of enrichment material available for the faculty member's use.

Acknowledgements

The authors acknowledge with great appreciation the numerous comments, notes, memorandums, and observations that a variety of colleagues from many institutions have provided us. Their input has helped us replace a wrong formula, identify typographical errors, and correct misspellings.

The previous edition of the book was reviewed by several individuals. Their suggestions have been incorporated in this edition. Thanks to Denny Rutherford, Washington State University; Ed Bushaw, Jefferson Community College; Jesse Clemons, State Technical Institute at Memphis; Nancy Cook, Newbury College; David Howell, ITHRA, Niagara University; and Susan Sheridan, University of Houston.

Who Are the Authors?

It is not unusual for a professional text to be coauthored. However, it is rare that the two authors are father and son. Jerry Vallen, the father, launched the book in 1974. Gary Vallen, the son, pursued several degrees and a dozen years in hotel management before becoming a joint author of the fourth edition. In this edition, he steps forward as the lead author.

Dr. Gary K. Vallen. Gary K. Vallen is Associate Professor in Hotel Management at Northern Arizona University. He joined the faculty there after 12 years in the industry in a variety of jobs: hotel manager, casino dealer, sales manager, and financial analyst. He has been a field representative for a ski magazine, and he worked in private clubs.

Dr. Vallen received his undergraduate degree in Hotel Administration at the University of Nevada, Las Vegas. Despite the long hours of industry, he simultaneously worked and earned an MBA degree at the University of Nevada, Reno. Later, after entering the field of education, he was awarded the EdD degree with an emphasis in hospitality management from Northern Arizona University.

The author has a consulting business with several specialties, including visitor analysis for festivals, fairs, rodeos, and ski slopes. He has developed criteria and carried out enumerable secret shopper evaluations for hotels and restaurants. His location in the southwest has enabled Dr. Vallen to consult with many Native American groups, including the Hopi and Navajo. He is also well known for his work in rural tourism.

Dr. Jerome J. Vallen. Jerome J. Vallen was the founding Dean of the College of Hotel Administration, University of Nevada, Las Vegas, and served in that capacity for 22 years. He now is a permanent faculty member at UNLV and holds that college's William F. Harrah Distinguished Chair. Following retirement from administration, he spent several terms at two universities in Australia and then became the Founding Dean of the Australian International Hotel School, Canberra, an affiliate of the School of Hotel Administration, Cornell University.

After earning a baccalaureate degree at Cornell University, Jerome Vallen entered the hotel industry, carrying with him the food experience gained from the family's small chain of four restaurants. For a period of several years, Vallen taught and worked in industry. Dr. Vallen also earned a master's degree in Educational Administration (St. Lawrence University) and a doctoral degree from Cornell's Hotel School.

Dr. Vallen has authored and edited several texts, including a text in hotel management and a work on the legal basis for obtaining gaming licenses in the state of Nevada. He has served as a consulting editor for textbook publishers, a consultant to the U.S. Department of Commerce, an outside examiner for the University of the West Indies, president of a consulting company, and a member of the board of several public and private companies.

Dr. Vallen has been the recipient of awards from such diverse groups as the University Alumni Association, The National Restaurant Association, and the Educational Institute of the American Hotel & Motel Association. Dean Vallen has served as President and Chairman of The Council on Hotel, Restaurant, and Institutional Education and was awarded that organization's prestigious H. B. Meek Award. He is listed in the American biography, *Who's Who In the West,* and has been cited in the *Congressional Record.*

Contents in Brief

Contents

SECTION I

The Hotel Industry

The lodging industry is maturing rapidly. It has aged more in the past 20 years than it did in the previous 2,000 years. The changes seen over the past two decades all suggest the same premise: a successful hotel or chain must remain flexible and adaptable to an evolving society.

Changing travel patterns have matured the lodging industry as much as any other societal impact. The highway hotels of yesteryear have become the airport hotels of today. And as guests speed across the sky traveling from New York to London in minutes instead of days, so too are major lodging chains speeding across cultural differences and establishing international subsidiaries at a faster rate than ever before.

Heterogeneity is another characteristic of a maturing industry. When the Model T Ford was first introduced, the customer had only three choices of color: black, black, or black. Today, there are many more colors as well as literally hundreds of automobile models to choose from. The lodging industry has had a similar history. In the homogeneous marketplace of the 1950s and 1960s, all hotel rooms had identical features, but this has given way to the enormous variety of lodging products of the 1990s. These lodging products have been designed to attract an increasingly diverse and sophisticated traveler. One visitor books a standard room; another buys a full-service suite. One customer needs a single night; another an extended stay. One traveler returns to the corporate hotel; another to the attractions of the resort.

Another proof of maturation of an industry is the presence of a continuous restructuring of ownership and competitive advantage. Independent and mom-and-pop lodging operations, the backbone of the hotel business several decades ago, are becoming less and less significant as they are eclipsed by giant lodging chains. Even small hotel chains of 5,000 to 10,000 rooms are quickly absorbed by megachains that boast upwards of 200,000 rooms under their brand affiliation. Yet this is a boon for banks and lending institutions, who were hurt by the industry's downturn in the 1980s; they are returning with anticipation as they seek new loans and financial opportunities in the renewed and burgeoning hotel industry.

CHAPTER 1

The Traditional Hotel Industry

Chapter Outline

Hotelkeeping is a historic industry with an open-ended future. It has survived and flourished throughout centuries of change. Whereas other industries have come and gone, innkeeping has adapted its traditional services to the demands of modern life. The present-day hotel evolved from the relay houses of China, from the khans of the Middle East, from the tabernas of Rome, from the road houses of Europe, and from the taverns of America. The industry has emerged from this rich cultural background with a special place in society. Today, hotelkeeping is an integral part of tourism's worldwide boom, a major player in the global outreach of business, and a continuing presence in the social, political, and cultural life of the community.

The Scope of the Industry

Mass travel is a modern phenomenon.[1] Historically, travel was a rarity because transportation was limited and individuals were neither economically nor politically free to move about, but advancements in means of transportation as well as expansion of economic and political freedom has been occurring over the past 200 years. Modern means of transportation have emerged from the industrial and electronic ages. Subsequent political and economic freedoms have helped to shape the modern travel industry.

A Look Back

Early guests shared their accommodations with strangers and often set their own rate of payment. Hotels remained small for thousands of years—rarely exceeding three-dozen rooms. Such small establishments were adequate for the times because guests arrived singly on camel, horse, or by stagecoach, all of which held only a few people. It took the steel of the Industrial Revolution to build upward, the finances of the corporate form of business to fashion the large-scale enterprise, and the size of modern transportation to carry the guests.

The modern hotel, with its exciting architecture (see Exhibit 1–1), has to some become a destination in itself—but that wasn't always the case. The historical role of innkeeping has been one of response, intended to provide services along the traveler's route. So long as the traveler's course, method of transportation, and travel time were restricted, there was no need to differentiate the inn. This was true even for the highway motels that dominated the American scene from the 1950s to the 1980s.

For 5,000 years, even the ultimate destination was predetermined. So innkeepers located themselves along the traveler's path and waited for the call for service. The range and quality of accommodations reflected the innkeeper's inclination, not the needs of the guests.

Providing shelter and an opportunity to rest from bone-wearying travel was the major service of the early inns. Food and lodging were the basic products then, even as they are today. Tomorrow may be another story altogether—it may bring an era in which the hotel's basic goods and services will be something other than food and shelter.

Palaces of the People

Many magnificent hotels were built in America between the Civil War and World War I. Serving guests from all walks of life, these hotels truly reflected the uniqueness of American democracy. The hotels of the era served as home and office, meeting site and social gathering place. Calling these American inns *palaces* was a play on the size and splendor of the structures as well as on the more restricted use of hotels by the aristocracy in Europe.

The word *hotel* appeared in London about 1760, and it began to be used in the United States some three decades later. It was Anglicized from the French *hotel garni,* "large, furnished mansion." The name change signaled a worldwide shift from an industry based on roadside accommodations to one located within the city.

EXHIBIT 1–1

The Luxor Hotel. The architecture of a hotel can be an attraction in and of itself.

Courtesy: The Luxor, Las Vegas, NV.

The third building to be erected in the new U.S. capital, following the White House and the Capitol building, was a hotel, the Union Public Hotel. Its physical structure resembled that of a palace, but its name guaranteed it to be a palace of the people. This was reaffirmed by the opening of another hotel in that same year, 1793, in New York City. The City Hotel was financed by a public stock offering, permitting the public to own the palace.

After World War II, when American currency was strong and American business was dominant, U.S. hotel companies expanded around the globe. They carried with them both the American approach to business and the American culture. The situation reversed in the 1980s when the dollar weakened. Foreign hotel companies, chiefly British and Japanese, found many hotel bargains within the United States, especially in those properties that were poorly financed and real estate dependent.

Hotels continue to link the world's cultures. Tourism plays one role; businesses that use hotels in developing lands as company offices, meeting places, and temporary residences play another.

The Service Culture

The latter half of the 20th century has been dubbed ''the age of service'' or ''the service society.'' This contrasts with the agricultural age of the 18th century and the industrial age of the 19th. The hotel industry, along with many other businesses (medicine, banking, retailing) carries this service label. As with many labels, there is sometimes confusion. All hotels do not offer the same level of service and, consequently, do not charge the same rates. Although we speak of one industry, it has many, many parts with but a single commonality: courtesy. That's what the service label is all about.

Consumerism, legislative regulations, and legal challenge are all part of the service society. Products and services are no longer determined by an isolated innkeeper along the post road but by a highly mobile and fickle consumer in partnership with government. As the first two chapters of this book explain, the hotel industry has responded rapidly, vigorously, and innovatively to this growing demand for choice.

What Is the Hotel Business?

The lodging industry is so broad an endeavor worldwide, divided into so many pieces, that a single definition is not practicable. A single theme is not apparent, and an accurate measurement is not possible. Nevertheless, many declare it to be among the world's largest industries. Undoubtedly, lodging is a major segment of the international economy. As a major component of world tourism, it helps drive the economic engines of developing countries and accounts for a great deal of investment dollars.

How Hotels Count and Measure

Once every five years, the Bureau of the Census issues a report (SC series) on the number of lodging establishments in the United States. The *1987 Census of Hotels* sets that figure at 40,424 and the number of hotel rooms at 2,872,338. Other agencies also count. The World Tourism Organization (WTO) estimates the global number at 10,167,000 rooms, of which the United States has 27 percent, or 2,739,000. The two figures are close enough to suggest that they are reasonably accurate. Both estimates are supported by the **American Hotel & Motel Association (AH&MA),** which counts 44,800 properties and 3.2 million rooms for 1992. Coopers & Lybrand, a national accounting firm, reckons the number at 3.08 million.[2]

Tourism requires an infrastructure adequate enough to meet the needs of the traveler. Therefore, tourism development always goes hand in hand with construction. For example, the 5,000-room MGM Grand Hotel and Entertainment Park (Las Vegas) spent a billion dollars in construction costs alone! Together, tourism and construction accelerate both the economic rise and the economic downturn of a tourist area.

With the collapse of the real estate market, hotel construction came to a standstill in the decade between 1984 and 1993. That period coincided with a serious decline in occupancy (see Exhibit 1–2). Hot spots such as Singapore, Las Vegas, and the Gold Coast of Australia marked exciting exceptions to the trend.

EXHIBIT 1–2

The collapse of the real estate market was reflected in the low occupancy decade of 1984–1993.

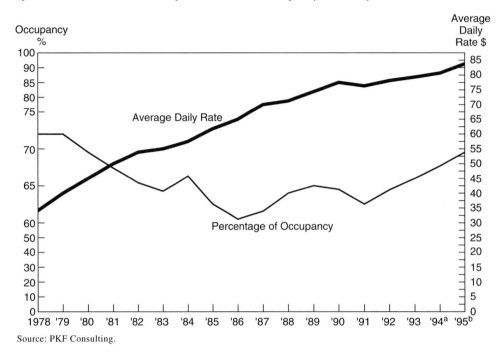

Source: PKF Consulting.

Occupancy.   Since three to five years is the normal span between planning and opening, few new hotels are expected on line before the year 2000.[3] At the same time, a decade of poor business has accelerated the removal of antiquated and worn-out hotel rooms. These old hotels were extended beyond their normal life span by the real estate boom and its accompanying income-tax benefits. With room construction now at a near standstill and bulldozed properties increasing in number, the supply/demand relationship should turn sharply in the industry's favor. That relationship, expressed as Number of Rooms Occupied (Sold) ÷ Number of Rooms Available for Sale, is called **occupancy, percentage of occupancy,** or **occupancy percent.**

Occupancy can be computed by one hotel for one night, one month, or one year. Citywide occupancy, regional occupancy, or national occupancy (Exhibit 1–2) can be—and are—tracked by hotels, consulting companies, convention bureaus, and state tourism offices. Everyone becomes engrossed with occupancy figures when companies such as Sheraton announce that a 1 percent rise in occupancy represents a $20 million improvement in profits.

Sales per Occupied Room.   Occupancy measures the hotel's ''share of the market,'' so it measures quantity. The quality of the business is measured by the amount of dollars received for the sale. **Sales per Occupied Room,** often called **Average Daily Rate (ADR),** is this second statistic. ADR is derived from the fraction Room Sales (as measured in dollars) ÷ Number of Rooms Occupied (Sold). Note that Number of Rooms Occupied appears in both formulas.

The health of the hotel business depends on the combination of occupancy and price. For some time, even after the decline in occupancy began, the ADR continued

EXHIBIT 1–3

Percentage changes in Average Daily Rate (ADR) are contrasted with percentage changes in consumer price index (CPI) during a decade of industry downturn.

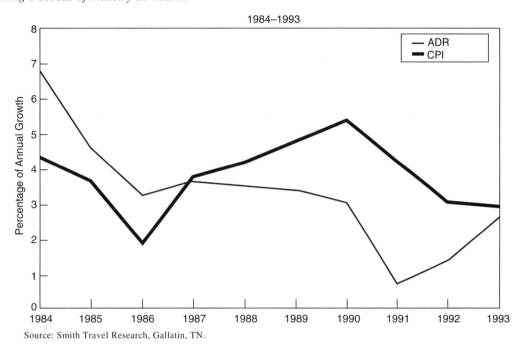

Source: Smith Travel Research, Gallatin, TN.

to climb (see Exhibits 1–2 and 1–3), even faster at times than the consumer price index (CPI). Room rates are price sensitive like other commodities. As more and more vacancies occur, prices level off because front-office managers hustle to keep competitive.

Special Characteristics of the Hotel Business

The room manager's ability to maximize the number of rooms sold or to increase the average daily rate obtained is limited by several industry characteristics. Some of these are also found within the airline industry.

Perishability.   Even the newest recruit to the hotel industry knows that an unsold room cannot be sold again. Hotel rooms, like airline seats, cannot be shelved, cannot be stored, cannot be saved, and cannot be used again.

Location.   Ellsworth Statler coined the expression "Location, location, location" to emphasize its importance to the hotel. Good economic locations are difficult to find in urban America. Changing neighborhoods and shifting markets sometimes doom a hotel whose original location was good.

Unlike the airline seat, there is no way to change a hotel's location. So management has learned to depend less on desirable real estate and more on marketing and sales; less on drive-by or walk-in traffic and more on central reservation systems.

	Percent
Monday	100%
Tuesday	100
Wednesday	90
Thursday	90
Friday	40
Saturday	20
Sunday	20
Total	460
Average per seven days	66%

Fixed Supply.   Not only is the location of the hotel fixed but so is its supply of (the number of) rooms. Airlines can adjust the number of seats by adding or removing planes from the route. With hotels, what you see is what you get.

High Operating Costs.   Unlike manufacturing industries, which offset labor with large capital investments, hotels are both capital- and labor-intensive. The result is high fixed costs (a *large nut* in the jargon of the industry), which continue whether or not the hotel has business. Thus, a high percentage of occupancy is needed just to break even.

Seasonality.   Throwing away the key is a traditional practice when a new hotel is opened. The act signifies that the hotel never closes. Yet hotelkeeping, even for commercial hotels, is a very seasonal business. The cyclical dip strikes the commercial hotel every seven days as it struggles to offset poor weekend business. The federal holiday law, which assigned long weekends to national holidays, reinforces this negative pattern.

The overall decline in room occupancy (Exhibit 1–2) can be attributed in part to poor weekend business. The business hotel represents a large portion of the total hotel business. Poor weekend business at commercial hotels has a large mathematical impact on the national occupancy figure. Given the usual occupancy of the downtown hotel (see Exhibit 1–4), it is difficult to achieve really high occupancies.

Annual cycles compound the problem. Commercial business is down even in midweek between Thanksgiving and New Year's Day and from May through Labor Day.

The ultimate solution is difficult to comprehend. Hotels in urban areas may someday operate on the same five-day week that their customers, their employees, and their purveyors do. They will respond to corporate demand cycles by closing the hotel on weekends and holidays. Managers will no longer symbolically "throw away the key."

The resort pattern is the opposite of the commercial pattern. Weekends are busy and midweek less so. The slack period of the commercial hotel is the very season of the resort. At one time, resorts opened Memorial Day and closed Labor Day. This 100-day pattern made the hotel's success dependent on the weather. Two weeks of rain are devastating when the break-even point is 80 days of near-full occupancy.

Although the dates of the winter season differ, there are still only 100 days between December 17 and March 15.

Both winter and summer resorts have extended their seasons with **groups,** conferences, and special activities. Hotels that operate on the four-day season may be worse off now than those on the four-season year. At least the latter have a higher **double occupancy** (two persons to a room).

Traditional Classifications

The inns of old evolved from private homes. Today's hotel, even the mom-and-pop variety, is not represented as anyone's home. It is either a point of destination or an accommodation for those in transit. Yesterday's tavern offered the family meal to all who came. Dining today is a created experience in design, decor, and menu. The old inn was almost indistinguishable from its neighbors. Today's edifice is a sharp contrast in style and packaging.

Although the basic concepts of food, shelter, and hospitality remain, their means of delivery have changed. These changes have been marked by shifting terminology: hostel, tavern, public house, inn, guest house, hotel, resort, motel, motor lodge, motor inn, bed and breakfast, airtel, boatel, hometel, skytel, and condotel.

Despite the speed of change, several traditional classifications have withstood the test of time. Some have more objective measures than others. None are self-excluding: Hotels can fall into every category or into only some. Moreover, there are degrees of belonging. One property may be well within a classification, whereas another may exhibit only some of the characteristics. Each category has an impact on the scope and function of the front office.

Size

The number of guest rooms is the measure of a hotel's **size.** Building height, acreage, gross sales, and net profit are ignored, although there is an obvious relationship between them and the number of guest rooms. Other relationships (number of employees, cost of replacement, etc.) are also evident.

Although size is the most objective of the several classifications, there is uncertainty even here. Often, more rooms are advertised than are actually available for sale. Old hotels have many rooms that are just not salable. Even newer properties may have rooms converted for other uses such as offices leased to businesses and associations. Still others are converted for storage or other operational facilities as unanticipated needs become evident. Generally, the older the hotel, the fewer the available rooms in relation to total rooms.

Hotels are grouped by size for purposes of study, for financial reporting, and for membership dues. The Bureau of the Census groups them this way as well. Although the latter uses several categories, a quick and easy classification considers 100 rooms or less to be a small hotel, between 100 and 300 rooms an average size, and over 300 rooms a large property.

Most of the industry's statistics depend on computations prepared by accounting/consulting firms—for example, Coopers & Lybrand, Pannell Kerr Forster, and Smith Travel Research. Each has its own classification system for presenting data, which makes the interchange of information almost impossible.

Exhibit 1–5

A baker's dozen. The largest hotels in the United States stand as strong testimony to the growing importance of gaming to the hotel industry.

MGM Grand Hotel	Las Vegas	5,000
Excalibur	Las Vegas	4,025
Flamingo Hilton	Las Vegas	3,525
Las Vegas Hilton	Las Vegas	3,175
The Mirage	Las Vegas	3,050
Treasure Island	Las Vegas	3,000
Bally's	Las Vegas	2,825
Circus Circus	Las Vegas	2,800
Imperial Palace	Las Vegas	2,600
Hilton Village	Honolulu	2,525
Luxor	Las Vegas	2,525
Stardust	Las Vegas	2,450
Hilton	New York	2,125

Note: Figures rounded to 25 rooms.

The Small Business Administration (SBA) has defined ''small'' for hotels seeking government business loans as properties doing $3.5 million or less in annual receipts.

Hotels and motels have been getting larger. The American Hotel & Motel Association reports the average size of its member hotel to be increasing. Still, their reported size of less than 150 rooms is surprising. These small properties are difficult to visualize when one thinks in terms of the Waldorf-Astoria in New York City (1,852 rooms) and the New Otani in Tokyo (2,057 rooms) (see Exhibit 1–5).

Motels.   Attempts to distinguish hotels, motels, and motor inns (motor hotels, motor lodges) by size were abandoned long ago. Many motor hotels have in excess of 300 rooms and many hotels less than 25. Even the Census Bureau allows each property to assign its own classification rather than attempting a nationwide definition. Still, people usually assume that motels are smaller than hotels.

At one time, the American Hotel & Motel Association excluded motels and clung to the term *American Hotel Association.* The City of Palm Springs, California, still insists there is a difference and has a law to prove it. City ordinances prohibit any of the 200-plus resort properties from using *motel* in advertising and display signs. *Hotel, lodge,* and *inn* are the only terms acceptable to the city fathers.

An opposite viewpoint is taken by the Canadian Provincial Conference on Tourism. It has developed three working definitions: A hotel is a commercial establishment in which the units (rooms) are accessible from the interior; motels have units that are accessible from the exterior; and motor hotels (or motor inns) have units that are accessible from both the interior and exterior.

Many years ago, the Florida tourism department offered a cash prize for a workable definition of *hotel* and *motel.*[4] The money is still waiting. A more recent tempest was averted when AT&T agreed with an AH&MA recommendation to list hotels, motels, and resorts separately in the Yellow Pages of the directory. The telephone company had planned to consolidate the three because a survey showed that nearly three-fourths of AT&T's customers looked under ''Motels'' when in need of accommodations.

Mom-and-Pops.   There are certain economics of size that account for the decline of the small hotel. They start with financing and construction and involve every aspect of the operation from marketing to purchasing. Size determines the quality of management that the property can afford. A motel with less than 100 rooms cannot budget management talent at the same level as a competitor with 300 rooms or a chain controlling several 100-room properties in the same area.

How then does the **mom-and-pop** establishment (the small, family-owned and -operated motel) continue to survive? It does, in the same way that small grocery stores and tailor shops do. It offers individual attention by the owners and their families. Guests receive the personal attention that is impossible with any other kind of organization. Labor costs are almost nonexistent, because the proprietor and the family babysit the establishment 24 hours per day, 365 days per year.

As the mom-and-pops become less able to compete for location and financing and less willing to serve the unremitting demands on their time, their numbers decline.

Class

Hotels are ranked or graded into distinct **classes.** There are two objective methods of making the divisions, but properties are also classified subjectively. One often says or hears that a particular hotel is a ''first-class'' (or ''fourth-class'') property. Nothing measurable is used to arrive at the conclusion—it's just sensed. Fortunately, more objective measures are available, but even these are far from perfect. One approach uses the Average Daily Room Rate; the other, a worldwide rating system.

Average Daily Rate (ADR).   In large measure, the price that the guest pays for the room is the best criteria of class. Delivering elegance and service costs money. Large rooms, costly construction, and expensive furnishings mean larger finance costs, depreciation, taxes, power usage, and so on. All of these are recovered by higher room rates. If towels are elegantly large and thick, the higher costs of purchase and laundering (by weight) are recovered by higher room rates. Similarly, a high level of maintenance, 24-hour room service, sauna baths, and other extra services represent both a better class of hotel and higher room rates.

Average Daily Rate has been increasing (Exhibit 1–3), but the increase is not solely a measure of increased service or elegance. Increased operating costs (particularly of labor, energy, and interest) must also be recovered. Although increased efficiency and better planning have offset some of the increases, costs have been met in the main by increased room rates.

Inflation, as well as cost recovery, accounts for some increases in room rates. It is a mistake, therefore, to equate an increase in ADR with an increase in class if the comparison is being made over time. However, at a given time and with a judicious concern for the size and the type of hotel, the ADR seems to be a fair measure of class.

Full Service to Limited Service.   Hotel/motel facilities are as diverse as the traveling public. Handling this enormous range of guests has created a very heterogeneous industry, from the plush, full-service high rise to the squat, limited-service motel.

On the one hand is a group of operator–investors who maintain that guests want nothing more than a room with a good mattress and a clean bath. Guests get along nicely without swimming pools, lobbies, or closets, according to this viewpoint. This hotelier offers limited service at a limited charge. There is such a market, of course, served by the $40 to $50 room rate of the budget motel.

One hundred and eighty degrees away is the full-service, upscale hotel. Not only does this hotel include superior facilities, it also offers a full complement of employee services. Expense-account business executives patronize the full-service hotel, although something less costly may be as satisfactory when traveling with the family.

Between the two extremes lies the bulk of the industry, adding services where competition and costs allow, paring them as market shifts and acceptable self-service equipment appear.

Part of that in-between market is the all-suite hotel. Commercial and leisure travelers alike have been attracted to all-suite accommodations like Embassy Suites (Promus Hotels) and Residence Inns (Marriott). By locating on less costly real estate and reducing the amount of public space, all-suites offer more guest room space at lower prices than the luxury properties.

Reorganizing the room design provides the unique privacy of several rooms within the single unit (Exhibit 3–13). That product seems to have meshed perfectly with guest demand. All-suites have moved from a curiosity of the 1970s to a 5 percent chunk of lodging's room inventory.

Number of Employees.   Almost by definition, **full service** and **limited service** refer to the size of the hotel's staff. Therefore, the *Number of Employees per Guest Room* (Number of Employees ÷ Number of Guest Rooms) becomes another measure of class. As with room rates, the measures range all across the board.

Budget properties, which have no restaurants, no bars, no room service, and no convention space, score as low as .25 employees per guest room. But after all, that is the product that they are selling.

The in-between class uses an in-between number of employees per room. The ratio ranges from 0.5 employees per room to a little better than 1:1. A 100-room hotel would have somewhere between 50 and 100-plus employees. Hotels with theater shows, acres of grounds, casinos, and 24-hour service require extra personnel and hence have a higher ratio.

Asian properties offer the best service. Labor is less costly, and the number of employees per room is the world's highest. At the Bangkok Shangri-La, for example, 1,073 staff members handle 697 rooms—a 150:100 ratio. The Peninsula Hotel in Hong Kong ranks better still, with 600 staff members for its 210 guest rooms.

Another ratio for comparing operations is that of *Revenue per Employee*. The output of service-industry workers cannot be measured in the same terms that heavy industry uses, which is the number of products manufactured. So the comparison is made in dollars of revenue per worker. This *Revenue per Employee* (Total Revenue ÷ Number of Employees) is a measure of productivity (see Exhibit 1–6), not a measure of class.

Rating Systems.   Hotel classifications have been standardized somewhat using formal rating systems. Most members of the World Tourism Organization have adopted the WTO's five recommended classifications. From the top, these are deluxe (or luxury) class; first class—which is not top-of-the-line despite its name—and tourist class, sometimes called economy or second class. Third and fourth classes,

EXHIBIT 1–6

Shown are the most productive chains in 1992 as measured by sales per employee. Several include revenues from gaming, which skews the results.

Sales per Employee	
Orient-Express Hotels Inc.	$104,048
Caesars World	94,948**
Queens Moat Houses	70,058
Bass (Holiday Inn)	61,654*
ITT Corp. (Sheraton)	59,777*
Circus Circus Enterprises	59,705
Forte Plc	53,965*
Club Med Group	45,602
Marriott Corporation	41,242
La Quinta Motor Inns L.P.	41,102
Stakis Plc	40,379*
Manor Care (Choice Hotels International)	35,455
ShoLodge (Shoney's Inn)	33,360
Hongkong and Shanghai Hotels (Peninsula)	33,277*
Ladbroke (Hilton International)	25,270*
Promus (Embassy Suites, Hampton, Homewood)	23,855*
Mandarin Oriental Hotel Group	21,931
Canadian Pacific Hotels & Resorts	19,325
Journey's End Corporation	17,418
Hilton Hotels Corporation	13,055*
Four Seasons Hotels Inc.	12,866

Courtesy: Hotels Magazine and Cahners Publishing Co.

*Hotel division only.

**Now owned by ITT Corp. (Sheraton).

which usually have no private baths, centralized heat, or even carpeting, are not for international tourists.

Each country implements its own categories. Local inspectors tend to be quite subjective in their ratings. If a pool is on the premises, it will meet standards, whether or not it is clean. An elevator adds to the ratings, whether or not it works. Government rating systems also fall prey to bribery, politics, and bickering within the trade association.

International travelers soon learn to limit stays in Africa or the Middle East to deluxe properties and to discount the deluxe category that many Caribbean properties give themselves. However, in Europe, first class is a perfectly acceptable level.

Worldwide.   Worldwide, there are about 80 rating systems. They range from the self-evaluation plan of Switzerland to the mandatory grading plan of South Africa, where tax incentives encourage properties to upgrade. Sometimes, however, rating systems work in the opposite way. Some deluxe Parisian hotels closed their dining rooms because it allowed them to pay taxes at the lower rates of first-class hotels. Many Italian hotels are underrated for the same reason.

Europe's four- and five-star hotels always have restaurants and bars; those with three stars may or may not. Two-star properties almost never do. **Garni** means that no restaurant is available, but a continental breakfast is usually served. In England, *hotel garni* is the American version of bed and breakfast.

The French have broadened the five categories. Two-star N (French for *nouveau,* ''new'') has been inserted to represent hotels under renovation, on their move up. Four-star L is now the epitome of *luxe* (luxury) at the top of the scale. Israel goes one better by using a six-star category.

The Swiss Hotel Association now uses five criteria instead of the single measure (price), which was its original category for classification. The Swiss system is unique because it is a private organization evaluating itself.

Mexican hotels are trade association graded, using the WTO's five classes, plus a luxury class, Gran Turismo.

Spain, too, has standardized its *paradors* (''stopping places'') despite their great range of physical facilities and furnishings. This government-operated chain of nearly 100 inns maintains approximately one-third at the four-star level. All but a few of the remaining group are in the two- or three-star category.

Japanese **ryokans** (pronounced LeoKan) are rated according to the excellence of guest rooms, kitchens, baths, and—of all things (to Western values)—gardens. These very traditional hotels usually serve two meals, which are often taken in the uncluttered guest rooms that open onto gardens. Over 1,000 ryokans are identified and registered (approved for international visitors) by the Japan Travel Bureau.

Korea also has budget-priced lodgings, *yogwans* (or inns). Most yogwans have Western-style accommodations, including private baths. Higher class yogwans can be identified because their names end in *jang* or *chang*.

The People's Republic of China (PRC) also adheres to WTO guidelines. Ratings are performed by the National Hotel Evaluation Committee, which operates under the China National Tourism Administration.

Stars are not universally used. Britain uses ''ticks'' for grading Holiday Parks (upscale caravan parks), and before the war, Yugoslavia had an alphabetical system. L, luxury, denoted a deluxe property. Expectations ranked downward from A, first class, to D, which promised no more than hot and cold water.

The alphabetical grading system once used by the Irish Tourist Board, Bord Failte, has been replaced by a star system of classification. The new system indicates the presence of particular facilities rather than a subjective ranking of their quality. This brings Ireland into agreement with the position of the European Community, which is to list, not rank, accommodations. European directories identify which hotels have elevators, laundries, air conditioning, and so on. They also classify facilities according to location: seaside/countryside; small town/large city. European auto associations add a little extra by classifying properties as privately owned or government run.

The U.S. Experience.   In a uniquely American way, U.S. ratings are done by private enterprises like Mobil and the American Automobile Association (AAA). Individual hotel companies have informal, self-rating systems, which emerge as a by-product of their efforts at market segmentation. For example, Choice Hotels International has (top to bottom) Clarion Hotels, Resorts, and Suites; Quality Inns, Hotels, and Suites; Comfort Inns and Suites; and Rodeway Inns, Sleep Inns, Econo Lodges, and Friendship Inns (see Exhibit 2–7).

Membership in Preferred Hotels, a loosely knit affiliation of independent hotels, requires ratings of superior or above average from one of the recognized services.

Mobil and the AAA distribute the two most popular consumer publications. Michelin is not as well known in the United States as it is in Europe. Zagat is a newer publication that uses the consumer as part of the rating process. There are many other publications available—bed and breakfast guides, or limited geographic sectors—but their coverage is narrower. The Mobil Travel Service covers North America only, but the AAA has expanded to include Mexico and the Caribbean.

Mobil, like Michelin, uses stars; AAA uses diamonds (Exhibit 1–7). Both organizations are stingy with their five-level ratings, awarding only two to three dozen nationally, although each looks at some 20,000 properties annually.

Not all guides are consumer oriented. Several list conference and meeting facilities, an American specialty. Others are important to travel agents and meeting planners. Among the trade publications are the *Official Meeting Facilities Guide* and the *Hotel & Travel Index.*

Type

The third traditional classification for lodging is **type.** It has three traditional subdivisions: **commercial, residential,** and **resort.** Like the definitions of hotel and motel, the distinctions have never been sharp. By consensus, the commercial guest is seen as the backbone of the lodging industry. Tourism is changing this, so the statement may not be true by the year 2000. Indeed, the traditional designations used here are becoming less and less descriptive of a changing industry. They make no provision for the airport hotel, the miniprice or budget hotel, or the condominium. Neither do they provide for the host of new entrants that have appeared in the past decade. These are classified in the emerging patterns of the following chapter.

Commercial Hotels.   This, the largest category of American hotels, could well be categorized as the **transient hotel** (see Exhibit 1–8). It is a hotel for short-stay guests who come for many reasons, but chiefly commercial ones. The business traveler, the conventioneer, the company executive, the consultant, and the engineer have replaced the "drummer" (salesperson) of a previous era—but not entirely; the commercial hotel, and the smaller motel as well, still rely heavily on the small-business traveler.

A true commercial hotel is located close to its market—the business community, which means an urban area. As the population center has left the downtown area, so has the commercial hotel. Arterial highways, research parks, business parks, airports, and even suburban shopping centers have become favorite locations. This helps explain the poor weekend occupancy (businesspersons are not working) of the urban hotel. Attempts to offset this weekend decline with tourists, conventions, and special promotions have been only moderately successful.

Transient hotels are usually full-service hotels. Until recently, businesspersons have been expense-account travelers who wanted (and could afford) four- and five-star accommodations. Lately, the travel offices of many businesses have begun to monitor travel costs more closely. Travel costs do impact a business's bottom line! Furthermore, Congress has enacted several restrictions on the amount that may be taken as tax-deductible meal costs (currently 50 percent).

From suite hotels to upgraded budgets, everyone is after business travelers, even though they are value shopping more diligently than ever before. Still, the commercial hotel remains the business center, catering to the various groups that have been enumerated, hosting trade shows, and serving as company training centers and meeting places.

Residential Hotels.   In contrast to the transient commercial guest, the residential guest takes up permanent quarters. This creates a different legal relationship between the guest and the landlord and may be formalized with a lease. In some locales, the room occupancy tax is not payable for a residential guest in a transient hotel.

EXHIBIT 1–7

Representative criteria are used to rate properties. Unlike other countries, which have governmental rating systems, the United States relies on private enterprise.

The key criteria are cleanliness, maintenance, quality of furnishings and physical appointments, service, and the degree of luxury offered. There will be some regional differences, as customers have different expectations for a historic inn in northern New England, a dude ranch in the Southwest, and a hotel in the center of a major city.

★

A one-star establishment listed in the Guide should be clean and comfortable and worth the prices charged when compared to other accommodations in the area. If they are below average in price, they may receive a checkmark for good value in addition to the one star. They offer a minimum of services. There may not be 24–hour front desk or phone service; there may be no restaurant; the furniture will not be luxurious. Housekeeping and maintenance should be good; service should be courteous; but luxury will not be part of the package.

★★

Two-star accommodations have a little more to offer than one-star and will include some, but not necessarily all, of the following: better quality furniture, larger bedrooms, restaurant on the premises, color TV in all rooms, direct dial phones or 24–hour switchboard service, room service, swimming pool. Again, luxury will usually be lacking, but cleanliness and comfort are essential.

★★★

Three-star motels and hotels will almost always include all of the facilities and services mentioned in the preceding paragraph. If some are lacking, and the

place receives three stars, it means that some other amenities are truly outstanding. A three-star establishment should offer a very pleasant travel experience to every customer.

★★★★

Four-star and five-star hotels and motels make up a very small percentage (less than 2%) of the total number of places listed; therefore they all deserve the description of ''outstanding.'' Bedrooms should be larger than average; furniture should be of high quality; all of the essential extra services should be offered; personnel should be well trained, courteous, and anxious to provide customers with everything they need and expect. Because the standards of quality are high, prices will often be higher than average. A stay in a four-star hotel or motel should be memorable. No place will be awarded four or five stars if there is a pattern of complaints from customers, regardless of the luxury offered.

★★★★★

The few five-star awards go to those places which go beyond comfort and service to deserve the description ''one of the best in the country.'' A superior restaurant is required, although it may not be rated as highly as the hotel or motel. Twice-daily maid service is standard in these establishments. Lobbies will be places of beauty, often furnished in fine antiques. If there are grounds surrounding the building, they will be meticulously groomed and landscaped. Each guest will be made to feel that he or she is a Very Important Person to the employees.

EXHIBIT 1–8

The urban hotel serves several markets, chiefly business and convention guests, and reflects the importance of location.

Courtesy: The Westin Bonaventure, Los Angeles, CA.

Some residential hotels accommodate **transient guests** and some transient hotels have **permanent guests,** with and without leases. The Waldorf-Astoria (New York City) is a good example of this combination: its Towers house many permanent guests. About two-thirds of all U.S. hotels reported both transient and permanent guests in the last census.

Apartment hotels are another type of residential hotel. They offer very few services, so kitchens are provided in the apartments. Front desks are limited or nonexistent in residential and apartment hotels.

Extended-Stay Hotels.   *Extended-stay* facilities offer more than a mere hotel room but are not the same genre as residential hotels, which connote permanency. *Extended stay* merely means long term.

Extensive travel and suitcase living quickly lose their glamour. Something different is needed for those persons moving locations or having extended business assignments away from homes and home offices. Keeping workers comfortable and productive takes more than a traditional hotel room. Extended-stay hotels provide kitchens, grocery outlets, office space—even secretarial support and office equipment, fireplaces, exercise rooms, laundry facilities, and more, but all with maid service.

The extended-stay hotel goes all out to make the stay-away as comfortable as possible. The all-suite hotel had its origin in this segment of the travel market. The all-suite/extended-stay distinction is blurred today because the same building caters to the long-term business traveler and to the other market segments (families, in-room meetings, interviews) to which the all-suite appeals.

Resorts.   Transient hotels cater to commercial guests, residential hotels to permanent guests, and resort hotels to social guests—at least traditionally they do (see Exhibit 1–9).

Economics has forced resorts to lengthen their operating period from the traditional summer or winter season to year-round operations. Resorts have marketed to the group and convention delegate at the expense of their social guest. As this began happening, the commercial hotel shifted its design and markets toward the resort concept, dulling once again the distinctions between types. What emerged is a mixed-use resort. Sometimes these resorts are found in residential areas as part of a master-planned community.

Many believe that the modified resort is the hotel of the future. It is in keeping with the nation's move toward increased recreation and compatible with the casual air that characterizes the vacationer. Unlike the formality of the vacationer of an earlier time, today's guest is a participant. Skiing, golfing, boating, and a host of other activities are at the core of the successful resort.

The Megaresort.   The megaresort, one of the lodging industry's newest segments, contains such a large variety of entertainment and recreational facilities that it is a self-contained unit. Guests need not leave the property during their entire stay. Size distinguishes the megaresort from similar self-contained properties like the Club Meds.

Although the megaresort is a feature of Las Vegas (Exhibit 1–5), it is not special to that location alone. Hilton's Hawaiian Village in Honolulu and the 640-acre Ko'Olina (Oahu's West Coast), which contains rooms, condos, and retail and office

Exhibit 1–9

The venerable Grand Hotel represents perfectly the traditional destination resort. Guests and supplies come to the island by boat, restricting operations to the summer season and to the American plan.

Courtesy: Grand Hotel, Mackinac Island, MI.

space, as well as a marina, also represent this genre. So does the 900-room Marriott Desert Springs and Spa near Palm Springs in California.

On the other hand, single feature specialty resorts have also proven quite successful. They appeared earlier than the hotel industry's general move toward segmentation. Tennis clubs (all types of sports clubs), spas, and health (diet) resorts opened and flourished. Club Mediterranee became the prototype of a new style of resort—one that featured an all-inclusive price, tips included.

Weather plays a key role in every type of resort. So geographic location is to the resort hotel what commercial location is to the transient hotel and population location to the residential hotel.

Plan

The **plan** is the basis for making the room rate charge. It identifies which meals, if any, are included in the rate. There is much less ambiguity about the hotel's plan than about its size, class, or type. Almost every hotel in the United States operates on the European plan.

European Plan. Rates quoted under the **European plan (EP)** apply to room accommodations only. Extra charges at prevailing menu prices are made for each meal taken. Evidence of the widespread use of the European plan is the lack of designation. Quoted rates always assume the European plan unless otherwise stated. The European plan is sometimes offered as an alternative when guests object to other plans.

Because European hotels usually offer some form of breakfast as part of the room charge, the pure European plan is less common in Europe than it is in the United States.

American Plan.   Rates quoted under the **American plan (AP)** include room and all three meals: breakfast, luncheon, and dinner. The AP (sometimes called **bed and board**) had its origin in colonial America when all guests ate at a common table with the host's family. The plan was still in use when the affluent resorts of the Northeast began opening a century later.

Because they were isolated—serviced by the railroads—resorts held onto the American plan for another century. Better roads and better cars gave guests the mobility that spelled the end of the American plan. Conference centers and some resorts still use it, but call it ''an all-inclusive package.''

In Europe, **full pension** (pen-si-own) or **en pension** is almost equivalent to the American plan. A Continental breakfast, not a full American breakfast, is one difference. *En pension* is the term used by European residential hotels (pensiones)—that's the main difference. The pension of Europe is the *guest house* or *boardinghouse* of Britain and the United States.

Because pensions are usually long-stay facilities, they are limited in services, and the guest almost becomes a member of an extended family. **Inclusive terms** is another phrase used to designate this plan in Europe.

Labels frequently add to the confusion. For example, the United Kingdom gathers statistics under the headings of hotels, guest houses, and other tourist accommodations. The U.S. Bureau of the Census uses hotels, 25 rooms or more; hotels, less than 25 rooms; motels, motor hotels, and tourist courts; and other lodging places (trailer courts, rooming and boarding houses, etc.).

Modified American Plan.   The **modified American plan (MAP)** is an astute compromise by which the hotel retains some of the AP advantages, and the guest feels less restricted. Guests get breakfast and dinner as part of the room rate quote, but not luncheon. This opens the middle of the day for a flexible schedule of activities. Guests need not return for an inconveniently scheduled luncheon nor suffer the cost of a missed meal. The hotel retains the obvious benefits of a captive market for the dinner hour.

In an effort to make the difference clear, some APs are now called FAP—full American plan.

Half pension or **demi-pension (DP)** is the European equivalent of the MAP. It includes lodging, breakfast, and one other meal. Granting either luncheon or dinner gives the guest still greater flexibility.

Continental Plan.   Under the **Continental plan (CP)**—mainland Europe being the Continent—breakfast is included with the room rate. This continental breakfast, consisting of coffee or chocolate, roll, and a bit of cheese (cold meat or fish in Holland and Norway), is on the wane even in Europe. (A hearty English breakfast is served in Ireland and the United Kingdom. It usually includes cereal, eggs with a choice of meat, toast with butter and jam, and tea or coffee, but no juice. However, it is rarely included in the room rate.)

In some parts of the world, this abbreviated breakfast goes under the name of *bed-breakfast.* With the same line of reasoning, the modified American plan becomes **half-board.** Neither should be confused with the **Bermuda plan,** which includes a full breakfast in the rate.

Café complet, a midmorning or afternoon coffee snack, is sometimes mistakenly called a continental breakfast. The distinction is neither the time of day nor the menu items, but the manner of payment. *Café complet* is not included in the room rate.

The appearance of late afternoon tea as a pleasant supplement to the overworked happy hour is certain to bring further confusion in terminology. Many top U.S. hotels have latched onto that quintessential British ritual, **afternoon tea.** Delicate sandwiches and small sweets served with tea, or even sherry, comprise this light snack. It is not to be confused with **high tea,** which is a supper, a substantial meal almost always served with meat. High tea is a rarity today, even in British hotels.

Continental Breakfast.   **Continental breakfast** has many meanings. A coffee urn with sweet rolls and juice left in the lobby when the dining room closes is often called a Continental breakfast. A similar setup at a group registration desk or at the rear of a meeting room during a speaker's talk appears on the program as Continental breakfast. Juice is included in the United States or when the delegates are Americans, but it is not usually served in Europe.

All-suite hotels have eliminated full-service dining rooms because they are expensive to operate. To accommodate overnight guests, who almost always want breakfast before departing, all-suites provide a full breakfast without charge as part of their marketing strategy. It is a revival of America's view of the Continental plan, which took form in the 1950s with the opening of the no-dining-room motel. In-room coffee makers, coffee in the lobby, or coffee and sweet rolls in the small proprietor's kitchen were all touted as Continental breakfast.

Bed and Breakfast (B&B).   **Bed and breakfast** surged onto the American scene so strongly that one might think it to be a whole new concept in hotelkeeping. It's hardly that. Bed and breakfast in the United States takes its cue from the British B&B, the Italian pensiones, and the German *zimmer frei* (room available)—lodging and breakfast offered by families in their own homes. The Japanese version of the U.S. B&B is *minshuku.*

B&B is a modern version of the 1930s roominghouse, once called the tourist home. The bed and breakfast was reborn for much the same reasons as its Depression-era predecessor—the landlord's need to supplement income and the lodger's hunt for less costly accommodations. Of course, for some innkeepers, it is an adventure, and for others, a hobby. The acceptability of the B&B gets a boost from the experience of a generation of owner–renters sharing living accommodations and time-share facilities.

Under the plan, guests take rooms with private families, who often furnish camaraderie along with the mandatory breakfast. The lack of privacy—shared bath, conversation at breakfast—forces the host and guest into a level of intimacy that brings new friendships along with the business relationship.

Like the rest of the industry, change is part of the B&B's vocabulary and no one definition fits all the parts. There are many subcategories because the business

Exhibit 1–10

Bed and breakfast (B&B) facilities operate under a variety of names like B&B Inns (chiefly California) or Country B&Bs (chiefly New England).

Eagles Mere Inn
Eagles Mere, Pennsylvania

EAGLES MERE "The Last Unspoiled Resort"

Eagles Mere, elevation 2,100 feet, in the "Endless Mountains" of Northeastern Pennsylvania, was developed in the 1800's as a resort for wealthy Philadelphians. They came to the mountain for the cool, clean air and crystal clear waters of the mile long lake. They built turn-of-the-century Victorian "cottages".

Built in 1878, it catered to the craftsmen who built the cottages and large hotels. The old hotels are gone and today the Eagles Mere Inn remains as the last country inn built for guests of the 1800's.

Courtesy: Eagles Mere Inn, Eagles Mere, Pennsylvania.

is very individualized and localized. The *B&B Inn* is a product of California, for example. It is a larger version (over half the B&Bs in the United States are 8 rooms or less!) and is usually the owner's means of livelihood. The conventional bed and breakfast is a personal residence and generally is not the operator's primary occupation.

Some observers see the *Country B&B* (see Exhibit 1–10), another subcategory, as an upscale boardinghouse because it serves all meals, not just breakfast. Its origin is New England. B&Bs, like other small businesses, lack staying power. Advertising, even a sign in the window, may be ruinous where zoning laws prohibit ''rooms for let.'' One positive sign is the Yellow Pages listing of B&B referral organizations under *B&B* rather than under their previous categories of *hotels, motels,* and *tourist homes.*

In one way, B&Bs are no different from other American hotels. They fight for business and rely on themselves for referral. In Europe and Japan, government tourist agencies make referrals to B&B establishments and in many cases even rate them by price and accommodations. The French call them *café-couette* (coffee and quilt), and the rating system uses coffee pots (three to six), not stars.

Since the U.S. government has never entered the tourist-rating business, several private rating and reservation systems have emerged. Like the B&Bs, the rating/referral systems come and go quickly, for they too lack staying power.

Boutique Hotels.   *Boutique hotels* are a different species altogether. They are very small inns, 10 to 30 rooms, perhaps with all the amenities of a fine hotel but without the size and bustle. The phrase ''European-style hotel'' is commonly used in reference to these establishments. Boutique hotels are ''fashionable,'' and that means they are found in a very good urban location. Hence, they are also called *urban inns,* or *baby grand hotels* in Britain.

Urban hotels are full-time businesses requiring substantial capital investment. Traditional financing for so risky an adventure is difficult to find. Moreover, earning a fair return on this unconventional investment pushes rates upward toward the level of other four- and five-star hotels. Since the volume on which costs are prorated is small, boutique hotels are unlikely to be profitable. They are, therefore, often designated *trophy hotels.* Their owners have the property as a personal achievement (a trophy) rather than as a viable business enterprise. Listing these unique buildings in the National Register of Historical Places provides special tax relief if the hotel results from the conversion of a historical site, as it often does.

Summary

The hotel business has survived and flourished over centuries because it has adapted to the changing conditions of its environment. Today, it serves as an integral part of the business and leisure industries by providing over 10 million rooms to travelers worldwide.

Even as the industry changes, it retains some traditional measures, limitations, and identifications. The quantity of its business is measured in room occupancy; the quality is measured in Average Daily Rate. To maximize both of these, management must overcome several limitations that are inherent in the business. These include perishability of product, a single location, a fixed supply of inventory, a high break-even point, and a seasonal operating period.

Retaining the industry's traditional identifications (size, class, type, and plan) helps identify the important permutations (all-suites, bed and breakfast, budget) that keep the industry exciting and economically sound. As the changes continue, new categories are needed. These are enumerated in the following chapter.

Queries and Problems

1. Using appropriate guides (for example, *OAG Travel Planner, Hotel & Motel Red Book* or *The Official Hotel & Resort Guide*), identify two or three U.S. hotels that quote rates on the full American or modified American plans. Is there any commonality among them? Identify your sources.

2. Create a checklist of two dozen items that could be used by an evaluator inspecting guest rooms for a national rating system.

3. Through personal observation on the site and an examination of advertising media (telephone directory, billboards, etc.), classify one hotel/motel in your home area as to type, plan, class, pattern, and affiliation. Itemize any other sources that you used and explain the conclusions that you drew.

4. Even as the number of mom-and-pop establishments is dwindling, the number of bed-and-breakfast establishments is increasing. Are these developments

contradictory? Why are mom-and-pops on the decline? Why are bed-and-breakfasts gaining in popularity?

5. How many rooms does the MGM Grand Hotel need to sell annually if it budgets on a yearly occupancy of 88 percent? (Hint: see Exhibit 1–5.)

6. Select one of the hotel chains identified in Exhibit 1–6 and, through research, determine the number of domestic rooms controlled by that company. Approximately what percentage of total U.S. hotel rooms does that figure represent? Cite your sources.

Notes

1. In 1992, an estimated 476 million international travelers spent some 278 billion U.S. dollars. *Compendium of Tourism Statistics,* 13th ed. (Madrid: World Tourism Organization, 1993).

2. *Census of Service Industries: Hotels, Motels and Other Lodging Places* (Madrid: World Tourism Organization, 1993); *Lodging Industry Profile* (New York: AH&MA, 1992); as cited by *Meetings,* May 1992.

3. The Chicago Stouffers, which was announced in 1982, opened in 1991.

4. A very early definition was offered by Howard E. Morgan, *The Motel Industry in the United States: Small Business in Transition* (Tucson: Bureau of Business and Public Research, University of Arizona, 1964).

The Modern
Hotel Industry

Chapter Outline

Travel has a long history that closely follows human development. Driven by the elements, by the need for food and shelter, and even by curiosity, people expanded their horizons almost from the beginning of time. Historians suggest that these aimless wanderings became purposeful around the year 4,000 B.C. The invention of the wheel and the introduction of money into trade are both attributed to the Sumerians (the ancient Babylonians), who lived on the eastern Mediterranean. Ur, the home of the biblical Abraham, was part of ancient Babylon, and it was here that tourist homes were first recorded.

Much of the very early travel was done by ship, so there was no need for the shelter of an inn. Later, in response to the needs of land travelers, came the caravansaries (stopping places for caravans in eastern countries), the mansiones (large hostelries located on the roads of ancient Rome), and the inns of Dickens's England.

Travel was flourishing in the Orient as well as in Europe. Although the adventures of Marco Polo were said to have opened the way to the East, the emperors of China were on the move a thousand years before the birth of Christ. Early Dutch explorers touched Japan in the first century A.D. Government-run houses with Western accommodations were built for them and became the prototype for business and governmental travelers. Since occidental and oriental lifestyles differed so widely, special inns serving each culture began to develop side by side—a coexistence that persists today.

Although physical accommodations have changed dramatically in 6,000 years, their origins remain surprisingly constant. Today's traveler is still driven by the elements: Seeking new business is the modern counterpart to foraging for food and shelter, and tourism is the modern equivalent to the Great Crusades.

A New Array for Lodging

Throughout the centuries, innkeepers—be they oriental or occidental, free or slave, family or giant corporation—have reacted to the demands of the traveler. Seldom—until now—have they created the product or generated the demand. Until as recently as the 1950s, hotels served primarily as the storage arm of transportation, carefully locating along the traveler's route.

The industry's traditional focus on location has not been abandoned. Current patterns, which reflect a new sensitivity to market forces, have supplemented the old focus, not replaced it. No longer is there just one route for the traveler, who wings around the globe at the speed of sound. There is, instead, an array of choice. Rather than a fixed destination along a predetermined route, the hotel of the 21st century is a fixed destination along no one's route and along everyone's route. Identifying, attracting, and holding the guest requires a new sensitivity to consumer needs.

An explosion of choice has taken place in all the goods and services that Americans buy. From bottled water to investment options, the consumer finds a rich array of products. Such is also the case in the lodging industry, which has joined the movement by introducing its own new products and options.

The permutation from the traditional to the new has been made in small, almost indistinguishable steps. The book has shown this by mixing some new ideas (e.g., the boutique hotel) into Chapter 1's traditional identifications and some of the older listings (e.g., conventions) into Chapter 2's modern identifications.

There are numerous divisions and subdivisions that can be used to visualize the complexity of the modern lodging industry (see Exhibit 2–1). Some of the new patterns emphasize marketing; some have more meaning for ownership and finance; and some are concerned with operations and management. All have significance for growth and profits.

Marketing Patterns

Guests take lodging for many different reasons, but actually for only one of two purposes. Either the hotel is their ultimate destination, or it offers them accommodations in transit. Although there are similarities, this transient-destination category is not the same as the commercial-resort grouping discussed in Chapter 1.

A transient hotel is a passing-through facility. Guests are en route to somewhere else: tourists en route to a national shrine, business executives to a corporate meeting, families to weddings, or ball teams to the destination of a big game. Rarely does the transient hotel hold the guest beyond one or two nights.

In contrast, the destination hotel is the objective, the very purpose of the trip. It is the hotel that houses the convention or corporate meeting. It is the family's

EXHIBIT 2-1

Segmenting the lodging industry presents an array of divisions and subdivisions.

Segmented by location
    Airport
    Highway/Collar
    Urban/Center city

Segmented by price
    Deluxe
    Midscale
    Budget

Segmented by type
    Commercial
    Resort
    Residential

Segmented by financing
    Public—Corporate
    Private
    Joint venture

Segmented by themes
    All-suite
    Bed and breakfast
    Boutique

Segmented by activity
    Casino hotel
    Conference hotel
    Golf (tennis) resort

Segmented by ownership
    Chain
    Condominium/Timeshare
    Mom-and-pop

Segmented by rating systems
    Five-star
    Four-star
    Three-star

Segmented by markets
    Business
    Convention
    Leisure

Segmented by plan
    American plan
    Continental plan
    European plan

Segmented by service
    Full service
    Moderate service
    Limited service

Other segmentations
    Mixed use
    Collar
    Franchise

temporary residence while they seek housing in their new locality. It is the best location near the medical center for persons visiting the sick. More and more, the destination hotel is part of the destination resort complex, often a megaresort, which is typified by the Disney properties.

Location helps fix the classification. The hotels of Acapulco and Miami Beach are unquestionably destination points. Equally certain is the transient nature of many a motor inn. There, on the outskirts of town near the freeway, it awaits the traveler en route to the megalopolis still a day's ride away. Most hotels are not so clearly of one type or another—those of New York City, for example.

The role of any hotel changes from guest to guest. In this context, the transient hotel is obviously not the commercial property of our previous chapter. Nor is the destination hotel necessarily a resort. So certain destination guests (say, first-time international travelers) of a commercial hotel might be interested in the American plan, more so than would be the transient guest at a resort. From our historical review, it is clear that the destination hotel is the new kid on the block of lodging.

Marketing to the Group.   Although groups occasionally use a hotel for transient purposes, the hotel more often serves as their destination site. Like individual travelers, groups come both as tourists and as businesspersons.

Tourist Purposes: The Tour Package.   Rising disposable income and broader travel horizons have made travel appealing to every level of American society. As the relative cost of travel and accommodations decline, the market potential grows ever larger. The travel and hotel industries have finally embarked on the same kind of mass production that has brought increased efficiency to the manufacturing industries. The delay was unavoidable because the large hotel is of recent origin, and only the large hotel is interested in and able to service large groups. Now that it is here, there is a new awareness of and a new concern for the mass movement of travelers.

Group tours are **packaged** in a variety of wrappings, some reminiscent of the old American plan. Indeed, the very **breakage** that the guest objects to in the American plan is accepted with fervor in the tour package.[1] Room, food, beverage, entertainment, and, in some cases, transportation, are packaged in with tips and baggage handling for one price. Breakage profits materialize because guests do not take every meal and drink nor use every service provided by the plan.

A new entrepreneur, the wholesaler—another party in the distribution system—has emerged during the past decade to handle the mass movement of travelers. Entrepreneurs are risk takers, and wholesalers are certainly that! Wholesalers buy blocks of rooms (commitments to take so many rooms for so many nights) from the hotel, blocks of seats from the airlines, and blocks of seats from the bus company. Then the wholesalers try to sell their packages, which now include transportation, ground handling, and baggage along with whatever else they are able to get from the hotel (see Exhibit 2–2). Breakage accrues to the wholesaler.

Quantity buying gives the wholesaler a good airline price. Special room and meal rates are negotiated with the hotel under the same umbrella—quantity discounts. With the promise of year-round, back-to-back charters, the hotel sales manager and accountant sharpen their pencils. One sale books hundreds of rooms. One correspondence confirms all the reservations. One billing closes the books. There is no commission to credit card companies, and there is a minimum loss from bad debts. It is a bargain buy for the traveler, a profitable venture for the wholesaler, and a basic occupancy for the hotel, which also gets free advertising.

Mass marketing has introduced many new customers to travel. Some have come despite the lack of individual service and attention. Others might have come because of it: Inexperienced travelers find comfort in the safety and security of the group; experienced travelers find irrefutable savings.

Mass packaging enables the customer to buy the services of the airlines, the ground transportation companies, the tour operators, the hotels, and the restaurants at a fraction of their separate, individual costs. But there is a loss of guest identity. Even the hotel feels a reduced responsibility when guests deal through third parties.

Almost any destination hotel can host a tourist group if it can attract the group to the site. It must meet the price of a very competitive market to appeal to the wholesaler. And it must be large enough to accommodate the group and still handle its other guests. Hotels in out-of-the-way places cater to bus groups. They're a broader market because the number of guests is smaller and almost any hotel can handle them. With bus tours, hotels provide a mix of destination and transient service.

Business Purposes: The Convention.   Our propensity to form business groups has produced an astonishing number of organizations. People come together under many umbrellas: business, union, fraternal, social, historical, veteran, health and medical, educational, religious, scientific, political, service, athletic, and on without end. For short, the industry uses the acronym SMURF: societies, medical, university, religious, fraternal. Each classification translates into numerous organizations,

EXHIBIT 2–2

A sample tour-operator advertisement is shown in which vacations are packaged for one price. (Hotels also package, but without the airfare.)

Courtesy: MLT Vacations, Minnetonka, Minnesota.

societies, clubs, and associations. Each of them meets, holds shows, and stages conventions. Functioning at local, state, regional, national, and international levels, these groups offer business to a variety of destination facilities.

Conventioneers assemble to promote their common purposes. These aims are as diverse as the list of associations that hold conventions. During the gathering of two, three, or four days, papers, meetings, speeches, and talks are given on a range of topics. Some are professional and some merely entertaining. The members also interact individually, discussing common goals and problems. Professional conventions may serve as formal or informal job-placement forums.

Both urban and resort properties vie for convention business as the growth of mixed-use facilities spreads.[2] To be competitive, the convention hotel must provide a range of self-contained facilities. Meeting space with appropriate furnishings and equipment and food facilities large enough to accommodate the groups at banquets are the minimum facilities needed. Conventioneers are a captive audience for the program and the planned activities. The more complete the property, the more appealing the site.

Sports activities, a change of scenery, and isolation from the hubbub of busy cities are touted by a resort's sales department. Urban properties respond with theaters, museums, and historical locations. Urban areas may have the advantage of publicly financed convention halls.

Hotels sometimes combine facilities with those of nearby competitors when the convention size is too large for one property. Although not the rule, conventions of 50,000 to 100,000 delegates have been recorded, usually when combined with trade shows.

Business Purposes: The Trade Show.   Trade shows are exhibits of product lines shown by purveyors to potential buyers. Conventions and trade shows are often held together. Shows require a great deal of space, particularly if the displays are large pieces of machinery or equipment (see Exhibit 2–3). Space requirements and the difficulty of handling such products limit shows to a small number of hotels. The city convention bureau has a role here. It builds halls to accommodate the exhibits, leaving the housing and guest service to the local hotels.

Goods of small compass—perfume shows, for example—can be housed in almost any hotel. Although less common today, assigning several guest floors to such a trade show and converting guest rooms into exhibit space is still done. The purveyor also occupies the room as a registered guest.

Business Purposes: The Single Entity.   The *single entity* is neither a tour package nor a convention/trade show. Here's why. Tour-package rooms are reserved as a block, and guests pay their own way, although indirectly through the tour organizer. Convention attendees may be reimbursed by their employers, but they reserve the rooms individually and pay the hotel directly. With the single-entity group, rooms are reserved in a block and the entire bill is paid by the entity. Businesses, institutions, or incentive planners—not the individual members of these groups—are the entities.

Hotels cater to various kinds of single-group bookings. A visiting athletic team is the best example. The team, not the players, books the rooms, and the team (the entity), not the players, pays the bill. Company sales and technical meetings, new product line showings, and training sessions exemplify the range. Hotel casinos have their own form of single entity, the gambling junket. Airlines promote single-entity

Exhibit 2–3

Hotels and convention centers accommodate trade shows that sometimes number in the tens of thousands of delegates.

Courtesy: Plastics Fair–Atlanta, November 9–11, 1993, produced by Advanstar Expositions.

charters, but the transportation arrangements are unimportant to the hotel except as arrival and departure times affect the work of the front office and the readiness of rooms.

Incentive tours are special kinds of single entities. Many businesses run incentive programs to encourage sales and production workers to improve output. A cash bonus, a prize, or an incentive trip—for example, a free vacation for two to a destination resort—is the reward for those who meet the announced goals.

Hotels like to book incentive tours because all the participants are winners and only the best accommodations are chosen. Unfortunately, the deals for these facilities are frequently negotiated through intermediaries—incentive (tour) companies, which have emerged as still another player in the sale and distribution of hotel rooms. Incentive companies negotiate for hotel rooms and deliver them to clients, the companies holding the incentive programs. Often, the incentive companies are also the consultants handling the clients' incentive programs.

Incentive companies represent many client–enterprises. This gives the incentive companies a great deal of leverage when they negotiate with the hotel. Everyone bargains tough when accommodations for several groups are at stake. It is the very same pressure that hotels experience when dealing with the quantity purchases of the tour-package companies. Price and quality are the differences: Cost is critical for the wholesaler; quality for the incentive buyer.

Tours, be they single entity, incentive, or as yet unnamed, are the group markets of tomorrow. One can foresee a growth of vertical integration with one large holding company owning the means of transportation, reservation system, tour wholesaler, incentive company, and hotel/resort. U.S. airlines might move in this direction again—they all owned hotels at one time—when the airline business recovers. JAL and ANA, both Japanese carriers, have already done so. The incentive is a simple premise: one **bed-night** sold by an integrated company is worth multiple times more than a single room sale made by a stand-alone hotel. The future is clear!

Marketing to the Individual.   Individual guests, not groups, were the focus of the early hotel. Chapter 1 explained the role of the transient hotel as an accommodation for the traveler on the move. Similarly, the early resort flourished by providing recreation and leisure for the individual party (''individual'' meaning family, servants, or friends coming as a unit). Both types of hotels still cater to the individual guest, but there are some new twists.

The Inclusive Tour Package.   The popularity of the wholesaler's tour package did not escape the notice of hoteliers. After all, why leave all the profits to the wholesaler? Eliminating the airfare and the portage reduced the package to the hotel's portion only, thereby eliminating the high risk otherwise associated with the *inclusive tour* (IT). Everything else remained: room, meals, drinks, and so on. Free use of the tennis courts (putting green, swimming pool, playground, shuffleboard, or table tennis) and free admission to the theater (formal gardens, exhibits, animal habitats, or exhibition matches) broaden the package without increasing the price. The product looks even better if small fees are normally paid for such services.

Breakage belongs to the hotel when the hotel creates the IT. Sometimes it markets the IT through the media directly to the public. Sometimes travel agents make the sale. Then, of course, the hotel pays the standard 10 percent commission. Since the packages does not distinguish room charges from other elements, the commission is paid on the full package price. Otherwise, the commission is paid on the room rate only.

One hotel may offer several packages: a weekend package, a run-away package, a holiday fling, and so on. Packages must be marketed carefully because the hotel competes with itself. It sells discounted rooms with extra services at a lower price than the **rack rate** of the very same room.[3] (Later chapters dealing with yield management and room rates again raise this issue of self-competition.)

The Business Guest.   Businesspersons need to be at a given place at a given time. Therefore, price is less important—not unimportant, but less important—to the business guest than to the leisure traveler. Businessmen and women are not apt to cancel a trip because of high rates, and they are not apt to make a trip because of low rates. Theirs is an *inelastic* market—there is very little change in demand to a change in price. The response from leisure guests is more dramatic: High rates repel them and low rates attract them. By responding to price changes, leisure guests represent a more *elastic* market.

All guests demonstrate some degree of elasticity. Leisure guests may be inelastic, they just have to be there—a wedding, a funeral, and so forth—and business guests may be elastic, rescheduling or postponing their meetings. Companies with travel desks, which schedule and buy travel (air, hotels, and car rentals) for their personnel, are more price sensitive. With someone other than the traveler doing the planning, businesses have shifted toward the elastic side. This shift helps explain the buyer's focus on value. Thus, all-suite hotels have grown in popularity, and expensive five-star properties suffered during the decade-long downturn in business.

Business guests may need special services such as in-room computers, private telephone lines for messages and faxes, and business centers with secretarial support. Specific requirements like these reduce the businesspersons' options, and this means still less elasticity. Meanwhile, the hotel industry struggles to decide how worthwhile expensive, business-oriented investments are in attracting this single segment of the market.

Ownership/Financing Patterns

At the same time that the lodging industry has been coping with numerous marketplace changes, it has been undergoing major shifts in ownership structures and methods of financing.

Historically, the inn was a family affair with the host–guest relationship paramount. That view began to change in the 1950s, when ownership and management became different activities. As that separation widened, hotel chains concentrated on managing. Other entities, the new owners, focused on the real estate—the building and the land on which the property stood. Federal income-tax laws and skyrocketing inflation encouraged real estate speculation.

Decades of Turmoil: State of the Industry. From the 1970s through the 1990s, hotel real estate has been in turmoil as real estate speculators entered the business. Tax laws provided large cash flows from the real estate although the operating hotel was not very healthy (Exhibits 1–2 and 1–3). In addition, there were large profits to be made when the hotel building was sold. Inflation drove up building prices (quoted in dollars per room) from tens of thousands per room to hundreds of thousands per room.[4] Hotel companies with well-known names generally remained aloof from this speculative cycle, leaving the "play" to nonhotel investors.

The Role of the Global Village. The appearance of the *global village* (shorthand for shrinking political differences and interlocking economic interests worldwide) coincided with the boom in hotel real estate. The value of the American dollar on international markets was weak during the midperiod (late 1970s and early 1980s) of the real estate spiral. That exacerbated the situation. Foreign investors found great real estate bargains in the United States even at inflated prices. U.S. real estate was cheap when compared to costs at home.

International investors purchase U.S. hotels with American dollars. To do this, they must first buy those dollars. When the dollar is weak, fewer units of the strong foreign currency are needed to buy the necessary greenbacks. This makes the purchase price an attractive bargain to an international company with a strong currency.

Furthermore, international investors differentiate, even more than U.S. developers, between the hotel as an operating company and the hotel as a piece of real estate. Buying the hotel to get the real estate is a long-run view, and international companies have a longer business horizon than do domestic companies.

Political stability is still another factor. An investor from Hong Kong, for instance, faces serious financial loss from political uncertainties and upheavals. Better to invest in the United States even if the price is high or the economic risk chancier because there is no political risk: The U.S. government is not likely to confiscate or nationalize the property.

The purchase and consolidation of the domestic hotel industry is not a factor of globalization alone. Many perceive lodging to be a mature industry. For them, the acquisition of existing properties is a better business play than the riskier move of new development and construction.

Global Village Examples.   The business arena in which hotel companies play stretches across the globe in every direction.

Stouffer Hotels, based in Ohio, owns and operates properties in the United States, Mexico, and the Caribbean. Stouffer was actually owned by Nestlé, a Swiss company. The 15,000-room chain was sold by Nestlé to a Hong Kong-based operator, New World Development Company. New World is the parent company of a one-time American chain, Ramada International (124 properties), whose North American headquarters is in Miami, and of New World Hotels (11 properties in Asia).

Inter-Continental Hotels, formerly a subsidiary of Pan Am Airlines (United States), is another example. It was purchased by Grand Metropolitan of Great Britain. Soon thereafter, it was sold to Seibu Saison Group, a Japanese retail and leisure conglomerate. Not long afterward, it was sold again. This time it went to Scandinavian Airline Systems (SAS). Within a very brief period, an American hotel company with hotels in 50 countries was involved with the British, the Japanese, and the Scandinavians. That's globalization!

Globalization is not limited to the hotel business but includes the lodging industry's important partners. Many airlines and travel agencies have multinational ownerships. KLM (Royal Dutch Airlines) has a major interest in Northwest Airlines (United States). Swissair, Singapore Airlines, and Delta (United States) have interlocking ownerships. Carlson Travel Group (United States), which is a subsidiary of the same company that owns Radisson Hotels, has controlling interest in a British counterpart, A. T. Mays.

Market patterns as well as ownership/management structures have also gone international. Some 100,000 U.S. corporate groups (about half of whom are involved in incentive travel) meet overseas annually.

Name changes have kept pace with the growth of the overseas movement. Best Western became Best Western International, and Quality Inns became Quality International and then Choice Hotels International. Other familiar names are Holiday Inns Worldwide and Marriott International. Even without the global terminology, hotels operate easily across national borders, and the flow goes both ways. For example, two Paris-based companies have spread internationally—Accor into 65 countries and Club Med into 35. Spain's Occidental Hotels are in a dozen lands, and Brussels-based SAS International Hotels are in about the same number.

The Improving Health of the Industry.   Chapter 1 highlighted the poor economic period (1981–1991) that hurt the industry for better than a dozen years. That experience was worldwide, and it was caused by a combination of low customer demand and high rate expectations. It was abetted in the United States by special income-tax benefits, which Congress then eliminated. Good room sales were needed to pay off the loans from expensive real estate transactions. But as occupancy fell (too many rooms and too few customers), so did rates. Hotel buyers were unable to meet the interest and loan repayments demanded by the banks. Estimates approximate that two-thirds of all hotel properties were in some level of financial distress.

As one real estate deal after another collapsed, so did the banking industry, which provided the loans. (All real estate, not just the hotel industry, suffered during this period of overbuilding and overspeculation.) With no payment flow, the banks were as badly off as the real estate investors. America's Savings and Loan Associations (banks) obtained the money to make these bad loans from their depositors, of course. These depositors were insured by the Federal Deposit Insurance Corporation (FDIC), an agency of the federal government. As a result of the credit emergency, all the hotels (and other real estate, too) that were unable to meet their bank obligations ended up in the hands of a new federal agency established to bail out the sick banks. This Resolution Trust Corporation (RTC) assumed control of the banks and began selling off the sick hotels (see Exhibit 2–4), which were the security for the loans. It was a fire sale—hotels were sold at substantial discounts from the original loan values. Although it hurt a great many hotel owners, it helped to speed up the recovery!

The recovery started in 1993, and it brought optimism to hoteliers for the first time in better than a decade. Business travel began improving, pushing up demand. Low inflation kept borrowing costs and operating expenses steady. Most important, distressed hotels had either gone out of business (reducing supply) or had been repurchased at low per room costs, which brought mortgage repayments down, well into reasonable ranges. Increasing demand without an increase in room supply—repentent lenders and disappointed speculators have not rushed in to build anew—pushes room rates up faster than inflation, so the industry becomes healthy again.

Ownership Alternatives.   The long down period forced the industry to reassess its approach to project financing. Hotel chains no longer provided their own financing as they did through the 1960s. Developers and speculators were simply unable to obtain mortgage loans. As the usual financing sources evaporated, two new alternatives appeared. Both had the same orientation—get the money from the guests!

Condominiums and Timesharing.   Both condominiums and timesharing had their beginnings in the destination resorts: geographically in Florida, the Caribbean, and Hawaii; conceptually in other vacation locations and skiing villages throughout the country. The condominium idea preceded timesharing by some 20 years. Condominiums were nurtured in the same income-tax environment that caused the real estate bust just discussed.

Despite their surface similarities, there is little likeness in the two patterns. *Condominium* units are real estate purchases, first of all. Guests own them as they own any home. Common space and common grounds are also owned, but as part of the group association. Each unit is complete with all the amenities, kitchen and general family space included. Owners furnish their units and maintain them according to personal preferences.

Since the owners are not always on-property, units are placed in a common rental pool. This requires on-site management to rent and service the units. Profits, if any, are paid to the owners on a pro rata basis. The complex might be part of a large resort facility that is operated by a well-known hotel chain or management company. Or, the condo owners might employ their own staff to operate and manage the units.

There are endless permutations to the basic plan. In its simplest form, the guest owns the condominium, reserves so many days per year for personal use, and—if the guest wishes—places the unit into the rental pool for the balance of the time.

Actually, condos are an unusual mix of functions. The owners finance the facility for the developer; then they occupy the units as guests, sometimes guests of

EXHIBIT 2–4

A composite ''For Sale'' advertisement placed for a typical property in default of its bank loan, which the RTC assumed when it took control of the failing bank.

RESOLUTION TRUST CORPORATION
*Resolving The Crisis
Restoring The Confidence*

SEALED BID

The Winter Hotel
137 Room Hotel

North Avenue
Missoula, Montana
Brochure #111

- Operating Restaurant/Bar
- Pool, FF&E, Practice Ski Hill
- On 5.1 acre site, approximate
- $1,000,000 + Estimated GOI, 1993

VIEWINGS:
Apr 25, 27 • May 2,   11am–1pm

This property is appropriate for all investors including small investors or small investor groups.

Broker Participation Welcome
Cash Only Sale

Bid Deadline:
May 17, at 3:00pm CST
To request property specific information, please call:

1-800-555-5555

*Coordinated by the RTC Kansas City Sales Center and National Real Estate Clearinghouse, JV.
Event ID Number: 111-11111*

themselves, since they also hire the management company that services their stay. Mixed use may prove to be the resort of the future. On the one property would be transient hotel rooms, all-suite extended-stay facilities, condos, and timesharing units.

Timesharing is not a real estate purchase! One does not buy the real estate but only the *right to use* the facility for so many days each year over some fixed period. Hence, the term *interval ownership* is also used. The more desirable the period of use (in season versus off season versus **shoulder** season[5]), the higher the initial timeshare fee. Additional housekeeping fees are also charged during the weekly occupancy of each holder. Contracts range from 10 to 40 years of use. At the end of the contract, ownership remains with the developer, in contrast to the condo, where ownership passes to the buyer right up front.

The developer tries to sell each unit 52 times, once each week. In practice, a week or two is held back for repairs and maintenance. Unlike the condo, repairs and maintenance, furnishings, and services are supplied by the developer since the space—sometimes just a single hotel room—is not owned by the occupants.

Timesharing started out with a very poor reputation. Because timeshare sales were not considered to be real estate sales, the states remained aloof and the industry was unregulated for many years. After numerous complaints about misrepresentations and unethical methods of selling, the real estate commissioners of the states established timeshare standards. This brought credibility to the industry, as did the recent appearance of companies like Disney and Hilton, as well as Marriott, which first entered the market in 1984.

Timeshare guests purchase a lifetime of vacationing at the same place and during the same season each year. To overcome this negative factor, clubs have been formed to swap times and locations. Of course, this adds still another fee. Other reciprocal arrangements like transferable memberships have been offered to widen the sales appeal. As well-known chains with properties worldwide enter the timeshare market, guest options widen and improve.

Also, new variations are being invented (vacation ownerships, club memberships, fractionals) as permutations of the basic theme. Among them is a move by noncondominium, nontimesharing resorts to sell some facilities in pieces. There are many advantages to the seller (the resort) and less risk to the buyer–owner (the guest).

The down payment from the condo or timeshare buyer becomes a new source of capital to the resort's current owner. The capital is used to refurbish and upgrade or to pay off outstanding debt. Sometimes, it just goes into the pockets of the old owner. With the basic occupancy promised by a group of permanent guests (who now are partial owners), profits improve. Less advertising represents savings. Less housekeeping and fewer repairs may be required, depending on the agreement. If kitchen facilities are provided, food and beverage costs are reduced. If not, higher occupancy produces higher food and beverage revenues.

The Joint Venture.   In several ways, the joint venture is similar to a partnership arranged between two or more individuals. However, with the joint venture, the individuals are one of several entities: corporations, partnerships, individuals, and even governments. For example, privately owned Radisson Hotels formed a three-way venture with the Russian Ministry for Foreign Tourism and a publicly owned American business-center company, Americom. They opened the 430-room Radisson Slavjanskaya.

Joint venture members invest in, share in, and create a new legal entity. Each participant brings its special capabilities to the joint effort: finance, marketing, operations, and so on. Since the joint venture is usually not taxed, each member reporting its own share of income, the duplicate taxation that the typical corporation faces is avoided.

Rising costs (land and construction), huge enterprises (megaresorts and developments), and specialization (finance and management) make the joint venture a perfect vehicle for the current business climate. A joint venture some years ago between Choice Hotels International and AIRCOA illustrates the point. The asset-management capabilities and real estate expertise of AIRCOA were merged with Choice's extraordinary sales, marketing, and reservation capability.

New and creative variations of the joint venture are on the horizon, hurried along by the explosion in gambling. Gaming management is a skill that new developers (Indian tribes, municipalities, and others) lack. Still, they want to retain the benefits that casino ownership represents. Joint ventures are the obvious compromise: Bring the skills and monies of the gaming management companies to the joint enterprise, while other members provide the sites, licenses, and political muscle.

Management Patterns

Our historical review has made it clear that the era of the small innkeeper and the individual entrepreneur is waning. Erecting large, expensive buildings and competing in international markets require the management talent and the capital funding that only large, public companies—the hotel chain—can provide.

Growth of the Chain.   The very act of traveling evokes the unknown, the strange, the unfamiliar. Within such an environment, travelers must select a rather personal service—a bed for the night. Examining or evaluating the experience beforehand is not possible. So the hotel's reputation or its membership in a chain or affiliated group become the primary reason for the guest's selection.

Overseas, the environment is stranger still. Brand recognition is even more critical to the selection. That is why American hotels developed abroad when the United States dominated the world's business scene. With international trade now more evenly balanced, foreign chains are appearing in the United States for the same reasons.

The combination of brand recognition and the inherent strengths of size and savvy management account for the chains' popularity and growth. And grow they have. The AH&MA publishes an annual *Directory of Hotel & Motel Companies* (chains). It defines a chain as any group of two or more properties operated under a common name (see Exhibit 2–5). Chain-controlled hotels now dominate the U.S. hotel industry. Some 75 percent of hotel rooms are under the umbrella of one chain or another. That figure was only 37 percent in the early 1970s, and there are almost 10,000 additional hotels today!

Modern business practices give chains an enormous operating advantage. Among their basic strengths are (1) expertise in site selection; (2) access to capital; (3) economies of scale (purchasing, advertising, reservations, etc.); (4) appeal to the best management talent; and (5) brand recognition.

As this chapter has stressed, hotel chains are no longer hotel builders. Just as often, the builders are not the owners, and the owners are not **hoteliers.** So it is to the hotel chain that the builder/developers and owners turn for the management

EXHIBIT 2–5

This is an alphabetical baker's dozen of the nation's best-known hotel names. Some chains are owned by other companies. Some names on the list own their hotels; others merely license (franchise) their names; still others operate under management contracts. Many do all three.

Best Western
Days Inns
Hilton
Holiday
Hyatt
Inter-Continental
La Quinta
Marriott
Quality
Radisson
Ramada
Renaissance
Sheraton

skills. It is to those same management skills that the institutional lenders trust the likelihood of the loan's repayment.

There are five different parties involved in the development and operation of a hotel. The confusion is compounded when one of the participants wears two or three hats. The *developer* (party number 1) sees the opportunity and puts the plan together. That developer could be one of the hotel chains—Marriott, for example. The hotel might be part of a larger development—one element in a shopping mall, or a business park, or a resort complex.

Financing is arranged from a bank, insurance company, pension plan, or other source. The *financier* is party number 2. As with all the participants, financing could come in total or in part from one or more of the other parties. The developer or the hotel management company might participate in the lending but more likely in the equity.

The equity—that is, the *ownership*—is party number 3. This party could be any of the others, a public corporation, a joint venture between one or more of the parties, or a separate entity making a passive investment.

If none of the participants is familiar to the consuming public as a hotel company, there will be no brand recognition. Then it is desirable that the group that manages the operation—the *management company* (party number 4)—have a recognizable logo. If the management company does not have a strong marketing presence, a franchise is licensed from a company (party number 5) that does.

A hotel chain such as Marriott or Sheraton is likely to be a combination of all five parties who help with the development and the financing, own a piece of the action, and supply the management talent along with the name recognition and reservation system that are so critical to the successful hotel. Just recently, Hyatt announced it would begin franchising for the first time.

The other extreme is a development by the local business community in a small town. That group may be the developer–owners, but the financing, the management, and the franchise are all a apt to be different parties.

The Management Contract and the Management Company.   A management contract is an agreement between the hotel owner and the management company (see Exhibit 2–6). If the hotel has been repossessed, it is likely to be the bank that

EXHIBIT 2–6

This is an alphabetical baker's dozen of the nation's best-known hotel management companies. Although these chains manage many hotels, they own only a few and franchise almost none (there is no name recognition).

Company Name	Approximate Number of	
	Guest Rooms	Properties
Amerihost Properties	6,000	50
American General Hospitality	14,500	70
Beck Management Group	13,000	90
Hostmark Management Group	14,000	60
Interstate Hotels	18,500	50
John Q. Hammons	8,500	40
Lane Hospitality	7,000	30
Larken, Inc.	14,500	70
Prime Hospitality Corp.	13,000	85
Richfield Hotel Management	33,500	175
Sage Development Resources	7,500	50
Servico Hotels & Resorts	8,000	35
Winegardner & Hammons	13,500	70

negotiates the contract. Indeed, the large number of hotel bankruptcies during the 1980s proved to be good business for the management companies. Having no hotel management experience, banks needed management services until the properties could be sold.

Management contracts are complicated legal instruments. In simplistic terms, the management company operates the hotel within the limitations and guidelines outlined in the contract. The management company enjoys rapid, inexpensive expansion because it provides neither financing nor equity. There is a positive side to the profit potential, with almost no risk.

It's good for the owner also. The owner acquires the professional management that institutional lenders like to see. Under experienced management, borrowing capacity improves, as do profits.

The contract can be negotiated at any time. If early in the development, the management company may provide expert advice during construction. Contracts expire or are cancelled and renegotiated throughout the life of the property. Terms vary at each stage as the condition of the venture changes. Falling revenue within the industry and increased competition among the management companies have driven down management fees, which approximate 4 percent of total revenues or about $750 per available room per year.

Management companies are paid to operate the hotel whether the hotel is profitable or not. Profits and losses accrue to the owners, who pay management fees as they pay other expenses such as insurance, taxes, and interest. The management fee is great for the management companies when business is poor. When business is good and profits high, a lease may be negotiated. Then the management company pays a rental to the owner for the privilege of operating the hotel. Profits and losses accrue to the management company. Both plans provide incentive percentage payments in addition to the flat fee or rental. The management lease will reappear again when the industry rebounds.

Rarely does the chain follow one pattern exclusively. In one instance, it might own and operate hotels. Or it might operate the hotels in joint venture with other

EXHIBIT 2–7

This is an alphabetical baker's dozen of the nation's best-known franchise companies. Name recognition enables them to license (franchise) their names. Some also operate under management contracts; some own the properties. Many do all three.

Company Name and Brands	Approximate Number Under Franchise:	
	Guest Rooms	*Properties*
Admiral Benbow Inns	2,000	20
Best Western International	275,000	3,500
Carlson Hospitality Group (Colony, Country, Radisson)	77,500	350
Choice Hotels International (Clarion, Comfort, Econo, Friendship, Quality, Rodeway, Sleep)	240,000	3,500
Forte (Forte, TraveLodge, Viscount)	50,000	600
Hilton Inns	45,000	175
Holiday Inns Worldwide	350,000	1,750
Hospitality Franchise System (Days, Howard Johnson, Park Inns, Ramada, Super 8)	400,000	3,500
Hospitality International (Downtowner, Master Host, Passport, Red Carpet, Scottish)	25,000	375
ITT Sheraton	55,000	250
Marriott (Courtyard, Fairfield, Marriott, Residence)	40,000	250
Microtel	1,500	350
Promus (Embassy, Hampton, Homewood)	55,000	400

owners. Still another option would be to manage, for a fee, the facilities owned by another. The chain may also franchise its name.

The Franchise.   *Franchising*—selling the right to a name, a product, and a system along with exclusivity for a specific area—is not a new idea nor is it special to the hospitality business, not even to the hotel and restaurant businesses. Tires, speedy printing, diet clinics, and more are all franchised these days. Franchising allows the small-business person (the *franchisee*) to operate as an independent, but provides many of the benefits of the chain. The **franchise** concept serves large, absentee owners and small, owner–operators equally well.

For a fee, the hotel adopts the name and trademarks of the seller (the *franchisor*), and receives services in turn. The franchisor helps with feasibility studies, site selection, financing, design, and planning. Almost all the advantages of the chain are available for the franchise fee—mass purchasing, management consultation, wide advertising, central reservations, and systems design.

The franchise and the parent company are so alike that the guest cannot distinguish between them (see Exhibit 2–7). This works to the advantage (or disadvantage) of both. Only the ownership–management structure is different. The chain (the franchisor) does not own the franchise property, the franchisee does; the chain does not manage the property, the franchisee does. (Under a separate management contract, the franchisee could hire the chain to manage its property.) The success or failure of the franchisee is still determined by individual business acumen, except that now there is the support of the chain.

EXHIBIT 2–8

Franchise fees. Franchisors charge franchisees a variety of fees, which are expressed here in different terms.

Item	Representative Terms	Alternative Terms
Initial fee	The greater of $35,000 or $300 times the number of rooms.	A lesser fixed amount plus a per room fee over, say, the first 100 rooms.
Royalty	4% of room revenue.	3% of gross revenue; *or* a minimum per room per night, say, $1.80.
Advertising fee	1.5% of room revenue.	1% of gross revenue; *or* a minimum per room per night, say, 50¢.
Sign fee	1% of gross revenue plus continuing expenses: local licensing, insurance, repairs.	None, except initial cost of installation plus continuing expenses.
Training fee	0.5% of gross revenue, plus cost of schooling.	None, but franchisee must bear costs of transportation and meals for employees sent to school.
Reservation fee	3% of room revenue, plus $2 for each reservation.	$4 for each reservation booked; *or* a minimum per room per night, say, $1.50.
Computer terminal fee	$400 per month.	None; *or* 0.5% of room revenue.
Preferred guest program	0.5% of room revenue.	May be included with advertising fee.

For this support, the franchisee pays both an initial franchise fee and a continuing charge of so much per room per night. But that's not all. The franchisee also pays a rental for the company sign; a percentage-of-volume fee (or a per room basis) for advertising; a fee for access to the reservation system; and a per reservation fee for each room booked (see Exhibit 2–8). In addition to this, the parent company also charges each time the franchisee buys required logo amenities.

Both the franchisor and the franchisee pursue independent goals. Each develops separately within terms of the franchise contract, although they appear to the public to be one company. Some owner–franchisees control more rooms or hotels than the parent company that issues the franchise. Similarly, owners with multiple properties may have each hotel franchised by a different national company.

Referral.   The growth of the chains and the franchises, with their interlocking **reservation** systems and single identity, put independent operators at a competitive disadvantage. For a long time, the independent hotel has struggled to maintain its freedom. Of late, the question has shifted from if and when to affiliate to how to choose the right organization.

Even the European hotel business, which is comprised chiefly of small, family inns, has begun examining options and affiliations. Almost three-fourths of European hotels are still unaffiliated. This new role for Europe's fiercely independent hoteliers reflects the globalization movement and the appearance of the American franchise overseas.

The **referral** organizations offer a way to fight back with less loss of identity than the franchise. Referrals are cooperatives structured to provide one service only—marketing. Common reservation systems, standardized quality, joint advertising, and a recognizable logo were the original, limited objectives of most referral groups. There is no interlocking management, no group buying, no common financing—nothing but a unified sales effort. But this effort has proved successful enough for some referrals to broaden their activities.

The referral is a means by which the small entrepreneur can compete. It has been especially popular with small motel and motor lodge operators. After a while, they began to seek additional advice and assistance from the referral group. Some organizations expanded beyond their original intent, offering support in financing, technology, and management. They have retained their co-op structure, however, and some referral groups continue to operate as not-for-profit organizations.

A Segmenting Industry

Chapter 2 is really all about choice. Modern times and modern businesses offer a range and a variety of alternatives in every aspect of life. Guests, owners, and managers have taken advantage of this multiplicity by shaping and molding the business of lodging into interesting new patterns.

Segmentation, which started in the 1980s as a "brand stretching" movement, continues changing the face of the hotel business and the business's guests. Segmentation cuts up the identifications of the operation and of the guest into smaller and smaller pieces. It makes the industry vibrant and competitive, but it makes identification of the whole more and more difficult.

Segmentation of the Product Line

Segmentation had its source, as did so many other recent industry changes, in the decades of turmoil that were discussed earlier. As business conditions worsened, hotel chains sought methods of broadening their markets—of finding new customers. Upscale chains moved into more moderately priced operations. Marriott introduced its Fairfield Inns, for example. Hotels in the middle range had the advantage of going both ways. Choice Hotels stepped upward with Clarion properties and downward with Sleep Inns (see Exhibit 2–9).

Other chains shifted horizontally as well as vertically in a desperate attempt to reverse the erosion of occupancy. Holiday Corporation went upscale with its Crown Plaza properties, which meant shifting from traditional highway locations to compete against the Hyatts and Hiltons in urban markets. Likewise, most of the commercial chains stretched into the resort business. Some of these changes put new products onto the market; others merely put new faces onto older properties whose logos were no longer an asset.

If nothing else, the range and rate of new product introduction proved how dynamic the lodging industry is. New products have taken hold and outstripped the expectations of even their most ardent supporters. Chief among these are the economy (budget) properties, the all-suite hotels, and the casino hotels.

The Economy Hotel.   The history of the motor court, the original economy hotel, is a story of **amenity creep.**[6] The first motor courts (1930s) were limited-service, roadside facilities. Kemmons Wilson founded Holiday Inns as a clean, no-frills competitor, but existing motor court operators saw the Inns as amenity creep. Since the process is ongoing, Holiday Inns itself eventually faced the creep of competition. It responded by creeping further.

EXHIBIT 2–9

Segmentation of selected companies.

Company Name	Low End	Midscale	Upscale	Suites
Choice	Comfort Inns EconoLodge Friendship Inns Rodeway Inns Sleep Inn	Quality Inns	Clarion	Comfort Suites Quality Suites Clarion Suites
Holiday Corporation		Holiday Inns	Crowne Plaza	
Hyatt	Hawthorn Inns		Regency Park Hyatts	Hyatt Suites Hawthorn Suites
Marriott	Fairfield Inn	Courtyard Residence Inn	Marriott Hotels & Resorts	Marriott Suites
Promus	Hampton Inns		Harrah's	Embassy Suites Homewood Suites
Nonsegmented Hotels Are Offered for Contrast (do not read this group horizontally)				
	Motel 6 Red Roof Inns	La Quinta Hilton Inns	Hilton Sheraton	Lexington Suites Radisson Suites

Note: Each listing makes reference only to other hotels in the same chain. The chart is not designed for vertical comparisons: Holiday's upscale property is not being compared to Hyatt's upscale property.

Little by little, small rooms grew larger. Direct-dial telephones were installed where there had been none. Free television replaced coin-operated TV sets. Expensive but infrequently used swimming pools were added. Air conditioning, in-room coffee makers, and dual lavatories became standard.

Each upgrade pushed room rates higher. Hotel companies that started in the economy segment (Holiday Inns, Ramada, Days Inns) found themselves in the mid-range. Undoubtedly personal egos played a role in upgrading the chains. So did the introduction of franchising. Franchise fees are based on room revenues. As amenity creep pushes up room revenues, franchise fees to the parent company also increase.

As room rates inch upward, new chains fill the void at the lower end. (Some date the start of this rotation from 1964, when Motel 6 entered the market.) The new companies forgo new amenities but most include accommodations that are by now basic requirements. Telephone, remote television, acceptance of credit cards—even breakfasts and frequent-stay programs—are seen as fundamentals today. How is it being done? There are three techniques: fewer amenities, better value in construction, and attention to operations.

Newer and newer rounds of economy chains employ newer and newer techniques. Rooms smaller than the standard 300 to 325 square feet are being offered now. (Microtel rooms are 178 square feet.) The chains are selecting less costly land, and they are building on smaller sites, 1.5 acres or less for 100 rooms. Nonbasic amenities such as pools, lobbies, meeting space, and restaurants have been eliminated once again. (Providing free continental breakfasts is actually less costly than operating a restaurant that loses money. Besides, budget hotels/motels are almost always located near outlets of national restaurant chains, with one restaurant often serving several competitors.)

The latest round of budget hotel/motels has focused on savings in design and construction. Economy is coming from standardized architectural plans and from using a limited number of qualified builders. Structures have low ceilings and improved insulation. Costs of initial construction have been reduced, and so have later operating expenses.

Some budgets employ less than 20 employees per 100 rooms, almost 60 percent less than the traditional figures suggested in Chapter 1. Eliminating the dining room is just one technique for reducing labor. Hanging the guest room furniture and providing a shower but not a tub increase the productivity of the housekeeping department. Automating telephone calls and assigning extra duties (including laundry operations to the night clerk) improve productivity on that side of the house.

Planned savings like these require new, well-designed facilities. And these were built—and succeeded—during and despite the 1981–91 decline in hotel construction. Because it takes about 250 properties to ensure market identification, some emerging chains acquired old mom-and-pop operations at fire sale prices in order to establish themselves as viable budget operators. Days Inns was one such company.

Hard Budgets.   The economy segment remains the most profitable division of the lodging industry. Like the parent industry, this segment is itself divided. The entire low-end segment is called economy, budget, limited service, or simply the low-end segment—all are euphemisms for ''inexpensive.'' Adding to the jumble of names and affiliations is a secondary classification of the budget segment. There are upscale budgets (La Quinta or Susse Chalet), intermediate budgets (Red Roof Inns or Econo Lodge), and low-end budgets (Motel 6 and E-Z 8 Motels). There is still a fourth category, best called hard budget, which includes capsule rooms and truck-stop facilities.

The hard budget properties are located at airports and at the hundreds of truck stops that dot the interstate system. Airports in Los Angeles and Honolulu offer 75 square feet for rest, showers, and stopovers between flights. Capsule rooms, which are somewhat like railroad sleeping berths, are smaller still, with head room only to sit. Although of larger dimension, self-service hotels—get your own linens and make your own beds—also fall into the hard budget category. Employees clean the rooms only between guests; no other services are provided.

All-Suite Hotels.   As the market of this new genre of hotels has changed, so has its terminology. Today, extended-stay hotels (see Chapter 1), all-suite hotels, and suite hotels are different names for the same type of operation.

Suite hotels were the brainchild of Robert Wooley, who created the first chain, Granada Royale Hometel. The idea was born in Phoenix in 1969, but it grew up in the years of the Texas oil boom. Extended-stay facilities were an important service to the transient oil economy. The idea was innovative—some say the best in a generation—but it borrowed from the traditional: the apartment hotel and the residential hotel.

Holiday Inns acquired Granada Royale Hometel, renamed it, and became the largest all-suite chain in the nation. It tested this segment of the market with two logos. Embassy Suites, which was spun off to Promus (1990) when the Holiday Corporation broke up, was and is a top-of-the-line, all-suite facility. Residence Inn was Holiday's other all-suite logo. In need of cash, Holiday sold the chain to Marriott in 1987.

Aztar

Bally

Caesars

Circus Circus

Hilton

ITT Sheraton

Mirage

MGM Grand

Pratt

Promus

Resorts International

Showboat

Trump

Many new players entered the market as the all-suite became the darling of hotel developers, and many chains jockeyed for position. The lure has been good occupancies and good rates, both made possible by the high value that the customer perceives. So once again, the pattern of proliferation prevailed with new names, new operators, and new products (Exhibit 2–9). Economy, midmarket, and upscale units emerged as they have done within other segments (economy, for example) and for the entire industry. Even the original concept of extended stay (*Home*tel) is no longer a determinant.

Some all-suite brands franchise, some do not, and some only franchise. Several have two or three brands: Clarion, Quality, and Comfort Suites are all by Choice, and Marriott has added Marriott Suites to its Residence Inn. By so doing, Marriott distinguishes between the extended stay, which Marriott defines as five consecutive nights or more, of its Residence Brand, and the transient accommodations of its Marriott Suites.

Extended stay was the original concept, and corporate users the target. The extended-stay hotel was designed for executives and their families who were being relocated. It was for training and educational sessions and for employees on long-term, but not permanent, field assignments. Private entrance, kitchenettes, and separate living–sleeping facilities are the attractive features.

Separate living–sleeping accommodations (Exhibit 3–13) are attractive to personnel interviewers conducting interviews, to women executives, and to others who require private space outside the intimacy of a bedroom. That's why the market turned away from the exclusive extended-stay use. The living space contains a sofa bed and sometimes a second bath. That opened still another market: traveling couples and families seeking economical accommodations.

The kitchenette is to the all-suite as the swimming pool is to the motel. Everyone looks for the amenity, but few use it. So we might get still another variation. That is the most exciting part of the hotel business. New patterns continue to emerge as new market niches are identified and new entrepreneurs shake up the establishment.

The Casino Hotel.   The casino hotel (see Exhibit 2–10) has shaken up the established industry as nothing before in this generation. As legalized gambling (gaming) spreads, this unique type of destination resort shows signs of becoming the most important economic player in the entire industry. That is no surprise when one hears that all of Hilton's 1992 growth and over one-half of its total profits were attributable to its domestic gaming division. That is from just five properties and 11,000 rooms (the chain has about 260 hotels and about 96,500 rooms)!

Gaming has swept across the land, in part because the national psyche has changed. Gaming is viewed now as another type of entertainment rather than as a vice. Moreover, direct gaming revenues from taxes, and indirect revenues to the locality from tourism, have become essential to the economies of several states. The biggest surprise, perhaps, has been the location of these new resort destinations. Biloxi, Mississippi, the heart of the Bible Belt; South Dakota's worn-out mining area, Deadwood City; and the Mashantucket Pequot Nation, Connecticut's Indian Tribe, have become major tourist draws and boom centers.

The operating profile of hotel casinos differs from that of the traditional hotel. Gaming revenues, not room sales, become the major income producer. Therefore, having rooms occupied (potential casino players) is more important than the price for which those rooms sell. To generate casino volume, room rates are lower at casino hotels; single and double occupancy are the same rate—more players; and food and beverage are often viewed as loss leaders—means of attracting traffic into the casino.

About 30 percent of the states now license casinos. That number is certain to rise throughout the balance of the century as the hotel casino takes its place in a segmented industry.

Other Hotel Segments.   The dynamic nature of the hotel business—out with the old and in with the new—has kept it viable and changing. New segments and new adaptations of older ideas are taking shape continuously.

Some hotels have joined up with elderhostel, a program designed to fill vacant dormitory beds during the summers. In this program, retired persons stay in hotels near a campus, where they choose from a variety of courses offered by distinguished professors.

On the other side of the age spectrum is Camp Hyatt, a children's camp operating within the Hyatt hotels. The camp caters to the children while the parents are at work or play. Hyatt even offers a frequent-stay program for the kids.

Because of the manner in which they ring the city, suburban hotels have been dubbed *collar* hotels. These hotels have followed industry from the high-rent, downtown districts to the open spaces of the suburbs. Beltway roads, which collar the city, have made the transition possible. Suburban hotels are narrowly segmented with few opportunities to add to the customer pool other than from the industries that they followed to the suburbs.

The Conference Center.   **Conference centers** are specialized "hotels" that cater to meetings, training sessions, and conferences of all types. Unlike the typical convention hotels, conference centers usually take no transient guests. Food service is also restricted to the in-house groups. Catering to this special market, conference centers provide a complete line of audiovisual materials, special seminar rooms and theaters, closed-circuit television with interactive teleconferencing, and simultaneous translation capabilities.

There are other operational differences that distinguish the conference center from the hotel. Double occupancy may be higher even among guests who are senior executives because the design encourages a greater familiarity, which is often a goal of the conference. The bundled price (rooms, food, and beverage quoted as one figure)—sometimes called a *corporate meeting package* (CMP)—is standard at most conference centers. Obviously, it is a modern version of the American plan because conference centers are the offspring of a marriage between the convention hotel and the old resort of tradition. Despite that lineage, conference hotels warrant a place in the emerging patterns.

Segmentation of the Customer

The market to which a hotel appeals and the guest (the customer) who is attracted to that particular property are interdependent. The guest's very presence at a given hotel simultaneously suggests the market segment of the hotel and the profile of the customer.

The Guest Profile.   Different guests have different needs and different expectations from their stay. Indeed, the same person presents a different profile when traveling for different reasons: business versus pleasure, expense-account versus family travel, and so on. Looking at the guest under various circumstances enables the industry to build and manage for specific, market-directed segments.

Guest profiles have been developed by trade associations, governmental agencies, rating firms, purveyors, external consultants, magazines, and the hotel companies themselves.[7] The typical study focuses on demographic profiles. Age, income and job, gender, residence, education, and the number of travelers in the party are all determinable with a good degree of accuracy. Knowing the guests is the starting point for servicing them.

Consider the economy market. Price-sensitive buyers form the core of the budget customers. Who are they? Governmental employees on a fixed per diem (per day) allowance make up one segment. Retirees, whose time is more flexible than their budgets, will go to the less convenient and less costly locations that economy properties require. International tourists, who have different expectations than domestic tourists; small-business persons sensitive to travel costs; and family vacationers help round out this segment.

Guest profiles tell us who the guests are and what they do after arrival. Business guests are mostly men;[8] tourists are mostly couples. Almost everyone watches TV from the bed. Some 20 percent actually rearrange the furniture! Business travelers use the telephone, the shower, and the TV movie more often than tourist travelers do. Tourists hold the edge on pool and recreational use. The leisure segment tends to be 5 to 10 years older than the business group. They make reservations less often and pay less for their room than the business traveler.

Globalization requires special attention to the profile of the international guest. Although foreign travelers are less important to the U.S. market (about 15 percent) than to the worldwide market (about 50 percent), they are still big business. International guests stay longer than domestic guests. Their typical six-day visit is more than half again as long as the usual domestic guest's stay. International visitors to the United States help the U.S. balance of trade, representing $20 billion in export equivalents.

Japanese visitors to Hawaii, for example, spend three times that of the U.S. tourist to Hawaii. Japanese visitors almost always tour in groups, even when they are honeymooning. Office groups (women), ski groups (men), business groups (99 percent male), and silver groups (retired couples) are the profiles of the Japanese traveler.

Some patterns take their lead from profiles less measurable than demographics. Developers differentiate between what have been called upstairs/downstairs buyers. Upstairs buyers are more oriented toward the room. These guests want large sleeping and bathing facilities and comfortable work space. For this, they will sacrifice theme restaurants, bars, banquet facilities, and exercise rooms. Not so the downstairs guests, who want public space above all else.

Businesswomen present still another profile pattern. They are the fastest-growing segment of the commercial hotel market, numbering about one-third of all business travelers. The latter description is a demographic measure. How best to please that market is uncertain. That's a psychographic factor. Psychographic profiles detail personality traits, desires, and inner motivations. Every demographic or psychographic profile is necessarily flawed because no individual guest is ever 100 percent of the composite study. Besides, the guest who stays at the hotel—the one whose profile the industry develops—is often not the person who bought the room initially.

Nonguest Buyers.   Vast numbers of hotel rooms are being sold to buyers who act as intermediaries for the actual occupants. Section II, which deals with the reservation mechanics, sharpens the distinction for the reader; so does Chapter 9, which discusses room rates.

Room rates are one focus of the pattern. Groups like the American Automobile Association and the American Association of Retired Persons have negotiated special member rates with many hotel chains. So widespread is the practice that almost every hotel entertains the request for discount, whether negotiated or not, in order to stay competitive.

Special travel clubs—Amoco Traveler and Encore Travel Club are among the best known—have arranged similar discounts for their members. The clubs specialize in second-night-free deals.

Another side of the reservation picture paints the third party as a buyer, not merely a rate negotiator. Business travel arrangements are often made by company travel desks, which may or may not be part of the traveler's business. Either way, paring travel costs is the mission of these tough negotiators. The range of third-party buyers is broadened further by the list that was detailed earlier in this chapter: Group tours, incentive firms, and wholesalers are making huge space commitments, but someone else actually uses the room.

Similarly, travel agents commit the hotel to room bookings—but the travel agents don't come; their clients do. Franchisees rely heavily on the franchise reservation system, but the system is just another third party, which may not be owned even by the franchisor! In every instance, the guest who actually arrives is different from the third party who made the reservation.

Airlines and auto-rental companies are also in the business of booking reservations. New companies are springing up locally, nationally, and internationally to reserve, buy, and resell hotel rooms. Each of these interposes a third party between the guest and the hotel. Allied with the broader picture of third-party buyers are the numerous frequent-guest programs.

Frequent-Guest Programs.   No one is really certain whether or not frequent-guest (-flyer) programs (FGP) actually increase market share. It is a difficult determination to make when everyone is using the technique. The programs are popular with (and costly to) Hyatt, Westin, and Hilton on the high end and Best Western, Super 8 Motels, and Red Roof Inns on the low end. In between are Holiday Inn's *Priority Club* and Best Western's *Gold Crown Club.*[9]

FGPs are costly to administer (their cost is estimated at $10 per room per night), and they saddle the chain with unused travel-credit liabilities. They add to the garble of names that segmentation has already muddled (Hilton's *HHonors Club,* Hyatt's *Gold Passport,* and Marriott's *Honored Guest Award*).[10] FGPs exacerbate the already sensitive balance that exists between franchisor and franchisee. But they have their positive aspects, too.

Guest profiles are one positive aspect. Vast amounts of information can be gathered about guests who must report in and signal their travel patterns in order to get posted for the prizes. Frequent-guest prizes are what entice guest loyalty, and it is the direct-mail contact to interested participants that entices the chains into the program. Having the demographic and preferential profiles of their guests is the trade-off to the hotels. Several boast membership rosters of more than 1 million names.

Gifts range from the simple to the expensive. Many are services that are available even to nonmembers under certain circumstances. Among them are check cashing, room upgrade, daily newspaper, late check-out, express check-in and check-out, toll-free reservation number, and guaranteed rates. Other gifts are specials: room discounts, discounts with travel partners such as airlines, auto-rental companies, or local tourist companies; health club membership; and free accommodations in exotic destinations. Tie-ins with credit-card companies often mean double or triple points earned.

Some hotels give travel-related awards like those just discussed. Others, sensing the guest's travel fatigue, offer premiums instead. U.S. savings bonds, upscale gifts from special catalogs, and membership in national organizations have all been tried. Travelers really get motivated to rack up points when a Jaguar is on the gift list! Below the surface is an ethical issue. Should the hotel issue bonds, gifts, and awards to the guest when the room rate is paid by a third party, the traveler's company?

FGPs can be seen as win–win situations. Guests win with prizes and discounts. Hotels win with improved marketing capability. FGPs can also be seen as win–lose propositions, just another form of rate cutting. Furthermore, they cause problems with the corporations that pay the bills. In spite of these problems, no one is daring enough to close a program. The parallel to the plight of the airlines' frequent-flier programs is apparent, and the solution for both is elusive.

Amenities.   Some might see the whole frequent-guest program as just another amenity. **Amenities** are extra products or services that add to guest comfort or convenience. Over time, these products or services creep from amenities to basic expectations. Fundamental accommodations like television and telephone were once sought-after amenities. The corridor ice machine may be viewed as an amenity by management, but the guest sees it as basic equipment.

Nonsmoking rooms are a good example of amenity creep. What was a ''special'' just a brief time ago has become a basic service of every hotel chain, and the guest's preferred amenity in most. Nonsmoking rooms have graduated to nonsmoking floors—even to entire hotels.

Until very recently, amenities meant a handful of mismatched toiletries that management viewed as basic necessities. Plastic shower caps, shoeshine cloths, facial tissues, and bottle openers were scattered about the room. Now amenities are tailored, color-coordinated, professionally packaged takeaways. They are marketing tools intended to make the guest feel good about the price–value relationship.

Amenities are being upgraded, supplemented, and presented in a variety of ways. The typical package includes hand, bath, and deodorant soap, with or without fragrance; toothbrush and toothpaste with mouthwash; shampoo and conditioner; and hand and body lotions. Of course, there are the old standbys—sewing kits, shower caps, shoehorns, and shoeshine cloths. Other items—suntan lotion or towelettes, cotton balls or swabs, combs, aspirin, and petroleum jelly—are included where cost is not a factor.

During the past decade, amenity creep pushed the cost of toiletries to as high as $5 to $6 per room per night. Then, cost-conscious hoteliers went to work. Cutting in-room amenities in half saved nearly $750 per room per year! Most every hotel still makes these extras available—but on request, not as bathroom giveaways. Even the biggies, like the Waldorf-Astoria, have eliminated shoehorns and sewing kits.

The shift downward in toiletries carried over to the contents of in-room bars. After expensive candies, nuts, and drinks (including nonalcoholic beverages) were ignored by cost-conscious travelers, hotels replaced them with popular-priced brands.

Except at the five-star properties, opulent bathroom amenities have lost favor with both the operator and the customer. In their place are more practical accoutrements, ranging from expensive electronic gadgets to the return of in-room coffee makers.

The New Amenities.   High-tech services are the latest amenity. Special bedside panels are a good example of this shift toward electronics. From here, the guest controls lighting and temperature, radio and television, electric curtains, and even the do-not-disturb signal on the entrance door. Among the electronic gadgets that hotels, especially business-oriented hotels, are providing are in-room faxes, with dual lines so simultaneous telephone usage is possible; in-room computers; electronic check-in and check-out; in-room films on call at any hour; and private in-room telephone voice mail.

Hyatt began an intensive advertising campaign after studying its guest profile. Now, its business travelers are provided those very items just mentioned: in-room faxes, phone access without charge, printers and copiers, an express breakfast, and a workstation.

Each hotel has its own version of an amenity. One offers a pet for company overnight; another a free shoeshine; a third, a jogging map. Both economy and all-suite chains have added microfridges, a combination of refrigerator, freezer, and microwave oven. Chapter 3 discusses amenities further as part of its section on bathrooms.

A New Look at an Old Amenity.   Food service is the oldest amenity of innkeeping. Yet hotel dining rooms are not favored by the traveling public today, and for certain they are not profitable for the host hotel. Nevertheless, industry watchers were surprised when first the motels and economy hotels and then the all-suites eliminated restaurants. Many felt it to be a poor business decision. After all, travelers had to eat. The decision proved to be just the opposite, because alternatives were offered.

All-suite hotels provided breakfast, the meal most travelers eat in the hotel. And all hotels began locating near free-standing restaurants.

Hotels entered into partnerships, some formal and some informal, with independent restaurants. (Although not successful, the idea was first tested by Howard Johnson in the 1950s!) Working with neighboring facilities to accommodate their guests, even with room service in some cases, hotels were able to close their non-profitable food outlets and improve their earnings picture. The next move, one that is going on right now, was to invite these independent restaurants into the hotel building. Larger hotels have done that. Hamburger, chicken, and pizza franchises have opened in the lobbies—usually with street access also—of some very major hotels. Not only do they offer the type of food service that today's traveler prefers, but they pay rent as well!

Even hoteliers who have not given up their dining facilities have borrowed a page from the successful restauranteurs. Pizza and other fast foods are being offered by the hotels. Some are using catchy new names, while others are holding onto corporate logos.

Summary

The modern hotel industry, the topic of this chapter, builds on the characteristics of the traditional hotel industry, the topic of Chapter 1. Market sensitivity is the major difference between the old and the new. As traveling consumers become a more diverse group and more identifiable as specific market targets, the industry responds in kind. It offers each group of users—but not to the exclusion of all others—a particular configuration, segmenting itself into a variety of products to meet the market's profile. The range of special accommodations is overwhelming: megaresorts and all-suites; convention hotels and tour properties; conference centers and casino hotels. There are so many new amenities being offered that even major segments (economy hotels, for example) have segmented into their own subdivisions (hard budgets).

Marketing emphasis is but one of lodging's modern patterns. Global dependence, tax legislation, franchising, and new room-buying intermediaries, among others, have introduced exciting changes into the lodging industry. Novel means of ownership such as timesharing, and new methods of operating such as the use of management companies, have emerged in response to the continual need for change and adaptation.

As one would expect, these shifts in pattern have wrought changes in hotel organizations, hotel designs, and front office responsibilities. Chapter 3 examines the contemporary structure of the hotel industry and concludes the text's introductory section.

Queries and Problems

1. Identify the advantages and disadvantages to the personal career of a student who takes a job after graduation with a Hilton Inns franchise, and passes up an offer from Hilton Hotels, the parent company.

2. The discussion on amenities (see pages 50–51) suggests that savings in amenities of up to $750 per room per year are possible. Show the mathematics that explain such a figure.

3. Someone once said, "If you try to be all things to every guest, you'll likely end up as every guest's second choice." Is that an accurate statement? Why or why not?

4. Why would the text say that the destination hotel is the "new kid on the block of lodging"? Explain, using historical reference.

5. A traveler driving along Interstate 36 stops at two different hotels on successive evenings. Explain, and differentiate between, the signs posted by the front desk in terms of the text discussion about ownership, management, franchising, and joint ventures.

> Hotel A: This Hampton Inn is owned by Jerome J. Vallen and Sons, Inc., under license from Promus. Richfield Hotel Management.

> Hotel B: This Hampton Inn is owned by Promus. Jerome J. Vallen, General Manager.

6. Obtain a copy of a management contract from a local hotel, or review a book in the library on hotel management contracts. Discuss three terms (for example, life of the contract, payment, maintenance of the property, or investment by the management company) that intrigue you.

Notes

1. *Breakage:* The gain that accrues to the hotel or tour operator when meals or other services included in a package price are not used by the guest.
2. Convention delegates are good business, spending an average of $638 each event, approximately 60 percent of which goes to the hotel. *Meeting News,* February 1994, p. 5, quoting a June 1993 International Association of Convention and Visitor Bureaus study.
3. *Rack rate:* The standard amount set and quoted by the hotel as its room charge—not a discounted rate.
4. The Mauna Kea Beach Hotel on Hawaii's Big Island was built in the 1960s for approximately $100,000 per room and sold some 25 years later for approximately $1 million per room!
5. *Shoulder:* The business period between peak volume and the lowest valley of the off season.
6. *Amenity creep:* The phenomenon in guest perception that makes special services become standard expectations over time.
7. One chain recently identified its typical guest as a 44-year-old male with a median income of $51,600. This typical guest, who travels by air and switches to an automobile at the destination, spends 4.9 room-nights per month in hotels. This definition fits most of the hotel industry's business travelers (see note 8).
8. Businessmen, age 35–49, with an average household income of approximately $54,000, account for nearly two-thirds of these room-nights. They usually travel alone and almost always make reservations. *Lodging Industry Profile* (New York: American Hotel & Motel Association).
9. These are registered trademarks.
10. Ibid.

CHAPTER 3

The Structure of the Hotel Industry

Chapter Outline

Hotel organizations are structured—put together—in many different ways. That's because the organizational structure is a method of arranging the work force to carry out the goals and functions of a particular company. And what a variety of goals, functions, and companies! Certainly, Chapters 1 and 2 made clear the immense range of operations, segments, markets, and locations that structure the numerous organizations under the single umbrella of the lodging industry.

Each organization takes final form from the patterns that make up the hotel industry. That's why the 1,000-room, chain-operated, convention hotel is no more like the mom-and-pop highway motel than is a seasonal, skiing resort like a casino hotel. And all these differ again from the conference center, the economy property, or the commercial hotel whose towers house residential guests.

Just as each hotel type calls for a different organizational structure, each calls for a different building structure, too. The ski lodge will likely have individual cottages or condos hidden in the woods. The resort may be a series of low-rise outbuildings surrounding the swimming pool. How different are these structure from the urban commercial giant, squeezed by high land costs, that adopts a high-rise configuration for its building design.

Differences notwithstanding, both the organizational structure and the building structure adhere to similar blueprints. Although differences distinguish the properties' lines, the basics are the same: the staff structured to serve the guest; and the guest room—the hotel's major product line—structured to accommodate the guest.

The Organizational Structure

Hotels employ a vast number of persons with a variety of skills. Hotels have plumbers and accountants, bartenders and cooks, grounds managers and water purification experts, telecommunication specialists and computer troubleshooters. The larger the hotel, the more specialized the tasks. Indeed, large hotels have bigger resident populations and provide more services than do many small towns.

Hotel organizations follow the pattern of other business or social institutions. They break up the work force into separate *departments,* with each department entrusted with a share of the duties and services. Modern management techniques try to minimize the differences among the various departments because any one of them can destroy the best efforts of all the others. Coordinating the whole, unifying the different specialties, and directing their joint efforts is the job of the general manager.

The General Manager

Management titles vary from hotel to hotel, just as their organizations do. The large hotel chains use titles at the corporate level that are similar to other American businesses: CEO (chief executive officer), CFO (chief financial officer), and COO (chief operating officer).

General manager (GM, or **The GM**) is the favored title at the unit level—that is, for the individual hotel. This person is responsible for everything that happens in the hotel: for all the departments (see Exhibit 3–1) and for the general profitability of the whole works!

If the general manager is also part of the corporation that owns the hotel, the title might be *president* (of the corporation) and *general manager* (of the hotel), or *vice president and general manager.* The manager who sits on the board of directors of the corporation could be *director and general manager,* or even *managing director,* but neither one is used often. Managing director has a European flavor (*directeur* is French for manager), so that term may be used as much for ambience as for organizational clarity. If the manager and family own the hotel, *owner–manager* is used. Standing alone, *general manager* implies no ownership affiliation. Such an individual is then the ownership's most responsible employee.

When several properties of the same chain are located in one city and all are supervised by one person, the GM term might be assigned to that person rather than to the executives of the individual hotels. Chains use other titles as appropriate: *area vice president for operations; regional director of marketing;* and *food and beverage manager, eastern division.*

Exhibit 3–1

Shown is an organizational chart. The rooms manager (resident manager, hotel manager, or house manager) is to the lodging segment of the hotel as the food and beverage manager is to the food service segment.

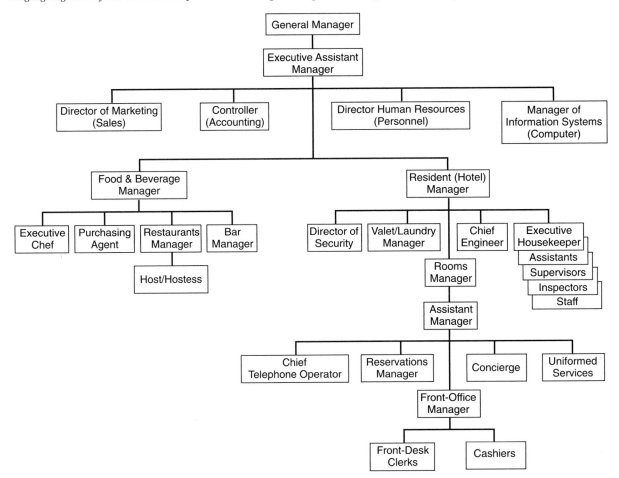

Whatever the specific title, the top executive of the hotel reports to ownership directly or through other divisional executives. Ownership vests its authority in that top executive and holds that person responsible for all that happens.

Hotel organizations support the GM with specialized departments, and sometimes with an assistant, the *executive assistant manager.* Like the general manager, the executive assistant has complete jurisdiction over the entire house. That distinguishes the executive assistant position from that of the *assistant manager* (Exhibit 3–1), which is a rooms department position only.

Hotels never close, and that places great demand on the energy and time of all hotel executives, but especially on the GM. Night, weekend, and holiday periods are covered in some hotels by rotating the entire management staff into a position called *executive on duty.* Every department head (Exhibit 3–1) takes a turn. Thus, the reservoir of management talent is deepened and the experience of the individual manager is broadened.

The Support Departments.   The issues with which hotels contend multiply almost exponentially, it seems. Each new matter requires more knowledge and necessitates more expertise. Support staffs have grown apace with the issues: legal issues, employment issues, environmental issues, tax issues, zoning issues, and on without end. The support departments furnish the knowledge and expertise to the management team and to the operating departments. On occasion, support departments even make guest contact, as when accounting communicates with a guest about an overdue bill or engineering dispatches a TV repairperson to the guest room.

Marketing, human resources, purchasing, legal, and management information systems are part of a long list of support departments. The functions of some of these departments cross into the interests of the operating departments. For example, the rooms manager looks to human resources for help in filling job vacancies; to sales for help in filling empty rooms; and to accounting for help in credit-card control and settlement. Other support departments are not quite as pervasive, but every department looks for assistance from every other department at one time or another.

Food and Beverage Department.   Service made directly to the guest is the responsibility of two major departments. The rooms department, which is the thrust of this text, will be discussed in detail. Food and beverage is the other major operating department.

This department is headed by a *food and beverage manager* (Exhibit 3–1) and divided into several subdivisions. Food preparation, which is the responsibility of the chef, is one of these. Food service falls under the jurisdiction of the restaurants manager (sometimes called the maitre d'hotel). The bar manager heads another area of this division, and the food and beverage purchasing agent still another.

Each of these department heads has one or more assistants who are responsible for certain areas of operation. The chef has a *sous* (under) chef and a steward (sanitation). Subordinate to the **maitre d'** are hosts and hostesses, who supervise the dining rooms. Bars are managed by head bartenders. So the organization grows, becoming larger and larger as lower organizational levels are added. At the bottom rung, doing the essential work, is the pot washer in the kitchen, the dining room attendant, the banquet porter, the kitchen runner, and the refuse handler.

The Hotel Manager

The *hotel manager* is the front-of-the-house counterpart of the food and beverage manager. All operating departments, except those dealing with food and beverage, report to the hotel manager. *Resident manager, hotel manager,* or *house manager* are the names most often used to designate this position. The jurisdiction may range from two to three departments in a medium-size hotel to a half-dozen and more in a large property.

Exhibit 3–1 outlines the divisions of the front of the house and positions the hotel manager in relation to the balance of the hotel organization. Every department that deals with the guest falls within the hotel manager's purview. The job is one of coordination—presenting the services of several different departments as those of one company.

Housekeeping.   The manager of the housekeeping department, who is called the *housekeeper* or *executive housekeeper,* is one of several department heads reporting to the resident (or hotel) manager. In some instances, the housekeeper reports directly to the general manager. This might happen in a small hotel without a house manager, when the GM wants to emphasize housekeeping, or when additional duties are given to the housekeeper—responsibility for the laundry, for example. It is this kind of variation that accounts for the differences among hotels even though there is a standard organization that everyone follows. All hotels have housekeepers.

The housekeeping department has the largest number of employees.[1] It is charged with the general cleanliness of guest rooms, corridors, and other public space. Housekeeping in the food and beverage department is not normally the responsibility of the housekeeping department—that is assigned to the steward.

Working with the housekeeper (Exhibit 3–1) are assistant housekeepers, floor supervisors, inspectors, and, at the end of the chain of command, guest-room attendants. Special attendants may be assigned to public washrooms, parlors, and bathhouses. Housepersons are available to do the heavier work and to move equipment.

Coordination between the front office and the housekeeper is essential. Hundreds of persons arrive at and depart daily from a large hotel. Rooms must be serviced quickly to placate waiting guests. Information on the status of rooms must be furnished accurately and immediately to the room clerks, who use the reports to make new room assignments.

The housekeeping department handles lost-and-found items, visits the sick, maintains linen storage and inventory, makes linen repairs, and issues uniforms to other departments. It handles all housekeeping assignments from dry-cleaning draperies, to disinfecting after animals have been in residence, to the cleanup that follows a fire.

Uniformed Services. The ranks of the service department—or uniformed services or bell department—are on the wane. At one time, this department included baggage porters, transportation clerks, and elevator operators for both guest and service cars. Now, it is composed chiefly of bellpersons and door attendants, and even these are decreasing in number.

There are several reasons for this decline. Changing travel habits and licensing requirements have eliminated the service department's role in travel arrangements. Secondly, guests travel lighter today than they did a generation ago. Suitcases are built lighter (and many have wheels), and shorter stays mean less clothing. Self-service is expected in many facets of American life, so many guests carry their own luggage.

The decline in the number of uniformed employees has another explanation: management cost-cutting. Today, everyone must be paid minimum wage, whereas tips alone constituted the salary of an earlier era. Reducing the staff cuts labor costs and with them fringe benefits, which add as much as one-third more to direct labor costs. So the hotel that services the entrance door around the clock is rare, and the motel without bell service is the norm.

The service department makes first contact with the arriving guest through the attendant at the door, sometimes as early as the van driver, who is also in the service crew. Parking, garaging, and auto service are offered at this time, although more and more urban hotels lease their garages on concession. (This is still another reason for a smaller department.)

Handling baggage for arriving and departing guests, including groups, is the major function of the service department. Laundry and valet service, ice, and transportation were once part of the department's duties, but they are less so today. Once roomed, few guests use bell service. Loudspeakers, telephones, and computer systems have even preempted the paging and message-service roles of the department.

In small hotels, bellpersons handle room service and lobby cleaning along with their other duties.

Not surprisingly, the modern title of the manager of the service department is *manager of services,* sometimes *superintendent of services.* These are not as romantic as the more traditional terms **bell captain** or, as a shortened form, *captain.* Recently, but still tentatively, responsibility for the department has been shifted to the concierge.

Telephone.   Modern telephone equipment has reduced the size of this department, just as automatic elevator equipment has reduced the size of the service department. Outgoing local and long-distance calls are handled by automatic, direct-dial equipment. Calls between guest rooms or from guest rooms to departments such as room service no longer require an operator. Still, the number of telephones in a large hotel often exceeds the number found in small cities throughout the United States.

Supervising this department is the head operator or *chief operator,* sometimes called the telephone supervisor. Additional crew might include message operators, shift supervisors, and toll (long-distance) operators. Automatic equipment has reduced the billing and charge duties of this department as well as the mechanical duties that it once performed. In no other area of the hotel has the introduction of costly and complex computer equipment been so rapid and so complete, and worked so well.

The telephone department is responsible for all telephone calls and message service, including **morning wakeup calls** (also automated). Incoming calls must be handled correctly and pleasantly, for often the caller's sole contact with the hotel is the disembodied voice of the operator. With the rapid introduction of fax service and the need for 24-hour coverage, some hotels are assigning fax locations to the telephone department.

Other Departments.   Security is another of the resident (or hotel) manager's responsibilities. It may be one person walking night fire watch in a small hotel or a full-time police force, including plainclothes officers, in large properties. As crimes against persons and property increase, larger and better-trained security forces appear. The security department is charged with the protection of the guest and the employee. It is responsible for the property of both the hotel and the guest. Safety, including fire control and prevention, is the department's major responsibility. Casino hotels have additional security needs.

Security helps the credit manager with lockouts and luggage liens. It also handles drunks and prostitutes, makes security reports on accidents, and carries out investigations, including deaths and suicides, when necessary. Uniformed security serves first as a deterrent, then as a restraint, and only rarely as a police force.

The swimming pool is another responsibility of the hotel manager, but pool sanitation is left to the engineering department. Lifeguards and pool attendants, who furnish towels, rafts, and lounge chairs, make up this department. There may be a pool manager in some of the larger operations.

The hotel manager handles day-to-day relationships between the hotel and its many tenants: stores, shops, offices, business centers (public stenographer), house physician, and airline ticket desks. Negotiating the lease contracts and rental arrangements by which these relationships are established is part of the hotel manager's wide range of responsibilities.

The Structure of the Front Office

What Is the Front Office?

Physically, the **front office** is an easily identifiable area of the lobby. Functionally, it is much less so despite constant reference to it as the "hub" and the "heart" of the hotel. The overuse of such terms should not detract from the real importance of the front office. It is in fact the nerve center of guest activity. Through it flow communications with every other department; from it emanate instructions for the service of the guest; to it come charges for final billing and settlement.

Organizational interdependence is not the only reason for the preeminent position of the front office. It is equally a matter of economics. Room sales produce over half the total revenue of the average hotel. For budget hotels, they produce all the revenue. And for others, much of the revenue that comes from food and beverage originates in meetings and convention groups, whose search for site selections begins with rooms. More revenue (about 66 percent) is derived from room sales than from the total of food, beverage, and telephone.[2] Furthermore, rooms are more profitable than these departments. Every dollar of room sales produces approximately 70 cents in departmental profit. Food and beverage combined average out to less than 20 cents departmental profit per dollar sale.

Hotel guests relate with the front office, and this adds to its importance. Guests who rarely see their housekeepers, who never see the cook, who deal with sales only on occasion, know the hotel by its desk. They are received at the desk and they depart from the desk. It is toward the desk that guests direct complaints and from the desk that they expect remedies. Guest identification, as much as profit or interdepartmental dependence, accounts for management's overriding concern with the front office.

Better to define the front office as a bundle of duties and guest services rather than as a fixed area located behind the lobby desk. Some divisions of the front office—reservations, for example—can be located elsewhere without affecting their membership in the front-office structure. Computerization's instant communication has reduced the need for all front-office segments to be within physical hailing distance of one another.

Someone once said that the front office was so named because it was close to the front door. Simple enough, but many hotels are substituting the term **guest-service area** in an effort to better define the role of the front office. By extension, the front-office manager becomes the guest-service manager. This adds to the confusion of titles and responsibilities.

Managing Rooms and the Front Office.   How the front desk is managed and staffed depends upon the hotel's pattern, its market segment, and its size. The organizational structure of a full-service hotel, for example, requires a very complete staff. Although few hotels have as complete an organizational structure as the full-service house, it serves as a model.

Full-service operations have three management positions on the hotel side (as differentiated from food and beverage or the support departments). The first of these positions, hotel manager (house manager, or resident manager) has already been discussed. Second is the *rooms division manager,* and then the *front-officer manager.* The front-office manager reports upward to the rooms division manager, who reports upward to the hotel manager, and thence to the general manager (Exhibit 3–1).

When the organization is so complete, job responsibilities grow narrower down the organization's line. At the top, the hotel manager has responsibility for all operational functions except food and beverage. Included are departments that have not been discussed such as maintenance and engineering, or laundry and valet. The hotel manager assigns responsibility for just the room functions to the rooms manager. That includes reservations, bell services, telephone, and the front office. The front-office manager takes control of the front office—clerks, mail and messages, guest information, credit, and so on. Some properties add yet another management level, the front desk. The front-desk manager is a supervisor usually responsible for a single shift (see Exhibit 3–2).

Most hotels do not need three or four management positions, so the responsibilities of these positions may be handled by fewer people. This chapter has followed reality by describing some of the rooms manager's duties under the headings of the hotel manager and the front-office manager. Remember: Many hotels just have one management level, or even none at all, between the employee on the desk and the general manager.

Whatever the manager's title, front-desk procedures require attention to detail. One study of the front-office manager indicated that performance and production are as important to success as is skill in dealing with people. The fact is that performance and dealing with people are both the same at the front desk, since handling details is the best means of attending to customer and employee needs.

Front-Office Clerks.   The front-office clerk is still another organizational level. Many different titles have been used for this position in an attempt to describe the job and to fairly represent the importance of the post. One hears room clerk—a once-popular term; receptionist—favored outside the United States; front-office agent; guest-service agent; front-desk clerk; and other similar combinations.

Titles aside, the front-office clerk has a host of duties that concentrate in four functions: room sales, guest relations, records, and coordination (see Exhibit 3–3). The front-office clerk is part salesperson, part psychologist, and part bookkeeper. Moreover, as first-line employees, front-office agents must carry out the policies that are established.

If an increase in room rates is mandated, it is the front-desk clerk who must sell up to a price-conscious guest. It is the front-desk clerk who adjusts minor problems and buffers management from the first blasts of major complaints. It is the front-desk clerk who brings together the guest's reservation, the housekeeper's room availability, and the proper record of the guest's account.

A new position, which is an extension of the front-office clerk, is appearing on the scene. The job has not yet been named, and it may disappear before it ever gets a title. With the introduction of computer-terminal registration, guests are able to bypass the front office and room[3] themselves. To encourage reluctant guests to give self-service a try, hotels have moved a rooms agent to the front side (the lobby side)

Exhibit 3–2

This is a position description of the front-desk or front-office manager. An industrywide restructuring during the early 1990s eliminated this position from some organizations.

Position Description: FRONT DESK MANAGER

RESPONSIBILITIES: The main responsibilities of the Front Desk Manager fall into the 12 categories described below:

1. FRONT DESK OPERATIONS—Front Desk Managers have the ability to perform all Front Desk duties in accordance with Corporate and Local SOP's [Standard Operating Procedures], supervise and maintain a smooth running shift, and develop an effective team.

2. BUDGET ADMINISTRATION—Front Desk Managers have the ability to read and comprehend budget worksheets, operating statements, and other financial reports, and take responsibility for adhering to, if not exceeding, budget commitments in the areas of sales, average room rate, occupancy, manhours, and wages.

3. PERSONNEL ADMINISTRATION—Front Desk Managers interview, orient, and train new employees; coach, counsel, and objectively evaluate all employees; and prepare payrolls and employee schedules. Front Desk Managers have a knowledge of benefit programs and the policies pertaining to AA, EEO, Guarantee of Fair Treatment, and termination.

4. GUEST RELATIONS—Front Desk Managers assist in the development, implementation and maintenance of effective guest relations and handle guest problems and complaints in such a way as to serve as role models for all employees.

5. TRAINING—Front Desk Managers identify employee training needs and then conduct or monitor appropriate training or cross-training programs. They also develop hourly and supervisory personnel and assist Management Trainees with their training programs.

6. COMMUNICATIONS—Front Desk Managers must be able to write effectively, speak clearly and concisely, listen attentively, maintain communication with all departments of the hotel, conduct effective (productive and informative) meetings, and keep the Front Desk staff informed of pertinent information.

7. LOSS/ACCIDENT PREVENTION—Front Desk Managers maintain a working knowledge of emergency procedures and loss prevention policies and procedures. They also must be able to effectively investigate, report, and follow-up on employee and guest accidents and be aware of the impact of these accidents on the Profit and Loss Statement. In addition, the Front Desk Manager must ensure participation of Front Desk personnel in all property safety awareness programs.

8. PLANNING AND ORGANIZING—Front Desk Managers utilize goal setting tools to achieve long and short range objectives and time management skills to meet job requirements and responsibilities. They schedule Front Desk personnel, taking into consideration both guest satisfaction and budget constraints, and effectively delegate departmental responsibilities.

9. LEGAL—Front Desk Managers must be knowledgeable of Corporate, Federal, State, and Local Regulations pertaining to the operation of the hotel.

10. INTERDEPARTMENTAL RESPONSIBILITIES—Front Desk Managers are knowledgeable about all departments within the hotel and how each affects the Front Desk operation in order to develop and maintain a productive relationship with all departments of the hotel. In addition, Front Desk Managers understand the functions of the Executive Committee.

11. TECHNICAL KNOWLEDGE—Front Desk Managers possess a working knowledge of all Front Office areas so that they can effectively supervise them in the absence of the Front Office Manager (or Assistant Front Office Manager). They know how to operate all Front Office equipment and how to report malfunctions should they occur. Front Desk Managers conduct quality control audits, enforce credit policies and procedures, and monitor selling procedures. Also, Front Desk Managers know the procedures and responsibilities of the Night Audit staff.

12. PERSONAL DEVELOPMENT—Front Desk Managers are responsible for consistently making progress on a ''Personal Development Plan'' which they establish for themselves.

Courtesy: Marriott Corporation.

EXHIBIT 3–3

This is a typical job description for a front-office clerk. Publications such as the Occupational Outlook Handbook, *the* Career Information Center, *and the* Professional Career Sourcebook *are standard career references and include many job descriptions.*

Job Title: Hotel Clerk

The hotel is personified by its clerks. The clerks receive the guests, service them throughout their stay, and handle their departures with efficiency and aplomb.

Acts as host(ess) and receptionist.

Accepts reservations.

Quotes rates and sells rooms.

Keeps records of vacant and occupied rooms.

Registers arrivals and assigns them rooms.

Ascertains creditworthiness of hotel guests.

Controls and issues keys.

Coordinates activities of both the bell service department and the housekeeping department.

Helps protect the guest's person, and the guest's and the hotel's property.

Responds to guest inquiries and gives information about and directions to the hotel and the locale.

Dates, sorts, and files incoming mail, messages, packages, and telegrams.

Receives and acts on guest complaints.

Maintains guest bills by posting charges and credits to individual guest accounts.

Collects in cash or credit from departing guests.

Uses telephones, telewriters, pneumatic tubes, switchboards, video display terminals, and other computer equipment.

---

of the desk. Slowly walking guests through the process a time or two reduces the pressure at the desk in the long run.

More than any other individual, the front-office clerk is the hotel in the eyes of the guest. This same visibility subjects the clerk to an inordinate amount of criticism. On the one hand, desk personnel are the hotel's best public relations representatives, and on the other hand, the source of much complaint. The supercilious attitude that is often ascribed to agents on the desk makes the reception an irritating, frustrating experience for the seasoned traveler and a frightening one for the inexperienced. Patient, gracious, and diplomatic desk clerks make friends for themselves as well as for the hotel.

Other Front-Office Duties.   There was once a front-office position called mail, key, and information clerk. Modern circumstances have eliminated the job and even some of the functions. What remains has been taken over by the front-desk clerks, or is now done electronically.

Today, for example, most mail comes by fax; guests don't stay long enough to get letters through the traditional post. Heavy metal hotel keys (and the front-desk traffic once generated by guests dropping them off and retrieving them later) have been replaced by electronic locks using disposable keys. Similarly, information and personal messages are handled today by electronic mail; in-room, closed-circuit television; and automated kiosks.

Electronic kiosks supply road and street maps, bus schedules, stock market quotes, theater offerings, weather reports, and information about events in town and activities within the hotel. Guests who have never used a computer keyboard are comfortable making one-touch inquiries, and hotels that have never staffed a concierge now have an electronic one in the lobby.

EXHIBIT 3–4

This concierge is at the lobby location in the Westin Benson, Portland, now a Westcoast Grand hotel.

Courtesy: Front Magazine, Westin Hotels.

Concierge.   A new front-office position, **concierge,** has been introduced in the United States. The concierge has always been popular overseas, especially in France.[4] (In Britain, where the front office is called the front hall, the job title is head hall porter.) Like a French idiom, however, translating the nuances of the job into Americanese leaves something to be desired. Many guests are not certain what the position does, let alone how to pronounce it (kon ṣyerzh).

The word comes from the Latin *con servus,* meaning "with service," and from the French. The *comte des sierges* was in charge of prisons, making him the keeper of the keys under the French monarchs.[5] The European concierge was a door attendant, and therefore keeper of the keys, and porter, a giver of service.

These duties are still part of the European concierge's job, particularly in the small hotels. Controlling the keys enables the concierge to watch the comings and goings of guests and thus to furnish a bit of extra protection and information. This is not the American interpretation of the job, except when a hotel offers a concierge floor, or luxury floor. Even then, the added security is a secondary objective.

The keeper of the door, the lobby concierge (see Exhibit 3–4), provides all types of miscellaneous information and a variety of personal, but minor, services. Information and service shape the basic description of the concierge's job. Travel information, messages, tickets and reservations to a broad range of events, babysitters, language translation, and secretarial sources all fall within the purview of the concierge. Guests may ask the concierge to arrange for pet care, to provide extra chairs, to arrange flower delivery, to find lost items, to get medical care in an emergency, to recommend hair stylists, anything. On some occasions, the concierge functions as an internal ombudsman.

As hotels retrench some services and automate others, the post of concierge becomes increasingly important. Guests can no longer turn to transportation desks, floor clerks, and elevator operators for questions and services. Those jobs no longer exist.

The *concierge floor* is one amenity not discussed in Chapter 2. It is an extra service facility available at an extra charge. The concierge service is limited to guests on that special sleeping floor. Continental breakfast and evening cocktails are usually provided. As a premium floor, there are other extras. A terry cloth robe is furnished for the bath, shoes are shined, rooms are larger, arrival and departure procedures are expedited, and security is enhanced.

Access to the floor is limited and requires a special key for the elevator. The concierge is usually seated by the elevator, adding security as the floor clerk's position did before World War II.

All the upscale chains have concierge floors. Hilton calls theirs Towers after the famed Waldorf-Astoria Towers, which is part of the Hilton Chain. Hyatt uses Regency Club; Radisson, Plaza Club; and Omni/Dunfey, Classic Floors. Add these names to the frequent-guest programs, and the confusion of name segmentation increases dramatically.

The Asian invasion of the U.S. hotel business has brought pleasant additions to the concierge service. A floor butler, or floor steward, is available around the clock to handle personal services, including unpacking. Upscale Asian hotels have room bells or switches on the bed console to summon the butler.

Room Reservations.   Reservations are requests for rooms from prospective guests who intend to arrive sometime in the future. These are received, processed, and confirmed by the reservations department. A *reservations manager* supervises the day-to-day activities and reports to the rooms manager (Exhibit 3–1).

Reservations arrive by letter and by fax sometimes, or even directly across the desk on occasion, but most often they are made by telephone. Reservation inquiries may come directly to the hotel's reservation office. More likely, they are made through the chain's or franchise's central reservation office, the 800 number. Chapter 5 explains the procedure in detail.

The reservation department keeps records of who is arriving, at what time, and for how long. This information, including the type of facilities wanted, must be communicated to the front-desk clerk (in anticipation of the guest's arrival).

Tracking the number of rooms sold and the number available for sale is the biggest responsibility of the reservation department. Groups and individual guests must be balanced to achieve a **full house**[6] without overselling (committing more rooms than are available).

Reservations are maintained on a day-to-day basis for a year and in less detail for three to five years. Much of this information is now computerized, as Chapter 4 explains.

Cashiers.   Cashiers are actually members of the accounting staff. Their location in the front office and their relationship to many of the front-office positions place them in direct contact with the front-office manager, who exercises control on a day-to-day basis.

Billing, posting (recording guest charges to accounts), and handling cash and credit-card transactions are the major duties of this position. As the front-office clerk is the guest's first contact, the cashier is usually the last. The cashier's window has

EXHIBIT 3–5

The modern front desk of a small hotel is open to the lobby to encourage a feeling of hospitality and to improve security.

Courtesy: Jerome B. Temple and Lodging Magazine.

been a frequent point of irritation because of lengthy delays and long lines. With computer capability, management has corrected much of that bottleneck.

Several banking services are handled by this department. Checks are cashed, advances and loans are processed, safe-deposit boxes are provided, and cash is collected.

Design of the Front Office

Like so many other aspects of the front office, its design and location are also undergoing change. The bank teller look of the old-fashioned office has given way to an open style that is less formal and more inviting (see Exhibit 3–5).

New, computerized systems have reduced the amount of paper and much of the clutter that typified the old.

The Lobby.   Front-desk computers have also shrunk the amount of floor space previously needed for the front office. This has encouraged new designs and configurations, which are coming at the same time that the lobby itself is enjoying a renaissance. For decades, the lobby was once the gathering place for business and social activities.[7] Hotel lobbies are providing that service again after a half-century of designs that limited usage and discouraged lingering.

Face-lifts and exciting interiors—interior architecture has gained new advocates among hoteliers—have shrunk the front office and introduced food, drink, and comfort to once sterile lobbies. The lobby is returning to its position of grandeur and to its role as a meeting place for all types of activities.

New or old, the desk must serve its several purposes. It must be accessible to the guest but take a minimal amount of costly lobby space. Heavy pedestrian traffic and the high-priced realty that hotels occupy make ground-level shops important income producers. The more space taken for clerical use by the front office, the less

EXHIBIT 3–6

Shown is a front-office schematic, not to scale. Letter references key the positions and equipment to an older version shown in Exhibit 3–7.

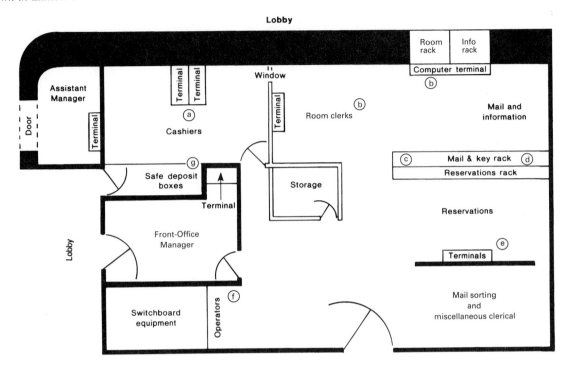

available for rental. Good economics and better systems have shrunk the floor space of the front office.

Increased computerization will minimize the registration desk still further by furnishing each station with a complete set of electronic tools. Functions may even be separated—general front-office services from registration, check-out from information.

The Desk.   The desk must be comfortable. The standard front-desk counter is about 3.5-feet high and approximately 2.5-feet across. The employee side of the desk is lower by one-half foot or so, providing a working shelf for clerical duties and allowing the equipment to site below the eye contact so critical to host–guest relations (Exhibit 3–5). Some hotels, notably Westin's hotel at the San Francisco Airport, have experimented with lobby pods where both employees and guests sit during the transaction.

Security is another important consideration in desk design. The cashier must be secured (see Exhibit 3–6), and the desk must be positioned to monitor the traffic in the elevator bays. Security is enhanced by a design that provides front-office personnel with an unobstructed view of the lobby.

Internal communications is another consideration in the design. Despite the many new marvels in communication, face-to-face interaction behind the desk remains the chief means of handling the day's business. Most designs center the

EXHIBIT 3–7

This is a schematic presentation of the content and furnishings of a precomputerized front office—see Exhibit 3–6.

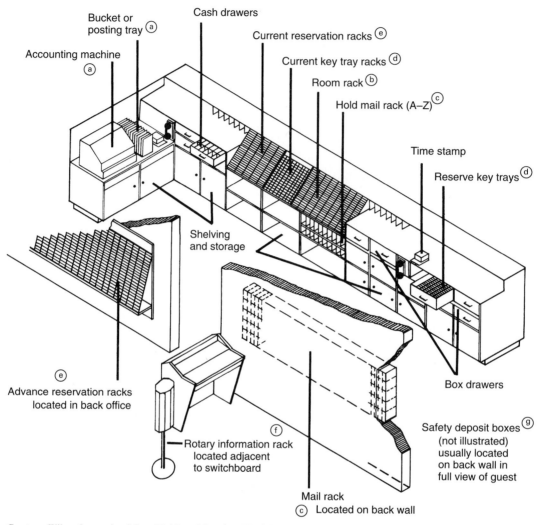

Bucket or posting tray ⓐ

Cash drawers

Current reservation racks ⓔ

Accounting machine ⓐ

Current key tray racks ⓓ

Room rack ⓑ

Hold mail rack (A–Z) ⓒ

Time stamp

Reserve key trays ⓓ

Shelving and storage

Box drawers

ⓔ Advance reservation racks located in back office

ⓕ Rotary information rack located adjacent to switchboard

Safety deposit boxes ⓖ (not illustrated) usually located on back wall in full view of guest

Mail rack
ⓒ Located on back wall

Courtesy: Wilcox International, Inc., Division of American Hotel Register Co.

front-office clerk as the hub of activity. Exhibits 3–6 and 3–7 locate that position in the middle of the desk.

From this advantageous location, clerks coordinate the flow of business, from reservations to cashiering. Group arrivals are the exception. Hotels with heavy group business often build satellite reception desks where busloads of arrivals can be accommodated without interfering with front-office traffic. Indeed, agencies handling group business are asking this of hotel companies.

Aesthetic as well as practical work space is the aim of modern desk design. Using lighting, form, and materials, architects must convey the image of the hotel: comfortable, open, organized, and professional.

EXHIBIT 3–8

These are the typical working hours of a hotel front office. Overlapping jobs are sometimes scheduled in 15- to 30-minute intervals to ensure consistency during shift changes.

Day shift	7:30 AM–3:30 PM
Swing shift	3:30 PM–11:30 PM
Graveyard shift	11:30 PM–7:30 AM

Working Hours of the Front Office

Hotels never close. The legal definition of a hotel requires that they do not. Therefore, work schedules must provide around-the-clock staffing—at least at the front desk; other departments (personnel or accounting) work a more normal workweek. Work schedules must also provide for the peaks and valleys that bring daily, sometimes hourly, fluctuations to the volume at the desk.

The Shift (or Watch).   Most desk employees work an eight-hour shift, five days per week, with two successive days off. That creates three equal shifts per day. Although there are variations, the model (see Exhibit 3–8) follows the pattern of other businesses.

The day shift is preferred by most employees because it follows the usual workday. Bellpersons opt for the swing shift, when arrivals and tips are the heaviest. Even senior front-office clerks choose the swing shift if tips are customary, as they especially are at resorts.

The graveyard shift has the least guest activity, but it is during this shift that the night audit is completed. The night audit is more specialized than the other front-office duties. Thus, night auditors cannot take advantage of the general policy that allows senior employees to select their shifts. Few workers prefer graveyard, which is one explanation for the shortage of night auditors.

A special effort is needed to maintain morale during the graveyard watch. Graveyard work should be covered by formal policies. Employees must know that they are not locked into a career of night work. They are rotated when openings appear in the more desirable shifts. In the meantime, salary supplements are paid for night work, and careful attention may be paid to night meals in those hotels where the kitchen staff tends to shortchange the night crew's menu.

Rotating personnel and shifts whenever possible, and where union contracts allow, enables employees to know one another. It also reduces the chance of collusion among employees who always work together. Sometimes day and swing shifts are switched en masse. This is done at the start of each month as employees' days off allow. It is unwise to make the switch on two successive workdays. The swing shift would close at 11:30 PM, and the same employees would report for the day shift at 7:30 AM the following morning. Not only is this a burdensome procedure in a large city, where employees need commuting time, but it may also be illegal under state labor laws. Shift rotations should always follow the clock: day, evening, graveyard, off; day, evening, and so forth.

Most front-office positions follow the same work pattern. Cashiers, clerks, and even supervisors change shifts in concert. A 15-minute overlap offers a continuity that is lost with an abrupt change of shifts. If there are several persons in each job, individuals could leave in 15-minute intervals. If not, complementary jobs could be changed every quarter hour. Cashiers might change at 3 PM and billing clerks at 3:15 PM, for example.

Forecast Scheduling.   Proper scheduling begins with a forecast of business for the next week or longer, depending on the period of the work schedule. This information is a by-product of the reservation forecast discussed in Chapter 6. Schedules can be prepared once the demand on the front desk is known.

With forecasting and advance scheduling, employees are given their days off during the slowest part of the week. Several may be off on one day, and none on a busy day. Part-time personnel can cover peak periods, or hours of the workday may be staggered. Each technique is designed to minimize payroll costs and maximize desk coverage when required.

The amount of help needed varies during the day and even within the same shift. Cashiers are busy in the morning handling check-outs and are less busy in the afternoon when the front-office clerks are busy with arrivals. Cashiers at a commercial hotel are slower on Mondays, when clerks are busier, and busier on Thursdays, when clerks are slower. An employee can be hired as a cashier for some days and as a clerk for others. Buyers of computer hardware should be certain that registration terminals are interchangeable with cashier terminals if job assignments are to be scheduled in response to traffic patterns.

The Split Shift.   The use of the split shift is limited to small and isolated hotels. But then it is not restricted to the front desk. The kitchen, the dining room, and the housekeeping departments schedule that way as well.

Unionization, wage-and-hour laws, and just plain physical distance have seen the decline of the split shift. Seasonal resorts still use it where wage-and-hour laws exempt seasonal workers. These resorts have remained free of unionization because of the short employment period and the transient nature of the work force. Moreover, employees live on the resort property or nearby so that the major disadvantage of commuting is alleviated.

The split shift has a real advantage for the small resort where only one person staffs the desk. Employees need not be relieved for meals, but eat either before or after their shift. Exhibit 3–9 illustrates the long and short day commonly used at the resort desk. It is customary for employees A and B to switch shifts daily or weekly. The night auditor does not rotate watches.

Resorts that do **turn-downs**—replacing bathroom linen and preparing the bed for use—may require the room attendant to return in the evening for another variation of a split shift. In upscale, urban hotels, turn-downs are handled by a second shift. It's a nice touch if the night attendant leaves on the pillow all the messages that came in that day.

The Building Structure

As this chapter's introduction implied, there is a good deal of similarity between the hotel's organizational structure and the structure of the building that is the hotel.

EXHIBIT 3–9

This is the typical split watch of resort hotels. It is used where allowed by labor laws. Employees A and B swap shifts weekly.

Employee A	7:00 AM–12:30 PM
Employee B	12:30 PM–6:30 PM
Employee A	6:30 PM–11:00 PM
Night Auditor	11:00 PM–7:00 AM

Both contain similarities property to property. That is, both the staff and the guest room are the fundamental, and hence, common attributes of every hotel. Yet, the differences that exist among the hotels, differences in organizational staffing and differences in physical buildings, are what distinguish the many properties and segment the industry into numerous parts.

The Old versus the New

Differentiating between hotels that were built before midcentury and those built afterwards (since World War II) is not difficult to do. Today's hotels take far more land—a *large footprint* is the real estate terminology—because they are more open and because the individual rooms are much larger. Exhibits 3–10 and 3–11 make clear the contrast. Some very famous hotels in the genre of Exhibit 3–10 still exist today. Best known among them are the Waldorf-Astoria (New York), the Drake (Chicago), and the Biltmore Hotel (Los Angeles).

The open design of the world's new hotels, including the megaresorts of Las Vegas, is represented in Exhibit 3–11. Guest rooms in hotels like these are very much alike, both among the hotels and within the individual structure. Older designs produced a wide range of room sizes, shapes, and locations (Exhibit 3–10). Hence, older hotels required many room rate classes to differentiate the variety of offerings. Current designs have reduced the number of rates from a dozen or more in the 1950s to three or perhaps five rate classes a half-century later.

The Old: Inside Rooms.   Inside rooms have followed the semiprivate (shared) bathroom (1930–50) and the public (served the entire floor) bathroom (previous century) into oblivion. Rooms 58 to 97 in Exhibit 3–10 form a **U** shape of inside rooms around the light court. As illustrated, inside rooms are enclosed by wings of the building. Contrast this inside view to the outside rooms, numbered 02 to 28 and 72 to 98, or to the entire design of Exhibit 3–11.

The view from the inside room is down, and the roof on the lower floor is often dirty and unsightly. Inside rooms are affected by the changing position of the sun, which casts shadows into these rooms even early in the day. The light courts produce some unusually shaped rooms—rooms 60 to 66, for example. Of course, smaller rooms and inside rooms are more economical in construction and land costs.

The New: Suites and All-Suites.   The hotel suite has changed in meaning since the introduction of the all-suite concept. The traditional suite is a parlor (living room) with one or more bedrooms, illustrated in the modern hotel by Exhibit 3–12 and in the more traditional hotel by Exhibit 3–10, rooms 72 and 74.

Larger suites add second or third bedrooms and additional living space. More luxurious accommodations include kitchens and formal dining rooms, saunas or

EXHIBIT 3–10

Shown is a representative floor plan of a 1925 hotel, which offered upscale accommodations in rooms smaller than today's budget inns. Light courts created odd-shaped rooms (44, 61, 63). (The building is no longer a hotel.)

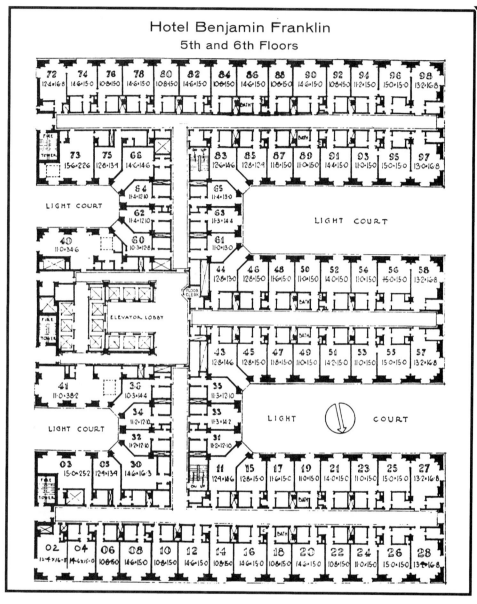

Courtesy: Benjamin Franklin Hotel, Philadelphia, PA.

EXHIBIT 3–11

This is a floor plan of a 21st-century hotel which is typified by the sweep of the open design and the standardization of guest rooms.

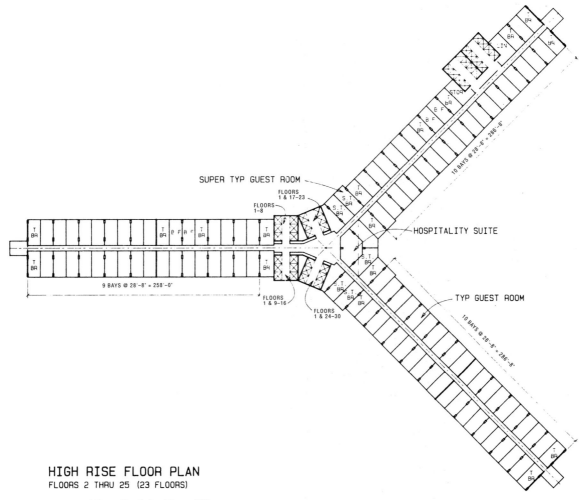

HIGH RISE FLOOR PLAN
FLOORS 2 THRU 25 (23 FLOORS)

Courtesy: Mirage Hotel, Las Vegas, NV.

swimming pools, and even libraries. Almost every suite contains a wet bar. Balconies and patios (lanai suites) are also common amenities. In the proper climate, suites have fireplaces. For a truly opulent experience, some hotels, especially casino hotels, offer a two-floor suite.[8] So does America's heartland: The two-floor suite of the Netherland Plaza offers a panoramic view of Cincinnati.

Specialty suites are named, although they may also be numbered as standard suites are (Exhibit 3–12). The *bridal suite,* the *presidential suite,* and the *penthouse suite* are common terminology. Historical figures or local references that emphasize the theme of the hotel—for example, the Kit Carson Suite—are other bases for choosing names.

Suites in all-suite hotels are a different product altogether. They are designed for a different market and a different use (Exhibit 3–13). The intent is for the all-suite to compete against the standard hotel room, not against the hotel suite. To

EXHIBIT 3–12

Here is a floor plan of a one-bedroom suite with the possibility of connecting a second bedroom. It is not a corner.

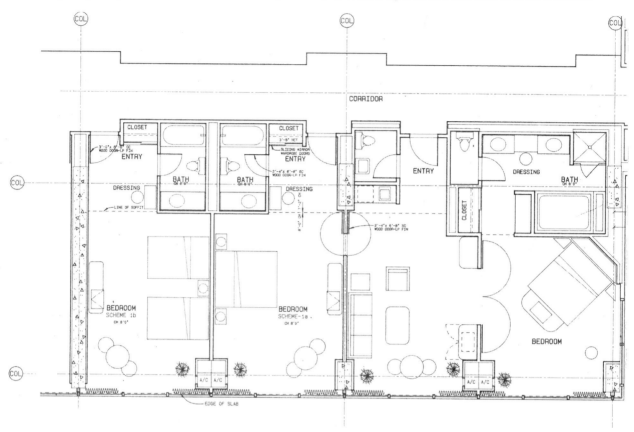

TYP END SUITE & GUEST ROOM PLAN
SCALE: 1/4" = 1'-0"

Courtesy: Mirage Hotel, Las Vegas, NV.

compensate for the extra square footage offered by the all-suite unit, public space is reduced. Forty percent of the typical hotel building is allocated to public areas. The all-suite hotel cuts that figure back by at least half.

All-suite and standard hotels alike employ a building technique that was invented by Ellsworth Statler in 1923. **Back-to-back** utility shafts reduce the amount of runs for piping, electrical, heating, and communication lines. There is economy in both the initial construction and continuing maintenance. It is not always possible, but kitchenettes, baths, and wet bars should be so constructed. Exhibits 3–10 and 3–12 show the baths back to back.

The Corner Room.   **Corner rooms** are the most desirable rooms on the floor. They offer a double exposure and therefore command a premium price. To enhance the price differential, corner rooms get preferential treatment from the architect. They are usually larger rooms, and they are frequently incorporated into the suite. Corner rooms were an integral part of the older hotel because its design created

EXHIBIT 3–13

The large square footage of all-suite facilities make them very appealing to the modern traveler, especially when a sofa bed (left room) adds to the accommodations.

Courtesy: Guest Quarters, Washington, DC.

them (Exhibit 3–10). Modern hotels have fewer building corners and thus fewer corner rooms; round hotel buildings have none at all.

Numbering for Identification

Everyone uses the guest room number for identification. Certainly guests depend on the number to locate themselves. Desk personnel address guests by name, but within the front office, identification is always by number and then, if at all, by guest name. Hotel rooms are identified first by floor number and then by room number.

Floor Numbering.   Floors are numbered upward sequentially, but most Western hotels omit floor 13. New York City's Plaza Hotel is an exception: It has both a 13th floor and a room 13. Numbering systems reflect the culture of the hotel's location. Four is to the Orient as 13 is to the Occident. One never finds four in Asia as a room number, and sometimes not even numbers that add to four. Seven is a lucky number in the United States, as it is, along with six, in the Far East.

Americans number the first sleeping floor as floor one regardless of the number of levels between it and the ground. Mezzanine, upper-ground floor, and shopping level are interspersed without any standard order. The sequence adds an array of nonnumerical elevator buttons that confuse anyone who isn't a lifetime employee of the hotel. *M* is for mezzanine; *MM* is for the second mezzanine floor. Try to decipher *LM, SB,* and *S2* (lower mezzanine, sub basement, and sub basement 2).

The rest of world begins numbering with the ground floor as floor number one. Even without the intermediary floors, what would be the 10th floor in the United States would be the 11th floor elsewhere.

A different numbering system needs to be used if the hotel is comprised of several low-rise buildings. Identically numbering each low rise unit of, say, three or four stories is one technique. Then each building is given a different name, and the keys for each are color coded. Others prefer to number the floors sequentially moving in order from one building to the next. Guests get confused because only one unit has its ground floor numbered as floor one. Ground floors of the other units will have numbers in the teens or even 20s.

Hotels that have two or three towers have the same options. Either the towers are differentiated by name (the river tower) or direction (the east tower) with room numbers identical in each, or the floors are numbered sequentially with the bottom floor of the second tower using the next floor number in sequence.

Room Numbering.   Assigning numbers to rooms is far more arbitrary then going up floor levels. Each hotel has a unique design, and that design determines where to begin numbering and what sequence to use. Sequential numbering is not even possible in an old floor plan like the one in Exhibit 3–10—too many corridors run at right angles to one another.

Rooms are frequently numbered odd and even along opposite sides of the corridor. The numbering might begin at the elevator bay and progress upward as the sequence marches down the corridor: 101, 103, 105 along one side; 102, 104, 106 and so on along the other. Of course, there is no rule that requires this. An atrium hotel like Loew's Anatole in Dallas has rooms on only one side of the corridor and the numbering is sequential. All-suite hotel rooms are numbered in the usual manner because every room in the hotel is a suite.

Different floor designs present different numbering problems and require good signage. If the elevator empties into the center of the sleeping floor, the logic of any system begins to break down. The numbering system gets very confusing when a new wing or ell is added to the original structure. Rarely is the entire floor, old rooms and new, renumbered in sequence. The new wing may be numbered sequentially from the old, without concern about the interface with the old numbers. Sometimes the old numbers are duplicated in the new wing by adding an identifying suffix or prefix, like *N* for north wing.

Care in using certain numbers such as four and nine apply equally to room numbering as to floor numbering, as mentioned earlier. In Asia, correct positioning is also important. Many hoteliers there employ a fung shui (or feng shui) master who helps position the location of everything from doors and windows to desks and files and helps decide the most auspicious date to open a new hotel, a new dining room, or whatever.

Adjoining or Connecting Rooms.   Rooms that abut along the corridor are said to be **adjoining rooms.** Using the numerical sequence discussed above, 101, 103, and

105 would be adjoining rooms, as would 102, 104, and 106. If there is direct room-to-room access (a door between the rooms) without using the corridor (Exhibit 3–10, rooms 53, 55, and 57), the rooms are said to be **connecting.** Obviously, every connecting room adjoins, but not every adjoining room connects.

Room Shape and Size

The guest room is the hotel's product. Therefore, its shape and size are critical to customer satisfaction. Size, especially, separates the industry into the several classes. Small rooms are associated with hard budget properties; huge rooms with deluxe accommodations. As the rate discussion of Chapter 8 points out, setting the different rate classes within the hotel also depends in part on the differences in the physical rooms.

Room Shape.   There has been little overall change in the shape of guest rooms. As concave, square, and round structures are built, corresponding changes occur in the interior shapes and dimensions. Research may eventually show advantages in guest satisfaction or in reduced wear from certain shapes. Until then, the parallelogram remains the classic favorite, with the depth of the room approximately twice the width. The first increases in room size are made by adding to the depth. Width is improved next by increasing from 12 or 13 feet to 16 feet, which is a luxury-class room.

Other shapes, which might look interesting from the outside, present certain internal problems. A round building of small diameter produces rooms without parallel walls. The outer wall is circular, and the inner walls are angled to accommodate the bath and the central service core within the limited cross section of the small diameter.

The presence of full or false balconies and French or sliding doors gives a sense of spaciousness to any room. Balconies are often part of a facade that adds interest to the outside of the building.

Room Size.   Room shape is primarily an architectural decision; room size is derived from financial and marketing factors. Although the trend has been toward larger and larger rooms, the economy segment has capitalized on smaller accommodations and smaller rates.

In the final analysis, the market determines the rate structure and consequently the average size room. That market varies from hotel to hotel, so that the twin double beds of the family-oriented hotel might be unacceptable to a property servicing the business traveler.

A comparison of international accommodations points up the differences in facilities. Japan's capsule rooms are stacked tubes, 5 feet high and 5 feet wide by less than 7 feet deep. Guests change in common locker areas and crawl into their own capsules for sleeping. Rooms in these capsule inns (a grand marketing euphemism) are less than 4 square feet. Japanese hard budget inns offer a 14-square-foot room.

Most budget facilities are larger. The Ibis chain (a European entry into the American market) builds rooms of approximately 130 square feet. Econo and Super 8 have rooms of about 190 square feet. Days Inns adds almost another 100 square feet.

The surprise comes when comparisons are made between today's budget accommodations and the rooms of the Benjamin Franklin hotel (Exhibit 3–10), which was a first-class facility in its era. The 150- to 175-square foot room of the prosperous 1920s was smaller than many of today's economy facilities, such as Choice International's Sleep Inn, at 210 square feet.

The Far East contributes to the other end of the scale as well. It has many of the world's opulent hotels, with large rooms and many extras. Hong Kong's Shangri-La Hotel offers a 500-square-foot facility (bath included). That size is immediately recognized as super luxury. (Guests do not get a feeling of luxury until the room size passes 400 square feet.)

The Four Seasons, a New York City hotel, compares favorably with luxury properties worldwide. Its rooms are 600 square feet (about 55.75 square meters), including the bath. The standard American room measures between 250 and 350 square feet (approximately 23.2 to 32.5 square meters). So the Ramada International, another recently built New York hotel, is right on target at 350 square feet.

All-suite hotels provide a contrast in size, both to one another and relative to the standard nonsuite property. All-suite properties are segmented into economy, midmarket, and upscale, and that is reflected in room sizes. Guest Quarters pioneered the all-suite hotel with a 650-square-foot unit that has now been downsized to 450 square feet. All-suite hotels include bedroom, parlor, bath, and kitchenette, making a unit, rather than a room, the standard of measurement. AmeriSuites' budgets offer 380 square feet. Park Suites measure some 480 square feet. Fireplaces carry Homewood Suites to 550 square feet.

Different kinds of guests use rooms in different ways. Within the same dimensions, a destination hotel furnishes proportionately more storage space than a transient property. A transient property allocates more space to sleeping and less to the living area than a destination facility. Such would be the case with New York City hotels, where the average use of the room is eight hours. Very cold or very hot climates increase the usage of the room.

The use of the room also dictates the kinds of furniture required. A destination resort wouldn't need a desk, but the hotel rooms in China and the Middle East serve as company offices and are furnished as such.

Designers have become quite successful in making small rooms look larger. For example, night stands can be eliminated by mounting bedside lamps on the wall. Mirrors do a good job of creating a perception of space. Wall-to-wall draperies and fewer patterned materials throughout the room add to the feeling of roominess. Nevertheless, it takes about 20 square feet (1.86 square meters) to justify each rate increment if spaciousness is the only criterion for the increase.

Clearly, there is no standard room. The hotel industry is moving in several directions at once. Miniprices use module units that measure 12 feet from center to center. Luxury operations opt for 15-foot centers and lengths of 30 to 35 feet. (The standard carpet sizes of 12 and 15 feet dictate the dimensions unless the plan calls for a custom job.) Costs of energy, borrowed money, and labor limit expansion even as competition pushes for more space. Comparisons, therefore, begin with the marketplace.

Bed and Bath

The increasing size of the bed—Americans are getting bigger—accounts in part for the increased size of the guest room. The new role of the bath—as a weapon in the competition wars—also contributes to the creep in total square footage.[9]

The Bath.   The hotel bath has undergone many changes throughout this century, but its position as a sound barrier between the room and the corridor remains. That location, abutting the corridor, saves construction costs and leaves the desirable outside walls for windows or balconies.

The bath accounts for about 20 percent of the room size. Thus, the baths in hard budget inns measure about 35 square feet and in midrange properties about 70 square feet. The luxurious Four Seasons, mentioned earlier, has a bath of 120 square feet. What a contrast this is to the hotel of a century ago, when public baths served whole floors or entire wings. (Very early hotels had all their baths in the basements because the mechanics of pumping water to higher floors was not yet in place.)

Stall showers, which occupy little space, gained favor as old hotels converted from rooms without baths. They fit easily into old, large closets or corners of renovated rooms. Tub and shower combinations were installed next when lifestyles changed again. Having both meets the cultural needs of all guests. The Japanese, for example, definitely favor tubs, just as they choose twin beds over all other choices. The bidet, which is installed in many other countries, has not found acceptance in the American home, and thus, not in the American hotel.

Upscale properties have cut back on low-cost amenities like soap and shampoo. Strangely, they have gone all out in building larger bathrooms with expensive appointments: in-floor scales; in-bath telephones, electric shoeshine equipment, adjustable no-fog mirrors, and plush bathrobes. The Palmer House Hilton in Chicago, which was renovated several years ago, has 300 guest rooms with his-and-her bathrooms. The same Four Seasons mentioned above features bathtubs that fill in one minute!

Not only is the bath larger, but the ancillary space has grown as well. Dressing areas and second lavatories outside the bath proper have also increased the overall dimensions. Replacing closets with open hanger space has helped compensate. Consolidating furniture also saves space. One vertical piece incorporates several horizontal space users. Into armoires, for example, have gone television sets, bars and refrigerators, writing desks with telephones, and several drawers for clothing. Reflected in the new design is the two-night stay and garment-bag luggage of today's traveler.

Beds and Their Symbols.   Bed types and sizes also follow fashion—from favoring double beds, to twin beds, to the queen-size period that we are now experiencing. As the choice of models expands, we can anticipate an increasing variety of beds. One day, guests will have a choice of mattresses: foam, spring, hard, soft, orthopedic, adjustable, and vibrating; and a selection of newcomers: flotation and futons.

Beds are being lowered as well as lengthened. The usual height of the mattress and box spring is 22 to 24 inches, in contrast to the average chair of some 17 inches. Lowering the bed to 17 inches makes the room appear larger because all the pieces are on the same horizontal plane. It also makes the bed easier to sit on, and lower hotel beds are used for that purpose. Adequate seating is needed to reduce the heavy wear on mattresses when beds are used as chairs. It is a real conflict: Lowered beds make the room appear larger, but the mattresses don't last as long.

If every hotel room were a replica of every other room, front-desk personnel would know immediately what facilities the room contained. The hotel industry has moved along that direction, but competition suggests that it will never arrive at such a destination. It is customary, therefore, for computers and front-office staff to use shorthand symbols in designating bedding and accommodations.

Bedding and accommodations are not always the same. *Single* or *double* refers with equal ambiguity to (1) the room rate, (2) the number of guests housed in the room, (3) the number of persons the room is capable of accommodating, or (4) the size and type of the beds. It is possible to have a single occupant in a double bed being charged a single rate although the room is designated as a double, meaning it could accommodate two persons.

A single occupant in a twin room sometimes needs assurance that no additional charge is being made for the unused bed. The single room configuration—that is, one single bed for one person—is unknown today. Thus, to the innkeeper, "single" means single occupancy or single rate.

Single Bed.   A **single** bed, symbol *S,* sleeps one person. A true single is 36 by 75 inches but is rarely used—it is too small. Instead, single rooms (rooms for one person) are furnished with one twin bed or one double bed. When the room is furnished with one twin bed, the symbol *S* is still used.

Single beds must measure at least 39 by 72 inches to win an AAA rating.

Twin Beds.   A **twin** room, symbol *T,* contains two beds each capable of sleeping one person. (Two persons could also be roomed in a double, a queen, or a king bed.) Twins measure 39 × 75 inches each and use linen 72 × 108 inches. The 75-inch mattress length has been replaced (in all bed sizes) with a longer length called a **California length.** The width measure of 39 inches remains, but the length is stretched to 79, 80, or 81 inches. An additional 5 inches is added to the linen length as well.

Because of their flexibility, twins once accounted for 60 to 70 percent of total available rooms. The trend shifted as twins were replaced by **double-doubles** and queens, and then by the queen-doubles. Business travelers prefer two beds: one for sleeping and one for spreading papers.

Because the double-double or queen-double sleeps four persons, it is also called a **quad** or a **family room.** Motel owners sometimes sell twin-doubles to a couple at a reduced rate with the stipulation that only one bed be used. A survey done by Sheraton's franchise division showed that the second bed of a double-double was used about 15 percent of the time.

Double Bed.   *D* is the symbol for **double bed.** The width ranges from 54 to 57 inches by 75 inches long, or the California length of 80 inches. Linen size would be 90 to 93 inches wide with the California 113 inches in length.

Half a double bed is only 28 inches or so, narrower than a single bed. And that explains its loss of popularity for double occupancy.

Queen and King Beds.   The **queen** and **king** beds (symbols *Q* and *K*) are extra wide—60 inches for Q and 72 inches for K—as well as extra long, California length. Although designed for two persons, some families squeeze in three or even four.

Both beds require larger rooms (the critical distance between the foot of the bed and the furniture—a three-foot minimum—remains) and larger sheets, 108 by 122½ inches. Since laundry costs are calculated by weight, larger sheets mean larger laundry bills. A larger room with extra laundry costs can only mean a higher room rate even without consideration for the extra, up-front costs of the larger bed, mattress, and linen.

Hollywood Bed.   Twin beds joined by a common headboard are referred to as a **hollywood bed.** A hollywood bed uses the twins' symbol, since that's what they are. They are difficult beds to make, because the room attendant cannot get between them. To overcome this, the beds are placed on rollers and swung apart, resulting in rapid carpet wear. Because the total dimension of these beds is 78 by 75 inches (two twins), they can be converted into a king by replacing the two mattresses with one king mattress laid across both springs.

Studio Bed (Room).   A **studio bed** is a sofa by day and a bed by night. During the day, the bed is slipcovered and the pillows are stored in the backrest. There is neither headboard nor footboard once the sofa is pulled away from the backrest to create the bed. Today's guest room serves a dual bedroom–living room function, so studio rooms should be popular with business guests. They once were. Studios are not popular anymore because the beds are not comfortable and the all-suite hotel serves the same dual purpose.

The studio room, once called an executive room, has been used to redo small, single rooms in older hotels. *UP,* undersized **parlor,** is one of the symbols used for studios. In Europe, a parlor that has no sleeping facilities is called a **salon.**

Sofa Bed.   A **sofa bed** is similar in function to a studio bed. It is a sofa first of all, which makes sitting more comfortable. It is usually 17 inches off the floor, whereas the studio bed may be as high as 22 inches. Unlike the studio bed, which rolls away from its frame, the sofa bed opens in accordion fashion from the seat. Since it unfolds, the sofa bed is less convenient and requires more space than the studio.

Parlors are generally equipped with sofa beds as part of a suite (Exhibit 3–12), but a studio bed is usually a room unto itself. Sofa beds can be single, double, or even queen size, although the single is more like a three-quarter bed (48 by 75 inches).

Sofa beds are often called *hide-a-beds* and, thus, carry an *H* designation. Large rooms that contain both standard beds and hide-a-beds are **junior suites.**

All-suite rooms usually contain a sofa bed in the parlor portion of the unit (Exhibit 3–13).

Rollaway Bed (Cot).   A **cot** or **rollaway** is a portable utility bed that is added to the usual room furnishings on a temporary basis. A rollaway sleeps one person, and a comfortable one measures 34 by 75 inches and uses twin sheets. Cots usually come smaller—30 by 72 inches, with linen 63 by 99 inches.

Setting up cots is costly in housekeeping time. First of all, the cots are rarely located conveniently. Cot storage never seems to be high in the designer's priority.

Water Bed.   In two decades, *water beds* jumped from a novelty to a hot item and then fell back again. The bed is rarely found in hotel rooms, although it offers an alternative to inner-spring and foam mattresses. The bed has a long history, dating back to the nomadic tribes of pre-Christianity, who filled goatskins with water. It was rediscovered by a Californian who first tried starch and gelatin as a filler. The water bed is still primarily a phenomenon of the western states.

Broader usage can be expected. Manufacturers have reduced the size and weight of the bed and overcome the wavelike motion with stabilizing chambers.

Futon.   The Japanese **futon,** which is a cotton-quilted ''bed,'' is another addition to the American sleeping design. Futons come in regular mattress sizes. The thick layers of batting are easily stored and readily adapted to service as a couch or bed.

And for the future? Possibly air beds—air cushions that support the sleeper without bedframe, mattress, or linens.

Summary

Hotels need structure to carry out their historical assignment—selling and servicing accommodations. Chapters 1 and 2 outlined the variety of lodging accommodations that have emerged as innkeepers labor to meet these marketplace expectations. Hoteliers do this in part by altering both the structure of the hotel's organization and the physical room being offered for sale. Although the size, design, and accoutrements of today's room would surprise the historical innkeeper, the basic commodities of accommodations and service have remained unchanged.

The modern guest is housed in a hotel room of some 300 square feet of floor space, of which about one-fifth is assigned to the bath (the bathroom). Segmentation means even a simple generalization like this one is difficult to make. On the upscale side, room size exceeds 600 square feet, with suites measuring upwards of 2,000 square feet. The hard budget end of the continuum offers room sizes of less than 150 square feet. (Outside the United States, square meters—there are .093 square meters per square foot—are the standard measure.) Similarly, upscale baths have sunken marble tubs, in-bath television sets, and dual lavatories, while hard budgets have no tubs, plastic bath curtains, and few amenities.

Hotel managers have looked as carefully at their staff structure as at their room structure. New societal expectations have wrought changes in service even as the increased physique of the modern traveler has changed the size of bedding. Guests are less willing to pay for, or wait for, individualized care, electing instead a degree of self-service. Less service demanded and less service offered have slashed the ranks of the uniformed services department; automation has reduced the need for telephone and elevator operators. Electronics permit self-check-in and check-out, altering further the duties of the front office.

Organizational changes do not always mean staff reductions. Security departments have been enlarged again and again as concern for guest safety grows. Attending to governmental and environmental regulations requires staff attorneys where there had been none before. Changes in the work force, in its size and in the laws that govern labor, necessitate large human resource departments, whereas a single personnel officer had handled the job a decade or two ago.

Some organizational changes have shifted responsibility rather than altering departmental size. Cashiers must deal with debit cards; concierges have been invested with new service responsibilities; integrated reservation systems with telephone and fax linkages have significantly altered the role of the reservations department. Indeed, reservations is probably the most dynamic of all the hotel departments. The function of the reservation system and the electronic-highway linkage that is its modern structure is discussed next, in Section II.

Hotelkeeping has mutated and restructured over time. So long as the momentum continues, so long as the industry continually reorganizes and reinvents itself, it remains competitive and successful.

Queries and Problems

1. With special attention to front-office activities, prepare a list of duties carried out by one (or more) of the fictional staff in the book *Hotel* by Arthur Hailey (Garden City: Doubleday & Company, Inc., 1965; also available through Bantam Books).

2. Interview a manager or operative employee of a hotel and then prepare a job description using the formats of Exhibits 3–2 and 3–3 for guidance.

3. Construct the organizational chart of an actual hotel (or use the chart in another text). Compare that organization to Exhibit 3–1. Identify and explain the differences.

4. Either as part of your travels this term or as part of a field trip, contrast the size, shape, bedding, price, and characteristics of two or more hotel rooms. Discuss.

5. Roughly sketch the lobby and front-office area of a nearby hotel/motel. Comment on the efficiency of the

design regarding traffic flow, security, reception, communications, employee work area, and space utilization.

6. Using the typical occupancy pattern of an urban hotel (see Exhibit 1–4), plot the biweekly work schedule for the desk of a 300-room hotel that has separate room clerk and cashier positions. The switchboard is not at the desk. Strive for efficient coverage with minimum payroll costs. All full-time employees receive two successive days off and work an eight-hour day, five days per week.

Notes

1. The housekeeping staff of the 4,000-room Excalibur Hotel (Las Vegas) numbers 750 persons.
2. The sequence is different in casino hotels, where casino revenue accounts for 60 percent of the gross and rooms only 15 percent. Food is 12 percent, beverage is 9 percent, and other is 4 percent.
3. *To room; room* (verb): The procedure of getting a guest housed in the room assigned, beginning with the initial greeting at the desk and concluding when the bellperson surrenders the key after escorting the guest to the room.
4. The International Union of Concierges was founded in Paris, France, in 1952 and in the United States in 1978. Members wear the Golden Keys (Les Clefs d'Or) that are their symbol of professionalism.
5. The prison in Paris's Palais de Justice is the Conciergerie prison. Marie Antoinette was imprisoned there during the French Revolution.
6. *Full house:* 100 percent occupancy; all guest rooms sold.
7. President Ulysses Grant (1869–77) frequently walked from the White House to the Willard, now an Inter-Continental Hotel, to have a cigar and a drink. Petitioners waiting to argue their constituents' positions hovered in the lobby; thus, the term *lobbyists.*
8. The two-floor Governor's Suite of the Fontainebleau Hilton (Miami Beach) is 20,000 square feet (the size of a dozen average homes) and has five bathrooms.
9. *Bath:* The bathroom, the room that houses bathing (including the bathtub), toilet, and washing facilities.

SECTION II

The Reservations Process

Nowhere is evidence of a maturing lodging industry so apparent as in the realm of reservations. From the smallest independent property to the largest of chains, the breadth and depth of reservation technology has impacted the very core of hospitality operations. The manner in which a hotel handles its reservations dictates the entire spectrum of automation found elsewhere in the operation. With increasing amounts of reservations made through travel agents, national sales offices, and corporate accounts, no property can successfully remain unconnected or unautomated.

At the chain or corporate level, central reservations offices (CROs) have matured at a dizzying pace. Although the intent of the CRO remains the same as 40 years ago—to sell as many hotel rooms as possible at the highest rate possible—the processes of booking the actual reservation, quoting the rate, and searching room availability are drastically different. Today, sophisticated central reservation systems offer real-time connections to each of the hundreds or thousands of individual hotels that comprise a chain. Through seamless connectivity technology, travel agents, airlines, and even end consumers can access a given hotel to check room availability, identify rate schedules, and ultimately make a reservation—all without speaking to a reservationist at the CRO or the property. Such technology is a definite sign of a maturing industry!

From the customer's viewpoint, the industry is maturing as well. Where reservations were once as simple as placing a toll-free phone call to a national CRO, they have become even easier to place with the introduction of customer-direct access through one of America's on-line subscription computer services. In addition, the increasing sophistication of yield management technology is making the cost of a hotel room a true bargain for guests who are able to travel during off-season, on the spur of the moment, or for those who are able to plan trip dates far in advance.

Reservation Data

Chapter Outline

Reservation Data

Reservations are a contract of sorts between the hotel and the guest. In accepting a reservation, the hotel agrees to provide a certain type of room for a specific length of stay at a predetermined rate. In turn, the future guest agrees to arrive on the chosen date and purchase the hotel room within the reservation parameters established.

Because of their contractual nature, reservations clearly state the terms of the understanding between the two parties. The agreed-on terms are simple enough and generally include rate, date, room type, method of payment and guarantee, guest name and address, number of guests, number of rooms, applicable discounts, and special needs or requests. Even when the two parties are represented by third parties (say, when the travel agent represents the guest and the central reservations system represents the hotel), the basic content of the reservation is the same.

Basic Reservation Content

The reservation process and especially the information obtained during the reservation are designed to improve the effectiveness of the front office. The facts communicated through the reservation form a valuable starting point from which the front-desk clerk can understand the guest's needs.

Effective reservationists can give and receive a great deal of information in a relatively rapid time frame. Indeed, the entire process is usually wrapped up within just two or three minutes. During these few minutes, the reservationist has put the guest at ease, answered all of the guest's questions, and received answers to the basic questions required by the hotel.

Today, the vast majority of reservations are taken directly on a computer keyboard. Guests who listen closely can often hear the tapping of keys as they provide the reservationist with such data as their address, date of arrival, or the spelling of their last name.

The computer not only provides rapid input, it also prompts the reservationist to ask essential questions. As one question is completed, the lighted computer cursor automatically moves to the beginning of the next question. In this way, essential information cannot be overlooked. In fact, if the reservationist attempts to enter an incomplete reservation into the system, the computer will audibly beep and the cursor will blink at the beginning of the incomplete information field. Refer to Exhibit 4–1 for a glimpse at an actual reservation screen.

Essential Information

Arrival and Departure Dates.   In the reservations centers for national chains, the questions of arrival and departure come third, after ''What city?'' and ''What hotel?'' Telephone time is not used to gather the details that follow unless the clerk is certain that space is available at the time and place requested.

Number of Nights.   This bit of redundancy forestalls later problems if the guest's count of nights is not in agreement with the time between the arrival and departure dates. A common miscommunication occurs when the guest counts the departure day in the number of nights.

Number of Persons.   The number of persons in the party and its structure help to clarify the kind of facilities needed. Two unrelated persons need two beds; a married couple could get by with one bed. Are there children? Is a crib required? A rollaway bed?

Number of Rooms Required.   Based on the size of the party and the types of rooms the hotel has available, additional rooms may be required. Most reservationists are authorized to handle requests for up to 10 rooms or so. As the number of required rooms increases above 10, the hotel's group sales department usually becomes involved.

Type of Rooms Required.   The question of room type is closely linked to the rate the guest is willing to pay. As the room type increases in luxury and sophistication, the corresponding rate increases as well. Although the specific rate the guest wants to pay is the real question being asked, the reservationist certainly can't just offer

EXHIBIT 4–1

A blank reservation screen or ''mask'' awaits input of guest data by the reservations agent.

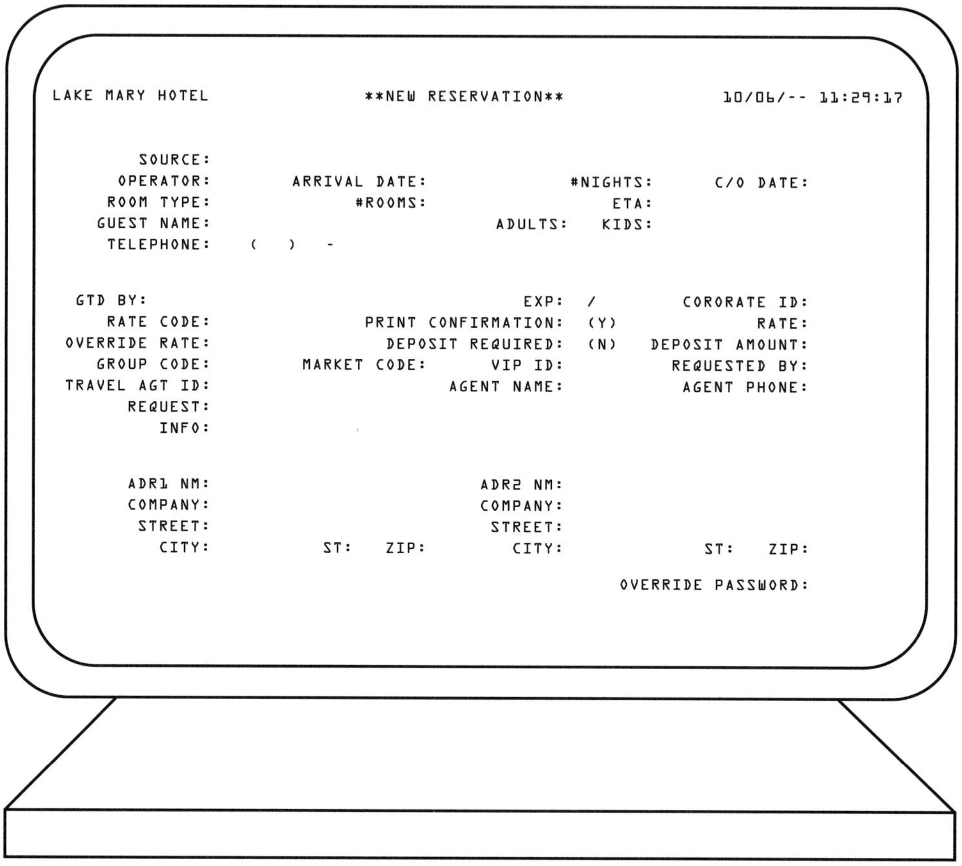

```
LAKE MARY HOTEL              **NEW RESERVATION**              10/06/-- 11:29:17


         SOURCE:
       OPERATOR:         ARRIVAL DATE:           #NIGHTS:       C/O DATE:
      ROOM TYPE:            #ROOMS:                 ETA:
     GUEST NAME:                          ADULTS:   KIDS:
      TELEPHONE:     (   )  -


    GTD BY:                             EXP:  /         CORORATE ID:
      RATE CODE:           PRINT CONFIRMATION:  (Y)            RATE:
  OVERRIDE RATE:             DEPOSIT REQUIRED:  (N)   DEPOSIT AMOUNT:
     GROUP CODE:      MARKET CODE:       VIP ID:         REQUESTED BY:
  TRAVEL AGT ID:                 AGENT NAME:            AGENT PHONE:
        REQUEST:
           INFO:


        ADR1 NM:                       ADR2 NM:
        COMPANY:                       COMPANY:
         STREET:                        STREET:
           CITY:      ST:  ZIP:           CITY:          ST:   ZIP:

                                             OVERRIDE PASSWORD:
```

a series of rates. That would be gauche. Instead, the reservationist offers a series of room types.

Generally, the reservationist attempts to sell from the top down. This is accomplished by offering the guest the most expensive room type first and then waiting for the guest to agree or decline before moving down to offer the next most expensive room type.

Price.   The reservation (the sale) could be lost by the rate quotation. The agent may have no negotiating room if the yield management system has eliminated lower-priced options. Quoting the price is not enough. Distinctions between the prices must be accompanied by descriptive matter intended to entice the buyer to the better rate.

Identification.   The name, address, and telephone number (home and office) of the party and of the caller (travel agent, friend, secretary, spouse) is requested. If unrelated persons share a room, both identifications are requested. When several names are involved, the one under which the reservation will be claimed must be ascertained. The confirmation is normally mailed to that address.

Quality of the Reservation.   The three quality types of reservations available—nonguaranteed, guaranteed, or advance deposit—are determined either by the guest or the reservationist. The reservationist, for example, may be restricted from accepting nonguaranteed reservations as a function of policy or unusually high business levels for the hotel. Similarly, the guest may not have a credit card with which to guarantee the reservation or may have a card but not be inclined to use it. In either case, the reservation may fail to materialize because of disagreement at this stage in the process. See Chapter 6 for a complete discussion of the quality of the reservation.

Nonessential Information.   Depending on the reservation system in place, the amount of reservation activity occurring in the reservation center at the time of the call, or any number of other factors, certain reservation information may not necessarily be required for each reservation. This less important information is categorized as nonessential or ''nice-to-know'' data. Examples of nonessential information include estimated time of arrival, special guest requests or needs, discounts or affiliations, and smoking or nonsmoking room preference.

Although essential information must be complete for a reservation to be accepted into the computer system, nonessential information is not required. The computer will allow the input of a completed reservation into the system when nonessential data is missing. In fact, some computer screens display essential data in one color (say, red) while displaying nonessential data in a secondary color (say, yellow). If time permits, or some other factor is present, the reservationist may request this additional data. Otherwise, it is often overlooked.

Estimated Time of Arrival.   By knowing the guests' estimated time of arrival (ETA), the hotel can properly schedule front-desk clerks to assist with check-in, van drivers to retrieve guests from the airport, and bellpersons to room them. More importantly, hotels that are filling to capacity can be certain to save rooms for guests who are going to be especially late.

Special Requests.   Guest requests or needs run the gamut from simple, rather nonessential requests to extremely essential guest needs. That is why most reservationists provide guests with an opportunity to request any other items of importance before the close of the reservation process. If the request is essential (e.g., a handicapped guest requesting a specially equipped room), the guest is usually certain to state the need. In other cases, the request (ocean view, near the Smith's room, below fifth floor) may be forgotten by the reservationist and the guest. That is the responsibility of the front-desk clerk—to handle each request on a case-by-case basis at the time of check-in. Indeed, reservationists generally explain, ''I'll note your request on the reservation, but I cannot promise you will get it.''

Discounts or Affiliations.   Corporate, AAA (American Automobile Association), AARP (American Association of Retired Persons), or similar discounts or affiliations are usually handled during the room type and rate discussion earlier in the reservation. In fact, many such organizations (AARP, for example) require the guest to state his or her discount as a part of the reservation process. In such cases, the discount is void if the guest forgets to request it at the time of reservation.

EXHIBIT 4–2

A computer-prepared reservation acknowledgment (confirmation). The same information is in the computer and can be used to prepare the registration card prior to arrival.

				PLEASE CHECK FOR ACCURACY	
				Your Reservations Have Been Confirmed	

HOT WIRE HOTEL
Shocking Behavior Drive
Electric City, Washington 77777-7777

Accommodations Requested

Arrival	Time	Departure	No. Guest	Room Type	Rate
6/11/9-	GTD	6/14/9-	2	DELUXE KING	120

Special Request: OCEAN VIEW | Group Affiliation: WESTERN ATHLETES CONFERENCE

We require credit to be established prior to or at registration.
For your convenience we accept the following credit cards:
VISA, Master Card, American Express, Carte Blanche, Diners
and Discover Card.

If your requested rate is unavailable we will assign the next available rate.
Special requests have been noted and will be fulfilled upon arrival if available.

PAUL D. LIGAMENT
1234 ACHILLES TENDON WAY
WOUNDED KNEE
SOUTH DAKOTA   00000-0000

A Guaranteed Payment Reservation:
Unless cancelled, you will be responsible for
payment of room accommodations reserved for one
night with the remaining days being cancelled.

A 6:00 pm Reservation:
Room accommodations and all remaining days
will be cancelled at 6:00 pm unless a deposit
of $100.00 per room is received in advance.

Reservation #9821-017   **Toll Free Reservations 800-555-5555**

Check in time is 4 pm
Check out is at 12 noon

Smoking or Nonsmoking Preference.   As the world becomes increasingly health conscious, this reservation information may change from nonessential to essential data. Most hotel reservation systems provide a separate entry record for smoking and nonsmoking preference. Certain older systems still include this information under the entry for special guest requests.

Acknowledging the Reservation

Most reservations are confirmed on the spot as part of the telephone conversation. If there is sufficient lead time, a written acknowledgment may follow. The format of the written notice is much the same from company to company (see Exhibit 4–2). If the written confirmation proves to be a simple postcard, it is unconnected to the internal reservation process. Many systems still are at this stage of computerization.

The reservationist closes the conversation by furnishing the caller with the reservation confirmation number obtained from the computer. In many cases, there is actually order to what appears to be a random number. First on the screen is the scheduled arrival date, from 1 to 365. February 5, for instance, is 36. Then the individual hotel of the chain is identified by its own code. The agent's initials follow. Identification of the reservation concludes with the next confirmation number in sequence. The number, with the pieces set apart, may appear as 36 141 ABC 2366.

Not every company follows this sequence. The reservation code might start with the first three letters in the guest's last name, and the clerk's identity might be dropped: VAL 36 141 2366. Or the number may be nothing more than the next digits in the sequence (Exhibit 4–2), accumulated by the month or year. In still other systems, the confirmation number is so cumbersome it is almost impossible to decode.

Storing and Filing the Reservation

Just as the reservation represents a promise to deliver a specific room type on a certain date in the future, the reservation itself is represented by some type of file. Without an accurate filing system, reservations could not be tracked and errors would occur. Indeed, even in hotels with efficient reservation filing systems, there are still misplaced or lost reservations.

No matter the size or level of sophistication of the property's reservation system, all reservations are filed according to their date of arrival. In an automated **property,** the file is electronic in nature; in a manual property, it is a **hard-copy** paper file. Entering or filing the reservation into the computer system requires a mere push of the button. And then ''presto,'' the reservation is electronically filed. It is as easy as that!

Once entered into the system, the reservation appears electronically in a myriad of formats and printouts until the date of arrival. On that date, the reservation changes from a future reservation to an arriving reservation. On the date of arrival, the overall responsibility for the arriving or incoming reservation changes from the reservations department to the front-office staff.

While the electronic filing system is simple and relatively small, the manual paper trail filing system is complex and cumbersome. As a result, manual filing systems were often frought with inconsistencies and errors. The reservation was handwritten, filed according to date, and physically filed on horizontal **racks** as the day of arrival approached. Exhibits 4–3 and 4–4 provide photos that offer a glimpse into the cumbersome and complex nature of manual reservation offices from another era.

The Manual Filing System.   Throughout this textbook, the automated computer approach has been supplemented by a glimpse at the manual systems in place just a few short years ago. In this way, the student can understand not just the electronic approach but also how a manual system would be implemented when the computer was unavailable. After all, who knows when the computer might have **downtime** or whether the hotel is so small or remote a manual system is chosen over an automated one.

If there is no computer, all reservations are processed by pencil and typewriter at the hotel. A reservation packet is created as a means of tracking the reservation. Included in the packet is a reservation data form that is used for both telephone and mail requests when there is no computer. Correspondence from the guest or other agency (travel agent, hotel rep, etc.) is attached. If the reservation was made by telephone, there would be no correspondence, but there may be a telephone reservation number to be included.

The confirmation is not automatically printed, as it is with a computer. A written confirmation must be prepared in duplicate by typewriter. The first copy is mailed to the guest, and the second copy, sometimes called the hard copy, is added to the reservation packet. The completed correspondence packet is filed by date of arrival in the appropriate file drawer.

A series of duplicate references and cross-references must be created with a manual system. Each reservation is supported by at least two records. One is the correspondence packet, which is filed alphabetically under the anticipated date of

Exhibit 4–3

Exhibits 4–3 and 4–4 are photos of outdated manual reservations racks. Like these racks, today's computer systems store reservations both alphabetically and by date.

Exhibit 4–4

arrival (Exhibit 4–3). The second record, the **reservation rack** (Exhibit 4–4), provides the reservation office with a broad view of activities. Material filed in a drawer or cubbyhole does not offer a wide enough perspective.

A reservation rack slip is prepared at the same time as the reservation confirmation. Reservation rack slips are racked in daily, alphabetical sequence. Reservations can then be located by date of arrival (the reservation correspondence packet) or by name (the alphabetical listing on the reservation rack).

The Computerized File.   A complete computerized system has neither cubbyholes nor vertical racks. All the reservation information is stored in the computer's memory and can be recalled for viewing on the computer screen if either the guest name or the date of arrival is known (see Exhibit 4–5). In a perfect world, the reservation or confirmation number would be known, and that also would bring the information forward.

An arrival list (Exhibit 4–5) is printed by the automated reservation system each night for the following day's anticipated check-ins. The transfer of data is delayed until registration. The material is keyed in by the room clerk, and the transfer completed, but only after the guest arrives. Unlike the manual system, the computerized reservation system generally does not have a supporting correspondence file. Almost all supporting data is electronic in nature. Only under unusual circumstances will there be hard-copy support. Examples of these circumstances include reservation requests by mail or fax rather than telephone. Hard copies are also needed if the chain's reservation system is not **interfaced** with that of the hotel's, because communication is manual, not electronic. (Refer to Chapter 5 for a more thorough understanding of the impact of this example).

Altering an Existing Reservation

Although the majority of reservations remain undisturbed until the date of arrival, a great number of reservations are changed. Common alterations to reservations include a changed date of arrival or length of stay, a changed guest name (as when an existing corporate reservation is to be claimed by a different employee), a changed room type or discount request, and a cancellation.

No matter what the alteration may be, the reservationist cannot make a change without first accessing the preexisting reservation. In an electronic reservation system, the reservation is usually accessed by inputting the guest's name, date of arrival, or reservation confirmation number. In a manual system, the reservationist must physically retrieve the reservation correspondence packet from its filing place.

In either system, manual or automated, the preexisting reservation must be found. Only under unusual situations is the existing reservation difficult to locate. Difficulty in finding an existing reservation occurs when either the guest or reservationist has made a clerical error. Common clerical errors include incorrect date of arrival or incorrect spelling of the guest's name.

In many cases, these errors are found and rectified. In other instances, the existing reservation cannot be located. If, for some reason, the reservation cannot be found, the reservationist may actually take a new reservation. This is risky, because chances are there will now be duplicate reservations in the system.

Advance Deposits.   Guaranteeing the reservation by means of an **advance deposit** has grown more popular and less popular at the same time. If the request is for cash

Exhibit 4–5

Computer display of expected arrivals (reservations) list. Identical hard copies are provided on the day of arrival to the desk, the uniformed services, and even to the dining room if it is an American plan hotel.

```
EXPECTED ARRIVAL 4/4/ MAGNA ONE HOTEL
PAGE 4
```

RES #	NAME	CONV GRP	NO. RMS	TYPE RM	RATE CAT	RES TYPE	ARRIV	SPL SVC
0261	ONITO, RANDAL		2	K	2	4		
0005	OTTA, M/M ALPREDO		1	S	2	2	11:00P	25
0616	OUVIA & FMLY, MRS JACK		1	D	3	2	11:00P	
R111	RAMLETT, M/M JOHN		1	K	2	2	8:00P	
R260	ROADWATER, M/M REX		3	S	1	2		26 13
R312	RODEY, M/M FRED	ZTUK	1	K	3	2		23
R406	ROWN, M/M MIKE		1	K	2	2	7:00P	
R234	RUCHER, WM/SON		1	D	3	1	10:00P	63
				W/KNIGHT				
R400	RUDNICK, M/M DUANE		1	D	2	3		
R422	RUNKER, M/M WM	00E	1	D	1	1		
R713	RURNSTEIN, M/M SCOTT		1	K	2	2		
R646	RYANT, MS CISSY		1	K	1	2	5:00P	
R456	RYER & FAM, M/M WAYNE		1	K	2	2		
S121	SAMPBELL, M/M KRONE		1	K	1	2		
S216	SAPP & PTY, M/M DONALDO		1	K	1	2		
S200	SAREY, TOMITHAN		1	S	4	2		
S617	SARNIVELE, NICHOLAS	JOIN	1	S	4	1		
S836	SARPENTER, MRS JULYE	WK	1	D	2	1	12:31P	
				W/BROWN				
S855	SASTELLI, MONSIEUR		2	K	C	4		14
T202	TATO, D/M LOUIS	ITUK	1	K	2	2	3:15P	
T008	TENTER & FAM, M/M DEAN		2	S	2	3	5:00P	25
T361	THANDLER, MR HAL		1	S	2	1		

```
**MORE**
```

(check), the procedure has become less popular. Handling cash or checks requires a disproportionate amount of clerical time and postage relative to the economic gain.

The initial reservation procedure is similar whether a deposit check is requested or not. The reservation is confirmed, but only tentatively, since it contains notice that a reservation deposit is required. Two copies of the reservation slip are mailed. The extra copy is to be returned with the check in the nonstamped, preaddressed envelope that is enclosed.

Most hoteliers feel that the cost, time invested, and delay make the procedure unwarranted. This is especially true considering the widespread availability of credit cards.

Guaranteeing by credit card is a procedure that has gained in popularity. The reservation clerk takes the credit-card number over the telephone and records it with the reservation. Nothing needs to be processed at this time. The charge will be forwarded only if the guest is a **no-show,** and then only if the hotel believes that collection is justified. In the usual sequence, the guest appears as expected and credit is established at registration.

Processing the credit card entails a fee that is not part of the cost of cash deposits. However, the fee isn't paid unless the charge is made. Check deposits have their own risk—they bounce.

Experienced travelers soon realize how much of a game the reservation process has become. Busy properties almost always insist on credit-card guarantees rather than on a 4 PM or 6 PM hold. Credit cards reduce the number of no-shows.

At the same time, guests know that many properties do not actually charge the card at the time of the reservation. With such properties, the guarantee is not processed until the expected night of arrival. A card that is charged at the time of the reservation requires another credit entry if the guest cancels in a proper and timely manner. So, to avoid making additional credit entries, many hotels wait to process the card until the night of arrival. The hotel's delay (laziness) provides the traveler with a winning technique that costs the hotel unless the rooms manager is alert to what is happening.

Some unethical travelers play a credit-card game. They provide the hotel with an inaccurate credit-card number. In this way, if they fail to show, the hotel cannot charge them. On the other hand, if they do arrive and their false credit-card number is challenged, they can blame it on poor communication or a clerical error: They invent the false credit-card number by changing the sequence of one or two digits on their real credit card, which makes for a fairly believable excuse. For example, if their Visa card number was 4567 890 123 456, they could simply change the number to 4567 809 123 456. Now they have a believable excuse in the event they do show up for their reservation—but a fictitious number in the event of a no-show.

Many hotel chains and individual properties are wise to this game and intercept ''errors'' at the time of the reservation. They accomplish this by having an automated reservations system that is interfaced directly to a credit-card clearing center. During the several minutes the guest is on the telephone with the reservationist, the credit-card number is input and an approval verification is received. If the approval is denied, the reservationist gives the guest another opportunity to read the correct credit-card number.

Cancellations.   **Cancellations,** like advance deposits, are special cases of reservation changes. They do not create unusual problems unless they are handled improperly. Handling anything at the front desk in an improper manner generates problems as well as bad public relations.

Encouraging cancellation calls is in the best interest of the hotel. Such calls reduce the no-show rate. Fewer no-shows generate more room revenue from **walk-in** guests and reduce complaints from the antiservice syndrome of **overbooking.**

The cancellation number, which is formulated like the confirmation number (discussed earlier), is the only major difference between a cancellation call and any other reservation change. Even then, its importance is limited to guaranteed reservations. The system must protect the guest who has guaranteed the room with a credit card (or other guarantee) from being billed if the reservation is cancelled in a timely manner. The cancellation number is important when the process breaks down and the guest is billed as a no-show. If the guest is not billed, the number isn't needed or used. Nonguaranteed reservations are not generally provided with a cancellation number.

The cancellation number is important to the reservation count. Cancellations always affect room availability counts. Reservation changes involving dates, number of rooms, and types of facilities also affect room availability counts. There are other reservation changes that do not alter the count projections. Into this category fall the hour of arrival, the exposure, a request for a rollaway bed, and others.

Linking the Reservation with the Front Desk

The reservation's journey ends at the front desk. Sometimes the journey is long, as when the reservation was made a year in advance. In other cases, the reservation lead time is extremely short, as with reservations made minutes before arrival. In any case, the front desk serves as the final stopping point in the reservation's journey.

The first step in linking the reservation with the front desk is to change the status of the reservation from future reservation to arriving reservation. At the beginning of every new day, some set of future reservations becomes today's incoming reservations. In a computerized system, this change occurs automatically, either as the clock strikes midnight or as a step in the night audit process. In a manual system, the appropriate reservation racks are physically moved to the front desk to reflect today's incoming guests.

It is at this moment that guests' special requests and needs become the concern of the front desk. Armed with the knowledge of which rooms are available, which rooms are due to check out, and which rooms are staying over, specific room assignments are developed in accordance with guest requests. Even in an automated property, the assigning of special rooms to match special requests is a manual operation. It is the clerk, operating with good judgment, who ultimately determines which requests can be met and which requests will be declined.

Special Coding.   Whether operating under a manual or computerized system, certain reservations are different from the rest. They may be different in their method of payment, in the guests' specific requests, in the fact that they are **commissionable** to a travel agent, in their time of arrival, or in their affiliation. Whatever the case, the front-desk clerk needs to be alert and to treat these reservations differently.

The difference is generally highlighted somewhere on the reservation. In a manual system, the difference is visually apparent, usually through the use of a color-coding system. Advance-deposit reservations are one color, travel agent reservations another color, and so on. In an automated system, colors are not the common method. Instead, a numerical coding system is usually used. In this case, advance-deposit reservations will be indicated with one code number (see Exhibit 4–6, which uses code #40) and travel agent reservations another code (Exhibit 4–6 uses code #55).

A listing of special codes might include some of the following (this is a rather incomplete list): advance deposits, late arrivals, credit card guarantees, corporate guarantees, convention delegates, travel agents, VIPs, permanent reservations, and riding reservations.

EXHIBIT 4–6

Example of a possible computer reservation code. Code numbers communicate on the computer screen the information provided manually by colored slips in the reservation rack. See right column of Exhibit 4–5.

Code	System Meaning	Print Out on Guest Confirmation
11	VIP	
12	Group buyer	
13	Honeymooners	
14	Comp	
20	Connecting rooms	Connecting rooms, if possible
21	Adjoining rooms	Adjoining rooms, if possible
22	Rooms on same floor	Same floor, if possible
23	Need individual names	Please advise names of individuals in your party
24	PS	Petit suite
25	RS	One-bedroom suite
26	LS	Two-bedroom suite
30	Send liquor	
31	Send champagne	
32	Send flowers	
33	Send gift	
34	Send fruit	
40	Require deposit	Please send one night's deposit to guarantee your reservation
41	Due bill	
42	No credit, require advance payment	
43	Walk-in	
50	Special rate	Special rate
51	Airline rate	Airline rate
52	Press rate	Press rate
53	Convention rate	Convention rate
54	Nonconvention rate	Convention rate applies to convention dates only
55	Travel agency	Travel agency
60	Cot	Cot will be provided
61	Crib	Crib will be provided
62	Bedboard	Bedboard will be provided
63	Wheelchair	Wheelchair will be provided
70	Casino guest	
80	See correspondence for very special instructions	
99	Print special message	(Whatever that message is)

Advance Deposits.   Reservations with an advance deposit need to be specially noted. If the deposit arrived, the front-desk clerk needs to be certain to post the credit on behalf of the guest. If the deposit never arrived, the front-desk clerk will probably cancel the reservation if the hotel is nearing capacity.

Late Arrivals.   If front-desk personnel know a given reservation is due to arrive late, they will be less likely to assume it is a no-show as the evening progresses. Also, most **late arrivals** require a guarantee of some sort to hold the room past the normal 6 PM time frame for nonguaranteed reservations. (See Chapter 6 for a full discussion of the quality of the reservation regarding nonguaranteed and guaranteed reservations.)

Credit-Card Guarantee.   Rooms guaranteed with a national credit card are theoretically held for the guest all night long. If the guest fails to arrive, the night auditor will charge the credit card for one night's room.

Corporate Guarantee.   The right to guarantee rooms with a corporation's good credit must be prearranged with the hotel. In case of a no-show, the room charge is billed to the corporation's city ledger account.

Convention Delegate.   *Group affiliation* is a better term than *convention delegate* because the members of a group need not be part of a convention. Hotels cater to tours, company delegations, wedding parties, and other groups that need to be identified. Several codes are needed when several groups are booked at one time.

Travel Agents.   Special-coding **travel agent (TA)** reservations expedites the internal office procedure. After the guest departs, the hotel pays the travel agent commission. (In those circumstances where the travel agent owes the hotel—an *account receivable*—the hotel bills the balance less the travel agent's commission.) When the reservation is placed, the agent identifies the agency, providing name, address, and **International Association of Travel Agents (IATA)** code number. Some hotels will not pay commissions, and the reservationist needs to explain that. If the customer wants that particular hotel, the agency will book the room and forgo its commission. Even if the hotel pays a commission, it may not do so on certain types of bookings. Deeply discounted rates (corporate or governmental, for example) are sometimes not commissionable.

Reservations are confirmed to the agency, not to the guest. In some cases, the hotel lacks the guest's address until registration time. To maintain accountability with the agency, the wise hotel manager sends a notice whenever one of the TA's clients fails to appear.

VIPs.   **Very important persons (VIPs)** are generally coded. These may be well-known dignitaries, celebrities, other hoteliers, or important members of an association that the hotel hopes to book later. VIP designations are made by a member of management or by the sales department. **Star reservation** is also used. A *contact reservation* is a VIP that should be met (contacted) and escorted to his or her room by the management.

Permanent Reservation.   Guests who return to the hotel periodically make a permanent reservation. Frequently, a particular room favored by the guest is saved for a given night or nights each month. Commercial travelers use this type of reservation.

Riding Reservation.   Reservations for which the date of arrival is vague are allowed to "ride." The probable date is booked and then the reservation is carried until the guest shows or an allotted period of time passes, usually less than one week.

Determining When to Deny the Reservation

Despite the large number of rooms that are available on an annual basis, every reservation request is not accepted. The decision depends on space availability and rate ranges available for the specific dates. An occupancy **forecast** determines the space situation for the day or days in question. Even if only one day of the sequence is closed, the reservation is refused and an alternate arrangement is offered. This is unfortunate if the declined reservation represented a request for a number of days. It is especially unfortunate if the period in question has only one sold-out date. Then, the hotel is essentially trading a profitable, long-term reservation against a potential overbooking situation for one sold-out date. In many cases, the reservationist would override the system and book this type of reservation. Obviously, such a decision would be considered on a case-by-case basis.

In other situations, the salesmanship of the reservationist comes into play. The telephone provides a two-way conversation during which the reservationist can gauge the behavior of the guest. Some guests can be convinced to reserve their chosen date at a slightly higher nightly rate. Other guests' minds can be changed towards a slower occupancy period with the offer of reduced rates.

In any case, guests who cannot be accommodated represent lost revenues. The reservationist attempts to salvage lost reservations in a number of ways—offering premium rates during almost sold-out periods, offering different dates when rates are not as high, or even offering another sister property of the same chain in a nearby community. When all else fails, the reservationist can only thank the caller and ask him or her to try again another time.

Yield Management in Theory

Requests for accommodations are sometimes denied even if the house is not full. Most of the hotel's advertised packages are refused if the forecast shows that the house is likely to fill at standard rack rates. The inverse of this is also true. Reservationists must be taught to sell discounted packages or other reduced rates (weekend, commercial, governmental) only on request or when encountering rate resistance.

With a full house, requests from travel agents, to whom the hotel pays a commission, may be regretted. A low priority is assigned to requests from agents who are slow in paying. All reservations are refused if the caller has a poor credit rating, regardless of the occupancy forecast. Busy hotels give preference to higher-paying multiple-occupancy requests over single occupancy.

Casino hotels give preferential treatment to those who are likely to gamble, even to the extent of granting them free accommodations in preference to paying guests who don't play. Noncasino hotels do the same, allotting their scarce space to reservations from certain areas or markets that the hotel is trying to develop. Seasonal resorts quote **in-season** and **off-season rates** and frequently require a minimum length of stay on holiday weekends.

Controlling the rates and restricting the occupancy to maximize gross revenue (**yield**) from all sources has long been a tool of the hotel manager. Now the process is being systematized into an occupancy–price strategy called **yield management.**

Yield Management Factors.   Like other businesses, hotel prices (room rates) have become more sensitive to customer wants and expectations. Yield management is market oriented, responding to sharper segmentation of guest identification. Until recently, hotel rates have been driven by financial and operating considerations alone (see Chapter 9). Rates were, and still are, expected to cover operational and capital costs and yet fall within the range of competition. Yield management adds another dimension to the approach.

Yield management has an economic rationale. It assumes that all customers are price conscious—that they are aware of the existence of and the significance of price variations. Furthermore, it assumes that customers are price sensitive—that their buying habits respond to increases and decreases in price.

All things being equal, the guest is motivated by lower prices. Theoretically, when a similar room type is available for a significantly lower rate at an otherwise equal hotel, the guest will select the lower priced accommodations. In addition, guests who might not have left home at rack rate are inclined to visit hotels when rates are low. As a result, low occupancy periods are generally accompanied by lower average room rates.

The Airlines' Role.   Lodging has adopted yield management concepts from the airlines. Airline rate discounting was widespread in the early 1980s, and that contributed to the array of prices that the airlines found difficult to track. They began experimenting with adjusted rates based on demand forecasts. Discounted tickets purchased far in advance were used to establish a minimum level of seat occupancy and to forecast overall demand. Low and seasonal periods were also discounted. As the plane filled and departure time neared, higher and higher fares were charged. Full price was eventually charged for the remaining seats—a price that would have been virtually impossible to charge when the plane was empty.

Airlines and hotels are much alike. Both have a relatively fixed supply of product (seats and rooms), and both have products that perish with the passage of time. In the 1980s, airlines had one extra edge—large computer capability that was in place and was functional. It takes the capacity of these large systems to simultaneously track occupancy (seat or room) and the variety of price options that both industries market.

Price-sensitive concepts have been employed by hoteliers for a long, long time. Refining the practices and developing them into a program with rules and triggers, with a knowledge base and a strategy, awaited the superior computer capability of the airlines. Today, most major lodging chains have developed (or are currently developing) an automated yield management system. These systems rival the best airline yield management systems in sophistication.

Market Demand.   Airlines and hotels did differ in one respect—their view of the guest. Hotels had previously operated on the belief that their customer was not a discretionary traveler. The guest who came, hoteliers felt, was someone who had to come. Guests did not come merely because the price was reduced enough to lure them into the purchase. Urban hotels, which cater to the least flexible guest, the

EXHIBIT 4–7

This is a normal corporate traveler reservations booking pattern. Although some corporate guests book 30 (or more) days in advance, the majority reserve rooms within a few days of arrival. This is a 275-room hotel that receives approximately 60 percent of its business from corporate guests.

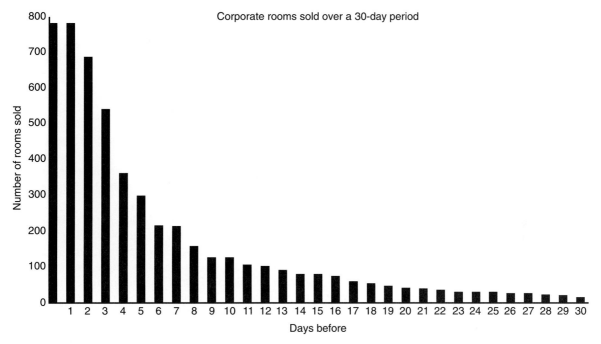

commercial traveler, first evidenced the change. In desperate need of weekend business, these properties began to market weekend specials to discretionary buyers. The march to yield management had begun.

Each customer class has different degrees of price consciousness and price sensitivity. Earlier discussions on segmentation indicated the wide range of guests to whom the industry appeals. In simple terms, these are the business class, the leisure user, and the group buyer.

The *business client* is less sensitive to price—not unaware of price, just less sensitive to it. Businesspersons must travel when the need arises; they will not go merely because the price is reduced.

Business arrangements may be made only a few days or hours before arrival (see Exhibit 4–7). Location is very important, both to save travel time and to present the proper image. Business travelers need to be near the business center, which means high-priced real estate and high room rates. These travelers are away from home a good deal. They seek and probably merit a higher level of comfort than the occasional leisure traveler. In summary, business guests pay higher rates because they are less price sensitive. They have to be where they have to be at a given time, and that arrangement is often made suddenly, with little advance planning, and therefore little opportunity to obtain discounted rates.

The *leisure guest,* as the name implies, is 180 degrees away. Lead time is long. Reservation bookings are well planned, with adequate time to shop for the best room rates. This class of guest is flexible as to the time of the trip, the destination of the trip, and the stopping places. These guests may not even use a hotel. High prices might drive them into camping or park facilities. Poor price value might send them to the homes of friends or family. When prices of accommodations, fuel, toll roads, and gasoline are too high, this guest will just stay home.

Leisure travelers have been the major beneficiaries of the yield management approach offered by both the airline and the hotel industries. The leisure travelers' flexibility with regard to travel dates and itineraries allows them to take advantage of deep discounting during off-season and slow demand periods. It is not uncommon to find hotel rooms discounted between 50 and 80 percent during slow periods. A $250 hotel room in Australia's Kakadu National Park in the tropics, for example, may cost only $100 or so during the rainy season; a $400 golf package in Palm Springs may be discounted to $175 in the heat of the summer.

Group business, the last of the three general classifications, exhibits characteristics from both of the other two categories. That's because the group market forms from components of the business and leisure classifications. From the leisure category come social, fraternal, and hobby associations. From the business segment come professional, union, and governmental groups.

Both types of groups—leisure and business—have their own idiosyncracies. Generally, business-oriented groups are sensitive to date and place while being less sensitive to rate. That is because business groups usually meet the same week every year. Leisure-oriented groups are more rate sensitive and therefore tend to be somewhat flexible with regard to date and place. Profits can be increased if the sales department, based on good forecasting, can steer the business to the right (right for the hotel) time, place, and rate.

Yield management has changed the interface between the sales department and the group buyer. Based on information from the yield management program, sales must decide to take the business, reject the business, or try to negotiate a different time at a different rate. Saturday arrival for a group might actually prove more profitable at $90 per night, for example, than a Monday arrival (which replaces full rack rate corporate guests) at $115 per night. A well-programmed yield management system should provide the answer.

At issue is whether the discounted room rates requested by the group, plus the value of the group's meeting room and banquet business, is valued at more or less than the forecasted income from normal guests who will be turned away. Yield management systems can answer that question. The discretionary decisions still remain for the salespersons to evaluate. For example, is other new business likely to spin off from this meeting? Is this a single event, or are we doing business with a meeting planner who controls 100 or more meetings per year?

Yield management means that function rooms are no longer booked on a first-come, first-served basis. Neither are guest rooms; there must be a price–occupancy mix.

Price–Occupancy Mix.   Yield is the product of occupancy times Average Daily Rate (ADR). Yield can be increased by raising rates when occupancy (demand) is high. Rates are raised by refusing packages, requiring minimum lengths of stay, and charging groups full rate without discounts. When occupancy (demand) is low, prices are dropped by promoting the packages, seeking out the price-sensitive groups, and creating special promotional rates.

EXHIBIT 4–8

Price–occupancy mix: Yield is the product of occupancy times rate. Management decides whether a higher rate (price) or a higher occupancy is preferable. This exhibit assumes 250 rooms and a 31-day month. Potential revenue assumes 100 percent occupancy at an $80 ideal rate.

Company	Average Daily Rate	Percent of Occupancy	Monthly Gross Revenue	Potential Revenue	=	Yield Percentage
A	$ 75	65.00%	$377,812.50	$620,000		60.9%
B	$100	48.75%	$377,812.50	$620,000		60.9%
C	$ 50	97.50%	$377,812.50	$620,000		60.9%

Since yield is the product of the two elements, equilibrium is obtainable by increasing one factor when the other decreases. Exhibit 4–8 illustrates the mathematics. Yield in all three cases appears to be identical. With the same room revenue, a management choice between high ADR and high occupancy needs to be made.

All managers will not view the values in Exhibit 4–8 as being equal. Some would prefer the higher occupancy over the higher rate. Higher occupancy means more persons. More guests translate into more food and beverage revenue, more telephone usage, more calls for laundry and dry cleaning. More guests mean more greens fees, more amusement park admissions, or more money spent in the casino. For these reasons, some hotels charge the same rate for occupancy by one or two persons.

Another group of operators would prefer to strengthen their Average Daily Rate. These managers feel that ADR is a barometer of a property's service and quality levels. With the lower occupancy that accompanies higher ADR in this yield management theoretical discussion, hotels save on variable costs like power, wear and tear on furniture and equipment, and reduced levels of staffing.

Clearly, the price–occupancy mix is not a simple, single decision. Dropping rates to increase occupancy might not be the choice of every manager. Indeed, the manager might take that option at one hotel but not at another. Variations in the facilities of the hotel, in its client base, and in the perspective of its management will determine the policies to be applied.

Forecasting.   Yield management relies on the ability of the computer system and the forecast team to balance the several segments of the market (Exhibit 4–9) with the array of rates that hotels now offer. Computers have the capability of offering a distant horizon—5 to 10 years ahead—and a continuing update of data. The discretionary input of the forecast team is still required, but historical data and future bookings are amassed as individual entries are recorded for reservation purposes. Technology has provided computer programs that can learn from the past in order to project into the future. These artificial intelligence systems refine their knowledge bases as new data are entered. Whatever the system, forecasting is the essential element of yield management. More on forecasting comes in Chapter 6.

EXHIBIT 4–9

Hypothetical market mix for Atlantic City hotels.

Hotel	Percent Occupancy	ADR	Marketing Mix Percentage					
			Individual	Casino	Convention City	and	Group Hotel	Wholesale
A	91.0%	$ 72.12	51.0%	47.0%	2.0%			
B	99.6	86.90	54.0	36.0				10.0%
C	100.1	107.25	100.0					
D	89.9	51.62	54.0	6.2	8.5		5.0%	26.3
E	99.4	84.12	60.7	10.1	19.1		4.1	6.0
F	89.9	49.75	45.5	14.6	8.8		30.1	1.0
G	99.9	55.63	24.2	11.8	6.1		9.6	48.3

Yield Management in Practice

Automated yield management systems are available to a wide spectrum of lodging operations. Most chains have some form of yield management in place through their central reservation systems. Although the benefits to the property from a chain-centered yield management system are probably less impressive than an in-house yield management system, there is little initialization cost.

On the other hand, some properties (even those affiliated with a chain) choose to install their own systems. The cost of such a system may be $100,000 or more, but the benefits from increased room revenues far outweigh the investment.

Yield management is most appropriate for hotel properties that demonstrate some or all of the following characteristics:

1. Demand can be clearly segregated into distinct market segments.
2. A large percentage of room reservations have a long lead time.
3. The property provides a variety of different room types and room rates.
4. Demand fluctuates significantly between periods of high and low occupancy.

The actual increase in room revenues experienced by a given hotel is greatly dependent on the characteristics listed above. Depending on the hotel, yield management systems may enhance the average room rate by some 2 to 10 dollars. For a 250-room property with 68 percent occupancy, a $2 increase in the average room rate would translate to $124,100 in extra room revenues per year. At that rate, even a $200,000 investment makes sense!

Expert Systems. Yield management systems allow for instantaneous response to changing conditions. Seven days a week, 24 hours a day, the system compares actual performance with forecasted assumptions and adjusts rates accordingly. To make these changes, advanced computer systems utilize either standard logical functions or state-of-the-art artificial intelligence operations. Artificial intelligence (AI) or expert systems use stored data that has been developed over a period of time to form rules that govern yield management decisions.

Today's expert systems are truly artificial intelligence. They literally think through demand, formulate decisions, and provide the user with an opportunity to talk with the computer. Below is a list of the special features generally found in an expert yield management system. The expert system

1. Is able to deal not just with quantitative facts but with qualitative data as well.
2. Includes an analysis of incomplete data when formulating a decision.
3. Explains to the user how a given conclusion was reached.
4. Allows a two-way communication interface with the user.
5. Maintains a database of historical facts.
6. Applies programmable rules and triggers to its set of facts.
7. Can override basic rules and triggers when additional decision criteria warrant.

Rules and Triggers.   The computer compares actual reservation activity with budgeted forecasts. When a particular date or period falls outside of the rules for that time frame, the computer flags it. Once flagged, most systems will print a management report identifying time periods in exception to the forecast. In addition, expert systems will automatically change rates and other sales tools. The immediacy of the expert system is a major advantage. Hundreds and even thousands of dollars may be lost in the time it takes management to approve a given rate change. The expert system acts first and takes questions later.

In order to establish rules or triggers for the system to use, management must first segment the room count into market types. For example, a typical 250-room property might **block** 25 rooms for discounting to government guests or IT packages, 50 rooms for transient guests, 100 rooms for business customers, and the remaining 75 rooms for sale to tour groups and convention business.

Different guidelines are then placed on each of these market segments. To illustrate, assume management expects 25 percent of the transient room block to fill by, say, 181 days out (days before arrival). It also expects that 91 days before arrival, transient rooms will be 60 percent sold, and by 61 days out, the entire block will be 90 percent reserved. These are the parameters management has forecasted for transient rooms; its expectations for business rooms may be completely different. Once these triggers are identified, they are programmed into the yield management system. The computer then evaluates the effects of changing demand and acts accordingly. If, for example, 181 days out the transient room block is 35 percent reserved, the computer would **flag** the date as a potentially busy period and increase rates for all remaining rooms. How much the rates increase is also subject to advanced programming.

Common Sales Tools.   Aside from simply adjusting the room rate, hotels have several other tools with which they work. One common tool is **boxing** the date. Boxing dates (no through bookings) is another control device open to the reservations manager. Reservations on either side of the *boxed* day are not allowed to spill into that date. For example, if Wednesday, April 7th, is anticipated as a heavy arrival date, we might box it. Rooms sold for Monday or Tuesday must check out by Wednesday; Rooms sold for Thursday or Friday cannot arrive a day earlier. Dates are blocked in anticipation of a mass of arrivals, usually a convention or group movement, that could not be accommodated through the normal flow of departures. With such heavy arrivals, no one is permitted to check in before that day and stay through the boxed day, even though there is more than enough space on those previous days.

Another tool available to the reservations department is closing a specific date to arrival. Dates that are closed to arrival allow the guest to stay through by arriving on a previous date. Closed to arrival is utilized as a technique for improving occupancy on preceding nights before a major holiday or event.

A final example of reservations sales tools is the minimum length of stay. This technique is designed to improve occupancy on nights preceding and following a major event or holiday by requiring guests to book a minimum number of nights. For example, if New Year's Eve has a three-day minimum length of stay, the hotel will probably improve occupancies on December 30th and January 1st.

Fenced Rates.   A relatively new addition to the list of reservations sales tools has recently migrated to hotels from the airline industry. Fences or **fenced rates** are logical rules or restrictions that provide a series of options to the guest. Guests are not forced to select these options; their rate is determined by which (if any) options they choose.

As with the yield management systems themselves, the airlines originated fenced rates. Examples of airline fenced rates might include the passenger who chose a lower but nonrefundable fare, a customer who purchased the ticket at least 21 days in advance to receive a special rate, or someone who stayed over on a Saturday night to take full advantage of the best price.

Fenced rates are relatively new to the lodging industry. However, the few chains using them seem quite satisfied with their results. It will probably be standard practice in the future to offer discounts for advanced purchases and nonrefundable and unchangeable reservations.

Summary

Because reservations are in a sense contractual agreements, the hotel or corporate reservationist must be careful to document all pertinent information. Some reservation information, such as the date of arrival, number and type of room, and guest's name and rate, is essential to the hotel. Other information, such as estimated time of arrival, special requests, and discounts, is less important to the reservation and may therefore only be collected in certain cases or by request of the guest.

Once the reservation has been agreed upon between the customer and the hotel or corporate office, its journey begins. In some cases the journey is short, as with those reservations made a few hours or days before arrival, and other times it is a long journey, as with reservations made many months—even years—in advance. Along the way, confirmation numbers are provided, advance deposits can be requested, and alterations or cancellations may be forthcoming. The length of the reservation's journey, or lead time, is a key factor in yield management.

With yield management (yield equals average room rate times the number of rooms sold), room prices change as a function of lead time and demand. Vacationing families, tour groups, and seniors often know as far as a year in advance their exact date and location of travel. These customers generally book early enough to take advantage of special discounts or packages; yield management works to their advantage. Conversely, corporate travelers frequently book accommodations at the last moment. In their case, yield management works against them by charging maximum rates to last-minute bookings when the hotel is nearing full occupancy.

Queries and Problems

1. The quality of the reservation (6 PM, guaranteed, and advance deposit) is a major factor in determining no-show rates. Knowing that 6 PM reservations have the greatest likelihood of becoming no-shows, why would any hotel ever want to accept 6 PM reservations? For that matter, why not simply install an ''advance deposits only'' reservations policy? Explain why most chains accept 6 PM reservations (and require their member properties to do the same).

2. Corporate management has asked its new trainees, of which you are one, to devise an incentive plan that would encourage guests to cancel unneeded reservations and thus reduce the no-show percentage. Be certain that your scheme does not open the hotel to various scams.

3. Develop a list of fenced rate restriction possibilities. This list may include those currently used by airlines, or create your own possible restrictions.

4. Many hotels are apprehensive about charging corporate guaranteed reservations if the traveler fails to arrive. Even though a room was held and revenue was lost, the hotel is afraid to charge the no-show back to the corporation for fear of retaliation and loss of future business.

   Develop a series of strict—but fair—reservations policies that protect the hotel's interests while at the same time minimizing conflicts with the corporate account.

5. Discuss the merits of higher rates with lower occupancy versus lower rates with higher occupancy if you were the manager of (a) a budget economy property, (b) a commercial convention property, or (c) an upscale resort property.

6. Yield management programs often discount rates to the benefit of one segment of guests but charge full rack rate to others who book at the last moment. With attention to the rewards and penalties that such policies carry, discuss a proposed policy that (a) deeply discounts rates for noncancellable reservations made 30 days in advance and (b) discounts rates for standby guests who are willing to wait until 7 PM for vacancies.

CHAPTER 5

Making and Taking the Individual and Group Reservation

Chapter Outline

Making and Taking the Reservation

The electronic age is changing the way industries do business. For lodging, the change is most pronounced in the reservation process. Completing a reservation takes three elements: someone to make the reservation, someone to take the reservation, and some means for the two to communicate. Each has undergone substantial changes. Third parties have entered the communications flow on both sides. The reservation maker, for example, may not even make the reservation, and the reservation taker also relies on agents. The third parties have interposed themselves between the maker and the taker, and so many have appeared that the ultimate takers (the hotels) have developed special marketing procedures and reservation facilities to accommodate the demand from third parties. The gap between the hotel and its guests has widened as an unexpected consequence of these new distribution channels.

Finally, the reservation itself materializes in a variety of ways. The telephone is no longer the communication device of choice for all parties. Today, the telephone

EXHIBIT 5–1

This chart shows the many possible combinations through which reservations are ultimately made. Arrows represent typical communication patterns. The electronic age is changing many of the ways we do business—hotel reservations are no exception.

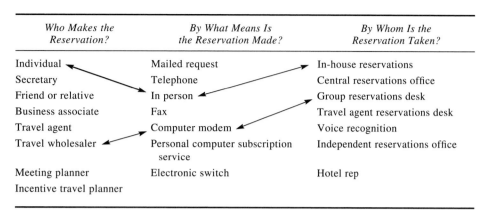

Who Makes the Reservation?	By What Means Is the Reservation Made?	By Whom Is the Reservation Taken?
Individual	Mailed request	In-house reservations
Secretary	Telephone	Central reservations office
Friend or relative	In person	Group reservations desk
Business associate	Fax	Travel agent reservations desk
Travel agent	Computer modem	Voice recognition
Travel wholesaler	Personal computer subscription service	Independent reservations office
Meeting planner	Electronic switch	Hotel rep
Incentive travel planner		

has been supplemented with on-line reservation systems between major suppliers, on-line modem communication for electronic users, fax machines for corporate guests, and a list of additional options to other users (see Exhibit 5–1).

Who Makes the Reservation?

Reservations can be made by a number of different parties. For example, the individual guest may contact the reservation center personally, thereby eliminating any other parties. On the other hand, a second party may become involved, as when the travel agent contacts the reservations system on the guest's behalf. Indeed, some reservations are made blindly without any specific guest in mind. An example of these "blind," or "unspecified" bookings might be when a company books 100 award trips to Hawaii as incentive prizes for a sales contest. The reservations are created long before the winners' names are ever known.

Depending on who actually creates the reservation, these contacts with the reservations system can be segregated into three distinct categories: first-person, second-person, and third-person contacts.

First-Person Contacts.   A first-person contact is personally initiated by the guest. Generally, reservations made by a particular individual for his or her own personal use are first-person reservations. These represent a large percentage of all the reservations made each year.

A corporate traveler calls the hotel she frequents and speaks with a familiar reservationist to book a room next week. The father of a family calls the central reservations system and checks hotel availability at a nearby amusement park for the July 4th weekend. Or, a bride-to-be reserves the honeymoon suite at her favorite ski resort. These are all examples of first-person reservations.

Second-Person Contacts.   A second-person reservation is one that is made by a friend, associate, relative, or travel agent on another individual's behalf. With second-person contacts, the reservation is made specifically with the guest in mind. The guest's hotel preference, dates of arrival and departure, rate sensitivity, and related likes and dislikes are all considered by the second party during the creation of the reservation.

Second-person reservations are extremely common and represent the bulk of reservations for many chains. A corporate hotel often finds secretaries calling for reservations on behalf of their bosses. A resort property works with a number of travel agents who reserve rooms with specific guests in mind. And rooms at local hotels are often booked by friends and family of the guest. These are all examples of second-person contacts.

The Travel Agent.   Travel agents are one of the major sources of second-person reservations. Travel agent bookings represent about 15 percent of all hotel rooms booked. Hotels pay a 10 percent commission—more in off-seasons to generate volume—for all rooms booked by a travel agency. Fees are not regulated. Amounts paid vary from property to property and even within the same property over time. **Overrides,** additional points of 10–15 percent, are paid to encourage high levels of business from one agency.

Guests pay no direct charge to the agency for its service, although some agencies have started to charge service fees. Neither do they pay for airline bookings made by the agent in the guest's name. Two areas of contention emerge from this relationship. One is a marketing problem, the other a bookkeeping problem.

There are several marketing problems. Hotels complain that travel agencies (TAs) send business chiefly during the hotel's busy periods. Additional reservations are not needed then, and certainly not if they require a commission. According to the agents, hotels befriend them only when there is no business and ignore them and their customers—who incidentally are also hotel guests—as soon as volume recovers.

If the travel agent's repeat bookings are few and widely spaced, commission checks are small. Hotels find the cost of processing such checks greater than the commission. Hotels also have problems with some of the bookings when they originate with unknown agencies whose credit status is unproven. For these and for other accounting reasons that are reviewed in a later chapter, commission payments are not as prompt as TAs would like them to be. It is prompt, accurate payment that heads the agenda of every travel agency–hotel meeting.

Other key topics include the hotel's willingness to honor reservations and the reliability of its reservation system, including the frequency of overbooking. TAs are frustrated by these issues and by uncollected commissions, which they maintain total as much as half of all debt due. Whereas travel agencies actively solicit airline business, they maintain that hotel bookings are made chiefly to accommodate their clients. That's hard to believe when one looks at the figures.

The macro view is rosier. Lodging industry payments to the travel industry increase each and every year. Hotels pay billions of dollars annually to the tens of thousands of individual agencies. Unfortunately for the client, those payments dictate which hotel the agency selects. If the guest has no preference (most do), the hotel that pays commissions promptly will be the one the agency selects.

The system operates through a patchwork of informal relationships. Few formal agreements are in place. Many hoteliers believe that they are in direct competition with the travel agent, fighting for the same business and paying a commission to boot. That kind of thinking is being supported by the appearance of powerful mega-agencies and consortiums of agencies. Large-volume dealers stand toe-to-toe with national hotel chains. By securing the travel contracts of small and large corporations, these mega-agencies squeeze discounted rates from the national hotel chains anxious to get or retain a piece of the business.

Third-Person Contacts.   A third-person reservation is one that is made without a specific guest in mind. Such reservations are generally created in large room blocks without prior knowledge as to exactly who will occupy each room. Instead, a block of rooms is reserved against future guest specifics.

A travel agent or travel wholesaler who negotiates a special package does so without actually knowing who will fill those rooms. An incentive travel planner arranges a series of vacation prizes before the winners of the contest are determined. And, a convention meeting planner books several hundred rooms on behalf of the convention delegates who have not even decided to attend the event. These are all examples of third-person contacts.

Who Takes the Reservation?

Just as there are numerous individuals and representatives making the reservation, there are a number of places accepting the reservation. An affiliated hotel not only accepts its own reservations but has a series of additional centers taking reservations on its behalf. These additional centers are designed to expedite the reservation process in a number of ways.

In-House Reservation Center.   No matter what their affiliation or level of automation, all hotels have some system for accepting direct or in-house reservations. In certain properties, the number of in-house reservations is quite minimal. In other operations, however, the bulk of hotel rooms are sold through the in-house reservation center. This is especially true with nonaffiliated, independent hotels where there is no central reservations system (CRS) or where the CRS represents a small percentage of all reservations.

Direct or in-house reservations are also taken in quantity by those hotels that host a large group sales business. Such business is generated by the hotel's own sales department, and those bookings bypass the CRS. For this reason, in-house reservationists have been incorporated into the sales departments of several hotel chains.

Experienced shoppers often call the hotel directly. The reservationist is more informed about the property. He or she has one hotel, whereas the CRS agent has hundreds or even thousands. If the hotel is full, reservations might be refused by the central reservation office but still be accepted on site.

A reservations manager, or supervisor, heads the division, which might number as many as a dozen persons. Large operations permit a degree of specialization, but the size scales downward until the room clerk alone carries out the function. Reports and room status computations may be the responsibility of one group of employees, and others may tend solely to tour groups. More often, several of these jobs are combined into one or two positions.

Central Reservations System.   The central reservations system (CRS) has historically been referred to as the central reservations office (CRO). Although there is a distinction between these two terms, today's jargon has made them almost fully interchangeable. Most managers refer to their central reservations center as the CRS.

In reality, the central reservations system (CRS) is the entire system, including all of the link-ups, software, switches, and nuances that will be described in this chapter. The central reservations office (CRO) is the hotel chain's portion of this overall system. The CRO is the actual office or site at which the chain's reservationists operate (see Exhibit 5–2).

Historically, most chains maintained one central reservations office. Guests accessed the office simply by dialing the 1–800 toll-free number the chain advertised (see Exhibit 5–3, which shows an alphabetical list of some of the major chains' 1–800 phone numbers). It was not uncommon for one central reservations office to receive several million phone calls per year. That is a lot of telephone activity!

Therefore, CROs needed to locate in an area with a great capacity for telephone volume. This area was the Midwest. The Midwest, especially Omaha, Nebraska, developed into a major central reservations' hub because of the excess equipment in the area. The Bell System had unused capacity as a result of the massive defense grid built to accommodate the armed forces. With a promise of exceptionally good service and the support of the telephone system, hotel companies began opening reservation centers in the late 1960s. This created a specialized labor pool, making the area even more attractive.

Even today, midwestern cities such as Omaha and Kansas City house a large percentage of the nation's CROs. However, as call volumes rose in the 1980s, most chains found themselves establishing several CROs scattered nationwide. Today, the numbers are staggering. Some of the larger lodging chains boast over 2 million calls per month and book well in excess of 1 million reservations per month.

Processing the Call. Reservation agents receive the incoming calls and process them at slightly more than two minutes each. They are assisted with in-coming telephone calls by sophisticated telephone switching equipment. During busy call volume periods, automated telephone systems answer the call and may segregate the caller according to a variety of options. The caller is asked to listen to the options and then select by pressing a specific number on the telephone keypad. Large chains use the telephone system to segregate callers according to the hotel brand in which they are most interested. Another common way to separate callers is according to whether their reservation is for a domestic hotel property, a European hotel, an Asian property, a Latin American operation, and so on.

Once callers have been properly routed, they may be placed on hold for the next available reservationist. During the holding period, a recording provides information about the chain, special discount periods, new hotel construction, and the like. Automatic call distributor equipment eventually routes the telephone call to the next available reservationist.

Time is money, with labor and telephone lines the primary costs of CROs. So the reservation manager battles to reduce the time allotted to each call. A sign in one office read: "Talk time yesterday 1.8 (meaning minutes). During the last hour, 2.2. Yesterday, 2.1." Actually, more sophisticated devices are available. Some computer-management systems monitor each agent, providing data on the number of calls taken, the time used per call taken, and the amount of postcall time needed to complete the reservation. However, employee evaluations must not be judged on time alone. Systems should evaluate the percentage of the agent's calls that result in firm bookings and the relationship of the agent's average room rate to the average being sold by the entire center (office).

Res centers charge a fee for each reservation booked. Since the center is usually a separate subsidiary of the corporate parent, even company-owned properties pay the fee of several dollars per booking. Franchisors often get more than just the booking fee. A monthly fee on each room plus a percent of gross room sales may

EXHIBIT 5–2

A national reservations center (CRO), which may employ hundreds of reservationists.

EXHIBIT 5–3

An alphabetical list of 10 national chains' 1–800 phone numbers. See also Exhibit 14–5 for more creative 1–800 numbers.

1. Best Western International	1–800–528–1234
2. Choice Hotels International	1–800–221–2222
3. Days Inn Hospitality Franchise Systems, Incorporated	1–800–325–2525
4. Double Tree Hotels Corporation	1–800–222–8733
5. Holiday Inn Worldwide	1–800–465–4329
6. Hyatt Hotels and Resorts	1–800–233–1234
7. Marriott Corporation	1–800–228–9290
8. Omni Hotels	1–800–843–6664
9. Radisson Hotels International	1–800–333–3333
10. ITT Sheraton Corporation	1–800–325–3535

also be charged. Franchisees complain about the fee schedule, but the reservation system is the major attraction of franchising. This appeal might diminish as franchise properties develop their own computer capability and hook into link-up systems.

Last Room Availability.   The old-fashioned central reservations offices of the 1960s through 1980s required constant manual updating of room availability between the hotel and the CRO. The hotel in-house reservations department was responsible for manually tracking the number of rooms sold by the CRO and calculating how many rooms still remained available for a given date. The CRO would continue blindly selling rooms until it was notified by the hotel to close room sales. In other words, the CRO never knew how many rooms were available at the individual property; it only knew that the hotel was still open with regard to room availability.

This placed an important responsibility on the in-house reservationist to notify the CRO when room availability was tightening. This notification became an exercise in timing and forecasting; as often as not, mistakes were made. Sometimes the hotel's in-house reservationist closed rooms with the CRO too early; other times, rooms were closed too late. If the reservationist closed rooms with the CRO too early, there were still rooms available for sale and those remaining rooms became the responsibility of the in-house reservations department. Many times, the reservations department did not have enough in-house reservation activity and the date would come and go with several rooms remaining unsold. On the other hand, if the in-house reservationist closed the rooms too late, the hotel was overbooked.

Commonly referred to as last room availability or full-duplex systems, today's CRSs offer on-line, two-way communication with all affiliated hotels in the chain. No longer a hit-and-miss game of guessing when the last room will be sold, modern CRSs can literally sell the very last room at any hotel. This is because the CRS now has on-line real information about the actual status of rooms at every hotel within the system. This is a significantly more efficient system because it allows the CRS more opportunities to sell every room without either underselling or overselling the hotel.

In addition, last room availability technology is a necessary first step in providing an automated yield management system to the chain. Without on-line, full-duplex communication, a hotel's room rates are difficult to update. In fact, some older systems required the hotel to publish rates 18 months in advance without allowing changes throughout the entire year. The hotel literally had to forecast its levels of business and live with those forecasts no matter what might occur. As a result, the only way a hotel could alter its rates upward or downward during busy or slow periods was to close room availability with the CRO. Once closed, all rooms had to be sold through the in-house system, and rates could be changed as warranted. Today's on-line, last room availability systems allow the property to update rates with the CRS as often as necessary.

The Hotel Representative.   Although not normally done, hotels might maintain sales offices in distant cities, sending reservations from these offices to the hotel. Casino hotels usually maintain such offices in nearby cities: New York for Atlantic City, Los Angeles for Las Vegas. Reservations are among the services provided.

Hotels more often establish their presence in other locations through the use of a representative (rep). This person, or company, functions much as the traditional product representative, as a spokesperson and salesperson for many noncompeting brands. Utell International is one well-known rep.

When many noncompetitors (same-quality hotels from separate cities) associate with one particular rep, another alternative emerges: The independents band together to market the membership under one umbrella. Preferred Hotels and Resorts and Leading Hotels of the World are good examples of this group. These are not-for-profit affiliations.

The rep and the hotel negotiate a fee schedule, although a fee plus commission is not unusual. There may also be an initial membership fee. For that charge, the rep provides many sales and marketing services, including trade-show representation. Most important, the rep provides the central reservation office that the independent hotel lacks. Some international reps even service chains because the international rep provides language operators overseas and settles with travel agents in the currency of the local area. These are capabilities that the chain reservation office may not have.

Technology, with its access to travel agencies, transportation facilities, and company travel departments, is the key to the reservation business. Reps maintain their own systems, which they interface electronically with one or more airline computer systems, something the independent hotel cannot do.

Independent Reservation Services.   Membership in a central reservations system is one of the major advantages chain-affiliated properties have over independent operations. The CRS provides each affiliated property access to sophisticated airline distribution systems, tens of thousands of travel agents, a convenient toll-free telephone number for potential customers, automated rate and inventory data, and a wealth of other automated benefits. Yet CRSs are extremely expensive, and the cost of developing a CRS is prohibitive for most small chains and independent operations.

Smaller chains can provide better guest service at a lesser cost by leasing the reservation service. Leasing from an independent reservation service is commonly referred to as *outsourcing*. It makes sense for independent properties and small and new lodging chains. For example, Ritz Carlton's reservations are handled by Covia; Fairmont, Meridien, and about 28 other chains use TeleService Resources; Preferred Hotels and Resorts uses Trust II; and Ramada International and Movenpick Hotels use ResCom Communications. (Interestingly, ResCom Communications is a subsidiary of the Holiday Corporation.) However, leasing arrangements do place another nonguest buyer between the hotel and the guest.

One plan relinquishes the whole system to a res-center-for-hire. It is a new concept for hotels, but sharing telemarketing companies is not a new idea. Hotel clients are something that companies like J. C. Penney Telemarketing (Motel 6 and Hawthorne Suites) need to get used to. For hotel rep companies—Utell International, for example—the move is a natural extension of their primary role and should represent economies for each of their clients. UtellVision is a computerized reservation system for Utell member hotels. The system simultaneously displays two screens. The top screen is a series of high-resolution pictures of the member hotel and maps of the surrounding areas; on the bottom is an on-line reservations availability screen.

Independent hotels and small chains that join a private reservation service expect to gain efficiency and economies of scale, and they generally do experience a number of money-saving benefits. They save significant investment in hardware and software by joining rather than developing their own system. They save operating and training costs. Reservation processing is more efficient due to the massive computer capacity of the independent reservation service. And salesmanship is enhanced by joining a group of professional trained agents.

Hotel chains have tried other, less dramatic restructuring in their search for electronic links and economy. Various affiliations have been tested as a means of broadening the market and spreading operating costs over a wider base. The affiliates have been other travel and lodging companies, but the umbrella has often been that of an independent entrepreneur. Some, like the Caribbean Hotel Reservation Service, have tried to develop space banks for an entire geographic area. Others are operated for one specific group: business travelers in luxury hotels, for example. Still others are quasi-public agencies such as tourist or convention bureaus.

How the Reservation Is Made

As we have seen, there are a number of possibilities with regard to both who makes the reservation and who takes the reservation. There are also a number of possibilities with regard to how the reservation is made.

The majority of all reservations are still communicated by telephone. Even as newer, more exciting technologies emerge, the telephone continues to play a crucial role in communicating the reservation. In fact, it will probably maintain its importance to the reservations process for many years to come. Even today, with the numerous automated options available to travel agents, more than half of all travel agent reservations are still communicated by telephone. New applications for the telephone strengthen its importance into the next century.

Voice Recognition.   Amazing progress has been achieved in the area of automated voice recognition. Currently, there are systems in place that can recognize hundreds of common words spoken by a host of various users. (IBM's personal dictation system is able to recognize 32,000 words.) There may come a time in the near future when simple first- and second-person reservations are handled electronically by voice-recognition and voice-synthesis (talking) systems.

The biggest argument in favor of such a labor-saving system is the overall repetitiveness of the reservationist's job. As unique as each reservation might seem, there are more commonalities than differences. Each reservation communicates the city, date, room rate and type, and other basic data. These are functions that a computer system could logically handle.

The voice-recognition reservations program would generate a series of questions for the guest to answer. With each response, the program would acknowledge the answer, allow the guest to make changes as necessary, and generate a new series of questions based on the previous response. In those situations where the computer could not recognize the guest's voice due to a strong accent or other impairment, a fail-safe system would be in place—the guest might press the zero button twice on the telephone keypad, for example, to alert an operator that personal assistance was needed.

The computer system could check availability, quote rates, suggest alternate dates, and thank the guest in a manner similar to the reservationist. Of course, such a system would be significantly less personal than dealing with an actual reservationist. On the other hand, it would surely be less expensive in terms of labor costs, and the computer system would never call in sick!

Facsimile Machines. Facsimile (fax) machines also utilize telephone lines to communicate the reservation request. However, with a fax machine, no operator answers the telephone call. Instead, the communication is machine to machine. The originating fax machine transmits information to the receiving machine. The receiving machine then prints the information onto a paper copy. For a reservation request, the information is then entered by a clerk into the computer system and the reservation is established.

Indeed, the fax machine is less an example of telephone usage than it is an example of mailed communication. Where mail (and telegram) played a role in communicating the reservation request many years ago, they represent an extremely small number of reservations today. That is due in part to the changing way in which the world conducts business. Few people are inclined to write a letter and wait for a response when a simple phone call generates immediate confirmation. That is why the facsimile approach never gained popularity in terms of reservations communication.

A new facsimile application has recently been introduced by both Apollo and Sabre, two of the major airline central reservations systems. Rather than creating a hard-copy paper document, this new application is an electronic fax transmission. Similar to electronic mail, both formats allow the central reservations system to electronically interpret the request without requiring the manual involvement of an operator or the generation of any paper. If the rooms request is available, a return message is electronically generated, telling the guest a reservation was created.

Personal Computer Subscription Services. One of the fastest growing means for personal access to the information superhighway is on-line subscription services. Such on-line companies as Prodigy, CompuServe, and On-Line America provide a direct link between the user and the server. Timely news and sports information, consumer and cinematic reviews, product ordering, and games are just a few of the common applications available to the on-line subscriber. Hotel reservations is another common application.

One of the more popular reasons for joining an on-line subscription service is to access major reservations systems (see Exhibit 5–4). Prodigy, for example, allows the subscriber a direct link to the Sabre network. Sabre, American Airlines' central reservations system, is able to provide useful information on most major airlines, hotels, and car rental companies.

Once on-line with Sabre, for example, the user can check air, rooms, and car availability; rates and discount plans; flight schedules; and additional pertinent data. After the guest has played with the options and made a decision, entering the reservation request is simply a matter of following the computer-generated prompts.

That is surprising to some users, because they wonder how the system can provide the same computer prompts when it is accepting reservations for a number of central reservations offices. For example, the input codes and data required for a Marriott reservation are quite different from the codes and data needed for a Sheraton reservation. The answer to this query lies in the sophisticated technology surrounding the switch.

The Electronic Switch. The hotel industry owes much to the airline industry. The airlines have frequently experimented and developed automated applications that were then altered to fit the hotel industry. Central reservations applications, yield management technology, and integrated property management systems all owe some

EXHIBIT 5–4

A graphical representation of the vertical integration of the modern reservations network.

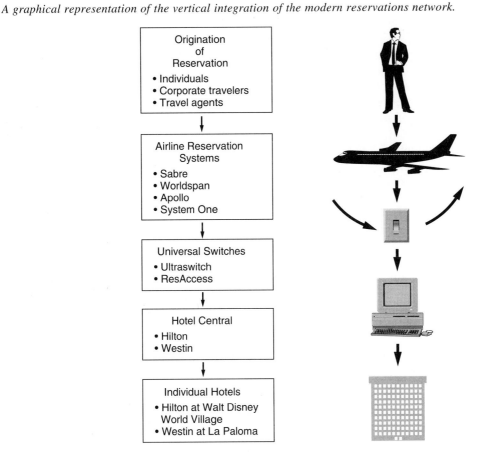

aspect of their success to the airlines. The electronic switch is the most recent example of airline industry technology serving the hotel industry. Thanks in part to the switch, these two industries are completely interconnected and entwined today. Reservations for hotels can be made through airline reservation systems, and vice versa.

History. Travel agents have had direct access to airline reservation systems for several decades. Major airline systems such as Sabre, Apollo, Gemini, Amadeus, Abacus, and Pars (see Exhibit 5–5) established electronic links to major travel agent offices for a number of reasons. Once on line, the travel agent was then able to check availability, compare prices, schedule convenient flight times, and ultimately book the air travel directly from the convenience of the travel agency. Today, due to a number of mergers and joint ventures, there are only four major airline reservation systems: Apollo, Sabre, Worldspan, and System One.

The systems were expensive, and though the airlines offered a number of avenues to access the terminal for relatively little cost, the number of terminals in a

EXHIBIT 5–5

A sampling of airline central reservations systems. The sheer size and cost make it impractical for one airline to own an entire CRS.

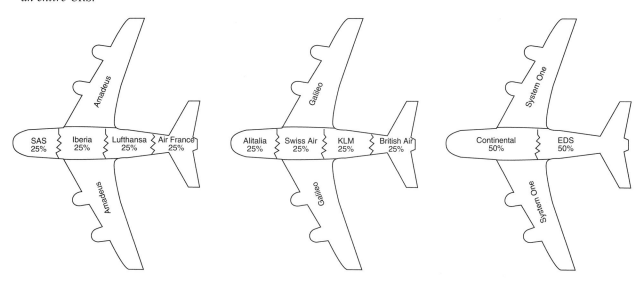

given office was still a function of the size and booking strength of that travel agency. Smaller travel agents had fewer terminals and thereby had fewer direct booking options than larger agents. However, the travel agent was always able to contact an airline by telephone to book the trip. Therefore, travel agents had two choices—book the business directly on the airline's CRS terminal (if available) or book the airline by telephone. Reservations by computer terminal rapidly grew in popularity.

A few years later, major hotel and car-rental chains joined forces with the airline reservations centers. The travel agent was then able to sell the complete trip, including air, ground transportation, and lodging.

However, things did not always run smoothly. Many major lodging chains were not connected to airline reservation systems. Although they were able to join, some lodging chains thought the costs were prohibitive. A single hotel property in the chain would have had to pay three separate commissions for a single reservation: The hotel would have to pay the travel agent a 10 percent (or higher) commission; the airline would take a fee for access to the airline reservations system; and the hotel chain would take its normal fee for booking through the chain's CRO. Those chains that chose not to join the airline reservations system were still available to the travel agent by telephone, but in many cases telephone reservations just were not made.

To address this problem, many hotel chains began providing more efficient telephone reservation services to travel agents. In an attempt to encourage telephone bookings, hotel chains established private 1–800 toll-free numbers exclusively for travel agents. These private phone numbers were staffed by experienced reservationists who could answer questions and book reservations very quickly. As efficient as this may sound, to many agents the telephone approach was not as appealing as the direct-access airline computer terminal.

Another issue that was apparent during these years was the fact that the hotel information listed on the airline reservations system was old news. Just as the hotel chain's CRO was not full-duplex at this stage, neither was the airline system. Hotels still needed to close availability when a number of rooms remained, they were still not able to alter rates at a moment's notice, and they were still only able to offer a few basic rate categories. In fact, many airline reservations systems only allowed a set number of changes to hotel information per day, and they required several hours' lead time. As a result, the risk of overbooking through the airline reservations system was high.

With the old-fashioned, one-way downloading of rates and availability, hotel chains and airline systems were constantly updating information. Not only was that labor intensive and prone to errors but it created time lags between the creation of new data and its appearance on the CRS.

Switch Technology.   Just as the hotel CROs have begun using last room availability, full-duplex, on-line systems, so have the airlines. Often referred to as *seamless connectivity,* today's travel agents can book on-line hotel rooms in real time. All of the benefits to the travel agent and hotel that accrue through last room availability systems are becoming available through airline reservations systems. Now, the travel agent is literally looking at the same hotel reservation data as the in-house reservationist; if there are special rates or packages, the travel agent can quote them as readily as the hotel's in-house reservationist. This is adding a new level of credibility to travel agents, who have often complained that their outdated data makes them look unprofessional to the customer.

This major leap forward took an enormous investment—billions of dollars according to some experts. It also took a new way of looking at an old problem. The difference between the old system and the new electronic switch technology is that instead of merely downloading hotel and rental car information into the airline reservations systems, the switch literally allows an interconnection between the airline systems (which are in most travel agents' offices) and the hotel chains' central reservations systems. This full connection from the agent's terminal through the airline system through the electronic switch to the hotel central reservations system is truly seamless connectivity!

Another major advantage of the switch is the ability of the travel agent to learn just one set of procedures and to input just one set of codes. Switch technology functions as a translator as well as a real-time communicator. It translates codes into one hotel central reservations system or another. Now, when the agent is interested in booking a room with, say, two queens, the agent does not need to remember the exact input code. One chain might identify two queens with a QQ code, another chain might use 2Q or DQ for double queen. The electronic switch allows the user one system of codes and translates that information across the regularities of each member hotel chain's central reservations system on the switch.

There are four major electronic switches in varying stages of development. The first system, THISCO, was developed by 11 major lodging chains (Best Western, Choice, Days Inns, Hilton, Holiday, Hyatt, La Quinta, Marriott, Ramada, Sheraton, and Forte) in conjunction with Robert Murdoch's electronic publishing division. THISCO, which stands for The Hotel Industry Switching Company, was originally introduced in the early 1990s and is still programming roughly one hotel chain per month into its system. Anasazi, Internal, and WizCom are the other three switches currently in use (see Exhibit 5–6).

Guest History Databases.   Another advantage of a fully integrated reservations system is the ability for hotels to share guest history information. Database information is currently only utilized within chains. As the switch technology improves, guest history data may actually be shared across chains.

Even within the chain, hotels rarely take advantage of their wealth of data. Most property management systems allow a guest history function. Standard information required for the reservation becomes a marketing tool, if properly administered. After all, the hotel already knows the guest's name and address, the dates of the last visit, the rate paid, the room type, the number of guests, and the method of payment. Add a bit of marketing information like the type of discount package purchased, the special rate or promotion used, and whether the reservation was over a weekend or was a weekend getaway package, and the manager has an enormous amount of marketing data.

CD-ROM Reservation Technology.   Another technological opportunity available to hotels through some of the airline reservations systems is CD-ROM. Both Sabre (through SabreVision) and Apollo (through Apollo Spectrum) offer CD-ROM technology to their listed hotels. CD-ROM is a high-tech way to see visual images of hotels and their surrounding communities.

Imagine a guest walking into a travel agent's office and asking to see pamphlets of hotels in Hawaii. Instead of merely showing pamphlets, the travel agent displays CD-ROM technology on the computer terminal. Now the guest is able to see color images of several hotels, maps of the surrounding community, and even take a tour through corridors, restaurants, and various features of the hotel. That is exciting, and many agencies experience booking rates three to four times higher with CD-ROM visuals.

Though rather expensive, the future looks bright for this new-wave technology. It allows the guest to make an involved and interactive hotel selection. And, it saves on brochure printing costs!

Accommodating the Group Reservation

Group rooms business, in all its varied forms, represents an enormous percentage of revenues to the lodging industry. For convention properties, group business may represent upwards of 90 percent of all lodging revenues. On the other hand, smaller lodging operations or certain transient and destination hotels receive relatively little revenue from group rooms activity.

Incentive travel, tour groups, conventions, and trade shows have become mainstays of hotel sales in the United States and abroad. Such gatherings are clearly defined as group business. Likewise, business meetings and corporate retreats, though smaller in scale, are also included in this broad definition.

Depending on the hotel, however, still smaller gatherings lose the distinction of being classified and tracked as group business. A small wedding party requiring only five or seven rooms, for example, may be considered an individual rather than a group reservation. Several executives meeting in a conference room for a few days are often handled through the hotel's in-house reservations department as individual

EXHIBIT 5–6

*A partial list of major
hotel chains and the
electronic switch to
which they are currently
linked.*

Company	Link
Best Western International	THISCO
Days Inn Hospitality Franchise Systems, Inc.	THISCO
Four Seasons Hotels and Resorts	Anasazi
Hilton Hotel Corporation	Internal
Holiday Inn Worldwide	Internal
Hyatt Hotels and Resorts	THISCO
ITT Sheraton Corporation	THISCO
Marriott Corporation	Internal
Nikko Hotels International	WizCom
Radisson Hotels International	WizCom
Westin Hotels and Resorts	THISCO

rooms. Indeed, even a convention meeting planner visiting the property several weeks before the convention is probably handled as an individual (though complimentary) room. Technically, the meeting planner's accommodations should be tracked as part of the overall convention count.

Group reservations are handled differently from basic individual reservations. One difference is the central reservations office (or reservations link-up) may not be entitled to handle the group. Many chains require that group accommodations deal directly with the specific hotel property. Even at the hotel property, larger operations remove group reservations from the responsibility of the in-house reservations department. Most large properties have a group sales department designed to handle (among other tasks) group rooms reservations. Finally, depending on business levels, policies, and property characteristics, large groups may be granted special rates and discounts. These special deals are negotiated between the group's representative and the hotel's sales manager, with final approval granted by the general manager of the property.

Because of differing policies and definitions, group business is handled and characterized differently across various hotels and chains. Therefore, it is difficult to know exactly how great is the impact of group rooms activity on the lodging industry. A fairly large number of group activities are never counted. However, the convention industry (including conventions, expositions, corporate meetings, incentive travel, and trade shows) is conservatively estimated at $75 billion annually in the United States alone. According to the U.S. Department of Commerce, that places the convention industry 17th in comparison to all industries in the United States! Of that $75 billion, roughly 66 percent of the revenues come from conventions and expositions, 30.5 percent come from corporate meetings, and 3.5 percent come from incentive travel (see Exhibit 5–7). Each of these categories of group travel has its own demographics and spending patterns. Some details related to convention visitor spending are shown in Exhibit 5–8.

The Importance of Group Business

The importance of the ratio of group room sales to total room revenues depends on the type of hotel operation. Some properties—conference centers, for example—are exclusively group-oriented in nature (see Exhibit 5–9). Other operations choose to accommodate groups during slow periods and off-seasons. There are very few hotels that entirely refuse to accommodate group business.

EXHIBIT 5–7

The group revenues pie demonstrates that two-thirds of all group rooms revenues come from convention and exposition business.

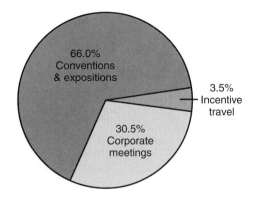

EXHIBIT 5–8

Delegates spend sizable sums on lodging and related expenses when visiting hotels on group business.

How the delegates' dollars are spent

5% Admission to shows, recreation, sporting events, and sightseeing
13% Retail stores
6% Local transportation, auto rental, and gasoline
3% Other
46% Hotel rooms
3% Hospitality suites
12% Hotel restaurants
12% Other restaurants

Delegate spending per trip by affiliation

Affiliation	Spending
Medical	$851
Trade show	$734
Educational	$625
Social	$561
Veteran	$507
Governmental	$449
Social service	$418
Religious	$358
Military	$322

Source: International Association of Convention & Visitor Bureaus.

Refusing Group Bookings.   The number of full-service properties that refuse to accommodate groups has dwindled in recent years. The group business is a lucrative market, and few properties can afford to scoff at this form of business. Of course, smaller, limited-service properties have less opportunity to attract and handle group business. But there are some sizable operations that deliberately refuse group room bookings.

Not too many years ago, select resort operations were less inclined to accept group business than they are today. They refused group bookings for a number of reasons. The primary reason was because the group alienated nongroup guests staying at the property. That is still often the case. Staying in a hotel that is almost entirely occupied by a large group can be disconcerting to the individual, nongroup guest. Walking the halls, playing tennis, eating a meal, or sitting in the lounge can be rather self-conscious activities when the nonaffiliated guest is surrounded by loud and boisterous group delegates. Some exclusive resorts disdain subjecting their individual guests to such an uncomfortable situation.

Hotels may be less interested in group business for several other reasons as well. Group business requires a certain investment from the hotel—there is the need for public meeting space, audiovisual equipment, tables and chairs, food serving

EXHIBIT 5–9

Conference and meeting facilities come in all shapes and sizes. These two examples range from a cozy roundtable conference room at the Adam's Mark Hotel in St. Louis to the 27,000-square-foot Plaza International Ballroom at the Peabody Orlando. Used with permission.

equipment, and so on. Also, there is the requirement of additional labor. Group hotels require a sales department staffed with one or more individuals, a convention and catering department staffed with one or more setup persons, and food production areas. Finally, groups often negotiate discounted room rates. Hotels that find themselves in the enviable position of having strong year-round occupancy may be less interested in discounted groups.

Casino Hotels.   Casino hotels are an interesting breed in themselves. Casino hotels generally only accept groups that have a high likelihood of gambling. All things being equal, the casino manager may prefer a group of sanitation engineers, bottling managers, or morticians over a group of doctors, lawyers, or school teachers. In fact, the hotel may prefer a few empty hotel rooms over a hotel full of nongamblers. Therefore, even when space is available, certain groups will be refused by casino hotels.

Assuming that the sanitation engineers are considered to be good gamblers, the casino must decide how much they are worth. The question that must always be answered is, Will the group produce more casino revenues than the individual tourists the group is displacing? If the group has a strong reputation for casino play, it will be able to negotiate a better discount than a group with a lesser (or unknown) reputation.

Reasons for Accepting Group Business.   Primarily, there are three reasons why most hotels are actively involved in seeking group rooms business:

1. Group business is a sizable market.
2. Groups provide certain economies of scale.
3. Group delegates spend more dollars.

The enormous size of the group business market was addressed earlier in this chapter. However, group economies of scale are an interesting bonus for the hotel operator.

Most items produced in mass quantities benefit from reduced per-item production costs. The same is true for the hotel industry. Selling a bulk of group rooms provides the operator with specific economies of scale. The sales department benefits from the reduced work in booking one large group as opposed to booking numerous smaller visits. The reservations department benefits from having a block of rooms set aside for the group. Even the front office, housekeeping, and uniformed services benefit from group room bookings.

With group arrivals and departures, business levels are clearly understood. With a five-day convention, for example, the front office is especially busy on the first and last days: During the first day, the front office is busy with heavy check-ins; on the last day, it is busy with check-outs. The middle days, however, are relatively slow for the front-office staff. During these slower middle days, the hotel saves labor costs by reducing its normal staffing levels. The same is true with the housekeeping and uniformed-services departments. In many hotels, the housekeeping department spends less time cleaning **stayover** rooms than it does cleaning check-outs. Likewise, the bell staff is busiest when assisting guests with luggage at check-in and check-out. Uniformed-service positions are very slow during the middle days of a convention.

Another reason hotels like group business is that group delegates have a higher worth than individual guests. No one understands this quite as well as the casino hotels. Interacting with other conventioneers often puts group delegates in a festive mood. The trip is not just business—in many cases there is fun and excitement in the excursion. And what better way to have fun than with an all-expenses-paid trip (see Exhibit 5–8).

Many convention, exposition, and related group delegates are visiting the event at no personal cost. Their company or business has probably funded most or all of the trip. Once at the hotel, delegates have a high likelihood of spending additional money. After all, their basic expenses (meals, lodging, transportation, and convention registration) have been paid. Therefore, they may buy the round of golf they might not ordinarily purchase if they were paying for the trip on their own. They may have an extra cocktail or two and buy more expensive brands. They may select a souvenir from the gift shop or even a painting from the gallery. And, of course, they might gamble a few extra (or a lot of extra) dollars. Even when delegates attend a convention at their own expense, there are favorable tax deductions that often reduce the real cost of the trip.

Types of Group Business.   The need to communicate an ever increasing amount of information has given extra strength to the convention market. Even as the information superhighway is being paved, the conventions market is larger than ever. Meeting and speaking with other delegates face to face offers certain benefits the impersonal computer or telephone cannot provide.

Even as the convention market is growing, so is the group tour and travel market. Lacking the expense account and tax advantages of the conventioneer, the group tourist seeks economy above all else. Group rates are often substantially lower than rack rates.

Whereas convention business is sold as a group and guests are handled individually, tour business is sold as a group and guests are handled as a group. One sale, one reservation, one registration,[1] one service, and one billing provide the savings on which the tour concept is built.

The Convention Group.   Arrangements for the convention are made by a representative or committee of the organization and confirmed to the hotel with a contract of agreement. Large associations have permanent, paid executives in addition to the annually elected officers. These account executives are so numerous that they have their own organization—**ASAE, the American Society of Association Executives.**

If the organization is large enough to have a paid executive, he or she negotiates the arrangements with the hotel's sales staff. Details focus on many areas, including housing, meals, and meeting facilities. The organization (club, association, union) contracts with the hotel to buy meeting space, banquet facilities, and rooms to house its own staff. It negotiates with the hotel for a block of guest rooms, but it does not pay for those rooms. Members deal individually with the hotel for accommodations.

The association sells function tickets to its membership for such events as banquets, cocktail parties, and luncheons. The money collected from these events is paid to the hotel at the negotiated price. If the association charges a higher ticket price, it will make a slight profit over the hotel's charge.

In addition, the group may also benefit from breakage if it sells more tickets than the number of delegates who actually show for the event. On the other hand, if it guarantees a number higher than the number of delegates who show, then the hotel will reap the benefit of breakage.

The organization is responsible for its own entertainment (although it may hire people through the hotel), its own speakers, films, and so on. For this, it charges the attendees a registration fee. Although some of the fee goes toward the costs of the program, the association usually profits here again.

Further gains may be made through the room rate arrangements. Sometimes organizations require the hotel to charge the attending members more than the negotiated room rate and to refund that excess to the group treasury. This raises many ethical concerns, particularly if the convention guest is unaware of the arrangement.

In no way does the association contract for rooms, except for those directly related to association headquarters, such as officers' and speakers' rooms. Room reservations are individually contracted between the hotel and each delegate. Billing is handled the same way, and collections become a personal matter between the conventioneer and the hotel.

Trade Shows.   Trade shows have many characteristics similar to conventions. In fact, trade shows are often held in conjunction with large conventions. The association (or trade-show entrepreneur) acquires space from the hotel or convention center and leases that space to exhibitors. Those managing the trade show invite guests, exhibitors, and shoppers.

The average guest stay is longer with a show because the displays, which are costly and elaborate, require setup and teardown time. Otherwise, reservation and front-office procedures are the same as for a convention or an individual guest. More city ledger charges (delayed billing) may occur because the exhibitors are usually large companies that request that type of billing.

The Tour Group.   Tour groups are very convenient for the hotel, but that convenience comes at a price. Tour operators demand deep discounts. They get them because the entire burden is on the tour operator, with only minimal risk for the hotel.

The hotel deals with one party, the group tour company or wholesaler. The wholesaler leases the bus or plane, books the rooms, commits land transportation and entertainment, and then goes out to sell the package. Travel agents are the wholesaler's major sales outlets. Each agent receives a commission for the sale, and the wholesaler combines them into one group. In so doing, the workload of the front office is reduced considerably.

As much as 40 percent of the tour operator's original room estimate may be lost between the start of negotiations and the date of arrival, perhaps as long as one year later. Consequently, tour operators may be given the right to **sell and report** until as close as 7 to 14 days before arrival. Sell and report, also called *status control,* allows the wholesaler or tour operator to sell rooms and report back periodically. The right to this **free sell** is changed to sold-out status at the discretion of the hotel's forecast team.

Careful control is maintained over the right to sell and report because several agencies might be in that mode simultaneously. Specific dates are closed when the hotel is full and others may be closed to arrivals. Within the terms of the contract with the wholesaler, the hotel's forecast team can alter the closeout date for the tours, asking for the final rooming list one week, four weeks, or even five weeks before arrival. Nowhere in this process is the hotel's in-house reservation office involved. The wholesaler and that company's team of travel agents do all the selling.

The deals are negotiated by the hotel's sales office, and the central reservations office is not involved in any manner whatsoever.

Managing the Convention Reservation

Associations book their shows and conventions as much as 5 to 10 years ahead. Two to three years' advance planning is the norm.

A **blanket reservation** is negotiated between the hotel and the group. As the date approaches, perhaps five to eight months before the convention arrives, the total room commitment is reviewed and the number and type of rooms are identified. These are estimates based on the group's historical experience with its convention.

About two months before the event, the association distributes the hotel's reservation form (Exhibit 5–10) through its mailing list, which could number anywhere from dozens of persons to thousands. These self-addressed postal cards piggyback the general convention mailing that details the program, the activities, and the cost.

The Blanket Reservation.   As individual requests arrive at the hotel, they are charged against the blanket reservation. The hotel and the association reexamine the room commitment 45, 30, and 20 days before the convention begins.

Reservations received after the closeout date, 20 to 30 days before the convention starts, are accepted only if space remains—on an **availability basis only.** Reservations are confirmed individually, with an additional copy sometimes going to the association for count control.

Overflow Hotels.   Some hotels require an advance deposit from convention delegates. This is especially true of isolated resorts where there is little chance that walk-ins will fill no-show vacancies. It is also true of overflow hotels.

Conventions are often too large to be housed in just one hotel. Therefore, the association finds additional properties to supplement the rooms available at the main or headquarters hotel. These supplemental properties are commonly referred to as overflow hotels.

Overflow hotels often require an advance deposit sufficient to cover the cost of all nights booked. This is because overflow properties may lose occupancy to the headquarters hotel during the second or third day of the convention. Because of cancellations and no-shows, the headquarters hotel often has vacancies at the outset of the convention. Rooms available at the headquarters hotel are very appealing to delegates housed at overflow properties. After all, for roughly the same rate, they can stay in the main hotel with all of the exciting hospitality suites and activities it has to offer.

Therefore, overflow properties need to protect themselves against delegates who check out the second day and move to the headquarters hotel. Overflow properties protect themselves by charging full advance deposits equal to the entire number of nights the delegate initially planned to stay. They may also change their cancellation policy to reflect 48 or 72 hours advance notice.

Refining the Count

Convention hotels usually cooperate by furnishing each other historical information about the group—numbers, no-shows, and the like. They do this because conventions usually move annually. A hotel in one section of the state or nation is not

Exhibit 5–10

Group confirmation cards showing run-of-the-house (flat) rates (left) and spread rates (right). Spread rates offer a range of choices not provided by the flat rates. (The hotel's address is on the other side of the card.)

Associated Tailors of America

Associated Tailors of America

May 4-8

**Herald Square Hotel
Reservation Department**

Please make the following reservations quoted on European Plan.

Reservations must be received by Herald Square no later than April 15.

☐ Guest Rooms—Single $82

☐ Guest Rooms—Double $88

☐ Suites: Petite $110
       Deluxe $135

Will Arrive _____ Time _____

Will Depart _____ Time _____

Name _____

Address _____

City _____

State _____ Zip _____

Reservations will not be held after 6 P.M. unless otherwise requested

---

Associated Tailors of America

May 4-8

**Herald Square Hotel
Reservation Department**

Please make the following reservations quoted on European Plan.

Reservations must be received by Herald Square no later than April 15.

☐ Guest Rooms—Single $72 $78 $84 $90

☐ Guest Rooms—Double $78 $84 $90 $96
       (Please circle rate choice)

☐ Suites: Petite $110
       Deluxe $135

Will Arrive _____ Time _____

Will Depart _____ Time _____

Name _____

Address _____

City _____

State _____ Zip _____

Reservations will not be held after 6 P.M. unless otherwise requested.

---

competing with another if the organization has already decided to meet in another city. Similar information is available through local convention or tourist bureaus, which report to and have access to the files of the International Association of Convention and Visitor Bureaus (IACVB). The IACVB gathers data about the character and performance of each group handled by the member bureaus.

Reservation problems occur despite the best predictive efforts of the marketing and reservations departments. Association memberships change over time, and certain cities prove more or less appealing than previous sites. The **casualty factor** (cancellations plus no-shows) also varies from group to group, reducing the value of generalized percentage figures. Two special cases help defeat the best-planned approach to group reservations: the unidentified conventioneer and the IT package.

The Unidentified Conventioneer.   Many conventioneers make room reservations by telephone or on business stationery rather than using the reservation postal cards. One of two things may happen with these unidentified conventioneers: (1) the reservation might be denied (the convention block is open, but general reservations are closed), and the guest goes elsewhere; (2) the reservation might be accepted as a nonconvention guest (both the convention blanket and the nonconvention categories are open). This second option leaves the hotel with duplicate space.

The situation takes a different twist when the conventioneer accepts space outside the blanket count because all the convention spots have been filled. Once housed, this guest argues to get the special, reduced, convention rate. Too many situations like that, and the carefully balanced yield management system goes awry.

The IT Package.   The Inclusive Tour (IT) package is the hotel's move into the lucrative group market. Except for the transportation, the hotel combines the housing, food, and entertainment to offer an appealing two- or three-night stay at greatly reduced rates. The IT package affects group bookings, but it is not a type of group business.

IT packages can and do compete with convention reservations. For large conventions, the yield management committee closes the remaining rooms to all but high-priced rates. When relatively few rooms of the hotel are assigned to the convention, all rate classes remain available, including the package, priced at less, and offering more, than the convention rate. Keen convention shoppers book the IT package.

Convention Rates

Convention rates are a curiosity. Convention organizers bargain hard to obtain the best possible rates. Yet it is the individual conventioneer who actually pays the tab.

In part, the room rate is determined by the number of food and beverage functions that the group buys. The slower the business period, the more the sales department is willing to negotiate to ensure the booking. Both sides look at the total package before reaching an understanding.

Comp Rooms.   Complimentary (**comp** or ''free'') rooms are one part of the total package. Complimentary rooms for use by the association are included at a rate of about 1 comp unit per 50 sold. The formula applies to both convention and tour groups.

Many hotels are beginning to take a hard look at how the comps are earned and used. No-shows and cancellations are no longer counted in the computation. Credit is given only for the number of rooms actually sold; understays do not contribute to the count.

The use of comps is also being restricted. Comps are meant to be used by convention executives and staff during the dates of the convention and possibly several days immediately preceding or following the event. Comps are not designed for use months later as a personal vacation for the convention executive!

Rate Quotes.   Rates are quoted as **flat** or **spread** (Exhibit 5–10). Under the flat rate, sometimes called single rate, all guests pay the same convention rate, which is usually less than the average rack rate. Except for suites, rooms are assigned on a best-available basis, called **run-of-the-house.** Some pay more for the room than its normal price, and others pay less. Run-of-the-house implies an equal distribution of room assignments. If half the rooms have an ocean view and half do not, the convention group should get a 50–50 split with a run-of-the-house rate. One Hawaiian hotel advertises ''run-of-the-ocean'' rates. A fair distribution includes an equitable share of standard, medium, and deluxe accommodations.

A spread rate, sometimes called sliding rate, uses the standard rack rate distribution already in place. The level is reduced several dollars below the rack rates. Assignments are made over the entire rate spread according to individual preference and a willingness to pay. The range of wealth and interest among the attendees makes spread rates more attractive to large groups.

Convention management companies, which sell all types of services to the association buyers, are flourishing as part of the trend toward third-party intermediaries. Their fees are paid by the hotel as a percentage of room rates, just as travel agents are compensated. Such commissionable rates reduce the rate-negotiating leverage that the convention group can exercise on the hotel.

Housing Bureaus

Once the convention or show outgrows the capacity of a single hotel—conventions of over 100,000 delegates have been recorded—a central reservations center is required. Publicly funded convention and visitor bureaus (CVBs) usually take on the job without charging a fee. The San Francisco CVB, for example, processes some 250,000 **room-nights** per year for that city. It offers its services once the convention size reaches 1,000 delegates using three or more hotels.

Each hotel commits rooms toward the blanket reservation and a citywide commitment is made to the association. Rates remain the prerogative of the individual properties.

Reservation request cards (Exhibit 5–10) are returned to the CVB's housing bureau rather than to the individual hotel. The bureau relays to the hotel the guest's first, second, or third choice, depending on which hotel still has space. The hotel replies, and a copy of the confirmation goes to the housing bureau as well as to the association's headquarters.

Two properties may join forces if the convention is too large for one hotel but does not need a citywide commitment. The property that booked the business becomes the headquarters site and the booking office, with the second hotel (the overflow hotel) honoring the negotiated convention rate. This practice is now considered a violation of the antitrust laws. Joint housing of delegates is permissible, but each property should negotiate its own rates.

Handling the Tour Group Reservation

The workload of the reservations department is affected relatively little by the demands of the tour group. Both the initial sale and the continuing contact rest with the hotel's marketing and sales department. That department may have a position called the *tour and travel desk*.

Yield management coordination is the major role for reservations during the time before the group arrives. Hotels doing a large tour and travel business maintain four-month horizons. Sell-and-report authorities are adjusted as forecasted demand equals, exceeds, or falls short of historical expectations.

Tour groups are almost always given shares-with rooms, since a premium is charged for single occupancy. The hotel gets a rooming list that shows each pairing. The entire block of rooms is preassigned. If the tour company brings in back-to-back groups, the very same rooms may be used again and again. Keeping the block together in the same floor or wing expedites baggage handling and reduces noise and congestion elsewhere.

Special group arrival sections, even special lobby entrances, reduce the congestion as the group arrives or departs. Transportation is by bus, even if only to the airport. These transfer costs are part of the fee and are arranged by the tour company. Bell fees are also included, levied by the hotel over and above the room charge.

Summary

Sophisticated automation is changing the method in which reservations are requested and accepted. Never before have hotels had reservations coming into their properties from so many varied directions. The introduction of last room availability technology has started a revolution in hotel reservations management.

Last room availability is real-time communication between central reservations offices and property-level reservations systems. With last room availability, the CRO can identify room types and rates at a member hotel and can literally sell to the very last available room. Electronic switch technology has afforded other segments of the industry the same access to member hotels. Travel agents, airlines, and subscription on-line services are all able to electronically access a property's reservations system.

While electronic reservations are gaining popularity for individual bookings, group reservations continue to require personal discussions with the property sales department. This remains true even as group business swells in importance to the industry. Unlike the individual reservation where most requests are straightforward, a personal touch is required for groups negotiating bulk rates, dates, meeting requirements, meal functions, and other hotel services.

Queries and Problems

1. On busy nights, it is not uncommon for a front-office manager to remove several rooms from availability. Usually, the manager creates a fictitious reservation, thereby ''selling'' the rooms and removing them from availability. By holding onto a few rooms, the manager feels in a better position to accommodate a special guest or request when the hotel is sold out.

   Granted that the reason management holds rooms may be very honorable, do you believe this practice undermines the very basis of last room availability technology? Explain your answer.

2. The chapter examined reservations in three distinct ways. It looked at who makes the reservation, who takes the reservation, and how the reservation is made. Developing as many assumptions and predictions as you like, brainstorm new technologies that might arise in the future. How will your new ''inventions'' change the way in which reservations are taken?

3. Central reservations systems are extremely expensive. Research and development, equipment, and staffing can easily run into hundreds of millions of dollars. How has this prohibitive cost structure changed the hotel industry? How will it change business in the future? And what options are available to the smaller and start-up chains in the industry?

4. Several studies indicate quite clearly that reservation calls made to a travel agent, or to the res center, or directly to the hotel may result in three different rate quotes for the same accommodations at the same period of time. Explain.

5. As a prominent hotelier, you have been asked by the CVB to appear before the county commissioners during a CVB budget-review session. The commission is angry that the local CVB spends public funds to maintain a convention housing bureau, and that those services are provided without a fee. Do the necessary research to provide hard facts to support your testimony in favor of the CVB.

6. One hears, ''IT packages are self-competing; I would never have them.'' Explain when this statement has a foundation and when it does not.

Note

1. Massachusetts was the last state to pass legislation
   allowing preregistration of groups. Prior to 1975,
   each member of the group had to register separately.

Forecasting Availability and Overbooking

Forecasting Availability

When a reservation has been accepted by both parties, the hotel and the guest, there is a high expectation that everything will materialize according to plan. The hotel expects that the guest will arrive on the scheduled date and pay for the requested room. Likewise, the guest expects that the hotel will have a clean room available for the agreed-on rate and with the amenities and features originally promised. When both parties are satisfied that the promise has been delivered, the reservations process is successful.

In the vast majority of cases, the reservation promise is fulfilled by both parties. The guest ultimately arrives as scheduled (or at least cancels the reservation in plenty of time), and the hotel delivers the agreed-on room type (or possibly a higher quality upgraded room). In a small percentage of reservations, however, things do not progress according to plan. The world is filled with uncertainty and change, and the reservations department is no exception. The guest may become ill, business plans may change at a moment's notice, the flight may be cancelled, or a number of other problems may materialize. Therefore, guests do not always arrive as planned.

Likewise, the hotel may have problems providing the room. There may recently have been a catastrophe that prevents the hotel from providing available rooms—for example, a fire, a flood, an earthquake, or a tornado. The computer system may have gone down, or some error of fact may have caused the hotel to accept too many reservations. Business plans may have changed, and a number of executives who were due to depart decided to occupy their rooms for another night. Therefore, hotels do not always provide available rooms as planned.

In either case (the guest not arriving or the hotel not having enough rooms), management enters the picture and makes decisions. Management's decisions regarding reservations are made while considering two principles: the desire to maximize occupancy and rate on behalf of the hotel, and the desire to maximize satisfaction and minimize problems on behalf of the guest.

Simple, Unadjusted Approach to Room Count

The concept behind rooms inventory is simple enough. There is a one-to-one match between rooms in the hotel and reservations accepted. Each reservation reduces the inventory until there are an equal number of reservations matched with available rooms. At that point, the hotel is sold out.

However, as additional factors begin to materialize, the simplicity is quickly complicated. Some rooms stay over, others check out earlier than expected. Some reservations cancel in advance of their arrival, others never show up to claim their reserved accommodations. Indeed, some reservations arrive a day or two early and still expect to receive their rooms. Add to these circumstances the chance for simple human error—''Oh, I thought he said July 14th, not July 4th''—and the situation is further complicated.

To fully understand the internal functions of the most complicated approach, it is important to start with the basic room tracking systems of yesteryear.

Historical Tracking Systems.   There were a number of manual tracking systems in previous decades. Each of these systems had one major factor in common—they were cumbersome and filled with potential errors.

Blocking individual rooms was the simplest of the several methods used to track reservations. The room was blocked with an appropriately colored flag at the time the reservation was accepted. The block was placed in the rack weeks or months before arrival.

As the number of reservations grew, it was desirable to supplement the individual room block with a day's journal. Without the journal, it was difficult to visualize all the reservations because the blocks were hidden behind the current room rack slips. Even with the journal, reservations were not in perspective. It was graphically difficult to visualize a long visit when each day of the reservation was documented on a separate page in the journal (see Exhibit 6–1, top).

The sequence is easier to follow when the reservation appears on a reservation chart (Exhibit 6–1, lower illustration). Charts can be hung from the wall, but size limits their use to smaller hotels. With the chart, rooms are listed vertically down the left side of the page and described by internally defined rack symbols. Listed horizontally are the days of the month, with several months in sequence. Special dates are flagged in color. Each reservation is plotted on the chart as soon as it is confirmed and assignments are made immediately. The total picture is apparent at once, and new requests can be honored by reference to the chart.

Another thing each of these manual tracking systems had in common was the way they reserved rooms. Each of these systems reserved rooms by room number— they actually reserved (blocked) a specific room against future arrival the very

EXHIBIT 6–1

These are two examples of obsolete manual reservations tracking systems. These systems reserved rooms by specific room number rather than by room type. Small, noncomputerized hotels have long used manual reservations systems in which the reservations were recorded on separate pages (top) or on charts (bottom).

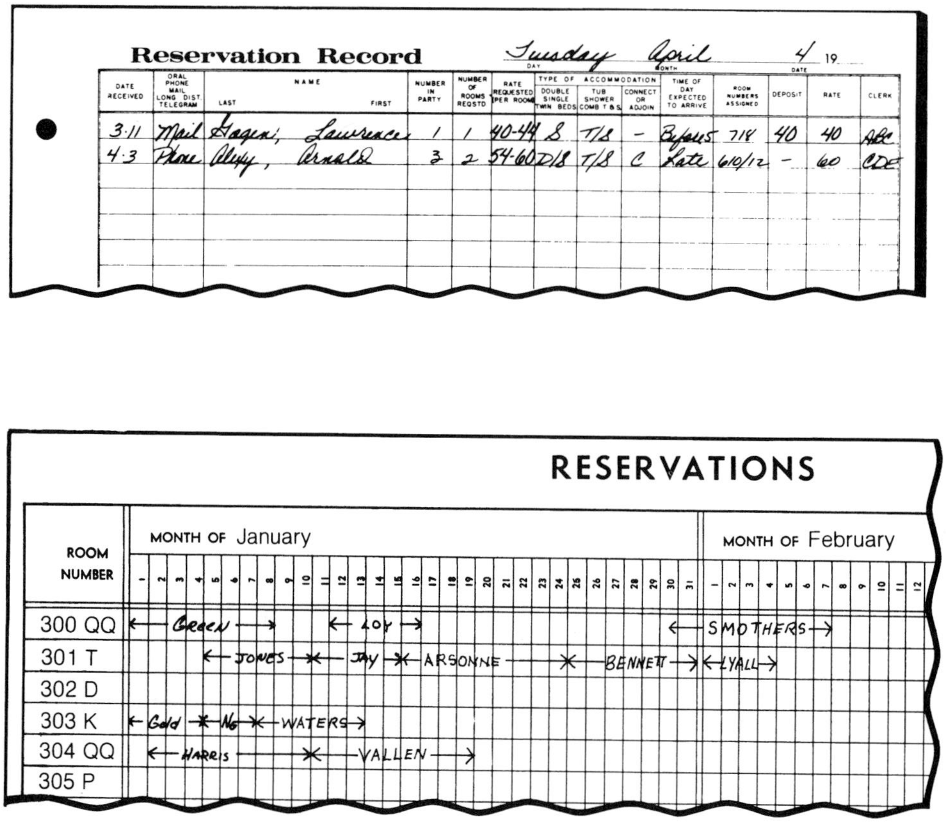

moment they were taking the reservation. Weeks in advance of arrival, the hotel had already blocked the exact room the guest would occupy. That proved to be too much detailed information for the hotel to manage weeks ahead of arrival.

Modern systems find this approach much too cumbersome. Many things can change during the several weeks prior to arrival. Therefore, modern systems prefer to reserve only the room type in advance. They saved the actual assignment of a specific room number until the guest arrives at the hotel.

Computer Tracking Systems.   To fully understand the computerized approach, it is interesting to first illustrate a sophisticated manual system. This system, commonly referred to as a density chart or density board, actually mimics the computer process.

The automated system isn't visible; if it were, the electronic system might look like the manual one illustrated in Exhibit 6–2. As the reservation is made, the appropriate room type is checked off. Like Exhibit 6–1 (top), each day of Exhibit 6–2 is represented by a separate page. To indicate the carry-over, X marks sometimes are used for the first day of the reservation and slash marks (/) thereafter.

EXHIBIT 6–2

A manual density chart tracks reservations by room type totals with a separate page for each day. A manual density chart performs in much the same way as a computerized density chart.

Day **SATURDAY**   Date **JULY 7**

Executive Suites

67	66	65	64	63	62	61	60	59	58	57	56	55	54	53	52
51	50	49	48	47	46	45	44	43	42	41	40	39	38	37	36
35	34	33	32	31	30	29	28	27	26	25	24	. . . .	3	2	1

Corporate Parlors

44	43	42	41	40	39	38	37	36	35	34	33	32	31	30	29
28	27	26	25	24	23	22	21	20	19	18	17	16	15	14	13
12	11	10	9	8	7	6	5	4	3	2	1				

King Deluxe

72	71	70	69	68	67	66	65	64	63	62	61	60	59	58	57
56	55	54	53	52	51	50	49	48	47	46	45	44	43	42	41
40	39	38	37	36	35	34	33	32	31	30	29	. . . .	3	2	1

Double Queens

57	56	55	54	53	52	51	50	49	48	47	46	45	44	43	42
41	40	39	38	37	36	35	34	33	32	31	30	29	28	27	26
25	24	23	22	21	20	19	18	17	16	15	14	. . . .	3	2	1

Standard Kings

40	39	38	37	36	35	34	33	32	31	30	29	28	27	26	25
24	23	22	21	20	19	18	17	16	15	14	13	12	11	10	9
8	7	6	5	4	3	2	1								

Standard Queens

36	34	33	32	31	30	29	28	27	26	25	24	23	22	21	20
19	18	17	16	15	14	13	12	11	10	. . . .	3	2	1		

Exhibit 6–3

An example of one of the many computerized status reports available to the reservations department. The upper half of this report provides availability, stayovers, group rooms, and so on by room type. AB and ST are towers of the hotel, while PAR (parlor), SUI (suite), and so on are specific accommodation types. The lower half of this report displays aggregate room count information for the week. Note that the first line of the weekly report beings with today's totals from the upper half.

```
*** SCREEN # 26/ PRINTER # 5  7:17:14  6/16/
    BOOKINGS BY ROOM TYPE - 06/16/     SAT

        AVAIL   O/M   % OCC   STAY   C/O   C/I   GRP   #GST
   AB      27     0    92.3    310    45    18     0    562
   ST      20     0    96.2    430   100    78     0    851
   PAR -    1     0   104.5     22     0     1     0     36
   SUI      4     0    92.3     35     6    13     0     81
   AMB      1     0      .0      0     0     0     0      0
   PRS      1     0      .0      0     1     0     0      0
   PNT      0     0   100.0      1     0     0     0      6
   TOT     52     0    94.5    798   152   110     0   1536


*** SCREEN # 26 PRINTER # 5  7:17:21  6/16/
    DAILY BOOKINGS FOR PERIOD BEGINNING=06/16/

   DATE     AVAIL   O/M   % OCC   STAY   C/O   C/I   GRP   #GST
   SAT 16      52     0    94.5    798   152   110     0   1536
   SUN 17 -    31     0   103.2    386   525   605     0   1542
   MON 18 -    35     0   103.6    805   186   190     0   1535
   TUE 19 -    43     0   104.4    880   115   123     0   1532
   WED 20     199     0    79.2    594   409   167     0   1220
   THU 21     337     0    64.8    417   344   206    39    984
   FRI 22 -    21     0   102.1    368   255   613    70   1626
```

Courtesy: Sahara Hotel, Las Vegas, Nevada.

The Automated System. Even with the memory capacity of a computer, the approach remains the same. Reservations track the total number of rooms by type; individual persons are not assigned to specific rooms until they arrive.

The computer is a density chart that functions very rapidly. The total number of rooms is fed into the system by types. As reservations are made, the computer subtracts the sale from the availability (see Exhibit 6.3). When a given room type is requested, the computer reports the status.

A Simple Room Count.   Whether the reservations tracking system is manual or automated, exact room counts are performed several days prior to the actual date of arrival. By taking a more precise look at the next several days, the reservations department prepares itself for problems that may lie ahead. In fact, several room counts may be taken throughout the day of arrival. Common times to readjust the day's room count are just after the check-out hour (around 11 AM for many properties) and immediately before and after 6 PM for hotels that allow nonguaranteed (6 PM) reservations.

A simple room count taken during these times provides management with a true understanding of the rooms inventory status for the day. If the hotel has rooms available for sale (a plus count), it is important to know the number and types of these rooms. Armed with this information, the reservations department and the front desk can better sell the remaining rooms in the hotel. Maximum rates are charged against the last few rooms available (a yield management approach).

Likewise, the hotel needs to know when there are no rooms remaining (an even or zero count). It is especially important to be forewarned when the hotel finds itself

EXHIBIT 6–4

A simple, unadjusted room count.

Given

A 1,000-room hotel had a total of 950 rooms occupied last night. Of those 950 rooms, 300 are due to check out today. In addition, there are 325 reservations for today. There are five rooms out of order.

The following table shows the calculation for this simple, unadjusted room count:

Rooms available in hotel		1,000
Occupied last night	950	
Due to check out today	300	
Equals number of stayovers		650
+Today's reservations		325
Total rooms committed for today		975
=Rooms available for sale (room count)		25 (with five OOO)

Occupancy percentage is 975 ÷ 1,000 or 97.5 percent.

in an overbooking situation (a minus count)—when there are more reservations and stayovers than there are rooms available. With advance knowledge, the hotel can arrange supplementary accommodations at other hotels, alert its front-office staff to handle the sensitive situation, and encourage the reservations department to accept cancellations if and when they occur.

Even in a computerized system, where the room count is available at a moment's notice, managers still need to understand the components that form the total rooms available count. Specifically, managers wish to know the number of rooms occupied last night, rooms due to check out, and reservations due to arrive.

Committed Rooms. The entire process works on commitments. The hotel is committed to guests staying over from last night and to guests due to arrive today. If the total of these (stayovers plus reservations) is less than the total number of rooms in the hotel, then there is a plus count. If the hotel has more commitments than rooms available for sale, then there is a minus count (overbooked).

Refer to a simple example in Exhibit 6–4. The numbers in this example will be used throughout the remainder of this chapter. Exhibit 6–5 shows an adjusted room count. It is based on the same information provided for Exhibit 6–4 but incorporates statistical adjustments to the simple formula presented in Exhibit 6–4.

Adjusted Room Count Projections

Mathematics carries an aura of exactness that deceives any reservation department that relies on unadjusted figures. Most of the figures must be modified on the basis of experience. The reservation department collects data over the years, and this information allows for more precise projections. But even the adjustments change from day to day depending on the day of the week and the week of the year. Percentages change with the weather, with the type of group registered in the house, and even with the news. Gathering the data is the first step and interpreting it is the second.

Each element in the formula can be refined by using additional data. Recomputing the formula with the more accurate figures can change the final results several times over.

Rooms Available in the Hotel. The actual number of rooms in the hotel (1,000 in the continuing example) can change from day to day. For a number of different

Exhibit 6–5

An adjusted room count.

Given

A 1,000-room hotel had a total of 950 rooms occupied last night. Of those 50 rooms, 300 are due to check out today. In addition, there are 325 reservations for today. There are five rooms out of order.

Historical Adjustments

The hotel has developed the following historical adjustment statistics: understays, 6 percent; overstays, 2 percent; cancellations, 2 percent; no-shows, 5 percent; and early arrivals, 1 percent.

The following table shows the calculation for this adjusted room count:

Rooms available in hotel			1,000
Occupied last night		950	
Due to check-out today	300		
Understays (6 percent)	+ 18		
Overstays (2 percent)	− 6		
Equals adjusted number of rooms to check out today	312 ⟶	312	
Equals adjusted number of stayovers		638 ⟶	− 638
Today's reservations	325		
Cancellations (2 percent)	− 7		
No-shows (5 percent)	− 16		
Early arrivals (1 percent)	+ 3		
Equals today's adjusted reservations	305 ⟶		− 305
Adjusted total of rooms committed for sale			− 943
Adjusted number of rooms available for sale (room count)			+ 57 (with five OOO)

Occupancy percentage is 943 ÷ 1,000 or 94.3 percent.

reasons, rooms that were available for occupancy one day may be closed to occupancy on another day. If the removal is unexpected, removing the rooms from inventory can have an impact on the hotel's ability to accommodate guests with reservations.

When rooms are removed from availability, they are designated as being in one of two distinct categories: **out of order** or **out of inventory.** The difference between these classifications is of critical importance to management.

Out of Order.   A room placed out of order is generally repairable within a relatively short time. A minor problem such as poor television reception, a clogged toilet, a malfunctioning air conditioner, or a broken headboard is enough to classify a room out of order (OOO). Out-of-order rooms pose a special problem to management because in sold-out situations they must be repaired and returned to the market within a rapid time frame. In periods of low occupancy, management may wait several days before returning such rooms to the market.

Out-of-order rooms are, by nature, minimally inoperative—the problem that placed the room out of order is slight. As a result, in some situations out-of-order rooms are actually sold to the public: If the hotel is facing sold-out status and the few remaining rooms are out of order, management may choose to sell these rooms "as is" for a reasonable discount. A broken television may warrant a $10 discount; an inoperative air conditioner may warrant a $30 discount. No out-of-order room would ever be sold if it posed a hazard to the guest.

Because out-of-order rooms can be repaired and returned to the market, they are included in the rooms-available-for-sale total. In calculating room count statistics, out-of-order rooms are treated as if there were nothing wrong with them. Likewise, when calculating occupancy percentages, out-of-order rooms are left in the denominator as if there were nothing wrong with them.

In the continuing example, note that five rooms are out of order. Because out-of-order rooms are not removed from inventory, there are still 1,000 rooms available for sale in the hotel. The occupancy of 97.5 percent has demonstrated no change in the 1,000-room denominator.

Out-Of-Inventory.   Out-of-inventory rooms cannot be sold "as is." Out-of-inventory rooms have significant problems that cannot be repaired in a rapid time frame. Examples of major out-of-inventory (OOI) situations might include a flood that destroyed all carpet and floorboards in the room, a fire that has blackened the walls and left a strong odor, a major renovation that leaves half of the wallpaper removed as well as no carpet or furniture, and a murder investigation in which the police have ordered the room sealed until further notice.

By their very nature, out-of-inventory rooms are not marketable. The problem that placed them out of inventory is significant enough to remove the room from marketability until it has been repaired. These rooms, therefore, are not included in the rooms-available-for-sale total. In calculating room count statistics, out-of-inventory rooms are removed from the total of rooms available for sale. Likewise, when calculating occupancy percentages, out-of-inventory rooms are subtracted from the denominator.

In the continuing example, note that five rooms are out of order. To illustrate the points addressed above, let's see what happens if we pretend those five rooms were actually out of inventory. Remember, out-of-inventory rooms must be removed from the available-rooms inventory. As a result, there will now be only 995 rooms available for sale in the hotel (1,000 rooms less 5 out of inventory equals 995). The room count total of +25 will also change. There will now be only +20 rooms available for sale (995 rooms less [650 stayovers plus 325 reservations] equals + 20). Out-of-inventory rooms have an impact on occupancy as well. The rooms-sold numerator (975) remains the same, but the rooms-available-for-sale denominator would change to 995. The occupancy calculation (975 divided by 995) yields 98.0 percent. This is a different result from that in Exhibit 6–4, which showed 97.5 percent.

Exhibit 6–6 presents several additional examples of out-of-inventory and out-of-order computations.

Rooms Occupied.   Rooms occupied the previous night is an exact figure except in those hotels where comp (complimentary) rooms are not listed as being occupied. Where policy excludes them from occupancy counts, the number of comp rooms must be added to the "Rooms occupied last night" figure to avoid an error in the projection. Similar errors pop up when the computer is programmed to count suites as two-room units even when the suite is not divided. The mistake comes in counting either two rooms as occupied or two rooms as checked out.

Stayovers Today.   The number of rooms scheduled to check out today is not an absolute statistic. It is primarily based on the guests' initial plans at the time they were making their reservations. Even when a well-trained front desk reconfirms the departure date during the check-in process, changes still occur.

1a. A 200-room hotel sold 125 rooms last night. If there were ten OOO rooms, the occupancy would be as follows:

- Numerator (number of rooms sold):   125
- Denominator (number of rooms available for sale—remember, the denominator is not affected by OOO rooms):   200
- Equation: 125 ÷ 200
- Percent occupancy: 62.5%

 b. A 200-room hotel sold 125 rooms last night. If there were ten OOI rooms, the occupancy would be as follows:

- Numerator (number of rooms sold):   125
- Denominator (number of rooms available for sale—remember, the denominator is reduced by the number of OOI rooms):   190
- Equation: 125 ÷ 190
- Percent occupancy: 65.8%

2a. A 460-room hotel sold 375 rooms last night. If there were twenty-two OOO rooms, the occupancy would be as follows:

- Numerator: 375
- Denominator: 460
- Equation: 375 ÷ 460
- Percent occupancy: 81.5%

 b. A 460-room hotel sold 375 rooms last night. If there were twenty-two OOI rooms, the occupancy would be as follows:

- Numerator: 375
- Denominator: 438
- Equation: 375 ÷ 438
- Percent occupancy: 85.6%

Each property collects data with which to project its understays and overstays. This data is usually expressed in terms of a percentage of the rooms due to check out that day. For example, in Exhibit 6–5, the understay percentage is 6 percent (.06 times 300 rooms due out equals 18 understays) while the overstay percentage is 2 percent (.02 times 300 rooms due out equals 6 overstays).

Understays.   Some guests leave earlier than the hotel had expected; they are known as **understays.** They are also sometimes referred to as earlys. When calculating the number of rooms due to check out, any understays will be added to the projected check-outs.

Overstays.   Some guests stay past their scheduled departure date; they are referred to as **overstays.** They are also sometimes known as **holdovers.** When calculating the number of rooms due to check out, any overstays will be subtracted from the projected check-outs.

By including understays and overstays in the continuing example, the number of rooms due to check out today changes.

Occupied last night		950
Due to check out today	300	
Plus understays (6 percent)	+ 18	
Less overstays (2 percent)	− 6	
Equals adjusted number due to check out today	312	−312
Equals adjusted number of stayovers		638

In the simple, unadjusted room count shown in Exhibit 6–4, the number due to check out today was 300. Once understays and overstays are included in the computation, however, that number changes to 312, as shown in the preceding table and Exhibit 6–5. Likewise, the number of stayovers demonstrated in the simple, unadjusted room count of Exhibit 6–4 changes with the inclusion of understays and overstays. In Exhibit 6–4, there are 650 projected stayovers. In the preceding table and Exhibit 6–5, that number changes to 638 projected stayovers.

Today's Reservations.   The simple room count found in Exhibit 6–4 is also adjusted to reflect today's incoming reservations. Just as some departing guests change their plans and overstay or understay the scheduled visit, some arriving guests do not follow their original plans. As a result, guests often cancel reservations, arrive a day or two earlier than expected, and some simply never arrive. Each of these variables is assessed and adjusted to represent a closer approximation of reality than the simple, unadjusted room count affords.

No-Shows.   Some guests who hold reservations never arrive at the hotel. These guests are referred to as no-shows. No-shows may be caused by a multitude of factors. A change in business or personal plans, inclement weather or closed roads, cancelled or stranded flights, illness, or death may be some of the reasons a guest fails to arrive. Indeed, it is also possible that they simply forgot they had made a reservation.

No-shows present the hotel with a unique problem—namely, it is difficult to know when to classify the reservation as a no-show. For nonguaranteed reservations, the industry standard is 6 PM. Nonguaranteed reservations that fail to arrive by 6 PM are considered no-shows, and those rooms are remarketed to walk-in guests.

Guaranteed and advance-deposit reservations are another story. The very nature of these higher quality guaranteed or advance-deposit reservations suggests that the hotel will hold a room all night long. Therefore, it is literally impossible for a hotel front-desk clerk to determine when a specific guaranteed reservation changes from an expected arrival to a no-show. A front-desk clerk or night auditor can be fairly certain that a reservation that has not arrived by 11 PM, midnight, or 1 AM is a no-show. However, there is always the chance that the guest has been detained and will still arrive in search of the reservation.

Asking for an estimated time of arrival on the reservation is one partial solution to this problem. By documenting the guest's expected arrival time, the desk clerk is better equipped to make difficult decisions about possible no-show guests. The earlier such decisions are made, the better the hotel's chances of selling the room to a walk-in.

Cancellations.   Although cancellations mean additional work for the reservations department and the front desk, they are still infinitely better than no-shows. Guests who cancel on the day of arrival are providing the hotel with an opportunity to resell the room. The earlier the cancellation is received, the better the chance of reselling the room.

Cancellation policies usually require notice at least 24 hours in advance of the reservation's arrival date. Cancellations made on the day of arrival are treated like no-shows and charged one room-night. However, because cancellations (even last minute cancellations) provide better information to the hotel than no-shows, many properties waive the one-night penalty to cancelling guests. Even if the hotel charges a late cancellation fee of, say, $25, that is better for the guest than being charged one full room-night. That seems fair to all concerned, because a cancelled room has more opportunity to be resold than a no-show room.

Early Arrivals.   Cancellations and no-shows reduce the number of expected arrivals. **Early arrivals** increase the number of expected arrivals. Early arrivals are guests who arrive at the hotel one or more days prior to their scheduled reservation date.

There are a number of reasons why a guest might arrive at the hotel in advance of the expected reservation date. For example, the reservations department may have had a different date for the reservation than the guest understood, or possibly the guest's plans changed and he or she decided to arrive one or more days early. Whatever the reason, the front office will attempt to accommodate the guest.

Even in periods of 100 percent occupancy, the front office will strive to find accommodations for the early arrival. Not only is that good guest service, but early arrivals often represent a number of room-nights to the hotel—many early arrivals stay through the end of their originally scheduled departure. An early arrival who arrives two days early for a three-night reservation may very likely stay all five nights.

Adjusting Today's Reservations.   The continuing example in Exhibit 6–4 shows an unadjusted reservations count of 325. Assuming a cancellation rate of 2 percent, a no-show rate of 5 percent, and an early arrival rate of 1 percent, the numbers change significantly (see the following table and Exhibit 6–5):

Today's reservations	325
Less cancellations (2 percent)	− 7
Less no-shows (5 percent)	− 16
Plus early arrivals (1 percent)	+ 3
Equals adjusted number of reservations	305

A certain amount of mathematical rounding is necessary in these equations. A 2 percent cancellation rate with 325 reservations gives 6.5 cancellations. It is necessary to round 6.5 cancellations to 7. Likewise, no-shows round from 16.25 to 16 and early arrivals round from 3.25 to 3.

The Adjusted Room Count.   The ongoing room count example from Exhibit 6–4 has been fully adjusted and restated in Exhibit 6–5. Notice that rooms due to check out today have been adjusted by overstays and understays. Today's reservations have also been adjusted by cancellations, no-shows, and early arrivals.

The count of 57 rooms available for sale shown in Exhibit 6–5 is significantly higher than the count of 25 rooms available shown in Exhibit 6–4. With the same five rooms out of order, the hotel can now accept 57 rooms as walk-ins (assuming it quickly repairs the five OOO rooms).

Exhibit 6–5 could just as easily have projected a change in the opposite direction. Second-guessing the actions of the guest is the reservation department's burden. Projections are made from the data gathered for the property and forecasted on the basis of experience. At best, it is a composite of many previous days and may prove disastrous on any given day. A cautious projection with too few walk-ins accepted results in low occupancy and empty rooms despite guests who were turned away earlier in the day. An optimistic projection allows the desk to accept so many walk-ins that the reserved guest who arrives late in the day finds no room.

This, then, is the dilemma of overbooking: the need, on the one hand, to maximize occupancy and profits, and the pressure, on the other hand, to keep empty rooms for reservations who may never arrive.

Hotels with heavy walk-ins, similar to the airline's standbys, are more flexible than isolated properties. Selective overbooking, 5 to 15 percent depending on individual experience, is the hotel's major protection against no-shows, double reservations, and ''guaranteed reservations'' that are never paid. Conservative overbooking begins with a collection of data, made easier by a well-programmed computer and a regular update of projections.

Data collection must be structured and accurate so the reservations office can rely on the figures. The computer can furnish the information if the database for accumulating the report was planned for in the programming. Data must be accumulated in a chronological fashion, day of the week matching day of the week. It is important for the second Tuesday in April, for instance, to match the second Tuesday in April of last year, irrespective of the calendar dates of those Tuesdays.

Dates do have importance, of course. The Fourth of July holiday is a more important date than the day on which it falls. Similarly, the days before and after such a holiday must be identified with other before and after days of previous years.

Utilizing the Room Count Forecast. Forecasts are projections of anticipated room sales for a given period. Sales are always the product of the number of items sold (rooms) times the price (average rate per occupied room). So a forecast is the start of a budget.

Room forecasting starts with an annual projection and ends with an hourly report. In between are monthly, biweekly, weekly, three-day, and daily forecasts (see Exhibit 6–7). Ten-day reports are sometimes used in place of the biweekly projections, but most reservation managers prefer to see two weekends included in a report.

Every department of the hotel uses the projections, and each projection should be involved in their preparation. Forecasts are critical tools for labor planning throughout the entire hotel. Each department makes sales and labor forecasts from the anticipated room count. Most departments depend on room occupancy for their own volume. This is certainly the situation with valet and laundry, room service, telephones, and uniformed services.

Housekeeping's schedule is also a function of room sales. So, too, there is a direct relation between the number of breakfasts served and the previous night's room count. Early work scheduling helps build good employee relations, and the

Exhibit 6–7

A computerized reservation forecast provides management with a 10-day (two weekends) view of arrivals and departures as well as tentative and committed group rooms. Note: Under the caption total rooms, ''OOO'' are out-of-order rooms; ''OFF'' are out of inventory (called ''off-line'' or off-market rooms in this hotel).

Occupancy Forecast Report

```
Santa Rae Ranch                    Occupancy Forecast Report                      Page Number:    1
Ann Parker                    For the Period from 03-Jan-  to 12-Jan-          03-Jul-19   11:55 AM
(avl.forecast)           Percentages Include Out of Order and Off Market Rooms
                             Percentages Exclude Tentative Group Rooms
```

	FRI JAN-03	SAT JAN-04	SUN JAN-05	MON JAN-06	TUE JAN-07	WED JAN-08	THU JAN-09	FRI JAN-10	SAT JAN-11	SUN JAN-12
Total Rooms	236	236	236	236	236	236	236	236	236	236
- OOO	3	2	3	3	2	2	3	1	1	0
- OFF	0	0	0	0	0	0	0	0	0	0
Rooms Available	233	234	233	233	234	234	233	235	235	236
Rooms Occupied	94	90	83	44	33	27	21	30	42	27
- Non-Group Departures	11	18	34	14	4	5	17	2	13	4
- Group Departures	12	3	14	1	2	2	0	1	5	4
+ Non-Group Arrivals	18	13	9	4	0	1	15	14	3	0
+ Group Arrivals	1	1	0	0	0	0	12	0	0	0
Net In-House	90	83	44	33	27	21	31	41	27	19
+ Estimated Pickup	0	0	0	0	0	0	0	2	2	2
+ Excess Committed	82	60	1	0	0	0	19	9	14	0
+ Tentative Grp Rooms	5	0	0	0	0	0	2	0	0	0
Net Rooms Reserved	172	143	45	33	27	21	50	52	43	21
Net Rooms Available	61	91	188	200	207	213	183	183	192	215
Non-Group										
Projected Revenue	7113.00	6527.50	3438.50	2757.50	2446.00	1810.00	1341.88	4265.37	3415.99	2913.49
Avg. Rate	103.09	101.99	88.17	95.09	97.84	86.19	70.63	137.59	162.67	171.38
Group (Reserved)										
Projected Revenue	1064.00	965.00	221.00	175.00	47.50	0.00	1148.00	1100.50	590.00	190.00
Avg. Rate	50.67	50.79	44.20	43.75	23.75	0.00	95.67	100.05	98.33	95.00
Group (Excess Committed)										
Estimated Revenue	5340.00	3925.00	20.00	0.00	0.00	0.00	1945.00	845.00	1280.00	0.00
Avg. Rate	61.38	65.42	20.00	0.00	0.00	0.00	92.62	93.89	91.43	0.00
Group (Tentative)										
Estimated Revenue	375.00	0.00	0.00	0.00	0.00	0.00	150.00	0.00	0.00	0.00
Avg. Rate	75.00	0.00	0.00	0.00	0.00	0.00	75.00	0.00	0.00	0.00
Group (Totals)										
Projected Revenue	6779.00	4890.00	241.00	175.00	47.50	0.00	3243.00	1945.50	1870.00	190.00
Avg. Rate	59.99	61.90	40.17	43.75	23.75	0.00	92.66	97.28	93.50	95.00
Totals										
Projected Revenue	13892.00	11417.50	3679.50	2932.50	2493.50	1810.00	4584.88	6210.87	5285.99	3103.49
Avg. Rate	76.33	79.84	81.77	88.86	92.35	86.19	84.91	121.78	128.93	163.34
% Occupancy Reserved	38.63	35.47	18.88	14.16	11.54	8.97	13.30	17.45	11.49	8.05
% Including Commits	73.82	61.11	19.31	14.16	11.54	8.97	21.46	21.28	17.45	8.05

	TEN/DEF	FRI JAN-03	SAT JAN-04	SUN JAN-05	MON JAN-06	TUE JAN-07	WED JAN-08	THU JAN-09	FRI JAN-10	SAT JAN-11	SUN JAN-12
American Building Consult	DEF	30/0	20/0								
Bavarian Bakeoff	*DEF	0/1									
Bob's Boblo Island Tour	*DEF	5/4	0/3								
Brady Tours	DEF							5/0			
Cardinal Group	DEF	1/0	1/0	1/0							
Cups & China	DEF	10/0									
Honda	DEF							25/11	20/11	20/6	
MIPS	DEF	6/5	5/5								
Micro Data	TEN							2/0			
Presentations Now	DEF	5/0	5/0								
Sky Line Displays	TEN	5/0									
US Clowns Inc.	DEF	25/2	25/2								
US Water Polo Team	DEF	12/1	12/1								

* - This group's commitments must be cleaned up or all availability reports will be out of balance.

Courtesy: Geac Computers, Inc., Tustin, California.

EXHIBIT 6–8

Manual forecast of space availability (similar to electronic forecast of Exhibit 6–7). Forecasts that depend on the cumulative results of previous day's forecasts (see arrows) grow less reliable day by day.

ROYAL HOTEL
Weekly Forecast for February 3 to February 9

	3	4	5	6	7	8	9
Rooms available for sale	1,206	1,206	1,206	1,206	1,206	1,206	1,206
Rooms occupied last night →	1,121	1,190	1,193	890	480	140	611
Less anticipated departures	444	396	530	440	350	55	20
Stayovers	677	794	663	450	130	85	591
Reservation expected	498	386	212	25	10	501	552
Estimated out of order	3	3					
Rooms committed	1,178	1,183	875	475	140	586	1,143
Estimated walk-ins	12	10	15	5		25	63
Rooms occupied tonight →	1,190	1,193	890	480	140	611	1,206

Group Arrivals

	3	4	5	6	7	8	9
National Water Heater Co.	80	140					
Play Tours of America			68				
Chevrolet Western Division					5	183	
PA Library Association						251	396
Chiffo-Garn wedding party							23

two-week forecast is usually used for that purpose. A two-week lead time may be required in those hotels covered by union contracts.

The reservation department should have its closest partnership with marketing and sales. Without that alliance, the property has little opportunity to maximize yield management policies. For example, how many discounted rooms has the sales department committed to wholesalers during a high-occupancy (thus, high-rate) period? The marketing department should be able to help reservations adjust no-shows, walk-ins, early arrivals, and so on as they pertain to a particular group. Group figures differ from independent guests and may vary from group to group.

Periodic Recounts. The longer the period between the preparation of the forecast and its use, the less reliable it is. Without periodic updating, all the departments, but especially the desk, act on information that is no longer accurate. The three-day forecast permits a final push for sales and a tightening of labor schedules throughout the property to maximize occupancy and minimize costs.

By the time hourly projections are being made, responsibility has moved entirely to the front office. Overbooking problems, additional reservations, walk-ins, and stayovers are being resolved by the front-office executives.

Periodic or hourly forecasts improve the system in two ways. Obviously, the information is more current (see Exhibit 6–8). Less obvious is the increased accuracy in percentage variations as the day wears on. Were it known, for example, that

80 percent of all the check-outs were usually gone by noon, a better guess of understays and overstays could be made at noon each day than at 7 AM. Similar refinements are possible with cancellation percentages, no-show factors, and so on. In fact, it is possible to improve the accuracy of no-show forecasts by separating the total reservations into three categories—advance deposit, guaranteed, and nonguaranteed—before applying a no-show percentage.

Further Adjustments by Reservation Quality.   Returning to the continuing example illustrated in Exhibits 6–4 and 6–5, an improved adjusted room count is possible by separating nonguaranteed reservations from guaranteed and advance-deposit reservations. Instead of merely stating that 325 reservations are due in, it is more valuable to understand that 100 reservations are nonguaranteed, 175 reservations are guaranteed, and 50 reservations are advance deposit.

If the hotel maintains statistical history by reservation quality or type, the accuracy of the entire projection is enhanced. In such hotels, the no-show percentage might be changed from the flat 5 percent for all reservation types to something more detailed. Assume that 10 percent of all nonguaranteed reservations are no-shows, 4 percent of all guaranteed reservations are no-shows, and 1 percent of all advance deposits are no-shows. The total number of no-shows would now change from 16 in Exhibit 6–5 to 18. This is calculated by taking 10 percent of 100 nonguaranteed reservations (10), plus 4 percent of 175 guaranteed reservations (7), plus 1 percent of 50 advance deposit reservations (1).

This same logic can be applied to early arrivals and cancellations. The more detailed the statistical history gathered by the hotel, the more accurate the daily projections will be.

Accuracy can also be improved by attention to the character of the market. The type of group clues the reservation department to the no-show percentage. For example, teachers are very dependable. Tour groups are nearly always full because volume is as important to the tour operator as to the innkeeper. That generalization must then be balanced by knowledge about specific tour companies. Allocations versus utilization should be computed individually on wholesalers, incentive houses, associations, and other group movers.

Market research may prove that bookings from certain localities are more or less reliable depending on transportation, weather, distance, and the kind of guest the hotel is attracting. Commercial guests have a different degree of dependability than tourists, who differ again from conventioneers or referrals. A large permanent guest population needs to be recognized in any percentage computation involving stayovers and anticipated departures.

The overall goal of any room count projection is to forecast the number of rooms available for sale. This is especially critical during high-occupancy periods. When the hotel is nearly full, it is important to forecast the number of rooms that may become available for sale due to understays, no-shows, and cancellations. By understanding the interrelationship of these adjustments, the front office has a better chance of filling the hotel.

However, these are only projections. Anything can happen on a given day. A hotel that historically expects a 5 percent no-show factor might one day experience a 0 percent no-show factor. In the continuing example of Exhibit 6–5, this would mean the hotel might find itself 16 rooms overbooked!

Overbooking

Overbooking—selling more rooms than are available—is a bona fide technique of reservation management. By employing this tool, management assumes a degree of legal risk as well as possible damage to its public relations image. Being refused accommodations despite a confirmed reservation is probably the most aggravating experience to which the hotel can subject its customers.

Hotel Policies

The burden of **walking** an arriving guest—sending that person away— falls to the room clerk. Too often management leaves it at that, making no provision to train the clerk, and no provision to house the guest. Where this is a frequent affair, the staff grows immune to the protests and even finds a bit of humor in walking one guest after the other. In doing so, the staff reflects the apparent attitude of an unconcerned management. This is not the case in properties where quality assurance programs are in place. The situation is never treated lightly, even if a number of guests were walked that day.

Antiservice in Overbooking.   A common approach for many clerks is to act as if the reservation never existed. The clerk's pretense is what guests find the most frustrating part of the experience. To play out the charade, the clerk consults with co-workers, massages computer keys, and examines hidden room racks. Finally comes a proclamation. To the hotel, the guest is a nonperson without a record and one for whom the hotel is not responsible.

To the dismay of the entire industry, certain properties give no attention to the matter of overbooking. They set a low priority on the loss of goodwill because they either have little repeat business or they have more business than they can handle. What is unimportant to these properties is of grave concern to the majority of hotelkeepers. The majority act to minimize the frequency of overbooking. The minority deem the problem unreconcilable and stand ready to face the legal consequences.

A Legal Contract.   Courts consider room reservations to be legal contracts. The request constitutes the offer, and the promise of accommodations represents the acceptance. Either the promise to pay or the actual transfer of a deposit is the third important element of a contract: consideration. The parties are competent; the transaction is legal; and there is a mutuality of interest. All the elements of a binding contract are in place.

If one party breaches the contract, the innocent party should be compensated for the injury. This has been the situation for many years. Recovery by either party has generally been limited to the natural or expected costs that the parties anticipated at the time of the agreement.

There have been few legal cases involving breach of reservation contract. That is because there is little to be gained by bringing suit. If the guest breaches the contract by failing to show up for the room, the hotel may have an opportunity to resell the accommodation. Even if the room cannot be resold, the monetary loss to the hotel is minimal. Similarly, if the hotel breaches the reservation contract by failing to provide a room, the guest is free to seek accommodations elsewhere. Even if a room cannot be found, the actual cost to the guest is still quite small (possibly

Our Pledge to You

We will not knowingly offer for rent, space on which we already have an advance deposit or credit-card guaranteed reservation from a customer. If, for any reason beyond our control, a room should not be available for a customer who has either an advance deposit reservation or a credit-card guaranteed reservation, we shall arrange for at least comparable accommodations at another hotel or motel in this area.

The Management

Courtesy: American Hotel & Motel Association.

limited to taxi fares and telephone calls expended in search of alternate accommodations). And courts are not willing to compensate the guest for inconvenience and depression.

In very few cases have negligence or fraud in room reservations been alleged and then proven. The threat remains, however, especially for those hotels that overbook as a matter of operational policy. If the complaining guest can show that the hotel consistently overbooked, there might be adequate grounds to recover in a tort action.

This is also true in cases where the plaintiff can demonstrate foreseeable damage. For example, if the hotel overbooked and walked the guest during a sold-out period in the city (say, during the Olympics or the World Series, if either was being held in the city), then the hotel could reasonably foresee the difficulty the guest would have in finding an alternative room. After exhausting all possibilities, if the guest decided to sleep in his or her car and was subsequently attacked and harmed, the hotel might be found liable for significant damages.

The Threat of Legislation.   Severe cases of overbooking, especially in isolated resort areas where no other accommodations were available, triggered initial interest by the Federal Trade Commission (FTC) about a decade ago. Action by the FTC was held off, in part, by the industry's decision to act. The problem was acknowledged, responsibility was accepted, and a program to educate the public was initiated.

Yield management may renew the government's interest—this time, probably at the state level. Several state attorneys general have already commented that hotels are playing the same game as the airlines did. Overbooking by the airlines led to federal regulations and penalties for failure to comply. Regulatory legislation can be expected for hotels, too, unless a combined effort at industry policing, improved reservation systems, and public relations can avert it. Florida has already enacted such legislation. In addition to monetary penalties, the law requires the hotel to reimburse guests for prepaid reservations whether paid directly to the hotel or to a travel agency. New York requires travel agents to warn clients in the form of a rubber-stamped message that, "this hotel has been known to overbook in the past." (See Exhibit 6–9.)

Others at Fault.   Although states such as New York and Georgia have legislated mere refunds for unaccommodated guests, Pennsylvania, Michigan, and Florida permit punitive damages. Hawaii and Puerto Rico have enacted an eviction law permitting the physical ejection of guests who overstay their reservation. That puts the ball in the hotel's court. No longer can the excuse for overbooking be laid on other guests.

The fault for overbooking is not the hotel industry's alone. Tour operators who earn commissions, conference committees who pledge room blocks, and individual travelers who don't show are all to blame. Each, the hotel included, attempts to maximize its own position at the risk of overbooking.

Tour operators who bring planeloads of tourists to a town contribute to the overbooking problem. The group is usually divided among several hotels, with the guest's selection of a particular hotel determining the cost of the tour. The tour operator is playing the odds, estimating that a given number of guests on each plane will choose hotels in the same ratio that the tour operator has committed rooms. When too many people select one property and too few select another, the hotel is blamed for overbooking. Guests are unaware that the hotel and the tour operator had agreed on the numbers months before.

Convention executives must be hounded to keep their numbers current. No-shows are reduced if the number of rooms saved for the convention is adjusted to the group's history at other hotels. If possible, convention groups should pair their members at the meeting site as the individuals arrive. This reduces the number of single rooms created when previously paired delegates do not show. Failing this, the hotel can levy a compulsory room charge for no-shows.

Guests, too, are to blame! They are notorious no-shows. Guests will make reservations in more than one hotel and, if they do show, will change their length of stay without notifying the desk. The reservation department is always second-guessing guests' moves, and this means occasional errors no matter how carefully previous statistics and experiences are projected.

No-Show Policies. Any overbooking discussion invariably gets around to no-shows—people who make reservations but never arrive and never cancel. No-shows, which reach as high as 25 percent in some cities on occasion, run about 8 percent industrywide.

No-shows can be penalized for their oversight in failing to cancel the reservation. The penalty may include either forfeiture of the advance deposit or collection against the method of guarantee. Guaranteed reservations are held against either a credit card or a corporate account. Collecting against guaranteed reservations is often quite difficult because guests are unwilling to pay the charge against their credit card or corporate account. This disagreement often results in a fight between the guest and the hotel over the amount of one night's lodging. Even when the hotel wins it loses because the guest may forever be lost as a valued customer.

Cancellation policies are another source of irritation to guests. After taking the time to contact the hotel and cancel the reservation, many guests are told they will still be charged one room-night. If the guest fails to contact the hotel within the limits established by the cancellation policy, the guest is still liable for one night's room charge.

Cancellation policies differ by chain, hotel, market, and destination. In addition, the cancellation policy often reflects the quantity of walk-ins experienced by the hotel. The most liberal cancellation policies allow the guest to cancel up until 6 PM on the day of arrival. Such liberal policies are generally found at corporate and chain-affiliated properties. If the guest fails to cancel within the time frame established, a one-night charge may be assessed. In contrast, many resorts and isolated destination properties mandate more stringent cancellation policies. Some request the guest to notify the hotel 24 or 48 hours in advance. Others require as much as 7 to 14 days notice. Indeed, more stringent cancellation policies may carry a weightier penalty: Some resort properties are known to charge the full prepaid stay.

Possible Solutions

Actually, there are no solutions to the problem of overbooking. As long as hotels overbook to compensate for last minute changes in occupancy and no-show guests, the problem will remain. Although eliminating overbooking is not a possibility, minimizing its impact may be.

To minimize the impact of overbooking, the hospitality industry needs to improve its stance in three critical areas. The first of these is the development of uniform industry standards for handling overbooking situations. The second area that will improve the overall situation is the increased use of impartial third-party guarantees. Similarly, the third area suggests increased utilization of advance-deposit reservations.

Industry Standards.   An industrywide policy of self-policing and public relations would minimize the incidence of overbooking and diminish the outcry from those cases that do occur. Success requires the support of each hotel and chain. A visible and concerted effort may serve to ward off renewed interest by the FTC. Apparently, governmental agencies perceive the issue more strongly than does the public. An AH&MA study on customer satisfaction ranked overbooking 19th in the frequency of guest complaints against hotels.

No matter how well managed the hotel, no matter how well made the forecasts, overbooking will occur. Preplanning for overbooking reduces guest irritation and even offers some chance of retaining the business.

Arranging substitute accommodations elsewhere is what the clerk should do. Providing the training to anticipate the incident is what management should do. Preparation includes preliminary calls to neighboring properties as the situation becomes obvious. Many satellite properties depend on this type of overflow for business.

Less ethical arrangements kick back payments to the clerk for each guest walked to the satellite property. This is very detrimental to the referring house, because clerks then have an incentive to direct guests elsewhere even when rooms are available.

Significant dollars can be attributed to walking a guest from those properties that have a quality assurance, guest-oriented policy in place. The hotel pays the round-trip cab ride to the substitute hotel. It underwrites the cost of one or more long-distance telephone calls. It also pays the room charge, regardless of the rate, at the alternative property. Some hotels give an outright gift (champagne, fruit basket, etc.) to apologize for the inconvenience. Others give a free room on the next visit as a means of bringing back a walked guest.

Assuming those figures are cab, $20; telephone, $7; and room rate, $73, each incident costs $100. This computation ignores the value of lost sales in the other departments. Overbooking is not an everyday affair. If three guests per night are turned away 10 times per year, the hotel spends $3,000 (3 × 10 × $100) in remedies. Walking guests does not make economic sense. The cost of failing to achieve 100 percent occupancy on the 10 nights is certainly less expensive than the overbooking outlay.

Exhibit 6–10

Citywide electronic referral service ties together participating hotels for improved guest service by helping individual properties maximize walk-ins and accommodate overbookings elsewhere.

HOTELEX LAS VEGAS						AREA CODE (702)
CAESARS 3570 L V BLVD **731 - 7110**	**MGM GRAND** 3799 L V BLVD **891 - 1111**	**MIRAGE** 3400 L V BLVD **791- 7111**	**TRSRE ISLND** 3300 L V BLVD **894 - 7444**	**BALLY'S** 3645 L V BLVD **739 - 4111**	**DESERT INN** 3145 L V BLVD **733 - 4444**	**L V HILTON** 3000 PARADISE **732 - 5111**
SAHARA 2535 L V BLVD **737 - 2111**	**SANDS** 3355 L V BLVD **733 - 5000**	**TROPICANA** 3801 L V BLVD **739 - 2222**	**ALADDIN** 3667 L V BLVD **736 - 0111**	**RIO SUITES** FLMNGO & VLY VW **252 - 7777**	**STARDUST** 3000 L V BLVD **732 - 6111**	**FRONTIER** 3120 L V BLVD **794 - 8200**
HACIENDA 3950 L V BLVD **739 - 8911**	**MAXIM** 160 E FLAMINGO **731 - 4300**	**GOLD COAST** 4000 W FLAMINGO **367 - 7111**	**HLTNGRNDVCTN** 3575 L V BLVD **697 - 2900**	**HOLIDAY INN** CASINO / STRIP **735 - 2400**	**D REYNOLDS** 305 CNVENTION CNTR **734 - 0711**	**CSNO ROYALE** 3411 L V BLVD **737 - 3500**
CROWN PLZA 4255 PARADISE **369 - 4400**	**LA QUINTA** 3970 PARADISE **796 - 9000**	**RESDNCE INN** 3225 PARADISE **796 - 9300**	**HOLIDAY** 325 E FLAMINGO **732 - 9100**	**BLAIR HOUSE** 344 E DESERT INN R **792 - 2222**	**ALEXIS PARK** 375 E HARMON **796 - 3300**	**ST TROPEZ** 455 E HARMON **369 - 5400**
LADY LUCK 206 N THIRD **477 - 3000**	**4 QUEENS** 202 E FREMONT **385 - 4011**	**FREMONT** 200 E FREMONT **385 - 3232**	**GOLDEN NUGGET** **386 - 8121**	**FITZGERALDS** 301 E FREMONT **388 - 2400**	**L V CLUB** 18 E FREMONT **385 - 1664**	**NEVADA PLCE** 5255 BOULDER HWY **458 - 8810**
PALACE STN 2411 W SAHARA **367 - 2411**	**BOULDER STN** 4111 BOULDER HWY **432 - 7777**	**DAYS INN** 4155 KOVAL **731 - 2111**	**SHOWBOAT** 2800 E FREMONT **385 - 9123**	**SAMS TOWN** BOULDER HWY **456 - 7777**	**BOOMTOWN** BLUE DIAMOND RD **263 - 7777**	**HARD ROCK** 4455 PARADISE **693 - 5000**

HAVALEX, INC.
P.O. Box 5286
REDWOOD CITY, CA
(415) 369-4171

MONITORS: CAESARS, DESERT INN, GOLDEN NUGGET

DATE: 03-01

CHANGE: ADD HARD ROCK HOTEL
FILE: LAS0395

Courtesy: Hotelex Systems, Redwood City, California.

Ignored in the economic computation is the cost of public relations. The iceberg effect of one extremely unhappy guest can add up to untold costs. Plagued by bad publicity from overbooking, the Bahamas Hotel Association (BHA) formalized an areawide policy. The BHA recognized that being stranded on an isolated island without a room was not going to encourage tourism. The new policy carried the cab ride one step further, guaranteeing air taxi to another island if all accommodations in the host area were fully booked. A $20 cab ride is cheap compared with the cost of an air taxi!

Other localities have established programs to help themselves and the unaccommodated guest. Chambers of commerce or tourist authorities have set up hot lines. Many metropolitan areas have adopted a system that hooks participating properties together electronically and displays the city status on a lighted board (see Exhibit 6–10). Each morning and periodically during the day, the separate properties indicate their availability status. Referrals are easily made by reference to the lighted board; a light on means rooms are available; a light off means that particular hotel is full. Equally important, the desk can monitor what is happening throughout the city and adjust its own walk-ins based on citywide conditions.

Clearly, steps can be taken to ease the impact of overbooking. The real problem lies with properties that do nothing. They are the true culprits. Even the FTC noted that it was not overbooking per se that concerned the commission. It was what the hotel didn't do to help when the guest was turned away. The FTC was criticizing the antiservice syndrome.

Third-Party Guarantees.   Guaranteed reservations are less secure than many people realize. This is because hotels are reluctant to charge guests who fail to honor their reservation. Insisting on payment from a corporate account creates more lost business and ill will than the value of one night's room charge. For many hotels, a corporate guarantee is merely a courtesy, because should the guest fail to show, the hotel has no intention of charging the corporate account.

Credit-card guarantees are less of a courtesy. Unless the customer is well known to the property, a credit-card guarantee will be charged in the event of a no-show. Unfortunately, charging the credit card does not always equate to receiving payment. In many instances, the guest will dispute the charge.

When such disputes arise, third-party involvement by the credit-card company is necessitated. The credit-card company usually requires the guest to issue a statement in writing. Such statements as ''I never made that reservation'' or ''I cancelled that reservation well in advance'' are difficult to prove. Once the statement is in hand, the third-party credit card company usually issues a temporary credit to the guest (and an off-setting debit to the hotel). This means that, temporarily, the guest does not have to pay the charge and the hotel does not receive the income.

At this stage, the statement is copied to the hotel and the property has an opportunity to respond. Many hotels stop at this point, believing that the case will never be settled in their favor. If the hotel chooses not to respond, the guest automatically wins the decision. Even when the hotel does respond, the case is still found in favor of the guest much of the time. Some critics of the system believe that credit-card companies uphold the guests because they want to keep them as customers. Today, as never before, there is intense competition among credit-card companies. Should guests be charged for no-shows and not be supported by their credit-card companies, they will likely change credit-card vendors.

Travel Agent Guarantees.   A different type of third-party guarantee utilizes the travel agent. When a guest makes the reservation through a travel agent, the hotel removes itself from dealing directly with the customer. In the event of a no-show, the hotel receives payment directly from the travel agent. Whether or not the travel agent then charges the no-show customer is the travel agent's problem.

The only weakness with this system is that the hotel must have a credit relationship with the travel agent. In today's fast-paced travel environment, there is rarely enough lead time for the travel agent to send a check and for the hotel to clear the funds.

What is now emerging is a third-party reservation from the travel agency, and a third-party (actually a fourth-party) guarantee for the settlement. The guest makes the reservation through the travel agent, and the travel agent pays the hotel with a check (a voucher) guaranteed by Citicorp, MasterCard, or Visa. These companies stand behind the creditworthiness of the voucher, so the hotel accepts it as cash.

EXHIBIT 6–11

Third-party money orders can be used to guarantee reservations. The hotel draws the check, which is used as a reservation deposit, leaving the collection to be made by the third party.

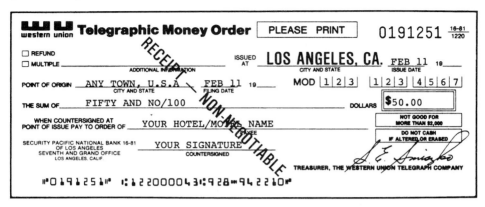

Courtesy: Western Union.

Trouble with the reservation and trouble with collection from the guest are problems for the other parties, not for the hotel.

Third-Party Advance Deposits.   Another method that removes the hotel from dealing directly with a no-show guest is the use of third-party advance deposits. In this case, a third-party (Western Union, for example) fronts the money to the hotel on behalf of the guest.

When the hotel signs on with Western Union (or some other agency), it receives an inventory of blank checks drawn on the participating agency (see Exhibit 6–11). The checks are made payable to the hotel. They need only be countersigned by an authorized member of the hotel staff to become negotiable. That happens when the guest wants to guarantee the reservation.

The guest calls the agency (Western Union, for instance) and requests that payment for the reservation be made to the hotel. The amount of the deposit plus a service fee is charged to the guest's credit card (Visa, for example). This relieves the hotel of the collection hassle whether or not the guest shows. Western Union calls the hotel and authorizes the check. The check is written and deposited into the cash drawer, and the reservation passes through the system in the usual manner.

Advance-Deposit Reservations.   Probably the best of all methods for reducing the industrywide problem of overbooking is to encourage advance deposits. Advance-deposit reservations (also known as paid-in-advance reservations) have historically maintained the lowest percentage of no-shows. Guests who pay a substantial amount in advance (usually the first-night's room charge, although some resorts charge the entire payment up front) have a strong motivation to arrive as scheduled.

However, advance-deposit reservations carry an extra clerical burden not found with other types of reservations. The reservation department, for example, has a tracking burden. If the guest responds by sending a deposit, the reservation must be changed from tentative to confirmed. If the guest doesn't respond, the reservation office must either send a reminder or cancel the reservation. Sending a reminder starts the tracking process all over again.

Handling the money, usually a check, involves bank deposits, sometimes bounced checks, and accounting records. Refunds must be made in a timely manner when cancellations are requested. Processing and writing any check represents a measurable cost of operation.

For many hotels, these operational burdens are inconsequential compared to the benefits that accrue from advance-deposit reservations. However, even those hotels using advance-deposit systems would likely switch if and when new guarantee systems become available. And that is apt to happen as new electronic systems and new innovations in money substitutes appear.

Summary

Accepting a reservation is really only half the battle. Tracking the reservation and forecasting house availability are also important components in a successful reservations department. Forecasting room availability is as much an art as it is a science. It is a simple matter to count committed rooms (those sold to stayovers and incoming reservations) as a means of forecasting the number of rooms available for walk-ins and short lead-time reservations. However, such a simple approach as counting committed rooms leaves a number of costly variables untended. Yet when the reservations manager begins to consider the potential for no-shows, cancellations, early arrivals, and understays and overstays, the art of forecasting becomes a bit like guesswork.

An error in predicting the number of cancellations and no-shows may prove disastrous to a nearly full hotel.

Guests will be overbooked and eventually walked to a nearby property. When this is a rare occasion, the employees treat the situation with compassion and the walked guest is a satisfied one. However, when walked guests become a routine daily occurrence, the hotel is showing greed by purposely overbooking each day in order to compensate for the maximum potential no-shows and cancellations. In such cases, employees become jaded, guests receive little concern, and dissatisfaction inevitably results.

In reality, the lodging industry has done a superior job reducing overbooking complaints in recent years. Partially from fear of government regulation (as with airline overbooking policies), and partially from a desire to create lasting relationships and repeat business in a highly competitive industry, few hotel overbooking complaints have become public scandals in recent years.

Queries and Problems

1. What is the difference between out-of-order and out-of-inventory rooms? Explain why one of these designations affects the occupancy count while the other has no bearing.

2. Prepare a simple unadjusted plus count from the following scenario:

   A 700-room hotel had a total of 90 percent of its rooms occupied last night. Of those occupied rooms, 260 are due to check out today. In addition, there are 316 reservations scheduled for arrival today and 10 rooms are currently out of order.

3. The rooms forecast committee is scheduled to meet later this afternoon. You have been asked to prepare remarks on group no-shows. Contrast the likelihood of no-shows for (*a*) business groups, (*b*) tour groups, and (*c*) convention groups. How would your remarks

differ if the group reservation had been made by (*a*) the vice president of engineering, (*b*) an incentive travel company, or (*c*) a professional convention management company?

4. The rooms forecast is a tool for managers throughout the hotel; it is not for the front office alone. List and discuss how some other nonroom department (housekeeping, food and beverage, etc.) would use the rooms forecast.

5. A chain's corporate office launches a national campaign advertising its policy of honoring every reservation. Each property is notified that overbooking will not be tolerated. What policies can be implemented at the hotel level to meet corporate goals and still generate the maximum occupancies on which professional careers are built?

6. Two hours before the noon check-out hour, a walk-in party requests five rooms. The following scrambled data have just been completed as part of the desk's hourly update. Should the front-office supervisor accept the walk-ins?

General no-show factor	10%
Rooms in the hotel	693
Group reservations due (rooms)	250
Number of rooms departed so far today	203
Rooms occupied last night	588
Total reservations expected today from all sources (including group rooms)	360
No-show factor for groups	2%
Understays minus overstays as a percentage of occupied rooms	8%
Early arrivals expected	2
Nonsalable rooms and rooms that are out of order	7
Total forecasted departures for the day	211

SECTION III

Guest Service and Rate Structures

In the life cycle of an industry, the maturation phase is characterized by numerous competitors offering similar yet slightly differentiated products. In such broad markets, customers face a wide range of product purchasing decisions. And if the products offer the same basic utility (e.g., all hotel rooms provide a bed and a shower), customers base their purchasing decisions on their perceptions of value and service. This is a maturing trend found in the lodging industry—guests select hotels that offer the highest levels of service at the most competitive rates.

Customer service has become the linchpin around which guests' purchasing decisions are made. Aware of the importance of customer service as a means of gaining competitive advantage in a maturing marketplace, hotel managers are searching for new and better ways to train their staff, empower them with decision-making autonomy, and provide enhanced personal recognition to the guest. Today's guests are finding that more hotels are utilizing guest history databases as a means of tracking their visits and providing the ultimate service at check-in, throughout their stay, and on return trips to the property. Hotel employees are also reaping benefits. Not only do today's employees receive improved customer-service training, they have also been empowered to act in a quasimanagerial capacity, handling guest complaints and making lower-level decisions without prior approval.

A maturing industry competes on the basis of price as well as service. The hotel industry is no exception, having demonstrated many instances of rate-cutting practices in highly competitive markets. With sophisticated travelers, hotel operators need to understand the role the room rate plays in the guest's purchase decision. At the same time, the operator's loyalty ultimately belongs to the owners and stockholders. Therefore, the correct room rate needs to be attractive to the guest while profitable to the owners—and that's walking a fine line, indeed!

CHAPTER 7 Managing Guest Service

Chapter Outline

Locating the discussion of guest-service management right in the middle of the book is not accidental. Every topic that precedes this chapter and every one that follows carries a message, implicit if not always expressed, about the importance and meaning of guest service.

From the start, the text discusses the business of lodging in industrywide terms. The first impression is one of high-tech communications. But innkeeping remains a high-touch enterprise, its global distribution systems and national reservation offices notwithstanding. Globalization has pushed lodging into the category of big business. Chain hotels, which control thousands of rooms and employees, serve to emphasize, not disparage, the importance of the industry's historical culture: guest service. Hoteliers have begun managing guest service once again, though differently, of course, than they did when hotels were owner-managed.

The evolution that brought this reversal was traumatic because all of it occurred in a very brief period. A rollercoaster ride of economic ups and downs highlighted many false premises that held sway during the final quarter of the 20th century.

Seeking solutions, hoteliers have looked inward toward operations, for the first time in many years. So now, to face a new millennium, the industry returns to an old premise: improved guest service. Quality in service has long been a measure of quality in innkeeping.

A Brief History of Quality Management

The introductory chapters have enumerated the many macrochanges that the modern hotel industry has introduced. What a contrast these are to the micromanagement skills required for guest service. For managers who had risen through the ranks of accounting and taxation, mass marketing and real estate financing, the shift is an abrupt one. Within a brief decade, hoteliers have seen the introduction, maturation, and influence of human resources departments when there had been none before.

From the mid-1970s through the mid-1980s, the lodging industry passed through a period of rapid real estate growth and expansion. Hotels were targets of intense speculation, fueled in part by favorable federal tax legislation. Eventually, the heady expansion period waned and collapsed as tough economic times and changing tax laws, in part, took their toll. Hotelkeeping, like much of American business, was reengineered—an apt euphemism for the self-inspection and rethinking that followed.

As the industry struggled to avoid wholesale bankruptcy, it abandoned its view of the hotel as a building and returned to its view of the hotel as a service business. Operations replaced financing as the focus of the 1990s. Hotel managers concentrated as never before on two aspects of operations: how to trim costs and how to build volume. From both needs came one answer: Attend to the guest.

Sensitivity to consumer needs and expectations is not special to innkeeping—it is a standard for all businesses. In one manner, then, lodging is like all business, just one industry among many. In other aspects, however, the hotel business is very different from heavy industry and even from other service industries.

Quality Management in Manufacturing

Worldwide markets, the advantage of globalization, come at the cost of worldwide competition. That competition grew intense throughout the 1950s, 60s, and 70s as the world's economies blended into one. During this period, the quality of American-made goods came into question. A reputation for quality, which the United States had held since the end of World War II, passed into other hands. Nearly a quarter century elapsed before the movement reversed again. A return to quality for all American industries was signaled by Ford Motor Company's advertising slogan, ''Quality Is Job One.''[1]

The now popular emphasis on quality had its American origins in the manufacturing industries. The decline in the reputation of American-made goods forced manufacturers to reexamine production techniques and the people—the workers—responsible for that production. American manufacturing responded, but it did not originate the movement toward quality management (QM).

Some work hard at tracing the origins of the quality management movement to Greek philosophers and Chinese mystics. Others attribute the entire concept to W. Edwards Deming, an American. Like so many evolving ideas, neither is all this nor all that. Indeed, quality control circles,[2] which are most important for the service industries, and ''total quality control,'' originated with the Japanese.

Japan and Germany have been America's primary competitors in quality. Since much of Deming's work to upgrade quality took place during the 1950s in Japan, which was infamous then for very poor workmanship, Deming remains a central figure in the whole movement. Deming urged his disciples—and that term is warranted because of the intensity of his adherents—to follow the 14 points that he promulgated. Some of his points focused on the process and the product, others on the workers and the environment.

Check In, Check Out does the same. First, it is a process-oriented text, dealing with how-to: how to track reservations; how to set rates; how to improve yield management; how to expedite guest registration; how to record and control the sale of guest services; and how to facilitate guest departure. All of this is presented in sequence with electronic technology as one means of improving the product and the process. In this manner, the book concentrates on one of Deming's concerns.

A chapter on guest service in the middle of the text acts as a fulcrum, balancing the how-to with the other elements of quality service—the guest and the staff. Attending to the employee, and through the employee to the guest, is an important part of front-office management, as well as the second part of the QM process.

Quality management (QM), quality assurance (QA), or **total quality management (TQM)**—the terms seem to be interchangeable now—originated in management's efforts to differentiate its property from competitors. In so doing, QM was viewed as another industry measure to distinguish one hotel from another. Traditionally, such measures have been location, size, and class. The distinction hasn't held up for quality management because quality management has become a standard, a norm, rather than a novelty.

Hoteliers have brought many innovations into the business. Bathtubs were added to hotel accommodations before they appeared in the White House. At one time, fans, radios, televisions, elevators, telephones, clocks, and swimming pools were unique products, installed in leading properties to attract guests. They are standard expectations today. To the credit of the hotel industry, TQM is viewed similarly. Quality management was an innovation when it first came to the hotel industry. Today, it is thought to be so basic an accommodation that no hotel can operate without it. Thus, the standard of the whole industry moves upward just as it does when every hotel room has a personal computer and fax.

Quality Management in Innkeeping

Hotels may not have embraced TQM terminology as early as manufacturing did, but the lodging industry has always been sensitive to guest service. Guest service is an industry fundamental, although management's attention to it waxes and wanes over time. Industrywide interest in guest service peaked anew when the Ritz-Carlton Company, a hotel management company, won the 1992 Malcolm Baldrige National Quality Award. The award itself was new, established by Congress only five years earlier. It recognizes American companies that achieve excellence by emphasizing quality. As the first hotel company to win the award, the Ritz-Carlton Company reawakened the entire industry to one of its basic tenets: Service the guests.

Winning an award in 1992 required the company to commit to excellence far earlier. Although the Ritz-Carlton Company set the pace, many other hotel companies also initiated formal quality management programs. The AH&MA held the first Quality Assurance Conference in 1988, and in that same year the Educational Institute of the AH&MA published the first text on the subject, *Managing Quality Services*.[3] Both the text and the conference flowed from the 1981 annual meeting when the AH&MA decided to create a *Quest for Quality* program. From that beginning, much of the industry came on stream.

Sheraton's Guest Satisfaction System (SGSS) began in 1987. Some Sheraton executives attribute part of the chain's increased occupancy and profits since then to the staff's heightened sensitivity to quality. The fundamentals of many of the programs are like Sheraton's. They begin with an emphasis on hiring the right people. SGSS calls that *HireVision;* the Ritz-Carlton Company calls it *Talent Plus*. All programs entail training, the delegation of increased authority to operative-level employees, and incentive awards to lubricate the smooth flow of the machinery. These are the standard attributes of quality management programs.

Radisson was another early convert to QM. It began a well-structured effort to implement a guest-service training program. Called "Yes I Can!" the program was installed in all Radisson-owned and -franchised properties. Radisson stretches its program of quality management beyond the guest, asking that each employee extend the same guest-oriented service to every other employee. Whether greeting or servicing a colleague, each staff member is to behave as if the other staff member were a guest.

Broadening the basic quality management program to other employees and even to purveyors is part of the explanation for the emergence of the term *total* quality management. TQM views everyone as part of the program: guests, staff, and purveyors. Companies that employ the TQM philosophy treat their purveyors as part of the excellence team but demand of them the same performance levels as the hotel itself is striving to achieve.

Each chain gives the basic idea, improved guest service and attention, its own twist. Ramada's "You're Somebody Special" program was launched in 1987. Doubletree calls its program *continuous improvement*. Lane Hotels prefers the term *employee entrepreneurship* to illustrate its empowerment of employees. To empower employees is to give them the authority to settle a matter at their own organizational level. The Arizona Biltmore goes one step further: It provides each employee with a small budget that can be used to implement the empowerment.

Empowering employees has another advantage: Fewer supervisors are needed if staff members have the authority to decide on their own. But for this concept to work, better trained employees are needed to carry out the empowerment—and therefore, better salaries will need to be paid. There is no evidence yet that the hotel industry has accepted that rationale.

Whether a chain or an independent property, a conference center or a franchise company, most of the industry has adopted some form or process that could be called quality assurance. Formal quality assurance programs are expensive, ongoing, and successful only when top management is committed for the long haul. That commitment often waivers over time because, like advertising, QM costs are easily measured but results are not.

What Is Quality Management?

QM begins with strategic planning and includes hiring the right persons, training them properly, soliciting their help through problem-solving teams, establishing standards, reviewing performance, and rewarding success. The preceding brief historical review hinted at how some companies are trying to achieve some or all of these goals.

Quality Management Defined

Trying to define quality or quality management is as difficult as trying to deliver it. Basic to the problem is the range of facilities and services highlighted in Chapter 1's discussion of segmentation. The industry is very fragmented, and so is its customer base.

Telling anecdotes—brief stories that exemplify the idea—is one approach to defining quality. Illustrations of this type are legend: A desk clerk makes sure an important letter gets typed for a guest after hours; a bellperson delivers a forgotten attaché case to the airport just in time; a housekeeper takes guest laundry home to meet a deadline; a door attendant lends black shoes to a guest for a formal affair.

Despite the difficulties, formal definitions are the vogue. Everyone gives it a shot—the authors try their hand a few pages on—even if the results are incomplete. Along with hundreds of other publications, *Managing Quality Services,* cited earlier, says that, ''QA is a management system that ensures consistent delivery of products and services.'' Another puts it this way, ''TQM is a way to continuously improve performance at every level of operation, in every functional area of an organization, using all available human and capital resources.''[4] Both of these descriptions, which represent the general run of QA definitions, fail to emphasize the duality of the issue: QM involves both the buyer–receiver of the service and the seller–giver.

The quest for quality and the search for quality come from both the buyer and the seller. Each sees the issue from a different perspective, however. Since neither one nor the other is monolithic, variations abound in the delivery and receipt of service and consequently in its definition. Quality has no objective substance, so definitions are vague, evaluations imprecise, and delivery inexact.

The Buyer's View.   From the guest's viewpoint, quality is the degree to which the property delivers what the guest expects. If the guest is surprised by a better stay than anticipated, the hotel is perceived as high quality. If the visit fails to meet expectations, the property is downgraded.

Advertising, word-of-mouth comments, price, previous visits, publicity, and more create a level of expectation within the guest. Of course, that barrage of communications is received differently with different perceptions by almost every guest. Moreover, those very expectations change over time and place, even within the same guest. Influencing the guest's expectations are components that may be outside the hotel's control: a late flight, a rude cabdriver, a bad storm.

Guests hold different expectations about different hotels, even different hotels within the same chain. Quality is measured against the expectation of that particular property at that particular time more than against different hotels in different categories.

Driving up to an economy property with a loaded family van and a pet but without a reservation carries one expectation. Flying around the world to an expensive resort—a trip that a couple has planned for and saved for over many years—creates a much different level of anticipation. Coming to a busy convention property with a reservation made by the company's travel desk evokes still a third level of expectation. Each expectation must be met by the hotel with a delivery at the highest level appropriate for the circumstances. Quality assurance attempts to do just that. It is a big, big order.

Consider two hypothetical properties. The first, an economy hotel offering minimal services, charges half its neighbor's rate. The neighbor, an expensive, upscale property and not a true competitor, has it all.

The economy hotel offers the following conveniences:

- No bellservice, but parking is convenient and many luggage carts are in the lobby.
- No room service, but the hotel is located near a well-known restaurant chain and has an exceptional choice of vending options.
- No health club, but the swimming pool is clean, open at convenient hours, and has a good supply of towels.
- No concierge, but the room clerk is knowledgeable and affable.

The upscale neighbor offers the following conveniences:

- Bellpersons, whom guests are urged to call on. But this hotel never schedules enough staff, resulting in long delays.
- Room service, but it is offered at limited times. This hotel suggests a pizza delivery company as an alternate.
- A well-reputed health club, but it is on lease, which means that this hotel charges for admission.
- A concierge, but the concierge has a recorded message that puts the guest on hold.

Extreme as the illustrations are, the point is obvious—quality is in the eye of the beholder. Managing for quality, therefore, must include standards set from the consumer's perspective. Doing so gives credence to the buyer's view of quality management.

Establishing measurements of performance against those buyer-derived standards is a necessity of every QM effort. So, too, is setting the goals for reaching those standards. A successful QM program, then, matches the buyer's standards with the seller's ability to deliver results. A good match will result in high quality.

The Seller's View.   Quality management, like all policy positions and operating practices, originates with management. Either management makes deliberate decisions to implement particular ideas or it passively accepts ongoing procedures. So it is with quality assurance. Management creates and carries out a program of enhanced guest service or there is none.

Delivering quality requires management to focus on both employees and guests. The two are intertwined. Increasing guest services to satisfy the buyer's side of quality management requires special attention to operational issues, the employees' side of quality management. Staying close to the customer means stressing customer wants, ensuring consistency, remedying the mistakes that do occur, and concentrating on the whole with a passion that hints of obsession. But all of these are also operational concerns. None can be accomplished without equal attention to those entrusted with the delivery.

Leadership.   Adopting QM as a company philosophy forces major changes in the definition of management. Traditionally, management is said to involve a series of functions: Planning, organizing, staffing, directing, and reviewing is the long-used list of management's responsibilities. QM adds another element—leadership. Managing as a leader requires a change in both the style of management and the composition of the work force being managed. When both components—management and work force—focus on delivering quality above all else, the company is said to have a *service culture.*

With a leadership style, managers shift from their traditional position of review, which requires corrective action after mistakes are made, to a proactive style of supervision. Errors must be corrected, of course, but a proactive stance aims at error avoidance. Minimizing errors, whether on a production line or a registration line, is what QM is all about.

This fundamental shift in management style requires a closer relationship between staff members, who are ultimately responsible for the errors—or, preferably, the nonerrors—and the leadership. Bringing employees into the action requires that they be "in the know." Management must make available operational information that at one time was considered confidential. Furthermore, the scope of employee interest and responsibility is enlarged. An awareness about and a sensitivity to the jobs of other departments, especially when those departments overlap, is fundamental to the QM concept.

Overlapping interests are reinforced through **quality circles (QC),** which involve employee representatives from several departments. (Quality circles are discussed later in this chapter.) For example, QCs for the front office have representatives from housekeeping, telecommunications, sales, and accounting. Each of those contributors may then sit on QCs within his or her own department. Soon the entire property is networked. Standards are developed with input from other departments, goals reflect the realities of the entire operation, and performance rewards are achievement driven.

Empowerment.   Once so much of management's guarded interests are opened to the operating staff, the next step is almost anticlimactic: Some of management's power is given away, delegated down the line. Operative employees are authorized to make their own decisions so long as these fall within the scope of the individuals' job assignments. Entrusting the employee to act responsibly requires management to give that employee the authority to take the requisite action. Giving the work force appropriate authority is empowerment.

The first response to empowerment is individual action by the single employee. A rate misquote is settled on the spot by the cashier. Apologies for an unmade room are expressed with a basket of fruit ordered by the desk clerk. Such individual acts of delegated authority bring immediate responses from the guests who experience them. But empowerment for quality assurance reaches far beyond guest relations.

Quality circles are being given more responsibility and broader authority to act. The original charge of identifying problems and recommending solutions has expanded. Some successful programs are asking the teams to help implement their ideas. With the responsibility of carrying out the change comes the empowerment to do so.

Quality circles tackle two types of problems. One kind deals with guest relations, usually how-tos. The group considers how to speed check-ins and check-outs, how to reduce errors in charges or reservations, how to expedite group baggage handling, and more.

The second type of QC issue also has an impact on quality service, but the relationship is less guest-oriented. The attention is on in-house procedures (moving linen without tying up the service elevators), cost reductions (chargebacks by the credit-card companies), or operational irritations (maintenance's negative response to requests for guest-room repairs). None of these has anything to do with immediate guest service, but all of them have everything to do with quality management.

The Employee.   Convincing supervisors to adopt a leadership style of management is but half the battle. QM requires the employees themselves to take on responsibilities, to accept the empowerment offered. Just as every supervisor does not believe in empowerment, so every employee does not seek it. Indeed, many prefer not to have it.

Similarly, the employer's willingness to share information about the business may not be matched by the employees' willingness or capacity to know what is being said—or, knowing what is being said, the ability to then participate.

Leadership in business requires followers; good leadership requires inspired and motivated followers. The composition of the hospitality work force—multifaceted with vast differences in language, education, and cultural expectations—necessitates the development of the followers as well as of the leaders.

The hospitality work force also carries the burden of turnover. Employees, and the term includes the hotel's supervisors and managers as well, come and go at a costly pace. Turnover at the lowest levels of the organization exceeds 200 percent per annum (every employee is replaced twice each year!). Less dramatic but equally disturbing turnover occurs among managers. Establishing, maintaining, and improving a service culture is often put aside in favor of gathering and replacing a turnstile staff.

Managing guest services through employee empowerment is a pervasive task. It reaches beyond the immediate delivery of services, stretching backward to employment and forward to retention. Delivering quality service begins with the hiring process. How else can the right person be in the right place? The hotel industry know this, so the personnel office has been the launch site for most QA programs. Hiring intelligent, participative, and sensitive employees is fundamental to managing for guest service.

Finding the right person even some of the time is a major hurdle that the hospitality industry does not always clear. Once found, retaining the right worker, like keeping the right customer, would seem to be a priority. Strangely, staff retention sometimes gets less attention than the original search. Yet retaining both the customer and the employee are the essence of QM and are less costly in time and money than attracting either of them from the start.

Even the right persons make mistakes in implementing whatever empowerment has been delegated. Chastising employees after the error has been made undermines the whole quality concept. Employees must take responsibility for their own actions, of course. However, QM replaces negative discipline with positive coaching, with direction and suggestions for the next time. In keeping with the whole concept of error-avoidance, the need for coaching declines as up-front training increases.

Continuous training is one response to high turnover. Training brings about changes in behavior. One type of training improves work skills—better use of the front-office computer package, for example. Another type of training enhances interpersonal skills—meeting and greeting the arrival across the desk. Managing for service requires industry executives to provide both types of training. Providing them on a continuing basis, at no small cost, is a measure of management's commitment to a quality service philosophy.

Hiring and training accomplished, incentives are needed to complete the initiative. Rewards are built into every successful QM program. At operative levels, where salaries are smaller, dollars and cents are the major rewards. Although managers, especially supervisory managers, are not above such incentives, the hotel industry has another reward to offer: time. Long hours cause many personal difficulties for nonhourly staffers. Incentives for supervisory managers may be nothing more than an additional day off!

Good staff at all operational levels is the thread of the quality assurance weave. The commitment to finding and holding those people is reflected in salaries paid, training offered, and incentives rewarded. A company that concentrates on better human resources ensures a better delivery of services.

The Authors' View.   There's an aphorism that has grown up within QA culture: "The answer is 'yes,' now ask me the question." That clearly represents the type of employee (and management) attitude that QM programs are supposed to instill. Applications of the adage apply equally well to employee–guest interactions, employee–management interfaces, and employee–employee contacts. Under an umbrella of so broad a coverage, this brief saying offers a simple definition of total quality management.

Closer inspection proves TQM culture to be very similar to the carefully cultivated culture of the concierge. With both, the attitude is expressed in Radisson's "Yes, I can!" Hotels that promote QM understand that the concierge is not a department, not even a staff. It is an attitude, the kind that one hopes all employees in a quality management program hold. Hence, the first part of the authors' definition: *Quality management is an attitude that has every employee acting like a concierge—*

Several times throughout this chapter the duality of quality assurance has been emphasized: The guest side (the display side) of the QM equation is balanced by the employee side (the operational side). Thus, the second phrase of the authors' definition of QM:—*and thinking like a manager.*

> *Quality management is an attitude that has every employee acting like a concierge and thinking like a manager.*

Quality Management Denied

The hotel business is part of a vast hospitality industry that includes food, beverage, and entertainment facilities. Within that definition, hotel leaders see their industry as a service industry, their product as hospitality, and their customers as guests. Because this position has been verbalized so often, hotel patrons are confused by the antihospitality-antiguest-antiservice syndrome that is part of some hotels.

Guest expectations, one component of quality delivery systems, were reviewed earlier. Guests recognize that every property is not charged with the same level of product despite its grouping under the common umbrella of lodging. But guests do not understand why minimal service means antiservice, and why a lack of personnel means a lack of courtesy. Management's failure to distinguish minimal service, justified by minimal rates, from antiservice, shown by employee negativism, has led to the antiservice syndrome that some hotels demonstrate and many guests experience.

Quality assurance is the industry's response to antiservice. QA programs are designed to ferret out the problems, to train for the solutions, and to reward those who demonstrate the right response. Sometimes, however, the very structure of the operation thwarts the best of intentions.

Who Knows Why?   Every organization develops standard operating procedures. They are to businesses as personal habits are to individuals. Some of them are new and meaningful; some are bad and in need of change. Guests encounter the old and the useless along with the new and the good. Hotels that insist on keeping the useless procedures irritate their guests unnecessarily and undermine the concepts of quality management. Some procedures seem to be intentional, as if inconveniencing the guest is easier than fixing the problem.

Examples of such procedures include the following:

Dining room dress codes that are more rigid than accepted social standards.

Check-out hours that are set around the housekeeper's schedule, rather than the guest's comings and goings.

Multiple occupants in one room being provided with only one key.

A pool that closes during the hours that most guests are in the hotel and opens when most are away.

Specific instructions to guests not to bring room towels to the beach but providing no other towels for this purpose.

Managers who take the best parking spaces, forcing the guest to walk an extra distance.

Housekeepers who tap on the door hours before they come to clean the room.

Guests being charged for incoming faxes despite the fact that thousands of incoming telephone calls are placed without a fee.

Unexplainable restrictions that are "explained" by company policy.

Implementing Guest Service

The modern hotel services mass markets. How different that is from the individualized attention that was the norm a century ago. Smiling, courteous, concerned employees working in a democratic culture have replaced the rigid, serve-food-from-the-left, clear-drinks-from-the-right, white-gloved autocracy of a past era.

Hotel companies have shifted from the formal to the informal; from pretense to expedited service; from rigid procedures to empowerment. Much of the change can be explained by the public's new attitude toward service. Cognizant of labor costs, functioning in a self-service environment themselves, sensitive to the employees' expectations of equality, today's guests no longer expect a subservient attitude. And employees no longer deliver it. Guests do expect—and are entitled to receive during each encounter—a friendly face, an attentive ear, and a twinkling eye. After all, quality service, as previously defined, is an attitude that shines through.

Exhibit 7–1

Moments of truth are the opportunity points at which the service provider and the service buyer meet.

Number of rooms in the hotel			300
Percentage of occupancy			×.70
Number of rooms occupied each night		210	
Percentage of double occupancy			×.33
Number of guest-nights		280	

Moments of Truth

Arrival	1		
Inquiry at the desk	1		
Bellperson	1		
Chambermaid	1		
Telephone operator	1		
Coffee shop host(ess)	1		
Server/Busperson	2		
Cashier	1		
Newsstand	1		
Total encounters per guest-night		× 10	
Daily number of moments of truth			2,800

Measures of Guest Service

Chapter 1 discussed the several measures with which the industry evaluates itself. Occupancy, as measured in percentages, is the basic quantitative measure. Average Daily Rate (ADR), as measured in dollars, is the basic qualitative measure. One could argue that changes in occupancy and ADR reflect guest satisfaction with the service encounter. They do, undoubtedly, in the long run. Occupancy and ADR rise and fall as guest satisfaction and dissatisfaction have an impact on sales volume. Both measures reflect many other, nonservice factors, however—the state of the economy, for one. Waiting for poor service to show up in low occupancy and poor ADR may be a matter of waiting too long.

Moments of Truth.   Several years ago, a study was undertaken to fix the costs of poor service.[5] Specific amounts of dollars and cents lost were calculated for each missed opportunity. As expected, overbooking, lost reservations, misplaced luggage, and discourtesy led the list of charges against the front office. Although one incident doesn't make a bankruptcy, poor service is insidious. Single episodes mushroom from minor, miscellaneous costs to staggering totals per week, per month, per year. Antiservice comes at a high cost.

Guests and staff interact more frequently in a hotel environment than in any other business setting. Hotel employees are asked to deliver an exceptional level of service over and over and over again each day. Exhibit 7–1 highlights the cumulative impact of having one's customers in residence.

With 70 percent occupancy and a double occupancy of 33 percent, employee–guest contacts number 2,800 per day. The figure soars to over 1 million per year for a hotel of only 300 rooms! The number multiplies even faster with full-service hotels, where more operating departments mean more employees. Not only are service expectations higher at the full-service property, so are the number of service contacts.

Opportunities for meeting guest expectations—or failing to meet guest expectations—have been called ''moments of truth.''[6] It is during these encounters, when the service provider and the service buyer meet eyeball to eyeball, that the guest's perception of quality is set. Some say the first 10 minutes are the most critical.

How does the staff respond? Does the final guest of the shift receive the same attention as the first arrival? For many, only a smile and an appropriate greeting are needed. More is expected by the next guest: the one with the problem, the one with the complaint, the one with the special need. If the employee is empowered to act, to respond with alacrity, to evidence concern, it is a shining moment of truth.

Total quality management requires similar moments of truth between supervisors and staffers. Employees will not shine outwardly unless there is an inner glow. Supervisors will not get positive moments of truth if they always second-guess subordinates who have been empowered. Supervisors will not get positive moments of truth if staffers are irritated, say, by late work-schedule postings that frustrate personal plans. Good results from service encounters begins with a good working environment. Shining moments of truth come best from a total quality program.

Quality Control.   Quality control (QC) is a critical element of quality assurance. QC helps management maintain standards in every property of its far-flung enterprise. Guests rely on these standards, identifying them through corporate logos. To ensure the consistency promised by the logos, chains use inspectors to make on-site visits and evaluations. Quality control has become more commonplace, therefore, as the size of individual properties grows and the range of franchising spreads.

Some chains have their own inspectors; others hire outside firms. Visits from the home company are both announced and unannounced. External inspectors usually come anonymously. Although there for a different purpose, inspectors from AAA, Mobile Travel Guide, and others are also on the road. In most cases, the inspectors provide a verbal report to the unit manager before filing the formal, written document with central headquarters. Tit for tat, managers may also file reports on inspectors. Generally, standards are enforced more stringently in company-owned or managed hotels than in franchised properties.

Each chain has its own policies. Hilton aims for three inspections per year. Choice Hotels International sets a minimum of two visits; Super 8 Motels, four visits per property per year. Franchise contracts also differ, allowing the franchisee a range of 30 to 180 days in which to remedy serious defaults before the franchise is cancelled. Radisson culls from the bottom up, using several criteria, including the comment cards that will be discussed soon. Differences among the chains account for the variations in procedure. For example, about 90 percent of Radisson's hotels are franchised, compared to, say, the 75 percent or so of Hilton's.

Quality control has many parts. One is an inspection of the physical facility. This involves a wide range of issues, from the maintenance of the grounds, to the quality of the furniture and equipment, to the cleanliness of the property. Are there holes in the carpets, burns in the bedspreads, paper in the stairwells? Checksheets used by the inspectors deal with a variety of details: working blow driers, cleanliness of air vents, number of hangers in the closet, and even the rotation of mattresses.

Food is tasted and drinks are sampled in all the food and beverage outlets, including room service. Large properties require several days for the full visit. Mystery shoppers, as inspectors are sometimes called, also check employee sales techniques. Does the room clerk sell up? Does the bellperson promote the facility? Does the telephone operator know the hours of the cabaret?

Security is another QC point. Both guest security (keys, locks, chains, and peepholes)[7] and internal security (staff pilferage from the hotel and theft from guests) come under scrutiny during the visit. Do bartenders ring up every sale? Does cash paid to room service waiters reach the bank deposit? Security shopping is designed to uncover dishonesty and criminal acts. That's far different from the intent of the typical inspection visit and may even require special state licensing.

Mystery shoppers are not police. Neither are they consultants or critics. They are reporters of the scene. Evaluating service and employee attitude and testing the staff's mettle during moments of truth are the QA purposes of quality control. Quality assurance is maintained when management acts on the QC reports, using them to reinforce good habits. Training, not punishment, follows when reports are negative. When that really is the intent of the practice, the staff learns about the mystery shoppers in advance, and the inspectors' evaluation sheets are made available to all. How else will the standards that management hopes to establish be known?

Quality Guarantees

Quality guarantees (QGs) reinforce quality assurance commitments and strengthen promises of empowerment. In the vernacular: QGs put the company's money where its advertising mouth is. Guaranteeing a satisfactory level of product and service takes gumption. It contradicts the not-my-fault phenomenon currently evident across the United States. Service guarantees take responsibility for everything that happens. QGs announce unequivocally to customers and employees alike that management is confident enough to stand behind its advertising. It is a courageous stand and a sign of management's confidence in the programs it has implemented. Sure, it backfires at times.

QGs are not like discounted rates, used and discarded as occupancy declines and recovers. Quality guarantees become part of the operating philosophy of the business: They are the very essence of the operation. Such a potent tool must be introduced carefully as the ultimate result of an ongoing and successful program of quality assurance. Guarantees fail miserably when they evolve from an advertising need rather than an operational plan.

Several years ago, a well-known hotel chain jumped on the QG bandwagon with a promise of ''complete satisfaction.'' No modifiers or limiting exceptions—just complete satisfaction guaranteed. An incident arose when a guest relying on that policy stopped at one of the properties. There was no hot water for a shower on the morning of departure. Citing the well-advertised guarantee, the guest asked for a free room or an allowance against the standard charge. The member property declined, explaining that the malfunctioning boiler was beyond its control. So much for a guarantee of complete satisfaction.

QGs need to be narrowly defined at first. Once a standard is established, the guarantee can be aimed at a target and delivered accordingly. Implementing guarantees in stages, by specific expectations within certain departments as capabilities come on line, announces to guests and staff that service quality is in place. Marriott, for example, guarantees to deliver room-service breakfast within 30 minutes. Failure to do so means a free breakfast. Wrapped up in this simple promise is an advertisement, a departmental promotion, an employee empowerment, an assurance of quality, and a willingness to be measured.

Other hotel companies offer different guarantees—the no-overbooking policy of Westin's, for example. Each Westin hotel keeps open enough empty rooms to ensure the property's compliance. Strict enforcement minimizes cash restitutions because guests are almost never walked. Obviously, there is still the cost of empty rooms that might have been rented. From a practical side, however, the guarantee is inexpensive to deliver. Hotels do not reach full occupancy very often. When they do, careful counting can almost always accommodate every reservation. Only on a few occasions will rooms be left vacant in order to meet the guarantee.

Quality guarantees are a two-edged sword. Failing to pay off after announcing a guarantee alienates guests far more than the incident itself. Guarantees must be unambiguous, limited in scope, and focused on specific objectives that are easily understood. With such guarantees, a failure to deliver is evident to all. There is no quibbling about payment, which—when made promptly—leads to guest loyalty and positive word-of-mouth advertising.

Nothing highlights operational weaknesses more than having to pay off guarantees that arise from legitimate complaints.

Americans with Disabilities Act.   The **Americans with Disabilities Act (ADA)** is a quality standard that government legislated in 1990 to become effective in 1992. It provides for changes in physical structures and hiring practices to accommodate the disabled. The ADA applies to all American businesses, including lodging, which is covered by Title III of the act. The law essentially provides civil rights protection for some 43 million disabled Americans and establishes stringent penalties to ensure compliance.

The federal government's ADA and the lodging industry's TQM converge on the same two subjects: Both treat guest and employee issues. The one legislates changes and the other implements them as a matter of good business. Hotel companies hired handicapped employees long before the law was enacted, although very little was done to accommodate disabled guests. Radisson was an early employer of the disabled, and so was the Ritz-Carlton Company. Holiday Inn, especially its Worldwide Reservation Center, was still another. Companies like these now include ADA awareness and training as part of their quality assurance efforts. Embassy Suites calls the ADA segment of its TQM program "Commandments of Disability Etiquette."

All departments of the hotel are affected by the legislation and the ensuing regulations. Front offices have made changes in work conditions to accommodate employees and in lobby and guest room designs to accommodate guests. Eliminating physical barriers is the major change for accommodating guests. Accommodating workers requires additional provisions. Included here might be modification of equipment or the acquisition of different equipment, enhanced lighting, and even power to recharge wheelchairs. Hiring practices and nonphysical adjustments are sometimes harder to implement than special equipment. Included in these human resources issues are special approaches in training, job restructuring, testing, position descriptions, and more.

Most changes attend to physical barriers because they are easy to see and remedy. Moreover, ADA regulations have itemized these in mathematical terms (door threshold—less than 0.5 inches; roll-in shower—a minimum of $36'' \times 60''$) that are impossible to misunderstand. Exhibit 7–2 offers a list of accommodations that fall within the purview of the law.

EXHIBIT 7–2

Shown are accommodations that lodging establishments must make to meet the requirements and intent of the Americans with Disabilities Act. (See the Americans with Disabilities Act Accessibility Guidelines—ADAAG.)

Communications

Telephones for the hearing impaired

Public telephones at proper height

Telecommunication Devices for the Deaf (TDD)

Guest rooms telephones

Visual alert to a ringing telephone

Easy dialing for those with reduced muscle control

Large telephone buttons or replacement pad

Voice-digital phone dialing

Safety Equipment

Visual alert to smoke detectors

Visual alert to door knocks, bells, and sirens

Visual or vibrating alarm clocks

Low viewports on doors

Low location of room locks

Lighted strips on stairwells

Contrasting color on glass doors and handrails

Dual handrails on ramps

Automatic door openers

Slower times on elevator door closures

Access

Handicapped parking spaces

Ramp access to and within the building

Minimum thresholds

Adequate door access

Levered hardware, or adapters

Bathroom access (see Exhibit 7–3)

Lowered drinking fountains with accessible controls

Closed caption decoders for TV and VCR

Assisted listening systems for meetings

Mattresses on frames rather than pedestal beds

Lower light switches and thermostats

Two-level reception desks

Curb cuts in sidewalks

Replacing high-pile carpeting

Accommodating seeing eye and hearing ear animals

Closet rods and drapery controls accessible

Extension cords for recharging wheelchairs

Lifts: elevators, vertical and incline platforms

Portable devices when facilities are not permanent

Eggcrate cushions for arthritics

Graphics

Size, color, and illumination

Braille and raised lettering in elevators

Braille and raised lettering behind guest room doors

Recessed or projected graphics where appropriate

Verbal recitation of bill denominations when making change

Guest bathrooms remain high on the unsatisfactory list. Redoing baths is an expensive proposition, so hotels prefer waiting until that need is evident before making wholesale changes. Exhibit 7–3 provides a summary of bathroom changes being implemented throughout the industry. Hotels built after 1992 are required to have 5 percent of the rooms for the physically impaired, 5 percent for the vision impaired, and 5 percent for the hearing impaired.

Innkeepers were not pleased with the passage of the Americans with Disabilities Act. It levied heavy remodeling costs on the industry despite the bill's supporters' saying it would not. Hotels that lagged in compliance faced fines and punitive lawsuits by the disabled. As was the case with similar legislation—the Occupation and Safety Administration (OSHA), for example—the ramifications of ADA's passage will not be known for years until the regulations and legal interpretations work their way through the bureaucracy of the government and the delay of the courts.

Complaints

Trying to quantify guest unhappiness is comparable to computing the costs behind moments of truth. Neither offers any mathematical accuracy, but they both make

Exhibit 7–3

Listed are alterations to standardized bathrooms required of lodging establishments to meet the provisions of the Americans with Disabilities Act.

Building roll-in showers with folding seats.

Replacing faucet knobs with lever hardware.

Installing grab bars in tub and toilet areas.

Elevating sinks to accommodate wheelchairs.

Insulating pipes on the underside of the sinks.

Raising toilet seats.

Lowering towel bars.

Enlarging bathrooms to provide turnaround space.

Providing transfer seats at the tub.

Designing clearance space to get through the door.

Lowering mirrors.

Including hand-held showers with adjustable height bars.

cogent points. Putting a dollar value to the cost of complaints begins with an assumption—a somewhat baseless figure bantered about the industry but one that is frequently quoted: It is said that 10 percent of guests would not return to the property of their most recent stay. Using the same values as Exhibit 7–1, that 10 percent represents 21 guest-nights per day, or 7,665 guest-nights per year for a hotel of 300 rooms.[8] Based on the nation's approximate Average Daily Rate of $61, the failure of guest encounters might be valued at $467,000 per year (7,665 guest-nights multiplied by the $61 ADR). The figure stretches into the stratosphere—$4,670,000—when a hotel like the 3,000-room Treasure Island (Exhibit 1–5) is considered.

Some argue, moreover, that labor-intensive industries such as lodging increase productivity only by improving service encounters. The failure to do so represents additional labor costs as well as costs from lost business. Here, too, there is not much empirical evidence to support the hypothesis.

Every complaint has an impact on the bottom line, but not every complaint takes dollars to resolve. One major investigation reported just the opposite: Only one-third of all written complaints involved a financial issue. Money is more often at stake with face-to-face encounters. Exhibit 7–4 offers another tidbit: Better to spend a bit to hold that guest than to invest five times the amount soliciting a new customer.

Still Another Calculation.   Still another calculation is shown in Exhibit 7–4. Like the others, it begins with a bunch of widely quoted but vaguely grounded assumptions. Still, the conclusions are startling.

Premise 1: 68 percent of nonreturning guests stay away because of indifferent service. (Deaths, relocations, competition, and poor products account for the other 32 percent.)

Premise 2: 5 percent or less of dissatisfied guests actually voice their unhappiness. There is an iceberg effect here. Below the surface floats the vast bulk of complaints, never voiced and never resolved. Of this silent majority, it is said that well over half will not patronize the hotel again. Worse yet, they will tell 9 to 10 others not to do so; some tell as many as 20 others.

Premise 3: About two-thirds of the icebergs can be warmed and won over by resolving the complaint. About one-third of complainers can be converted

EXHIBIT 7–4

*Here are some widely
quoted but rarely
referenced figures
dealing with complaints
and complainers.*

Loss of Guests

68% of nonreturning guests quit because of indifferent service.

32% is lost to death, relocation, competition, and poor products.

Complaints

Less than 5% of dissatisfied guests speak out—and for every one that does there are two who do not.

Over half of the silent majority refuse to return—an iceberg floating beneath the service.

Noncomplaining guests do complain to friends and acquaintances.

- 9 to 10 others will hear of the mishap.
- 13% of the group will gripe to 20 others.

Two-thirds of the iceberg could be won over if they were identified—about half of these could become boosters.

Costs

It costs over $10 to write a complaint letter (including the time to write it, follow-up, and postage).

It costs five times more to get a new customer than to keep an existing one.

---

from blasters to boosters if their complaints are handled quickly and properly. Implicit here is the guest's willingness to speak up. Guests will when they are very angry or when management creates an environment that encourages guests to register complaints.

Preventing the Complaint.   Identifying the reluctant complainer is a challenge. It will not be met by asking departing guests the rote question, "How was everything?" Desk personnel and managers from all operational and organizational levels must ask direct and specific questions. That means talking to guests, whether in the lobby, by the pool, or elsewhere. The dialogue may start with pleasantries: an introduction, a comment on the weather, an inquiry about the frequency of the guest's visits. But then the conversation must elicit the negatives, if there are any. "Did you use room service?" opens a chain of related questions. "How was the bed?" directs the conversation in a different direction. "Can you tell me about any especially pleasant (or unpleasant) experiences you have had here?"

Issues that flow from these solicitations are not complaints in the truest sense, but they give management direction for improving service and preempting complaints from someone else later on. More important, they bring out the guest's concerns and give the hotel the opportunity to redirect the dynamics and make friends. Many of the issues raised require no immediate actions, no costs, no allowances. They form the base for operational changes and they build the relationships that promote returning guests, especially if the questioner follows the brief interview with a letter of thanks to the candid guest.

Early Warning.   Complaints can be forestalled if the hotel staff is up front with the guest and tells it like it is. Alerting guests to bad situations allows them to decide whether or not to participate. So, the reservation department explains that the pool is closed for repairs during the dates under consideration. A request for connecting rooms is impossible to promise, so the request is noted but no guarantee is made by the reservationist.

Similarly, sales executives must warn small groups about other large parties in the house during the anticipated booking period. Room service reports elevator problems and thus some delay before the order will be delivered. Room clerks offer special rates in a certain wing because ongoing renovations there are noisy at times and create extra dust.

Complaint management acknowledges how the "squeaky wheel" gets the best results. Promptly attending to the squeak may mean better service for all. Observant guests often side with the hotel when an obnoxious complainer rolls up to the desk. They will cede their priority in line to get the pest out of the way. Similarly, handling families with tired or irritable children outside the sequence actually improves service for others.

Preventing the complaint by anticipating the problem and providing unsolicited, accurate information is far preferable to assuaging angry guests after the fact. Explaining the circumstances makes guests feel better about the situation and forestalls their complaints. "The maid will not get to the room before luncheon, so we can accommodate your early arrival but not before 1 o'clock."

If a policy of candor works wonders in reducing complaints, the opposite is also true: Misleading information, either directly or by implication and omission, enrages guests who feel they have been cheated—as they have.

Comment Cards. An ongoing debate continues about the effectiveness of guest comment cards. But the battle to improve guest service needs every weapon that can be mustered. Comment cards are just another device for getting guest input. Like other information-gathering techniques, they have advantages and disadvantages. Innovative approaches to this old standby strengthen the instrument and improve its quality. The better the questionnaire, the more information available for managing guest services.

Hoteliers complain that guests use questionnaires to gripe. Guests do not balance the good and the bad, hoteliers protest, but concentrate their comments on operating weaknesses. Actually, that's good. Uncovering and remedying shortcomings is what QM programs are all about. As noted earlier, too few guests ever bring their concerns to the hotel's attention. Guest comment cards help overcome the iceberg effect, the reluctance of the complainer to complain. Management's grumbling about the disproportion of positives and negatives has its origin in promotion and bonus decisions, which often include comment-card data.

Critics attack the validity of comment cards on the basis of very low response rates, typically 1 to 2 percent of the guest population. Long, detailed questionnaires account for some of the low numbers. Guests just won't take time to answer. Small cards with a narrow focus, one that changes periodically, improve the overall response rate. Monthly themes that focus on single issues produce better results than full-blown questionnaires that are never answered. Areas of special concern can always be tested more frequently.

Just asking guests to participate increases the number of returns. Some of the best results come during the check-out procedure, when response rates improve tenfold. Locating touch-screen terminals in the lobby near the cashier solicits direct responses from departing guests. Marriott's Fairfield Inns call it the Score Card System. Strategic placement encourages adult use and dissuades random input from children, another criticism often voiced.

Participation rates increase when guests have an incentive for completing the cards. The rate of return goes up with every dessert coupon the desk issues. (It also gets guests into the coffee shop.) Similarly, room upgrades for the next visit combine incentives with room promotions. Immediate upgrades are given when the solicitation is made during registration.

Awarding elaborate prizes from a drawing of comment-card participants is another incentive for guests to complete them. It also flags the importance that the property attributes to quality assurance. Moreover, contest information enables the hotel to match guest names with comments. That isn't always possible otherwise because some guests prefer anonymity.

Many American companies, including some in lodging, advertise toll-free 1-800 numbers to disaffected consumers. The significant cost of doing this is more than balanced by the demographic information gathered. Moreover, immediate attention to consumer complaints builds enormous goodwill and does it quickly. It is a unique combination of quality management and modern electronics.

However done, management gathers the information and analyzes it for trends in operating weaknesses and strengths. A good system does more than establish customer goodwill. It helps measure service and identifies functions that are working well or poorly. Checking off complaints over a given period on a simple spreadsheet highlights those areas that appear over and over again on the comment cards.

Every comment card should receive an immediate and personal response. Letters and telephone calls indicate the property's level of concern and often elicit further details. Internal implementation of corrective action may also be immediate—purchasing more hand towels, providing maps of the area, or repositioning training sessions.

Some information has strategic value and involves serious budget restraints. Building additional elevators or buying new computer systems may be requested by the comment cards but such implementation may need to wait.

As this discussion has suggested, using various techniques improves response rates to comment cards and also their validity. Summarized, these techniques involve the following:

1. Actively soliciting the questionnaire by personal appeal, especially at check-in or check-out times.
2. Paying a bounty—an upgrade, a free in-room movie, or a glass of wine with dinner.
3. Downsizing the questionnaire by reducing the demographic and marketing questions that often ride shotgun over issues of service.
4. Asking specific questions that allow quick check-off responses but providing space for guests who wish to comment.

After going to all that trouble, management sometimes fails to get its money's worth. Without careful policing, employees and their friends may complete the forms, or even tell the guests what to say. Other times, the form is shortstopped somewhere: Housekeepers throw away those left in rooms; desk clerks pocket those that reflect poorly on them; and/or unit managers withhold those with negative information. Providing postage-paid cards with the chief executive's address helps circumvent incorrect handling and emphasizes the questionnaire's importance to the company.

Quality Circles.   Quality circles, or quality teams, are still another method of getting information. Circles are small groups of employees that meet regularly as quasi-permanent teams to identify issues in delivering quality service. The terminology differs, but guests are occasionally added to the teams (this is especially appropriate at resorts). If the circle catches problems before complaints are registered, TQM is working perfectly. Sometimes the remedies come after the fact, arising from management's referral of a series of complaints.

Quality circles in the service industry are very much like those in manufacturing. Small, continuous improvements—creative changes—are the goals. Spectacular breakthroughs or innovations are not customarily part of the circle's design. Consequently, the group's composition is taken from all levels and across departmental lines. Delays in room service at breakfast, for example, may prove to be housekeeping's fault—moving linen between floors ties up the elevators just when room service demand is the highest!

Total quality management requires each employee to service other departments as if they were guests. A cross-departmental team, therefore, has members who are internal customers of one another. Teams may function in several capacities, or different teams may be organized for specific, corrective action. In addition, there are quality improvement circles, focus groups (short-term, one-issue teams), or on-going self-managing units.

American culture emphasizes the individual and not the group. Circles have been very successful in some hotel environments and have flopped terribly in others. Like comment cards or lobby interviews or 1–800 toll-free calls, the circle serves as another piece in the whole quality mosaic. It is both a source of information on which to act and a means of finding the solution with which to act.

Handling the Complaint.   Quality assurance aims for error-free service, but that is a goal more than a fact. Experience keeps a tight rein on reality, making complaint-free environments desirable but very unlikely—only the number, timing, or place of the complaint is uncertain, not whether one will occur. As QM programs reduce the number and focus the place, the remaining complaints gain in importance. Besides, not all complaints are subject to quality management solutions. Systems, procedures, and training aside, the unexpected will always happen—door attendants do lose car keys.

Preparing for Complaints.   Preparing for complaints begins by acknowledging their likelihood. Training programs must first emphasize the probability of a complaint. Employees with a proper mindset, those not caught unaware, recognize the importance of attitude in receiving and resolving complaints. Proper preparation minimizes the impact and cost of the complaint. Preparing properly means making the best of the worst. Readying employees to receive and resolve complaints has become an integral part of quality management programs.

Although the specifics differ, complaints follow a theme in each department. This gives quality circles an effective role in training. Within the circle, members share their individual experiences and solutions, and the group adopts the best ideas as departmental standards. Employee empowerment, the authority to accept responsibility and to remedy the situation, is implicit.

For front-desk employees, common themes spring from specific encounters. What is the proper response to a departing guest who protests a **folio** (guest bill) charge? What should be done with an irate arrival whose reservation has been sold to another? What accommodations can be made if the guest tenders a travel agent's coupon that is not acceptable to the hotel? Common situations all, playing themselves out time and again in a fixed pattern if not an exact duplication. None are rare, unexpected encounters. A series of options must be readied and employed as needed.

One typical option instructs employees to direct certain situations to higher management. Even empowerment programs limit employee authority to certain decision levels. Preparing employees for the complaint must include information about when and why and to whom to refer the matter. Rarely do the sessions train for the next (frequently necessary) step: What is to be done when the next level of authority is not available? Leave the fuming guest to wait . . . and wait . . . and wait?

Complaints may arise because the spread between guest expectations and service delivery widens dramatically after arrival. But complaints are not always of the hotel's doing. Hotel staff may just be the most convenient recipient of the guest's bad day. Tired and grumpy travelers, those who have done battle with family members or business associates, who have fought against cancelled flights and lost luggage, may find the hotel employee—especially an inexperienced one who dithers and dathers—an ideal outlet for a week of frustrations. Preparing for the complaint means understanding this.

Preparing for the complaint means putting up with drunks and being tolerant of the show-off and the braggart performing for the group. Preparing for the complaint allows one to overlook exaggerations, sarcasm, and irony. Preparing for the complaint recognizes that senior persons sometimes berate younger staff in a replay of the parent–child relationship. Preparing for the complaint means understanding that some persons can never be satisfied whatever the staff may try.

Responding to Complaints.   No complaint is trivial. Treating one as if it were explodes an easily resolved issue into a major brouhaha. What is perceived as trivial often emanates from a series of small, unattended issues that smoulder until management blows hot air onto the fire.

Complaints are communicated when complainers speak and listeners give ear—*receive the complaint.* Careful listening is the basis for resolving every complaint. Full attention to the speaker moves the problem toward prompt resolution even before the explanation is complete. Experienced complaint-handlers never allow other employees, guests, or telephone calls to distract them from hearing out the complainant.

Complainers do not always begin with the real issue—which is true, of course, with many conversations. Questions are appropriate provided they are not judgmental, but interrupting unnecessarily angers the speaker and pushes the conversation to another level of frustration before all the facts are in hand.

Listening requires good eye contact and subtle supportive body movements. Appropriate nodding, tsh-tshing, mouth expressions, and hand movements encourage the speaker and convey attention, sympathy, and understanding. It is important to remain in contact with the speaker and empathetic toward his or her experience throughout the recitation.

Small mishaps end in court cases when the listener makes short shrift of the incident and of the individual voicing the aggrievement. Lawsuits are the invariable results of leaving the resolution of small accidents entirely to the security staff. Aggrieved guests want management's attention and evidence of its concern. They want a sympathetic listener to hear them out.

Guests do not like being rushed along; they want the whole story to come out. The listener must be sensitive to his or her own body language, careful that negative signals are not halting the complainer or dropping a cold blanket over the encounter. Watching for the guest's nonverbal signals helps interpret the guest's readings of one's own signals.

Complainers who grow hostile or who become overly upset, loud, or abusive must be removed from the lobby. Shifting to a new venue should be done as quickly as possible once the issue intensifies or the time commitment grows inordinate. Perhaps the pretense can be that of comfort—let's sit down in the office.

Walking to the new location offers a cooling-off period. It provides an opportunity to shift the topic and to speak in more conversational tones. Walking changes the aggressive or defensive postures that one or the other might have assumed in the lobby. The office location adds to the manager's authority and prestige.

The louder the guest growls, the softer should come the response, which usually brings an immediate reaction: Loud complainers quiet down to hear replies that are given in near whispers. A harsh answer to abuse or to offensive language only elevates the complaint to a battle of personalities. Above all, the hotel wants the guest to retain dignity. Divorcing the interaction from personalities helps do that. The facts are at issue, not the individuals; certainly not the employee, who may be the original target of the guest's ire.

Ultimately, the manager may refuse to discuss the issues further unless the guest modulates language and tone. The hotelier tells the complainer that he or she is being addressed politely and the listener expects the same courtesy. In a worst-case scenario, say with a drunk or drug-crazed guest, the hotel may need to call the police.

Asking permission to *record the complaint*—take notes—indicates how seriously management views the matter. It also allows the guest's complaint to be restated and recorded with accuracy—at least, accurate from the guest's point of view. The hotel's representative gets an additional opportunity to express concern and sympathy as the issues are restated aloud. It also slows the conversation, helping to cool emotions. Contributing to the written report makes the complaining guest sense that already something is being done. Thus, the stage is set for resolving the problem.

Front offices maintain permanent journals of the day's activities, including complaints. These logs improve communications with later shifts since the issues often carry over. The documentation helps the participants recall the incident later, provides a basis for training, and supports legal proceedings if the matter goes that far. Serious accidents are documented again by security and by the hospital or the police, depending on circumstances.

The recordkeeping goes further. Getting the guest's folio, registration card, or reservation data helps the manager understand what happened. Calling an employee into the office or on the telephone in the guest's presence broadens the investigation, clarifies the facts, and mollifies the complainer.

Once registered, the complaint must be *settled*—resolved and closed. The complainant expects some satisfaction or real restitution for the embarrassment. The hotel wants to keep the customer, strengthen the relationship, if possible, and send the guest forth as a booster who tells the world how fairly he or she was treated. Still, the hotel doesn't want to give away the house atoning for mistakes that caused no harm and little damage.

Apologies are free—we can give away as many as needed. And, indeed, only an apology may be needed. Apologies are in order even if the complaint seems baseless or unreasonable. The effectiveness of the apology depends on the guest's reading of the manager. Is the hotelier truly contrite or merely mouthing niceties as a means of getting a quick solution? There are different ways of apologizing, but none are effective unless they ring true.

The standard, "I am sorry, and I apologize on behalf of the hotel," goes a long way toward settling minor issues quickly and satisfactorily. "I am sorry" can take on different nuances with different levels of emphasis—"I *am* sorry"—additional words—"I am *so* sorry"—or deleted words—"I'm sorry."

Guests listen for subtle connotations in words and voice. Voices can be shaped and honed through practice to carry just the right intonations and emphases. Concern, belief, and self-disparagement can be communicated irrespective of the words. Other standbys, although often repeated, have a proper place in the list of apologies: "I know how you must feel"; "Yes, that is distressing"; and "I would have done the same."

Although it is not necessary to fix blame for the incident—and doing so may be counterproductive—the hotel's staff clearly may be at fault. When pertinent, admitting as much helps to set the tone, as long as the admission doesn't include minimizing the incident or offering lame excuses. Use a simple statement about "our" mistake.

Managers who want to go beyond the apology send gifts to the room. The traditional fruit basket, or a tray with wine and cheese, or even a box of amenities serve this function. Apologies appear on the card once again.

Complaints that are settled with apologies are the least expensive kind and often prove to be the most satisfying for both sides. Subsequent telephone calls or letters reinforce the apologies that were expressed during the face-to-face encounters.

After hearing out the guest, quieting down the situation, and offering appropriate sympathy, the hotel manager must provide *restitution* and lay the issue to rest. The quicker the problem can be resolved, the better. That is what happens with most complaints. But serious items are not settled that easily. Smashed fenders, dentures broken on a bone, or snagged designer's dresses are not remedied on the spot. Insurance companies, or law firms in more serious instances (a fall in the tub), work their wares slowly. Nevertheless, sympathy, concern, and prompt, on-the-spot action reduce the longer-run consequences and costs.

More concrete solutions are needed when apologies are not enough. A list of options should be identified for the hotel's representative as part of the preparation process. Heading the list are items that cost the hotel little or nothing, as would an upgrade. Even here, there are degrees: Should we upgrade to another level? To the concierge floor? To an expensive suite? The upgrade is offered for this visit or for another. If for another, the manager's card with a direct number—"call me personally and I'll arrange it"—reinforces the special nature of the solution. Some managers preface every offer by hinting that the arrangements are special. By implication, deviating from standard procedure recognizes the guest's importance and the hotel's desire to make things right.

Annoying but inconsequential incidents can be handled with small gifts. Tickets to an event that is being held by the hotel are welcome. Athletic contests (tennis tourneys), presentations (distinguished speakers), theater-style entertainment, and the like are almost without cost if seats are plentiful.

Admission to the hotel's club or spa, tickets to local activities such as theme parks or boat rides, or transportation to the airport in the hotel's limousine are other options. Cash refunds are the last choice, but they may be the only appropriate response. Damage to property requires reimbursement, and extraordinary circumstances necessitate an allowance against folio charges.

Usually, the situation is less serious. The guest has twice before reported an inoperative television set. Or, the guest's request to change rooms has been ignored. Or, the long delay in getting a personal check cleared for cashing is irritating and embarrassing. Complaints of this type need fast and certain action. Once the solution is resolved, a wise manager explains what is to be done and how long it will take. Better to overestimate the time—then a more rapid turnaround will impress the guest with the hotel's sincerity.

Guest demands soften if the episode is handled well and the guest feels that the treatment is fair. If the interview seems to be moving that way, the guest can be brought into the decision loop. Carefully, the hotel's representative elicits the guest's expectations, which often are less than the hotel's, and draws the guest into formulating the remedy. The complainer becomes part of the solution, and the process gains momentum toward a quick and satisfactory conclusion.

All of which is easier said than done. Standing near an experienced complaint-handler—listening to what is said and how it is said—is the best learning experience the manager can have. It is especially helpful if the claim is denied.

Customers are always right! Except sometimes they aren't. The first reference is to the attitude with which management hears the guest's complaint; the second reference is to the context of the complaint. Management can listen attentively, sympathize completely, and communicate caringly, but still *say no* to outrageous requests based on nonevents.

Refusing compensation—remember, apologies are always in order—may cost the customer's patronage. It is a fine judgment call, as repeat patronage may already be lost. In denying restitution, inexperienced managers resort to ''company policy'' as the reason. Company policy is a great turnoff! Better to explain the answer in terms of fairness, of safety, of service to other guests, of economic reality, or of past experience.

Unhappy guests may request the intervention of higher authority. If that is appropriate, the next manager must be formally introduced and the issue recapped aloud to expedite the meeting. Thereafter, the first interviewer remains silent unless questioned and allows the second conversation to progress without interruption.

Complaints that are resolved quickly and equitably make friends for the hotel. Resolved or not, management's attitude, as expressed in words and movements, goes far toward minimizing (or aggravating) the damages.

Summary

Managing guest services requires management vision and a box of tools. If history is any guide, the jargon of the tools—quality circles, quality control, total quality management—will soon fade away.[9] Such is the experience with other management terminologies. Fads in management, like other fashions, come and go. The hotel industry must retain the vision and principles of guest service even as the jargon changes.

A global momentum toward the service sector and toward the meaning of service accounts for the popularity of the total quality management movement. Lodging, which has been in the service industry for 3,000 years, has rediscovered much of its heritage in a return to the service mode.

Managing guest service focuses on process and product, on employee and work environment. From these fundamentals come operating and managerial principles: the enhancement of the service encounter—the moments of truth; a pledge of commitment from each member of the organization; empowerment—the assignment of authority to the employees who make things happen; and the hiring, measuring, monitoring, and rewarding processes.

Quality management has as many definitions as it has proponents. The essence of managing for quality is simple to express and difficult to implement. Above all else, managing for guest service means responding to guest needs. QM means running the hotel about customer needs and not about the products of the hotel. It is a shift from what management wants to offer to a product that the market wants to buy. As that happens, the guest perception of quality and the reality of quality move closer together.

The success of the quality management structure finds voice in the manner that the hotel treats complaints, provides for the disabled, and stands on its promise to deliver at given, measurable levels. Hopefully, the experience learned during the low dips of the 1980s and 1990s will not be forgotten as the industry recovers in the 21st century.

Queries and Problems

1. Prepare a tally sheet—a spreadsheet—that could be used by the front desk to analyze complaints that are registered there or forwarded there from the executive offices.

2. Develop a dialogue for the hotel staff to use during the following situations:
   a. The ski resort is empty and no wonder—there hasn't been any snow for two weeks. A telephone call comes in requesting a reservation for a party of six couples for two days hence.
   b. A wildcat strike was launched by the housekeepers midmorning, well before most of the departures had gone. Obviously, few rooms have been remade, although supervisors and managers from all departments are frantically attempting to fill the void. By early afternoon, the lobby is full of displaced arrivals—many individuals and a group tour, all within earshot. A VIP, guest of the marketing director, arrives and approaches the desk.

3. Prepare and briefly discuss a list of six quality guarantees that are defined narrowly enough to be communicated easily and achieved successfully (for example, room service delivered within 30 minutes).

4. The training emphasis this month deals with employee–guest and employee–employee interaction. Management wants to help lower-end employees feel comfortable during greeting occasions. Train some fellow classmates to initiate a series of greetings under the following circumstances:
   a. The employee meets a new, unfamiliar staff member at the time clock.
   b. The employee encounters the general manager in conversation with another person.
   c. The employee unexpectedly encounters a guest, as might occur in a corridor or entering or leaving an elevator.
   d. The employee almost collides with a deliveryperson as they both pass along the employee-exit corridor.

5. Working with a colleague, practice saying aloud the three statements that follow. Tape yourselves, listening for and explaining the changes in your voices after you have repeated each statement 10 times.

   "I'm sorry the pool is temporarily closed for repair."

   "Good morning, may I help you?"

   "I'm sorry, but your room has been sold; we have made arrangements for you at another property not far from here."

6. Establish a list of rewards (and measures for earning the incentives) for desk clerks. For bellservers. For reservationists.

Notes

1. Trademark of the Ford Motor Company.
2. Quality circles are employee teams.
3. Stephen J. Shriver, *Managing Quality Services* (1988).
4. Ibid, p. 3; Bruce Brocka and Suzanne M. Brocka, *Quality Management: Implementing the Best Ideas of the Masters* (Burr Ridge, IL: Richard D. Irwin, 1992).
5. Stephen Hall, *Quest for Quality: Cost of Error Study* (American Hotel & Motel Association, 1984).

6. The term *moments of truth* has been attributed to Jan Carlzon, former chairman of SAS Airlines.
7. To be approved for inclusion in AAA's lodging guide, hotel rooms must have deadbolts, automatic locking doors, and peepholes, and provide facilities for the disabled.
8. A guest-night, sometimes called a guest-day or room-night, is one guest for one night. Three guests staying two nights represents six guest-nights.
9. Jargon is the language of a profession.

The Guest Arrival Process

Chapter Outline

The Guest Arrival Process

In many hotels, the guest arrival process appears to be a simple affair. The guest is greeted, information is verified, payment is initiated, and a room is selected. Most guests move through their arrival and registration process without a second thought to the intricacies and choreography of the front-office functions involved. Yet the entire check-in process is important enough to be evaluated as a substantial part of the hotel's overall rating by both Mobil and AAA. Exhibit 8–1 gives a glimpse of the complexity of the guest arrival process.

An ideal check-in goes unnoticed by the guest because all hotel and front-office functions flow smoothly. From the valet attendant who parks the car to the door-person who greets the guest, from the bellperson who handles the luggage to the front-desk personnel who handle the arrangements, all systems work in unison. Within just three to five minutes, the guest is happily on the way to the room.

Aside from the actual reservation (which may or may not have been made first person by the guest), this is the guest's first opportunity to see the hotel in action.

EXHIBIT 8–1

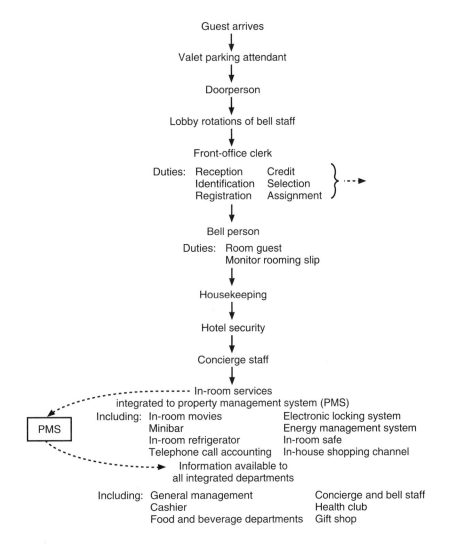

First impressions are critical, and that is why the arrival and check-in process is often referred to as a moment of truth. The front-office staff does not get a second chance to make a good first impression.

First Impressions

Various types of hotels offer differing levels of service. At no time is this difference in service as pronounced as it is during the arrival and check-in process. Limited-service properties offer no employee interaction between the front door and the front desk. In a limited-service property, the guest may not see or speak with any employee other than the front-desk clerk.

Full-service hotels, on the other hand, place several ranks of employees between the front door and the front desk. The guest may encounter a valet parking attendant, a doorperson, and a bellperson before ever arriving at the front desk.

Exhibit 8–2

Shown are doorpersons ready and waiting at the Wedgewood Hotel in Vancouver, British Columbia, Canada.

Valet Parking Attendant.   The first employee that guests often encounter in a full-service hotel is the valet parking attendant. The parking attendant greets the guests as they pull their vehicles under the porte cochere, opens their car door(s), may assist with placing luggage on the curb, and takes responsibility for parking and securing the vehicle (Exhibit 8–1).

Valet parking is an amenity or service provided by many fine hotels. However, not all full-service hotels offer valet parking. It is most commonly found in urban, city-center hotels where space is at a premium and guest self-parking is inconvenient.

This department is a revenue center for many hotels. By charging the guest a fee for parking each day, the valet parking department generates income to help defray the costs of maintenance and insurance on the parking lot or parking structure. The parking fee (which runs as high as $50 or $60 per day in some hotels) is added directly to the guest's folio or account. In addition, many guests tip the attendant each time their car is returned.

Many hotels lease or subcontract the operation of this department to a private parking company. With leased operations, a private company takes the responsibility for parking the guest's car, insuring it against damage, and staffing the department. In such cases, the guest is unaware that valet parking is a contracted department.

Doorperson.   As with valet parking, not all full-service hotels offer a doorperson. For one thing, the position of doorperson is expensive to staff. This is especially true when you realize this is not a revenue-producing department. As a result, generally only the finest hotels can afford to provide doorpersons.

To many guests, no position represents the hotel quite like the doorperson. The uniformed services position of doorperson is part concierge, part bellperson, part tour guide, and part friend all rolled into one. The doorperson may offer the guest suggestions, point out interesting historic sites, explain difficult directions, and locate a taxi. For newly arriving guests, the doorperson assists with removing and securing luggage from the car until the bellperson retrieves it for delivery. In addition to all of these tasks, the doorperson also opens doors! See Exhibit 8–2.

Guest Registration

After being greeted at the curb and the front door, the guest arrives at the front desk (Exhibit 8–1). In a small property, the desk itself is small and probably staffed with just one or two clerks. Each of these clerks is capable of handling the full range of functions the guest requires. In larger properties, however, the front desk may be literally hundreds of feet long, with 20 to 30 or more clerks working. In large hotels, each clerk has a distinct responsibility. Although each line or queue is clearly marked with a sign, arriving guests are usually on their own in deciding which clerk to approach or in which line to stand. For arriving guests, the sign might say ''reception,'' ''registration,'' ''check-in,'' or ''arrivals.''

Two types of guests present themselves at the front desk—those with reservations and those without. Those with reservations are generally handled without problem. The clerk reconfirms the accommodations requested, the guest signs the registration card, a method of payment is secured, a room is selected, and some pleasantries are exchanged. In a computerized property, the entire reception process can be handled quickly—say, in two or three minutes.

Guests holding reservations may encounter two problems: no record of the reservation and no space available. The arrival and reception should go quickly, even if the reservation has been misplaced, provided space is available. As unobtrusively as possible, the clerk elicits the reservation information again and makes the assignment. No reference to the missing paperwork is made. Far more composure is necessary if the clerk is to successfully handle an overbooking situation. With proper training, the emergency procedures described in Chapters 6 and 7 are implemented, and the moment of truth is achieved without incident.

A lower level of expectation exists for guests who have no reservations. If space is available—and in most hotels there is space—the procedures take a little longer. Information that was available to the clerk from the reservation must now be obtained and checked against availability for the first night and succeeding nights. The same questions posed by the reservationist must be asked by the room clerk. How many nights? How many rooms? How many in the party? Like the reservationist on the telephone, the room clerk offers the walk-in alternative accommodations, rate, or length of stay, if the exact request cannot be met.

Blocking the Room.   On busy days, reservations and VIP rooms are blocked at once. Walk-ins and even some reservations are accommodated only on a first-come, first-served basis. On close counts—the desk is never positive who will or who will not check out—a guest may be kept waiting for hours, only to be told that there are no rooms after all.

Just a Reminder

_____ Room _____

You indicated upon checking in that you would be departing today. Your room is reserved for an incoming guest and your check-out time is 12 noon.

Should you need to stay in New York City an additional day, please contact our assistant manager, located in the main lobby or on Ext. 123. The assistant manager will make the necessary arrangements to reserve a room for you in a nearby hotel, as all our rooms have been reserved for today.

You can also make reservations for your next hotel stop before departure through our worldwide central reservation service.

Thank You.

To force departing guests to leave, a card explaining that the room is reserved and that the guest is expected to vacate on the stated departure date is placed in the room or hand delivered at registration time (see Exhibit 8–3). Some properties ask the guest to sign a statement or place initials next to the check-out date on the registration card. However, notifying an in-house guest that it is time to leave and forcing the guest to vacate are two entirely different matters. Although the hotel is thought to have legal standing, most hoteliers will refrain from ejecting a guest who has overstayed the reservation contract.

Registered, Not Assigned.   Very early arrivals, especially those who appear before the day's check-out hour, may be required to wait until a departure creates a vacancy. Even then, the room must still be cleaned. Baggage-check service is offered to all guests who must wait, and a complimentary beverage may be given to some if the hotel is responsible for the wait. In anticipation of an upcoming vacancy, the clerk may have the guest register. The account is marked **RNA (Registered, Not Assigned)** and kept handy until the first appropriate departure takes place. The assignment is made but the guest is kept waiting until housekeeping reports the room ready for occupancy—guests are not sent to unmade rooms.

Guests who arrive after the room is vacated but before it has been cleaned by housekeeping—a status called **on change—** are assigned at once but not provided with a key until the room has been cleaned and inspected. This is not an RNA.

RNAs occur whenever the hotel is very full with simultaneous arrivals and departures of large conventions, or when tour groups overlap. Busy holidays cause RNAs at the type of resorts where arrivals come early and departures stay late.

Waiting for the room is a distressing experience, especially as the hours tick away. On some occasions, it may be necessary to assign guests temporary rooms, changing them to a permanent assignment later on. This type of costly duplication should be avoided except in special circumstances. Most front-office systems, including computerized ones, allow RNAs to create charges even though no room identification is possible.

The Registration Card.   Registration is not essential to the common-law creation of a legal guest–hotel relationship. In several states it is not even a statutory requirement. In contrast, other countries not only require registration cards but use them as police documents. Guests furnish foreign innkeepers with passports and a great deal of personal information that has value only to the authorities (see

东方宾馆外国人临时住宿登记表
Tung Fang Hotel Registration Form of Temporary Residence for Foreigner

姓　　名 Name in full	中　　文 In Chinese		性　　别 Sex	
	原　　文 In original language		生　　年 Date of birth	
国　　籍 Nationality		来华身份或职业 Identity or occupation		
签 证 或 旅 行 证 号 码 及 期 限 Visa or travel document number and date of validity				
停 留 事 由 Object of stay		抵 达 日 期 Date of arrival		
何 处 来 何 处 去 Where from and to		拟 住 日 期 Duration of stay		
房 号 或 住 址 Room number or address				

Exhibit 8–4). Indeed, hotel registration in Brazil requires the guest to fill in the names of both mother and father. Age, sex, date of birth, next destination, previous stop, and nationality are never found on registration cards in the United States. Whether legally required or not, registration remains the best means of acknowledging the guest's arrival and of recording and processing the guest's stay.

Manual (nonautomated) properties still utilize registration cards as part of the overall registration process. The arriving guest is handed a blank ''reg'' card (see Exhibit 8–5) and pen, and asked to complete the required data.

Today's automated **property management system (PMS)** has reduced the need for manually collecting information. (A more thorough discussion of the PMS is found in Chapter 13.) Automated properties preprint registration cards from the information collected at the time of reservation (see Exhibit 8–6). Now instead of burdening the guest with completion of an entire card, the front-desk clerk merely asks the guest to verify accuracy of information and sign at the bottom of the card.

The standard registration information required is generally consistent across both manual and automated hotels.

Name and Number in the Party.   The number of registration cards used to register a party depends on the character of the group more than on its size. Except for an immediate family, a separate registration card is prepared for each person. Thus, two adult brothers sharing a room register separately, but one card handles the registration of a husband and wife. Married women whose names are different than their husbands' names also get second registration cards.

Like the rest of society, innkeepers face the dilemma of new social mores toward sex and marriage. They find themselves in the compromising position of accommodating unmarried couples even though it opens them to prosecution under the laws of many states. Still, few police agencies would act so long as the innkeeper does not run a disreputable property.

Unless the room clerk is absolutely certain from some information that the desk possesses, it is unwise to challenge a represented relationship on the mere suspicion that the couple is not husband and wife or brother and sister. Most innkeepers would

EXHIBIT 8–5

This old-style manual registration card shows business affiliation and method of payment. It is part of a packet including the rooming slip (shaded area). Note the number of guests, the split rate, the clerk's identification, and the folio cross-reference. (Western International Hotels is now named Westin Hotels and Resorts.)

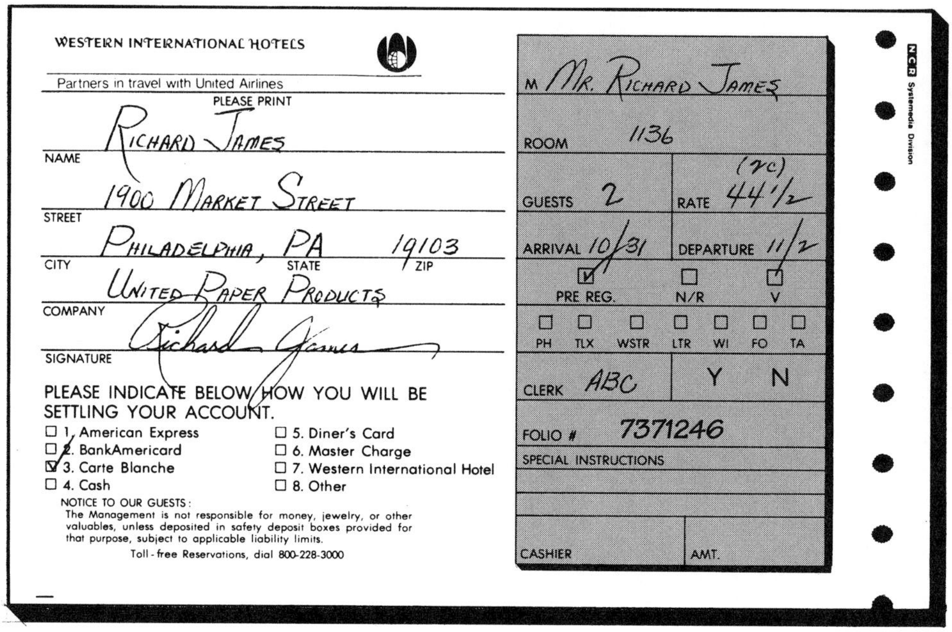
WESTERN INTERNATIONAL HOTELS

Partners in travel with United Airlines

PLEASE PRINT

NAME Richard James

STREET 1900 Market Street

CITY Philadelphia, STATE PA ZIP 19103

COMPANY United Paper Products

SIGNATURE Richard James

PLEASE INDICATE BELOW HOW YOU WILL BE SETTLING YOUR ACCOUNT.

- ☐ 1. American Express
- ☐ 2. BankAmericard
- ☒ 3. Carte Blanche
- ☐ 4. Cash
- ☐ 5. Diner's Card
- ☐ 6. Master Charge
- ☐ 7. Western International Hotel
- ☐ 8. Other

NOTICE TO OUR GUESTS:
The Management is not responsible for money, jewelry, or other valuables, unless deposited in safety deposit boxes provided for that purpose, subject to applicable liability limits.

Toll-free Reservations, dial 800-228-3000

M Mr. Richard James

ROOM 1136

GUESTS 2 | RATE (rc) 44½

ARRIVAL 10/31 | DEPARTURE 11/2

☒ PRE REG. ☐ N/R ☐ V

☐ PH ☐ TLX ☐ WSTR ☐ LTR ☐ WI ☐ FO ☐ TA

CLERK ABC | Y N

FOLIO # 7371246

SPECIAL INSTRUCTIONS

CASHIER | AMT.

NCR Systemedia Division

Courtesy: Arizona Biltmore, Phoenix, Arizona.

take the couple in unless they blatantly flout the relationship. Under today's standards, it seems better to admit them than to challenge them.

The number of persons (the house count) has importance for statistics that are developed during the night audit. In addition, the number of persons in the room determines the rate charged. When indicating the number of guests in the room, many hotels separate adults from children. This is especially true in an American plan hotel that probably charges less for young children's meals than for adult meals.

Address. An accurate and complete address is needed for credit and billing and for the development of mailing lists for future sales promotions. A complete address includes such things as ZIP codes, apartment numbers, and even state of residence, for the names of many cities are common to several states. Commercial hotels often ask for the patron's business address and organizational title in addition to the residential address (Exhibits 8–5 and 8–6).

Greater credit can be extended to a guest whose address has been verified through an exchange of reservation correspondence than to a walk-in. Whereas those intent on fraud will use false addresses, vacant lots, or temporary box numbers, unintentional skippers (people who forgot to check out or inadvertently left a portion of their folio unpaid) can be traced, billed, and subsequently collected from if an accurate address is on file.

Room Number. Even as the hotel industry seeks higher levels of courtesy and guest service, the guest is known as much by room number as by name. Once the guest is registered in the property management system and a room number has been assigned, all subsequent transactions are referenced and billed to the room number rather than to the guest's actual name. The room number is the major means of locating, identifying, tracking, and billing the guest.

Exhibit 8–6

Shown is a computer-prepared registration card. (A carbon might serve as a rooming slip.) Note credit and liability statements.

```
2059                M/M Paul D. Ligament      6/14/9-        RATES DO NOT INCLUDE TAXES
Room                Name                      Depart         Res. #  122 ABC 9821

DLX K               Western Athletes          6/11/9-
Type                Firm or Group             Arrive         Group # WA

ABC
Clerk ID                                                     Deposit


                    Address          Rate Plan
                                     160         ⚡ HOT WIRE HOTEL
Street 1234 Achilles Tendon Way                    Shocking Behavior Drive
City/State Wounded Knee, SD 00000-0000             Electric City, Washington
Company Horsn Around, Inc.                                77777-7777
Date Departure  6/14/9
Signature  Paul D. Ligament

I agree that my liability for this bill is not waived and I agree
to be held personally liable in the event that the indicated
person, company, or association fails to pay for the full
amount of the charges.                              NOTICE TO GUESTS:
                                                    This hotel keeps a fireproof safe and will not
                                                    be responsible for money, jewelry, documents
I would like to handle my Account by:               or other articles of value unless placed therein.
☐Cash/Check ☐Master Card ☐VISA                      Please lock your car.
☐Diner's Club ☒American Express
☐Discover
```

Date of Departure. The guest's expected date of departure is of critical importance during the check-in process. By double-checking the guest's departure plans, the front office ensures the accuracy of future room availability figures.

As indicated earlier, many front offices require the guest to sign a statement or initial the registration card next to their date of departure. This is especially true for busy periods when a scheduled departure is necessary to provide the room to a newly arriving reservation. Of course, plans change, and some percentage of guests will invariably depart earlier or later than they originally thought. In such cases, the front office strives to accommodate the guest. There is usually no extra charge for early departures and most unscheduled stayovers are accommodated.

Corporate Affiliation or Discounts. Another issue resolved during the check-in process is the guest's corporate affiliation or qualified discounts. The corporate affiliation (if applicable) is often logged and tracked by the front desk on behalf of the sales and marketing department. This corporate information is critical to the sales department because many companies have accounts with individual and chain properties. By tracking corporate guest visitation, the sales department is able to continue offering discounts and special rates to companies who frequent the property.

Even when a corporate guest's company has not negotiated a special room rate, the hotel is usually willing to grant a standard corporate discount. Such discounts range from 10 to 20 percent or higher depending on the type of hotel, the date, and season of visitation.

Even noncorporate guests may qualify for discounts. Transient guests are often members of national or worldwide organizations such as AAA or AARP. AAA (American Automobile Association) and AARP (American Association of Retired Persons) are two of the largest membership organizations in the world. Most hotels grant AAA and/or AARP discounts to qualified guests. A complete discussion of rate discounts is found in Chapter 9.

Clerk Identification.   The front-desk clerk who checks the guest into the hotel is identified in both the manual and property management system documents. In the property management system, the clerk identification is automatically assigned from the password the clerk used when logging onto the computer. In a manual system, the clerk is identified either by initials or code.

Clerk identification is important in case a problem or other issue arises. By knowing who checked the guest in, management can return to that clerk and ask related questions. Possibly the guest was pleased with the process and complimented management on the clerk's performance. On the other hand, maybe the clerk provided an insufficient discount, was rude to the guest, or forgot to establish a method of payment.

Folio and Folio Number.   All hotels assign a unique folio number to the guest's account. In a computerized property, this account number is provided at the time of reservation. The number is assigned early in case the guest sends advance payment. The folio (or account) number references the guest's automated file just as readily as the room number or guest name. In a manual property, the unique folio number is not assigned until check-in, when the next sequentially numbered folio is removed from the top of the stack.

Numbered registration cards and numbered guest folios are more important in smaller hotels than in larger ones. Numbering serves as a control device when one employee is clerk, cashier, and supervisor all in one. It is possible for such an employee to sell the room as clerk, pocket the money as cashier, and cover the discrepancy as night auditor. When the staff grows large enough to permit a separation of duties, numeric form control becomes less important.

Numbered registration cards actually become burdensome as the front-office staff grows larger. Care must then be exercised to account for missing numbers without the offset of a control function. Besides, sequentially numbered forms are more expensive than unnumbered ones.

Another major advantage to the property management system is the ease of storing records. While according to some management consultants the standard is seven years (three years for registration cards), many properties find themselves storing folios, registration cards, and accounting records for even longer periods. In an electronic hotel, storage is easy when daily records are downloaded onto tape or disk.

In a manual property, storage consumes considerably more space. Used folios are filed in numerical sequence (which almost corresponds to chronological order) and used registration cards are filed alphabetically by month or period. If the guest's name is known, it is possible to locate the folio by cross-referencing the account number printed on the registration card.

Disclaimer of Liability.   Almost every registration card carries a statement concerning the hotel's liability for the loss of guest valuables. Examples of such disclaimers are shown in Exhibits 8–5 and 8–6. The form and content of the statement are prescribed by state statute and, consequently, these vary among states. If the innkeeper meets the provisions of the statute, and public notice on the registration card is usually one such provision, liability for the loss of valuables is substantially reduced. Were it not for the dollar limits set by state legislatures, innkeepers would have unlimited liability under common law.

Common law is far more stringent than statutory law; it makes the hotel responsible in full for the value of guests' belongings. Most states, but not all, limit the innkeeper's liability to a fixed sum even when the guest uses the safe provided. Other statutes prevent recovery against the hotel if the guest fails to use the safe, provided the hotel has complied with every provision of the law (see Exhibit 8–7).

State legislatures have extended this principle of limited liability to checkrooms and to goods that are too large for the ordinary safe—salesperson's samples, for example.

States get a quid pro quo for their protection. Notices, which must be posted in the rooms, must include the maximum rate charged for the room (Exhibit 8–7). Charges sometimes exceed that figure when a yield management system is in operation or when rates are changed several times during the course of a couple of years. The hotel may charge what it wishes, but there is a danger in not changing the permanent rate schedule posted in each guest room.

Pets.   Registering pets has some serious potential costs, including the discomfort of other guests. Some hotels refuse all animals except Seeing Eye dogs. Others seek pet owners as a distinct portion of their market. Most pet owners appreciate the innkeeper's problems and make restitution for damages. Additional protection is provided when a contract is signed by the owner agreeing to pay for any damages that occur.

Additional Contents.   The registration procedure is completed quickly when there is no waiting line. Empty spaces and lines on the registration card are filled in by the guest (name, address, and signature), or by the clerk (dates of arrival and departure, room and rate assigned, and clerk identification). With a computer, much of the data is preprinted during the quiet hours of the previous night, so there is even less to do at registration.

Even as management strives to expedite the process, extra reading matter is being added to the registration card. The content of these extra messages differs among hotels and chains. Each has different problems and legal experiences. The presence of the messages meets legal requirements, but it is doubtful whether any guest actually reads messages during the hurried moments of registration. The message is repeated on the rooming slip, however, and that slip is left with the guest (see Exhibit 8–8).

Legitimate misunderstandings— for example, about the rate of the room or the date of departure—occur quite often. For this reason, some hotels have guests initial the registration card indicating their agreement to its content. The check-out hour is frequently included, with a notice of additional charges for overstaying. Misunderstandings are not eliminated by the system; the hotel just gains the satisfaction of blaming the guest (the antiservice syndrome in action). Printing the messages in

EXHIBIT 8–7

Shown is a posted notice to guests effectively limiting the hotel's liability. Such a notice must be properly completed (showing the room rate at the bottom of each card) and posted in each room.

NOTICE TO GUESTS
ARIZONA INNKEEPERS' LAWS

NOTICE is hereby given of the provision of Section 33-302 of the Arizona Revised Statutes provided as follows:

§33-302.   Maintenance of fireproof safe .

A.   An innkeeper who maintains a fireproof safe and gives notice by posting in a conspicuous place in the office or in the room of each guest that money, jewelry, documents and other articles of small size and unusual value may be deposited in the safe, is not liable for loss of or injury to any such article not deposited in the safe, which is not the result of his own act.

B.   An innkeeper may refuse to receive for deposit from a guest articles exceeding a total value of five hundred dollars, and unless otherwise agreed to in writing shall not be liable in an amount in excess of five hundred dollars for loss of or damage to property deposited by a guest in such safe unless the loss or damage is the result of the fault or negligence of this establishment.

C.   An innkeeper shall not be liable for loss of or damage to merchandise samples or merchandise for sale displayed by a guest unless the guest gives prior written notice of having and displaying the merchandise or merchandise samples, and acknowledges receipt of such notice, but in no event shall liability for such loss or damage exceed five hundred dollars unless it results from the fault or negligence of this establishment.

D.   The liability of an innkeeper to a guest shall be limited to one hundred dollars for property delivered to this establishment to be kept in a storeroom or baggage room and to seventy-five dollars for property deposited in a parcel or checkroom.

NOTICE is hereby further given of the provisions of Section 33-951, and 33-952, Arizona Revised Statutes, as amended, which provided as follows:

§33-951.   Lien on baggage and property of guests

Hotel, inn, boarding house, lodging house, apartment house and auto camp keepers shall have a lien upon the baggage and other property of their guests, boarders or lodgers, brought therein by their guests, boarders or lodgers, for charges due for accommodation, board, lodging or room rent and things furnished at the request of such guests, boarders or lodgers, with the right to possession of the baggage or other property until the charges are paid.

§33-952.   Sale of property; notice

A.   When baggage or other property comes into the possession of a person entitled to a lien as provided by §33-951 and remains unclaimed, or the charges remain unpaid for a period of four months, the person may proceed to sell the baggage or property at public auction, and from the proceeds retain the charges, storage and expense of advertising the sale.

B.   The sale shall not be made until the expiration of four weeks from the first publication of notice of the sale, published in a newspaper once a week for four consecutive weeks. The notice shall contain a description of each piece of property, the name of the owner, if known, the name of the person holding the property, and the time and place of sale. If the indebtedness does not exceed sixty dollars, the notice may be given by posting at not less than three public places located at the place where the hotel, inn, boarding house, lodging house, apartment house or auto camp is located.

C.   Any balance from the sale not claimed by the rightful owner within one month from the day of sale shall be paid into the treasury of the county in which the sale took place, and if not claimed by the owner within one year thereafter, the money shall be paid into the general fund of the county.

NOTICE is hereby further given of the provisions of Section 12-671; and 13-1802; Arizona Revised Statutes, as amended, which provide as follows:

§12-671.   Drawing check or draft on no account or insufficient account with intent to defraud; civil action; definition of credit; prima facie evidence

A.   A person who, for himself or for another, with intent to defraud, makes, draws, utters or delivers to another person or persons a check or draft on a bank or depositary for payment of money, knowing at the time of such making, drawing, uttering or delivery, that he or his principal does not have an account or does not have sufficient funds in, or credit with, such bank or depositary to meet the check or draft in full upon presentation, shall be liable to the holder of such check or draft for twice the amount of such check or draft or fifty dollars, whichever is greater, together with costs and reasonable attorneys' fees as allowed by the court on the basis of time and effort expended by such attorney on behalf of plaintiff.

B.   The word "credit" as used in this section shall be construed to be an express agreement with the bank or depositary for payment of the check or draft.

C.   Proof that at the time of presentment, the maker, issuer or drawer did not have sufficient funds with the bank or depositary, and that he failed within twelve days after receiving notice of nonpayment or dishonor to pay the check or draft is prima facie evidence of intent to defraud.

D.   Where a check, draft or order is protested, on the ground of insufficiency of funds or credit, the notice of formal protest thereof shall be admissible as proof of presentation, nonpayment and protest and shall be prima facie evidence of the insufficiency of funds or credit with the bank or depositary, or person, or firm or corporation.

E.   "Notice", as used in this section, means notice given to the person entitled thereto, either in person, or in writing. Such notice in writing shall be given by certified mail, return receipt requested, to the person at his address as it appears on such check or draft.

F.   Nothing in this section shall be applicable to any criminal case or affect eligibility or terms of probation.

§13-1802.   Theft; classification

A.   A person commits theft if, without lawful authority, such person knowingly:

1.   Controls property of another with the intent to deprive him of such property; or

2.   Converts for an unauthorized term or use services or property of another entrusted to the defendant or placed in the defendant's possession for a limited, authorized term or use; or

3.   Obtains property or services of another by means of any material misrepresentation with intent to deprive him of such property or services; or

4.   Comes into control of lost, mislaid or misdelivered property of another under circumstances providing means of inquiry as to the true owner and appropriates such property to his own or another's use without reasonable efforts to notify the true owner; or

5.   Controls property of another knowing or having reason to know that the property was stolen; or

6.   Obtains services known to the defendant to be available only for compensation without paying or an agreement to pay such compensation or diverts another's services to his own or another's benefit without authority to do so.

B.   The inferences set forth in §13-2305 shall apply to any prosecution under the provisions of subsection A, paragraph 5 of this section.

C.   Theft of property or services with a value of one thousand dollars or more is a Class 3 felony. Theft of property or services with a value of five hundred dollars or more but less than one thousand dollars is a Class 4 felony. Theft of any property or services valued at two hundred fifty dollars or more but less than five hundred dollars is a Class 5 felony. Theft of property or services of one hundred dollars or more but less than two hundred fifty dollars is Class 6 felony. Theft of any property or service valued at less than one hundred dollars is a Class 1 misdemeanor, unless such property is taken from the person of another or is a motor vehicle or a firearm, in which the theft is a Class 6 felony.

THE MANAGEMENT

RATES ON THIS ROOM

THE ABOVE RATES ARE SUBJECT TO ADJUSTMENT FOR SPECIAL NEGOTIATED OR SEASONAL RATES.

EXHIBIT 8–8

Partial list of regulations and marketing appeals that appear on U.S. rooming slips for the guest who takes time to read them.

Informative
Floor plan of the property
Aerial view of the property
Telephone directory of services
Kinds of lobby shops
Foreign language capabilities of the staff
Airline, taxi, and limousine telephone numbers
Local sites to see and things to do
Airport bus: times of operation and rates
Currency exchange capabilities
Map of the city with highway designations

Marketing
List of restaurants: prices, hours of operation, and menu specialties
A message of welcome or a note of appreciation
WATS number for other hotels in the chain
Recreational facilities: tennis, golf, pool, sauna

Regulatory
Check-out hour and check-in hour
Rate of gratuity applied to the room charge
Regulations for visitors
Limitations on pets
Dress code

Availability of the safe for valuables
Settlement of accounts
Expectations for guaranteed reservation holders
Deposit of room keys when leaving the property
Fees for local telephone calls

Identification
Clerk's identifying initials
Identification of the party: name, number of persons, rate, arrival and departure dates
Room number
Key code—where room access is controlled by a dial system key

Instructional
Express check-out procedure
Electrical capacity for appliances
What to do in case of fire
How to secure the room
Notification to the desk if errors exist on the rooming slip
How to operate the in-room films; their cost
How to operate the in-room refrigerator; cost
Rate of tax applied to the room charge

several languages accents both the cautionary attitude of management and the hotel's quest for foreign business.

Frequently included now is a statement by which the guest agrees to stand personally liable for the bill if some third party (the company, the association, or the credit-card company) fails to pay (Exhibit 8–6).

Completing the Registration

At registration time, many things are going on simultaneously: The reservation is being located; the guest is being welcomed; accommodation needs are being determined or reevaluated; some small talk is taking place; the clerk is trying to sell up; the guest's identity, including the correct spelling of the name and address, is being verified; certain public rooms or services in the hotel are being promoted; the anticipated departure date is verified; both the guest and the clerk are completing their portions of the registration card; the credit card is being validated; and mail or messages are handed over. Finally, a bellperson is called and the guest is roomed.

All this normal activity notwithstanding, the clerk must remain alert to several special cases. Room clerks collect the coupons that accompany each IT package, and there could be a dozen of them. Room clerks are the point position for advertising contracts (rooms traded for advertising), for travel agency vouchers (the guest has paid the travel agency that booked the room), and for special rates. Conventions, for example, sometimes have reduced rates before and after the convention dates and sometimes they don't.

Throughout the procedure, which could take anywhere from 1 to 15 minutes, the clerk must remain calm, dignified, and friendly. Some feel that the clerk's attitude is the most important part of the whole registration and reception procedure.

The Room Selection Process

Before deciding which rooms will be assigned to arriving guests, a house count is required. The first house count is conducted early in the morning, soon after the day's first shift begins. By comparing the housekeeper's report against the property management system (or manual room rack), the clerk identifies all available rooms, those currently vacant as well as those due for check-out. A determination is made at this point as to how many additional walk-ins will be accepted. That decision may be revised several times throughout the day (see discussion in Chapter 5).

Selecting Rooms to Block.   Blocking, or preassigning rooms to guests, ensures a high level of certainty that special requests will be accommodated. When the house count identifies a high plus count (lots of rooms available to walk-ins), few rooms will be preblocked. For example, there is no purpose in blocking a standard queen reservation when there are numerous standard queen rooms available. Conversely, when the house count is tight (few rooms available to walk-ins) all incoming reservations will be blocked against the list of available rooms. In this way, the few unblocked rooms remaining are easily identified for walk-in customers. In the event that the house count is negative (the hotel is overbooked), a priority list is established. Management-made reservations, VIPs, and guaranteed reservations head the priority list—the rest of the reservations will probably be filled on a first-come, first-served basis.

Regardless of projections, a careful rooms manager always blocks special cases early in the day. Included in this category are connecting rooms, early arrivals, handicapped rooms, special rates, no-smoking rooms, guaranteed reservations, management-made reservations, suites, and VIPs. If the house is very crowded, even special request assignments may need to wait for check-outs. The desk knows who the anticipated departures are, although it's never really certain. The desk does not know what time the departures are leaving relative to the arrival of the new guests. So special requests are assigned first to vacant rooms (if the rooms meet the requirements of the request), and then to rooms as the guests depart.

The numbers of the preassigned rooms are entered into the PMS. This prevents the room's assignment to another arrival. It also provides immediate display for the clerk when the guest approaches and requests the reserved accommodations. Changes in the original assignments are made throughout the day as new information surfaces. If the arriving guest reports a change in the size of the party, or in the date of departure, or if the party appears before the preassigned room has been vacated, changes will need to be made.

The Room Assignment.   Even with preassigned or blocked rooms, the front-desk clerk reconfirms reservation information with the arriving guest—number in the party, length of stay, and so on.

Whenever possible—and it's possible more than it's practiced—the clerk should attempt to *sell up*—to sell the guest a higher-priced room than was originally reserved. Good selling is the key to rooms profits. (See Exhibit 9–14.)

The best way to sell up (or up-sell) the product is to show it. At resorts, where longer stays are the norm, guests may prefer to see the room before signing in. That can be done—and has been done—with a screen monitor at the desk. In the not-too-distant future, the image will be projected into the home to sell the reservation directly to the buyer via the personal computer. The use of a front-desk photo album is another common way to demonstrate to the guest the various differences in room types.

Obviously, the better the clerk knows the product, the more rapidly and satisfactorily the assignment will be made. It has been jokingly said that the fewer the rooms available, the easier it is to make assignments. With few rooms, the guest must take what's offered or have nothing.

Computer Algorithms.   The computer uses an algorithmic function to search its memory for appropriate room assignments. Algorithms are a series of "if-then" statements by which the computer arrives at the proper response. The algorithm comes into use when the computer displays an arrival list, an over-the-credit-limit report, or similar statements. It does the same with room assignments, but the program is more sophisticated.

Suppose a double-double is to be assigned to the arriving party. The system can be made to display the first choice (the computer's first choice), and the room is then assigned. Or, if the clerk wishes, the screen will display all the double-doubles, including those ready, those on change, and those that are out of order. Management can control the display—the first double-double displayed is the one that management wants sold first, and the final room on the list is to be sold last. In this manner, management controls rooms to accomplish any of several goals: to rotate room usage equally; to concentrate occupancy in newly refurbished rooms at a higher rate; to restrict wings or floors to save energy; and others.

Room Assignment Variations.   Generally, the room assignment process is straightforward. The guest requests a specific type of accommodation at time of reservation, the front desk blocks an appropriate room early on the day of arrival, and the guest receives exactly what was expected. This is the standard process, though there are variations.

Upgrading.   **Upgrading** an assignment—giving a better room at the original rate—is one technique for resolving complaints. It has other applications as well. Upgrades might be given to frequent-guest program members, to VIPs, to businesspersons from companies with negotiated corporate rates, and even to guests as a reward for patiently queuing.

Upgrades are also used if there are no rooms available at the rate reserved. In such cases, a well-trained (and motivated) front-desk clerk tries to up-sell the guest. More frequently, the guest is given the better room at the lower rate, but the upgrade is explained. If the differential is significant, the guest is moved the following day when the lower rate opens. The costs of moving, to both the guest and the hotel, warrant leaving the upgraded assignment for a few nights if the rate spread is small.

Did Not Stay.   A party that registers and leaves is a **DNS**— a **did not stay.** Dissatisfaction with the hotel or an incident with a staff member may precipitate the hasty departure. The guests might seek remedy first, or they might leave without saying why. The cause might not be the hotel. Emergency messages might be awaiting their arrival, or a telephone call might come in soon after the assignment. As a courtesy and to ensure good guest relations, no charge is levied if the party leaves within a reasonable time after arrival, even if the room was occupied for a short period.

As a control device, DNS situations are referred to and approved by a supervisor. Weaknesses in the reservation system or in hotel service may thereby be uncovered.

Paid in Advance.   Although all guests are asked to establish credit at check-in, few actually pay their bills in advance. Instead, most guests imprint a credit card or utilize their corporate account to establish credit against charges to be incurred during the visit. Only a small percentage of guests choose to pay cash (or a cash equivalent like a traveler's or personal check) at check-in.

Under the law, hotel room charges may be demanded in advance. In addition, the law provides innkeepers with the right to hold luggage for nonpayment. This prejudgment lien is under court challenge. Rather than testing the issue, hotelkeepers rely on the credit card and on their right to collect in advance.

Paid-in-advance guests are "flagged" to prevent charges being made from other departments. Once the room is paid in advance, other departments must collect cash for services rendered. Communicating that to the other departments is very difficult unless a PMS is in place.

Paid-in-advance guests may be checked out automatically the following day at the check-out hour unless other arrangements have been made. A prudent manager verifies the departure of the paid-in-advance guest before reassigning the space.

Important Guests.   Reservations may carry the designation VIP (very important person), SPATT (special attention required), Star Guest, or some other similar code. All these mean that the guest is an important person and the clerk should provide service in keeping with the visitor's stature. The guest could be the executive officer of a large association that is considering the hotel as a convention site, a corporate officer of the hotel chain, or perhaps a travel writer.

Such a designation sometimes requires the assistant manager to accompany the arriving guest to the room. It sometimes means that the guest need not register. It may also mean that no information about the guest will be given out to callers unless they are first screened.

There is a difference between a VIP and a DG (distinguished guest), according to one professional publication. The VIP represents either good publicity for the hotel or direct business, whereas the DG is honored because of position rather than economic value. Presidents, royalty, movie stars, and celebrities rate a DG designation. Meeting planners, company presidents, or committee chairpersons get the VIP treatment and then only during the tenure of their office. VIPs are treated to comp rooms, baskets of fruit, or bottles of liquor. Thoughtfulness and imagination sustained by personal consideration are more important to the DG than the amount of money spent.

Self-Check-In Terminals.   Even as hotels are striving to provide higher levels of guest service, automated devices enable the guest to perform more and more of the front office's functions. The best example of customers serving themselves is self-check-in/self-check-out terminals. Located in the lobbies of some of the finest hotels in the world, guest-operated terminals are no longer viewed as a reduction in service. Instead, self-check-in devices provide the guest another long-awaited option. Rather than queuing at the front desk for some undetermined length of time, today's sophisticated traveler can opt for a self-check-in (see Exhibit 8–9).

Integrated directly into the property management system, the self-check-in/self-check-out terminal offers choices much like a front-desk clerk would. The guest can select room numbers and room types from an on-line inventory of clean and available rooms. In addition, many of these machines are portable, thereby allowing the hotel to strategically locate the terminal in busy areas (say, for a large group check-in). Some hotels even locate the system in their shuttle vans for registration en route from the airport.

Prerequisites.   Most self-check-in terminals require the arriving guest to hold an advanced reservation and a valid credit card. Although that is the current standard, these prerequisites are changing. Some of the newest self-check-in devices now provide an option for walk-in customers. However, the self-check-in process is more detailed for the walk-in guest. All of the basic information obtained during the reservation process (name, address, length of stay, etc.) must be input by the guest into the terminal. Likewise, some self-check-in terminals are now accepting cash. These are especially popular in limited-service motels that continue to sell rooms after hours via automated terminals.

Provisions.   Some self-check-in systems display an electronic map of the property. In this way, guests can knowledgeably select rooms most convenient to them. In addition, it is possible for the terminal to display messages, promote certain aspects of the hotel, and even to up-sell the guest to a higher-priced room!

Most self-check-in/self-check-out terminals feature a built-in printer that provides the guest with a receipt of the transaction. This receipt may actually be used as a guest identity card during the stay. Some of the newer self-check-in systems even utilize touchscreen technology. Rather than using a keyboard or computer mouse for data entry, the guest need only touch the monitor. For example, if the computer provides a selected list of room types, the guest merely touches the list next to the room type of choice. Touchscreen technology has also been incorporated at the front desk for clerks to use as a supplement to the keyboard.

Self-check-in terminals also provide the guest with a room key. While some of the older systems required the guest to visit the key clerk at the front desk, most of the more recent terminals include an automated key function. At the end of the self-check-in process, the system instructs the guest to remove a blank key card from the stack and swipe it through the electronic key writing slot. As an added bonus, many systems allow guests to use their personal credit cards as the room key.

It is interesting to note one glaring omission of the self-check-in terminal—lack of the guest's signature. Although the legal relationship between hotel and self-registered guest would be difficult to dispute, is it in fact legal if the self-check-in device does not actually require the guest's signature. There is no signature with

EXHIBIT 8–9

A self-check-in/self-check-out terminal is activated by the guest's own credit card. The unit is linked to the hotel's property management system. An additional link encodes a blank key card that allows the guest entry to the newly assigned room.

Courtesy: CapData, Phoenix, Arizona.

the registration documents nor with the credit card. Possibly the light-pen, an electronic device whereby the user writes directly on the computer monitor, will be introduced as a solution to this oversight.

Establishing Guest Credit

Unlike many foreign countries, the United States does not issue national identity cards. State-issued driver's licenses, military identification cards, and even photo-bearing credit cards have come to serve that purpose. Identification at check-in is critical to both the welfare of the guest and the hotel.

Obtaining Guest Identification.   Accurate identification at check-in is so important as to be mandated by many local statutes. By accurately knowing the guest, the hotel protects itself and provides a valuable service to local law enforcement agencies. Information about transient visitors can be of critical importance. In Rhode Island, a guest was found murdered. The hotel had obtained no identification at check-in, and it took authorities many days to accurately identify the victim.

Proper identification also serves to protect the hotel. When cash customers are allowed to check in without producing identification, the hotel opens itself to a number of potential problems. A classic case in Arizona illustrates the point. A guest checked into a one-story motel, paid cash for the room, and signed the registration card with a phony name. In the dead of the night, the guest proceeded to load his van with all of the room's furnishings. The next day, the guest was gone, the motel room was bare, and the motel had absolutely no recourse, having failed to obtain proper identification. (And the room was truly bare. The guest had taken everything—the television, bed, and dresser, as well as the toilet, tub, and carpet!)

Even if the guest has no intention of stealing, securing guest identification aids the hotel in a multitude of ways. Accurately knowing the guest's name and address allows the hotel to return lost and found items, bill and collect late charges, and maintain a valuable database.

Identification Cards.   Hotels are just beginning to use small, internal, identity cards. The card, which includes the guest's name and period of stay, is issued along with the rooming slip at the close of the registration sequence. It may supplement the rooming slip with additional data (Exhibit 8–8) or it may replace it.

The card is used to validate the guest's identity at hotel facilities (pool, spa, tennis courts), or when signing charges (food, beverage, gift shop) to the room. Certain resorts enclose the card in plastic to protect it from water and sun.

Credit Cards.   Every registration card asks the guest to identify the method of payment (Exhibits 8–5 and 8–6). If a personal or company check is the answer, credit approval must be obtained from the assistant manager. More likely, a credit card is tendered. If there is a choice, the desk should always request the card for which the hotel has negotiated the best merchant fee (see Chapter 12).

An imprint of the guest's card is made on the proper credit-card charge form and the guest signs the blank form. With a PMS, the credit-card data are entered into the electronic folio either through the computer keyboard or by means of a credit-card reader. More recent automation has eliminated the time-consuming charge form, using instead an electronic printout that looks much like an adding machine tape.

Using a credit-card reader, the room clerk gets a simultaneous authorization about the validity of the card from the credit-card company. The terminal reads the magnetic strip and communicates that number electronically to the credit-card clearinghouse. Use of electronic credit-card scanners integrated with property management systems saves about 40 valuable seconds during the check-in process. The number can be punched in manually if the strip signal is damaged or inoperative. Back comes an authorization number (or a denial), which appears on the screen of the credit-card reader. This number is entered electronically into the computer or written manually on the charge form. It is needed only if there is some dispute later about the validity of the charges. The authorization number is the hotel's guarantee that the credit card is legitimate.

An approval number can also be obtained by telephone. The clerk talks either to a computer or to an actual person. The telephone method is time-consuming and prone to error. Forty digits must be verbalized, including the number of the card, the expiration date, the merchant's number, and the amount of the sale. Still, it is better than the technique used some 20 years ago in which the clerk scanned printed lists of invalid numbers before accepting the card. Under current procedures, the burden of approval is on the card company.

Part of the communication between the credit-card company and the hotel involves the amount of charges that will be added to the guest's balance. Limits exist for both the hotel and the individual. Chapter 12 explains these ''floor limits.'' That discussion also includes the next steps in the credit-card story: processing the card at departure and collecting from the credit-card company.

Other Guest Records.   Front-office records post departmental charges incurred by the guest against the credit established at check-in. Back-office records track those charges through the bank or credit-card company until payment has been received. Credit cards are just one of several records initiated by the front office but completed by the back office. Final settlement of travel agency bills clears through the back office, although the reservation and paperwork begin at the front. Frequent-guest records and frequent-flyer partnership records are another front-office/back-office relationship. The disposition of these various records is explained in Chapter 12. It is not a matter that concerns the clerk at the point of registration.

Recordkeeping for frequent-guest or frequent-flyer programs is a new job for the front office. It has just recently been incorporated into the PMS at many properties. Guests using automatic-teller registration may still be required to go to the desk to get frequent-guest credits. In many cases a manual 3-inch × 5-inch form is still used. The guest completes one part asking for name and program identification. The clerk completes the other part, including the flight number if it is an airline partnership program. Double-dipping is allowed, and one visit may require two forms—one for the hotel's frequent-guest program and one for the airline partnership credits. The guest is given one copy, similar to a credit-card receipt. Two copies of the form are sent to the back office for processing.

Rooming the Guest

While the guest registration process nears completion, a bellperson may arrive to escort the guest to the room. As the guest moves into the realm of the bell department, a number of critical functions are accomplished. The bellperson explains various locations and departments throughout the hotel, details a list of current hotel activities and promotions, and serves as final inspector before the guest prepares to occupy the room.

Even as the guest is being roomed by the bellperson, the front desk is completing the registration. In a manual property, there is a great deal of follow-through required of the front desk. The guest folio must be created, the room rack must be updated, and an addition to the alphabetical listing of hotel guests must be prepared. In an automated property, the computer handles these various functions and the front-desk clerk is immediately ready to greet the next customer in line.

Goodwill Ambassadors

The bell staff is part of a much larger department commonly referred to as uniformed services. Throughout the guest's visit, the uniformed services department attends to

EXHIBIT 8–10

AAA's Four- and Five-Diamond rating guidelines for bellpersons. This short list of bell staff guidelines is required by AAA for four- and five-diamond lodging operations.

Among the requirements for a Four- and Five-Diamond ranking by the American Automobile Association are the following services expected of bellpersons:

All Bellpersons Must
___ Be neatly uniformed.
___ Wear tasteful nametags.
___ Be friendly, courteous, and helpful.
___ Be knowledgeable of hotel and area.
___ Make good eye contact with guests.
___ Acknowledge the presence of guests (e.g., when passing in corridors).

On Guest Reception
___ Welcome guest to the hotel.
___ Address guest by name (should pick up on name from desk or luggage tags).
___ Explain Food and Beverage departments; recreational and other facilities.
___ Hang garment bag in closet.
___ Take out and set up luggage rack; suitcase should be placed on luggage rack, not on bed or floor.
___ Explain operation of lights, TV, and thermostat.
___ Offer ice at a 4-Diamond, expected to be automatic at a 5-Diamond.
___ Point out emergency exits or diagram.
___ Offer to open or close drapes.
___ Explain any unusual features within the room.
___ Explain turn-down.
___ Check bathroom supplies.
___ Offer additional services.

On Check-Out
___ Arrive promptly (wait should not exceed 10 minutes).
___ Check around room and in bathroom for belongings that might be left behind.
___ Offer to arrange for car delivery.

Source: ''Highly Effective Bell Staff Enhances Your Property's Image,'' *Hotel & Resort Industry,* May, 1988, pp. 84–89.

various needs and services (see Exhibit 8–10). Valet parking, doorpersons, concierges, hotel security, and the bell staff all play a key role in enhancing the property's image. No other department has the degree of personal one-on-one time with the guest as does uniformed services.

The bell staff, like all members of uniformed services, are goodwill ambassadors who turn an ordinary visit into a warm and personable experience. By developing close, professional relationships with the guest, a well-trained bellperson successfully promotes a number of hotel services. Suggestive selling and gentle persuasion are invaluable skills for a bellperson to possess.

Guest Communication.   Bellpersons, like all members of the uniformed services staff, are encouraged to engage the guest in conversation. Whenever staff members see a guest, they should make the effort to smile and at least offer a simple greeting (see Exhibit 8–11). By taking such steps, the guest comes to know and trust one or more members of the uniformed staff.

It is interesting to watch which uniformed personnel are attracted to which guests. Sometimes it is a matter of personality type or due to a relationship formed

EXHIBIT 8–11

*A uniformed bellperson
stands ready to room the
guest after check-in.*

Courtesy: The Fairmont Hotel and Tower, San Francisco, California.

during the rooming process. Whatever the reason, many guests develop a favorite among the bellpersons or other uniformed services staff. Such relationships, as long as they remain in the boundaries of professional behavior, are encouraged by management.

By developing such personable relationships, the bellperson is well situated to know when the guest's visit has gone awry. The bellperson can then approach the guest and solicit the complaint. Careful training places the bellperson in the critical role as bridge between the dissatisfied guest and the responsible department. When management works to keep open these lines of communication, the bellperson performs a key function in the hotel's quality assurance program.

Training.   Although a professional dialogue is encouraged, it is often difficult to monitor and maintain. All uniformed services staff (but especially the bellperson) have ample opportunity to speak with the guest on an intimate level. By design, bellpersons have a great deal of autonomy. Therefore, it is difficult for management to know what is actually being discussed with the guest during these one-on-one conversations.

There are numerous examples of bellpersons stepping over the line of acceptable behavior. Distraught with the job, a bellperson might bad-mouth the hotel or senior management to the guest. Disappointed with the lack of gratuities that day, a bellperson might boldly ask for a more generous tip from the guest. There are even cases where bellpersons dealt drugs and prostitution to the guest! Minimizing such occurrences begins with proper hiring and continues with constant training.

Secret Shoppers.   Because it is so difficult to assess the bellperson's professionalism while he or she is rooming the guest, many managers contract with secret shopper services. Such services work on the premise that employees act differently when they sense management is watching. On the other hand, a secret shopper posing as a hotel guest is able to truly observe the employee's professionalism on the job.

Secret shoppers visit the property and stay one or more nights. During this time, they attempt to engage employees in a number of usual and sometimes unusual activities. Although employees are probably forewarned that secret audits may be conducted, they usually have no idea they are being observed. As a result, secret shopper services are an excellent way to monitor the effectiveness of employee training.

The Bell Department

Several innovations have affected the uniformed services department's functions and means of earning income. Self-service icemakers and vending machines on the floor, and in-room refrigerators and minibars, have reduced the kind and number of service calls that bellpersons make. Group arrivals, in which individuals room themselves, further reduce the service functions of this department.

Rotation of Fronts.   Tips comprise the bulk of the bell department's earnings. According to a study done by the American Hotel & Motel Association, the bellperson's cash salary was the lowest of any hotel employee. Despite this, total earnings usually exceed that of other front-office employees, including some management positions. Each opportunity for earning a tip is carefully monitored.

The bellperson who comes forward to take the rooming slip and room the guest is called a **front.** Fronts rotate in turn. The one who has just completed a front is called a **last.** Lasts are used for errands that are unlikely to produce gratuities. Cleaning the lobby is a responsibility of the last. Lasts are also assigned dead room changes, with no chance of a gratuity, such as lockouts and moves carried out in the guest's absence.

Between the front and the last, positions rotate in sequence, moving forward in the rank as each new front is called. Each position in the sequence should be represented by a particular post in the lobby. One station might be by the front door to receive incoming luggage; another across the lobby; a third by the elevators. Staffing requirements for a full-service bell department run approximately one bellperson for every 40 to 50 estimated check-ins.

The procedure is much less formal today. Fronts wait by the **bellstand,** which is visible from the front desk. As the clerk completes the registration, the front is summoned to the desk by lights or signals or verbally by the clerk calling "Front!" Aware of the routine, the front rarely needs prompting.

With a property management system, remote printers located at the bellstand print the rooming slips, so the bellpersons approach the guests aware of their names. By coding the printout, the desk communicates additional information (VIP, light luggage, etc.) to the bell department. The PMS also maintains a record of fronts.

A record of fronts assures each individual of a proper turn, although the sequence may be altered if a guest requests a specific person or if a last is still away on some long-term errand. The record, maintained at the bell captain's desk, tracks the crew, which is the most mobile department in the hotel. By noting the bellperson's presence on various floors at various times, the record offers protection from accusations in the event of theft or other trouble. It fixes responsibility about the rooming procedure or lost luggage. The comings and goings of the bell staff, the purposes of their errands, and the times elapsed are recorded and maintained as a book, a card, or a duplicate of the rooming slip. All are timestamped.

Duties of the Bell Staff.   Depending on the level of service for the particular hotel, there may be no uniformed services department at all. In many small hotels, the bell staff is a catch-all department that performs a multitude of tasks. Small operations may ask the bellperson to drive the shuttle van, act as doorperson, make room-service calls, deliver cocktails to guests relaxing in the lobby, and even aid the front-desk staff during meal break periods.

Certain responsibilities are outside the scope of the bell department's duties. Bellpersons do not quote rates or suggest room assignments. They call the room clerk for a second assignment whenever the guest is dissatisfied with the room.

Bellpersons, or just the captains, share in other incomes. Auto rentals, tickets to local attractions, and bus tours are available at the captain's desk. Each of these companies pays a commission (10 to 15 percent) that more often accrues to the uniformed services than to the hotel. This may also hold true when the hotel contracts an outside laundry or dry cleaner for guest service.

Luggage.   The doorperson, or just as often the guest, carries in the baggage from the cab or car. It stays on the lobby floor until the guest is finished registering. The room clerk gives a rooming slip to the bellperson, who now takes over the guest's service. Jointly, the guest and the bellperson identify and retrieve the luggage and head toward the elevator. The guest, the bellperson, and the baggage might ride up together. Or the bellperson might leave the guest in order to transport the luggage on the service (rear) elevator, while the guest rides the guest (front) elevator. They meet at the elevator lobby on the guest's assigned floor.

Large hotels employ a different system of baggage handling. The luggage of arriving guests is taken at the curb by the doorperson, who gives the guest a baggage check. The luggage goes into a receiving area adjacent to the door and behind the bellstand in the lobby. There it waits while the guest registers. A room key and an extra copy of the rooming slip (the bellperson's copy) are given to the guest by the room clerk as the registration is completed. The guest gives the bell captain, or a clerk at the bellstand, one copy of the rooming slip along with the luggage stub obtained from the doorperson. The guest goes to the room unescorted. Later the baggage is delivered, after being matched at the bellstand using the stub delivered by the guest.

Final Inspection.   Rooming arrivals is the chief task of the bell department. Although many individuals room themselves, it is preferable to go in the company of a staff member. Guests who are in the company of a bellperson avoid the embarrassment of walking in on an occupied room. Service personnel always knock and wait before unlocking the door.

Once inside, the bellperson performs another inspection function. First, he or she hangs the guest's loose clothing and hefts the baggage onto the luggage rack or bed. Temperature controls are checked, and the room is inspected for cleanliness, towels, soap, toilet tissue, facial tissue, and other needs. Lights, hangers, television sets, and furnishings are examined. Special features of the hotel are explained—the spa or the operating hours of room service, for example.

Exhibit 8–12

A group arrival list showing names, room numbers assigned, arrival and departure dates, and affiliation. This list serves as the reference document for baggage, billing, and group communication.

HMS32G	FINNERMAN				VAIL SKI AREA HOTEL			2/05/9=
GUEST NAME		ROOM	GROUP	ARRIVAL	DEPART	COMPANY LINE	# PERS
ADAMS	ADAM	609	NEWMEX	2/05	2/08	NEW MEXICO ST. SKI TEAM	1
BROWN	BOB	607	NEWMEX	2/05	2/08	NEW MEXICO ST. SKI TEAM	1
CURTIS	CHARLES	612	NEWMEX	2/05	2/08	NEW MEXICO ST. SKI TEAM	1
DILARDO	DALE	612	NEWMEX	2/05	2/08	NEW MEXICO ST. SKI TEAM	1
EVANS	EVAN	616	NEWMEX	2/05	2/08	NEW MEXICO ST. SKI TEAM	1
FEINSTEIN	FRED	613	NEWMEX	2/04	2/08	NEW MEXICO ST. SKI TEAM	1
GRAY	GARY	604	NEWMEX	2/05	2/08	NEW MEXICO ST. SKI TEAM	1
HARRIS	HARRY	606	NEWMEX	2/05	2/08	NEW MEXICO ST. SKI TEAM	1
INGOLS	IAN	616	NEWMEX	2/05	2/08	NEW MEXICO ST. SKI TEAM	1
JEFFREYS	JEFF	606	NEWMEX	2/05	2/08	NEW MEXICO ST. SKI TEAM	1
KASTLE	KRIS	604	NEWMEX	2/05	2/08	NEW MEXICO ST. SKI TEAM	1
LEWIS	LOUIS	605	NEWMEX	2/05	2/08	NEW MEXICO ST. SKI TEAM	1
MORRISON	MORRIS	602	NEWMEX	2/05	2/08	NEW MEXICO ST. SKI TEAM	1
NEWTON	NEWT	605	NEWMEX	2/05	2/08	NEW MEXICO ST. SKI TEAM	1
O'REILLY	ORSON	609	NEWMEX	2/05	2/08	NEW MEXICO ST. SKI TEAM	1
POWELL	PAUL	607	NEWMEX	2/05	2/08	NEW MEXICO ST. SKI TEAM	1
QUAIL	QUINN	618	NEWMEX	2/05	2/08	NEW MEXICO ST. SKI TEAM	1
ROBERTS	ROBERT	602	NEWMEX	2/05	2/08	NEW MEXICO ST. SKI TEAM	1
						TOTAL PEOPLE:	18

Self-service items are pointed out—the ice machine, or the in-room refrigerator. Connecting doors are unlocked if the party is to share several connecting rooms. Unless there is a special request for service, the bellperson leaves the key and the rooming slip and accepts the proffered tip, if any. Before leaving, there may be a final sell for a particular dining room or lounge and a final "good day."

Group Baggage.   Tour groups are easy for the bell staff to handle and are generally quite profitable. Using the guest list furnished by the group, the desk preregisters the party (see Exhibit 8–12). Roommates, whom the tour company has identified, are assigned, and keys are readied in small envelopes for quick distribution (see Exhibit 8–13). Similar key envelopes are prepared for rapid distribution to airline crews when permanent reservations have been negotiated with the airline.

A property management system will print the key envelopes, coded by groups, the rooming lists showing who is with whom and where (so important to the tour guide or the company meeting planner), identification cards for in-house use, baggage tags, and every other form needed for a successful group meeting. All of these items are derived from the same basic information, which is fed into the computer only once.

Final instructions to the tour members are given on the bus. Communication is impossible once the captive audience is lost. Tour members are reminded that charges not included in the tour price will need to be settled individually with the

EXHIBIT 8–13

Shown are tour keys readied for distribution. Discount coupons, local merchants' materials, and convention/group information such as bus and meeting schedules might be included in the envelope.

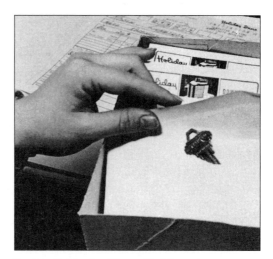

Courtesy: Holiday Inn, Minneapolis, Minnesota.

hotel. A notice to that effect is also included in the key envelope (Exhibit 8–13). The envelopes are distributed in the lobby by the desk, the tour coordinator, or sometimes the bell staff. Guests find their own rooms without help from the bell department while the baggage is being unloaded from the bus.

Group baggage can be a headache as well as a backache for the uniformed services if bags are improperly marked or hard to identify. Putting some procedures in place makes the task easier. The tour company should provide each traveler with brightly colored tags to attach to the luggage before departure. The color identifies the group, expediting baggage handling in and out of the airport. The individual's number is written on each tag, and that number corresponds to the individual's place on the master rooming sheet. (Copies of the list should have been given to every hotel on the tour.) The number, which is easier to read than a name, helps the bell staff match the bags with room numbers.

There is another variation: Each bag can be marked with the correct room number from a computer printed list of adhesive-backed labels. The bellperson removes the room number from the printed list and slaps it on the bag for delivery.

In some instances, baggage is delivered only to the floors, where the guests pick up their own bags. Assigning tour groups to one floor or one wing facilitates baggage handling.

Regardless of the method used, group baggage delivery takes time. Guests are impatient and the bell crew knows there is no extra tip coming. At best, the bag is placed in the room without the usual service.

The Rooming Slip.   The rooming slip serves as a vehicle for communication between the front desk and both the bellperson and the guest. The bellperson uses the rooming slip to better understand the guest and the rooming situation. The slip provides the bellperson with information related to the guest's name, the guest's affiliation or corporate name (if appropriate), the room number assigned, the guest's home address and city (great for making small talk), and the number of nights reserved. As explained earlier, the rooming slip also serves as a support document to prove the bellperson's whereabouts during a specific period in question.

EXHIBIT 8–14

The flip side of the European rooming slip serves as advertising media for noncompeting services.

Courtesy: Insel Hotel, Bad Godesberg, Germany.

Although not intended for that purpose, the slips have been used by the Internal Revenue Service. Estimating the average tip per front and counting the number of fronts according to the rooming slips provides a fair estimate of tip income. The estimate is then compared to that reported by the employee.

Content.   The guest uses the rooming slip for two purposes—as a receipt and as guest identification (in the absence of an identification card). As a receipt, the rooming slip provides the guest with an additional opportunity to verify the accuracy of information. For example, the rooming slip may show that the guest's name has been spelled wrong. Likewise, the room rate, date of check-out, or some other information may be inaccurate. Many rooming slips also restate hotel disclaimers as a means of strengthening the hotel's legal relationship with the guest.

Overseas hotels use the rooming slip as a sales tool for their own property and for local, noncompeting businesses (see Exhibit 8–14). American hotels haven't yet taken to selling ads. With their more extensive services and facilities, they need all the space themselves.

The American rooming slip is an interesting mix of selling, services, and legal safeguards. Depending on management's inclination, the rooming slip is either a simple slip of paper or a complete, elaborate sales tool in a variety of colors. Caesars Palace in Las Vegas has a rooming booklet of 20 pages! Exhibit 8–8 lists the range of information that a hotel might try to communicate to the guest.

Color-coded rooming slips, like Hyatt's Passports (Exhibit 8–15), may also serve as the guest identification card. The color tells the cashiers in the bars and dining rooms whether the guest is a paid-in-advance guest, a tour group member, a VIP, and so on.

The right half of Exhibit 8–15 illustrates another use of the rooming slip. Although the guest is just arriving, check-out information and a check-out form are provided in order to plan for a quick departure. Quick check-out has been in place far longer than self-check-in/self-check-out terminals. Innovative departure systems that did not need computer hardware were inaugurated as early as 1975. However, they all require the guest to use a credit card or other form of advance credit.

EXHIBIT 8–15

Rooming slip for Hyatt Hotels include advertising (on the reverse side) and express check-out.

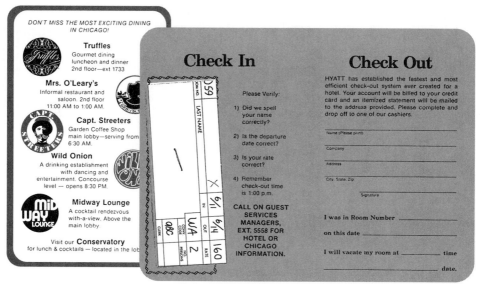

Courtesy: Hyatt Regency, Chicago, Illinois.

Summary

Arriving guests face a number of opportunities to meet members of the uniformed staff. Valet parking, the doorperson, front-desk clerks, and the bell department all play critical roles in the arrival process. The first impressions made by these employees create a positive (or negative) lasting effect on the guest's perception of the hotel operation.

The check-in procedure represents an especially sensitive segment of the arrival process. The front-desk clerk communicates with the guest in an unscripted fashion where few rules dictate their interaction. A wise front-desk clerk evaluates the guest and attempts to understand unique requirements. Too rapid a check-in and the guest leaves with a sense of rudeness or having been rushed. Too slow a check-in and the guest perceives inefficiency in the hotel operation. Add to this sensitivity the need for the desk clerk to retrieve payment, extract additional information, get a signature on the registration card, ask credit questions, and attempt to up-sell to a higher-priced room, and the check-in process can be a tense several minutes.

The bell department spends the last moments with the arriving guest. Rooming the guest is a complex process of small talk, suggestive selling, room inspection, and overall guest service. Oh yes—bellpersons carry the luggage as well.

Queries and Problems

1. Reorganize the following jumbled list of events, persons, and job activities into a logical flow from start to finish of the guest arrival process:
   a. Room selection.
   b. Establishing guest credit.
   c. Registered, not assigned.
   d. Bellperson.
   e. Valet parking attendant.
   f. Rotation of fronts.
   g. Room assignment.
   h. Obtaining guest identification.
   i. Rooming slip.
   j. Upgrading and/or up-selling.
   k. Rooming the guest.
   l. Preblocking rooms.
   m. Doorperson.
   n. Registration card.

2. Foreign registration cards often require significantly more personal information than is required for domestic registration cards. Some management personnel feel this extra data amounts to an invasion of the guest's privacy. Other managers, however, believe this extra information aids the hotel in providing better security and service levels to the guest. With whom do you side? Why might a hotel legitimately need to know your future and past destinations, your mother's maiden name, and your date of birth?

3. Intentional bias can be programmed (through computer algorithms) into the room-selection sequence of a property management system. Rooms will then appear in a prescribed order, rather than in sequence or at random. Certain rooms can be offered first, or not, depending on management's criteria. What criteria might management establish to decide which rooms appear in which sequence in order to direct the clerk's selection?

4. A local merchant, whose attempts to service the hotel's guest laundry and dry cleaning business have been frustrating, visits with the new rooms manager. (The laundry of this 600-room, commercial hotel does not clean personal guest items.) The conversation makes the rooms manager realize that she has never seen commission figures on any of the reports. She learns that the bell captain, who doesn't seem to do any work—that is, he doesn't take fronts—gets the commissions.

   The rooms manager initiates a new policy. All commissions from car rentals, bus tours, ski tickets, laundry, and balloon rides will accrue to the hotel. An unresolved issue is whether or not the money will go into the employee's welfare fund.

   A very angry bell captain presents himself at the office of the executive assistant manager. Explain with whom you agree (the rooms manager or the bell captain) and prepare an argument to support your opinion.

5. Some hotels upgrade corporate guests to nicer rooms when space is available. Usually, the guest need not even ask for this courtesy—it is offered as standard operating procedure. Managers of such properties believe the corporate guest appreciates the courtesy and the nicer room. And since the room is not likely to sell anyway, why not make someone happy?

The reverse side of this argument, however, suggests that the guest comes to expect this treatment and even feels slighted if only standard rooms are available. In addition, hotels that give upgrades away free are doing themselves a disservice in terms of up-selling corporate guests to a higher rate. After all, why should corporate guests ever select higher priced rooms (or concierge floor rooms) when they are given at no extra charge as a matter of standard practice? How would you respond to these arguments?

6. Ten weary, footsore travelers,
   All in a woeful plight,
   Sought shelter at a wayside inn
   One dark and stormy night.
   ''Nine beds—no more,'' the landlord said,
   ''Have I to offer you;
   To each of eight a single room,
   But number nine serves two.''
   A din arose. The troubled host
   Could only scratch his head;
   For of those tired men, no two
   Could occupy one bed.
   The puzzled host was soon at ease—
   He was a clever man—
   And so to please his guests devised
   The most ingenious plan:
   | A | B | C | D | E | F | G | H | I |
   In a room marked A, two men were placed;
   The third he lodged in B.
   The fourth to C was then assigned.
   The fifth went off to D.
   In E the sixth he tucked away.
   In F the seventh man;
   The eighth and ninth to G and H.
   And then to A he ran.
   Wherein the host, as I have said,
   Had lain two travelers by.
   Then taking one—the tenth and last,
   He lodged him safe in I.
   Nine single rooms—a room for each—
   Were made to serve for ten.
   And this it is that puzzles me
   And many wiser men.*

Does it also puzzle you? How was the ingenious host able to lodge ten men in only nine rooms?

*Excerpted from *Hotel News,* Winnipeg, 1935.

Factors in Determining Room Rate

Due to inflation, higher operating costs, improved room demand, and a number of additional factors, hotel room prices are rising at a pace that exceeds even the rate of inflation. Prices quoted today are substantially higher than just a few short years ago. Rising at an annualized rate above 3 percent, the average discounted corporate room rate in America is about $82.30.

This trend of room prices rising at or above the rate of inflation is relatively new. For a number of years, the lodging industry was a buyer's market. Rates remained relatively constant and deep discounting was the norm.

As the industry continues its rise out of the depression experienced in the late 1980s and early 1990s, rates are the primary vehicle for change. For the most part, today's lodging industry is a seller's market. As a seller's market, hotels are experimenting with their highest rates ever. Only the future will tell what will eventually happen with the rapid growth in room rates.

EXHIBIT 9–1

An example of rack rate categories. Note that there is no double occupancy charge for suite accommodations. Also, this hotel offers a family plan but charges for extra beds.

HYATT ✦ KINGSGATE SYDNEY

AUSTRALIA

AT THE TOP OF WILLIAM STREET
SYDNEY, N.S.W. 2011, AUSTRALIA
TEL: 357 2233 TELEX: 23114 FAX: (02) 356 4150 CABLE: HYATT SYDNEY
LONG DISTANCE AT LOCAL RATE 008-222-188

INDIVIDUAL RATES from 1 February
Australian Dollars

Room Type	single	twin/double
Standard	$135	$145
Superior Room	$150	$165
Deluxe Room	$165	$180
Regency Club Room	$180	$210
Regency Club Suite		$300
One-Bedroom Suites		$225
Two-Bedroom Suites		$300
Rushcutter Suite		$450
Paddington Suite		$575
Penthouse Suite		$750

EXTRA BED: $10.

TAXES/SERVICE CHARGE: Not applicable in Australia.

RATES ARE SUBJECT TO CHANGE WITHOUT PRIOR NOTICE.

FAMILY PLAN: Children under 18 years of age sharing room with parents at no extra charge.

GROUP RATES: Available on request. Applicable for groups of 15 persons or more.

Source: Hyatt Kingsgate Sydney, Sydney Australia. Used with permission.

Discounting the Rack Rate

All hotels have a rack rate against which other pricing structures are designed (see Exhibit 9–1). A hotel's rack rate is the quoted, published rate that is theoretically charged to full-paying customers. In essence, the rack rate is the full retail rate. However, just as customers rarely pay the sticker price for a brand-new automobile, guests rarely pay the rack rate for a hotel room.

Although reservationists try to offer the customer full rack rate, shrewd guests never accept it. Corporate discounts, affiliation discounts (AAA and AARP, for example), frequent-travel discounts, advanced and nonrefundable purchases, and a host of other possibilities have all combined to erode the hotel's ability to charge full price.

Proof of discounting is most evident in the Average Daily Rate computation. Hotels with an average rack rate of, say, $78 probably never actually attain a $78 ADR. Instead, the property's ADR is a reflection of the vast discounting taking place throughout the property. Corporate meetings, tour groups, discounted transient travelers, and corporate guests negatively impact the hotel's ability to sell rooms at rack rate. As a result, a hotel with an average rack rate of $78 probably receives an ADR closer to $68 in the end.

Discounted Rates.   Discounted or special rates come in a variety of shapes and sizes. Some merely provide a slight discount from the posted rack rate, as when a hotel offers a 10 percent price reduction for AAA or AARP members. Other special rates, such as volume discounting programs and seasonal price reductions, are quite significant, reducing the posted rate 50 percent, 75 percent, or even more.

Rate discounting is very widespread, visible in every category and classification of hotelkeeping. Rare is the guest who pays full rack rate. Still, the situation is not yet a desperate one for the hotel industry. Rates that have been too high for market conditions are merely being adjusted.

The reordering of rates is part of the shakeout of segmentation. Rates are a function of supply and demand, and these two variables are slowly moving toward equilibrium. However, for the short run, special rates—a term that is preferable to discounted rates—are in. The list of those entitled to special rates is limited only by the imagination of the marketing department.

One hotel chain has special rates for teachers; another for students. Most have discounts for senior citizens; almost all allow children in the room with their parents at no charge. The *Worldwide Directory* of Holiday Inns advertises a sports rate for U.S. amateur and professional teams. Special introductory rates are a common tactic for launching a new hotel. The same tradition that gives police officers discounts in the coffee shop gives other uniformed groups such as the clergy and the military discounts off the room rack. And so the list grows.

Travel agents and travel writers usually get free accommodations while they are on **familiarization (fam) trips.** At other times, the special rate is a standard 50 percent discount, unless, of course, they come during the height of the busy season.

Hawaii's *kamaiina* rate (literally, ''oldtimer's rate'') is an interesting case of special rates. A class-action suit was filed by a Californian on the grounds that the 25 percent discount granted to Hawaiian residents was discriminatory. The argument was denied by the court. The judge found that ''offering a discount to certain clients, patrons, or other customers based on an attempt to attract their business is [not] unlawful.'' The decision is important because it shows the other side of the issue. Rates that are raised to discourage business from certain persons might well be judged as discriminatory. Rates that are lowered to attract certain persons are viewed quite differently, at least by one court.

All rate discounts should be aimed at the development of new markets and should be phased out as that market stabilizes. It does not work that way in practice. Over time, many special rates become part of the established rate structure.

Seasonal Rates.   Posted rates can be changed, or they can include seasonal variations. Season and off-season rates are quoted by most resort hotels, with incremental increases and decreases coming as the season approaches and wanes (see Exhibit 9–2). The poor weekend occupancy of urban hotels has forced them to offer a seasonal rate of sorts—a discounted weekend rate.

EXHIBIT 9–2

The Boulders Resort in Carefree, Arizona, publishes its seasonal rate variations. Notice the wide differences in rates between the high season (January 19–April 30; December 22–January 1) and low season (May 29–June 25; September 1–27; December 10–21). Note also the supplemental charge for modified American plan.

SPLENDID SECLUSION

Nestled in the high Sonoran Desert foothills north of Scottsdale, The Boulders offers the enchantment of a dramatic location created by the forces of time. Spectacular rock outcroppings that captivate everyone who steps within their spell. Ancient saguaros silhouetted against the clear Sonoran sky. And a world-famous resort which blends so easily with nature that the local wildlife might never notice it was there.

The private country club features two 18-hole championship golf courses built right into the desert, as well as a tennis garden and the new Sonoran Spa…which offers a variety of signature body treatments using the natural herbs of the desert along with a fully equipped cardiovascular and weight room, aerobics classes, and a variety of nature hikes and other stimulating programs.

Just a short stroll from the resort is el Pedregal, a festival-style marketplace of intriguing shops, restaurants, and galleries. And all around The Boulders is the enticing tranquility of the lush Sonoran Desert with its breathtaking natural views.

RESORT CASITAS

At The Boulders there's no such thing as a typical guest room. Instead there are 160 guest casitas shaped into the dramatic terrain, each decorated with natural wood and Mexican tile. Among the pleasures of these individual casitas are fully stocked mini-bars, a woodburning fireplace for cozy evenings, and a private patio or balcony overlooking the spectacular desert terrain.

CASITA DAILY RATES

European Plan *(no meals included)*	Single	Double	Triple	Modified American Plan *(breakfast and dinner included)*	Single	Double	Triple
Jan 2–18, May 1–28, Sept 28–Dec 9	$325	$350	$375	Jan 2–18, May 1–28, Sept 28–Dec 9	$375	$450	$525
Jan 19–April 30, Dec 22–Jan 1	$425	$450	$475	Jan 19–April 30, Dec 22–Jan1	$475	$550	$625
May 29–June 25, Sept 1–27, Dec 10–21	$200	$225	$250	May 29–June 25, Sept 1–27, Dec 10–21	$260	$335	$420

PATIO HOMES

Patio homes at The Boulders are ideal for families or groups of friends who want to make themselves at home in a setting more spacious than one of the traditional casitas. Along with all the same services and amenities as the casitas, each Southwestern-style patio home features a fully-equipped kitchen, spacious dining area and living room, fireplace, private patio, laundry facilities and garage, with a choice of one, two, or three bedrooms.

PATIO HOME DAILY RATES

Dates	1-Bedroom Plus Den	2-Bedroom	2-Bedroom Plus Den	3-Bedroom
Jan 2–18, May 1–28, Sept 28–Dec 9	$450	$650	$700	$750
Jan 19–April 30, Dec 22–Jan 1	$550	$750	$800	$850
May 29–June 25, Sept 1–27, Dec 10–21	$325	$400	$450	$475

Courtesy: The Boulders Resort, Carefree, Arizona

Hotel capacity in many resort communities is vast, able to handle great numbers of tourists during periods of peak demand. Because of this glut of hotel rooms available for high-season demand, low-season rates are often deeply discounted—so steeply in fact, that many resort properties simply closed their doors during low-occupancy seasons. This practice changed some 10 or 15 years ago. Today, very few resort properties actually close for the off-season. The expense of reopening the facility, training and hiring new staff each year, and operating a skeleton crew to maintain the closed facility combined to change the economics of closing the property. Instead, resorts remain open though steeply discounted to value-conscious guests.

Weather or Not.   When it comes to negotiating group rates, even Mother Nature gets involved. A growing trend designed to reduce the length of the low or shoulder season at certain resorts is a weather discount factor. Credits or discounts against the rate are offered guests for each day it rains or stays unseasonably cool.

Obviously, this is risky business, and few resorts are yet offering such plans. But select Hiltons and Marriotts are currently on the bandwagon, and others are sure to follow. Indeed, at least one Marriott resort offers a "temperature guarantee" package that they have insured through Lloyd's of London!

Weekly Rates.   Weekly rates, which are less than seven times the daily rate, are offered occasionally and were very popular in the American plan resorts of New England. Improved forecasting and increased revenues in all of the other departments, including greens fees, food, and beverage, compensated for the reduction in room revenue.

Both the daily rate—assume $170AP—and the weekly rate—assume $1,050AP—are recorded by the clerk on the registration card and, later, on the guest bill. The $170 rate is charged daily until the final day, when a $30 charge is posted. In this way, the daily charge is earned until the guest meets the weekly commitment. If one-seventh of the weekly charge were posted daily, the hotel would be at a disadvantage whenever the guest left before the week was up, as frequently happens.

A variation on the weekly reduction discounts services such as valet, laundry, and greens fees but leaves the room rate intact.

Corporate Rates.   America's corporations do a great deal of business with the nation's hotels. The AH&MA estimates that figure at over $100 billion annually.

Corporations and hotel chains are synergetic. Corporations have offices and plants worldwide. Employees at all levels (management, personnel, sales, engineering, accounting) travel in vast numbers. They visit the very countries and cities in which the hotel chains have opened their properties worldwide. The synergism works when the employees of this corporation stay in the hotels of that chain. By guaranteeing a given number of room-nights per year, this corporation negotiates a better rate, a corporate rate, from that hotel chain.

Reducing room rates is only part of the discount. Reducing the number of rooms needed to close the deal is a more subtle form of discounting. Not many years ago, corporate rates required 1,000 room-nights per year. Recent figures place the level as low as 50.

The figures were pushed lower by the appearance of third-party negotiators rather than by the astuteness of corporate travel desks. Corporations with numbers that were too small to negotiate on their own were included under the umbrella of room consolidators. Third-party volume buyers who were in no business other than negotiating discounts with hotels (and airlines) represented numerous companies and developed a tough rate-negotiating base. Hotels responded by dealing directly with the corporate accounts, bypassing the travel agents and the volume buyers, who may be nothing more than travel agents in disguise.

Technology has altered the corporate discount picture. In the past, major corporations negotiated favorable rates by promising a large annual room volume with a given chain. However, no one really counted, and room volume (actual or anticipated) was never verified.

With the increasing sophistication of CRS systems, most major hotel chains are now able to accurately track a corporation's total room volume. Corporate room activity at franchised properties, parent properties, and through the CRS are all combined into a quarterly volume report. Stouffer Hotels, for example, produces quarterly reports for more than 1,800 of its major corporate accounts. These reports take the guesswork out of room rate negotiations and give both the hotel chain and the corporation an accurate picture of utilized volume.

Corporate rates are now one of the panels in the mural of discounting. But their implementation has left still another irritant between travel agents and hoteliers. Slashing rates low enough to compete for corporate business leaves the hotel with no margin for paying commissions. Travel agents get no commission when they book rooms for corporate clients who have negotiated special rates with the hotel. The agent who makes the reservation to accommodate the corporate client is in a dilemma. Either book the room and get no commission or tell the corporate clients to book their own rooms.

Commercial Rates.   Commercial rates are the small hotel's answer to corporate rates. Without the global chain's size to negotiate national corporate contracts, smaller hotels make arrangements with small commercial clients. Such understandings might account for 5 or 10 room-nights per year for a manufacturer's representative or salesperson traveling on a personal expense account.

Under the commercial rate plan, a standard low rate is negotiated for the year. This standard rate provides the commercial guest with two advantages. First, the rate is guaranteed. Even during periods of high occupancy, most small hotels honor the commercial rate. Secondly, when demand is mild, the commercial guest is granted an upgraded room accommodation at no additional charge. This small courtesy costs the hotel nothing yet generates substantial loyalty on the part of the guest.

Per Diem Rates.   Federal, state, and local governments reimburse traveling employees up to a fixed dollar amount. This per diem (per day) cap is made up of two parts—room and meals. Auto rental may or may not be included (see Exhibit 9–3). Reimbursement is made on the actual cost of the room (a receipt is required) but no more than the maximum. Anyone traveling on government business is reluctant to pay more than the per diem room allowance, since the agency will not reimburse the excess. (Meal reimbursement is a given number of dollars per day and generally requires no receipts.)

Key cities, those with higher costs of living, are given higher caps. The General Services Administration of the federal government publishes the per diem rates that apply to federal employees. This distinct market segment covers all federal civilian employees, military personnel, and, recently, cost-reimbursed federal contractors.

EXHIBIT 9–3

Per diem costs in 25 cities. Per diem costs include hotel (about 47 percent), meals (about 30 percent), and car rental (about 23 percent).

1.	New York City	$350.63
2.	Washington, D.C.	269.21
3.	Boston	256.62
4.	Philadelphia	244.83
5.	Newark	236.22
6.	Chicago	235.70
7.	San Francisco	224.30
8.	Honolulu	222.08
9.	Dallas	218.56
10.	Houston	214.01
11.	Los Angeles	212.26
12.	Phoenix	205.72
13.	St. Louis	205.63
14.	Detroit	205.31
15.	Atlanta	204.54
16.	San Jose, CA	202.22
17.	San Diego	201.06
18.	Cleveland	200.33
19.	New Orleans	194.83
20.	Stamford, CT	192.19
21.	Santa Barbara	191.24
22.	Tampa	190.35
23.	Tucson	189.97
24.	Minneapolis	189.67
25.	Baltimore	189.54

Source: *Corporate Travel/RIT,* April 1994.

Difficulties may arise when the per diem guest encounters the desk. Some chains accept the government rates, but individual properties may not. And if they do, the yield management decision may reject these heavily discounted rates for that particular period. Moreover, since per diems, like all special rates, are on a *space-available* basis, most central reservations systems will not quote the rate for confirmation. (Space available means that rooms are not confirmed in advance by reservation.) Over all these hurdles, the guest must then prove per diem entitlement. Without a standardized form, letter, or procedure, the individual room clerk makes a discretionary call based on whatever evidence the guest can provide.

Employee Rates.   Special rates are extended to employees of the chain when they travel to other properties. Indeed, for the large chains, this is actually a market segment. Substantial discounts from the hotel's minimum rate plus upgrade whenever possible result in a very attractive bargain. Special rates are always provided on a space-available basis. Employee–guests are accepted only if rooms are vacant when they present themselves. The Federal Deficit Reduction Law of 1984 reinforced this by taxing the employee for the value of any free room if paying guests were turned away.

Offering complimentary or discounted employee rooms is an inexpensive way for chains to supplement their employee benefits packages. Because such rooms are provided on a space-available basis, there is little associated cost (aside from house-keeping) to providing the employee a free or deeply discounted rate. And many chains find some real benefits in increased morale and motivation as employees take advantage of the chain's discounted rooms.

Indeed, some chains actually listen to their employees. They request visiting employees to fill out evaluation forms complete with comments and suggestions for improvement. If carefully monitored and tracked, such a "secret shopper" program can have enormous advantages to the chain.

Other Discounts.   There are an unlimited number of additional rate discounting possibilities. Large groups such as AAA, Discover Card members, or the like no longer have a monopoly on special rates. Indeed, any size group that can produce even a few room-nights per year is negotiating discounted rates.

One growing midsized market is bank clubs. Members of credit unions or banks and holders of numerous credit cards now find discounted hotel chain rates part of their incentive package. Some of these groups charge for the service, others provide it free as a means of attracting and holding bank customers.

Auctioning is a form of discounting that may gain popularity even at the smallest market level—the individual traveler. Auctioning will allow hotels, airlines, and rental car agencies to enter a product-available database marketed directly to the traveler through technology available to the travel agent. The guest—say, Carl Jones—decides where he is traveling to, the dates and times he wishes to travel, and any specifications (must be a four-star property, a midsized car, etc.) related to the trip. He is then asked to quote his own rate!!

If a hotel, airline, and/or rental car agency informs the database that this is a reasonable offer, Jones gets the deal as bid. He never knows until the offer is accepted which airline he will fly, which hotel will accommodate him, or which rental car he will drive. If the bid is too low, Jones places a time limit on his offer and waits to see over the next few days whether the various travel components in question will respond favorably.

Leading technology firms are in the early stages of developing auctioning. When it materializes, inventory auctioning will set a new standard for rate discounting in the industry.

Complimentary Rates.   Hotel managers should be as reluctant to give away complimentary (comp) rooms as automobile sales managers are to give away free cars. But both the perishability of the room and the low variable cost of housing an occupant change this reality. Comps are used for business promotion, as charitable giveaways, and as perks.

By custom, complimentary rates are extended to other hoteliers. The courtesy is reciprocated, resulting in an industrywide fringe benefit for owners and senior managers. Such comps rarely include food or beverage (costs are too high) even in American plan hotels. As mentioned earlier, another portion of the travel industry—travel agents and travel writers—are comped during fam trips. Deregulation permitted fam trip comps by the airlines, which have now joined the hotel industry in developing site inspection tours for the travel industry.

Site inspections are also made by association executives, who are considering the property as a possible meeting place. Site visits are comped (even though some association executives have been known to abuse the industry standard by using site inspection opportunities to vacation with their families). Comp rates as part of the group's meeting were discussed previously, and these are considered to be acceptable standard practice.

Comps are given to famous persons whose presence has publicity value. Comps are used as promotional tools in connection with contests in which the winners receive so many days of free accommodations. In gambling casinos, comps extend to food, beverage, and even airfare from the player's home. Parking is so difficult in Atlantic City that it too has become part of the high-roller's comp package. After all, in a brief period of table play, such individuals can lose many times the cost of this promotion, which on close inspection proves to be surprisingly inexpensive.

Posting the Comp.   Internal control of comps is important! In some hotels, the night auditor is required to submit a report of comps granted each day and by whom (see Exhibit 9–4). It is also desirable to include this information in the accounting records. To that end, the actual room rate is recorded in the rate block on the registration card and marked ''COMP.'' Daily, or at the end of the stay, the charge is removed from the folio with an allowance. Under this procedure, a daily room charge is made so that the room and the guest are both counted in the room and house counts. The total allowances at the end of the accounting period provide statement evidence of the cost of comps.

Some casino hotels have the comp paid by a paper transfer to another department (sales, casino, entertainment). The departmental manager has accountability, and the amount of comps appear on that departmental budget.

Recording no value in the rate square but only the word *COMP* is another method for handling free accommodations. No dollar value is charged each day and, therefore, no allowances are required to remove the charges. Neither is a permanent dollar record of comps available. Comps are not usually recorded in room and house counts under this procedure.

The Day Rate Room.   Special rates exist for stays of less than overnight. These are called **part-day rates, day rates,** or sometimes **use rates.** Day-rate guests arrive and depart on the same day.

Day rates obviously make possible an occupancy of greater than 100 percent. Furthermore, the costs are low. Nevertheless, the industry has not fully exploited the possibilities. Sales of use rates could be marketed to suburban shoppers and for small, brief meetings. Frequent airline schedules impeded the use of day rates at airport hotels, although capsule rooms at international airports have had some success. Airport properties have promoted their locations as central meeting places for company representatives coming from different sections of the country.

A new day rate market is becoming evident. Motels near campsites and along the roadways are attracting campers as a wayside stop during the day. A hot shower, an afternoon by the pool, and a change of pace from the vehicle are great appeals when coupled with the low day rate.

Check-in time is often early morning. Corporate guests prefer to start their meetings early, and truck drivers like to get off the highway before the 8 AM rush hour. If clean rooms remain unsold from the previous night, there is little reason to refuse day rate guests early access to the room. Indeed, they may order room-service coffee or breakfast as an added revenue bonus.

Since rooms sold by the day are serviced and made available again for the usual overnight occupancy, the schedule of the housekeeping staff has a great deal to do with the check-out hour. If there are no night room cleaners, the day rate must be

Exhibit 9–4

Shown is a special rate and complimentary rate authorization form. Note that all special rates or comps require an authorizing signature.

Hotel Stapleton
Special Rate Authorization
House Promotion Authorization

Name _____ Room _____

Affiliation _____

Reason for Special Rate or Comp _____

_____

Regular Rate $ _____ Special Rate $ _____

Other Comps: Food _____ Beverage _____ Other _____

Date In _____ Date Out _____

Authorized by: _____
                        (name)   (title)

closed off early enough to allow room servicing by the day crew. On the other hand, low occupancy would allow a day rate sale even late in the day. Nothing is lost if an additional empty room remains unmade overnight.

There are no rules as to what the hotel should charge for the day room. Some purists suggest that it must be half the standard rack rate. Others appreciate the extra revenue and are willing to charge whatever seems appropriate. Corporate hotels must remember that their day rate rooms compete with their convention and meeting facilities. A small group of executives might prefer meeting in the day rate guest room with its attached bath and access to room service rather than the larger impersonal convention meeting room. This can prove detrimental to the hotel if the meeting room sells for $100 per day and the day rate guest room is only $45!

Senior-Citizen and Related Discounts.   The senior segment of the nation's population has formed itself into numerous associations that are organized into retirement clubs, leisure clubs, and golden years clubs. The bulk of their membership is retired, fixed-income pensioners who are generally very price sensitive although economically comfortable. Hotels encounter the clubs as wholesale rate negotiators (the most popular of which is AARP), who promise travelers in large numbers, which they may not deliver, in return for discounted rates. The chains have responded with discounts. Additional discounts, as deep as 50 percent, are granted by giving a second night free if the traveler buys the first night at rack rates.

These specially negotiated rates and package plans need careful entry into the property management system. Package plans, for example, include entertainment, meals, and baggage transfer. The portions of the package are not broken out. Since the charge includes more than the room rate, the room clerk inputs the name of the package, no dollar amount, in the rate entry (''San Francisco Holiday,'' for example), leaving the distribution to the back-of-the-house accounting.

The night auditor prepares rate-discrepancy reports for management. They are a quick product of a property management system. The PMS has all the rack rates in memory. Every room assigned at a special rate is identified and reported.

EXHIBIT 9–5

Shown is a rate discounting equivalency table. Figures in columns 2 through 5 reflect the new occupancy rate required to gross the same revenues that were earned at the current occupancy rate without discounting.

Current Occupancy (%)	Percentage of Rate Discount			
	10	15	20	25
50%	55.56%	58.82%	62.5 %	66.67%
55	61.11	64.71	68.75	73.33
60	66.67	70.59	75.00	80.00
65	72.22	76.47	81.25	86.67
70	77.78	82.35	87.5	93.33
75	83.33	88.24	93.75	100.00

The Negative Perception of Discounting.   Room discounting is designed to increase occupancy at the cost of a lowered room rate. If the resulting occupancy increase is sufficient, it covers the lost revenues from reduced rates. In such a situation, both parties are happy—the guest pays less for the room and the hotel makes a higher profit from having created more room demand.

However appealing these potential profits are, rate discounting has a negative side as well. After becoming accustomed to discounted rates, customers perceive full rates as a very poor value. It is hard to pay $250 during a high-occupancy period when just a few weeks ago you received the same room for a $100 rate!

In fact, many experts believe hotel customers are becoming increasingly aware of the room rate discount game. Travel publications have written a number of articles touting the same bottom line to the customer—shop around for your best rate. Many customers have trained themselves to ask for the discount when booking lodging accommodations. This creates the image that standard prices are unfair and that the industry needs to discount the rate because the quality of the product does not warrant full price.

Discounts May Hurt Profits.   In fact, the whole idea of discounting rates to increase demand is somewhat suspect. Let's assume a given hotel property was operating at an annualized occupancy of 60 percent with a $70 ADR. Because the property decides it wants to increase occupancy, it establishes a rate discounting program. Exhibit 9–5 shows that for this example, a 10 percent rate discount (second column of Exhibit 9–5) requires occupancy to rise to 66.67 percent in order to gross the same revenues as previously earned.

An increase of 6.67 percent may not be easy in a community experiencing, say, only a 3.0 percent demand growth. In order to accomplish a 6.67 percentage point increase, some other lodging operation(s) will lose customers. Herein lies the biggest problem: As competing lodging properties catch wind of your discounting program, they too will begin to discount. Ultimately, a rate war will ensue, and the only winner will be the customer who pays the reduced rate.

Additional Variations of the Rate

Not all variations for the rack rate involve discounting. Factors such as the charge for additional guests in the room, negotiating a group rate years into the future where inflationary pressures must be considered, and periods of extremely high occupancy demand provide managers with opportunities to flex their rate muscles.

Premium Rates.   Some hotels find themselves in the enviable position of having too much business—too much demand during certain premium periods. These premium periods are generally characterized by a national or regional holiday, major sporting event, or other sizable attraction. For example, when Indianapolis hosts the Indianapolis 500, when New Orleans celebrates the Mardi Gras, or when Los Angeles enjoys the Rose Bowl, hotel rates rise dramatically.

Premium rates are charged when normal demand significantly exceeds room supply. In such cases, hotels have been known to charge several times their standard rack rate. Such rate adjustments may be based on "gut feel" and a knowledge of what other properties are charging, or yield management software may be utilized to assist with the decision-making process.

Indeed, rate alone is not the only adjustment the guest will be forced to accept. Other standard practices include closing specific dates to arrival and requiring certain minimum lengths of stay. By carefully following such practices, a manager can extend a sold-out day—say, Super Bowl Sunday—into a sold-out weekend or three-day event.

Double Occupancy.   *Double occupancy* refers to the use of the room by a second guest. Traditional rate making increases the single-occupancy rate by a factor (normally not twice) whenever the room is double-occupied. However, the price spread between single and double occupancy has been narrowing. One rate is being used more frequently because the major costs of a hotel room are fixed (debt service, taxes, depreciation). Having a second or third occupant adds relatively few incremental costs (linen, soap, tissue). Although far from universal, one charge for both single and double occupancy is gaining favor.

Convention rates are almost always negotiated with double occupancy at no extra charge. The more persons in the hotel, the more the hotel benefits from sales in other departments: banquet, bar, casino. Suite charges have also followed that pattern. The room rate is the number of rooms that comprise the suite, not the number of guests who occupy it. The room, not the guest, becomes the unit of pricing.

Several arguments support the movement toward a single room price. The fewer the rate options, the less the confusion, and the more rapidly the telephone reservationist can close the sale. Price is a critical issue in package plans or tour bookings, and rates can be shaved closely because the second occupant represents a small additional expense. A third occupant adds a still smaller incremental cost. The incremental cost is almost unnoticed if the extra person(s) share existing beds. That is what makes family-plan rates attractive. An extra charge is levied if a rollaway bed, which requires extra handling and linen, is required. Suite hotels are popular because the extra hideabed is permanently available.

Unless the family-rate plan has been quoted, a charge is generally made for the third and subsequent occupants to a room (see Exhibit 9–6). Even in hotels where single and double occupancy is charged the same rate, a third or fourth guest probably pays an additional fee. Usually, that added charge is a flat fee—say, $20 per extra person.

Many hoteliers find a flat $20 fee illogical in light of the numerous room types available at the property. Where $20 may be fine for a $100 standard room, it does not seem high enough for a $150 deluxe or a $200 executive parlor. Indeed, if the hotelier can make the argument that we charge for extra guests because they cost the hotel incremental expenses, then that argument is doubly true in premium rooms.

Exhibit 9–6

A circa-1958 article discusses the controversy surrounding the family-rate plan. Note in the third paragraph that rate-cutting (e.g., discounting) is referred to as "the most disagreeable word in the hotelman's language." Also note the names of old chains that are no longer in business.

Controversy is growing among American hotelmen about the Family Rate Plan method of basing hotel rates upon occupancy by adults only. Children of fourteen years or less, accompanying their parents, are not charged for occupancy of rooms with their parents. For example, one adult and a child are charged a single rate for the double occupancy of the room. Two adults and children are charged a double rate for a room, or two single rates if two rooms are engaged. There are various other modifications of the plan, but fundamentally it represents complimentary accommodation of children below a certain age level.

At least three leading hotel chains have adopted the plan and report great success from the higher occupancy attributable to it. Why, then, the controversy? Certainly when hotel chains of the stature of the Statler, Eppley, and Pick chains favor the Family Rate Plan, it is well on its way to becoming a standard practice for most other hotels in the country.

The controversy rests on the issue of whether this plan is a form of rate-cutting—the most disagreeable word in the hotelman's language. In this era of downward adjustment from high wartime levels of occupancy, naturally hotelmen are sensitive to any indirect methods of reducing rates. No hotelman wishes to see any kind of repetition of the rate-cutting practices of the 1930's.

In an attempt to evaluate the plan in its rate-cutting connotation, we believe that most hotelmen would be hardpressed to define a rate-cut in exact terms. For example, is the commercial rate to traveling men a type of rate reduction? Does a convention rate involve a hidden discount? We can remember the time when it was standard practice to compliment the wife of a traveling man, when a week's stay at a hotel resulted in having the seventh day free of charge, and when the armed forces, clergy, and diplomats got lower rates.

In our opinion, rate-cutting is practiced only when hotels depart from their *regular* practices and tariff schedules in order to secure patronage from prospects who are openly shopping for the best deal in room rates. If, therefore, it is regular practice for hotels to have special rates for group business, this does not seem to represent rate-cutting. And the same principle should apply to the Family Rate Plan. If this plan becomes widely adopted—as seems very likely—then it falls into the category of any other special type of rate for special business.

In some respects the plan is a form of *pricing accommodations by rooms instead of by persons.* In many resort hotels a room is rated regardless of its occupancy by one or two persons, and a similar concept is used in apartments and apartment hotels.

Although the arguments for or against the Family Rate Plan must be decided by hotelmen themselves, a strong point in favor of the plan is found in its adoption by other vendors of public service—the railroads and airlines. Family rates, weekday rates, seasonal rates, special-type carrier rates, etc., have been in vogue for several years. If the hotels adopt the Family Rate Plan, it seems that they will be falling into line with a national trend rather than venturing alone into a new and untried experiment in good public relations.

Source: The Horwath Hotel Accountant.

In a standard room, extra guests (whether the second, third, or fourth occupant) cost the hotel in a variety of ways, including extra water and electricity, additional amenities, more towels and linens, and, of course, some wear and tear. These costs are not identical from a standard room to a deluxe accommodation. Hotels outfit deluxe rooms with larger bathtubs, more expensive personal amenities, heavier quality linens, and higher quality furnishings. An additional person in a deluxe room has a higher incremental cost to the hotel than an additional person in a standard room.

A flat $20 rate represents a declining percentage of the rate as the quality of the room increases. In the $100 standard, $20 reflects a 20 percent surcharge. Yet in the $200 executive parlor, $20 reflects only a 10 percent surcharge. In fact, if the $100 standard guest is willing to pay $20 for an extra occupant, it makes sense that the $200 executive-parlor guest would be willing to pay something like $40 for an extra guest.

Quoting Convention Rates.   Just as the hotel manager is concerned with establishing rack rates, discounted rates, and premium rates for today, tomorrow, and the short term, there are pressures to forecast rates far into the future. These pressures are created by the sales and marketing department, which may be selling convention room blocks 5, 10, even 20 years into the future. And just as rate is an important factor to groups today, it is also a major criterion for selecting accommodations 20 years hence.

Room rate inflation is a major concern for group business. A $125 negotiated group rate today can easily become a $250 group rate in 15 or 20 years. Inflation is less the concern of the group than whether $250 will be a fair price in 15 years.

Sometimes the deal is struck but the final rate is left to be negotiated until both sides can get a sense of value. If a rate has to be given, management must protect against an unknown inflation factor. Yet the buyer is unwilling to commit to inflation-based rates like those of the late 1970s if the inflation rate is low, as in the mid-1980s.

Groups are asking for contract language that protects the room rate. Statements are stipulating that rates will be no more than X times the basic rate, or Y percent off the rack rate, or no more than the best rate (the lowest rate) charged at the time of the convention. All are terms, as are most rate quotes, that defy specific definition.

Time Is Money

While the actual date of arrival and departure is the primary consideration for establishing the guest charge, the actual hours of occupancy may someday play a role in rate determination. In simple terms, time is already a rate criterion in many hotels. For example, take a walk-in guest who arrives at two o'clock in the morning. If many rooms remain available, the clerk (night auditor) is likely to offer the guest a substantial discount for purchasing a room. And why not? At 2 AM, rooms have little chance of being sold at full rate.

Arrival Time.   The day of arrival is listed on the reservation, the registration card, and the guest folio. The time of arrival is also indicated on the folio by means of an internal electronic clock operating in the property management system. Assuming that the clock is accurate, the actual minute of check-in is recorded on the electronic folio.

The actual time of arrival is more critical to the American plan hotel, where billing is based on meals taken, than to the European plan operation. American plan arrivals are flagged with a special meal code.

The hour of arrival at a European plan hotel is less critical. An occasional complaint about the promptness of message service or a rare police inquiry might involve the arrival hour. Very, very late arrivals, such as a guest who arrives at 5 AM, are the exceptions. Somewhere in the early morning hours (5 AM–7 AM) comes the break between charging for the night just passed and levying the first charge for the day just starting.

If rooms are vacant, guests are generally assigned as soon as they arrive. A room vacant during the previous night can be assigned to a morning arrival the next day. Rooms that were occupied need housekeeping. With a noon or 1 PM check-out hour, the room may not be ready until that afternoon. To forestall complaints, check-in hours are established and publicized on reservation forms (see Exhibit 4–2), sometimes on the mailing envelope. Overseas arrivals often encounter a 1 PM check-in (as in London), with flights arriving early to mid-morning.

Check-out time: 1 PM

We would like to ask your cooperation in checking out by 1 PM so that we may accommodate travelers who are beginning their stay. If you require additional time, you may request a two-hour grace period (until 3 PM) from the assistant manager or the front-office manager. If you wish to check out later, we regret that there must be a $12-per-hour charge, from 3 until 5 PM, for this added service. An additional half-day rate will be charged to guests who delay their departure until between 5 PM and 8 PM. After 8 PM, a full-day rate will be charged. Of course, you are then welcome to remain until the following afternoon at 1 PM.

As an incoming guest, your comfort and convenience depends on these stipulations. We hope you will visit again soon.

Check-in hours are difficult to control. Guest arrivals are dictated haphazardly by travel connections and varying distances. The termination point of a night's lodging is more controllable, so every hotel posts an official check-out hour.

Departure Time.   Check-in and check-out hours are eased or enforced as occupancies fall or rise. Setting the specific check-out hour is left to each hotel. It might be established without any rationale, or it might be the same hour that nearby competitors are using. The proper hour is a balance between the guest's need to complete his or her business and the hotel's need to clean and properly prepare the room for the next patron.

Seasoned travelers are well aware that check-out extensions are granted by the room clerk if occupancy is light. Under current billing practices, the effort should be cheerfully made whenever the request can be accommodated. When anticipated arrivals require enforcement of the check-out hour, luggage can be stored in the checkroom for the guest's convenience.

Resorts are under more pressure than commercial hotels to expedite check-outs. Vacationing guests try to squeeze the most from their holiday time. American plan houses usually allow the guest to remain through the luncheon hour and a reasonable time thereafter if the meal is part of the rate. Some 90 percent of the resorts surveyed in an AH&MA study identified their check-out hour to be between noon and 2 PM, in contrast to the 11 AM–1 PM range used by transient hotels. These same properties assigned new arrivals on a ''when-available'' basis.

Special techniques in addition to that shown in Exhibit 9–7 have been tried to move the guest along. On the night before departure, the room clerk, the assistant manager, or the social host(ess) calls the room to chat and remind the guest of tomorrow's departure. Even today, this task could be assigned to a computer. A more personal touch is a note of farewell left by the room attendant who turns down the bed the night before.

Incentive Rate Systems.   Incentive rate systems have been suggested as a means of expediting check-outs. First, the check-out period for a normal day's charge would be established—say, between 11 AM and 1 PM. Guests who leave before 11 AM are charged less than the standard rate, and those who remain beyond 1 PM are charged more. Flexible charges of this type require a new look at the unit of service, shifting from the more traditional measure of a night's lodging to smaller blocks of time.

Exhibit 9–8

This exhibit demonstrates three different hotel room utilization times. The first guest checks in very late and checks out very early. The second guest follows the hotel's 2 PM check-in and 11 AM check-out policy. The third guest extends arrival and departure times by taking advantage of light occupancy and normal front-office courtesies.

	February 14th Arrival	*February 15th Departure*	*Total Hours*
Guest 1	1 AM	6 AM	5 hours
Guest 2	2 PM	11 AM	21 hours
Guest 3	8 AM	3 PM	31 hours

Unlike other service industries, hotels have given little consideration to time as a factor in rate. Arrival and departure times establish broad parameters at best. We can expect these to narrow as hotelkeepers become more concerned with the role of time in rate structuring. Taken to the other extreme, it is conceivable that the hour will eventually become the basic unit for constructing room rates. Under current practices, a stay of several hours costs as much as a full day's stay (see Exhibit 9–8).

The total length of stay may also be an issue in the guest's level of satisfaction with the hotel. Guests with few hours to visit scarcely get enough time to sleep and bathe. It is the guest with sufficient leisure hours who truly enjoys the property by taking advantage of relaxation and recreational activities (Exhibit 9–8).

A popular journalist once observed that the length of time you have in your hotel room is inversely proportional to the quality of that hotel room. When you arrive at, say, 1 AM and need to get some rest for a 7 AM flight the next morning, the room will be lavish—there will be vases of roses, trays of food and drink, soft music, a Jacuzzi tub, and candlelight. Conversely, when you have no time commitments and all day to spend in the hotel, it is invariably a poor quality establishment—there will be no restaurant or lobby, fuzzy television reception, and a drained swimming pool!

The American Plan Resort.   Meals are part of the American plan (AP) rate, as they are with the modified American plan (MAP). Accurate billing requires an accurate record of arrival and departure times. Arrivals are registered with a meal code reflecting the check-in time. For example, a guest arriving at 3 PM would be coded with arriving after lunch but before dinner.

A complete AP day technically involves enough meals on the final day to make up for the meals missed on the arriving day. A guest arriving before dinner would be expected to depart the next day, or many days later, after lunch. Two meals, breakfast and lunch, on the departing day complete the full AP charge, since one meal, dinner, was taken on the arriving day. MAP counts meals in the same manner, except lunch is ignored.

Guests who take more than the three meals per day pay for the extra at menu prices, or sometimes below. Normally, guests who miss a meal are not charged. That is why it is very important to have the total AP rate fairly distributed between the room portion and the meal portion. Meal rates are set and are standardized for everyone. Higher AP rates must reflect better rooms, since all the guests are entitled to the same menu.

AP and MAP hotels have a special charge called **tray service.** It is levied on meals taken through room service. European plan room service typically contains hidden charges as a means of recovering the extra service. Menu charges are greater than the usual coffee shop prices when the food is delivered to the room. This device is not available to the American plan hotel because meals being delivered to the room are not priced separately. Instead, a flat charge of several dollars per person is levied as a tray service charge.

Determining the Rate

Because a sound room rate structure is fundamental to a sound hotel operation, every manager is sooner or later faced with the question of what is the proper room charge. It is a matter of exceeding complexity because room rates reflect markets and costs; investments and rates of return; supply and demand; accommodations and competition; and, not least of all, the quality of management.

Divided into its two major components, room rates must be large enough to cover costs and a fair return on invested capital, and reasonable enough to attract and retain the clientele to whom the operation is being marketed. The former suggests a relatively objective, structured approach that can be analyzed after the fact. The latter is more subjective, involving many factors, from the amount of local competition to the condition of the economy at large. There is little sense in charging a rate less than what is needed to meet the first objective; there is little chance of getting a rate more than that limit established by the second.

Yield management, the balancing of occupancy and rate, has emerged as the number one component of rate making. Chapter 4 examined the questions with which a yield management system deals. Yield management deals with timing. At what occupancy level are discounted rates, or premium rates, triggered (Exhibit 9–5)? Yield management deals with volume: How many rooms should each rate class have, and what percentage of each should be shifted upward or downward? Yield management deals with marketplace: Shall we cater to the corporate guest or the golden club tour? Yield management deals with horizons: What decision is to be made six months out? Three months out? Today? Yield management deals with displacement: Is the group booked Saturday through Tuesday at a discounted rate displacing more or fewer dollars than the traditional business traveler of Monday and Tuesday? Yield management deals with lead time: What is the lead time of conventions (one to three years of lead time), groups (one to three months of lead time), and individuals (one to three days of lead time)?

Yield management has attracted attention because it introduces two new concepts to room pricing: (1) the industry is selling rooms by an inventory control system for the first time; (2) the pricing strategy considers for the first time the customer's ability and willingness to pay. This discretionary market, with a sensitivity to price, is itself a new phenomenon.

In years past, the rate structure was built from the standpoint of internal cost considerations. Yield management has not eliminated that focus. Important as they are, customers are not the only components of price. Cost recovery and investment opportunity are reflected there as well. Depreciation and interest as well as taxes and land costs are outside the hotel–guest relationship but not external to the room charge.

The more traditional components of rate deal with recovering costs, both operating and capital. They deal with profits and break-even projections. Mixed into the equation are competition, price elasticity, and rate-cutting. In the final analysis, the Average Daily Rate earned by the hotel will be determined by the ability of a reservationist or room clerk to sell up.

Rate Calculations

Hotel room rates are derived from a mix of objective measures and subjective values. Expressing room rates numerically gives an appearance of validity, but when those numbers originated as best-guess estimates, the results must be viewed with some measure of doubt or uncertainty.

Facts and suppositions combine together when hotel managers calculate the room rate. As useful and respected as these various mathematical formulas may be, they are still merely an indication of the final rate. Fine-tuning the formula, establishing corporate and double occupancy prices, and adjusting the rate according to the whims of the community and the marketplace are still the role of management.

The Hubbart Room Rate Formula.   The **Hubbart Room Rate Formula** offers a standardized approach that structures the decision criteria involved in assigning room rates. The Hubbart Formula proceeds from the needs of the enterprise and not from the needs of the guests. The average rate, says the formula, should pay all expenses and leave something for the investor. Valid enough—a business that cannot do this is short-lived.

Exhibit 9–9 illustrates the mechanics of the formula. Estimated expenses are itemized and totaled. These include operational expenses by departments ($1,102,800 in the illustration), realty costs ($273,000), and depreciation ($294,750). To these expenses is added a reasonable return on the present fair value of the property: land, building, and furnishings ($414,000). From the total expense package ($2,084,550) are subtracted incomes from all sources other than room sales ($139,200). This difference ($1,945,350) represents the annual amount to be realized from room sales.

Next (Exhibit 9–10, Schedule II), an estimate of the number of rooms to be sold annually is computed. Dividing the number of estimated rooms (38,325) to be sold into the estimated dollars ($1,945,350) needed to cover costs and a fair return produces the average rate to be charged ($50.76). The computations are simple enough; the formula is straightforward enough. Deriving the estimates is where the weakness lies.

Shortcomings of the Formula.   The Hubbart Room Rate Formula, like many such calculations, is only as accurate as the assumptions on which it was projected. Several such assumptions come immediately to mind for the Hubbart Formula: What percentage is ''reasonable'' as a fair return on investment? What occupancy rate appears most attainable? What are the cost projections for payroll, various operating departments, utilities, and administrative and general?

The formula leaves the rooms department with the final burden after profits and losses from other departments. But inefficiencies in other departments should not be covered by a high, noncompetitive room rate. Neither should unusual profits in other departments be a basis for charging room rates below what the market will bring.

EXHIBIT 9-9

Shown is the Hubbart Room Rate Formula, Schedule I. *This formula for transient and residential hotels is used to determine the amount needed from room sales to cover costs and a reasonable return on the present fair value of property.*

					Example	
Operating Expenses						
Rooms department					$467,400	
Telephone department					60,900	
Administrative and general					91,200	
Payroll taxes and employee relations					178,200	
Advertising and business promotion					109,800	
Heat, light, and power					138,900	
Repairs and maintenance					56,400	
Total operating expenses						$1,102,800
Taxes and Insurance						
Real estate and personal property taxes					67,200	
Franchise taxes and fees					112,200	
Insurance on building and contents					37,200	
Leased equipment					56,400	
Total taxes and insurance						$ 273,000
Depreciation (Standard Rates on Present Fair Value)	*Value*		*Rate*			
Building	$_____ at		%		168,750	
Furniture, fixtures, and equipment	$_____ at		%		126,000	
Total depreciation						$ 294,750
Reasonable Return on Present Fair Value of Property	*Value*		*Rate*			
Land	$_____ at		%			
Building	$_____ at		%			
Furniture, fixtures, and equipment	$_____ at		%			
Total fair return						$ 414,000
Total						$2,084,550
Deduct—Credits from Sources Other than Rooms						
Income from store rentals					14,850	
Credit from food and beverage operations (if loss, subtract from this group)					131,400	
Net income from other operated departments and miscellaneous income					(7,050)	
Total credits from sources other than rooms						$ 139,200
Amount to be realized from guest room sales to cover costs and a reasonable return of present fair value of property						$1,945,350

Courtesy: The American Hotel & Motel Association, Washington, D.C.

EXHIBIT 9–10

Shown is the Hubbart Room Rate Formula, Schedule II. *The computations are used to determine Average Daily Rate required per occupied room.*

		Example
1. Amount to be realized from guest room sales to cover costs and a reasonable return on present fair value of property (from Schedule I)		$1,945,350
2. Number of guest rooms available for rental		150
3. Number of available rooms on annual basis (item 2 multiplied by 365)	100%	54,750
4. Less: Allowance for average vacancies	30%	16,425
5. Number of rooms to be occupied at estimated average occupancy	70%	38,325
6. Average Daily Rate per occupied room required to cover costs and a reasonable return on present fair value (item 1 divided by item 5)		$ 50.76

There is some justification in having rooms subsidize low banquet prices if these low prices result in large convention bookings of guest rooms. (Incidentally, this is one reason why the food and banquet department should not be leased as a concession.) Similar justification could be found for using higher room rates to cover unusually high dining room repairs and maintenance, or advertising costs. The trade-off is wise if these excessive expenditures produced enough other business to offset lost room revenue resulting from higher room rates.

Additional shortcomings become apparent as the formula is studied. Among them is the projected number of rooms sold. This estimate of rooms sold is itself a function of the very rate being computed. Rate, in turn, is a function of double occupancy (subsequent increased rates for double occupancy are buried somewhere in the Hubbart rate). Neither component (the impact of rate on occupancy and the impact of double occupancy on rate) is projected.

The average rate that is computed ($50.76) is not the actual rate used by the hotel. Hotels use a number of rate classes, with various proportions of the total number of rooms assigned to each classification. The actual average rate will be a weighted average of the rooms occupied. Reflected therein are the range of accommodations the hotel is offering and the guest's purchase of them based on nearby competition.

Square Foot Calculations.   In order to compensate for the fact that the Hubbart Room Rate Formula provides no rate detail related to room type classifications, some managers employ a square foot calculation. The basis for this method is the fact that more expensive and higher quality guest rooms are invariably larger than standard hotel rooms at the same property. Therefore, rather than calculating the Hubbart Room Rate per room sold, this variation calculates the rate on a per-square-foot basis.

To illustrate, assume that the hotel presented in Exhibit 9–10 has a total 56,250 square feet of space in its 150 guest rooms. With occupancy of 70 percent, there would be an average of 39,375 square feet sold per day. With an annual required return of $1,945,350, the daily required return is $5,329.73 ($1,945,350 divided by 365 days). Therefore, each square foot of rented room space must generate $0.1354 per day ($5,329.73 divided by 39,375 square feet sold per day) or almost 14 cents in daily revenue. As a result, a 300-square-foot room would sell for $40.62 (300 square feet times $0.1354) and a 450-square-foot room would sell for $60.93.

Whichever system is used, the formula's average room rate ensures a minimum operating result. Management might well select another average room rate with corresponding levels of occupancy to achieve a different return on investment. There is a great interdependence between sound rate policy and sound operating policy. The Hubbart Formula is a guide through the complexities of rate structuring, but no single formula can replace balanced business judgment.

The Building Cost Rate Formula.   Time and repetition have created an industry axiom saying that rate can be evaluated by a rule of thumb (the **Building Cost Rate Formula**): The average room rate should equal $1 per $1,000 of construction cost. For a 250-room hotel costing $14 million (including land and land development, building, and public space but excluding furnishings and equipment), the average rate should be $56 ($14 million ÷ 250 rooms ÷ $1,000).

The building cost yardstick is about as reliable as an old cookbook's direction to the chef: "Flavor to taste." Despite some very radical changes throughout the years, the rule is still being quoted on the theory that rising construction costs are being matched by rising room rates. Higher construction costs are a function of room size as well as building materials and labor. This generation of rooms is 100 to 200 percent larger than rooms were even 25 or 30 years ago.

Cost of construction includes other factors: type of construction, location, high-rise versus low-rise buildings, and the cost of money. Luxury properties can cost five or six times as much per room as economy hotels. Land costs vary greatly across the nation. Comparing California and Arkansas is a lesson in futility. New York City may be stretching toward a $300-room-per-night rate, but that is not the expectation of the manager in Dubuque, Iowa.

Economy chains have stopped advertising a minimum national rate. Each locale has its own cost basis for building, borrowing, taxing, and paying labor. Budgets aim only for a percentage rate below that of local competitors. Advertising a single rate as part of the national company logo is no longer feasible.

Increases in room construction costs are startling. Marriott's typical room cost runs between $100,000 and $200,000 today. Its figure was $8,000 in 1957. Consider what has happened in Hawaii in 20 years. The Mauna Kea Beach Hotel was built there in 1967 at approximately $100,000 per room. In 1988, the Hyatt Regency Waikoloa came on line at $210,000 per room, for a total of 1,244 rooms at $261,000,000. The sales price of rooms being resold outstrips even construction costs. It is happening nationally, but especially in Hawaii, where international buying is very heavy. Twenty years after the Mauna Kea was built at $100,000 per room, it was sold at $1 million per room! And the hotel was 20 years older by that time.

The situation is the same in New York. Regent Hotels, a superluxury chain, has a 400-room hotel in New York with an average cost of $750,000 per room. With an actual Average Daily Rate of $400, the hotel is far from the $750 ADR dictated by the rule of thumb.

The Hotel Bel-Air in Los Angeles is another hotel that breaks the mold. With only 92 rooms, the property recently sold for a record $110 million (or approximately $1.2 million per room) to a Japanese hotel concern. In spite of the incredibly high Average Daily Rate ($375), the hotel earns far less than the $1,200 per average room-night that the Building Cost Rate Formula dictates.

These examples are special cases of ''trophy hotels.'' Such exorbitant prices cannot be explained in terms of weak–strong currencies alone. Viewing the trophy as an art asset, which gives satisfaction and pleasure to the owner, offers some perspective on the price. Like an art piece, these eyebrow-raising prices are justified as long-term investments and by their uniqueness (location). In retrospect, the excessive prices of a generation ago have proven to be good deals.

In fact, no one actually expects the Japanese hotel company that purchased the Hotel Bel-Air to make a profit. The only profits will come from selling the resort several years down the road. And that seems quite plausible—hotel real estate sales are up. The Japanese hotel company was one of four interested parties willing to bid in excess of $1 million per room for the Hotel Bel-Air. And the company that sold the hotel made an enormous profit, having purchased it just seven years ago for $22.7 million.

Trophy hotels are extreme examples that do not set the rule for the remainder of the industry. With economy hotels costing less than $30,000 per room, and standard properties less than $70,000 per room, advocates of the rule take heart. Lower costs and lower rate figures keep the spread between actual rate and rule-of-thumb rate close enough to keep the rule alive.

Conditions seesaw, first supporting the rule and then undermining it. The general rise in land and construction costs has been offset by improvements in design and reductions in labor force. The rise in financing costs has been offset by the lower costs of older hotels still in use. Since building costs are tied to historical prices, older hotels have lower financing costs (and probably lower real estate taxes, too) to recover. That is true, at least, until they're sold.

The Cost of Renovation.   The costs of additions, property rehabilitations, or new amenities (pool, exercise room) fall within the purview of the rule. First, the cost of the upgrade is determined on a per room basis. The installation of an in-room air conditioner might be priced at $1,500 per room. A general-use item, such as a sauna, would need a per room equivalent. The cost (assume $150,000) would be divided by the number of rooms (100) to arrive at the per unit cost.

Exhibit 9–11 illustrates an example of a major room rehabilitation program. This exhibit assumes a 225-room hotel spends $2,750,000 renovating its rooms, for an average cost of $12,222 per room. The problem assumes the hotel has a 15 percent cost of funds (interest rate). With a $12,222 expense per room at 15 percent interest and 15 years of debt repayment, $2,090.17 is the annualized cost of principle and interest per room per year. Therefore, the rule of thumb established in the Building Cost Rate Formula suggests that the hotel needs to charge an additional $2.09 per occupied room-night to compensate for the expense incurred when renovating its facility. With that kind of information, management can evaluate the likelihood of the additional investment being competitive in the eyes of the guest who is asked to pay the increased price.

Shortcomings notwithstanding, the rule is still widely quoted. Modernizing it, raising the room rate to $1.50 per $1,000, has been suggested as a means of making it more applicable. That attacks the problem from the wrong side. Rates have not kept up. If actual rates cannot achieve even the $1 rule per $1,000, they certainly will be no closer to reaching a $1.50 figure.

The Ideal Average Room Rate.   The firm of Laventhol & Horwath designed the **Ideal Average Room Rate** as a means of testing the room rate structure.[2] According

EXHIBIT 9–11

Calculating room rate impact from a major renovation project.

Basic Hotel Information
225 rooms in hotel
15 percent cost of funds (interest rate)
$2,750,000 total renovation project

Project Cost per Average Guest Room
$2,750,000 total project divided by 225 rooms equals $12,222.22 cost per average room.

Incorporate 15 Percent Cost of Funds (Interest) Rate
$12,222.22 project cost per average room is to be repaid over 15 years at a 15 percent cost of funds. The combined principal plus interest will be $2,090.17 per room per year.

Incorporate the Building Cost Rate Formula
$2,090.17 annualized cost per average room divided by $1,000 formula constant equals $2.09 rate increase per average room.

to this approach, the hotel should sell an equal percentage of rooms in each rate class instead of filling from the bottom up. A 70 percent occupancy should mean a 70 percent occupancy in each rate category. Such a spread produces an average rate identical to the average rate earned when the hotel is completely full—that is, an ideal room rate.

Exhibit 9–12 illustrates the computation used to derive the ideal rate. This formula assumes that each room type (standard, executive, deluxe, and suite) fills to the same percentage of rooms sold as every other room type. At a 70 percent hotel occupancy, 70 percent of the standard rooms will be sold, 70 percent of the executive rooms will be sold, 70 percent of the deluxe rooms will be sold, and 70 percent of the suites will be sold.

Once calculated, the manager is armed with a valuable figure, the Ideal Average Room Rate. As long as rates remain constant and the ratio of double occupancy does not change, the manager has a valid ideal rate. If the actual average rate is higher than the ideal average rate, the hotel has failed to provide a proper number of high-priced rooms. The market is interested in rooms selling above the average, so room types and rates should be adjusted upward.

An average room rate lower than the ideal, and this is usually the case, indicates several problems. There may not be enough contrast between the low- and the high-priced rooms. Guests will take the lower rate when they are buying nothing extra for the higher rate. If the better rooms do, in fact, have certain extras—better exposure and newer furnishings—the lack of contrast between the rate categories might simply be a matter of poor selling at the front desk.

Check-in at the front desk represents the last opportunity to up-sell the guest to a more expensive room accommodation. Good salesmanship coupled with a differentiated product gives the hotel a strong chance to increase middle- and high-priced room sales. Such comments as ''I see you have reserved our standard room; do you realize for just 12 more dollars I can place you in a newly refurbished deluxe room with a complimentary continental breakfast?'' go a long way towards satisfying both the guest and the bottom line.

A faulty internal rate structure is another reason that the ideal room rate might not be achieved. The options, the range of rates being offered, might not appeal to the customer. Using the ideal room rate computation, the spread between rates could

EXHIBIT 9–12

The Ideal Average Room Rate Formula.

Room Type	Number Rooms by Type	Percent of Double Occupancy	Single Rate	Double Rate
Standard	140	30 percent	$ 80	$ 95
Executive	160	5 percent	$105	$105
Deluxe	100	25 percent	$120	$140
Suite	75	70 percent	$160	$160
Total rooms:	475			

Calculation Steps

1. Multiply all standard rooms (140) by their single rate ($80) to get a product of $11,200. Then take the double occupancy percentage for standard rooms (30 percent) times the total number of standard rooms (140) to get 42, the number of double-occupied standard rooms. Next, take the 42 double-occupied standard rooms times the differential between the single and double price ($95 double rate minus $80 single rate equals $15 differential) to get $630. Finally, add the room revenue for standard rooms calculated at the single rate ($11,200) to the additional room revenue received from standard rooms sold at the double rate ($630) to get the full-house room revenue for standard rooms, a total of $11,830.

2. Follow the same procedure for executive rooms: 160 rooms times $105 equals $16,800. The differential between single and double occupancy for executive rooms is zero, so there is no added revenue for double occupancy. The full-house room revenue for executive rooms is $16,800.

3. Follow the same procedure for deluxe rooms: 100 rooms times $120 single rate equals $12,000. In terms of double occupancy, there are 25 deluxe rooms (25 percent double occupancy times 100 rooms equals 25 rooms) sold at a $20 differential ($140 double rate minus $120 single rate equals $20 differential) for a total double occupancy impact of $500. The full-house room revenue for deluxe rooms is $12,500.

4. Follow the same procedure for suites: 75 rooms times $160 equals $12,000. The differential betwen single and double occupancy for suites is zero, so there is no added revenue for double occupancy. The full-house room revenue for suites is $12,000.

5. Add total revenues from standard rooms ($11,830), executive rooms ($16,800), deluxe rooms ($12,500), and suites ($12,000) for total revenues assuming 100 percent occupancy—ideal revenues. That total ($53,130) divided by rooms sold (475) is the Ideal Average Room Rate of $111.85.

No matter what the occupancy percentage, the Ideal Average Room Rate remains the same.

Try this problem again, assuming, say, 70 percent occupancy. The end result will still be an Ideal Average Room Rate of $111.85.

Courtesy: Laventhol & Horwath, Philadelphia.

be adjusted. According to the authors of the formula, increases should be concentrated in those rooms on those days for which the demand is highest. That begins with an analysis of rate categories.

Rate Categories.   The discrepancy between the rates the hotel furnishes and those the guests require can be pinpointed with a simple chart. Guest demands and the hotel offerings are plotted side by side.

Guest demands are determined by a survey of registration card rates over a period of time. The survey should not include days of 100 percent occupancy when the guest had no rate choice. Special rate situations would also be excluded. Using elementary arithmetic, the percentage of total registrations is determined for each rate class. Exhibit 9–13 illustrates the contrast between what the guest buys and what the hotel offers. It also points to the rates that need adjustment.

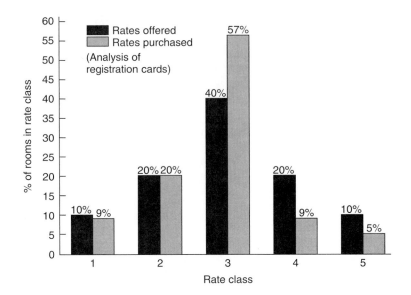

Exhibit 9–13 assigns 40 percent of the hypothetical hotel to the average room rate. Two additional categories of 20 percent and 10 percent, respectively, appear on both the lower and upper ends. Hilton Hotels use five categories, much like those in the illustration. However, eight rate categories were established when the company redid the Chicago Hilton & Towers. Fifteen different room types were identified, based on type of bedding, bath, furnishings, view, and location, for the eight rate classifications. Another example of rate categories is found in Exhibit 9–12.

The move toward fewer rate categories compensates for the increasing variety of special rates. Holiday Inn recently revised its classification, trying to hold to three types: economy, standard, and luxury. The Ramada Renaissance opened in San Francisco with 17 rack rates but adjusted to just three several years later. Similarly, Hyatt International announced six rate categories worldwide and eliminated its single/double differential. In contrast, 107 different rates were uncovered at the Roosevelt Hotel (1,076 rooms) in New York City during a major renovation.

Lower-priced rooms are in greatest demand. It is the sad history of our industry that hotels fill from the bottom up. This means that low occupancy is accompanied by a low Average Daily Rate. It is felt, therefore, that there should be more categories at the lower end of the price scale. These lower categories would be bunched together, while the higher rates would be spread over fewer categories. That might be the reason that Hilton advises its franchises to concentrate on the minimum single rate as the key in competition. (It also recommends that double occupancy be 50 percent higher than single rates.)

Additional Rate Components

It is not possible to quantify all the components that go into setting room rates. Some elements are just not subject to measure; other components are externally controlled. For example, the federal park service approves the reasonableness of room rates charged by concessionaires within the parks on the basis of the quality and price of private competitors outside the park.

The Competition Component.   Just as the Hubbart Formula establishes the minimum the hotel can afford to charge, competition sets the maximum it can expect to get. External competition from neighboring facilities prescribes the general price range. Internal physical differences within the rooms determine the rate increments.

Supply and demand, the degree of saturation, and the extent of rate-cutting in the community fix the rate parameters. Customers comparison shop, and hotel management should do the same. Differences in both the physical facilities and the range of services offered justify higher rates than the competition. The physical accommodations are easier to compare; they are there for the looking. Swimming pool, tennis courts, meeting rooms, restaurants, and a lobby bar head a long list of differences that give one property a competitive advantage over its neighbor. Room size, furnishings (bed and bath types), location, and exposure differentiate the internal product.

The condition of the facilities can offset the competitive advantage of their availability. ''Clean and neat'' sends an important subliminal message. Hotels with burnt-out bulbs in the hotel sign, wilted flowers in the planters, and dirty glass on the entrance door lose out to hotels with lesser facilities that look fresh and new.

Differences in service are more difficult to discern, but they add to the room rate charge as substantially as other components. Twenty-four-hour room service, pool guard on duty, and an extensive training program for employees begin another, less visible list of competitive advantages. Like the capital outlays of the physical accommodations, these costs must be recaptured in the room rate.

Up-Selling at the Front Desk.   The room rate policy, whatever it might be, faces a moment of truth when the line employee and the buying public come face to face. Fashioning a room rate policy is a futile exercise of formula building unless management simultaneously prepares its staff to carry out the plan. The selling skills of reservationists and clerks are critical to the Average Daily Rate until the house nears capacity. Since nearly full occupancy is a rare occasion, earning a consistently higher ADR on the 60 to 70 percent day is achieved only when a program for selling up is in place.

The hardest sell comes from the room clerk. A guest who approaches the desk with a reservation in hand has already decided to buy. Once committed, the new arrival is susceptible to a carefully designed and rehearsed sales effort (see Exhibit 9–14). The hardest job comes from the reservationist who doesn't even see the buyer. Too hard a sell, too firm a price, and the guest is lost early on. Teamed up, the reservationist and the room clerk deliver a one–two punch to the ADR, although they could be 1,000 miles and 30 days apart.

A firm sale begins with product knowledge. That's why good sales executives travel to the central reservation office to brief the operators there. On property, both the reservationists and the room clerks need continuous training about the facilities and accommodations of the hotel. This is rarely done. Few hotels ever assign 15 minutes per day for staff visits and inspections. Hotels spend millions of dollars upgrading rooms and modernizing facilities, but the room clerk never sees the changes. A simple and consistent training program assures management that reservationists and front-desk clerks know their product.

If the desk staff knows the product, a repertoire of reasons can be developed to up-sell. A 10 percent up-sell of $10 to $20 on a room of $100 to $200 is not a large increment. Since it all goes to the bottom line, it represents a large annual figure, even if only a portion of the attempts are successful. The focus might be to move

EXHIBIT 9–14

Mastering the basics of selling. Common sense advice from the Foundation of the Hospitality Sales and Marketing Association International's pamphlet entitled The Front Office: Turning Service into Sales.

Mastering the Basics of Selling

1. Impressing the Guests

- Maintain an appealing physical appearance, including good posture. Don't lean on or hang over the front desk. Bring to the job your own sense of spirit and style.
- Organize and keep the front desk area uncluttered.
- Get to know your property's every service and accommodation type thoroughly. Make frequent forays around the property to learn firsthand about each kind and category of room so that you can better describe the facilities to potential guests.
- Memorize or keep close at hand an up-to-date list of the locations and hours of operation of all food and beverage facilities; entertainment lounges; recreational and sports rooms; and banquet, meeting, exhibit, and other public areas.
- Learn the names and office locations of the general manager and all department heads, including directors of marketing, sales, catering, convention services, and food and beverages.
- Be friendly to guests, greeting them warmly and, whenever possible, by name and title. For instance, when requesting a bellman's service, ask him to take ''Mr. Smith to room 340.'' (To ensure the guest's privacy, be discreet in mentioning the room number to the bellman.) Call the bellman by name as well.
- Give guests your undivided attention.
- Answer all questions completely, but concisely and accurately, based on your in-depth knowledge of hotel operations. Refrain from boasting about accommodations and services; instead, offer simple, to-the-point descriptions of features.
- Assume a polite, patient manner in explaining the various options available—for example, the size of rooms, kinds of reservations (confirmed or guaranteed), and the terms ''American,'' ''European,'' or ''modified American'' plan.

2. Winning the Guests

- Expand prospects' accommodations horizons with descriptions of the room and service possibilities awaiting them. Potential guests may think of a hotel as simply a building filled with bedrooms, but you know better. So inform them about rooms with views, rooms near the health spa, twin-bed rooms, suites, rooms furnished according to a certain historical period, or ultra-modern accommodations with Jacuzzis. Lay everything out for prospects, dwelling on the positive, distinctive appeals of each choice. Throw in the tempting intangibles associated with each type of room; for instance, the prestige of having a room on the same floor as the hotel's exclusive club for special guests, or the pleasure of staying in a room equipped with a VCR or a fireplace.
- Attempt to sell a room to suit the client. Observe people and try to read their particular hankerings. If a guest is new to the hotel, a room with a nice view might be impressive. Business travelers might prefer a quiet room at the back. Guests with children, people staying for an extended visit, honeymooners, and celebrities are among those who might be interested in suites.
- Sell the room, not the rate. If a guest asks flat out for rates, avoid quoting a minimum or just one rate; instead, offer a range, portraying in detail the difference in accommodations that each rate affords.
- Should a prospect look unsure or reluctant to book a room, suggest that the guest accompany a hotel employee on a walk-through. A tour of the premises gives guests a chance to settle any doubts they might have and demonstrates the hotel's policy of good will and flexibility.
- Keep abreast of special sales promotions, weekend packages, and other marketing strategies, and dangle these offerings to prospects. (To make sure you're informed, you might ask your sales department to hold regularly scheduled presentations to front-office staff on their latest schemes.)
- Look for opportunities to extend the sale—there are many. If a guest mentions that he or she is hungry or arrives around mealtime, promote the hotel's dining facilities; if a guest arrives late, talk up the entertainment lounge or room service. As the person most in contact with guests throughout their stays, you are in the enviable position of being able to please both your guest and hotel management. You can delight guests merely by drawing their attention to the multitude of services your hotel offers, whether it's quick dry cleaning or a leisurely massage. And you can thrill the boss by advancing a sale and hotel revenues through your promotion of in-house features.

(continued)

EXHIBIT 9–14

Concluded

---

3. Wooing the Guests
- When a guest arrives, upgrade the reservation to a more luxurious accommodation whenever availability allows, ask whether the guest would like to make a dinner reservation, and ask whether he or she would like a wake-up call.
- Record and follow through on all wake-up call requests.
- Deliver mail and messages promptly.
- Avoid situations that keep guests waiting. For instance, if you're unable to locate a guest's reservation and a line is beginning to form on the other side of the counter, assume the hotel has plenty of the desired accommodations available and go ahead and book the guest. Finish registering anyone else who is waiting, and then search for the missing reservation.
- Should mishaps occur, whether a reservation mix-up or a housekeeping error, handle the matter with aplomb without laying the blame on any individual employee or department.
- Dispatch each departing guest with a favorable impression of the hotel. In other words, treat the guest with care and courtesy during check-out. Regardless of whether guests enjoyed their stay, they will remember only the hassles experienced at check-out if you allow them to occur. Therefore, don't. That is, be sure there are useful, comprehensive procedures for dealing with guests who dispute postings and payments, and follow those procedures with assurance and professionalism.

---

the commercial guest from standard service to a concierge floor. The weekend shopper of that commercial hotel needs a different approach. This discretionary buyer may turn away if the rates quoted at check-in fail to reflect the package plan originally booked at the time of reservation.

Each guest looks at the incremental dollars differently. And so does the employee. Management must be cognizant that the basic rate and the incremental up-sell are not modest to employees working for an hourly wage. Part of the training must attend to the employee's frame of reference. Having some type of incentive plan for the employee does help change attitudes.

Incentives to Up-Sell.   Motivated room clerks are better selling tools than cut rates and giveaways. They are less expensive too, even with an incentive-pay plan. And it takes a good incentive plan coupled with proper training to make the system work.

Incentive systems stimulate interest and emphasize the goals that management has enunciated. Rewards are especially important during heavy discounting periods when guests know that low rates are available and their resistance is high. Unlike some other places of the world, American clerks do not share in any mandatory service charge. A special cash pool is needed for incentive distributions.

Incentive systems require an accurate and easily computed formula. Flat goals can be established, or the focus can be on improvement from last year, or last month, or last week for that matter. Most front-office incentives are keyed to Average Daily Rate. Occupancy is a factor in total revenue, which suggests other bases for setting goals.

Most systems establish a pool that is shared by the team. Individual competition is restricted to the clerks, but selling up is a function of the reservation office, the telephone operators, the bellpersons, and others. That's why the team pool, with its spinoff in morale and teamwork, is preferred.

The cash pool is generated from a percentage—say, 10 percent— of room sales that exceed projections. Management projects either the total room sales or the Average Daily Rate. Management projections might be based on the ideal room rate (Exhibit 9–12) or the budget forecast. If actual sales exceed target sales, the bonus

Exhibit 9–15

Curve A represents a normal (elastic) demand curve. As the room rate is reduced, room demand increases. The leisure market is generally considered an elastic market. Conversely, corporate travelers are usually thought to be inelastic (represented by Curve B). Corporate travelers make reservations based on their need for a room on a given date; they are little concerned about the room rate.

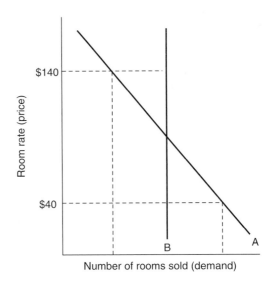

becomes payable. The bonus period is important. It must be long enough to reflect the true efforts of the team but short enough to bring the rewards within grasp.

Measuring the higher room sales attributable to the incentive system requires a standard—a yardstick—by which success can be computed. A trend line for previous periods or the full rack rate can be used. Then the measure is a ratio of actual total room sales to maximum revenues at full rack rates.

Elasticity of Demand.   Until quite recently, the lodging industry has considered the number of rooms sold—room occupancy—as the measure of success. It did so because room demand was thought to be inelastic, not sensitive to price changes (see Exhibit 9–15). The supposition was supported by actual experience. Room income (occupancy multiplied by Average Daily Rate) actually rose during the low occupancy periods of the past decade because increased room rates did not drive away significant amounts of sales (occupancy). It did not, goes the reasoning, because room demand is inelastic.

Elasticity is the degree of demand resulting from changes in price. Large demand changes that result from price changes mean that demand is elastic; no changes mean the demand is inelastic. Rate reductions in an elastic market generate new business; rate reductions in an inelastic market do not. The hotel industry has always believed that reductions in rate produce less new business than is lost from lowering the unit price, thereby suggesting that room demand is somewhat inelastic.

Elasticity of demand for hotel rooms is exceedingly complex. An inelastic property can actually increase rates during an economic slump with profitable results. Rate changes can be disastrous—or very beneficial—depending on the elasticity of demand and the direction of change chosen by management.

Different markets have different degrees of sensitivity. Tour properties are more elastic, and commercial demand is more inelastic. Hotels experience different degrees of elasticity throughout the year. That is what the demand pricing behind seasonal rates is all about. A given hotel may have numerous seasons throughout its annual cycle.

The industry began to rethink its position on inelastic markets during the first part of the 1980s. Hoteliers realized they were also retailers, and they moved toward incremental rates. Discounting, which swept the industry after it was introduced, meant that hotel executives were finally viewing their industry from a marketing perspective rather than from the traditional operational one. Thus, the rationale that selling a room for any price above the direct cost of the room (housekeeping, heat, linen, etc.) was better than leaving it vacant.

The change in the industry's approach to rate making between the 1970s and the 1990s was not a matter of smarter innkeepers. There was a very big change in customer profile, especially the appearance of the leisure market with its discretionary traveler. The airlines discovered price elasticity—it was a new market for them, too—after deregulation, and they set the direction for the hotel industry to follow. Both industries discovered that demand was elastic (for the leisure segment) and inelastic (for the business segment) for time as well as for price.

Elasticity in time and price is the fundamental on which yield management rests. But the success from discounting elastic markets could cloud the need to hold firm on rates directed toward inelastic markets. Dangerous spillover of discounting to the inelastic business market could undermine the whole rate structure.

Time–price elasticity differs with each group. Discretionary buyers are unlikely to risk a night without a room. Business buyers, who have little lead time, do not need a price inducement for last-minute shopping.

Rate-Cutting.   According to many industry experts, there is a distinct difference between rate-cutting and discounting. Rate-cutting functions in an inelastic market. Unwarranted rate cuts generate new business for one property only by luring the customer away from another property. Discounting attracts new customers to the industry, benefiting all properties. Discounting seeks out the stay-at-home customer, the visit-friends-or-family customer, and the let's-camp-out customer. Rate-cutting aims at the guest across the road or down the boulevard.

Competitors, who are the source of the new business, counter with rate cuts, and the price war is on. A decline in price per room and in gross sales, rather than the hoped-for increase in occupancy, is the net result. Some resort localities outlaw price wars by making it a misdemeanor to post rates outside the establishment. Printed rate schedules are permitted; it is advertising on the marquee that is not allowed. Conversely, other communities actually require room rates to be posted outside the property. In such cases, the lowest and highest posted room rates on the marquee establish the rate parameters the customer can expect to pay. This reduces the unsavory practice of ''sizing-up'' the walk-in guest before quoting a room rate.

The real test is whether the plan brings new guests to hotels or whether it diverts existing business from other hotels, with benefit accruing only to the bargain-hunting guest.

The long list of special rates proves that not all rate variations are viewed as rate-cutting. Perhaps they must merely stand the test of time. The family plan, in which all children roomed with their parents are accommodated without charge, caused dissension when it first appeared (Exhibit 9–6). It is today a legitimate business builder. So, too, is the free room given to convention groups for every 50 or 100 paid rooms. Like any good sales inducement, special rates should create new sales, not make the product available at a lower price. For once sold at a lower rate, it is almost impossible to get the buyer to pay the original price.

Once established, rates are not easily adjusted. Increases must be undertaken slowly if they are not to affect patronage. It does not matter that the rate was too low to begin with. Rate reductions will bring no complaints if the initial rates were too high. Opening with rates that are too high may do devastating damage before the adjustment is made. Excessive rates create bad word-of-mouth advertising that takes time and costly sales promotions to counteract.

Bed Taxes.   Another rate component over which hotel managers have little or no control is local lodging taxes. Also known as bed, room, or hotel taxes, these guest charges often provide significant revenues for the local municipality. Operating with increasingly tight budgets, cities are lured into the easy money available from taxing out-of-towners. After all, it appears politically correct to increase the tax revenue base without actually raising the taxes charged to local citizens.

But the reality of the situation is not so straightforward. Several concerns are not initially apparent. First is the ethical debate. Many antagonists of the hotel tax believe it is wrong to charge out-of-town visitors for city services and improvements that are not tourism-related. For example, how can one justify charging a bed tax that's earmarked for improving and building new schools and local sports field complexes? The visitor clearly does not benefit from the taxes paid—it is taxation without representation.

Secondly, several sophisticated studies have demonstrated that an increased lodging tax actually hurts the local economy. More revenue may be lost in other taxes than is actually gained in room tax. For example, New York City, with the highest lodging tax in America (currently an effective 16.25 percent rate) has suffered a decrease in convention business by as much as 30 percent. With 30 percent fewer convention visitors, that's 30 percent fewer purchases of souvenirs, arts and crafts, meals and drinks, clothing, and related purchases. Each of these purchases generates tax revenue (sales tax) in its own right. Therefore, an increase in the lodging tax can have negative repercussions—a decrease in related sales tax revenues.

How Much Is Too Much?   Although the individual traveler rarely considers the lodging tax rate when deciding where to stay, group business is becoming increasingly conscious of this premium charged against the room rate. A carefully negotiated room rate seems inconsequential when the city slaps an additional 21.25 percent lodging tax. (At one point, New York City's lodging tax was 21.25 percent, based on a $100 per night room rate.)

At some point, the bed tax rate becomes a deterrent to marketing a given city. Rates in the 10 to 12 percent range are probably acceptable to most consumers (the average lodging tax rate in the United States is 10.3 percent and is projected to reach 11.0 percent within a few years). However, rates above, say, 14 percent may be too high for certain groups and individuals. Cities such as Chicago, Columbus, Houston, and Los Angeles all have bed taxes in the 14 to 15 percent range (see Exhibit 9–16).

EXHIBIT 9–16

Shown are the five US cities with the highest hotel occupancy taxes.

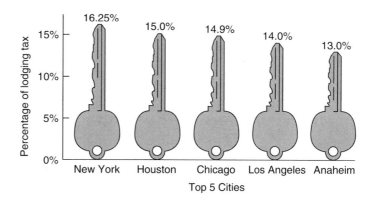

The trend may be changing, however. More and more hotel managers are joining together to battle rising bed taxes in their cities. By forming one cohesive and vocal group, hotel managers represent a formidable opponent to city councils bent on raising the tax. And with the domino effect that develops when fewer visitors come to the city, it is not difficult to garner additional support from local merchants.

Summary

A proper room rate is as much a marketing tool as it is a financial instrument. That's because the room rate needs to be low enough to attract customers while at the same time high enough to earn a reasonable profit. Easier said than done. Even in this day of sophisticated computer technology, calculating the room rate still involves plenty of guesswork and gut instincts. There is an unquantifiable psychology involved in the room rate. An attractive rate for one person may appear to be too high or too low to another guest. For some, high rates suggest a pretentious operation; for others, a low rate suggests poor quality.

Searching and working towards the perfect rate is difficult, indeed. Even after the rate has been determined and established, it is immediately changed. Rates fluctuate by season, they change according to room type, they vary with special guest discounts, and they shift as a function of yield management.

Although there are some well-established methods for calculating the proper rate, these should never be used to the exclusion of common sense and market demand. The Hubbart Room Rate Formula and the Building Cost Rate Formula are two of the most common means for determining the rate. In addition, the Ideal Average Room Rate Formula adds a dimension of retrospection to understanding the appropriateness of a rate in terms of the local marketplace.

Queries and Problems

1. Assume the ideal average room rate for a given property is $87.25. Month after month, however, the hotel consistently outperforms its ideal average room rate by at least $5 to $10. You are the general manager of the property, and you know you can extract much information from this data. Based on the fact that the hotel's actual ADR is consistently higher than its ideal average room rate, what do you know about the front-office staff's ability to sell rooms? What do you know about the price sensitivity of your customers? And what do you know about rate tendencies in the surrounding marketplace? Armed with this data, what type of action might you now consider?

2. Up-selling at the front desk is paramount to enhancing hotel profitability. Yet up-selling also has the potential to cause the guest discomfort and to appear pushy or aggressive. There is a fine line between professionally up-selling the room and appearing as if you are ''hustling'' the guest. How might you attempt to up-sell each of the following types of guests? Acting as the front-desk clerk, prepare a professional up-selling dialogue for each of these situations:

a. Standing before you is an executive on your corporate-discount plan. He is stretching and yawning from a hard day of air travel and local meetings.

b. About to check in is a mother with her three young children. She is alone—her husband doesn't arrive until tomorrow. The kids are obviously excited about the prospects of swimming and running around the courtyard.

c. Two gentlemen from a recently arrived bus tour are standing in front of you. Even though the rest of the tour group is housed in standard double queen rooms, these men are commenting that their room is much too small.

d. A female executive with an extended-stay reservation is currently checking in. She comments on the fact that she must stay in your hotel for at least 10 days. How can she possibly survive 10 days away from home?

3. A commercial hotel offers a deeply discounted rate on Friday, Saturday, and Sunday nights. Discuss what should be done or said in each of the following situations:

a. A guest arrives on Saturday but makes no mention of the special rate and seems unaware of the discount possibilities. The desk clerk charges full rack rate. On check-out Monday morning, the cashier notices the full rate charged for two nights, but the guest (after reviewing her folio) says nothing.

b. The situation is the same as that above in (*a*), but this time the guest does comment that she thought a discounted rate might apply.

c. A corporate guest stays Wednesday through Wednesday on company business. He receives a slightly discounted commercial rate for all seven nights, but his rate is still much higher than the special weekend rate available to anyone off the street. He knows about the special rate and asks that his three weekend nights be reduced accordingly.

d. Create a fourth scenario of your own.

4. Explain why hoteliers differentiate between discounting practices and rate-cutting. Create a list of similarities and differences between discounting and rate-cutting. Then conclude whether you believe they are substantially different activities or really two different statements for describing the exact same practice?

5. The Hubbart Room Rate Formula calls for an average room rate that will cover expenses and provide a fair return to the investors. Compute that rate from the abbreviated but complete set of data that follows:

Investment (also fair market value)	
Land	$ 3,000,000
Building	25,000,000
Furniture and equipment	6,000,000
Nonappropriated expenses, such as	
advertising, repairs, etc.	$ 1,200,000
Income from all operating departments	
except rooms, net of losses	$ 3,200,000
Rooms available for sale	563
Nonoperating expenses, such as	
insurance, taxes, and depreciation	510,000
Desired return on investment	16%
Interest on debt of $25,000,000	14%
Percentage of occupancy	71%

6. Using the data from problem 5, compute what the typical room charge should be according to the Building Cost Rate Formula.

Notes

1. *The Hubbart Formula for Evaluating Rate Structures of Hotel Rooms,* 1952, is available from the American Hotel & Motel Association, 888 Seventh Avenue, New York, New York 10019, and is used here with the Association's permission.

2. Used with permission.

SECTION IV

The Hotel Revenue Cycle

The lodging industry demonstrates maturity in its daily accounting practices. Unlike other functions of the rooms division, where change prevails and the landscape of the future looks quite different from yesteryear, basic accounting systems have changed little in these past decades. Indeed, a true characteristic of maturity is understanding the importance of keeping in place those practices proven over time.

Other than the introduction of automation to the city ledger, it has changed little over time. The basic categories of the city ledger remain the same: The customary 30-day billing cycle is still the standard, and credit collections are as much a function of human nature and the economy as ever before.

It is the same story with the transient ledger. Computer automation aside, the basic functions of the transient ledger remain unchanged. The buckets (and their associated hard-copy folios) have given way to internal computer memory. Telephoned room billing information requests from departmental cashiers to the front desk have given way to software interfaces between the property management system and point-of-sale terminals. And manual postings of guest charges have given way to automated electronic posting.

Cash-handling systems have matured even as cash becomes less common in lodging operations. Today, the lodging industry is less preoccupied with cash—especially in the corporate markets—than ever before. Credit cards and other city ledger transactions are growing in importance as cash and cash equivalents (such as traveler's checks and bank checks) decline in use. Bank and prepaid hotel debit cards, poised for rapid growth a decade ago, have actually shown little sizzle in the hotel industry. Yet as cash and checks become less common, fraudulent scams will be easier to perpetrate. Hotel cashiers, with little experience handling cash and checks, will be likely targets for the maturing white-collar criminals.

Billing the
Guest Ledger

Chapter Outline

There's a tempo, a rhythm, to the flow of guests through the hotel. Reservations sounds the first beat, then comes the arrival and registration procedure, followed by the stay and the eventual departure. Between check-in and check-out, guests enjoy the facilities of the hotel. That's what the hotel business is all about. Hotels sell rooms, food, beverage, and minor-department services such as telephone and laundry.

Because they register on arrival, customers (guests) are known to the hotel-keeper. Consequently, the sale of services can be consummated without an immediate monetary payment. The hotel simply charges the guest's bill for the service rendered. Hoteliers call that bill a *folio*.

The guest's folio—an accurate and current statement of how much the guest owes the hotel—is available at the front desk on demand. Whereas other businesses send their customers monthly statements, the hotel statement is ready on a moment's notice, even though the exact time of departure is unknown. Indeed, even the day of departure is often uncertain.

Hotels have evolved a system that can bring forth an accurate folio without delay. After all, the hotel is as anxious as the guest to have a ready and accurate bill. Incorrectly charged items delay the check-out procedure and create ill feelings.

Charges not on the folio statement are difficult to collect after the guest has departed. Collecting late charges by mail after the guest has checked out of the hotel is expensive and often causes additional ill feelings.

Accounts Receivable

Most commerce is carried on without immediate payment. Businesses buy and sell to one another without a direct exchange of money. Payment is delayed until a more convenient time in order to carry out the sale as quickly as possible. Hotels work that way as well. Guests are not disturbed during their sleep in order to collect for the price of the room. Instead, the guest is charged for the room and the collection is made later, usually at check-out time. During the period between the sale (the charge to the guest) and the payment (on departure), the guest owes the hotel and is known as an **account receivable.**[1]

Types of Accounts Receivable

Hotels have two types of accounts receivable. Guests who have outstanding balances with the hotel and are currently staying in the hotel are called *transient guests*—transient accounts receivable. Another class of accounts receivable is *city guests*—city accounts receivable—persons or companies that have outstanding balances with the hotel but are not registered guests (not presently occupying sleeping rooms).

Guests can and do change status from transient to city and even occasionally from city to transient. Accounts are sometimes maintained in each category. A transfer takes place, for example, when a transient guest settles the outstanding account by using a credit card at check-out. The debt is still owed, but the guest is no longer in the hotel. The transient debt owed by the guest has become a city ledger debt owed by the credit-card company.

The Ledger.   There are many guests in each of the two categories. In hotels as large as those in Exhibit 1–1 (the Luxor Hotel), there might be 5,000 guests or more, with 2,000 to 3,000 folios. Accountants call the aggregate of individual accounts receivable a *ledger.* The folios of transient guests—registered guests—are grouped together in the **transient ledger;** the folios of city guests—nonregistered guests—are grouped together in the **city ledger.** Terminology and timing are the chief differences between the ledgers.

The Transient Ledger.   *Transient ledger* is shorthand for the transient accounts receivable ledger. Hotel employees use other professional jargon to identify this transient ledger. Because the ledger is kept at the front office for easy access as registered guests come and go, it is often called the *front-office ledger.* Since it is comprised of registered guests, **guest ledger** is another frequently used term. By extension, the transient folio (the individual guest account) is called the *guest folio,* the *front-office folio,* the **account card,** or the **guest bill.** Room rates are the largest source of charges to guests' folios, so **rooms ledger** is still another term for the group of transient folios.

The City Ledger.   There are numerous subcategories of the city ledger (see Chapter 12), but there is but one general term: *city ledger.* That makes city ledger terminology easier to remember than the variety of labels used for the transient ledger (guest, front-office, or rooms ledger).

Other than the terminology and location (the city ledger is kept by the accounting office), timing is the chief difference between the ledgers. Charges are **posted** (recorded) immediately to the transient ledger, since the bill may be rendered at any time. City guests, having established credit in advance, are billed periodically. This permits some delay in posting charges. Like many other businesses, city accounts are billed monthly unless the nature of the charge calls for an earlier billing. To accommodate these variations in time, each ledger differs in form and in the posting–billing procedure.

What Is and Isn't Accounted For.   Each folio is the record of an account receivable, a statement about a guest with a debt to the hotel. Since folios deal with accounts receivable only, persons who pay cash for services received, as they might in a bar or restaurant, are not part of the front-office billing procedure. It makes no difference whether the person paying cash in the restaurant or bar is a stranger, a city ledger guest, or a registered guest. Those who pay cash are not accounts receivable! Hence, there is no front-office billing for them.

A hotel can sell services to its registered guest under three different categories: for cash (in the bar, for example); as a transient account receivable guest (for an occupied room posted to the front-office folio); or as a city charge (restaurant purchase, for example) when payment is made with a credit card. (The credit-card company, which now owes the debt, is not a registered guest). Only charges for services to transient guests involve billing at the front office.[2]

Two accounting events take place when transient guests buy services from the hotel: (1) debts are created by the guests for themselves, and (2) incomes (or sales) are earned by the hotel for the services rendered. Room sales, food sales, beverage sales, and telephone sales are the most common incomes. Eventually, the guest will leave and a third accounting activity will take place: (3) the settlement of the debt.

Recording Charges.   Familiarization with accounting and with its system of debits and credits assists the posting clerk (cashier) and the night auditor in carrying out their jobs. A knowledge of debits and credits is especially helpful in understanding how front-office records (the transient ledger) interface with back-office records (the city ledger). Unfortunately, many front-office staffers lack even a rudimentary knowledge of the subject. Therefore, front-office forms and other internal records are designed to ensure accuracy even if the staff is not accounting literate.

Debits and Credits.   Accounting language speaks of debits and credits. Meaningless in themselves, debits and credits represent the manner in which accountants increase and decrease the values of certain records. Some persons find it helpful to visualize the debit as the left side of a T-shaped account and the credit as the right side:

Account Receivable	
Debit	Credit

The format of some front-office bills may even reflect that design (see Exhibit 10–1).

EXHIBIT 10–1

Shown is a computerized folio. Visualize a ''T'' by focusing on the charges (debit) column as the left side and the credits column on the right. Mentally, draw the horizontal arm. Also note the folio heading, arrival and departure times (bottom of the page), and the final entry, which involves a direct billing to the sponsoring organization.

Daytona Beach
Hilton
Resort

2637 S. Atlantic Avenue
Daytona Beach. Florida 32118
904-767-7350

DB

			In	Out	Folio
Name:	VALLEN, JEROME	MR.	10/25–10/28/9		12977
				Rate 59.00	PAGE 1 A
Address:					Room 621

SECOND AVE.
DAYTONA BEACH, FL   02115   DRACDI
DABHINFXXOCT28A6NR   BEL   TRAVEL AGENCY

Date	Description	I D	Ref. No.	Charges	Credits	Balance
10/25/9	ISLANDER 01	XAQ	419354	9.00		
10/25/9	VID-COM	XAQ	E3	8.43		
10/25/9	VID-COM	XAQ	E5	8.43		
10/25/9	ROOM	XAP	621	59.00		
10/26/9	201-595-7796	XAQ	18:18	3.36		
10/26/9	VID-COM	XAQ	E5	8.43		
10/26/9	ROOM	XAP	621	59.00		
10/27/9	ISLANDER 01	XAQ	419995	19.62		
10/27/9	ROOM	XAP	621	59.00		
10/28/9	SUNROOM CAFE 01	XAQ	814544	7.31		
10/28/9	DIRECT BILL	BEL			241.58	
10/28/9	C/O TIME 08:16	BEL		.00		
10/28/9	DIRECT BILL	BEL			241.58-	
10/28/9	ADJUST MOVIE	BEL			8.43	
10/28/9	ADJUST PHONE	BEL			3.36	
10/28/9	DIRECT BILL	BEL			229.79	.00

Checked In 07:16 pm TDO   Checked Out 08:16 am BEL
CR: OT: AB: R:N HH: AL: A#:

Guest *Jerome J. Vallen*

Firm   Address

City   State   Zip

Rates do not include applicable sales. occupancy or other taxes.

Transfer to credit ledger
I agree that my liability for this bill is not waived and agree to be held personally liable in the event that the indicated person. company or association fails to pay for any part or the full amount of these charges.

Guest Signature

Courtesy: Daytona Beach Hilton Resort, FL.

Assets.   Under some circumstances, debits increase value and credits decrease value. Such is the case with a business's *assets*. An asset is something a business owns. Hotels own many assets: buildings, land, autos, kitchen equipment, and so on. Two assets are especially important to the front office: cash (money), and debts (accounts receivable) owed to the hotel.

Hotels show an increase to their cash holdings by debiting their cash accounts. Paying out cash requires hotels to decrease their cash—hence, a cash credit. The rules are: debits increase assets, and credits decrease assets.

The same holds true for the accounts receivable asset. When guests owe the hotel, the asset grows large, so we debit accounts receivable. As guests settle their folios, the asset, accounts receivable, is reduced, so we credit accounts receivable. The same rules apply: debits increase assets, and credits decrease assets.

Incomes.   *Incomes* (or sales) operate just the opposite from assets. That is, debits decrease incomes and credits increase incomes. The hotel's front office is concerned with many incomes, but they all follow the same debit/credit rule. When rooms income, food income, beverage income, telephone income, golf income, laundry income, valet income, and so on are earned—that is, when a sale is made—income is increased. Increasing income means crediting the specific income.

Sometimes, an income is decreased, as it is when a room that was charged to the guest (credit income) is complimented. The original income credit must be washed out, because no room charge is being made after all, and that takes a debit. The rules are: debits decrease incomes, and credits increase incomes.

Equality of Debits and Credits.   Each accounting event has two parts. For example, two things happen when a guest signs the bar tab, charging it to the room folio: The guest (an account receivable asset) owes the hotel more, and bar sales (income) has also increased. Apply the rules: To increase an asset, debit; to increase an income, credit. Thus, an accounting entry with two parts has been created. This system of *double entry* accounting always requires equal dollar amounts of debits and credits for each accounting event.

If the same guest paid the bar bill with cash (money), the entry is debit cash (to increase an asset, debit) and credit bar sales (to increase sales [or income], credit). Of course, such an entry would *not* pass through the front-office folio because the folio is an account receivable (the guest owes the hotel), and a cash sale does not involve accounts receivable.

Another example involves a departing guest who settles the unpaid folio at check-out time. As a result of charges to the folio—nightly room sales, or the bar charge just discussed—the guest is an account receivable. Accounts receivable are assets owned by the hotel and are, therefore, debits. Because the guest settles the account with cash, the hotel's cash increases (debit cash). The guest's account receivable decreases (credit accounts receivable).

Three rules of accounting have been met by this entry. The double entry is in balance: equal debits and credits. The two rules of assets have been adhered to: to increase an asset (cash), debit; to decrease an asset (accounts receivable), credit. The accuracy of every accounting entry can be verified by checking for three rules: (1) equality, and the proper rule of (2) debit and (3) credit.

EXHIBIT 10–2

These are components of a microcomputer installation: inputs (full-sized keyboard and 3 1/2-inch disk drive); outputs (video display terminal [VDT], 3 1/2-inch disk, and a printer [not shown]); and a central processing unit (CPU). This microcomputer is one of several linked together to form a Local Area Network (LAN).

Courtesy: Lodgistix, Inc., Wichita, Kansas.

The Individual Account Receivable

The transient (front-office) ledger contains a host of individual accounts receivable. Various names have already been suggested to identify these individual receivables: Folio, bill, guest account, guest account card, and guest bill are the most common. *Visitor's account* is the European version.

Location of the Folio.   Modern hotels have adopted computerized folios almost without exception. These computerized bills (Exhibit 10–1) are maintained in electronic memory and are visible only when printed. Therefore, only input/output devices (see Exhibit 10–2) are needed at the front desk. Older, handprepared, pencil-and-paper folios (see Exhibit 10–3) have to be physically stored at the front desk for immediate accessibility. That requires a good deal of valuable front-office space.

Whether electronic or handprepared, guest ledger folios are the responsibility of the front-office cashier (Exhibit 3–1). Handprepared folios generated such a large quantity of paper at the front desk that a billing clerk or posting clerk was often required to support the cashier. As this chapter explains later on, much of the posting is done now by computer terminals in the various food and beverage outlets. The result is fewer desk employees and fewer errors.

Number of Folios.   The size of the hotel determines the number of folios, more or less. Essentially, there is one for each room. There are exceptions, of course: Two friends sharing one room might request two folios, and a family occupying several rooms may need but one.

EXHIBIT 10–3

This and the following page illustrate handprepared, pencil-and-paper folios. (Refer to this illustration again at page 271, where the text explains two types of transfers: Room 407's credit is a transient ledger-to-transient ledger transfer; and room 409 is a transient ledger-to-city ledger transfer.)

ROOM NO.	409								E69080

m M/m Art E. Fishal
86 Bates Boulevard
Hitchcock, Texas 01020

ARRIVED	RATE	PERSONS	COT	REG. CARD #	PREV. INV. #	CLERK
12/23/	78	2	N/A	69080	N/A	SB

DATE	12/23/		12/24/															
BROUGHT FORWARD			84	24														
ROOM	78	–																
TAX	6	24																
RESTAURANT																		
''																		
TELEPHONES–LOCAL																		
–LONG DISTANCE																		
TELEGRAMS																		
LAUNDRY & VALET																		
CASH ADVANCES																		
''																		
NEWSPAPERS																		
TRANSFERS from 407 #69081			84	24														
TOTAL DEBIT	84	24	168	48														
CASH																		
ALLOWANCES																		
CITY LEDGER																		
ADVANCE DEPOSITS																		
CREDIT CARDS			168	48														
TRANSFERS																		
BALANCE FORWARD	84	24	–															

ALL ACCOUNTS ARE DUE WHEN RENDERED

(continued)

EXHIBIT 10–3

Concluded

ROOM NO.	407						E69081

m _BENNY FISHAL_
12345 Education Avenue
Reading, Pennsylvania 98765

ARRIVED	RATE	PERSONS	COT	REG. CARD #	PREV. INV. #	CLERK
12/23/	78	2	N/A	69081	N/A	SB

DATE	12/23/		12/24/													
BROUGHT FORWARD			84 24													
ROOM	78	–														
TAX	6	24														
RESTAURANT																
"																
TELEPHONES-LOCAL																
-LONG DISTANCE																
TELEGRAMS																
LAUNDRY & VALET																
CASH ADVANCES																
"																
NEWSPAPERS																
TRANSFERS																
TOTAL DEBIT	84	24	84	24												
CASH																
ALLOWANCES																
CITY LEDGER																
ADVANCE DEPOSITS																
CREDIT CARDS																
TRANSFERS to 409	#69080		84	24												
BALANCE FORWARD	84	24	—													

ALL ACCOUNTS ARE DUE WHEN RENDERED

The number of city ledger accounts is not determined by the number of rooms. In pre-credit-card days, large hotels had thousands of city ledger accounts—individuals and companies who wanted credit privileges with the hotel. Not so today, when almost everyone carries a national credit card. Now, the bulk of the city ledger can be accounted for in a half-dozen national credit-card accounts.

Two hard copies of the folio are printed on demand.[3] Usually, that takes place only once, when the guest checks out. One or both copies may be given to the departing customer. If a hard copy isn't needed, the folio can be viewed by the clerk on a front-desk monitor or by the guest on the television set in the room.

Master Accounts.   Tour operating companies, trade associations, conventions, and single entity groups incur charges that are not billable to any one individual. Business expenses such as these are billed to another folio called a **master account.** Master accounts allow group charges to be distinguished from personal charges. The master account is its own person, much like a business corporation has a legal identity separate from that of its individual owners. Master accounts are not city ledger accounts. So long as the group is in the hotel, its master account is a standard guest folio at the front office. Master accounts are often transferred to the city ledger for direct billing after the group has departed.

Decisions about master account billing are made well in advance of the group's arrival. The hotel and the organization settle sales and credit terms as part of the group contract. How the charges are distributed is decided by the group, not the hotel. A business company holding a sales meeting might have all the charges of every delegate billed to the master account. A convention has individual convention delegates responsible for room and personal charges, but the association covers banquet costs, cocktail parties, and meeting expenses. Costs such as these and rooms for visiting speakers are charged to the convention's master account.

Tour groups do just the opposite. The master folio covers all the room charges and whatever meals were included in the tour price. No individual room rate postings are made. Personal expenditures (bar drinks, greens fees, etc.) not offered by the tour package are charged to the guest's personal folio.

Each group and association has its own way of doing things. That makes for numerous variations in master account billing. Under one plan, the full room rate for everyone is included on the master folio, which the company pays. Another might include only the single rate. Then delegates with attending spouses would be charged the spread between single rate and double rate on their individual folios.

A flat dollar allowance per room is another modification. Onto the master folio goes a per diem allowance that includes any type of charge (room, meals, bar). Charges that exceed the lump-sum figure are entered on the personal folio. Additional complications arise from American plan billing, from compulsory service charges, and from room-based taxes.

Large companies and affiliated allied members are among the attendees of most conventions or trade shows. They cover the expenses of their own staffs with a master account, which is separate altogether from the master account of the group putting on the event. The hotel will have numerous, unrelated master accounts to track. Posted to these accounts are the expenses of the affiliated companies for cocktail parties and host suites, and even meals provided for the total convention by the sponsoring affiliate. Such sponsorship is an accepted means of public relations for the allied members.

Those responsible for the master accounts might settle the bill at check-out. More frequently, it is transferred to the city ledger and settled by mail and telephone over the next 30 days. Chapter 12 resumes the discussion at the point of transfer.

Split Billing.   The distribution of the charges between the master account and the guest's personal folio is called *split billing* or *split folios*. Both the master folio (often called the A folio) and the guest or B folio are standardized forms of the types illustrated throughout the chapter. A and B are used merely to distinguish the group entity from the individual person. The A folio is the major folio where the large charges of the association, tour company, or business are posted. Sometimes, the hotel itself is the A folio. Such is the case with casino comps and frequent-stay customers.

Casino Comps.   Casino hotels sometimes provide complimentary (free) accommodations to ''high rollers'' (big players). Split billing is used to account for the comps. To the A folio is posted all the charges that the hotel/casino will comp. Depending on the size of the guest's credit line, the comp could be for room only, or for room, food, beverage, and telephone. Even the airfare might be reimbursed. Items not covered are posted to the B folio, which the guest pays at departure.

Preferred-Guest Programs.   Preferred guest (or frequent traveler) programs employ the flexibility of split billing. Two different folios are opened when a guest turns in frequent-traveler points. The full rate of the room is charged on the A folio. On departure, the guest pays the nonroom charges, which have been posted to the B folio. The A folio is transferred to the city ledger, and either the parent company or the franchisor is billed. According to the frequent-traveler contract, one of these is now the account receivable obligated to pay the room charge.

The actual amount paid to the hotel under the preferred-guest program is always less than the rate quoted to the guest. Most programs pay full rack rate only if the occupancy of the hotel is above a given figure—90 percent perhaps. Below that figure—and the hotel is usually below that figure—the program reimburses the participating hotel for the operational expenses: linen, labor, and energy. So the reimbursement may be set anywhere from $20 to $30. No provision is made for recovering fixed costs such as taxes, interest, or fair wear and tear.

The burden falls heaviest on resorts. Where else would one expect the frequent traveler to use the points—at the same corporate hotels where the points were originally accumulated? Or at a luxury resort near friends, relatives, or a relaxing destination? The burden of Preferred-Guest Program redemption is especially onerous to resorts if the program reimburses, as some do, on a sliding scale based on the previous month's Average Daily Rate. Resorts discount rooms during the off-season or the shoulder periods. This produces a low ADR. Yet the next month, when the season starts and when the frequent travelers cash in their points, the parent company reimburses on the basis of the previous month's low ADR.

Posting the Charges

Because the hotel identifies each arrival through the reservation and registration procedures, it extends credit—the right to charge—to its guests. This chapter is about registered guests (accounts receivable) who buy with the credit that the hotel has extended to them.

Front-office folios are the records of these accounts receivable. Charge sales made by guests appear on their individual folios. (Debit accounts receivable; credit sales.) Folios do not reflect sales made for cash, or sales made with a credit card in any of the hotel's bars, restaurants, or other outlets. Cash and credit cards can be used at check-out to settle the account receivable that arises from charge sales made in these outlets. (Debit cash; credit accounts receivable.)

Rooms is the only department that always sells on account. Room rates are posted nightly as part of the night audit. (Debit accounts receivable; credit room sales.) So the guest awakens to find the folio balance larger by the value of the night's stay plus tax. As with other departmental charges, cash and credit cards can be used later to settle the account receivable that arises from the room sale posting. (Debit cash; credit accounts receivable.)

Overview of the Billing Procedure

Widespread use of the electronic folio didn't become apparent until the mid-1980s. Pencil-and-paper folios were the norm during the previous half-century. Progress during that period focused on the development of better carbon paper and then on duplicating paper without messy carbon. Stationery companies were able to package forms with the carbon and carbonless paper and reduce the duplication required when rewriting information over and over again. The computer does much the same. It retains the information in memory and prints it again and again as needed.

Preparation of the Folio.   The folio is created when the guest arrives and registers. Modern computers format the folio from the registration data entered by the desk clerk as the arrival procedure is being completed. Pencil-and-paper systems require an additional step to copy reg card information to the folio. The name and address of the arriving party, the room number assigned, the number of persons in the party, arrival and departure dates, and the room rate are the essential bits of information recorded on the top of every folio.

Time of arrival (Exhibit 10–1); clerk's identifying initials and the group affiliation, including the number assigned for its identification (see Exhibit 10–4, right top, ACCT # 20539); the reservation confirmation number; the hotel's logo, address, and telephone/fax numbers; and more appear on most folios.

Folios are numbered sequentially as a means of accounting identification and internal control. Folio numbers usually appear on the upper right corner of the folio.

As society grows more litigious, information of all kinds is being added to the folio to protect the hotel from unwarranted lawsuits. Notice of the availability of a safe for the protection of the guest's valuables is one such disclaimer. This fits better on the registration card (Exhibits 8–5 and 8–6), which the guest sees on arrival, rather than on the folio, which the guest normally sees only at departure.

Nearly every folio now carries at the bottom of the page a statement about liability for the bill (Exhibit 10–4). With so many persons (employers, associations, credit-card companies) other than the guests accepting the charges, hotel lawyers want to make certain that eventually someone pays. The odd part about the statement is how rarely the guest is asked to sign it.

Filing the Folio.   Electronic folios are maintained in memory. Pencil-and-paper folios are filed in the cashier's work area in a file box called a **cashier's well, pit,**

EXHIBIT 10–4

A computer-prepared folio shows group affiliation and group identification number, 6566; the clerk's identification, #54; and the guest agreement for liability of the bill.

Radisson Hotel Ottawa Centre

100 Kent Street, Ottawa, Ontario, Canada K1P 5R7 Telephone (613) 238-1122

LA RONDE
FINE CUISINE

CAFE TOULOUSE

Lautrec's

ROOM / CHAMBRE	NAME / NOM	RATE / TAUX	DEPARTURE / DEPART	TIME / HEURE	ACCT #
2228	STEIN, FRANK N.	75.00	14/10/		20539

TYPE / STYLE	FIRM OR GROUP / COMPAGNIE OU GROUPE	PLAN	ARRIVAL / ARRIVÉE		GROUP
1K1A	AMERICAN		09/10/ 12:29		6566

CLERK COMMIS: 54

75 HARRIS
P.O. BOX 12   DB
LANSING MI 90125-0012
ADDRESS / ADRESSE

METHOD OF PAYMENT
MODE DE PAIEMENT

DATE	REFERENCE / RÉFÉRENCE	CHARGES	CREDITS / CRÉDITS	BALANCE DUE / SOLDE DÛ
09/10	ROOM 2228, 1	75.00		
09/10	ROOM TAX 2228, 1	3.75		
10/10	TOUL POS 000000	17.12		
10/10	LNG DIST 315-386-	.57		
10/10	ROOM 2228, 1	75.00		
10/10	ROOM TAX 2228, 1	3.75		
11/10	ROOM 2228, 1	75.00		
11/10	ROOM TAX 2228, 1	3.75		
12/10	LNG DIST 315-386-	1.14		
12/10	LNG DIST 315-386-	1.14		
12/10	ROOM 2228, 1	75.00		
12/10	ROOM TAX 2228, 1	3.75		
13/10	TOUL POS 000000	9.86		
13/10	TOUL POS 000000	16.58		
13/10	ROOM 2228, 1	75.00		
13/10	ROOM TAX 2228, 1	3.75		
				440.16

FIRM / COMPAGNIE   ADDRESS / ADRESSE

CITY
VILLE _____ PROV._____ POSTAL POSTALE _____

ATTENTION _____

GUEST SIGNATURE
SIGNATURE DU CLIENT   X _____

I AGREE THAT MY LIABILITY FOR THIS BILL IS NOT WAIVED AND AGREE TO BE HELD PERSONALLY LIABLE IN THE EVENT THAT THE INDICATED PERSON, COMPANY OR ASSOCIATION FAILS TO PAY FOR ANY PART OR THE FULL AMOUNT OF THESE CHARGES.

IL EST CONVENU QUE MA RESPONSABILITÉ DE CETTE FACTURE N'EST PAS ABROGÉE ET JE CONSENTS À L'ASSUMER DANS L'ÉVENTUALITÉ OÙ LA PERSONNE INDIQUÉE, SOCIÉTÉ OU ASSOCIATION REFUSE DE PAYER LE MONTANT EN TOTALITÉ OU EN PARTIE.

Courtesy: Radisson Hotel Ottawa Centre, Ottawa, Canada.

Exhibit 10–5

Shown is the cashier's well, pit, or bucket. It is used to segregate pencil-and-paper folios or other papers (vouchers) by sequential room number. Automated properties often use the bucket to separate and locate preprinted folios more readily.

or **bucket** (see Exhibit 10–5). Within the well, folios are separated by heavy cardboard dividers. Guest accounts are kept in room-number sequence because room numbers are the major means of guest identification, even more so than names.

Not all hotels have done away with the cashier's bucket. A need for filing paper information by room number still exists even with electronic systems. The section on communications, which follows, explains this.

Presenting the Bill.   Common law protects the innkeeper from fraud by requiring guests to prove a willingness and an ability to pay. Credit is, therefore, a privilege that management may revoke at any time. Nervous credit managers do just that whenever their suspicions are raised. The folio is printed and presented to the guest with a request for immediate payment. Even the traditional delay until the guest checks out is revoked. Motor hotels may go one step further by collecting in advance either in cash or with a signed credit-card voucher.

Since most guests are not credit risks, bills are normally presented and paid at check-out time. It works that way for the vast majority of guests who stay several nights. Long-term guests are billed weekly, and they are expected to make prompt payment. Irrespective of the length of stay, bills are also rendered whenever they reach a predetermined dollar amount established by management. The class of hotel, which reflects room rates and menu prices, determines the dollar figure of this ceiling. Using the same ceiling set by the credit-card company for that particular property simplifies the process. Credit-card companies also have limits on the amount that the individual guest can accrue. Charges over that figure void the hotel's protection and cause the credit manager to present the bill.

Communications.   A guest can buy and charge services as soon as the folio is open, even before going to the room. Although this was always possible, electronic communications has increased the speed and accuracy of the process. This portion of the chapter explains how it used to be done and how it is done now.

Exhibit 10–6

Shown is a portion of a departmental control sheet, where guest vouchers are hand-recorded (as a protection against their loss) before being dispatched to the front office for posting.

		DEPARTMENT CONTROL SHEET		
NAME			DATE	
VOUCHER NO.	ROOM NO.	GUEST NAME	AMOUNT	MEMO.
			$	

KAYCO NCR FORM NO. 118   **THIS REPORT MUST BE SENT TO NIGHT AUDITOR BY 12 O'CLOCK EACH NIGHT.**

Courtesy: Kayco Systems, Lake Elsinore, CA.

Guests buy services from dining rooms, bars, room service, newsstands, and so on. Every one of these services is delivered some distance from the front desk where the folio is maintained. Getting the information from the point of the sale to the front desk is critical to the accuracy and completeness of the billing process.

Before the Age of Electronics.   With a pencil-and-paper system, the communication between the department making the sale and the desk recording the sale depended on close cooperation and fast footwork. As an example, let us follow the sequence of a guest who eats breakfast in the coffee shop and signs the check. By so doing, the guest requests the coffee shop to charge the meal to the folio. The coffee shop cashier verifies the guest's identity by looking at the guest's key or identification card (Exhibit 8–8). Sometimes, no verification at all is made.

As a precaution against the loss of the signed check, a handwritten record (a **departmental control sheet**) is prepared at the department (the coffee shop) selling the service (see Exhibit 10–6). The coffee shop check (now called a **voucher**), showing the amount of the charge, the room number, and the guest's signature, is sent by the coffee shop cashier to the front desk. The cashier/billing clerk at the front desk enters the amount on the proper folio. The coffee shop charge will be paid eventually as part of the entire bill when the guest checks out. Exhibit 10–12 shows the posting of such a charge from the "library bar."

Sending the voucher to the desk from the coffee shop is easier said than done. Handcarried charges are slow because they must await the availability of a runner (busperson, food server, bellperson). To minimize the inconvenience, the coffee shop cashier usually accumulates several vouchers before summoning the runner. Employees sometimes forgetfully pocket the voucher as they go off to do their regular jobs. Each of these communication problems results in delay at the front office and even a loss of revenue from unposted or late charges.[4]

With Electronic Systems.   The property management system (PMS), the hotel computer, has done away with vouchers, control sheets, and problems caused by runners. Communication is electronic. The distant department is tied to the front-office folio by means of the PMS. Cashiers in the dining rooms, bars, and room

EXHIBIT 10–7

Example of an electronic point-of-sale (POS) terminal. This POS, located at various revenue centers (restaurant, gift shop, lounge, etc.) would be interfaced with the PMS. In this way, the cashier can electronically verify and post transactions to the guest room.

Courtesy: Qantel Business Systems, Inc., Hayward, California.

service enter the guest check into an electronic, **point-of-sale (POS)** cash register (see Exhibit 10–7). Instantaneously, the information enters computer memory. The guest's folio is always current and late charges are minimized. Moreover, the PMS gives the departmental cashiers additional capability to verify guests' identities and their right to charge.

Property management systems with point-of-sale terminals are expensive installations. Management might make an economic decision to leave certain minor departments, which generate a small amount of revenue, without POS capability. Therefore, some hotels have a mixture of electronic and pencil-and-paper systems.

Charges or Debits

Debits (increases to accounts receivable) and credits (decreases to accounts receivable) are posted (entered on the folio) to keep the guest account current.

Debits, or charges, originate in services that guests buy from one of the many hotel departments. Rooms, food, and beverage generate most of the charges. Telephone, laundry, and valet are minor departments. Depending on the type and pattern of the hotel, and on what is and what is not included in the rate, charges are generated also by other departments. Among these are greens fees, ski-lift tickets, garage or parking fees, saunas and health clubs, horseback riding, in-room films and bars, and more. Each sale results in a debit to accounts receivable and a credit to the particular income.

Understanding the Line of Posting.   Each folio posting requires an equality of debits and credits, as discussed earlier in the chapter. That equality is not immediately apparent on the guest folios illustrated throughout the chapter. Each departmental charge appears on a folio as a single line, rather than the two parts required for equal debits and credits. Exhibit 10–8 contains a variety of departmental charges (incomes), each illustrated by a single-line posting. Among these are room income (line 1), telephone income (line 4), and restaurant income (line 5, Woodlands).

The explanation is apparent once the folio is reexamined. The folio is an account receivable. The rules learned earlier require accounts receivable to be increased by debits. Each line that increases the amount of the folio balance in Exhibit 10–8 is a debit to the account receivable, known as room number 346.

Look at the similarity of Exhibits 10–1, 10–4, and 10–8. The postings are almost identical: room income, telephone income, restaurant income. Once again, the entry of each line is understood to be debit, accounts receivable (increasing the folio—the guest's debt to the hotel), and credit the particular income. (Remember the rule: Incomes are increased by credits.)

Getting the Posting on the Folio.   Charges are posted throughout the day as the guest uses a particular service. Often, a charge appears again and again, as it might for telephone, food, and beverage. Sometimes, a service is used but once a day, less frequently than that, or not at all. Laundry or in-room films (Exhibit 10–1, lines 2 and 3) are examples of less frequent charges. In every instance, the charge, which originates in the department, must be posted through the property management system (PMS) onto the guest folio.

If the hotel has point-of-sale terminals (POS), the communication is electronic. Such is the case with telephone calls and in-room films. At bars and restaurants, the departmental cashiers enter the charges into the PMS by means of POS terminals. If the particular department has no POS, a pencil-and-paper voucher must be delivered to the front-office cashier, who enters the charge into the PMS through a front-office terminal.

The Rooms Department.   The rooms department is an exception to the procedure. Room charges are posted but once each day. Room charges are posted at the desk by the night auditor during the early hours of the morning.

With a pencil-and-paper system, the night auditor removes each folio from the cashier's well, writes the room charge on each, and totals the account (Exhibit 10–3). This is a very time-consuming and error-prone procedure.

Property management systems keep the room rates in memory, post automatically, and total electronically when the folio is printed. When the night auditor initiates the program, the rate and tax are posted to the folio, as illustrated in Exhibit 10–8, lines 1, 2, 7, and 8, and in other illustrations throughout the chapter.

Three infrequent exceptions require the room rate to be posted during the day by the billing clerk or cashier. Day rates, when guests arrive and leave the same day, before the night audit takes place, are posted by the day crew. So are additional room charges made because of late check-out. The previous night's charge is posted

EXHIBIT 10–8

An electronic folio shows charge postings from different departments of the hotel, including room sales taxes and county occupancy taxes (lines 2 and 3; 8 and 9). Note the accounting references that follow each line entry.

STOUFFER WESTCHESTER HOTEL
80 WEST RED OAK LANE
WHITE PLAINS. NEW YORK 10604
(914) 694-5400

TOWNS, SEYMOUR	ARRIVAL	3/11/
	DEPARTURE	3/13/
123 NORTH STREET	NO. IN PARTY	2
WHITE PLAINS, NY	RATE	89.00
10601		

ACCT. NO.   801936   ROOM NO.   346

#	DATE	DESCRIPTION	AMOUNT
1	3/11/	ROOM/346/2/2/4	89.00
2	3/11/	SALES TAX/346/2/2/4	6.19
3	3/11/	COUNTY OCCUPANCY TAX/346/2/2/4 OCCUPANCY TAX	2.67
4	3/12/	LOCAL/LOCAL TOLL/346/3120XX4006/1/4 09:56/6987991	.75
5	3/12/	WOODLANDS/346/736334/1/4/113355	24.03
6	3/12/	LOCAL/LOCAL TOLL/346/312CXXX011/1/4 11:41/6987991	.75
7	3/12/	ROOM/346/2/2/4	89.00
8	3/12/	SALES TAX/346/2/2/4	6.19
9	3/12/	COUNTY OCCUPANCY TAX/346/2/2/4 OCCUPANCY TAX	2.67

                                              * BALANCE DUE *   221.25

ACCOUNTS PAST 30 DAYS SUBJECT TO **SERVICE CHARGE** OF 1 1/2% PER MONTH **(ANNUAL RATE OF 18%)**

PRINTED ON RECYCLED PAPER

COMPANY   STREET

                    CITY / STATE   ZIP

I agree that my liability for this bill is not waived and agree
to be held personally liable in the event that the indicated
person, company or association fails to pay for any part of   SIGNATURE _____
these charges.
                                                                            FORM # RC169

Courtesy: Stouffer Westchester Hotel, White Plains.

in the normal manner, but the premium for staying late is added by the cashier as the guest departs.

Guests who pay in advance are the third exception. Often, but not always, the room charge is posted at the same time the guest makes payment. With that procedure, the guest gets a receipt at check-in and does not usually return to the desk at check-out.

Although debits to accounts receivable (the posting that results from a departmental sale) are the more common, every posting is not a debit. As we shall soon see, some lines are credits to accounts receivable. Taxes collected by the hotel for the government are an exceptional debit to accounts receivable that needs further explanation.

Sales Taxes.   Taxes levied by local and county governments on room sales are a universal fact of business life. Adding insult to injury, the hotel is required to collect the tax and reimburse the government. Thus, a tax entry follows every time a room charge is posted. The hotel is acting for the government by making the tax charge. The entry is debit accounts receivable—increasing the guest's debt to the hotel—and credit sales taxes (payable).

Sales taxes payable is a debt that the hotel owes to the government. The tax is payable by the hotel. In other words, the hotel is an account receivable to the government just as the guest is an account receivable to the hotel. Logically enough, one becomes an *account payable* when situated on the other side of the owe-owed relationship. Collecting the tax from the guest for the government makes the hotel liable (owes) to the government. This liability is called an account payable or taxes payable. Exhibits 10–3 and 10–4 and others reflect those tax entries as debit accounts receivable and credit taxes (or accounts) payable.

Reference Numbers.   Nearly every hotel folio—certainly nearly all that are illustrated here—display a reference number as part of the posting description. There is no uniform numbering system among hotels, but there is within the single property because that identifying umber is an accounting reference. It is possible to draw some obvious conclusions even without knowing the systems.

Exhibit 10–8, for example, displays the account receivable debit immediately after the charge is described; that is, room 346, debit to the account receivable. That same conclusion is apparent also in Exhibit 10–9, with room 2315 the account receivable.

One might assume that the telephone references in Exhibit 10–8 (e.g., 346/3120 . . . 4006/1/4 . . .) are sequential numbering (to help resolve the bill that the telephone company will submit to the hotel) followed by the telephone number called. The reference number in Exhibit 10–1 might be the voucher number that gave rise to the charge. Note that the Islander Coffee Shop postings seem to be somewhat in sequence. These reference numbers probably identify the Islander check voucher used for that sale. It is different in Exhibit 10–9. Each restaurant outlet (Promenade Deck and Prince Court) has a repeating reference (5996 and 1382, respectively). These numbers reference the department in the hotel's chart of accounts. A chart of accounts is a coded numbering system by which the hotel establishes a hierarchy of income and expense departments. Each different department is referenced against the chart of accounts by a series of numbers. These numbers are unique to each property according to the number and extent of departments and the type of accounting system in place. Referring to Exhibit 10–9, the room charge was referenced with #518, excise tax with #519, and room tax with #520. In such a

EXHIBIT 10–9

An electronic folio illustrates an advance deposit made with a credit card. Note the debit (2315) and credit reference numbers (518, 519, 520, etc.) for each charge.

HAWAII PRINCE HOTEL

W A I K I K I

⊙ PRINCE HOTELS

Hawaii Prince Hotel, 100 Holomoana Street, Honolulu, Hawaii 96815
Telephone: (808) 956-1111   Facsimile: (808) 946-0811

A–STANDARD

DECAT, M/M BILL
1234 PENNSYLVANIA AVENUE
WASHINGTON, DC
56789-0000

ARRIVAL DATE	6/21/9
DEPARTURE	6/22/9
NO. IN PARTY	2
RATE	125.00

ACCOUNT NO. - 67877   ROOM NO. 2315

NUMBER	DATE	DESCRIPTION			AMOUNT
1	5/31/9	ADV DEP VISA MASTER	6	22 57	$130.21CR
		1NT RM/ST TAX		67877	
2	6/21/9	ROOM	2315	518	$125.00
3	6/21/9	EXCISE TAX	2315	519	$5.21
4	6/21/9	ROOM TAX	2315	520	$6.25
5	6/21/9	LOCAL PHONE	2315	621XXX9005	$.75
		13:57	9564902	67877	
6	6/21/9	PROMENADE DECK	2315	5996	$23.00
7	6/21/9	PROMENADE DECK	2315	5996	$3.00
8	6/21/9	PROMENADE DECK	2315	5996	$.96
9	6/22/9	PRINCE COURT	2315	1382	$18.00
10	6/22/9	PRINCE COURT	2315	1382	$2.00
11	6/22/9	PRINCE COURT	2315	1382	$.75
		* Balance Due *			$54.71

SIGNATURE

I AGREE THAT MY LIABILITY FOR THIS BILL IS NOT WAIVED AND AGREE TO BE HELD PERSONALLY LIABLE IN THE EVENT THAT THE INDICATED PERSON, COMPANY OR ASSOCIATION FAILS TO PAY FOR ANY PART OR THE FULL AMOUNT OF THESE CHARGES.

Courtesy: Hawaii Prince Hotel, Honolulu.

system, the number 5 (or 05) means front desk and 18, 19, and 20 are examples of three credit postings made at the desk.

To summarize: Every folio posting represents a dual event—a balance of equal debits and credits. Most folio postings represent the sale of services (charges) to the guest and give rise to a basic accounting entry of debit accounts receivable and credit the particular income—rooms, telephone, health club, and so on. Room sale taxes, which are levied on guests and remitted to the government, are an exception. The credit is a liability (a payable) that most American hotels and many abroad are required to collect from their guests.

Payments or Credits

As the guest folio is increased by charges or debits, so it is decreased by payments or credits. The accounting entry to do this is debit whatever means are used to settle the account (we'll discuss those momentarily) and credit accounts receivable. Paying the bill reduces the guest's account receivable, hence the credit. (Remember the rule: Credits reduce assets.)

As the chapter has already noted, charge entries occur and are posted many times throughout the day. Credit entries occur less frequently, usually at departure, although sometimes at the beginning of the stay. Irrespective of how and when the credit is given, the transient folio (the guest bill) must always have a zero balance after check-out! That is, total credits and total debits must be equal as the guest leaves. Whatever debt the guest incurs on the transient folio during the stay must be settled at departure.

Whereas there are many charges or debits to the folio arising from the hotel's sale of various services, there are only three methods of settling the account. That's a helpful rule to commit to memory. There are only three methods of payment, or credit to accounts receivable, although more than one payment can be used to settle the account. The methods are: (1) pay the bill with cash; (2) reduce the amount owed, using an **allowance;** and/or (3) transfer the debt to someone else, who then becomes the account receivable.

In accounting terminology, cash means money, including foreign currencies, traveler's checks, personal checks, and bank or cashier's checks. For a thorough discussion on paying the bill with cash, see Chapter 11.

Allowances. Just as retail stores allow the return of unsatisfactory goods, hotels give credit for poor service, misunderstandings, and mathematical errors. The retailer's exchange of merchandise is the hotel's allowance. Legitimate adjustments to guest complaints are considered so important that lease provisions usually give the hotel authority to grant allowances for unsatisfactory service by concessionaires renting space in the hotel.

Even computerized properties may use paper-and-pencil allowance vouchers (or **rebate** slips). A written record requiring an authorized signature highlights the issue both for the guest and for the company anxious to minimize errors in guest service (see Exhibit 10–10). Improving weaknesses in the operation starts with knowing what the failures are.

An allowance report is prepared daily as part of the night audit. As hotels empower employees (Chapter 7) to make decisions such as granting allowances, reports to management increase in importance as a control technique. Even so, a

EXHIBIT 10–10

Prenumbered allowance vouchers provide pencil-and-paper records of guest complaints and errors.

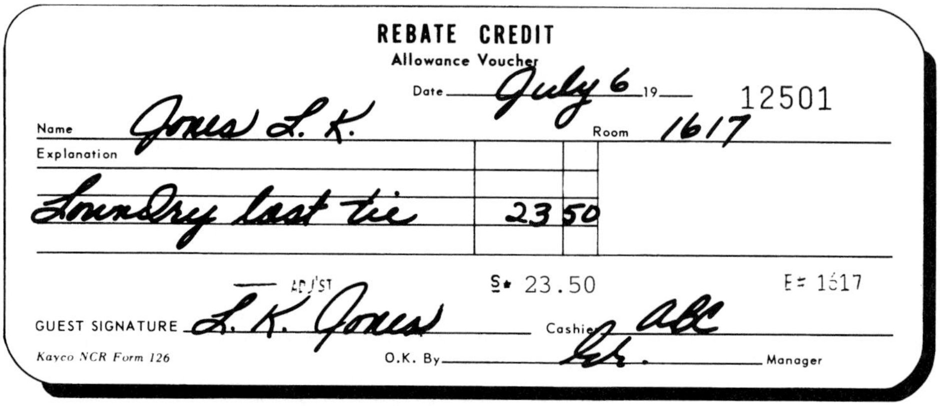

REBATE CREDIT
Allowance Voucher
Date July 6 19__ 12501
Name Jones L. K. Room 1617
Explanation
Laundry lost tie 23 50
ADJ'ST $* 23.50 E= 1617
GUEST SIGNATURE L. K. Jones Cashier abc
Kayco NCR Form 126 O.K. By ______ Manager

Courtesy: Kayco Systems, Lake Elsinore, CA.

manager's or supervisor's signature is required if the value of the allowance exceeds a given ceiling.

Allowances are given to adjust the bill after the fact. Problems brought to management's attention early enough will be corrected. Allowances are warranted only if it is too late to rectify the complaint. A range of circumstances require allowances: a higher room rate is posted than appears on the guest's rooming slip; a charge belongs on someone else's folio; a guest room never receives service from housekeeping; the hotel fails to deliver promised services or a basic commodity such as hot water; or a complimentary guest.

Comp Allowances. Only a few executives have ''power of the pen''—the authority to compliment rooms or other services. Comps are subject to abuse, and top management should require a daily compilation of comp charges. If, as is done in many instances, the guest is not recorded, not charged a rate, nor counted in either the house count or the room count, there is no accounting record of the stay and, consequently, no control. It is far better to charge the guest in full and grant an allowance at the end of the stay to cover the charge on the room.

Good accounting for comps starts with a daily posting of the full room rate. To allay the guest's concern, the rate that appears on the top of the folio is marked *comp*—for example, 140 COMP. At departure, an allowance—one of the three methods of settling (crediting) accounts receivable—is prepared. Since this represents an equal reduction in room income, the debit is to room sales, or to room sale allowances (debits reduce sales). This technique separates these courtesy comps from normal room allowances (adjustments) and from frequent-guest room allowances. The alternative, combining all room allowances on the night audit report, provides much less information.

Allowances for Poor Service. Who has not witnessed coffee poured into a customer's lap or a pair of hose snagged on a cocktail booth? A suit is lost by a valet; a shirt is scorched by the laundry; the cot for the child is never delivered. Countless irritating events are bound to occur in hotels that serve hundreds or thousands of visitors each day.

If the problem is not caught immediately, there is little management can do but reimburse for the loss. The account receivable is credited (reduced) and the department being charged (food, rooms, laundry) is debited (its income is reduced).

Allowances to Correct Errors. Handling small late charges is one of several clerical errors requiring correcting allowances. A late charge is posted to the folio of a guest who has already checked out. If the charge is large enough to pursue by mail, a transfer—soon to be explained—is used. If the late charge is too small to warrant the costs of collection, including guest annoyance, it is wiped off. Accounts receivable is credited and the hotel absorbs the error (debit the department from which the late charge originates).

Some errors are just carelessness in posting. Exhibit 10–11 shows the allowance for an additional 99 cents that was inadvertently posted as part of the room charge by the night auditor. Exhibit 10–1 (third line from the bottom) adjusts for a dual posting of an in-room film (lines 2 and 3).

Many errors originate in misunderstandings or lack of attention. For example, a couple arrives for several days but one spouse leaves early. Although the desk is aware of the situation, the double occupancy rate continues for the entire stay. An allowance is needed to reduce the debit balance by the difference between the single and double rates multiplied by the number of nights overcharged.

In theory, it should not happen, but sometimes a guest folio is carried one night beyond the actual departure day. An allowance corrects the error. This happens most frequently with one-night, paid-in-advance guests who do not bother to check out.

Every protested charge is not the hotel's error. This is why having old vouchers accessible to the cashier is helpful. When shown a signed voucher, guests often recall charges that they had vehemently protested only moments earlier. Large bar charges fall into this category when viewed with a sober eye the following day. This also happens when two persons share a room and one makes charges but the other pays. Especially when the first guest has already checked out is it necessary to prove to the remaining guest that the charge was made.

Although computers reduce the number of errors, they do not compensate for guest forgetfulness or for honest misunderstandings or mistakes.

Extended-Stay Allowances. Some resorts allow a reduction in daily rate if the guest remains an extended length of time. To make certain of the guest's commitment to remain, the full daily charge is posted and not the pro rata charge of the special rate. Either an allowance is given on the final day to adjust the weekly rate or the charge of the final day is reduced to meet the special weekly rate.

Recording the Allowance. Allowances, like the two other credits (cash and transfers), usually arise at the time of departure. Once the issue that triggers the allowance is resolved, a pencil-and-paper voucher might be completed and an authorizing signature obtained. The amount of the allowance is then credited to the folio. The guest uses the allowance along with either or both of the other methods of settling the bill (Exhibit 10–11) and checks out.

Each allowance will be charged (debited) against the department from which it originates—room, food, telephone, and so on—by the accounting department, not by the front office. The allowance vouchers or computer records serve as the basis for these charges, which, as debits, reduce the credit income accounts of the operating departments.

Exhibit 10–11

An allowance and a credit-card transfer illustrate two of the three means of settling an outstanding folio. Note the sequential folio number on the upper right side.

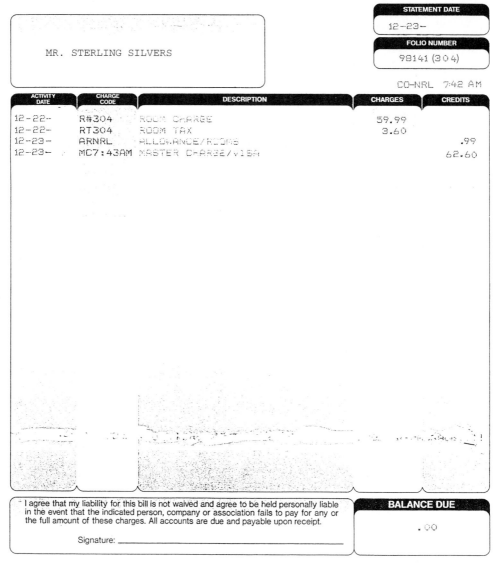

ORIGINAL

Transfers.   Transfers are the third and most common method of settling a folio at check-out. Credit-card settlements and other city ledger arrangements involve transferring the folio balance from the guest folio at the front office to the city folio in the back office.

A **transfer** is an accounting technique used to move a figure from one folio to another. One account receivable gets larger (debit) as the new amount is added. The balance of the other gets smaller (credit) as the amount is removed. Each account changes by the same amount, except one increases and one decreases. The rule is: Each debit transfer must have an equal credit transfer.

All or part of any account balance can be transferred. According to the circumstances, transfers are made between accounts in the same ledger (transient to transient), or between the ledgers (transient to city or city to transient).

Transfers between two transient folios located at the front office are easier to track because both folios are available to the front-office staff. Transfers between transient folios and city ledger folios appear incomplete to the front-office staff because one of the folios, the city ledger, is not available. The city ledger is maintained by the accounting office.

Both procedures involve the same accounting entry. Every transfer results in a debit to accounts receivable (one individual or company) and a credit to accounts receivable (a second individual or company).

Transient Ledger to Transient Ledger.   The two pages of Exhibit 10–3 illustrate transfers recorded on pencil-and-paper folios. Note that the two parties each had a folio and that each stayed over night on December 23rd (the first column). Each incurred a room and tax charge of $84.24. When the new day, December 24th—the second column—starts, each folio has an opening balance (''brought forward'') of $84.24. As the morning unfolds, however, Room 407 will give its charge (transfer) to Room 409. Room 409 will pay both charges.

Room 407 (folio number E69081) checks out, paying the account with a transfer. That is, the account receivable was reduced (credited) with a transfer that brought the folio balance to zero. Earlier, the chapter stressed that every check-out must have a zero balance: Debit charges must equal credit payments.

The previous section also stated that every credit transfer must have an equal and corresponding debit transfer. So it is in Exhibit 10–3. With room 409, the debit transfer of $84.24 is posted and included as part of the new debit balance. After the transfer, 409 has a balance of $168.48, the total of the two room-nights plus telephone and restaurant charges.

Exhibit 10–3 illustrates a transfer involving two pencil-and-paper folios, both of which are in the guest (or transient or front-office) ledger. Exhibit 10–12 also shows transfers, line 009, but on electronic folios. Line 010 of room 723 shows still another type of transfer—the final settlement by credit card.

Credit-Card Transfers.   The second folio in Exhibit 10–3, the one numbered E69080, is settled in full with a credit-card charge of $168.48. This, too, is a credit transfer. Both pencil-and-paper folios have been settled with credit transfers, but room 409's entry is a transfer to the city ledger. The city ledger's half of the transfer is not visible to the front desk, but the posting is a debit to a city ledger account receivable. That city ledger account receivable is now the credit-card company! No longer does the guest owe the hotel—now the debt is owed by the credit-card com-

EXHIBIT 10–12

An electronic transfer between two transient folios is illustrated on line 9 of each folio. Final settlement is by credit-card transfer to the city ledger, line 10 (see following page). Compare the electronic transfer postings with the pencil-and-paper method of Exhibit 10–3.

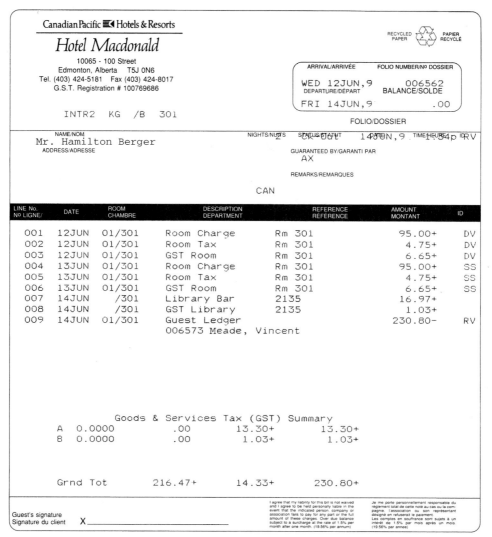

Canadian Pacific ◼◀ Hotels & Resorts

Hotel Macdonald

10065 - 100 Street
Edmonton, Alberta   T5J 0N6
Tel. (403) 424-5181   Fax (403) 424-8017
G.S.T. Registration # 100769686

ARRIVAL/ARRIVÉE	FOLIO NUMBER/N⁰ DOSSIER
WED 12JUN,9	006562
DEPARTURE/DÉPART	BALANCE/SOLDE
FRI 14JUN,9	.00

RECYCLED PAPER / PAPIER RECYCLÉ

INTR2 KG /B 301

FOLIO/DOSSIER

NAME/NOM   Mr. Hamilton Berger
ADDRESS/ADRESSE

NIGHTS/NUITS 2   STATUS/ÉTAT   14JUN,9   TIME/HEURE 4p   ID RV

GUARANTEED BY/GARANTI PAR
AX

REMARKS/REMARQUES

CAN

LINE No. N⁰ LIGNE/	DATE	ROOM CHAMBRE	DESCRIPTION DEPARTMENT	REFERENCE RÉFÉRENCE	AMOUNT MONTANT	ID
001	12JUN	01/301	Room Charge	Rm 301	95.00+	DV
002	12JUN	01/301	Room Tax	Rm 301	4.75+	DV
003	12JUN	01/301	GST Room	Rm 301	6.65+	DV
004	13JUN	01/301	Room Charge	Rm 301	95.00+	SS
005	13JUN	01/301	Room Tax	Rm 301	4.75+	SS
006	13JUN	01/301	GST Room	Rm 301	6.65+	SS
007	14JUN	/301	Library Bar	2135	16.97+	
008	14JUN	/301	GST Library	2135	1.03+	
009	14JUN	01/301	Guest Ledger 006573 Meade, Vincent		230.80-	RV

Goods & Services Tax (GST) Summary
A 0.0000   .00   13.30+   13.30+
B 0.0000   .00   1.03+   1.03+

Grnd Tot   216.47+   14.33+   230.80+

Guest's signature
Signature du client   X _____

I agree that my liability for this bill is not waived and I agree to be held personally liable in the event that the indicated person, company or association fails to pay for any part or the full amount of these charges. Over due balance subject to a surcharge at the rate of 1.5% per month after one month. (19.56% per annum)

Je me porte personnellement responsable du règlement total de cette note au cas ou la compagnie, l'association ou son représentant désigné en refuserait le paiement. Les comptes en souffrance sont sujets à un intérêt de 1.5% par mois après un mois. (19.56% par année)

(continued)

pany. Eventually, the credit-card company will pay the hotel and collect from the guest. Chapter 12 explains the mechanics of that sequence.

Exhibit 10–11 offers another view of the credit-card payment. Note here that two of the means of settlement are employed—allowances and transfers. Exhibit 10–12 shows computerized folios in which the credit transfer is to the credit-card company. Every such transfer carries a tacit assumption that an equal debit to one of the credit-card companies appears in the city ledger.

Direct City Ledger Transfers. Exhibit 10–3 shows old-fashioned pencil-and-paper folios. They are very helpful, however, because they identify the several kinds of transfers. Transfers are one of the three credits by which transient folios are bal-

Exhibit 10–12

Concluded

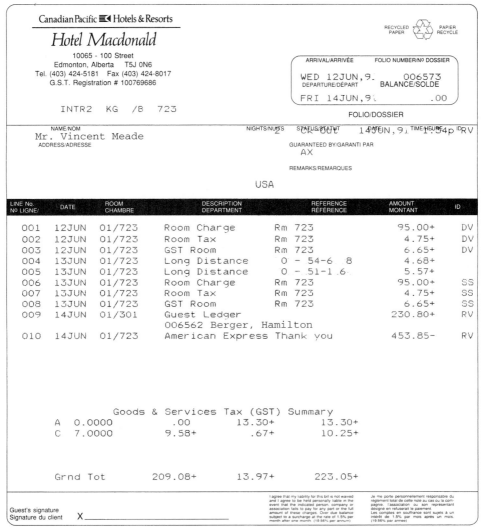

Courtesy: Hotel Macdonald, Edmonton, Canada.

anced. Cash and allowances are the other two. In Exhibit 10–3, one sees four possible transfer options. Type one, the second line from the bottom for room 407, is a transfer between transient accounts, described above. Type two is a credit-card transfer, which was also discussed. Type three are direct city ledger transfers, and type four are advance deposits.

Direct city ledger transfers are no different in form or procedure than credit-card transfers. The distinction lies in the debit posting to the city ledger. In the case of credit cards, the city ledger designation (debit) is Visa, American Express, and so on. Final settlement comes from one of the credit-card companies. Direct city ledger transfers result in a debit to a personal, city ledger account—an individual's, an association's, or a company's. Usually, such credit has been preapproved.

Master accounts are the best example of direct city ledger transfers. The firm, association, or group is billed at the conclusion of the event. Doing so saves the hotel the service costs of using a credit-card company. When the group leaves, the master account—the A folio in the transient ledger—will be credited (Exhibit 10–1) and the association's account in the city ledger is debited. In Exhibit 10–1, the $229.79 balance is credited (with a transfer credit) in the transient ledger and subsequently debited (with a transfer debit) to the association in the city ledger. Billing and collection then take place through the mail.

Direct city ledger transfers sometimes involve coupons. A guest who is booked by a travel agent or airline may pay the transient folio with a coupon. This is a receipt by which the third party, the travel agent, acknowledges that it has already been paid by the guest. By accepting the coupon, the hotel agrees to directly bill the travel agency or other third party. This is accomplished by transferring the transient guest's folio (credit) to the third-party's account in the city ledger (debit) and billing by mail.

Despite improved credit-checking procedures, hotels still experience **skippers.** Skippers are persons who leave **(skip)** the hotel without paying. Some skippers are accidental or the result of misunderstandings. The transient folio is transferred to the city ledger and billed. Since honest guests leave a trail of reservation and registration identification, collection takes place without difficulty.

Real skippers make their living by skipping. Their moves are intentional and deliberately planned even though the states have legislated skipping as a prima facie case of intent to defraud the innkeeper. Because it is a crime, a police report should be filed.

It often takes a day or two to verify the skip. Charges for additional room nights are posted during that period. It makes little difference, actually, since collection is rare. Once discovered, the room is checked out. The folio balance is transferred to city ledger and eventually written off as a bad debt.

Telephone companies usually rebate credit for telephone calls made by skippers and not paid. There are never too many, since the skipper has no wish to leave a traceable trail.

Advance-Deposit Transfers. Advance-deposit transfers flow in an opposite direction from the other two city ledger transfers. Credit-card and direct city ledger transfers shift the account receivable *from* the transient ledger *to* the city ledger, where billing occurs. Advance deposits are different. The balance starts in the city ledger. The movement is the *from* the city ledger *to* the guest ledger.

Guaranteed reservations require a one-night deposit, either a credit-card deposit or a cash deposit. Receipt of payment establishes an advance-deposit account in the city ledger. It must be in the city ledger because the guest has not yet arrived to open a guest account. Transient folios exist only for registered guests.

The reservation check is deposited in the hotel's bank account: debit cash (increase the asset); credit accounts receivable (the hotel owes the guest one night's lodging). The advance deposit remains as a city ledger credit account until the guest arrives, days or weeks later. Now the credit must be transferred *to* the transient ledger *from* the city ledger. The entry is a debit to accounts receivable advance deposits in the city ledger and a credit to accounts receivable *guest's* folio in the guest ledger.

Exhibit 10–13 illustrates the transfer (the first line) on a front-office folio. Like other transfers, the city ledger portion is not visible to the front-office staff. The guest begins the visit with the hotel owing the guest. The small amount still due at check-out is settled, with cash in this illustration.

EXHIBIT 10–13

An advance deposit paid with cash starts the folio with a credit balance. A cash payment at check-out completes the sequence, illustrating one of the three methods of folio settlement.

30 PITT STREET
SYDNEY NSW 2000 AUSTRALIA
TELEPHONE: (02) 259 7000
FACSIMILE: (02) 252 1999
TELEX: AA127792
A.R.B.N. 003 864 908

SYDNEY
RENAISSANCE
HOTEL

GUEST		
VALLEN, M/M J	ROOM	2003
EASTER PACKAGE	RATE	170.00
2ND AVE BEACHSIDE APPTS	No. PERSONS	2
BURLEIGH HEADS QLD 4220	FOLIO No.	152490
	PAGE	01
	ARRIVAL	04/12/
	DEPARTURE	04/16/
CH-A BUNNY	DEPOSIT	$680.00

DATE	REFERENCE No.		DESCRIPTION	CHARGES / CREDITS
19				
		00754	DEPOSIT	680.00CR
APR12	401	01859 99	LOCAL CALL	.70
APR12	011	02003 00	ROOM CHG	170.00
APR13	131	04071 61	BRASSERIE	22.00
APR13	401	02145 99	LOCAL CALL	.70
APR13	011	02003 00	ROOM CHG	170.00
APR14	181	02003 43	MINI BAR	2.50
APR14	011	02003 00	ROOM CHG	170.00
APR15	401	01736 99	LOCAL CALL	.70
APR15	011	02003 00	ROOM CHG	170.00
APR16	001	00001 23	PAID CASH	26.60CR
			TOTAL-DUE	.00

TRAVEL AGENCY
LOVE   TRAVEL
JENN
SH8   HIGH   ROAD
SOUTHPORT   QLD   4215

CHARGE TO

I AGREE THAT MY LIABILITY FOR THIS BILL IS NOT WAIVED AND AGREE TO BE HELD PERSONALLY LIABLE IN THE EVENT THAT THE INDICATED PERSON, COMPANY OR ASSOCIATION FAILS TO PAY FOR ANY PART OR THE FULL AMOUNT OF THESE CHARGES.

SIGNATURE

SYDNEY RENAISSANCE HOTEL - INSPIRED BY THE PAST, DESIGNED FOR THE FUTURE. SM.
FOR RESERVATIONS: AUSTRALIA (008) 222 431, IN SYDNEY (02) 251 8888 ● BANGKOK 02 236 0361
HONG KONG (852) 311 3666 ●   JAPAN (0120) 222 332, IN TOKYO (03) 3239 8303 ● KUALA LUMPUR
(03) 241 4081 AND (03) 248 9008 ● SEOUL (02) 555 0501

AUSTRALIA ● CANADA ● CARRIBEAN ● CENTRAL AMERICA ● CHINA ● EUROPE ● HONG KONG ● INDIA
INDONESIA ● JAPAN ● KOREA ● MALAYSIA ● MEXICO ● MIDDLE EAST ● PAKISTAN ● SRI LANKA
THAILAND ● UK ● USA   FORM No. FO 001 12/92

Courtesy: Sydney Renaissance Hotel, Sydney, Australia.

Another example is offered by Exhibit 10–9, but here the advance deposit was made with a credit card. Again, the visit starts with the hotel owing the guest. The final settlement of $54.71 brings us back to the beginning. The guest can settle up with cash, allowances, or transfers.

Summary

Selling services such as rooms, food, and beverage is the business of hotelkeeping. Most of these business transactions are made to registered guests, called transient accounts receivable. (An account receivable buys without immediate payment and, therefore, owes the hotel.) Hotels also do business with nonregistered accounts receivable, or city guests. Individual transient receivables are combined into the front-office, or transient, or guest ledger. Individual city guests are combined into the city ledger.

Receivables in both ledgers are increased by accounting entries called debits and decreased by accounting entries called credits. Explanations of business transactions are simplified when professional terminology like this is used. Each sale of service simultaneously produces income for the hotel. Incomes are increased by credits and decreased by debits. A dual-entry system of equal debits and credits emerges as a result. Each sale increases accounts receivable with a debit and increases income with a credit by the same value.

Individual accounts receivable are maintained on personal records called folios. Each registered guest has a folio that reflects the increases (debits) brought about by the guest's purchase of hotel services. This folio must be settled (credited) when the guest checks out.

There are three methods of settling a folio debt. Settlement is made by cash; by a reduction of the amount due (called an allowance); or by transferring (shifting) the bill to some other person or some other company (usually a credit-card company) to pay. However the settlement is made, every front-office folio is brought to a zero balance when the guest departs. Credits balance the debits that have been generated throughout the guest stay.

This chapter has focused on debits and credits developing from accounts receivable transactions. The next chapter looks at cash transactions, including their effect on accounts receivable.

Queries and Problems

1. Differentiate the following:
   a. Debit from credit.
   b. Master account from split account.
   c. A folio from B folio.
   d. Transient guest from city guest.
   e. Charge from payment.

2. Use a word processor to replicate the folio that would be produced when the Arthur Jones family checks out. Mr. and Mrs. Jones and their infant son, George, reside at 21 Craig Drive in Hampshireville, Illinois 65065. Their reservation for three nights at $125 per night plus 5 percent tax is guaranteed May 17 with a $200 cash (check) deposit for one night, indicating that they will arrive late. They check in at 10 PM on June 3rd and take one room (1233).
   a. Breakfast charge on June 4 is $12.90.
   b. Mrs. Jones hosts a small luncheon meeting for her company, and a $310 charge for the meeting room and meal was posted to the folio.
   c. The family decides to leave earlier than planned and notifies the desk of a 7 PM check-out.

   d. A long distance call of $8 is made.
   e. The family checks out. They raise the issue of no clean linen—the laundry had a wildcat strike—and argue for an allowance. One is given—$25. The rooms manager then charges 30 percent of the normal room charge for the late departure.
   f. Payment is made with an American Express Card, no. 33333333333.

3. Answer the following questions:
   a. How could a late charge occur with a POS terminal?
   b. How does the server in the gourmet room of the hotel's 43rd floor verify the identity of a guest who wants to charge the $813 bill to the room folio?
   c. How are the debits and credits visualized as an accounting entry when a guest charges a ski-lift ticket to the room account? The hotel does not own the ski lift; it is a concession.

4. Under which of the following circumstances would management grant an allowance? How much would

the value of that allowance be? What else might be done if an allowance were not granted?

a. Guest sets the room alarm clock, but it fails to go off, which causes the guest to miss a meeting that involves thousands of dollars of commission.

b. Same circumstance as (a) but the guest called the telephone operator for a morning call, which wasn't made.

c. Guest checks out and discovers the nightly room charge to be $15 more than the rate quoted two weeks earlier by the res center.

d. Same circumstance as (c) but the discrepancy is discovered soon after the guest is roomed.

5. How would the following transfers be handled? (Answer either by discussion, by offering the accounting entries, or both.)

a. A departing guest discovers that a $60 beverage charge that belongs to another guest, who is still registered, was incorrectly posted yesterday to the departing guest's account.

b. Same circumstance as (a) but the posting was made today.

c. Same circumstance as (a) but the other guest has departed.

d. Two days into a guest's four-day stay, the reservation department realizes the guest's advance deposit was never transferred to the front-office account.

e. Same circumstance as (d) but the discovery is made by the guest, who writes to complain about the omission one week after check-out.

6. In debit and credit terms, prepare these two entries:

a. The hotel pays the local government quarterly room sales tax, which amounts to $1,664.86.

b. The hotel receives a check from its parent company for $2,900, representing the total payment on several frequent-guest stays that resulted in room charges by the hotel of $8,600.

Notes

1. Remember the spelling rule for rec*ei*vables: Place *i* before *e*, except after *c*, or when sounded like *a*, as in *neighbor* or *weigh*.

2. Small hotels sometimes process city ledger entries at the front desk before sending them to the accounting office. Adding persons and stops to the sequence improves internal security, especially for a small property.

3. *Hard copy* is a computer term for material that has been printed rather than merely displayed on the computer screen.

4. A *late charge* is a guest's departmental charge that arrives at the front desk for billing after the guest has checked out.

Cash Transactions

Cash Transactions

In the front office, the term *cash* includes all transactions involving foreign currency, traveler's checks, personal checks, debit cards, as well as U.S. currency. Because cash is a negotiable commodity, cash transactions are documented separately from credit-card, direct bill, and other noncash activities.

Separate documentation gives management added detail with which to follow the cash trail. The amount of money involved, the guest's name, room number, date and time, and clerk identification are all details provided through the property management system. As an added control, hotels also require cashiers to reconcile their cash drawers on a shift-by-shift basis. This allows for timely discovery of errors. Discovery of errors, maybe so—but once the error is made, correction after the fact is difficult.

Not only are cash receipts from room guests handled by the front desk, but money received on behalf of other hotel departments is the cashier's responsibility as well. Money paid to the hotel for banquet and catering functions, valet laundry services, and vending sales are all examples of hotel or ''house'' receipts flowing through the front-desk cashier.

Paid-Outs

To complicate matters further, it is important to understand that cash is not always a credit transaction. Cash receipts (a payment made by the guest) are credits to the guest folio, decreasing the balance owed the hotel. Cash receipts (credits) increase the amount of cash in the cashier's drawer.

However, cash can also be a debit (a cash advance on behalf of the guest) to the guest folio, increasing the balance owed the hotel. Cash paid from the hotel on behalf of a guest is called a **cash advance** or a **paid-out.** Paid-outs (debits) decrease the amount of cash in the cashier's drawer.

Tips to Employees.   Tips are the most common cash advance. They are paid to an employee on the request of the guest. A signed check from the dining room or bar is the usual method of request. The amount of gratuity is added to the check by the guest when signing for the service. When the signed voucher reaches the clerk, the departmental charges are separated from the tip. The tip is posted under the cash advance category, not the food or beverage category. After all, the tip is not departmental income, so it must not appear under a departmental heading.

Acting on the guest's signature, the front-office cashier pays the tip to the server, who signs for the money on a cash advance voucher (see Exhibit 11–1). The cash advance voucher is then posted to the guest's folio along with the departmental charge (food, beverage, or whatever). At the end of the shift, this paid-out (in the amount of $12, as shown in Exhibit 11–1) will appear on the cashier's balance report as a reduction to the cashier's drawer.

Since the procedure is not an unusual one, a traffic problem could develop at the front desk if employees from all over the hotel came to collect their tips. To forestall this, tips are paid by the cashiers in the various dining rooms and bars. In a way, the problem handles itself. Most tips are added to national credit cards. Charges to national credit cards do not usually come to the front office. Only charges to the guest's folio, whether there are tips or not, flow through the front-office procedure. Even a credit-card charge (restaurant, bar) made by a registered guest will not pass through that guest's folio, but rather will be deposited as income directly by the department involved.

Front-office cashiers still process tips to front-of-the-house employees: bell, housekeeping, and delivery persons. Most hotels pay their employees' tips on receipt or at the end of the shift. This is wonderful for the employee, but it can often result in the hotel subsidizing its employee gratuities in three common ways: float (i.e., the time value of money), merchant discount fees on credit cards, and potential noncollectible accounts. Granted, it may be a minimal sum of money when considered on a per employee basis, but over time (and in large properties with hundreds or thousands of employees) it can easily add to a significant amount.

Float.   Because of the time value of money, it is expensive to prepay an employee's tip before the guest's bill is paid. Yet this is exactly what happens with many paid-out tips. To illustrate the point, let's follow the payment cycle for a newly arriving guest, Diane Green.

Exhibit 11–1

The signature of the recipient shows evidence of payment on this cash advance voucher. The voucher is posted on an old electromechanical machine, which is no longer in use.

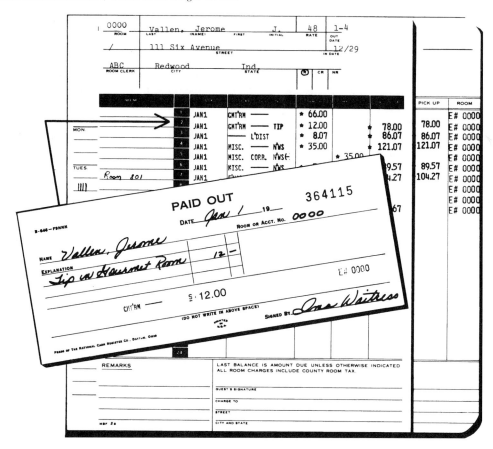

Upon arrival, Green asks the front desk to issue a $10 tip to the bellperson as a paid-out against her folio. Because this is the first day of a lengthy visit, let's assume Green's folio will not be settled for nine days. In this example, the hotel has ostensibly paid the bellperson with money it will not receive for nine days.

To add insult to injury, Green's bill will likely be settled by national credit card. Certain types of credit-card companies take weeks before they pay the hotel. It is conceivable therefore that the hotel has paid the bellperson a tip with money it will not receive for some 20 or 30 days!

Merchant Discount Fees.   National credit-card companies charge merchants a fee for accepting their credit card. The merchant discount fee may range anywhere from 2 to 5 percent depending on the sales volume of the hotel, the credit card in question, and a number of other variables (see Chapter 12). In Green's example, she settled the bill with an American Express Card. Let's assume the hotel pays a 4 percent fee for the use of American Express.

A 4 percent fee on all American Express Card sales means that the hotel receives $96 from American Express for every $100 charged at the hotel. Therefore, American Express will only reimburse the hotel $9.60 for the bellperson's $10 tip, which the hotel has already paid in full.

Although 40 cents sounds trivial, it adds up over time and volume. After all, that's 40 cents for just one tip to one bellperson; imagine dozens of tips to possibly hundreds of employees per day.

Noncollectible Accounts.   The most blatant example of subsidizing employee paid-out tips is when the guest folio becomes uncollectible. Whatever the reason for the uncollectible account, the hotel loses more than the departmental revenues. Whether the uncollectible folio was a direct bill account gone bad, a personal check with insufficient funds, or a fraudulent credit card, the hotel also loses the amount of the paid-out tip.

Some hotels attempt to collect paid-out tips back from their employees. But collecting from the employee months after the service was rendered is quite unlikely. In addition, it causes ill will to collect what the employee perceives as a rather trivial sum of money.

Cash Loans.   Loans to hotel guests are generally quite rare, occurring under unusual circumstances and only to those guests well known by the hotel's management. Advancing money to the guest as a paid-out (debit) against the folio runs the same risks discussed above (float, credit-card fees, and potential losses from uncollectible accounts). However, just as few hotels charge processing fees to employees who receive tips against credit cards, equally few hotels charge fees to guests desperate for a cash loan.

It is now more difficult to cash a check than it was to obtain a cash loan years ago. This is especially true on weekends when banks are closed. Some hoteliers believe that it is better to have a small loan skip than to have a large check bounce, so they grant the former if forced to choose. Companies that use the hotel on a regular basis may establish "loan" arrangements for their staffs by guaranteeing the advances. Preferred-guest programs provide just such check-cashing privileges.

Third-Party Sources.   A number of new options have surfaced as a result of the hotel industry's unwillingness to act as banker for the millions of domestic and international travelers. Among these options are automatic teller machines (ATMs), credit-card advances, and expedited money order services. Each of these options provides cash to the guest without jeopardizing the hotel or putting it into a business for which it lacks expertise.

Credit-card advances (e.g., Comcheck) and money order services (e.g., Western Union's FlashCash) transfer the related costs and risks of loaning money (float, credit-card discount fees, and potential losses from uncollectible accounts) from the hotel to the guest. In essence, guests send themselves money and pay their own costs. For example, by calling Western Union and using a national credit card, guests authorize payment to themselves. The guest gets the money, but Western Union, not the guest, is now the hotel's account receivable.

These financial services don't come free. Fees paid by the guest to the third parties range from 5 to 10 percent, depending on the amount and the company plan. Guests who would howl at the hotel for charging such usury pay up without a whimper.

Exhibit 11–2

Worldwide ATM machines are proliferating at a rapid rate. Most of the traveling public is close to a cash machine, but the high transactions fees dissuade many potential users.

Company	Number of Worldwide ATMs	Fee per Transaction
American Express	75,000+	2 to 5 percent of the transaction amount
Cirrus	100,000+	Rates set by the issuing bank
Diners Club	110,000+	4 percent of the transaction amount or $6
Plus	100,000+	Rates set by the issuing bank

Automatic Teller Machines.   By far the most common method used by today's guests for generating cash is the automatic teller machine (ATM). The use of ATMs is not limited to the United States either—ATMs are rapidly becoming the accepted norm for quick currency worldwide (indeed, two of them just opened in Moscow). The two most popular overseas networks, Cirrus and Plus, can be accessed by over 90 percent of the ATM bank cards in circulation in the United States. Another attractive benefit to using worldwide ATMs is that the ATMs' foreign exchange rate is often lower than the rate charged by local banks.

Corporate travelers are depending more and more on automatic teller machines. ATMs are available 24 hours a day, 365 days a year. And with hundreds of thousands of machines available (see Exhibit 11–2), an ATM is usually just a step away. This limits the amount of money corporate travelers need to carry for a long trip. In addition, it minimizes the risk of financial loss if the guest's wallet is stolen or lost.

Although this is the age of credit cards and electronic payments, travelers still need to carry cash for expenses such as taxi cabs, tips to skycaps or bellpersons, newspapers, and incidental items. Corporate travelers have historically received cash advances prior to departing on business trips. Yet cash advances are costly, running as much as $20 or more to process each advance because of the number of people involved. The traveler needs to fill out the cash advance request, the manager needs to approve it, an accounts payable clerk processes it, and a financial manager cuts the final check.

In recent years, many firms have begun using ATMs exclusively. The traveler uses the corporate credit card to secure cash for the trip, getting additional cash when necessary along the way. At the end of the trip, whatever cash remains unspent can be redeposited directly back to the ATM account. Even considering the fees charged by the ATM network, this is a considerably cheaper way of handling cash advances.

Despite their popularity elsewhere, ATMs are still relatively scarce in hotel lobbies. However, it is only a matter of time before these cash-vending machines regularly appear in hotel lobbies. There may even be a rental fee to the hotel for the space in the lobby. If nothing else, guests could be encouraged to pay bills by cash (getting the money from the lobby machine) and thus reduce both the hotel credit-card fee and the costly delay in collection that hotels now experience.

Paid-Outs to Concessionaires.   Full-service hotels often arrange for local merchants to provide guest services the hotel is unable to offer. These merchants may actually have an outlet inside the hotel (e.g., a beauty salon, florist, or gift shop), or they may contract services off-premise (e.g., a travel agent, valet cleaning, or a printing shop). These private vendors are commonly referred to as concessionaires; their shops are known as **concessions.**

The concessionaire–guest relationship often mandates that the hotel act as middleman. In circumstances where the hotel relays the goods on behalf of the guest (laundry is usually delivered to the guest's room by the bellstaff, for example) or where the concessionaire looks to the hotel for collection (say, when a guest charges her hairstyling to the room folio), the hotel is acting as an intermediary. As such, the hotel is sometimes entitled to a fee or commission for its part in the process. It is not uncommon for hotels to earn 10 to 20 percent of the laundry and dry-cleaning revenue (the other 80 to 90 percent accrues to the vendor) as their share of providing laundry bags, bellstaff pickups and deliveries, storage, and collections.

The hotel also finds itself stuck in the middle when dealing with problems or complaints. When a business suit has been lost or destroyed, the guest is not interested in learning that the laundry service is a private concession. Quality guest service dictates that the hotel solve the problem on behalf of the guest!

Posting the Paid-Out.   The hotel also acts as intermediary in terms of disbursing revenues to the concessionaire. Payment is made to the merchant when the service is completed and charged to the guest's folio as a paid-out. Specifically, the clerk debits accounts receivable (a paid-out to the guest's folio) and credits cash. At the end of the shift, the cashier's balance report reflects the reduction of cash in the money drawer. In essence, the hotel has loaned the money on behalf of the guest and awaits repayment when the guest checks out. Of course, all of the costs associated with float, credit-card discount fees, and uncollectable accounts are issues for negotiation between the hotel and the concessionaire.

Paying the concessionaire in cash each time the service is used is expensive and time-consuming, for the merchant as well as for the hotel, since the concessionaire must wait for the cash and sign the paperwork. In many cases, a different plan is arranged. The hotel bills the guest just as if the concessionaire were a department of the hotel, collects on check-out, and reimburses the merchant periodically. In such cases, the guest's folio looks a bit different as well. Rather than reflecting a paid-out posting (Exhibit 11–1), the charge instead is posted to an actual department (say, laundry or valet). The net effect—the guest owes the hotel—remains unchanged.

Refunds at Check-Out.   Although unusual, it is possible for the hotel to owe the guest at the conclusion of the guest's stay. This happens in one of several ways. Either there was a substantial deposit with the reservation, or a large payment on account was made on (or after) arrival. If the guest shortens the stay, or the hotel adjusts the rate downward, there could be a credit balance at the time of departure. Paid-in-advance guests who make additional payments to cover charges to their rooms (such as for telephone calls) also show a credit balance.

At check-out, the hotel pays the guest. Zeroing the credit balance of the account requires a debit or charge entry. A cash advance (paid-out) voucher is prepared for the guest's signature in the amount of the credit balance. At the end of the shift, the computerized cashier's balance report subtracts the amount of the paid-out from the total cash remaining in the money drawer.

Cash is never refunded if the original payment was not made in cash! The guest might have a credit payment as a result of an unused deposit made with a travel agency voucher or with a credit card. A cash refund, if any, should be made by the travel agent to the guest, and the clerk should so explain. The hotel would settle with the agency, the original source of the credit. If the guest's personal credit card were the source, the hotel would issue a rebate against the credit card.

Similarly, large cash deposits made by the guest may not be refundable on check-out. Before receiving the large cash deposit, the clerk should explain hotel policy regarding paid-outs. Some hotels restrict the size of the paid-out to, say, $100. Anything above that amount requires a check to be processed by the hotel accounting department and mailed to the guest's home. This prevents guests from depositing illegitimate traveler's checks, personal checks (discussed later in this chapter), or counterfeit money and then attempting to collect legitimate cash against that amount the following day.

Receipts

The same forces that have reduced the amount of cash paid-outs being handled by the front-office cashiers have similarly affected cash receipts. Very few guests use cash anymore to pay for anything, especially hotel bills.

Cash Receipts at Check-Out.   Cash reconciliations represent a very small percentage of total room check-outs. Most guests pay by credit card or direct bill account; few use cash, traveler's checks, or personal checks.

Posting cash paid to the folio has the opposite effect from posting a cash paid-out to the folio. Where the paid-out increases the amount owed by the guest (debit to accounts receivable), cash paid decreases the amount owed by the guest (credit to accounts receivable). In all cases, the amount collected from the guest is the exact amount required to reduce the folio balance to zero.

It is a quick procedure: The computerized property management system maintains a cumulative balance, which indicates the exact amount due. Some hotels display the folio on the computer screen for the guest to scan, others preprint hard copies of all departing guests' folios, and still others encourage self-check-out via the television screen (see Chapter 14).

Whatever the method, all cashiers are trained to inquire about very recent charges that may still be unrecorded. Catching unposted telephone or breakfast charges minimizes the number of late charges, with their high rate of uncollection and guest displeasure.

Cash Receipts on Account.   Payments may be requested at any time, not only on departure. Long-term guests are often billed weekly, as a means of improving the hotel's cash flow and keeping the guest as current as possible. Guests who exceed certain credit limits or guests who generate too many charges (especially items normally paid for in cash) are also billed on account. Sometimes, guests themselves decide to make payments against their accounts.

Departing guests normally receive a copy of their bill as receipt. Guests who make payment on account often receive something quite different. Although many computerized properties provide guests with a printed copy of their folio displaying the credit received from the cash payment on account, many other hotels utilize a simple cash receipt form (see Exhibit 11–3). This form is presented to the guest as a means of documenting the cash payment.

The desk is frequently faced with a guest—especially one who hasn't traveled extensively—who tries to pay on the day before departure. Because of possible late

EXHIBIT 11–3

Shown is a cash credit slip used to document cash payments made by the guest.

```
 _____
|                                                           |
|              CASH CREDIT              24901               |
|                                                           |
|                 DATE_____ 19_____                 |
|                                                           |
|  NAME_____       ROOM_____ |
|  _____ |
|     ACKNOWLEDGEMENT IS MADE OF RECEIPT OF AMOUNT PRINTED   |
|          BELOW.                                           |
|     THIS HAS BEEN CREDITED TO YOUR ACCOUNT.    THANK YOU.  |
|     CASHIER: – USE THIS RECEIPT IN THE FOLLOWING          |
|              INSTANCES: –                                 |
|         (1) IN CASE GUEST DOES NOT PRESENT WEEKLY BILL TO  |
|             BE RECEIPTED.                                  |
|         (2) PAYMENT TO APPLY ON ACCOUNT.                  |
|         (3) ADVANCE PAYMENT.                              |
|   _____  |
|  |                                                      | |
|  |                                                      | |
|  |_____| |
|                 (DO NOT WRITE IN ABOVE SPACE)             |
|  Kayco NCR Form No. 130         SIGNED_____   |
|_____|
```

Courtesy: Kayco Systems, Lake Elsinore, California.

charges, the desk tries to discourage guests from making payment too early. In fact, day-early payments require special attention by the cashier, who must be certain to collect enough to cover the upcoming room-night and room tax that will not be posted until the auditor arrives. So the employee convinces the guest to wait until the next day rather than paying in full the previous day in anticipation of an early departure. Naturally enough, guests who are so convinced find it incomprehensible that they are unable to conclude their business until the next morning. This is much less a problem in modern hotels, which provide the guest with a number of rapid automatic or self-check-out options.

Cash Receipts at Check-In.   All guests are asked to establish credit on check-in. With cash customers, and sometimes with guests who appear suspect (possibly because they have little or no luggage), the hotel asks for full payment up front. This is especially common in limited-service motel operations.

In such cases, a slightly different posting procedure may prevail. Rather than simply posting paid to the folio (credit to the accounts receivable folio and debit to cash) and leaving the credit amount in place until the night audit, some hotels post room and tax immediately and present the guest with a zero balance receipt.

No posting is required by the night auditor, but the guest is still listed on the audit of the arriving night. The guest is similarly counted as part of the room and house count, appearing on the departure list the following day. Other times, the cashier does not post the room charge and the guest is given a receipt such as that in Exhibit 11–3. To get a copy of the receipted folio, the guest must return to the desk at check-out time. That would also be the case with a computer-prepared folio. Posting the room during the night audit means the folio is incomplete until then.

Unless an additional deposit is made, no additional charges are allowed against a paid-in-advance guest, who usually leaves without stopping at the desk. An additional room charge is made and collected each succeeding day the customer remains. Unless this is received, someone on the desk automatically checks out advance payments by the check-out hour of the following day. Some economy motels, where all guests pay in advance, actually lock out guests who remain beyond the check-out hour. Less extreme measures, including telephone message lamps, are usually used to communicate with the paid-in-advance guest.

Automatic check-out of a paid-in-advance guest requires coordination and communication. The front desk must be careful not to prematurely show as vacant any room that was paid in advance. Prior to automatically checking the guest out, a bellperson or housekeeper must first inspect the room. Only after they communicate that the room is truly empty should the front desk check the guest out.

Reservation Deposit Receipts.   As previously explained, cash deposits (checks included) are not widely used. Credit cards are the most frequent means of guaranteeing reservations. Still, some hotels, particularly resorts in high season, require cash deposits.

Different hotels handle these deposits in different ways, usually as a function of their size and the sophistication of their accounting systems. The easiest but least businesslike method assigns the check to the front-office cash drawer. There it stays, unrecorded, until the guest arrives weeks or months later. The check is then applied to a newly opened folio as if the money were just received that day. This procedure simplifies the bookkeeping, especially if there is a cancellation, but it has little additional merit even for a small hotel. Lack of a proper record and the failure to clear the check through the bank indicate poor management of both procedure and funds.

Sometimes the actual folio that is to be assigned the guest on arrival is opened when the deposit check is received. This procedure is extremely cumbersome for manual or semiautomated properties that utilize prenumbered folios. In such cases, the posted folio may remain at the front office (in the cashier's bucket or well) for weeks or months.

However, in computerized properties, this procedure works quite satisfactorily. That is because one major difference between manual and computerized properties is the timing as to when they assign the guest folio. In a manual property (unless a reservation deposit is received), the folio is not assigned until check-in, which may be months later. In a computerized property, a folio identification number is assigned immediately, at the moment of reservation. Therefore, it is wholly appropriate for the front desk to post an advance-deposit payment to a preassigned electronic folio, but less appropriate to post an advance to a manually assigned folio.

Still another method of handling deposits is to create a special front-office folio called "advance deposits." Each advance deposit received is posted to this account (credit the special account and debit cash). This special account carries a credit balance, reflecting the fact that the hotel owes money (or service) to each of the advance-deposit guests. When the guest eventually arrives, it is a simple matter to transfer the credit balance to the newly opened folio. This is accomplished by posting a transfer debit against the special account and posting an offsetting transfer credit to the new guest's folio. In the end, the new guest folio shows the credit balance from the guest's original advance deposit, which may have been received weeks ago.

Establishing a City Ledger Account.   The most common method for handling reservation deposits uses the city ledger. An account is established in the city ledger for advance-deposit receipts. Guest deposits are credited to that account and later transferred to the folio on guest arrival. The city ledger account sounds exactly like the special advance-deposit account discussed above—and it is. The primary difference is a function of accounting control.

In the special advance-deposit account, control for both receipts (credit the special account) and disbursements (transfer debit the special account) is retained by the front-office staff. This is contrary to safe accounting practices, and it is the primary catalyst behind establishing a city ledger account for advance deposits. The city ledger account removes the potential for front-desk cashiers to embezzle from the hotel.

With a city ledger advance-deposit account, the front office (the cashier) sees only one side of the transfer, the credit made to the account of the arriving guest. The debit portion to the city ledger advance-deposit account is made by the accounting office, not by the front-office cashier. This contrasts with the debit and credit transfers both being done by the front-office cashier when the special account is maintained at the front office, as described previously.

As an additional control, the reservation office keeps both the cashier's cage and the city ledger accountant current with the names and amounts of advance deposits. Each day's anticipated list is compared to the actual arrivals, and oversights are corrected. Deposits applied that day by the front-office cashier become the basis of the city ledger debit entry made by the accountant. Unclaimed deposits serve as a subsidiary list to the advance-deposit account in the city ledger. Some unclaimed deposits will be returned because of timely cancellations. Others will be forfeited to pay for the rooms that were saved for the no-shows.

House Receipts and Expenses

Although the front-office cashier is primarily responsible for handling rooms-related revenues and disbursements, other responsibilities are assigned as a function of convenience. Due to the fact that the front desk is centrally located and accessible to all departments of the hotel, the cashier takes on a set of hotel-related cash responsibilities. Specifically, the front-office cashier is responsible for house receipts and expenses.

Assorted City and General Ledger Receipts. Some hotels, especially small properties that lack a full accounting staff, elect to funnel all cash and check receipts through the front office. This adds another person and record to the process, which strengthens the internal control. It also adds another set of responsibilities to the front-office cashier.

Examples of assorted city and general ledger receipts that are not affiliated with the rooms division include payments for meetings or banquet functions, reimbursements or rebates for overpayment to vendors, refunds or credits from taxes, and lease revenues from merchants or concessionaires. In small hotels, the front-office cashier might serve as dining room or lounge cashier. Magazines, newspapers, and candy may be sold across the desk. Coin collections from vending machines or sales of miscellaneous items such as kitchen fat (to tallow-rendering plants) or container deposits may all flow through the front desk. Meal tickets in American-plan resorts are also commonly sold at the front desk.

Depending on the accounting system in place, the cashier posts paid (credit) to some type of general account and it is reflected (debit to cash) in the cash drawer documentation. The specific detailing of the general account (each affected account must be updated) is later handled by the accounting department on an item-by-item

EXHIBIT 11–4

Shown is a typical petty cash voucher for use with imprest petty cash fund.

PETTY CASH

AMOUNT $ ___6 $\frac{37}{...}$___   DATE _Dec. 18_

FOR ___one hotel T-shirt —___

___Promotional gift to Sunshine Tours Leader___

_____

CHARGE TO ___Director of Sales and Marketing___

                    SIGNED ___Mary Noel___

KAYCO FORM NO. 1046

Courtesy: Kayco Systems, Lake Elsinore, California.

basis. For frequent transactions (say, meal tickets at an American-plan resort) the accounting department will establish an account number or code directly in the property management system. In this way, postings made by the front-office cashier are immediately reflected and updated in the account affected.

Assorted House Paid-Outs.   Just as the front-office cashier handles cash receipts from miscellaneous sources, petty expenditures for house expenses may be made there as well. And just as some of the cash coming into the desk may not actually be guest receipts, some of the cash flowing out from the desk may not be treated as guest paid-outs. The front-office cashier acts, on the one hand, as a depository for the accounting department and, on the other hand, as the accounting department's disbursing agent.

Unlike guest paid-outs, which have an impact on the cashier's drawer, house paid-outs do not. As such, house paid-outs are not posted to the property management system—guest paid-outs most certainly are. The reason house paid-outs do not affect the cashier's drawer is because house paid-outs (petty cash disbursements) are treated just like cash.

The person receiving the money (say, the bellperson who just purchased $30 worth of flour for the kitchen) signs a **petty cash** voucher (see Exhibit 11–4). The voucher is kept in the cashier's drawer and treated as if it were cash. It is cash, because the accounting department's general cashier will buy the petty cash voucher at some later point. The purchase of this voucher by the general cashier reimburses the front-office cashier and leaves the cash drawer intact—as if the petty cash disbursement had never been processed in the first place.

The Imprest Petty Cash Fund.   If the front-office cashiers are reimbursed daily, the petty cash fund is administered by the accounting department's general cashier. If the front-office cashiers are only reimbursed when the petty cash vouchers reach a sizable sum or at the end of the month, it is known as an **imprest petty cash** fund. An imprest fund authorizes the front-office cashier to hold petty cash vouchers in the drawer day after day.

House vouchers are then accumulated and kept in the cashiers' drawers as part of their cash count. Weekly, monthly, or on demand, the general cashier buys the vouchers from the front-office cashiers. No daily reimbursements are made.

A wide range of small expenditures are processed through the petty cash fund. Salary advances to good employees or termination pay to employees the hotel wants immediately off the premises might be paid by the fund. Some freight bills need immediate cash payment under ICC regulations. Stamp purchases, cash purchases from local farmers or purveyors, and other payments (Exhibit 11–4) are handled through the front office of a small hotel.

The Cashier's Daily Report

Every cashier in the hotel, whether at the front office, the dining room, the bar, room service, or the snack bar, prepares a daily cash report. With the report, the cashier turns in the departmental monies. These funds (plus any that clear through the general cashier) constitute the daily deposit made at the bank.

The daily deposit is supported by a flow of cash records. The records of the front-office cashiers (the cashier's balance report—see Exhibits 11–5 and 11–6, discussed shortly) are first reviewed by the night auditor. They are processed again the following day through the income audit. The income audit combines the front-office cash records with the records of the other departmental cashiers. This creates a support document (see Exhibit 11–7) for the bank deposit.

Preparing the Cashier's Report

The front-office cashier's report is much more complicated than standard cashier reports found in other departments. This is due to the bidirectional flow of the front-office cashier's responsibilities. Whereas departmental cashiers only receive payment from guests, front-office cashiers both receive funds and pay them out.

The Cashier's Bank.   Each cashier receives and signs for a permanent supply of cash, called the **bank.** The amount varies depending on the position and shift that the cashier has. A busy commercial hotel needs front-office banks of as much as $10,000, but the night cashier at the same hotel might get along with $250. It is partly a question of safety and partly a question of good financial management. Excessive funds should not be tied up unnecessarily; temporary increases can be made for busy periods.

A careful review of all house banks may release sizable sums for more profitable use. One major accounting firm reports that the total of house banks and cash on hand is about 2 percent of total sales (about $600 per room). An excessive percentage suggests that cashiers are borrowing from their banks or that daily deposits and reimbursements are not being made, which means that extra funds are required to operate the banks. There are other reasons, of course—infrequent reimbursement of the petty cash fund, for example, which makes the fund unnecessarily large.

EXHIBIT 11–5

A cashier's balance report shows cash, check, city ledger (credit card), and paid-out transactions (accounts). The code column references the hotel's chart of accounts. See Exhibits 11–6, 11–7, 11–8, and 11–9.

```
CASHIER:  Ardelle          REPORT DATE: 03/09/--              12:27:30

                          CASHIER'S BALANCE REPORT

CODE    ROOM    LAST NAME      FIRST NAME    ACCOUNT    RATE    TIME        AMOUNT

0001    217     JOHNSON        LINDA         CASH       RACK    06:57:23       48.52
0026    1171    VANLAND        TOM           VISA       GRP     07:11:10      179.37
0024    678     HARRISON       GEORGE        DSCV       TOUR    07:12:12       87.50
0025    456     LENNON         JOHN          MC         TOUR    07:16:44       87.50
0011    319     WILSON         BILL          CHCK       DISC    07:17:17       82.50
0011    337     ADAMS          JOHN          CHCK       RACK    07:21:50       67.21
0031    902     GREENBACKS     LOTTA         POUT       RACK    07:24:01      -17.50
0026    842     STUART         LYLE          VISA       GRP     08:10:15      161.40
0024    212     JONES          ROBERT        DSCV       DISC    08:34:20      242.59
0011    711     GREGORY        GARY          CHCK       TOUR    09:10:10      111.77
0011    315     GONNE          CONNIE        CHCK       RACK    09:44:30       96.20
0031    107     MOORE          MANNY         POUT       TOUR    10:10:15      -20.00
0025    371     ORTIZ          RAUL          MC         RACK    10:40:29       68.57
0011    211     JACKSON        ANDY          CHCK       DISC    11:04:41       46.31
0011    551     WASHINGTON     BOB           CHCK       TOUR    11:57:01    1,278.71
```

Cashiers lock their banks in the safe or hotel vault after each shift. Funds may not be taken from the bank for personal use. Surprise counts of cashiers' banks are made by the accounting office, which secures the cashier's safe deposit box closed and requires the cashier coming on duty to summon an auditor before opening the box.

Unfortunately, common banks for several employees to share are not unusual. These are seen in every department from the bar to the front office. Control is difficult to maintain, and responsibility almost impossible to fix. Custom and convenience seem to be the major reasons for continuing this poor practice, although it obviously releases extra funds as well.

Everyone handling money should be covered by a bond. Bonds are written to cover either individual positions or as blanket coverage, whichever best meets the hotel's needs.

The bank must contain enough small bills and coins to carry out the cashiering function. There is absolutely no value in having a $300 bank comprised of three $100 bills.

For the example that follows, assume a bank of $500.

Net Receipts.   **Net receipts** is the difference between what the cashier took in and what was paid out. Since only front-office cashiers are permitted to make advances, net receipts in the bar and coffee shop are the same as total receipts.

EXHIBIT 11–6

This is a cashier's report by code (chart of accounts). This portion of the report shows payment methods against which the cashier can reconcile cash, checks, and charges. This report shows payment activity by room. Other reports would also be printed showing activity by department (say, telephone, restaurant, or lounge).

```
CASHIER: Ardelle           REPORT DATE: 03/09/--                  12:28:41

                   CASHIER'S BALANCE REPORT BY CODE
========================================================================

CODE   ROOM    LAST NAME    FIRST NAME    ACCOUNT   RATE   TIME      AMOUNT

0001   217     JOHNSON      LINDA         CASH      RACK   06:57:23    48.52
TOTAL  CASH    0001                                                    48.52

0011   319     WILSON       BILL          CHCK      DISC   07:17:17    82.50
0011   337     ADAMS        JOHN          CHCK      RACK   07:21:50    67.21
0011   711     GREGORY      GARY          CHCK      TOUR   09:10:10   111.77
0011   315     GONNE        CONNIE        CHCK      RACK   09:44:30    96.20
0011   211     JACKSON      ANDY          CHCK      DISC   11:04:41    46.31
0011   551     WASHINGTON   BOB           CHCK      TOUR   11:57:01 1,278.71
TOTAL  CHECKS  0011                                                 1,682.70


TOTAL  AMERICAN EXPRESS   0021                                         0.00


TOTAL  CARTE BLANCHE      0022                                         0.00


TOTAL  DINERS CLUB        0023                                         0.00

0024   678     HARRISON     GEORGE        DSCV      TOUR   07:12:12    87.50
0024   212     JONES        ROBERT        DSCV      DISC   08:34:20   242.59
TOTAL  DISCOVER           0024                                       330.09

0025   456     LENNON       JOHN          MC        TOUR   07:16:44    87.50
0025   371     ORTIZ        RAUL          MC        RACK   10:40:29    68.57
TOTAL  MASTERCARD         0025                                       156.07

0026   1171    VANLAND      TOM           VISA      GRP    07:11:10   179.37
0026   842     STUART       LYLE          VISA      GRP    08:10:15   161.40
TOTAL  VISA    0026                                                  340.77

0031   902     GREENBACKS   LOTTA         POUT      RACK   07:24:01   -17.50
0031   107     MOORE        MANNY         POUT      TOUR   10:10:15   -20.00
TOTAL  PAID-OUTS 0031                                                -37.50
========================================================================
```

Exhibit 11–7

This cash receipts summary report recaps records of all departmental cashiers and serves as the source document for the income auditor's daily bank deposit. Information shown for the first front-office cashier (Ardelle) corresponds with Exhibits 11–5, 11–6, 11–8, and 11–9.

CLERK: Thomas

REPORT DATE: 03/09/--   12:39:17

CASH RECEIPTS SUMMARY REPORT

DEPARTMENT	CASHIER	CASH SALES	COLLECTION TRANSIENT RECEIVABLES	COLLECTION CITY LEDGER RECEIVABLES	TOTAL CASH RECEIPTS	PAID-OUTS TRANSIENT	PAID-OUTS CITY LEDGER	NET CASH RECEIPTS	ADD:OVERAGES LESS:SHORTAGES	TURN IN FOR DEPOSIT
FRONT OFFICE	ARDELLE		452.51	1,278.71	1,731.22	-37.50	0.00	1,693.72	-.76	1,692.96
FRONT OFFICE	BABETTE		1,171.14	622.50	1,793.64	-49.00	-25.00	1,719.64	1.20	1,720.84
FRONT OFFICE	CHARLES		850.19	1,460.51	2,310.70	-11.50	-5.00	2,294.20	0.00	2,294.20
FRONT OFFICE	DIANE		67.10	0.00	67.10	0.00	0.00	67.10	0.00	67.10
FRONT OFFICE	EDWARD		572.46	604.27	1,176.73	-12.90	0.00	1,163.83	-2.41	1,161.42
FRONT OFFICE	FRANCES		934.72	210.58	1,145.30	-18.65	-14.00	1,112.65	.87	1,113.52
GIFT SHOP	GARY	687.14	0.00	0.00	687.14	0.00	0.00	687.14	0.00	687.14
GIFT SHOP	HARRY	901.73	0.00	0.00	901.73	0.00	0.00	901.73	-1.47	900.26
LOUNGE	ILONA	1,262.85	0.00	0.00	1,262.85	0.00	0.00	1,262.85	1.01	1,263.86
LOUNGE	JEROME	2,411.59	0.00	0.00	2,411.59	0.00	0.00	2,411.59	0.00	2,411.59
RESTAURANT	KATE	816.44	0.00	0.00	816.44	0.00	0.00	816.44	-.25	816.19
RESTAURANT	LOUISE	1,017.55	0.00	0.00	1,017.55	0.00	0.00	1,017.55	-.61	1,016.94
SNACK BAR	MARC	469.68	0.00	0.00	469.68	0.00	0.00	469.68	2.71	472.39
SNACK BAR	NANETTE	371.02	0.00	0.00	371.02	0.00	0.00	371.02	0.00	371.02
DAILY TOTALS		7,938.00	4,048.12	4,176.57	16,162.69	-129.55	-44.00	15,989.14	.29	15,989.43

Net receipts at the front office are computed by subtracting total advances (paid-outs), city and transient, from total receipts, city and transient. House paid-outs and miscellaneous receipts are not included (as discussed earlier in this chapter).

For discussion, assume the totals of the front-office cashier's balance report to be:

Receipts	
Transient receivables	$2,376.14
City receivables	422.97
Total receipts	$2,799.11
Paid-Outs	
Transient ledger paid-outs	$ 107.52
City ledger paid-outs	27.50
Total paid-outs	$ 135.02

The front-office cashier accesses this information through the cashier's balance report (Exhibits 11–5 and 11–6). Some cashier's balance reports provide only summary data such as that described in this section—total transient ledger receipts, total city ledger (and general ledger) receipts, total transient ledger paid-outs, and total city ledger paid-outs. Other cashier's balance reports are very complete, telling the cashier exactly how much net receipts to have in the drawer.

Whether the system provides detail for net receipts or not, this figure is a simple number to compute. In this example, net receipts are total receipts ($2,799.11) less total paid-outs ($135.02) equals $2,664.09 in net receipts.

Over or Short.   No cashier is perfect. The day's close occasionally finds the cash drawer over or short. Sometimes the error is mathematical, and either the cashier finds it without help or it is uncovered later by the auditor.

Errors caused by poor change-making are usually beyond remedy unless they are in the house's favor. Guests may not acknowledge overpayments, but they will complain soon enough if they have been shortchanged. Restitution is possible if the cash count at the end of the shift proves this to be so.

Overages and shortages become a point of employee-management conflict when cashiers are required to make up all shortages but turn in all overages. Other systems allow overages to offset shortages, asking only that the month's closing record balance. Both procedures encourage the cashier to reconcile at the expense of ethical standards. Shortchanging, poor addition, and altered records accommodate these management requirements. It is a better policy to have the house absorb the shortages and keep the overages. A record of individual performance is then maintained to determine if individual overages and shortages balance over the long run. They should, unless the cashier is inept or dishonest.

Over or short is the difference between what the cashier should have in the cash drawer and what is actually there. It is the comparison of a mathematically generated net total against a physical count of the money in the drawer. The cashier *should* have the sum of the bank plus the net receipts. What money is on hand in the drawer is what the cashier *does* have. Over or short is the difference between the *should have* and the *does have*.

In our continuing example, the front-office cashier should have $3,164.09 on hand at the close of the shift. This is calculated by taking net receipts ($2,664.09) plus starting bank ($500) equals $3,164.09.

Should Have on Hand	
Net receipts	$2,664.09
Starting bank	$ 500.00
Total of should have	$3,164.09

Once the cashier knows how much should be in the drawer, it is a simple matter of comparing that total with the actual cash on hand. The cashier's drawer probably contains personal and traveler's checks, currency, coin, and petty cash vouchers. Credit cards are not included in this discussion of the cashier's drawer because they are often electronically deposited to the hotel's bank or handled by the accounting department as a city ledger accounts receivable. A full discussion of credit-card processes is included in the following chapter.

Does Have on Hand	
Checks (personal and traveler's)	$2,704.60
Currency	356.00
Coin	62.13
House petty cash vouchers	42.50
Total cash on hand	$3,165.23

The cashier apparently has more in the drawer than there should be. In such a case, the cashier has an overage. If the amount of cash on hand were actually less than what there should be, the cashier would be short. The amount of the overage or shortage is simple enough to compute—just subtract the amount there should be ($3,164.09) from the amount of cash on hand ($3,165.23). The net total ($1.14) is the amount of overage (if it is a positive net number, it is always an overage) or shortage (if it is a negative net number, it is always a shortage).

Cashier Turn-In.   When the cashier has calculated net receipts, determined the amount there should be, and counted the actual cash in the drawer, it is a simple matter to compute the **turn-in.** However, in many hotels, the cashier is not responsible for counting the drawer. In such operations, cashiers are not allowed to count the drawer even if they wish to.

When cashiers total receipts and count their drawers, they know exactly how much they are over or short. Overages can be very appealing to unscrupulous cashiers. If allowed to calculate the amount of overage, some cashiers will pocket the difference. That is troublesome, but it becomes double trouble when the cashier's calculations were in error. If the cashier bases the overage amount on an error and then steals that amount, the mistake (and the theft) is likely to be uncovered by the night auditor. This is a common way in which hotels uncover employee embezzlement.

For this reason, many hotels limit the employee's access and knowledge regarding the correct amount of the day's deposit. Instead, the employee rebuilds the starting bank with currency and coin and then deposits everything else remaining. In such operations, the front-office cashier functions no differently than a departmental cashier.

The Front-Office Turn-in.   The turn-in of the front-office cashier is more involved than the turn-in of the departmental cashiers. The front-office bank is used to cash checks, make change, and advance cash as well as to accept receipts. Assume, for example, that nothing took place during the watch except check cashing. At the close of the day, the bank would contain nothing but nonnegotiable checks. It would be impossible to make change the next day with a drawer full of personal checks. So, the cashier must drop or turn in all nonnegotiable items, including checks, traveler's checks, foreign funds, large bills, casino chips, cash in poor condition, vouchers for house expenses, and even refund slips for inoperative vending machines.

The objective of the cashier's turn-in is to rebuild the starting bank in the proper amount and variety of denominations to be effective during the next day's shift, and drop the rest of the contents of the cash drawer. Sometimes, there are enough small bills and coins in the cashier's drawer to rebuild tomorrow's bank quite easily. At other times, there are too many large denomination bills or nonnegotiable checks and paper to effectively rebuild tomorrow's bank. In such cases, the cashier must turn in all of the large bills and nonnegotiable paper, leaving tomorrow's bank short. That's OK, because the income audit staff will leave currency and coin in requested denominations for the start of tomorrow's shift. By adding these funds to the short bank, tomorrow's drawer will be both accurate and effective.

Our continuing example helps to illustrate the concept of turn-in or drop. Remember that the cashier has a total of $3,165.23 on hand, comprised of checks ($2,704.60), currency ($356.00), coin ($62.13), and house petty cash vouchers ($42.50). The cashier must turn in all of the nonnegotiable paper, including checks ($2,704.60) and house petty cash vouchers ($42.50), which equals a $2,747.10 total turn-in.

Due Bank.   At this point, it is quite obvious that the cashier does not have enough negotiable money to rebuild tomorrow's $500 starting bank. In fact, tomorrow's bank will be short by $81.87. This shortage is commonly referred to as the **due bank.** It is also known as the **due back, difference returnable, U-owe-mes,** or the **exchange.**

The due bank is calculated by taking the amount tomorrow's bank should be ($500) less the amount of money kept (currency of $356.00 and coin of $62.13) equals the amount the starting bank will be short ($81.87).

Due Bank Computation	
Original bank	$500.00
Cash on hand	418.13
Due bank	$ 81.87

Since the cashier always retains the exact bank, it is apparent that the turn-in includes the overage or allows for the shortage. The hotel, not the cashier, funds the overages and shortages. A due bank formula, which produces the same due bank

Exhibit 11–8

Preparation of the front-office cashier's report requires an understanding of the computations. This figure is based on a different set of numbers than those found on the preceding pages. It is based on the same numbers shown in Exhibits 11–5, 11–6, 11–7, and 11–9.

Given

1. The bank at $1,000

2. The cashier's balance report shows:

Cash receipts (both transient and city ledger)	$1,731.22
Paid-outs (both transient and city ledger)	$ 37.50

3. Count in the cash drawer at the close of the watch:

Checks	$1,682.70
Currency	821.00
Coin	177.26
House vouchers	12.00
	$2,692.96

Computation

1. Net receipts (gross receipts minus advances)

   $NR = \$1,731.22 - \$37.50 = \$1,693.72$

2. Overage and shortage (what should be in the drawer minus what is in the drawer)

   $O\&S = (\$1,000 + 1,693.72) - 2,692.96 = \$.76$ short

3. Turn-in (checks, vouchers, other nonnegotiable items and all cash except the bank)

   $TI = \$1,682.70 + 12.00 = \$1,694.70$

4. Due bank (amount needed to reconstitute the bank)

   $DB = \$1,000 - (821.00 + 177.26) = \$1.74$

5. Verification (the excess of the turn-in over the amount due)

   $DB = \$1,694.70 - (\$1,693.72 - .76) = \$1.74$

figure as the simple subtraction computation, mathematically illustrates the hotel's responsibility for the over and short.

Due Bank Formula

Due bank = Turn-in − (Net receipts ± Over or short)

Due bank = $2,747.10 − ($2,664.09 + $1.14)

Due bank = $2,747.10 − ($2,665.23)

Due bank = $81.87

To keep their banks functional, cashiers specify the coin and currency denominations of the due bank. There is little utility in a due bank of several large bills. For the very same reason, the turn-in may be increased with large bills to be exchanged for more negotiable currency. More often, the change is obtained from the general cashier before the shift closes, or from another cashier who has small change to exchange.

Exhibits 11–8 and 11–9 offer another example of the due bank and illustrate the completed cash envelope.

The Income Audit

Income auditors and hotel general cashiers are members of the hotel's accounting department. They usually perform the income audit each morning to process the cashier drops made the previous day. The purpose of the income audit is to verify that each department's (and indeed each shift's) cashier has accurately dropped (turned in) the amount indicated on the deposit envelope (Exhibit 11–9). Although

EXHIBIT 11–9

Shown is a cashier's envelope for preparing the turn-in at the close of the shift. Exhibit 11–8 (and Exhibits 11–5, 11–6, and 11–7) show the source of the figures that appear on the envelope, but note that the net receipts figure includes the $.76 shortage.

DEPARTMENT CASHIER'S REPORT

DAY *Tue*   DATE *3-9*   19

CASHIER *Ardelle*

DEPT. *F.O.*

SHIFT *8:00*   A.M. ☑ P.M. ☐   TO *4:00*   A.M. ☐ P.M. ☑

	AMOUNT		✓
CURRENCY $1.00			
" $5.00			
" $10.00			
" $20.00			
" $50.00			
" $100.00			
COIN 1¢			
" 5¢			
SILVER 10¢			
" 25¢			
" 50¢			
" $1.00			
BAR STUBS:			
PAID-OUTS:			
VOUCHERS AND CHECKS:			
New York Exchange-Wilson	82	50	
Cleveland Trust-Adams	67	21	
Chicago 1st Natl.-Gregory	111	77	
Bank America-Gonne	96	20	
Natl. Bank of St. Louis-Jackson	46	31	
First Interstate-Washington	1278	71	
Postage Stamp Voucher	12	-	
TRAVELER'S CHECKS			
LESS SHORT		76	
TOTAL AMOUNT ENCLOSED	1694	70	
NET RECEIPTS WITH O & S	1692	96	
DIFFERENCE	1	74	

Courtesy: Kayco Systems, Lake Elsinore, California.

this function is performed in a vault or safe room, there are several general cashiers present and the audit may even be videotaped as an additional safeguard.

The income audit generally has two distinct purposes: to verify that cashiers really turned in what they said they turned in, and to prepare the hotel's daily bank deposit. During this function, every deposit envelope from every department cashier is opened, verified, and added to the growing pile of cash, checks, traveler's checks, foreign currency, house vouchers, and so on. Every form of payment except credit cards is counted, totaled, and added to the hotel's daily deposit. Credit cards are the exception because hotels electronically deposit many national cards (e.g., Visa and MasterCard)—other credit cards are billed through the city ledger (e.g., American Express)—placing them directly in the hands of the accounting staff.

All cashiers are scrutinized by the income audit staff. This includes both front-office cashiers (who probably calculate the exact amount of their turn-in and know shift by shift whether they are over or short) as well as departmental cashiers (who may or may not actually precalculate their turn-in before preparing the deposit envelope). In the case of departmental cashiers who rebuild their starting bank and blindly drop the rest of their money, general cashier merely counts and verifies the contents of the drop. Whereas the general cashier attends to the actual count of the cash turned in, the income auditor focuses on the accuracy of the amounts reported by the various departmental cashiers. Together, the general cashier(s) and income auditor(s) make up the day audit team.

Paying Off the Due Back.   Many cashiers—front-office and departmental cashiers alike—turn in more money than necessary. The excess amount of their drop is the due back (due bank). As discussed above, due banks may be caused by a variety of factors: there may have been a large house paid-out that used most of the drawer's cash; there may have been too many large denomination bills and too few small ones to rebuild tomorrow's starting bank; or there may have been too many checks cashed to leave sufficient money for tomorrow. Whatever the reason, the income audit staff pays each cashier's due bank from the growing pile of turned-in cash before preparing the hotel's daily deposit.

Most operations use a signature and witness system to facilitate returning the due backs to each cashier. One main cashier (often a front-office cashier) is given a series of due bank envelopes with the name of each cashier to whom the envelope is owed. The departmental cashier then signs for the sealed envelope in the presence of the main cashier and adds the contents of the envelope to the department's starting shift bank. Of course, the sealed envelopes were prepared during the cashier audit and were therefore witnessed by several general cashiers as to the correct amount sealed inside. Though simple, these signature and witness systems are generally quite effective.

Paying Off the House Vouchers.   In hotels that utilize an imprest petty cash fund, front-office cashiers are asked to hold their house vouchers until they build to some predetermined amount (say, $25). When the front-office cashier writes a house voucher for a soda machine refund ($.75), a video game refund ($.50), and a tank of gas for the shuttle van ($19.50), these are kept in the cash drawer until they exceed the predetermined amount ($25). Even at the close of the shift, as the cashier is building tomorrow's starting bank, the vouchers are still kept by the cashier. Tomorrow, however, if the cashier writes a few more house vouchers (say, a gallon of sour cream was purchased from the grocery store for $4.59), the entire sum of all vouchers will be turned in.

In this example, the sum to be turned in is $25.34. The cashier turns in all of the house vouchers, not merely the one or two vouchers that put the total over the magic predetermined amount. The income audit staff counts the house vouchers as cash and credits the drop envelope with the amount of house vouchers. In some cases, a due back may be caused by an extremely large house voucher (say, a large C.O.D. shipment arrived).

Package Coupons.   Hotels that operate in busy tour and travel markets often incorporate the redemption of package coupons and certificates into their cash drawer procedures. Such coupons or certificates are primarily found in departmental cashier turn-ins, but front-office cashiers may also have an opportunity to redeem them under some circumstances.

Generally, package tours provide the guest with substantially more than just a hotel room. Breakfast each morning of the visit, two free rounds of golf, a discount in the gift shop, several free drinks, and a dinner show are all examples of products that might be included in a packaged tour. In order to identify themselves as members of the tour, guests are presented with a coupon booklet that contains redeemable certificates.

As an example, when a couple arrives at the dining room for breakfast, the waitstaff and cashier may not be aware they are tour customers. In fact, they are treated like any other customer until the end of the meal. Then, instead of paying for the breakfast in cash, credit card, or room charge, the tour couple need only redeem their complimentary breakfast coupons.

It's at this point that many accounting systems break down. Departmental cashiers forget to collect tour coupons with the same determination that they show when collecting cash. After all, the cashier thinks, the meal is complimentary; if the tour guest accidentally forgets the coupon booklet in the room, what's the harm? This employee logic overlooks the fact that someone is paying for the guest's complimentary meal (golf, drinks, or whatever). In fact, the redeemed coupon serves as documentation to the travel wholesaler for payment. Redeemed coupons are proof that goods (breakfast in this case) were exchanged and become the basis for the account receivable. That's why, depending on the accounting system, redeemed coupons often become part of the departmental cashier's daily turn-in.

Foreign Currency.   Foreign currency (see Exhibit 11–10) is not generally accepted in the United States. Overseas, U.S. currency is widely accepted. Even the Canadian dollar, with its stability and similarity of value, experiences exchange problems as it moves southward from the U.S.–Canadian border. But international tourism is growing at an amazing rate, with more to come in the years ahead. More foreign currencies are being tendered across hotel desks, and more language capability is being encouraged among front-office staffs.

Nevertheless, very few American hotels have followed their international counterparts into the foreign-exchange business. This is a service that U.S. hotels would prefer to have done by another agency. The growth in foreign-exchange facilities has been outside the hotel lobby.

Cities with large numbers of foreign tourists, such as New York and Miami, have developed adequate exchange facilities to accommodate the international tourists. These currency exchange companies, privately owned, have been supported by local tourist bureaus, chambers of commerce, and the U.S. Travel and Tourism Administration, which see the importance of the international tourist to the balance

EXHIBIT 11–10

Shown are most of the world's currencies. Conversion rates for major currencies are quoted daily in local newspapers and in The Wall Street Journal.

Country	Currency	
Austria	Schilling	
Belgium	Franc	
Czech Republic	Koruna	
Denmark	Krone	
Finland	Markka	
France	Franc	
Germany	Mark	
Greece	Drachma	
Hungary	Forint	**Europe**
Ireland	Punt	
Italy	Lira	
Malta	Lira	
Netherlands	Guilder	
Norway	Krone	
Poland	Zloty	
Portugal	Escudo	
Slovak Republic	Koruna	
Spain	Peseta	
Sweden	Krona	
Switzerland	Franc	
United Kingdom	Pound	
Argentina	Peso	
Bolivia	Boliviano	
Brazil	Real	
Chile	Peso	
Colombia	Peso	
Costa Rica	Colon	
Ecuador	Sucre	**Central and South America**
El Salvador	Colon	
Guatemala	Quetzal	
Honduras	Lempira	
Nicaragua	Cordoba	
Peru	New Sol	
Uruguay	New Peso	
Venezuela	Bolivar	
Egypt	Pound	
Ethiopia	Birr	
Ghana	Cedi	
Libya	Dinar	
Morocco	Dirham	**Africa**
South Africa	Rand	
Sudan	Dinar	
Tanzania	Shilling	
Zambia	Kwacha	
Australia	Dollar	
Bahrain	Dinar	
China	Renminbi	
Hong Kong	Dollar	
India	Rupee	
Indonesia	Rupiah	**Mideast, Far East, and Pacific**
Israel	Shekel	
Japan	Yen	
Jordan	Dinar	
Kuwait	Dinar	
Lebanon	Pound	

(continued)

EXHIBIT 11–10

Concluded

Country	Currency	
Malaysia	Ringgit	
New Zealand	Dollar	
Pakistan	Rupee	
Philippines	Peso	
Saudi Arabia	Riyal	
Singapore	Dollar	**Mideast, Far East, and Pacific (concluded)**
South Korea	Won	
Syria	Pound	
Taiwan	Dollar	
Thailand	Baht	
Turkey	Lira	
United Arab	Dirham	
Bahamas	Dollar	
Bermuda	Dollar	
B.V.I.	Dollar	
Curacao	Guilder	**Caribbean, Bahamas, and Bermuda**
Jamaica	Dollar	
Martinique	Franc	
Trinidad	Dollar	
Canada	Dollar	**North America**
Mexico	Peso	

of trade. Their presence allows the hotels to service the currency needs of the international guest with a reasonable ceiling on costs.

Servicing the guest is all that American hotels appear to do. It is a limited service at that—limited to a very few hotels that deal only in a few popular currencies because they have identified a well-defined international market segment for themselves. Overseas, foreign exchange is a profit center for the hotel. There is a profit to be made because both domestic and foreign hotels exchange currency at something less than the official rate. That's a double insult because even the official rate, which is determined by open market bidding, provides a spread between buy price and sell price.

Since it is not desirable to inventory money from all around the world, hotels do not provide for the reconversion of U.S. dollars into foreign funds as the visitor prepares to go home. Therefore, the hotel's concern is only with the bid rate. Money brokers quote both a buy (bid) rate and a sell (ask) rate. The desk buys foreign currency from the guest at a rate that is lower than the broker's bid rate, reselling later to the broker at the bid rate. The hotel might buy Canadian dollars, for example, at 25¢ less than it sells them for, although the official spread might be only 15¢. The extra spread between buy and sell may be further enriched by a supplemental exchange fee. This fee, which currency dealers call *agio,* provides the hotel with additional funds to pay for bank charges or to offset unexpected variations in foreign currency value. The latter makes it especially important to process foreign currency quickly and to include it in the turn-in every day.

Obtaining daily quotes and avoiding banks that are not brokers (i.e., middlemen) themselves will maximize foreign exchange profits. In fact, the hotel could become an intermediary broker by also converting funds for taxi drivers, bellpersons, and servers throughout the community in addition to its own personnel. Of course, this opens a whole new business with the large risks that accompany foreign exchange.

If the hotel is dealing in foreign currencies, the accounting office must furnish the cashier with a table of values for each currency traded (Exhibit 11–10). (Several airlines quote currency rates, including rates on foreign traveler's checks, as part of their res system service.) If currency values fluctuate over a wide range, a daily or even hourly quote is necessary to prevent substantial losses. More likely, the hotel will just refuse that particular currency.

Canadian currency poses less of a problem than most other kinds. It is similar in form, divisions, and value to the American dollar. Consequently, hotels close to the border have accepted Canadian dollars at a par with the American dollar. Although this practice involves an exchange cost to the hotel, it has been a good advertising and public relations gimmick that has more than offset the expense.

An Example from the Land of Nod.   Let's see what needs to be done when a guest from the Land of Nod tenders a N̶1,000 bill in payment of a $34 account. Each - N̶ (Nod dollar) is exchanged at 5¢ U.S. money by the hotel, although the official rate may be somewhat higher—say, 5.1¢. Therefore, the N̶1,000 is exchanged at $50, which is $1 less than the official rate of exchange. The cashier would return $16 U.S. in exchange for the N̶1,000 and the charge of $34. (Change is given only in U.S. dollars even if the cashier has Nod dollars.) If, on the other hand, the guest had offered only a N̶500 bill, the cashier would have collected an additional U.S. $9 to settle the $34 account in full. What if it were a N̶2,500 bill, and the cashier had on hand 1,500 Nod dollars? What would be the change? (Answer: The cashier would give U.S. $91 in change. Remember: Foreign currency is never returned even if it's available in the cash drawer. That would give away the profit earned on the exchange rates.)

Rare indeed is the hotel that will accept a foreign check. However, if payment were made by foreign check, the hotel makes an additional charge, passing on to the guest the bank's fee for foreign exchange. The amount of the fee is a function of both the size of the check and the variation in the rate of exchange.

Foreign traveler's checks (especially Canadian traveler's checks) are more readily accepted than personal checks. Although cashiers are cautioned to use the same level of scrutiny with foreign traveler's checks as they use with U.S. traveler's checks (accepting traveler's checks is discussed in depth towards the end of this chapter), there is an additional catch. Foreign traveler's checks look identical to U.S. traveler's checks, with one simple difference: Instead of stating "Pay to the order of (name) in U.S. dollars," the foreign traveler's check states "Pay . . . in Canadian dollars" (see Exhibit 11–11), or whatever currency. Many a time has a clerk accidentally cashed a foreign traveler's check thinking it was payable in U.S. funds. This can represent a considerable loss to the hotel.

Cash and Cash Equivalents

Although the use of cash and cash equivalents (personal checks and traveler's checks) is less prevalent in hotels today, the incidence of counterfeiting and forgery is at an all-time high. Therefore, though cash transactions represent a decreasing piece of the entire revenue pie, the need for caution and proper cash-handling skills is as critical as ever.

EXHIBIT 11–11

Foreign traveler's checks look quite similar to U.S. checks. There are some variations in color according to the currency payable. An untrained or unwary cashier can easily confuse currencies using similar denominations, especially dollars, which are traded in Australia, Canada, Jamaica, Hong Kong, and Singapore, for a start (see Exhibit 11–10).

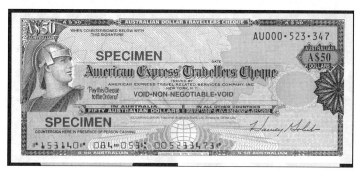

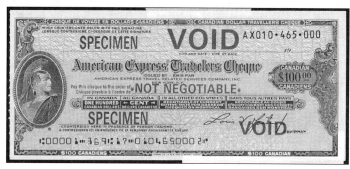

Courtesy: American Express Travel Related Services Company, Inc., Salt Lake City, Utah.

Counterfeit Currency

According to the U.S. Secret Service, there may be over $1 billion in counterfeit currency in circulation worldwide. In 1986, the problem of counterfeit U.S. currency was declared epidemic. Since that time, the passage of fake bills has actually accelerated.

Hotels are likely targets for professional counterfeiters for several reasons. First, hotels are often rushed with numerous small transactions, allowing the professional counterfeiter easy access and egress. Second, hotel cashiers are inundated with so many guests that they would probably have a difficult time remembering (much less describing or identifying) the professional counterfeiter.

Finally, hotels handle relatively little cash as a percentage of all sales volume. Although that may sound contradictory, counterfeiters often seek establishments that deal in little cash. That's because cashiers who handle lots of cash become very adept at spotting a phony. Conversely, hotel cashiers (who handle relatively little cash) are poorly prepared to spot fake currency.

Detecting Counterfeit Currency.   Exhibit 11–12 demonstrates the key points to examine when scrutinizing the authenticity of a bill. However, the information contained in Exhibit 11–12 is rapidly being supplemented by new, proactive technology.

In recent years, the government has been adding several additional counterfeiting safeguards to some of the larger bill denominations. Beginning in 1990, the Treasury Department developed new technology that embeds $100 bills with polyester grey thread to the left of the Federal Reserve seal and microengraves ''The United States of America'' above the portrait. The Treasury Department began with $100 bills, but expects to process $50 and $20 bills this way in coming years as well.

The grey thread can be seen when the bill is held up to direct light. The microengraving can only be seen with a magnifying glass. Both technologies are designed to thwart casual counterfeiters who easily create phony money with their high-tech copying and scanning machines. It is impossible for the casual counterfeiter to replicate the grey thread, and the microengraving appears quite blurry on counterfeited copies.

Hotel Cashier Applications.   Hotel cashiers may also be interested in a number of new and relatively inexpensive counterfeit detection devices that have hit the market in recent years (see Exhibit 11–13). These detection devices utilize two additional technologies in their search for counterfeit currency. One of the most popular devices is a detector shaped like a marker pen made by companies such as Dri-Mark Products of New York. This pen is popular with major retailers (such as Disney and Toys-''Я''-Us) because it is simple to use. In essence, it employs a chemical reaction to indicate whether the currency in question has authentic cotton fibers (all U.S. currencies use a cotton-based stock).

A second detection technology searches the bill for magnetic ink. Magnetic ink has been used by the Federal Reserve since 1932. The ink is found on the portrait and around the edges. Counterfeit currency created on copiers or printing presses lacks the magnetic ink (Exhibit 11–13).

Whatever their approach, hotels are urged to use caution when accepting currency. Counterfeit currency can cost the hotel a considerable amount of money in a relatively short amount of time because counterfeiters usually pass a number of bills in quick succession. Counterfeit bills are like ants, you never find just one! And when the hotel finally realizes what has happened and calls the police or the Secret Service, they are in for another shock—the counterfeit bills will be confiscated without restitution.

Check-Cashing Safeguards

Even in the smallest hotel, management cannot make every credit decision every hour of the day. Instead, it creates the policies and procedures that will minimize losses and retain customer goodwill. A credit manual or credit handbook is the usual manner of communicating management's position. Each company reflects its own approach in policies, but procedures for handling personal checks (and traveler's checks) are much alike from hotel to hotel and from handbook to handbook.

Hotels train their front-office personnel to be pleasant, courteous, and accommodating. Check scam artists are usually loud, rude, and threatening. By pushing in during rush hours, harassing the clerks who have been taught to ''take it,'' and pressuring for service, passers of bad checks walk away with millions. Losses can be reduced when certain procedures are put in place.

EXHIBIT 11–12

What clerks should do if they receive a counterfeit bill.

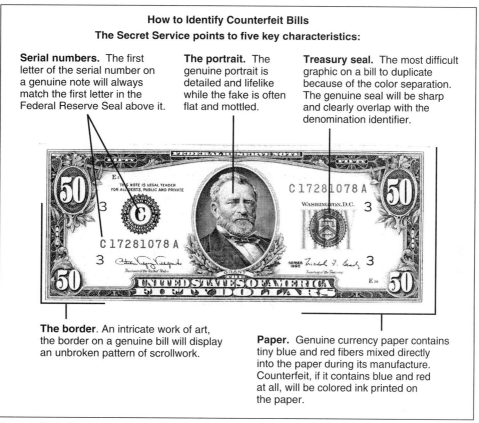

How to Identify Counterfeit Bills

The Secret Service points to five key characteristics:

Serial numbers. The first letter of the serial number on a genuine note will always match the first letter in the Federal Reserve Seal above it.

The portrait. The genuine portrait is detailed and lifelike while the fake is often flat and mottled.

Treasury seal. The most difficult graphic on a bill to duplicate because of the color separation. The genuine seal will be sharp and clearly overlap with the denomination identifier.

The border. An intricate work of art, the border on a genuine bill will display an unbroken pattern of scrollwork.

Paper. Genuine currency paper contains tiny blue and red fibers mixed directly into the paper during its manufacture. Counterfeit, if it contains blue and red at all, will be colored ink printed on the paper.

Source: U.S. Secret Service.

1. Don't return the bill to the passer. Many passers are amateur criminals and will probably become skittish. Some may even run from the lobby.
2. Delay the passer, if possible.
3. Observe the passer for a description. Note anyone with the passer and license number of any vehicles.
4. Call the police or the local office of the Secret Service.
5. Write your initials on the blank portion of the note.
6. Handle the note as little as possible to allow the passer's fingerprints to be lifted. Place it in an envelope as soon as possible.
7. Surrender the note only to a properly identified police officer or Secret Service agent.

EXHIBIT 11–13

New technology puts counterfeit currency detection at the cashier's fingertips. Shown here is the vistatector, which is capable of detecting magnetic particles embedded on the front of all U.S. paper currency.

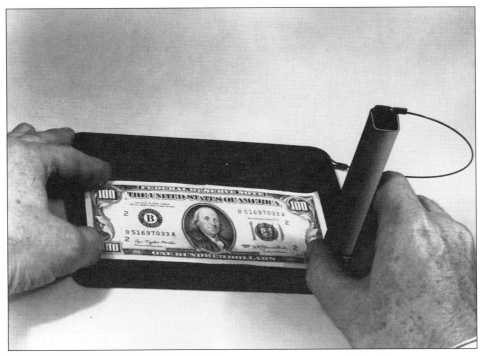

Courtesy: Vistatech Enterprises, Ltd., New York, New York.

Procedures for Minimizing Fraud.   Hotel operations are 100 times more likely to lose money to forged and fraudulent checks than they are to armed robbery! Using proper check-cashing procedures is critical to avoid significant losses from this form of robbery.

Computer technology has made forgery a simple crime for anyone to perpetrate. Basic desktop publishing and scanning equipment is all one needs to ably copy and alter personal checks. And since checks are paid by computer automation as well, the altered check will clear provided the account has sufficient funds.

Unfortunately, hotels that accept forged or worthless checks have little recourse. Banks are not responsible for losses incurred from bad checks passed against them. The hotel ends up holding the bag—prevention is the only cure.

The Old "One-Two-Three."   Prevention is as easy as "one-two-three." That's because the vast majority of faulty checks can be detected by front-office cashiers with three simple observations.

First, is the check perforated? All legitimate checks are perforated on at least one side (except for the small percentage of checks that are government checks, checks printed on computer card stock, and counter checks). Because perforation equipment is so bulky and expensive, few check forgers bother with this detail.

Second, does the Federal Reserve district number match the location of the issuing bank? Cashiers should compare the 1–12 Federal Reserve district number located between the brackets along the bottom of the check with the restated district number printed (in smaller type) in the upper right-hand corner of the check (see Exhibit 11–14, #9). Many check forgers change the Federal Reserve district numbers at the bottom of the check to a different district. In this way, the check is sent for clearing to the wrong district, gaining the forger several valuable days. Remember, if the numbers don't match, the check is a forgery.

Third, is the routing code printed in magnetic ink? The routing code found at the bottom of the check (Exhibit 11–14, #8) must be printed in dull, flat magnetic ink. If the ink is shiny, or you can feel the raised ink, the check is a forgery.

Although these are the three critical questions for a cashier to observe, there are others. A comprehensive check-cashing checklist has been developed and is discussed later in this chapter. It provides management with a more thorough understanding of the check-cashing process.

Some Simple Deterrents.   Every weapon available must be employed in the battle against check fraud. Closed-circuit television in banks and photographing procedures elsewhere affirm a hotel's right to use similar equipment. Dual-lens cameras, which simultaneously record a picture of the instrument being negotiated and of the check passer, are available. Other systems allow the development of latent fingerprints without the use of ink or other messy substances. Just a sign explaining that such equipment is being used serves as a deterrent, as does a printed warning citing the penalty for passing bad checks.

Other hotels collect a check-cashing fee, which is used to offset worthless checks. The rationale of penalizing honest guests is open to debate. It would be better to adopt and enforce a stringent procedure, irritating as it is to the honest guest, than to collect an unwarranted fee. The procedure may include a telephone call at the guest's expense to his or her office or bank according to the circumstances and time of day. Using a check-cashing service may cost the guest the same amount, but it puts the hotel in a better light.

Endorsements.   Procedural protection requires proper and immediate endorsement after the check is received. This is particularly true with open endorsements containing only the payee's name. The cashier should use a rubber stamp that reads as follows:

For Deposit Only
The ABC Hotel

The stamp should contain space for identification, credit-card number, room number, and the initials of the person approving the check.

A special endorsement is used for checks that are cashed. Otherwise, the hotel falls prey to an old trick. The guest cashes a check in the exact amount of the bill and then leaves without paying. When the hotel attempts to collect by mail, the canceled check is presented as evidence of payment. To avoid this, all checks could be taken as receipts on account. Any cash given for checks would appear on the folio as a cash advance. This roundabout procedure can be avoided by an endorsement that reads as follows:

Received in Cash from
The ABC Hotel

Invariably, bank endorsements blot out much of the information recorded on the rear of the check. The data is unusable when needed most, if the check comes

Exhibit 11-14

Fourteen locations flag a possible bad check: (1) Is the date current? (2) Do the routing numbers correspond to the magnetic numbers? (3) Has the account existed for some time? (4) Is the amount more or less than the statutory definition of grand larceny? (5) Are the values of the handwritten dollars and the numerical dollars identical? (6) Does the signature correspond to the registration card or the endorsement? (7) Are the account numbers in agreement with a bank card that is being proffered? (8) Is magnetic ink dull or reflective? (9) Is the number of the Federal Reserve Region accurate? (10) Does the bank directory list this bank as shown? (11) When was the account established? (12) How does the maker's identity compare with the hotel's records? (13) Is the check perforated? (14) Is the payee a third party, a corporation, or cash?

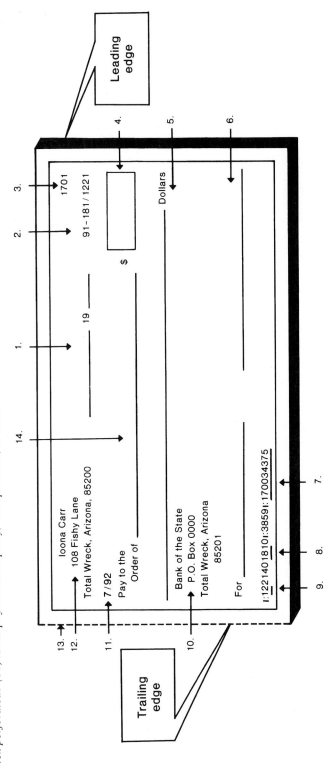

back. This issue, which was one that every industry faced, was addressed by Congress in 1988. The legislation that emerged assigned the first 1½ inches from the trailing edge of the check (Exhibit 11–14) to endorsements. In that space on the rear of the check go all the endorsements and whatever identification will fit into the area. The front of the check can still be used if more data is needed.

Debit Cards.   Debit cards provide the hotel with immediate payment through the guest's bank account. Rather than writing a personal check, the debit card electronically debits the guest's bank account and credits the hotel. Payment is immediate, and the risk associated with accepting personal checks is removed.

Although debit cards are starting to gain acceptance in many industries, the hotel industry has been slow to follow suit. This may be due to the fact that relatively few guest folios are settled with anything other than a credit card or a direct bill account, or perhaps it is because the hotel industry has historically lagged behind other industries in technological enhancements and innovations. Whatever the case, it is not likely that many guests will opt for immediate debiting of their bank account—not when they can continue to receive some 30 days float through their credit-card billing process.

A Check-Cashing Checklist.   No single set of rules covers every circumstance, but a list of limitations and restrictions is a helpful guide to those responsible for approving checks. Such a list follows. Modifications depend on the class of hotel, the source of authority, and the circumstances surrounding the particular request:

1. Accept checks only for the amount of the bill. Be particularly alert for the cashback technique, by which cash as well as services rendered are lost.

2. Allow no one to be above suspicion on weekends, holidays, and after banking hours.

3. Refuse to accept any check that is altered, illegible, stale (older than 30 days), postdated, poorly printed, or from a third party.

4. Be suspicious of checks slightly smaller than the statutory measure of grand larceny. If $100 separates petty larceny from grand larceny in the state, then a $107 check is less likely to be counterfeit than is a $94 one.

5. Compare the signature and address on the check with those on the registration card: Are they similar? Should they be? Compare the signature on the front with the endorsement on the rear. Ask the same questions!

6. Compare the age of the guest with the birth date on the driver's license. Has the license expired? Compare the person's listed height and weight, hair and eye color, and the photograph, if available, to the person standing before you. More and more state driver's licenses and identification cards are being manufactured with tamper-proof technology. When identification data has been altered, the card disintegrates in some conspicuous manner. For example, with Pennsylvania's driver's licenses, the state seal disintegrates if the card has been altered.

7. Pay special attention to endorsements. Accept no conditional, circumstantial, or restrictive endorsements. Challenge endorsements that are not identical to either the printed name (in the case of a personal check) or the payee (in the case of a third-party check).

8. Require endorsements on checks paid to the bearer or to cash. Require all endorsements to be made in your presence, repeating them when the check is already endorsed.

9. Refuse a check payable to a corporation but endorsed by one of the officers seeking to cash it.

10. Obtain adequate and multiple identification and record it on the rear 1.5 inches of the trailing edge along with any other information that can help if the check is refused: address, telephone number, credit-card number, license plates, clerk's initials.

11. Verify business names in telephone directories or listings such as Dun & Bradstreet, Inc. Obtain military identification. Call local references. Request a business card.

12. Create fictitious information or names of company officers and see if the guest verifies them.

13. Make certain the check is complete, accurate, and dated. Watch for misspellings and serial numbers of more than four digits.

14. Keep a bank directory and check the transit and routing numbers against it. Verify the name of the bank with the directory listing, giving special attention to the article ''the'' and the use of the ampersand (&) in place of the word *and.* ''City Bank of Laurelwood'' is not the same as ''The City Bank of Laurelwood''; ''Farmers and Merchants Bank'' is not ''Farmers & Merchants Bank.''

15. Check for perforations. All legitimate checks have at least one side that is perforated.

16. Remember, cashier's checks (a check drawn on the bank by one of its officers) are spelled with an apostrophe *s,* are full size, never pocket size, and are rarely prepared with a typewriter. Watch it! These checks can be stopped at the bank of issue up to 72 hours after being validated. (Trust companies issue treasurer's checks, not cashier's checks.)

17. Be cautious of certified checks, since most persons do not use them. Certification numbers are written or stamped, rarely typewritten.

18. Check the signatures on bank drafts (a check drawn by a bank on its correspondent bank) with the bank directory, and verify the bank's correspondent bank at the same time.

19. Note that, because of withholding, payroll checks are almost never even dollar amounts.

20. *Read* identification—don't just look at it! Ask questions: ''What does your middle *C* stand for?'' Don't offer the answer: ''Is your middle name *Charles?*''

21. Determine whether the guest is registered from the same city as the one in which the bank is located.

22. Be familiar with bank locations: The 12 federal reserve districts are numbered from 1 in the east to 12 in the west. Locate the magnetic code on the lower left of the check. The first two digits following the bracket (|:) identify the federal reserve bank handling the commercial paper. Numbers greater than 12 (the federal reserve districts) are fakes. This is not true of NOW accounts or similar noncommercial checks.

23. Watch the calendar: Most bad checks are passed during the final quarter of the year, the holiday season.

24. Expect the magnetic code to be dull; shiny numbers that reflect light have been printed with other than magnetic ink. Preestablish firm limits on the value of the checks to be cashed.

25. Question emergencies. If airfare is needed to fly home unexpectedly, why can't the airline take the check?

26. Ignore evidence of identity that consists of social security cards, library cards, business cards, or voter identification cards. These are easily forged or reproduced, and they generally carry no photo.

27. Personally deliver the check to the cashier without allowing the guest to retrieve it once it has been approved.

28. Watch check numbers. Low digits mean a new account where the danger is greatest. The larger the number, the safer the check. New accounts generally begin with number 101, and 90 percent of all ''hot'' checks are written on accounts less than a year old (numbered 101–150).

29. Look for the small date on the left upper section of the check (when available). This indicates the date the account was opened.

30. Do not write the check; insist that the check be written by the guest.

31. Machine, color-copied checks can be smeared with a wet finger; real safety-paper checks cannot.

32. Remember that bank cards do not cover cash losses, only merchandise purchased. Limit check cashing to the front-desk cashiers.

33. Note that credit managers have been known to eavesdrop on guest telephone calls.

34. Ask yourself how difficult it would be to create the identification offered.

35. Compare the numerical amount of the check with the written amount.

36. Watch the value of foreign traveler's checks. Foreign checks are issued in foreign currency. Don't cash 20 marks or francs as a U.S. $20 value.

Traveler's Checks. American Express (AmEx) pioneered the traveler's check, and it has retained its preeminent position ever since. Visa and MasterCard entered the field in the late 1970s and early 1980s as extensions of their credit-card business. Several banks and travel agencies round out the slate of participants. It is a competitive business.

Traveler's checks are purchased by the consumer prior to the trip. They are used as if they were cash, with the issuing company guaranteeing their replacement against loss or theft. The charge is usually 1 percent, but the checks are often issued without charge. Even without charge, there is plenty of competition for the business. Large sums of interest-free money are available for investing. The time lag (the float) between the purchase of the traveler's check and the use of the check might be months. Some 15 to 20 percent of traveler's check sales are never claimed. No wonder AmEx advertising encourages buyers to hold their checks for some distant emergency.

Buyers sign the checks at the time of purchase and countersign when they cash the instruments. Signature comparison is the main line of defense against fraud. Checks must be countersigned under the scrutiny of the cashier or resigned if they were initially endorsed away from the cashier's view. Some traveler's checks provide for dual countersignatures (usually to accommodate a husband and wife team), yet only one signature is required to cash the check.

Traveler's checks are very acceptable and some hotels will cash them even for nonregistered guests. Other hotels are extracautious and require additional identification or compare signatures to registration cards. Comparing signatures is all that's required. In fact, many issuing companies do not even want the cashier to ask for additional identification. That is because extra identification takes the cashier's focus away from the signature line. And the identification may also be invalid—in more than half the instances of stolen traveler's checks, the identification has also been stolen!

Prompt refund of lost or stolen checks is their major appeal. Hotel desks, with their 24-hour service, represent a logical extension of the issuing company's office system. Hilton entered into such an agreement with Bank of America. It is both a service to the guest and a marketing device for the chain.

Some Simple Deterrents.   The best defense is to carefully watch the guest sign the traveler's check. Cautious cashiers should never remove their eyes from the check being signed. Indeed, some cashiers never even remove their hand from the check, always holding onto one corner while the guest is signing. It is a simple matter for someone to produce a stolen traveler's check, pretend to sign it while the cashier's attention is focused elsewhere, and then quickly substitute a previously signed traveler's check with a well-forged signature.

Like their commercial brothers, traveler's checks employ a magnetic code on the lower left portion of the paper. The first digits are always 8000, which tells the clearinghouse computer that it is a traveler's check. The next portion of the code identifies the type. For example, 8000001 is Bank of America, 8000005 is American Express.

Although forgers can easily alter the clearinghouse transit codes, they cannot easily copy the high-quality, high-speed laser images major companies print in their traveler's checks. These images can be seen when holding the traveler's check to the light (don't confuse these highly detailed laser imprints with simple watermarks found in paper). MasterCard and Thomas Cook, for example, show a Greek goddess on the right side of the check. Similarly, Citicorp displays a Greek god's face on the right of the check. Bank of America uses three globes (which supplement the other globes already visible). And VISA provides a globe on the left with a dove in the upper right of the check.

American Express utilizes a somewhat different safety approach. Red dots are visible in the check if held up to the light, but a wet finger is the acid test. It will smear the check when applied to the denomination on the back left side, but will not smear the back right side.

The components of this chapter—cash, cash paid-outs, and cash equivalents—represent a small percentage of the transactions that occur at the front desk. Most transactions are handled by credit card or credit transfer to a city ledger account. In the next chapter (Chapter 12), the focus changes to the issues of credit. Because credit cards and credit equivalents represent the lion's share of front-office transactions, poor or lazy procedures can harm front-office profitability. Chapter 12 explains credit-handling procedures and cautions the manager to treat credit transactions with the same care as cash transactions.

Summary

Even as the quantity of cash circulating in hotels declines, the need for careful cash-handling practices increases. This is especially true for front-desk cashiers because they not only receive cash but pay it out as well.

Front-office cashiers receive cash from a number of potential sources. Guests may pay cash on their room folio at check-in, at check-out, or in the middle of their stay. Cash is also received at the desk on behalf of other departments (as when a customer pays for a banquet) and for auxiliary revenue centers such as soda machines or video games.

Cash is paid out by the front-office cashier for a number of reasons as well. On check-out, the guest who overpaid the folio may receive a refund. Employees may receive charged tips in cash, concessionaires may receive charged purchases in cash, and guests themselves may receive cash advances against the folio. Add to this list of paid-outs the use of an imprest petty cash account and the front-office cashier's job becomes a complicated and sensitive task.

To make the job even more difficult, cashiers must remain alert to potential check-cashing, credit-card, or cash transaction frauds. Hotel front desks are favorite targets for counterfeit currency, forged checks, or stolen credit cards. Front-office managers need to carefully train cashiers to identify situations where fraudulent practices are occurring.

Queries and Problems

1. Industry experts suggest the amount of cash in the banks of hotel cashiers should equal hotel's cashier banks equals some 2 percent of gross revenues, or about $600 per available room. For a 100-room hotel that grosses $3 million annually, this equals $60,000 in cashiers' banks.

   As a new general manager, you are concerned with the sizable amount of outstanding cash in the various banks. You know if it were released from the banks, the cash could return significant revenues or interest income.

   Be creative as you identify three distinct methods for identifying which banks have excess cash or other means for releasing some of the $60,000. However, please remember to maintain cash bank security as you brainstorm new methodologies.

2. An international guest tenders $171 in U.S. funds and #2,000 from his native land to settle an outstanding account of $206.20. #s are being purchased by the hotel for 51.50 per U.S. dollar. What must the cashier do now to settle the account? Assume the guest has more American dollars; assume he doesn't. The hotel cashier has no foreign funds in the drawer.

3. Explain how international tourism helps balance the trade deficit of the United States. How does international tourism worsen the deficit?

4. Sketch and complete a cashier's envelope for October 11 showing the details of the turn-in and the amount of due back. (City ledger collections are handled by the accounting office. No provisions are made for cash over or short; the cashier covers both.)

Given for Query #4

House bank	$1,800.00
Advances to guests	$181.15
House vouchers	$16.20
Vending machine refunds	$0.50
Collections from guests	$7,109.40
Cash in the drawer exclusive of other cash listings	$1,721.00
Traveler's checks	$2,675.00
Personal checks:	
Washington	$75.25
Lincoln	$310.00
Jefferson	$44.98
Carter	$211.90
Kennedy	$55.00
Others	$1,876.85
Bills of $100 denomination	10 each
Torn and dirty currency	$62.00
Silver	$680.14

5. *a.* Prepare a bank deposit slip for the morning of February 15 from the cash reports summarized below. Exchange is always handled in cash if possible.

   b. In general journal form, prepare a cash receipts journal entry.

6. Some hotels prevent cashiers from knowing their net receipts. Without knowing net receipts, the cashier turns everything in from the day's drawer. If the drawer is significantly over for the shift, the cashier is none the wiser and is not tempted to steal the amount of the overage. Do you support such a policy? Are there any drawbacks to not allowing cashiers access to their net receipt figures?

Given for Query #5

Cashier	Turn-In	Over or (Short)	Cash Sales	Accounts Receivable Advances	Accounts Receivable Collections
Abel	$43,060.00	$(4.00)		$756.00	$43,820.00
Baker	8,263.98	(.12)	$8,264.10		
Charleen	933.86		933.86		
Davis	21,800.88			19.00	17,350.88
Evans	9,116.26	16.00		800.70	9,400.50
Frankl	2,626.00		2,626.00		
Gray	64.00	(9.00)			73.00

Credit and the City Ledger

Chapter Outline

Social and economic shifts set the stage for the credit revolution that began during the second half of the 1900s. Credit in innkeeping predates the phenomenon by centuries. Colonial innkeepers and proprietors of the Roman mansiones issued tokens, like today's traveler's checks, redeemable on demand. The value of the tokens fluctuated with the creditworthiness of the hotelkeeper. Earlier still, knights used their signet rings impressed in wax to guarantee their payment. Freed from the need to carry coins, they traveled with greater ease along the dangerous roads where highwaymen lurked.

Buying on credit—promising to pay later—is how America does business. Both commercial and consumer transactions start out that way. Commercial businesses usually settle their accounts by check, but even that is changing as credit-card companies market new ''corporate procurement'' cards (MasterCard has BusinessCard, for example). Retail customers such as hotel guests usually settle their accounts with personal credit cards. With over 100 billion credit-card transactions each year, paying cash at the front desk is out of sync with the realities of the marketplace.

All businesses, hotels included, refer to unpaid customer purchases as accounts receivable. As Chapter 10 explained, hotels have some accounts receivable registered in the house—transient accounts receivable—and some that are not registered—city ledger accounts receivable.

Most city accounts start out as transient accounts. For example, a registered guest who uses a credit card to complete a speedy check-out becomes a city guest. So too does an association or company that transfers its master account from the front office to the city ledger with a request to be billed by mail.

Transferring front-office accounts to city accounts is one of three methods for settling the transient folio at check-out. Cash and allowances are the other two options. Chapter 10 discussed these and also explained how charges made by guests were posted to front-office accounts. In this manner, hotel guests buy on credit, just like other consumers. Each service purchased increases the guest's folio, the account receivable, and also increases the sale of that particular department—rooms, food, beverage, telephone, and so on. In keeping with this age of credit, most guests settle their folios with a credit card, transferring transient ledger accounts to city ledger accounts.

The City Ledger

Chapter 10 also explained that a ledger is a group of accounts or records. All accountants maintain a variety of such ledgers, grouping similar transactions together. Hotel accountants maintain a special grouping of nonregistered accounts receivable—a city ledger.

Major Categories of the City Ledger

Just as the front-office ledger is composed of many individual account folios, each identified by a room number, so the city ledger may be subdivided. City ledger accounts have no room numbers, but they do have account numbers for ease in identification and posting (Exhibit 10–11, line 4: "MC7:43AM").

No hotel merchant can do business without accepting credit cards. Consequently, even the smallest hotels maintain a credit-card category within the city ledger. If the small hotel accepts no other forms of credit, credit cards may be the city ledger's one and only category. That would work perfectly well, but it denies hotel credit to any party that is not using a national credit card. In that case, there would be no city ledger receivables in individual names, only in the names of the credit-card companies.

Few hotels work that way—most maintain several categories of city ledger accounts. Although they may not be actual, separate physical groupings, they can be viewed as if they were for discussion purposes.

Credit Cards.   Estimates of credit-card usage range from two-thirds to three-fourths of all food and beverage sales. More important than the actual figures is the upward trend in credit-card transactions. Even Europeans, who traditionally favor cash settlement, have started using cards.

A Brief History of Hotel Credit Cards.   Hotels were dabbling in credit cards as early as 1915, when Western Union (the telegraph company) and the railroads issued cards to preferred customers. In 1950, a New York attorney, supposedly embarrassed at being short of cash, founded Diners Club. Within a year, gross billings reached $1 million dollars. Before a decade had passed, American Express, Carte Blanche, and MasterCharge (MasterCard's predecessor) were doing business. The lodging industry's big chains trailed the rush, but not for long.

Credit cards issued by hotels (frequently called company cards or hotel cards) were short-lived. Costs of administration—especially computers, which were not a strength of the 1960–70 hotel chain—and of borrowing to keep the credit program afloat were too high. Besides, other broad-based cards were finding more general acceptance.

Hilton's experience is a good example of the ambivalence the industry held toward credit cards. Between 1959 and 1962, Hilton twice converted its system. All Hilton and Statler cardholders (Hilton bought the Statler chain in 1954) were switched to Carte Blanche and then back again to company cards only.

By the 1970s, the lodging industry had come to understand that credit cards were financial instruments and not marketing appendages for hotels. With some relief, the hotel industry left the credit-card business to the credit-card companies. So another intermediary between the guest and the hotel appeared on the scene. The credit-card company as a third-party intermediary plays a similar role in hotel operations to that of the third-party reservation agency, the third-party marketing group, or the third-party telephone company.

Kinds of Credit Cards.   All credit cards are not the same. Although their number and variety seems almost endless, credit cards can be classified into three general types: **bank cards, travel and entertainment cards (T&Es),** and all others. The differences between bank cards and T&Es grow less apparent as banking deregulation and competition force each to take on attributes of the other. Bank cards now charge an annual fee, although they were initially offered without cost. T&Es, which traditionally required the merchant to wait a long time for reimbursement, have introduced express deposits like the bank cards. Prestige cards with higher limits and special privileges have been added to the bank card lines to attract the affluent, long the purview of the T&E cards. Both are developing **smart cards** to broaden their use and reduce fraud. The battle has been joined!

Bank cards (e.g., Visa and MasterCard) are issued by banks to anyone, depositors and nondepositors alike. Initially, bank cards offered credit to economic groups unable to qualify for travel and entertainment cards. Competition has narrowed the gap between the two card classes, but the distinction between them remains.

With a bank card, purchases can be financed over time, but interest is paid on the balance due. Cardholders who make prompt payment avoid the high interest rates, up to 1.5 percent per month. Banks, being in the business of lending money, encourage cardholders to finance.

Banks administer the system by charging a discount fee to the merchants. Large-volume merchants such as hotel chains are able to negotiate smaller discount fees, which otherwise range from 1 to 2 percent on the low end to a high of 3 to 5 percent. Banks and merchants engage in other banking activities, and the volume of that business may also affect the credit-card rate that the bank charges its merchant customers.

Chains and franchises, which negotiate discount rates on their combined credit-card volume, have a competitive edge over independent properties. Efforts to umbrella independents have not been successful. The flat service charge levied by the

EXHIBIT 12–1

This diagram of the bank interchange system outlines the flow of records and fees as the credit-card charges pass through the system. Ultimately, the merchant hotel pays the total cost.

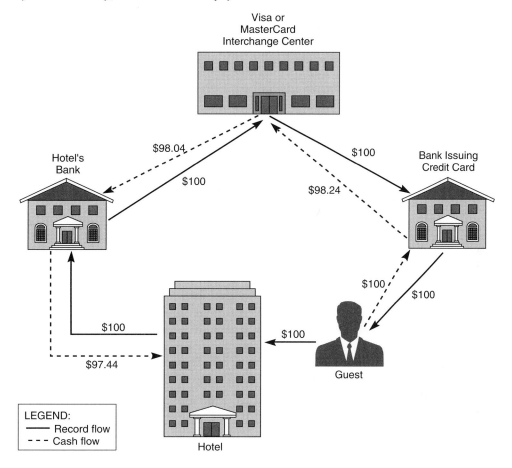

umbrella organization to administer the program offsets the savings made by renegotiating quantity discount fees. However negotiated, bank discount fees are lower than those charged by the travel and entertainment cards.

The American cards, Visa and MasterCard, are international in scope and are the volume leaders worldwide. Canada's en Route Card and Japan's JCB (Japanese Central Bank) card are the leaders outside the United States. Reciprocal agreements between U.S. and other international cards add customers and additional merchant outlets for all. The acceptance is more than geographic—it includes a wide variety of goods and services. Guests can complete an entire trip on credit and even obtain cash loans when an emergency arises.

Internationally or domestically, the system works much the same. The hotel deposits (manually or electronically) the sales records of its bank card transactions in its own local bank. The hotel's bank account receives immediate credit for the day's total, less the discount fee (see Exhibit 12–1). The hotel's bank gets reimbursed from the cardholder's bank, which may be some distance away. The transfer of funds takes place through an interchange system that Visa and MasterCard own and operate. These credit-card interchange centers function like the check-clearing facilities of the federal reserve banks.

Electronic communications facilitate the clearance procedures, especially internationally. Now, the information moves by way of wire from bank to interchange and back to bank. The system no longer requires the actual transfer of paper credit-card slips. Consequently, charge slips are no longer returned to customers. American Express, which uses lasers to reprint the charge slips, still does so as a customer service.

Largest and best known of the *travel and entertainment (T&E)* cards is American Express (AmEx). Diners Club and Carte Blanche are now under one ownership, both having been acquired by Citicorp.

T&E cards differ from bank cards, but the distinctions are narrowing. Nevertheless, T&E cardholders still face more stringent credit checks and pay larger annual fees. Intent remains the basic difference. Bank cards encourage delayed payment in order to generate interest for the bank. Travel and entertainment cards expect the user to make monthly settlement. Higher membership fees and higher discount rates from merchants counterbalance the loss of interest earnings. Of late, however, T&E cards are advertising extended-payment options as the lure of interest earnings grows more attractive.

Irrespective of which card type they're using, consumers prefer credit cards over cash. Cards provide a 30- to 60-day float[1] of interest-free money. T&E card companies also get a float—the period between collecting from cardholders and reimbursing merchants. (Bank cards take no float—the funds are available as soon as deposited.) Merchants (hotels) pay for everyone's float. Besides that, they pay larger discount fees to T&E companies and wait longer to be reimbursed. Waiting is a very real cost, especially in tight money markets. Extraprompt payment to the hotel can be negotiated, but at an additional surcharge over the usual 3 to 5 percent T&E discount fee.

As mentioned in an earlier chapter, discount fees are even paid on the tips that customers add for the servers. That's bad enough, but then the hotel is also out of pocket for the cash advanced to the employee if the credit card is dishonored and uncollectible. Employees are expected to refund tips under such circumstances, but what is good in theory may not work in practice. Staff turnover is rapid, and employees may be gone long before the protested charges are resolved.

Concessionaires cause similar problems if guests are permitted to charge purchases to their folios. If the folio is subsequently paid by credit card, the hotel pays the discount fee on the concessionaire's sale. This issue and that of **chargebacks**[2] from dishonored cards should be handled in the lease.

Because of the costs, hotels prefer bank cards to T&Es. In fact, three times as many merchants accept bank cards as T&E cards. T&E cards are fighting in a very competitive arena. Merchant boycotts have forced AmEx to reduce discount rates. Bermuda hotels resisted T&E cards for many years by acting in concert on the isolated island. The ban was eventually broken, although many small properties there still refuse the cards.

It seems like everyone has joined the crusade against T&E cards. Visa has announced a strategic plan to compete with American Express—not with MasterCard, its traditional rival. Banks now issue gold cards, which compete head to head with AmEx, after winning a 1988 lawsuit that AmEx started. Hotel and restaurant companies encourage customers to use non-T&E cards, although that is contrary to T&E contracts.

As part of the competitive battle, both card groups have broadened services. This includes a globalization effort, emergency services, higher credit limits, cash from ATMs, and reservation guarantees for hotel rooms. Cosponsored (cobranded) cards, such as Visa and Carlson Travel Network (parent of Radisson, Country Kitchens, and TGI Fridays) herald still wider appeal and accessibility as the nation marches toward the elusive era of the cashless society. Cobranded cards will be discussed shortly.

Hotels continue offering T&E cards and paying higher discount fees because some guests demand it. Despite grumbling by all merchants, especially restaurateurs, over excessive discount costs, the number of T&E outlets continues to grow, part of the general increase in credit-card usage.

The hotel's own company card is a private label credit card, like those of the big retail department stores. These retail credit cards are limited in use—few other merchants accept them. Promoting customer loyalty is their chief purpose, but the 1.5 percent monthly charge on overdue accounts cannot be dismissed. Since sales promotion rather than credit control is the objective, credit verification is minimal. There is no urgency for the hotel industry to return to such retail cards because frequent-guest programs provide the same marketing information.

Cobranded cards—those that carry two designations—are growing in popularity. Almost any organization that can offer the credit-card company an extensive mailing list can cobrand with the national card. Charities, professional associations, public television stations, and many others add their names to the already established brands of credit cards. Credit-card companies give these affiliates a small percentage of every sale (typically, 0.5 percent) that members charge to the cobranded card. Airlines encourage the use of cobranded cards by adding frequent-flier miles. This is a bonus for both the user and the airlines, which earn big cash flows from their cobranding partners.

General Motors (GM) is one example of the ultimate in credit-card come-ons. Points are earned toward the purchase of a GM car every time a consumer uses the card! Other well-known cards are AT&T's Universal Card and Sears's Discover Card. Sears, a retail and financial giant, was the first of the nontraditional cards to appear and then only after winning that right in a court battle. Discover Card is unique because it rebates cash to the users, rather than giving frequent-flier points or credits toward automobiles.

Debit cards are not a category of the city ledger, but they warrant inclusion here because we are going to see more of them as time goes by. Debit cards transfer funds electronically (through EFT, electronic funds transfer) as the card is swiped through the reader. The bank account of the user/buyer is reduced immediately. The process is very much like the ATMs (automatic teller machines) discussed in Chapter 11. With an ATM, the user gets the cash; with debit cards, the merchant gets the cash. So the merchant/hotel likes it. There is no time lag, no float, between the purchase and the payment, so the consumer doesn't like it and doesn't use it—at least, not yet.

Consumers will shift from credit cards to debit cards when certain obstacles are removed. Current regulations do not permit merchants (hotels) to levy surcharges on credit-card purchases. Moreover, rebates for cash payments are limited to 5 percent under current interpretations of usury and truth-in-lending laws. There is no means for a merchant to reward customers who use debit cards. Prices cannot be cut for cash, and prices cannot be raised for credit-card purchases. With no price differentials and with the 30-day float still in place, the consumer remains a credit-card fan.

Debit cards, the ultimate in the cashless society, are in place awaiting customer acceptance. EFT means savings in time, paper, accounting costs, and processing expenses, including the cost of bad checks. Everyone will benefit indirectly, but widespread use awaits more direct benefits to the customer. Convenience is one such benefit, and it accounts for the growing use of debit cards in supermarkets. Supermarkets, which may not accept credit cards—fees are too high for low grocery markups—are doing business with debit cards.

Master Accounts.   Master accounts, which may be viewed as if they were a separate city ledger category, are opened at the front desk for a variety of reasons. Under one grouping, the guest might not even be registered. Such is the case with banquet charges for events such as weddings, anniversaries, retirements, and class reunions, all of which are discussed later in this chapter.

More often, master accounts originate with registered guests—especially business executives, who use them to handle group functions.[3] Chapter 10 explained these group charges—rooms, entertainment activities, room service, food and beverage functions, and so on. Sometimes, even outside vendor charges (florist or band) are paid by the hotel and charged to the master account.

Because the amounts involved are considerable, the hotel wants prompt payment. To ensure this, the master account is carefully examined and discussed by the meeting planner or the association manager (the client) and the hotel. Functions that involve thousands of persons using rooms, rental space, and banquet facilities represent very large sums of money. Errors in master accounts may be substantial, but even meeting planners concede they are not always in the hotel's favor. Even so, there are several points of irritation cited by meeting planners. Four predominate: split billing, authorized signatures, chronology of posting, and room charges.

Meeting planners complain that billings are often incorrectly split between the master account and the individual guest folios. They claim this happens despite specific, written instructions. Charging VIPs on their own folios instead of against the master account is a typical error of this sort.

Authorized signatures are another irritant. Meetings and convention groups have many bosses. In addition to the elected officers, the board of directors, and the paid professional staff, there are informal leaders. Not all of these persons are authorized to sign charges, so a list of authorized signatures is furnished to the hotel. Nevertheless, charges originating from unauthorized signatures appear on the master folio.

The sequence in which charges are posted to the folio is important to the client. The breakfast of day 2 should not be posted before the dinner of day 1. It often is, so picky clients will require the entire bill to be reposted to show each event in sequence. Comparisons to the original contract and to the function sheets are thereby facilitated, and the meeting planner is happier.

Comp room charges are another common complaint. Complimentary rooms are given to the meeting according to a widely used formula: one free room for 50 paid rooms. Meeting planners complain that the hotel credits (deducts) from the master folio rooms at the lowest rate. The comp rooms are provided to VIPs, so it is the best rooms that are actually occupied. Therefore, say the clients, the best rates should be comped.

Although it is best to resolve differences while they are fresh, before the group leaves the property, it is not always possible to do so. Areas of agreement should be resolved and billed promptly without waiting for the resolution of the few differences. Otherwise, a paltry sum will keep thousands of unpaid dollars in the city ledger.

Groups and Packages.   Master account billing is also used for groups, packages, and single entities. The nature of the single entity (athletic teams, company product shows, or incentive groups, for example) means there is one buyer. One account receivable is responsible for the total billing. Accompanying the master account are the names and room numbers of the individual members. The group's affiliation is also part of the room rack identification—color on the old manual rack, code on the computer rack.

Incidental charges made by individual members of the group are treated in one of two ways: They are paid either by the individual or by the entity. If all charges (rooms, meals, and incidentals) are paid by the entity, posting is made to the master account. Split folios are needed if the individual is responsible for personal charges.

To ensure collection, notices (some of which are computer generated) are inserted in the key envelope (see Exhibit 8–13), reminding the guest that personal charges must be settled individually on departure. The master account is paid at departure or, more likely, transferred to the city ledger for collection from the single-entity organization.

Who pays for what is more clearly understood with tour packages. The package has been marketed and sold with certain services included or not. Services that are not included are posted to the guest's individual folio. Coupons are issued to the guests for those services included in the package. The coupons are color-coded and dated to limit their use to the particular package. Guests pay for breakfast, drinks, tennis—whatever is part of the prepaid package—with the appropriate coupon. Cashiers in the various hotel departments treat the coupons as part of their turn-in.

Coupons are charged to the tour operator's master account, so breakage accrues to the tour operator. That is, the tour operator collects from the guest for the entire tour but pays the hotel only for actual tickets returned to the master account. By not using the services they have purchased, guests create additional profit for the promoter.

In the hotel's own package—*inclusive tours* (ITs)—breakage comes to the hotel. The package is sold to the guest and the money is collected in advance, minus a commission if it goes through a travel agency. If the guest fails to use a coupon, it is the hotel that has gained. Hotels distribute the total prepaid package charge among the departments, allocating a portion of the total as room sales.

Travel Agencies.   Hotels and travel agencies have a strong love–hate relationship. In part, the antipathy springs from the hotels' view that travel agents, as third-parties in the reservation process, get paid for supplying hotels with their own customers. For the travel agents' part, getting paid is the whole issue. They say hotels fail to pay, and are unwilling to pay, fees that are rightfully due.

"Not so," is the response of the lodging industry. Holiday Corporation reports that travel agency requests for commissions are in error 80 percent of the time. Either the commission was paid, or the customer never stayed. Days Inns reports the figure closer to 90 percent. Moreover, according to one hotel leader, it is not a question of intent. Failure to pay, if that really happens, is not by design. Travel agency accounting has low priority in the accounting offices of the nation's hotels. It's one job that's just put off.

When animosities reach the boiling point, both parties act. The hotel refuses to accept reservation requests from certain agents. Tit for tat, the agents no longer book with that particular hotel. The travel agency is placed in the more difficult position. Either its guest is not accommodated, or the reservation is made indirectly and the commission ignored.

Paying or not paying commissions, soliciting or not soliciting travel agency business, are not city ledger issues. If accounting personnel are handling agency accounts, management has already made its decision. That decision, despite all the carping, is almost absolute throughout the whole lodging industry: Take the business and pay the commission.

This issue may prove to be moot. Rapid changes in technology are redefining the travel agency's role. In-home shopping, STPs (satellite ticket printers), and ticketless airline ticketing threaten to bypass the agency. Airlines spend almost as much in agency commissions as they do on airline maintenance! Agencies depend on airline commissions for their very survival. If the airlines devise ways to eliminate the travel agent, the travel agent will either diversify to new revenue sources or be gone—the hotel business alone will not support them. American Express has learned this lesson of diversification; today half of its revenue is earned from fees rather than commissions.

Other City Ledger Categories

City ledger credit-card and travel agency accounts emerge from the hotel's business with third parties. Many master accounts also involve third parties. In addition to tour groups, guests may be represented by convention planners or incentive companies. Although not equal to the dollar volume of third-party business, there are a number of city ledger accounts that derive from more direct sales to receivables.

Late Charges.   Departmental charges such as food and beverage that arrive at the front desk after the guest has checked out are called *late charges*. Late charges are irritants to both the guest and the hotel. Guests may need to modify expense accounts after the late charges arrive by mail, and hotels may need to absorb the costs because guests often refuse to pay after the fact. If the late charge is small enough, the hotel might not even bill: Processing the late charges might cost more than the amounts sought.

Collections are easiest with folios that have been transferred to the city ledger. Then the accounts are merely updated before billing. Such is the case with express check-outs. Folios are transferred to the city ledger, updated with late charges, if any, and billed several days later to the credit cards that the guests had tendered.

Adjustments are more difficult if the guest settles at the cashier's window with a credit card. If the credit-card company does not permit after-the-fact additions to a signed charge slip, the hotel will bill the guest directly, using the registration card address. This procedure gives the hotel a second chance at collecting, although it doesn't reduce the guest's anger. The same procedure is also used with guests who settle with cash, including checks and traveler's checks. Collection is less likely when a disputed charge originates with a nonregistered guest—no reg card and no address—using a credit card in the dining room or bar. Credit-card companies will not release cardholders' addresses and may not allow altered charge slips.

Late Charge Procedures.   Late charges are identified by *LC* (late charge) or *AD* (after departure). Small late charges—$15 and under, perhaps—are wiped off with an allowance. This is done by reopening the folio of the departed guest and posting the late charge. The new balance is immediately zeroed by means of an allowance, creating a permanent record of the transaction. (Debit departmental sales, and credit accounts receivable.)

A second procedure is also used. A new, separate late-charge folio is created, on which all small late charges are posted. Daily, the total late-charge balance is cleared with one allowance, obviously a less burdensome procedure for the desk. Either way, management should get a daily allowance report, which is one of the exception reports prepared during the night audit (see Chapter 13).

Notwithstanding these provisions for allowancing late charges, efforts to collect them should be conscientiously pursued. In that case, the late charge could be posted to the guest's closed folio and immediately transferred to the city ledger for billing.

Delinquent Accounts.   Into the delinquent (or bad debt) division of the city ledger go all receivables that are awaiting final disposition. Such is the case with large, uncollectible late charges, which were not treated as allowances. They, and other unrecoverable debts, are eventually written off—taken off the books—as bad.

Returned checks (bounced checks) also account for a portion of delinquent receivables. Rather than reestablishing the customer's old records, returned checks are viewed as new debt and tracked separately. Checks come back for many reasons. Chief among them are insufficient funds, no such account, account closed, illegible signature, and incorrect date. Since passing bad checks is a criminal offense, hotels should support the police in prosecuting offenders even when restitution is made.

Credit-card chargebacks, guests who skip (intentionally leave without paying), and judgmental mistakes in extending open credit comprise the remainder of the delinquent division. For most hotels, credit card chargebacks, skips, and open credit errors represent a negligible operating cost. Hotels that show significant costs in these areas should reevaluate their credit policies.

Executive Accounts.   Hotel executives can be city ledger receivables in their own hotel. Management people use the hotel for personal pleasure as well as for house business. Company policy dictates how charges are to be made. House entertainment might be distinguished from personal charges on the guest check by an ''H'' (house business) or an ''E'' (entertainment) added under the signature. Without these symbols, the accounting department bills the individual as a regular city account. Many times, though, the billing is only a percentage of the actual menu price, depending on the employment agreement.

Due Bills.   **Due bills,** sometimes called *trade advertising contracts, trade-outs,* or *reciprocal trade agreements,* are nothing more than barter deals. Hotels have traded room-nights for advertising on radio and television stations, billboards, newspapers and magazines, and even for capital goods since the 1930s.

A Rationale for Due Bills.   Airlines, theaters, arenas, and the media have highly perishable products. So do hotels. There is no means of recapturing an unsold airline seat or an unused television commercial. The same is true with the lodging industry: There is nothing to inventory. Once the night has passed, the product cannot be sold again. Swapping goods and services can be mutually beneficial when both parties have unsold, perishable products.

Reciprocal trade agreements swap free advertising for free hotel facilities. Their use may be restricted to rooms only, with food and beverage to be paid for in cash. This is understandable from the hotel's point of view. The cost of providing an otherwise empty room is minimal; the cost of food and beverage is high. Moreover, unused food and beverage, unlike unused rooms, can be sold the following day. The advertising media set restrictions too, making no promise as to where the hotel's ad will appear in print or at what time it will be heard on the airwaves.

Whereas the hotel would like to limit the due bill to rooms, to use by certain individuals, and to given days of the week with advance reservations required, the facts of life may be otherwise. It is a matter of negotiation.

Some due bills are so negotiable that they are traded on an open market. Discount brokers buy the bills from the original receiver, or negotiate directly with the hotel, at reduced prices. The due bills are resold to a third, or even a fourth party, each time with an additional markup. In due course, they are used at the hotel in lieu of cash. The hotel accepts the bills at face value, which is still greater than the price paid by the final user.

The concept works, and so does the series of marked-up resales, because two prices are involved. Both the hotel and the media (or other swapping party) deliver the due bill at retail prices but deliver the goods or services at cost. If the media accepts a $100 room for a $100 television spot that cost $40, the TV station can resell the room at $60 and still make $20. There is even greater impetus when we remember that the room and the air time would have gone unused anyway.

Due bills are favored during periods of low or moderate occupancy and are less popular during busy periods. The oil embargo of the 1970s and the poor economy of the early 1980s brought a rebirth of due bill usage.

Processing the Due Bill.   Due bill users must present the actual due bill agreement at the time of registration. This permits the clerk to assign the most expensive accommodations. (The hotel's cost of delivering an expensive room is almost the same as delivering an inexpensive one.) The clerk also verifies the expiration date of the agreement. Amounts unused after that date are lost to the due bill holder. When that happens—and it does frequently—the hotel gets the advertising (or whatever) but the media company never gets to use all of its due bill.

The due bill is attached to the registration card and the rate is marked ''Due Bill'' along with the dollar room charge. A standard guest folio, or sometimes one specially colored or coded, is used. The actual due bill is filed at the front desk during the guest's stay. After the value of the accommodations used has been recorded on the due bill, it is returned to the holder at check-out.

The transient folio, which was used to accumulate charges during the due bill user's stay, is transferred to the city ledger in the usual manner. However, the city ledger account is treated differently. There is no billing. Instead, the account is charged off against the liability incurred by the contract.

At the time of the agreement, a liability was created in the hotel's promise to furnish accommodations to the media or other trader. As hotel accommodations are furnished, that liability is decreased. It is balanced off against the city ledger account that was created from the transfer of the guest folio at the time of check-out.

Standard City Ledger Accounts.   In its simplest form, the city ledger represents a debt relationship between the hotel and its local customers. Those customers could

EXHIBIT 12–2

Shown is a miscellaneous charge order (MCO), a voucher used by airlines to pay hotel charges, particularly when the airline is acting as a travel agency.

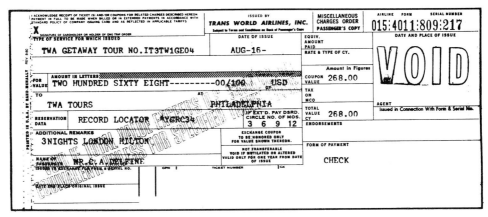

Courtesy: Trans World Airlines, Inc.

be anyone in the community. School officials, government offices, utilities, and even individuals are city ledger accounts. Local businesses might use the hotel's rooms for visiting executives and the hotel's public facilities for business meetings and social affairs. Once credit has been established, authorized signatories merely sign for the charges. The hotel's accounting office bills monthly.

Airline crews are sought-after city accounts even though competition forces down rates. Layover crews charge their rooms, and once a month the hotel bills the airline. Airlines also contract with hotels to accommodate stranded travelers with room and meal facilities. The airlines pay for those facilities with a **miscellaneous charge order (MCO)** (see Exhibit 12–2). This same coupon is used when airlines act as travel agents. Arriving guests, who have already paid the airline, present the MCO as evidence of the prepayment. The hotel accepts the order, credits the guest by transferring the folio to the city ledger, and bills the airline, net of commission.

Banquet Charges. There has been a decided reduction in the type of open-book credit (credit based solely on signature) that banquet charges once represented. Party givers and banquet chairpersons once expected to sign for the party while the hotel waited for collection. Catering managers still allow this when credit arrangements have been made in advance. When such arrangements have not been cleared, collection is made by a member of the catering department, who channels it through the front desk. The function charge is paid on the spot, with both the charge and the receipt posted at the desk.

When credit is extended, the signed food or beverage check is posted to a master account, transferred to the city ledger, and billed. Banquet accounts are usually billed within three days, which follows the pattern for other master account and speedy check-out billings.

Company-sponsored banquets are big business in the United States and even more so in Japan. Whether overseas or at home, company-sponsored affairs, and to a somewhat lesser degree private receptions (weddings, bar mitzvahs, etc.) are low-risk ventures: The responsible party is known.

Pay-as-you-go functions are much riskier affairs. The group may be known, but there is no financial identity behind the group. Included in this category are school proms, political dinners, charitable fundraisers, and other speculative functions that base payment on ticket sales. A portion of the estimated bill should be collected in advance, and a ticket accounting system should be part of the up-front agreement. The credit department should review the contract and establish the identity and creditworthiness of the responsible individual.

Managing Credit

Organizing and processing accounts through the city ledger, the first segment of this chapter, is but one component of credit. Management must attend to a long list of other functions, including bad debt management, check processing, internal procedures, and collections. But first of all, management must decide what its credit policies are.

A Cost–Benefit Decision

There is no perfect credit policy. Any business that extends credit is vulnerable to loss. Each credit decision weighs immediate, determinable benefits against possible, uncertain costs. Recognizing that, the hotel industry has reduced its level of open credit. More reliance is now placed on credit cards and credit investigations. Open credit still has traditional uses—for advances to concessionaires, outlays for tips, payments for C.O.D. packages, and even some convention/banquet sales.

Successful credit policy cannot be measured by accounting figures alone. Hotels with small amounts of bad debts (or small ratios of bad debts to accounts receivable) are not necessarily the best managed ones. A conservative credit policy will mean few credit losses, but it may also cause substantial losses from business that was turned away. Low credit losses are easily measured on the books; lost business has no entry. Profits might have been improved by taking the business that an ultraconservative credit policy denied. The conundrum is that the increase might not have been achieved; there's no way to know.

The issue is not black and white—always credit/never credit. Every full-service hotel offers some amount of credit. The question focuses on how much, when, and under what circumstances credit is offered. The answer is not always the same, even for the same credit manager in the same hotel. With different conditions, credit could be severely curtailed, moderately administered, or liberally issued, even to the same customer with the same credit standing (see Exhibit 12–3).

Good occupancy, the first item of Exhibit 12–3, permits the hotel to adopt a conservative credit policy. There is no reason to replace low-risk guests with those of uncertain credit standing. When occupancy is high, a bad debt loss is the sum of full rack rate plus administrative costs, not just the marginal cost of providing a room during low occupancy.

Food and beverage sales, which have a high variable cost, are different. Far more caution is needed to justify banquet sales during a low period than room sales during a low period. A banquet bad debt may well cost the hotel two-thirds or more of the bill (food, call-in labor, flowers, special cake, favors, etc.). Room losses are substantially less, both in percentage (25 percent) and in absolute dollars.

EXHIBIT 12–3

*Shown are issues
involved in the
determination of credit
policy. Factors other
than the
creditworthiness of the
guest explain why credit
tightens and eases over
time, even for the same
guest.*

Severely Curtailed	Moderately Administered	Liberally Issued
High occupancy	·	Low occupancy
In-season	·	Off-season
No competition	·	Price cutting
Established property	·	New hotel
High interest rates	·	Low interest rates
Reputable hotel	·	Disreputable hotel
Item of high variable cost	·	Item of low variable cost
Inexperienced lender	·	Low debt-recovery costs
Hotel overextended	·	Good credit rating

Hotels reduce rates when occupancies are low. These would also be the times for a more liberal credit policy. In fact, the more liberal credit policy might be traded for the lower room rates. Too dismal a circumstance, and the hotel will need to give both to get the business. Fighting for market share or competing with better appointed properties are additional reasons for liberalizing credit (Exhibit 12–3).

The most obvious cost of poor credit is the out-and-out loss from nonpayment. Bad debts generate other hidden costs, the loss of customer goodwill among them. Administrative costs such as recordkeeping, application forms, printing, credit checks, postage, telephone, and employee time are never charged against the debt and rarely are they toted up. In contrast, bank charges, attorney fees, and collection costs are usually identifiable. That fact does not make them any less expensive, however.

The offsetting benefit is that of expanded sales volume. There is also profit to be made from lending. If the hotel's credit rating is good, it can borrow at low rates, or even self-finance. Extending credit at 18 percent annually (1½ percent per month) provides an opportunity to profit from the interest spread.

The Management Function

Establishing and monitoring credit is a broad-based management function coordinated by the credit manager. If there is no credit manager, the controller takes on the task. Some responsibilities are handed off to other managers, who then form a credit committee. The rooms manager assumes an active role in front-office credit, and the sales/catering executives do the same for banquets and group business.

The credit manager/controller must support a credit policy that encourages a healthy marketing approach even as it strives for prompt payment and bottom-line returns. This is best done by viewing credit in three subfunctions: extending credit, monitoring credit, and collecting receivables.

Extending Credit to Arriving Guests. Prescreening for credit approval is not always possible in the lodging industry. Lead time may be inadequate, as it is with a walk-in guest; reservations may not originate with the hotel, which is the case with central reservation systems. Nevertheless, after-the-fact collections depend on before-the-fact procedures.

Collecting overdue accounts begins with identifying the receivable, either at registration or earlier. Credit management is a pervasive function that merely begins at the desk. Like marketing or security, credit is everyone's responsibility. House-keeping must report light or missing luggage, uniformed services must be wary of suspicious activities, and food and beverage personnel must obtain legible signatures and room numbers when guests sign for services.

A Reservation Arrival.   Identification is more reliable when the guest has a reservation that involved correspondence. Then, the name, address, and perhaps even the company identification have been verified by mail. At registration, complete name and address are reconfirmed. That means given name, not initials; and street address, not post office box, office building, or city alone.

Early suspicions can be confirmed quickly. ZIP code directories help identify false addresses. Some hotels have the bellperson record the guest's car license number on the rooming slip. Illegible scribbles on the reg card are clarified before the guest leaves the desk. An inexpensive telephone call to the guest's supposed office puts many issues in perspective.

Credit procedures put stress on the clerk–guest interchange. Specific information must be elicited but done under the quality assurance umbrella. Tact in selecting the right words and care in applying voice intonations—often ignored in training programs—must be taught and practiced. Many factors—a tired guest or a misplaced reservation—exacerbate an already awkward situation. If baggage is missing or light, the clerk will need to press for more complete details. If the guest is nervous or poorly dressed, the clerk may insist on photocopying a driver's license. The line between information gathering and invasion is a thin one, as is the line between guest understanding and anger. Front-office clerks need to be masters of diplomacy.

No magic formula separates safe risks from poor ones. But collection is possible only if the hotel can identify the person and the address. Returned checks, late charges, credit-card chargebacks, and other open accounts cannot be collected, regardless of the guest's sincerity, without these essential facts. Unlike most industries, innkeeping has the opportunity to get the data. Procedures should be in place to ensure its collection.

A Walk-In Arrival.   Because walk-ins pose additional credit risks, every hotel flags them with a special identification: *NR* (no reservation), *OS* (off-the-street), and *WI* (walk-in) are common symbols for alerting desk personnel. Recent telephone reservations, particularly those directed through the central reservation system less than 24 hours before arrival, must be classified as walk-ins for credit purposes.

The reg cards of walk-in guests are not always filed immediately. Some properties wait until the credit manager has inspected them. The credit manager uses telephone directories, credit-card companies, city directories, colleagues, and direct-dial telephone calls to verify information about guests, be they walk-ins or otherwise.

Suspicious guests can be required to pay in advance—credit card or not. Paid-in-advance guests are usually denied credit throughout the house. Extreme measures like these do not build guest loyalty. Few walk-ins intend to defraud the hotel. The extra caution needed to protect against some should not disintegrate into antiservice for all.

Three Means of Collection.   Unheard of a generation ago, it is now accepted practice to ask arriving guests to identify their method of payment. The question is standard on every registration card (Exhibits 8–5 and 8–6). Each of the three means listed there (cash, check, and credit card) has advantages and disadvantages to the house.

Cash.   Even cash is not trouble-free—counterfeiting plagues every retail register. Cash transactions also add to the hotel's internal control problems. Checks and credit-card slips are not as appealing to a cashier set on theft. The same holds true for short-change artists—they, too, focus on cash.

Checks.   Often, guests assume that permission to settle with cash means permission to settle with personal checks. Then guests, who are hurrying to depart, become greatly distressed when check-outs are delayed because of the special check verification procedures (Chapter 11) used by the credit managers. Not surprisingly, honest guests give an antiservice interpretation to the whole process.

If settlement is to be by check, the credit manager needs lead time during business hours to confirm the details. Appropriate telephone expenses are charged to the guest. Except in unusual cases, the approval is limited to the amount of the folio; no cashback is authorized.

Risk is reduced if the check writer offers a bank-guarantee card. The issuing bank guarantees the check below a given dollar ceiling—say, $250. Even then, the hotel must watch the expiration date of the card, verify the card number against the number on the guest's check, and match signatures. The cards are not much help for an industry that draws its clientele from outside the local area. That might change with the coming of interstate banking.

Charging a fee of $1 to $5 for accepting a check would not be unreasonable. The larger the check, the less costly the percentage fee would be. Guests already pay a 1 percent fee for traveler's checks. Hotels do not charge for check cashing because it is a financial service that they do not wish to offer. Usually, hotels only cash checks for guests, and even then there is a $50 or $100 ceiling limit.

Other options for handling checks are the check verification systems, trademarked under names such as Telecheck or Telecredit. Hotels pay a fee to the check-guarantee companies, which insure each check cashed. If a bank is involved, there is an annual fee plus a per use fee. Otherwise, only a larger per use fee is paid to the telecheck companies, which verify the checks through a computer interface system. By telephone or point-of-sale device (see Exhibit 12–4), front-desk personnel enter the guest's identification. The answer returns in less than a minute. Verification is by exception. The check is approved unless information on file triggers a negative response. An approved check is given a guarantee number—the hotel's claim number—which is written on the check's face.

Credit Cards.   Credit cards are the most desirable means of guest identification and payment. But even they are not trouble-free, and their advantages come only with substantial costs to the hotel. Chapter 8 treated the role of the credit card in the registration procedure. Although that procedure is the same for all cards, the fees paid to use them are not. T&E cards are more expensive to the hotel than bank cards, and verifying by telephone is more costly than using POS terminals. Hotels that use an electronic interface system at the point of sale, where the card is swiped through a reader (see Exhibit 12–5), pay the smallest fee but the highest cost for equipment lease or purchase.

Credit cards are verified through a credit-card authorization procedure. The approval that comes back verifies that there is such a card, that the line of credit is

Exhibit 12–4

Shown is a combined Touch-Tone and card swipe point-of-sale verification terminal.

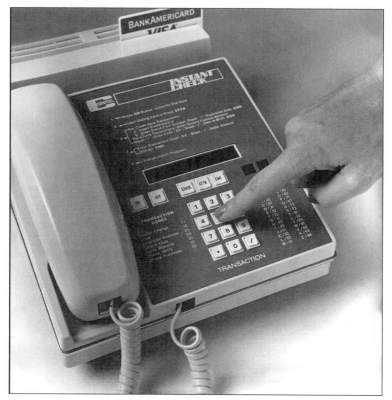

Courtesy: Centel Transaction Services, Las Vegas, NV.

Exhibit 12–5

This is a combined swipe-through credit-card authorization and check verification terminal.

Courtesy: Lodgistix, Inc., Wichita, KS.

sufficient to cover the charges, and that the card has not been reported missing. Whether the person presenting the card is the true cardholder is another matter altogether. Putting the user's photograph on the card has been one means of reducing that risk.

Fraud and mishandled credit cards are costly for the merchant/hotels but especially for the credit-card companies. Credit-card users are sheltered, because their responsibility is capped by law at $50. So antifraud efforts are concentrated in the credit-card companies with some help from the merchants.

Eliminating paper records was the start of the defensive battle. Discarded credit-card carbons had been used to match names and credit-card numbers as the first step in their fraudulent use. Embossing the credit-card number on both sides has also helped because it requires counterfeiters to make two alterations.

Long-term solutions lie in credit-card technology. Holograms that produce three-dimensional images, which display motion when moved from side to side, are widely used now. Unfortunately, the cost of reproducing these has dissuaded the credit-card companies as well as illicit users.

Hotels can help themselves by reducing the number of chargebacks. Hotels are given 30 days to respond to credit-card company inquiries about charges that guests protest. One study suggested that some 50 percent of those inquiries are never answered. By federal law, credit-card companies credit guests for unanswered charges, which means the hotels absorb the losses. Chargebacks are also initiated by the credit-card companies for procedural errors that hotel personnel may cause. In both cases, training the staff in a list of do's and don'ts such as the following checklist will reduce the number of costly chargebacks.

Checklist for Credit Cards

1. Be aware that every business is assigned a floor limit, which is the maximum dollar volume allowed on a single credit card without additional authorization.
2. Insist that employees know that limit, for, once exceeded, all charges, including those below the floor, are voided.
3. Do not split charges on two or more vouchers to avoid the floor limits.
4. Never give a cash refund if an unused advance deposit was made through a credit-card charge (or travel agency voucher, for that matter).
5. Bill credit-card companies promptly.
6. Refuse to post fictitious items in order to give cash against the credit card.
7. Get guest's telephone number on the form in order to trace legitimate errors.
8. Watch for altered cards, rearranged numbers, or replaced digits that will make a hot card usable. Clues are glue on the card, blurred holograms, color variations, or misaligned numbers. Compare numbers on the back and front sides. Watch for altered signature panels, which are made tamper-evident by repetitive designs on the panels.
9. Question credit-card signatures made with a felt-tip pen that could be used to cover an original signature.
10. Compare the signature on the departmental voucher with the signature on the credit card. If uncertain still, compare with the registration card signature.
11. Make certain the card imprints completely on all copies of the voucher; check the clarity of the signature.
12. Use the proper voucher form. Each company has its own and may not accept its competitors.

13. Anticipate employee misuse—changed figures or additional charges that permit the employee to pocket some cash.

14. Answer promptly chargeback inquiries from the card companies.

15. Cardholders agree to surrender the card on request, since it remains the property of the credit-card company. Agents of the hotel should exercise no force in retrieving a card, nor should they destroy the card or publicly humiliate the guest. Instruct employees not to apprehend anyone suspected of using an invalid card.

16. Carry insurance against false arrest based on incorrect information furnished by the credit-card company.

17. Refuse credit cards whose expiration date has passed the last day of the month specified. Watch on some cards for ''from'' dates; charges before that time will be rejected.

18. Compare the credit card and driver's license signatures when suspicious of the individual or the card. (Many states are treating their driver's licenses with a chemical process that disintegrates, changing the graphics if the data on the card have been tampered with.)

19. Teach cashiers that MasterCard uses numbers that begin with 5; Visa numbers begin with 4; American Express numbers begin with 3; and Discover numbers begin with 6.

Monitoring Credit.   For most guests, credit is monitored by means of credit cards, first on arrival and then at departure. A smaller number of guests are monitored more carefully either because of the hotel's credit policies or because of restrictions set by the credit-card companies.

Even guests who use national cards have two credit restrictions. One is the personal limit of their own credit line, and the other is the **floor limit** of the hotel. The floor limit is the maximum credit line that the hotel may allow to any one guest without seeking additional approval from the credit-card company. (The floor level should be as high as the hotel can negotiate.) If the card is approved at registration, the card company guarantees payment up to the floor—actually, it's a ceiling. Unless specific approval was requested and received for charges above the floor, the entire charge—floor and all—will be denied by the card company in case of default.

Hotels also act to protect themselves against the ceiling of the guest's own credit line. They freeze the amount the guest is apt to spend—the hotel's floor—to ensure collection. If the guest incurs less than the floor, and most do, the hotel is supposed to release the difference when the guest checks out. Few hotels do so, so the customer finds that his or her personal credit limit has been reached before that level of expenditure has actually been made. New York was the first state to outlaw this practice.

Losses could be substantial if the floor limit is breached without clearance. This is not an issue if the guest pays. There is a problem only when the guest doesn't pay and the hotel looks to the credit-card company for reimbursement. Hence, the frequent monitoring of folio balances, no less than once daily. The job is generally assigned to the swing or graveyard shifts.

In a manual system, the clerk flips through the bucket scrutinizing the folios' daily and cumulative balances. With a computer, the overlimit report, which is an exception report (see Chapter 13), can be screened many times during the day. Whether a manual or a computer system, the credit manager (or even the posting clerk) must project the current rate of spending as the folio balance nears the floor limit.

Questionable folios, and even some picked at random, are examined in detail. Is there a credit card for the room? Are the numbers legible? Is the expiration date still valid? Is the balance below the floor? Is an approval number on file? The total charges are examined, but especially the pattern of charges. Suspicious accounts are listed by the night clerk in a report, which the credit manager examines first thing in the morning.

Several situations mandate immediate action. The most serious is the credit-card company's refusal to increase the floor limit on a suspect folio. Paid-in-advance guests who exceed the deposit limit and guests with preapproved direct billing who exceed the agreed limit are additional examples. Actions that portend a skipper are probably the most immediate problem.

If discovered during the day, or as a result of the night clerk's report, the credit manager acts immediately to collect. If unable to collect, the credit manager may take the guest's luggage, lock the guest out of the room, or call the police in case of fraud. (State laws make skipping and bad-check passing prima facie cases of fraud.)

If the credit alert is discovered during the wee hours of the morning, common sense dictates waiting until a more reasonable hour. (Courts have ruled against hotels that lock guests out at unreasonable hours.) Wait too long, however, and the hotel might have a skip.

Credit Alert and Skippers.   Intentional skippers can be identified by the pattern of things they do. Indeed, the credit manager should develop a standard description much like airlines have done for the typical hijacker. The average skipper is male, 30 to 35 years old, a late walk-in with light baggage and vague identification. He is a heavy tipper and a quick new friend of the bartender. The skipper makes no telephone calls that can be used to trace him. His address is usually a well-known one in a large city, but it proves to be false. He writes his name and address poorly and offers no business identification.

Skipper alerts begin with light or worthless luggage. Guests become doubly suspect when they charge their folios with small items, which one normally pays for in cash. Skippers compound the hotel's costs by passing bad checks or using stolen credit cards. Bad-check passers concentrate on weekends or holidays when commercial hotels are understaffed and banks are closed. With ATM machines readily available, fewer and fewer hotels are cashing checks. Those that do should maintain a check-cashing record to alert other shifts of ongoing activities. Then a check-cashing report becomes part of the night audit activities.

Skippers and bad-check passers frequently work one area before moving on. A telephone or fax network among local hotels does much to identify the culprit even before his or her arrival. Photographs of suspects and identifying information, perhaps from the police, will undoubtedly be displayed someday on computer terminals.

Something needs to be done because crime has moved from the street into the hotel. Frustrating the criminal takes the combined efforts of all employees. Clerks, bellpersons, house police, cashiers, housekeepers, engineers, and room service waiters, too, must watch for and report the telltale signs. Large quantities of blank checks or money orders, firearms and burglary tools, keys from other hotels, unusual amounts of cash or gems, or just heavy traffic or loitering about a room indicate serious trouble is brewing.

EXHIBIT 12–6

The likelihood of collecting unpaid receivables diminishes over time.

Time Allowed for Account to Remain Unpaid	*Percentage Collectible Expected*
Due date	99
3 months	90
4 months	86
5 months	81
6 months	63
12 months	42
24 months	26
36 months	17
60 months	Less than 1

Source: Composite of hotel and nonhotel industries.

Collecting Receivables.   The city ledger is what receivables are all about. Every unpaid departure or charge (every account receivable) is transferred from the transient ledger to the city ledger: from the front office to the back office. Here is accumulated every category of debt: master accounts, travel agency coupons, skippers, credit cards, direct company billings, conventions, and banquet guests. How these debts are to be collected and by whom reflects on the hotel's cash flow and on its profit picture.

Billing and Chasing.   Hotels, like other retailers, bill non-credit-card receivables monthly. If the guest arrives early in the cycle and takes 30 days to pay after getting the bill, 60 days elapse before the hotel knows that it has a problem. Hotels are switching to 15-day billing cycles because the longer an account is unpaid, the less likely it is ever to be paid (see Exhibit 12–6). Other bills, like convention and banquet events, are going out three to five days after the function. Direct company billing and express check-out should be mailed one to three days after departure.

Second notices should follow soon after the first billing, usually at the end of the month. Routine notices twice during the next 30 days and telephone calls thereafter should inquire whether the statement has come, whether it is accurate, and when payment can be expected. Each notice should point up the additional interest charges that late payments accrue.

Chasing unpaid debts should not be a random effort—it must be in someone's job description. Otherwise, customers get the impression that the hotel has forgotten. Nor should the collector be apologetic—the late payer is the wrongdoer. Payment arrangements should be specific in both amounts and dates. Partial payments may be accepted with the same understandings, provided the periodic payment is not so small that its absence is overlooked. Each partial payment extends the statute of limitations.

What Next?   When faced with a delinquent account, the hotel has three courses of action: (1) it can continue with its own internal efforts to collect; (2) it can hire the services of a third party, such as an attorney or a collection agency; or (3) it can enter into an agreement with a factor.

Hotels that choose the internal option must be prepared to invest in the process. Without a full-time credit manager, the job is one more task added to the office of the controller. Even then, it has the costs that were itemized at the beginning of this chapter. Fees for credit-reporting companies need to be added to the administrative expenses. Federal and state legislation is another big hurdle. If the staff is insensitive to the rights of the debtor (and they have many legally protected rights), the process should best be left to a third party.

The worst of the bad debts end up with collection agencies. Oddly enough, their basic technique is writing letters, much like the hotel does. More than 90 percent of their collections are generated by simple dunning letters. Still, collections are light, especially for small accounts, which have the lowest priority with the collection agencies. Less than 25 percent of accounts turned over are collected. If no collection is made, there is no fee, but the fee takes 30 to 40 percent of what is collected.

Debtors usually pay up, because the demand for payment grows increasingly intense. They also feel the threat to their credit ratings. Most of all, the debtors know that the hotel is serious now, and they perceive the agency as relentless and threatening.

Most hotel receivables are credit cards. The balance is business credit—companies, travel agencies, and association debt. *Factoring* accounts receivable may involve additional services, but it is essentially the sale of the receivables. Factoring has never played a major role in lodging, as there isn't enough business volume. Moreover, the factor buys all of the business receivables, not just the bad ones. Sometimes, they won't take the bad ones. Hotels with a large convention business may find the sale of receivables desirable, especially if the hotel is in a cash squeeze and the receivables are of good quality. After examining the quality of the receivables, the factor buys them at something far less than face value.

The Mechanics of the Entry

City ledger accounts receivable originate from two kinds of transactions. In one, the individual front-office folio is transferred to the city ledger. This entry has been the emphasis of preceding discussions. Credit-card settlements, master accounts, and travel agency payments are examples of transient accounts receivable becoming city ledger accounts receivable by transfer.

A second type of city ledger transaction bypasses the front-office folio. Postings are made directly to the city ledger—there are no ledger-to-ledger transfers. This happens when guests, whether registered or not, use credit cards in food and beverage outlets. These do not appear on a folio, so they are processed differently.

Transfers from Guest Folios

Transfers *from* the guest folio *to* the city ledger reduce the folio receivable with a credit (Exhibit 10–1, final line) and increase the city receivable with a debit. Daily and cumulatively, the total transfer debits always equal the total transfer credits. As discussed previously, once the transfer is made, the accounting office bills by mail from the city ledger.

When settlement is received, the check is deposited (debit cash) and the individual account receivable in the city ledger is reduced (credit accounts receivable). For certain receivables such as convention master accounts, the city ledger record is actually closed. Other receivables—for example, credit cards—are continuing records with payments and new charges continually flowing in and out. This basic procedure is used for every city account: credit cards, late charges, master accounts,

EXHIBIT 12–7

This is a typical travel agency form for requesting reservations from cooperating hotels. Efforts to standardize a single form have not been successful.

Step 1. Agency types out as much of form as it can.
Step 2. Agency mails Parts 2 and 3 to hotel or completes form by phone.
Step 3. If Step 2 was done by mail, hotel fills out balance of form on both parts and returns

Part 3 to agency. If Step 2 was completed by phone, agency throws away Part 2.
Step 4. When form has been all filled out, remittance is attached to Part 4 and mailed to hotel.

Step 5. Part 3 is filed in client's folder and Part 1 is mailed or delivered to client.
Step 6. Part 5 is filed in date tickler for commission collection and/or is thrown out when commission has been collected.

AGENCY REQUEST FOR HOTEL/MOTEL ACCOMMODATIONS

CONFIRM TO AGENCY VIA ☐ RETURN MAIL ☐ AIR MAIL ☐ TELEPHONE ☐ WIRE

Date_____ ☐ INITIAL REQUEST ☐ CANCELLATION ☐ CHANGE

CATEGORY ☐ MINIMUM ☐ MODERATE ☐ DELUXE

CLIENT

AGT.

HOTEL/MOTEL

TEL. NO.

AGENCY LIABILITY SUBJECT TO CONDITIONS ON REVERSE SIDE HEREOF

CONFIRMED RESERVATIONS FOR:
_____ ROOMS _____ PERSONS _____ NIGHTS

HOUR   DAY   DATE   VIA   FROM

ARRIVE

DEPART

_____ SINGLE _____ TWIN _____ DOUBLE _____ STUDIO _____ SUITE _____ SEE BELOW
☐ NO FACILITIES ☐ PRIVATE TOILET ☐ PRIVATE SHOWER AND TOILET ☐ PRIVATE BATH AND TOILET

☐ NO MEALS(EP) ☐ CONTINENTAL BREAKFAST ☐ AMERICAN BREAKFAST
☐ DEMI PENSION (MAP) ☐ FULL PENSION(AP)

CONFIRMED FOR HOTEL BY _____ DATE _____

ROOM RATE $ _____

NO. OF NIGHTS _____

WHEN VALIDATED THIS VOUCHER HAS A VALUE OF
$
EXCLUDING TAXES AND CHARGES FOR SERVICE AND PERSONAL INCIDENTALS

PLEASE REPLY BELOW AND RETURN GREEN COPY TO TRAVEL AGENCY
☐ Quote rates in U.S. Dollars or specify currency exchange rate _____
☐ Advise cancellation date without penalty _____
☐ State if reservations are guaranteed _____ YES _____ NO
☐ May agency deduct commission if fully prepaid _____ YES _____ NO

COMM. $ _____

DEPOSIT _____

HOTEL/MOTEL TO COLLECT FROM CLIENT $ _____

Reply by Hotel/Motel:

THIS BOX FOR AGENCY USE ONLY
CK.   DATE
NO.   SENT

By _____ Date _____

Courtesy: Willow Press, Inc., Syosset, NY.

company accounts, travel agencies, banquet accounts, and executive accounts. Some of these require special handling.

Travel Agency Records. A good share of the antipathy that exists between hotels and travel agencies can be ascribed to poor recordkeeping on both sides. Accounting for the travel agency commission starts with the reservation. Commissionable reservations are flagged, and that identification is carried onto the registration card and the folio. Computer systems capture and track the travel agency guest more efficiently than manual systems. Whichever system is used, commissionable folios are segregated from noncommissionable folios, and immediate attention given to DNAs (did not arrive). A notice of nonarrival, frequently a postcard, is mailed to the travel agency. This forestalls a claim and the endless correspondence that follows.

How It Is Supposed to Work. There are so many hotels and so many travel agencies (more than 30,000 with a sales force of 200,000 in the United States alone) that the system works best on a prepaid basis. This requires the agency to support its reservation request with a check for the full amount less commission. Accompanying the check is a reservation form like that in Exhibit 12–7. By returning one copy of the form, the hotel confirms the reservation and awaits the guest.

The arriving guest presents his or her copy of the reservation form, now called a **coupon** or *travel agency voucher.*[4] The hotel gives full credit on the folio for the value of that voucher. Charges in excess of the prepaid amount are paid by the guest at check-out.

This procedure, where the hotel has the cash less commission before the guest arrives, is preferred. The travel agency has its commission, the hotel has its payment, and the guest is accommodated as arranged. The advantage from reduced paperwork is lost if the guest stays longer than planned (an additional commission) or shorter than planned (a rebate is needed).

In any case, settlement is handled by the back office through the city ledger. The travel agency's check is deposited (debit cash) when received, and the agency's city account is credited in the full amount of the room charges. (The difference between the smaller check and the full room charge is a debit to rooms commission expense.) Later, when the guest checks out, the unpaid folio balance is transferred to the city ledger and charged against the open account being maintained for the travel agency. A second transfer is needed if the guest pays for incidentals in excess of the prepaid room charge with a personal credit card.

Although at first it appears to be poor money management, some hotels hold the undeposited check at the front desk. This isn't done if the sum is large or if the reputation of the specific travel agency is bad. Clerical savings can be significant if the check is held. There is no need to maintain and post agency accounts in the back office. Cancellations are easily handled by returning the original check. And a good deal of record verification is reduced because the check and the coupon are processed together.

Why It Doesn't Always Work.   Rarely does the prepaid reservation procedure work as well in practice as it does in theory. First of all, the agency may not send the check. There may not be time if the reservation was made by telephone. Even if there were time, the agency may not have the check to send. A corporate account, for example, is customarily settled after the trip, not before. So rather than being prepaid, the guest tenders an IOU (the agency's coupon), naively expecting hotel credit for payment that has not yet been made to the agency, let alone to the hotel.

Unless a good credit relationship has been established with the travel agency, this arrangement is not to the hotel's liking. The hotel finds itself in the position of servicing the guest while attempting to collect from a third party. Quite naturally, the agency's voucher is refused unless the credit relationship exists beforehand.

A full house presents special problems even if the credit relationship is well established. Without a prepaid reservation, the guest finds himself without a room and without a refund. The deposit, if any, is still with the travel agency. Similarly, a guest who stays fewer days than the reservation stated gets no refund even if the room was prepaid; the excess is rebated to the agency.

Issues grow more intense when the guest is carrying a foreign voucher from an overseas agency. International tourists present vouchers with different formats, languages, and currency denominations. Front-office staffers are often unprepared to deal with them.

Help is available from the International Hotel Association (IHA), which publishes the *World Directory of Travel Agencies.* The IHA also circulates a list of problematic and late-pay agencies. Members who rely on the IHA's material can recover some debt through the association if an agency proves unwilling to pay.

Foreign-exchange companies—for example, Deak-Perera—have clearing-houses that facilitate international hotel–travel agency exchanges in both directions. For a small charge in addition to the exchange fee, they will handle the conversion of foreign travel agency deposits into U.S. funds. So will some of the airlines and some of the hotel rep companies.

Helping to Make It Work.   The clash between hotels and travel agencies is about up-front money. If the agency prepays the reservation, the system works as designed. If the reservation is not prepaid, everything depends on whether or not the hotel accepts the agency's coupon (voucher).

Two issues are involved in the acceptability of vouchers. First, they are not standardized, even within the United States. Unfamiliar forms, formats, colors, designs, and languages raise questions, which a busy desk finds easier to reject than to answer. Second, the problem is compounded when the creditworthiness of the travel agency issuing the voucher is unknown to the hotel. More often than not, such is the case.

Professional organizations such as the **American Society of Travel Agents (ASTA)** and the **Hotel Sales and Marketing Association International (HSMAI)** have worked hard to standardize vouchers. Despite good intentions, two major efforts failed to produce a mutually acceptable form. Later, ASTA issued its own form. It was unsuccessful, partly because it entailed a fee payable to ASTA and partly because it was a product of the travel industry, not lodging.

Lack of success at the national level was matched at the international level: The International Hotel Association (IHA) and the Universal Federation of Travel Agents Association (UFTAA) reached a similar impasse. Format was less a problem internationally—the issue floundered on the complexity of financial guarantees. Not only are there far more international travel agencies and hotels, none of which know each other, but they all use different currencies! Once again, the lodging industry turned to third-party intermediaries.

Visa and Citicorp have interposed their financial credibility between the hotel and the travel agency, just as they have done with credit cards. Previous attempts at standardization, even by companies as big as Hilton and Holiday, have floundered on the need for prepayment—hotels simply do not give credit willy-nilly to every unknown travel agency. **Worldwide Travel Vouchers (WTVs)** by Visa and Citicorp substitute recognizable logos and established credit for those of unknown origin. The hotel is paid by credit-card voucher (Visa) or by check (Citicorp). Payment is in U.S. funds (local currency in other nations) on a standardized and recognizable form.

WTVs shift the issue from hotel acceptability to travel agency policy. Will travel agencies use worldwide travel vouchers for room reservations if their clients—especially their important business clients—have not prepaid them? If not, the difference with WTVs is only in format. However, part of the worldwide travel voucher can be detached and used to deposit the commission due the agency. Savings in back-office accounting is real, and that alone warrants its use.

Each transaction with the credit-card company, such as depositing the travel agent's commission, involves a fee. That's why credit-card companies are in business. But transferring charges to the city ledger and cutting checks also cost the hotel.

If the reservation is prepaid, the TA takes the commission before sending the voucher to the hotel. Each WTV is numbered, so the reservation can be made by telephone and guaranteed using the voucher number. The travel agency deposits in its bank the guest's payment, less commission. The hotel eventually draws from its bank that same amount. It does this by depositing a voucher slip, which looks like a credit-card slip and functions similarly.

Citicorp's check-payment system has a variation on the procedure. The travel agent collects from the guest but pays a commission and an additional fee to the bank. (This system has no credit-card fee.) Since the hotel ultimately pays that fee, the check is written net to the hotel. The client carries the check/voucher to the hotel. At departure, the guest endorses the form, and the hotel endorses the attached check. Whereas a guest check might be suspect, the Citicorp check is guaranteed. It is taken into the cash drawer and the account is settled. Additional charges, including extra room-nights, must be paid by the guest in some other manner.

The guest is another issue—and perhaps the major one—in the hotel–travel agency relationship. International guests do not use credit cards as American guests do; they prefer to carry vouchers. Chains worldwide are moving to accommodate that cultural difference. Sales offices of such stalwarts as Holiday, Sheraton, and Hospitality Franchise Systems sell their own vouchers, usually in minimum packages of 25, at substantial discounts. The chain has use of the money. It has secured the business—no chance the guest will go elsewhere—and the hotels have avoided the hassle of unknown vouchers at the desk.

If hotels don't solve the problem, third parties, including possibly the Airline Reporting Corporation (ARC), which has immense document-processing capabilities, will grow more important as intermediaries. The whole issue might prove moot when smart cards reintroduce direct guest–hotel reservations and payments using interactive telephones/televisions/computers. Indeed, one projection suggests that travel agencies will all but disappear anyway, either replaced by smart cards and telecommunications or eliminated by the airlines, which seem unwilling to pay profit-draining commissions any longer.

Frequent-Guest Programs.   The rationale for frequent-guest programs (FGPs) has been discussed several times throughout the text. The mechanics of the programs are equally clear. By stopping at participating properties, guests earn points toward free room-nights and sometimes airline points as well. Each stay is validated electronically or by means of a manual voucher. The points are earned at properties throughout the chain or franchise, but they are generally used at resort destinations.

Usually, the hotel's parent company does not reimburse the full amount of the room rate. Rooms have a high profit margin and the parent company knows that. Besides, the hotel earns food and beverage sales from the frequent-guest visitor.

Split folios are used to process the coupons that the frequent guest tenders. Onto the B folio are posted all the incidental charges. The guest is responsible for these and pays them at check-out. The A folio, which contains the room charge, is transferred to the FGP account, a receivable in the city ledger. The chain is billed either for the full rack rate or the reduced rate agreed to in the FGP contract. An allowance (charged against rooms) reduces the amount due from the chain either before the bill is sent or when the check arrives. Only rarely does the hotel get full reimbursement at rack rate.

FGPs are marketing programs, so every hotel of the chain contributes on a per room basis towards the costs. From the fund come payments for rooms used as well as the sales and administrative expenses. Reimbursement for bad checks is one such expense. FGPs offer check-cashing privileges. Should the check bounce, the hotel transfers the unpaid amount to the chain's city ledger account and bills along with the reimbursable room charge.

Under some FGPs, the monthly amount due the hotel from the chain is offset against the monthly amount due the chain from the hotel: FGP fees and franchise fees. Others keep the several accounts separate, collecting from the FGP on the normal 30-day cycle of city ledger billing.

Transfers to Guest Folios

Occasionally, though not often, guests with unpaid city ledger accounts return to the hotel. The balance of that city account is then transferred to the transient folio at the front desk. Billing at check-out involves the total debt, but settlement may simply mean transferring the new total back to the city ledger.

Advance Deposits.   Advance deposits generate more frequent movements *from* city ledger accounts *to* transient guest folios. Shifting accounts in that direction is the opposite of all the other ledger-to-ledger transfers that have been discussed. That's because, technically, they are not the same thing. Advance deposits are not city ledger receivables in the strictest sense. The hotel owes the guest for prepaid services that have not yet been delivered. The hotel is the guest's account receivable. With other city accounts, the guest is the hotel's receivable.

Nevertheless, advance deposits are usually handled as city accounts. Viewed in a broad context, they are accounts receivable. It is a contrary relationship, however, so the advance deposit is sometimes called a contra (opposite) receivable. Even when advance deposits are carried as accounts receivable in the city ledger, they appear as liabilities—accounts payable—on the balance sheet.

The mechanics are simple. The guest or travel agent sends a check, usually one night's lodging plus tax, to confirm the reservation. The money is deposited in the hotel's bank account, debit cash and credit advance deposits, the contra account receivable. (Earlier discussions suggested other ways of handling the deposit.) There the sum remains until the guest checks in some time later. When the guest arrives, the balance is moved *from* (debit) the city ledger *to* (credit) the guest folio in the transient ledger (Exhibit 10–9, line 1). The opening credit balance starts the relationship with the hotel owing the arriving guest—which is, in fact, the situation.

Reservations guaranteed by credit cards are not advance deposits since the credit-card charge is processed after the fact and only if the guest proves to be a no-show.

City Ledger Postings without Transfers

Many nonregistered customers and many registered guests, too, use credit cards to pay for services such as food and beverage. Those credit-card charges become part of the departmental cashiers' daily turn-in (Chapter 11). As such, they go directly to the general cashier in the accounting office, bypassing the front office and the ledger-to-ledger transfers that would otherwise be required.

EXHIBIT 12–8

The traditional credit-card charge slip (top) is used by the individual guest, and the summary transmittal form with instructions (bottom and center) is used by the merchant hotel to batch and transmit the individual vouchers.

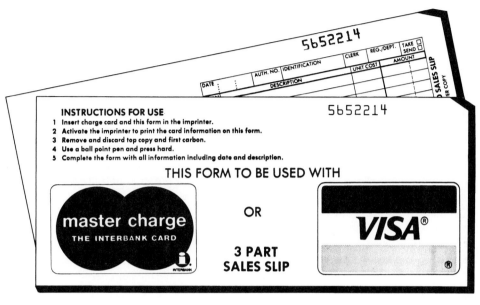

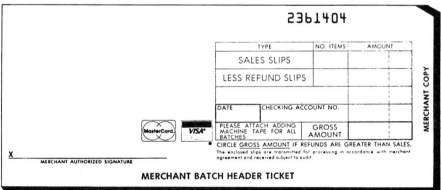

Courtesy: First Interstate Bank, Las Vegas, NV.

How the accounting office processes the credit-card charges depends on the type of credit-card system in place. Most properties have replaced the manual slips with electronic capture.

Manual Charge Slips.   If the hotel still uses the traditional credit-card form (see Exhibit 12–8), departmental cashiers process each on an imprinter, get the guest's signature, and turn in the slips at the end of the watch.

The vouchers are separated by type (MasterCard, Visa, etc.) in the accounting office. Then they are batched, or bundled, for posting to the city ledger accounts of the credit-card companies. Copies of the slips are forwarded to the credit-card companies, on transmittal forms (Exhibit 12–8) that combine 100 vouchers. The accounting entry is debit the particular credit-card company (an account receivable) and credit the departmental incomes (food, beverage, etc.) that generate the sales.

Periodically, the T&E credit-card companies reimburse the hotel, less commission. That generates an account entry: debit cash and debit commissions expense; credit the receivable of the particular credit-card company. With bank cards, the slips are deposited in the hotel's bank the next morning—no need to mail them off—so the funds are available immediately.

Chargebacks by the credit-card companies are usually maintained in a second city ledger account. This distinguishes problem accounts from standard accounts. Notified of a disallowed charge, the hotel transfers the standard account (credit) to the newly created account (debit). Unless the situation can be corrected, the new account may become a bad debt.

Electronic Draft Capture. The communication highway has wrought significant changes in the handling of credit-card charges. Guests encounter the manual charge slips less and less. Instead, the electronic verification of the card's authenticity is followed by an electronic printout of the charges. A slip of paper (see Exhibit 12–9), looking much like the tape of an old-fashioned adding machine, is presented for signature. One copy goes to the guest, and the second copy becomes part of the cashier's departmental control records.

What happens with the charge slips is more visible but less important than how it happens. Electronic draft capture (EDT) eliminates postage, paper sales drafts, and the batch handling and sorting that accompany manual city ledger posting. Electronic contact with the financial institutions through a processor also means quicker access to funds. Moreover, most banks give reductions in the interchange (merchant discount) rate for electronic transactions.

Speedy electronic information, most of it by laser imaging, represents additional float for the credit-card companies. The quicker the charge is on the guest's bill, the sooner the company can expect payment. All the cards discussed in this chapter, except Japan's JCB card, are now electronically captured by one of several means.

Dial and Touch-Tone terminals can still be used at registration for credit-card authorization. EFT-POS online processing is the other end of the technology. Swiping the card through the terminal obtains the authorization at registration and interfaces the hotel's computer (PMS) with the credit-card computer. Electronic billing and ultimate collection from the card issuer then follows. In between the dial and the on-line interface options are a series of electronic choices depending on what costs the hotel can absorb or counterbalance through savings. Whether purchased or leased, equipment and software costs must be absorbed, perhaps negotiated as part of the discount fee. Maintenance and repairs must be provided, but by whom and for how much is also at issue. In general, the more automatic the procedure, the higher the costs but the greater the savings in discount fees.

EXHIBIT 12–9

Pencil-and-paper forms (Exhibit 12–8) are being replaced by electronic terminals that process charge vouchers quickly and individually, even across the globe.

ANZ BANK NIGHTLINK
QUEENSTOWN PARKROYAL
BEACH STREET
QUEENSTOWN
PH 03 4427800 GST 5 -5 9 -65
HAVE A NICE DAY
TAX INVOICE
AMEX MERCHANT : 5   1 9 -7
BATCH: 000023

ACCOUNT NUMBER
3   0 7   2   00   AM
DATE-TIME   EXP. DATE
08DEC   17:55   09
TRANSACTION TYPE   APPROVAL CODE
SALE   3
REFERENCE/INVOICE NO.   TERMINAL NO.
000111   1 3   994
HOTEL/REST

TOTAL NZ$ 488.84
EST INCL
CUSTOMER SIGN BELOW

X *Jerome J Vallen*
 CARDHOLDER NAME
VALLEN JJ

 I ACKNOWLEDGE RECEIPT FOR GOODS AND
SERVICES AND LIABILITY FOR CHARGES AS
RECORDED HEREON AND WILL OBSERVE MY
AGREEMENT WITH THE CARD ISSUERS

Courtesy: Park Royal Hotel, Queenstown, N.Z.

Summary

Today's travelers prefer credit over cash. These modern customers see credit as their right rather than as a privilege granted by the sellers. Innkeepers accommodate this fact but with a keen eye toward managing credit and credit losses. Credit-card companies have the same objectives and, despite operational irritants between them, work closely with merchants (hotels).

Hotels track their credit guests through the city ledger, a group of records that accumulate accounts receivable. Accounts receivable are individuals, including companies and credit-card agencies, that owe the hotel for services. Hotels provide rooms, food, beverage, and other services to a variety of accounts receivable. Among these are banquet and convention groups, travel agencies, individual companies, and even the hotel's own executives. Most are individual, transient guests who convert their own accounts into credit-card receivables.

Modern electronic communications is replacing paper recordkeeping and speeding the whole process along the communications highway. Developing these capabilities is not the job of the hotel industry, so a variety of third-party intermediaries, including check-verification agencies, national credit-card companies, and banking institutions, have become inseparable from the hotel industry in the eyes of the credit user—the guest.

Queries and Problems

1. A front-office clerk attempts to get additional credit information from an arriving guest. Write two dialogues to be used in a training manual. Include the approach and the proper choice of words to be employed by the clerk as well as the kinds of information to be requested if the guest (*a*) has a same-day reservation but the information is incomplete, and (*b*) is a walk-in with no baggage.

2. Explain how the following transfers should be handled. Be specific, citing the location of the entry, the ledger or ledgers involved, and the debit or credit requirements.
   a. A transient guest checks out using a national credit card.
   b. The president and treasurer of a small company check in for a business meeting. The hotel has been carrying the unpaid balance of a charge generated by these officers at their last business meeting about three months ago.
   c. A couple departs and requests that the balance of the folio be charged to the couple's parents, who are registered in another room. The parents concur.
   d. An association completes its meeting and the association executive, after reviewing the balance due, requests billing to the group's headquarters.

3. In terms of the front office and of the city ledger, explain the quick check-out system used by numerous hotels.

4. Many older hotels in the area in which your resort is located have suffered for years from a seasonal influx of skippers and room burglary gangs operating with stolen keys. (Few of these old properties have modern locks.) The local hotel association has asked you to draft a plan for a security network that could be implemented before the next season. Prepare the plan, providing details of procedure by explaining the roles of the individuals or groups involved.

5. In terms of the front office and of the city ledger, explain how a reservation request from a travel agent is processed if (*a*) the agency has a good credit relationship with the hotel and the guest pays the agency; (*b*) the agency has no credit rating with the hotel, and the guest pays the agency; and (*c*) the guest makes no payment to the agency.

6. A noticeable squeeze on profits had brought the management team to a brainstorming session. One idea is put forth by the controller. Noting the large amount of credit-card business that the hotel is doing, the controller suggests that each tip charged to a credit card be reduced by 4.77 percent when paid to the employee. (That amount is the average discount fee the hotel is paying to all the credit-card companies.) The controller further suggests that an additional 1.1 percent be subtracted, representing the percentage of credit-card charges that prove uncollectible.
   What comments would the food and beverage manager be apt to make? The rooms manager?

Notes

1. *Float* is the use of uncollected funds during the transfer period in which the funds are in process.
2. *Chargebacks* are guest charges that the credit-card company refuses to accept either because of unanswered guest complaints (by the hotel) or because of technical problems between the card company and the hotel.
3. With 80 percent of its market in group/convention business, the Opryland Hotel processes about 80 to 90 group master accounts daily! (''Leaping Over the Paper Chase,'' *CKC Report,* July–August 1993, p. 7.)
4. Travel agent vouchers or coupons are different from such other coupons as marketing coupons (distributed as promotional discounts) and tour group coupons (used as tickets for admission or for meals).

SECTION V

Rooms Management Technology

Rooms management technology is relatively young in comparison to an otherwise mature hospitality industry. And the rapid pace of technological advances seen over the past two decades shows little sign of slowing. Instead, new devices are continually being introduced and proven forms of automation are constantly being refined. Not only are computers faster, smaller, and more powerful than ever before, but they are also less expensive. This affordability of computer systems has had a positive and maturing effect on the industry.

Because they are so inexpensive, practically all hotels have a property management system (PMS). And though some systems are older than others, the basic functions of the PMS remain unchanged. The night audit routine, automated posting of room and tax, and the printing of management reports are generally quite standard across all systems. The major changes to come in the future will be the utilization, storage, and speed of access of historical guest and hotel data. Powerful systems will put history at management's fingertips. This will provide a whole dimension of service never before tested—each subsequent reservation will provide more guest data to the hotel—favorite room type, birth date, favorite dessert or beverage, frequency of travel, and so on.

More expensive and therefore less common are automated guest-room interfaces. Not all hotels can afford to offer sophisticated telephone call accounting systems, electronic locking systems, or many of the guest-operated devices such as in-room entertainment, minibar, and safe systems. Yet these state-of-the-art PMS interfaces will surely be the amenities of the future. As the lodging industry matures, it competes on the basis of hotel differentiation, and automated guest interfaces are a very visible form of differentiation. Guests who once selected hotels on the basis of swimming pools, health clubs, and in-room amenities may soon make their choice based on which properties offer a sophisticated fire-safety system, state-of-the-art television-based entertainment, and in-room minibars.

The Night Audit

The night audit (which is sometimes referred to just as the audit) ends the hotel's day. Night auditors work the hotel's final shift, and the job they do closes the day's accounts. The audit reconciles the accounting activities of the past day and provides information for the issues of the following day. What is done and how it is done have changed dramatically during the past decade because electronic data processing has altered the focus and changed the procedures.

The Auditor and the Audit

As the previous 12 chapters explained, keeping records for a front office demands attention to the smallest details. Doing so with a mechanical system (pencil and paper) is a tedious task made more difficult as the hotel's size increases. The introduction of property management systems (computers) in the last half of the 20th century is analogous to the introduction of structural steel during the last half of the 19th century. The latter enabled hotels to grow larger by building upward. The former ensures the integrity of the records system no matter how large the property.

The Night Auditor

Despite the title, the night auditor is rarely a trained accountant and is an auditor only by the broadest definition. In general terms, an *auditor* is an appraiser—reporter of the accuracy and integrity of records and financial statements. One type of auditing, internal auditing, involves procedural control and an accounting review of operations and records. Internal auditing also reports on the activities of other employees. It is this final definition that best explains the role of the hotel night auditor.

No special knowledge of accounting or even of bookkeeping's debits and credits is required of the night auditor. Having this knowledge is helpful and desirable, but it is sufficient for the auditor to have good arithmetic skills, self-discipline, and a penchant for detailed work. Auditors must be careful, accurate, and reliable. The latter trait is an especially redeeming one because the unattractive working hours make replacements difficult to recruit and almost impossible to find on short notice.

Work Shift.   At large hotels, the audit crew arrives sometime between 11 PM and midnight, the traditional graveyard shift, and finishes generally about 7 or 8 AM the next morning. Since their work is the basis of the following day, they stay until the job is completed, regardless of the hour.

At a small property, the night auditor relieves the desk's swing shift (approximately 4 PM to midnight) and is, in turn, relieved by the day shift (approximately 8 AM to 4 PM).

General Duties.   The audit staff of a large hotel consists of a senior auditor and several assistants. A separate night crew handles the usual duties of the desk, freeing the auditors to perform their functions without interruption. In a small hotel, a single auditor relieves the entire desk, filling the jobs of reservationist, room clerk, cashier, telephone operator, and auditor. Whether or not auditors assume these front-office tasks, they must be conversant with them. It is those very duties that the night audit audits.

When the actual tasks are taken on, the night auditor is likely to be the only responsible employee on duty. The auditor assumes the position of night manager whether the title is there or not. The same range of problems faced by the day manager is involved, but to a lesser degree. Emergencies, credit, mechanical breakdowns, accidents, and deaths are some of the situations encountered by the night manager.

Security and incident reports must be filed by either the night auditor/manager alone or cooperatively with the security staff. Without a security contingent, the auditor may be the one who walks security rounds and fire watch.

Few hotels of less than 150 rooms employ a night engineer. Yet management has generally been lax in preparing the night auditor/manager for the problems that arise in this area of responsibility. Fire, plumbing problems, power failures, elevator mishaps, and boiler troubles are matters that take the auditor's time.

Equally time-consuming are guest relations: a noisy party going into the early hours of the morning; the victorious football team shouting in the lobby; a sick guest; visiting conventioneers in the 11th-floor suite; paid reservations yet to arrive and the hotel 100 percent occupied. Such are the nonaccounting matters for which the night auditor might be responsible.

Mature judgment and experience are needed to carry out these nonaudit functions. The combination of audit skills, working hours, and responsibility merit a higher salary for the night auditor than for the average room clerk, but the spread is not noticeably larger.

The Audit

For nearly a century, the industry relied on the manual night audit to uncover and remedy the numerous human errors that resulted from a pencil-and-paper system of accounting. The frequency and variety of errors declined as electronic recordkeeping was introduced. Consequently, the modern audit concentrates less on error discovery and more on management reporting.

Accounts receivable are the focus of the night audit. During the audit, the accounting activities of the previous day are reconciled, balanced, and closed. The audit verifies accounts receivable, recapitulates revenue data for the daily sales journal entry, monitors guest credit, and creates managerial and operational reports.

Reconciling Accounts Receivable.   Every business that extends credit to customers reconciles accounts receivable periodically. Whereas other retail establishments close and balance their accounts monthly, hotels do the job nightly. The accuracy and completeness of each guest folio is verified during the night audit.

Hotel auditors lack the luxury of time because hotelkeeping is a very transient business. Arrivals and departures keep coming and going without notice at all hours of the day and night. Each new day brings more charges and more credits whether or not the previous day has been reconciled. There is no holding a departing guest until the folio is ready. The night audit must make certain that it always is ready.

The pressure of immediacy is missing with city ledger guests. City ledger guests are not registered, so their billing cycle is more like the accounts receivable of other businesses. Depending on the nature of the original charge, city receivables are billed for the first time three days—sometimes 10 days—after the charge is incurred.

Both city and transient guests are receivables and, therefore, part of the night audit, which deals only with receivables. Cash sales are not posted to folios, as earlier chapters have explained. Cash sales are verified by the income auditor, sometimes called the day auditor, in conjunction with the general cashier. Receivable sales pass through the night audit to the same income audit. Both types of sales (cash and credit) are combined in the income audit and recorded ultimately in the sales journal.

The income auditor usually works the day shift completing the income audit early in the morning with a daily report to the manager. It replaces the preliminary report, which reflects charge sales only, that the night auditor leaves for the manager.

The Closeout Hour.   The night audit reviews the records of a single day. Since hotels never close, management selects an arbitrary hour, the **closeout hour** (also called *the close of the day*), to officially end one day and start the next. The actual time selected depends on the operating hours of the lounges, restaurants, and room service of the particular hotel. Each new charge changes the folio, so the audit is prepared when changes are infrequent—in the early morning hours when guests are abed. Departmental charges before the closeout hour are included in today's records. Departmental charges after the closeout hour are posted to the folio on the following date after the night audit has been completed.

A late closeout hour captures the last of the day's charges, but it puts pressure on the auditing staff, which needs to finish the job before the early departures begin leaving. Too early a closeout hour throws all the charges into the following day, delaying their audit for 24 hours. Standardized stationery forms list midnight as the closeout hour (Exhibit 10–6).

Posting Charges.   Posting (recording) room charges is one of the night auditor's major tasks. Before the advent of the property management system (PMS), which is the name the industry has given to the computer, postings were done manually. In order to post room rates and taxes, each folio had to be removed from one by one and returned to the cashier's well (Exhibit 10–5).

Exhibit 13–1 (see also Exhibit 10–3) illustrates the results on a manual folio. Once the room charge and tax are posted, the night auditor adds the column (including the previous day's total) and carries the balance forward to the next day. In this manner, a cumulative balance is maintained, and the manual folio is ready for the departing guest at any time.

Included in the total are departmental charges, which are posted in a similar manner, but not by the night auditor. Throughout the day, the cashier (or posting clerk) records these departmental charges (vouchers) as they arrive at the desk from the operating departments. Exhibit 13–1 shows these as bar, food (restaurant), and garage (paid-out) charges.

With a point-of-sale (POS) terminal (Exhibit 10–7), postings are done electronically. There are no vouchers arriving at the desk; indeed, there are no posting clerks at the front desk. In fact, there are no visible folios, everything being maintained in computer memory. Charges are posted directly to the electronic folio by the departmental cashier, who enters the charge at the point of sale (see Exhibit 13–2). Chapter 10 illustrates several of the electronic folios.

Manual System Errors.   In a manual system, figures are recorded again and again—on the voucher and the control sheet by the departmental cashier and on the folio by the front-office cashier. And that is not the end. The night auditor totals them by hand and rewrites them all once again on the transcript sheet. Writing and rewriting each figure creates numerous errors that a PMS with an on-line POS avoids.

Several errors are inherent in the manual system. Poor handwriting is the most obvious one. When handwritten, figures 1 and 7, 4 and 9, and 3 and 8 are often confused. Recopying also causes slides and transpositions. Slides are misplaced units, which may involve decimals. Saying 53 21 mentally or aloud may result in either 53.21 or 5,321 being recorded. Transpositions are similar errors, but the digits are reordered—53.21 may become 35.12.

Even simple addition causes problems. The auditor may create errors by incorrectly totaling the folios, the control sheet, or the packets of vouchers. Adding machines help, but there is no guarantee that the figures are accurately entered. Hand audits still require adding-machine tapes to allow comparison between the actual figures and those entered into the calculator.

Subtracting one total from another highlights the error. Errors of addition usually appear as differences of 1 in the unit columns. If the difference in the totals is 1 cent, 10 cents, $1, $10, and so on, the culprit is likely to be an error of addition. If not an error of addition, it might be a slide or transposition. Slides and transpositions are flagged when the difference in the total is evenly divisible by 9. For example, the difference between 53.21 and 35.21 is 18, evenly divisible by 9. Searching for mistakes begins by looking for errors of addition or transpositions and slides.

Exhibit 13–1

Two nights of room and tax postings have been made by the night auditor on this manually prepared (pencil-and-paper) folio. Food, bar, and garage (cash advance) postings are made during the day by the front desk. (Note the credit balance of October 6.)

THE CITY HOTEL
ANYWHERE, U.S.A.

NAME *B. M. Oncampus*

ADDRESS *1 Campus Rd., University City*

ROOM NUMBER *1406*   RATE *60*

NUMBER IN THE PARTY *1*   CLERK *ABC*

DATE OF ARRIVAL *10/5*   DATE OF DEPARTURE *10/7*

CHANGES: ROOM NO. _____ TO ROOM NO. _____ NEW RATE _____

DATE	10/5	10/6	10/7				
BAL.FWD		(19)	70				
ROOMS	60	60					
TAX	3	3					
FOOD	10	12					
BAR		6					
TELEPH							
LAUNDRY							
CASH DISBR GARAGE	8	8					
TRANSFERS							
TOT CHRG	81	70					
CASH							
ALLOWANCES							
TRANSFERS	100						
TOT CRDS	100						
BAL DUE	(19)	70					

Exhibit 13–2

A display menu or mask on the POS terminal guides the cashier through a posting sequence. Without a POS, the posting is done at the front office from vouchers sent there by the departmental cashiers.

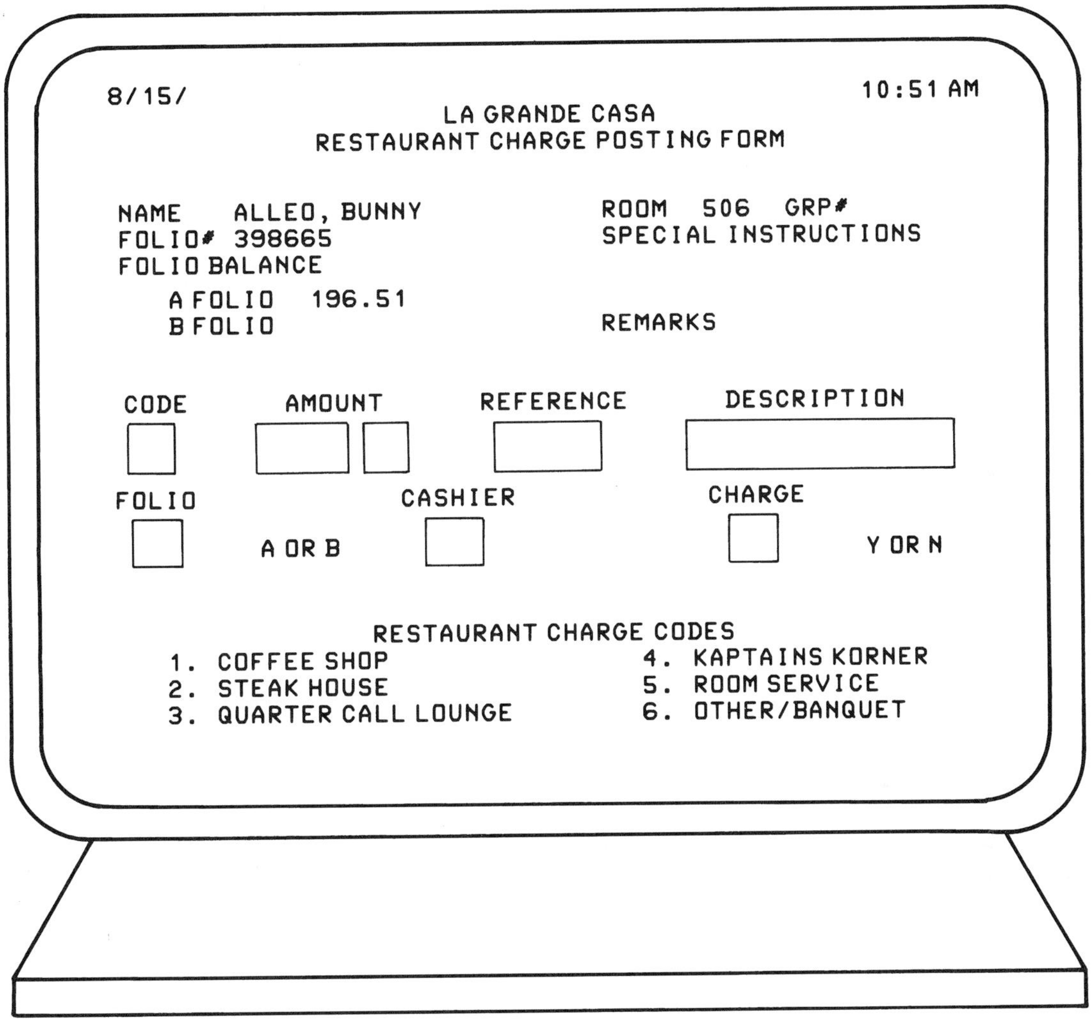

```
8/15/                    LA GRANDE CASA                    10:51 AM
                  RESTAURANT CHARGE POSTING FORM

     NAME    ALLEO, BUNNY          ROOM  506  GRP#
     FOLIO# 398665                 SPECIAL INSTRUCTIONS
     FOLIO BALANCE
         A FOLIO   196.51
         B FOLIO                   REMARKS


     CODE      AMOUNT      REFERENCE      DESCRIPTION
     [   ]   [      ] [  ]  [      ]      [                ]

     FOLIO              CASHIER           CHARGE
     [   ]   A OR B    [      ]           [   ]   Y OR N


                  RESTAURANT CHARGE CODES
         1. COFFEE SHOP          4. KAPTAINS KORNER
         2. STEAK HOUSE          5. ROOM SERVICE
         3. QUARTER CALL LOUNGE  6. OTHER/BANQUET
```

Other Room Charge Postings. Room charges are normally posted by the night auditor. The job is faster and easier when done with the computer because there is no bucket and there are no folios. Time is saved in not removing 500 to 1,000 folios from the well. Room charges with the appropriate tax have been programmed into the computer. Memory knows how much each room is to be billed, and the proper tax is automatically computed. Individual postings and folio totaling are not required. Activating the rooms program brings all the accounts receivable up-to-date in memory, although most hotels will also get a nightly printout, a *hard copy,* for emergency backup (see Exhibit 13–3).

In three infrequent circumstances, room charges are posted by the cashier, not by the night auditor. Part-day rates, late check-outs, and paid-in-advance folios are handled by the desk before the arrival of the audit team.

EXHIBIT 13–3

A computer-prepared report of guest folios summarizes the balance of each registered guest. Each column equates to a corresponding column of the pencil-and-paper transcript.

THE CITY HOTEL, ANYWHERE, U.S.A.   Page 1
03/16   Guest Ledger Summary Report

Room #	Name	Folio #	Open Bal	Charges	Credits	Close Bal
3004	Huent	0457	–0–	81.30	.00	81.30
3005	Wanake	0398	65.72	91.44	.00	157.16
3008	Lee	0431	132.00	101.01	.00	233.01
3110	Langden	0420	–0–	99.87	100.00	0.13–
3111	Nelston	0408	233.65	145.61	.00	379.26
3117	O'Harra	0461	789.75	121.10	.00	910.85
6121	Chiu	0444	32.60–	99.87	.00	67.27
6133	Valex	0335	–0–	165.30	.00	165.30
7003	Roberts	0428	336.66	109.55	.00	446.21
7009	Haittenberg	0454	19.45	87.43	.00	106.88
Totals			44,651.07	18,632.98	950.00	62,334.05

Guests who arrive and depart the same day (day-rate, use-rate, or part-day-rate guests) leave the hotel before the auditors come on duty. Room charges must be posted to those folios within the time frame of the guests' stay.

Extra room charges are normally made for guests who remain long after the check-out hour. Brief extensions are accommodated without charge when possible, but extraordinary delays incur late room charges. Here, again, guests leave before the arrival of the audit team, so the cashier posts the extra room charges.

Paid-in-advance guests, those with no baggage or no credit identification, pay room charges even before they occupy the rooms. Many hotels receipt such payments with copies of the folios showing the room charges, plus tax, and the balancing payments. So the cashier who accepts the payments also posts the room charges even though these guests will be registered during the night auditor's shift.

Recap of Revenue Data. Proving the balances of the individual accounts receivable means reconciling the total postings made to the folios with the charges arising from the various departments. By the time the audit begins, hundreds or even thousands of charges will have been made against guests' accounts. Included in these charges are food, beverage, local and long-distance telephone calls, laundry, valet, cash advances, ski tows, in-room charges (films, safes, bars), greens fees, sauna baths, and the like. Added to the day's list are the room and tax charges just completed by the night auditor.

The night audit makes certain that the daily *total* charged by each department agrees with the *sum* of the individual postings on each folio for that particular department. For example, bar charges are posted to the individual folios throughout the day. The night audit accumulates all the bar charges on the folios and compares that total to the total charges the bar reported making.

With a property management system, separating and totaling departmental charges are not difficult tasks—the computer does them. Charges are posted to the individual folio from the point-of-sale terminal and, simultaneously, accumulated by department: food, beverage, telephone, and so on. With one entry at the POS, the hotel charges the guest and tracks the sales of each department. As required, the computer spits out the information: the individual folio, the income of the single department, the total of all folio balances, and the total of all departmental incomes.

Manual folio systems are more demanding than property management systems. Each departmental posting (bar, restaurant, and paid-outs, for example [Exhibit 13–1]) is recorded on the folio, but there is no electronic total. Therefore, the night auditor must obtain that total by adding up the departmental postings made to the individual folios. What is done instantaneously by the electronic PMS is a long and tedious task when done by hand.

The Transcript.   The transcript separates the charges of the folios, just as the PMS does. Once separated—broken apart by departmental charges—it is a simple task to compare the totals of each department to the totals originating from that department, just as the PMS does. *Once separated* is the operative phrase.

Let's review the sequence of the manual audit. The night auditor comes on duty, posts all the vouchers that arrive before the closeout hour, posts the room charges and tax, adds the folios, and carries the balances forward (Exhibit 13–1). The transcript is the next step.

In room number sequence, each folio is copied onto a large spreadsheet (see Exhibit 13–4). Lines that appear horizontally on the folio (Exhibit 13–1) are vertical columns on the transcript. Thus, there is a transcript column for each department—rooms, taxes, food, and so on—just as there is a horizontal line for these departments on the folio. As each folio is copied across the sheet, the departmental charges are separated by the vertical columns.

When all the folios, including the day's departures, are copied onto the transcript—and that may take several transcript sheets—the night audit is back to the basic premise: Do the totals of the columns, which are the sum of the postings to the individual folios, agree to the charges originating in the departments, as shown on the control sheets?

Although the form of the control sheet differs somewhat in the several departments (in some instances, only the cash register tape is available), the method of proving departmental charges is identical department to department.

Vouchers from the various departments arrive at the desk all during the day. After being posted, each voucher is marked to lessen the chance of duplicating the charge. Next, the checks (vouchers) are sorted by departments—a job made easier with different colors for each department—and filed into pigeonholes. There they remain for the night auditor, who totals them on an adding machine. The adding machine tape is then attached to the pile of vouchers.

Three different totals are available to the auditor for each department:

1. The total derived from the departmental control sheet. Each time a guest charges a departmental service to the folio, the departmental cashier makes an entry on the control sheet. At the end of the day, this sheet is totaled and forwarded to the night auditor.

EXHIBIT 13–4

A transcript spreadsheet for a hand audit is prepared from individual folios. Column totals are verified against departmental control sheets, and totals are cross-footed to prove the mathematics.

DAILY TRANSCRIPT OF
ACCOUNTS RECEIVABLE

DATE __10/7_____ 19__

American Hotel Register Co., 224 W. Ontario St., Chicago, IL 60610   FORM 73

ACCOUNT NO.	ROOM NO.	NUMBER OF GUESTS	OPENING BALANCE DEBIT	OPENING BALANCE CREDIT	ROOMS	RESTAURANT	BEVERAGES	LOCAL CALLS	LONG DISTANCE	LAUNDRY	VALET	CASH DISBURSEMENTS	TRANSFERS	ROOM TAX	TOTAL DEBITS	CASH RECEIPTS	ALLOWANCES	TRANSFERS		CLOSING BAL DEBIT	CLOSING BAL CREDIT
8111	1812	3		1532	29 —		3 —	20		4 —				58	3678		— 20			2196	
8811	1817	2	6360		30 —	5 —			4 —					60	3960					10324	
8123	1824	1			1850	640						1 —		37	2677	37 —					1073
7184	1906	2	2193		2156									43	2199					4392	
7913	1907	2	3996		30 —		6 —						4796	60	8456					12456	

| Total | 40 | 51 | 76820 | 1532 | 67650 | 5210 | 6170 | 720 | 1840 | 4 — | 17 — | 4796 | 1353 | 89839 | 16750 | 210 | | | 49870 | 1703 |

DEPARTURES

8106	1616	3	4620		440								440	5060						
8007	1649	1	1887											1857	30					
7792	1924	2	3996			4 —	40	360					8 —			4796				

| Total | | | 10503 | | 440 | 4 — | — 40 | 360 | | | | | 1240 | 6917 | 30 | 4796 | | | | |

CITY LEDGER

| TOTALS | | | 87323 | 1532 | 67650 | 5650 | 6570 | 760 | 22 — | 4 — | 17 — | 4796 | 1353 | 91079 | 23667 | 240 | 4796 | | 49870 | 1703 |

Courtesy: American Hotel Register Co., Northbrook, IL.

2. The total on the adding machine tape of the individual vouchers, which have arrived at the desk one at a time. These are the communicative devices between the departmental cashier and the front-office billing clerk.

3. The total posted to the folio for that department. This total is the sum of the postings made to the folios. The auditor gets that value from the departmental column of the transcript.

If the system is working, the departmental control sheet (which records the event) has a total equal to the vouchers (which communicate the event) and to the folios (which are the ultimate record of the event). If the system isn't working, one or more of the totals will be out of balance. Then the night auditor goes to work.

If the three totals agree, the auditor moves on to the next department. When one of the figures fails to reconcile, the audit begins in earnest and the auditor must uncover errors. If two of the three totals agree, the search is concentrated on the unequal total, among several likely causes.

Mistakes in mathematics account for a large portion of the errors. The major ones—slides, transpositions, and addition—were explained earlier in this chapter.

When the control sheet figure is larger than the other two balances, the auditor searches for a lost check. If the check was posted and then lost, the check (voucher) total will be the smallest of the three totals.

Too small a transcript figure for several columns suggests a folio was left off the transcript, so its missing values are having an impact on all the departments. Simple oversights like this seem less simple in the early morning hours. Then, a check omitted from the departmental control sheet or a voucher filed before it was posted mean long minutes of searching by the weary auditor.

Vouchers posted to the correct department but to the wrong guest account will not be evident to the auditor. All three totals will agree even though the wrong guest account is charged. This is not so with the reverse situation—when the charge is made to the proper folio but to the wrong department. Then the audit total will be out of balance with the voucher total and the total of that particular departmental control sheet. Of course, the other department—the one that received the extra posting—will be out of balance by the same amount, providing a clue to the error.

One error, special to the pencil-and-paper folio, is particularly difficult to find. It occurs when a departmental posting is recorded in the column of a previous day. The posting clerk inadvertently posts a current charge to a previous day. Having been posted to a folio column that has already been balanced, the charge doesn't even appear on the transcript, which is a copy of the current day's folio column. Finding this error requires the auditor to list the departmental vouchers in room number sequence and search for the missing charge down the transcript sheets, which are also in room number sequence. Of course, reconciling balances is not the purpose of the audit; it is but one step in providing an accurate guest folio.

Proving Room Charges.   Unlike the charges of other departments, room charges originate at the desk. There is neither control sheet nor voucher since there is no interdepartmental communication. Instead, the transcript's room income column, which is the sum of the folios, is tested against the room rack data, which is summarized on a **room count sheet** (see Exhibit 13–5).

Room income, house count, and room count are verified by means of this room count sheet. **Room count**—the number of rooms occupied—and **house count**—the number of guests registered—also appear on the hand transcript (Exhibit 13–4). On the transcript, room count appears as column 2; house count as column 3; and room income as column 6. The room count sheet has the same information, but the rack is its source. They should reconcile because the rack and the folio (transcript) have the registration as a common source.

The room count sheet, which is also called a **daily rooms report,** a **night clerk's report,** or a **room charge sheet,** is prepared from the room rack. It is a permanent record of the rack at the close of the day. Three informational bits are gathered from the rack: the number of persons in the room, the number of rooms occupied, and the rate paid for each room. This information is copied onto the room count sheet.

The totals of house count, room count, and room income are now reconciled by comparing the values on the transcript with the totals obtained from the room

Exhibit 13–5

The manual room count sheet provides a permanent record of the room rack. Although a different format, a similar report is prepared by the computerized property management system.

OCCUPANCY AND ROOM REVENUE REPORT										Hotel Gary						DAY *Monday*		DATE *9-12-*					
EAST WING																							
ROOM	No Guests	RATE	ROOM	No Guests	RATE	ROOM	No Guests	RATE	ROOM	No Guests	RATE	ROOM	No Guests	RATE	ROOM	No Guests	RATE	ROOM	No Guests	RATE	ROOM	No Guests	RATE
3101			3319			3615			3910			4206			4501			4719			5016		
3102			3320			3616			3912			4207			4502			4720			5017		
3103			S3322	4	80	3617			3914			4208			4503			S4722			5018		
3104			3401			3618			3915			4210			4504			4801			5019		
3105			3402	2	66	3619			3916			4212			4505			4802			5020		
3106			3403	2	66	3620			3917			4214			4506			4803			S5022		
3107			3404			S3622			3918			4215			4507			4804			5101		
3108			3405	2	68	3701			3919			4216			4508			4805			5102		
3110			3406			3702			3920			4217			4510			4806			5103		
3112			3407			3703			S3922			4218			4512			4807			5104		
3114			3408	1	58 —	3704			4001			4219			4514			4808			5105		
3115			3410			3705			4002			4220			4515			4810			5106		
3116			3412	3	72	3706			4003			S4222			4516			4812			5107		
3117			3414	1	59 50	3707			4004			4301			4517			4814			5108		
3118			3415	3	66 —	3708			4005			4302			4518			4815			5110		
			3416			3710									4816								

3312			3606	2	66	3903			S4122			4418			4712			5007					
3314			3607	2	66	3904			4201			4419			4714			5008					
3315			3608	3	71	3905			4202			4420			4715			5010					
3316			3610	1	66	3906			4203			S4422			4716			5012					
3317			3612			3907			4204						4717			5014					
3318			3614			3908			4205						4718			5015					
TOTAL			TOTAL	57	3731 00	TOTAL			TOTAL			TOTAL			TOTAL			TOTAL			TOTAL		

count sheet. They should agree because both forms represent the actual occupancy status. The transcript reflects that status from a folio viewpoint and the room count sheet reflects it from a rooms-occupied viewpoint.

Housekeeper's Report. Further verification of room status comes from the **housekeeper's report.** Housekeeping forwards the report to the desk once or twice each day. Using a generally accepted set of abbreviations (see Exhibit 13–6), housekeeping reports the status of guest rooms to the desk. Occupied rooms are indicated by checkmarks or lines (see Exhibit 13–7). **Sleep-outs,** rooms with baggage but no occupants, are flagged with a *B.* Occupied rooms with no baggage or light baggage are shown with an *X* mark. Other codes (Exhibit 13–6) mix handwritten symbols with alphanumeric symbols, which have been adopted from property management systems.

Discrepancies between the housekeeper's report and room status at the desk are investigated by the front office or the housekeeping staff. Sometimes a bellperson is dispatched to look at the room and report back. The credit manager is especially interested in reports of light luggage, in discrepancies in the number of occupants, and in potential skippers—*X*-marked rooms.

The second report of the day, the afternoon report, is the chief means of uncovering sleepers, skippers, and whos. **Sleepers** are guests who have checked out, but are still being carried as if the room were occupied. *Skippers* are guests who have left without checking out, without paying. **Whos** are unknown guests—someone is occupying a room but the desk doesn't know who it is.

Three additional situations keep the housekeeper's report in use even if room status is being maintained electronically with a PMS. Internal control is difficult in

Exhibit 13–6

Shown is a list of terms and codes found on the housekeeper's report. Property management systems use only alphabetic or numeric symbols.

Baggage: no occupant (sleep-out)	B
Check-out: room on change	c/o
Cot	C
Do not disturb	DND
Double-locked room	DL
Early arrival	EA
No service wanted (Do not disturb)	NS
Occupied	√
Occupied, but dirty	OD
Occupied, with light baggage or no baggage	X
OK	ok
Out of order	O (also OOO)
Permanent guest	P
Ready for sale	/
Refused service	RS
Stayover	s/o
Stayover, no service	SNS
Vacant	V (also no symbol at all)
Vacant and dirty (on change)	VD

Exhibit 13–7

The housekeeper's report of room status is used by the room clerks to verify room status at the front office.

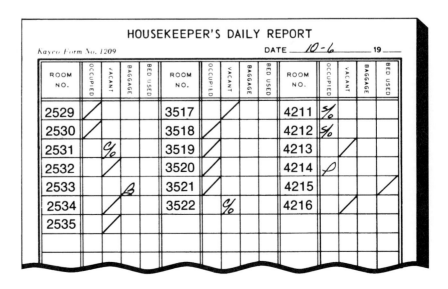

a small hotel, where the desk is staffed by one person who sells the room, collects the money, and posts the record. The housekeeper's report was originally furnished to the auditor. Having a second party compare the room status at the front office to the independently prepared housekeeper's report established a degree of internal control. It is still important for the small hotel! As front offices grow larger and departmentalize, the internal control function of the housekeeper's report diminishes.

Property management systems have helped eliminate the need for verifying occupancy by banging on the guest-room door. Indeed, the PMS has actually reversed the flow of the housekeeper's report. The *room occupancy status report* is prepared by the night audit for housekeeping, which gets its copy early in the morning. This preworkday report on the status of rooms speeds the work of the housekeeper. Room attendants are assigned early in the day, so they begin work immediately. With early knowledge of the room count, the housekeeper refines the work schedule, calling in extras or scheduling days off for full-time staff. The reverse housekeeper's report also communicates guest complaints, ensuring that they get attention early in the day.

The housekeeper's report alerts the desk to special circumstances. Among these are double-locked rooms (DL) and do not disturb rooms (DND) that remain unchanged between the morning and afternoon reports. Floor attendants mark these rooms NS, not serviced, or RS, guest refused service (see Exhibit 13–8). Wise hotel managers telephone such rooms before the day has passed to verify the condition of the occupant. If no one answers the call, the room is entered in the company of security or housekeeping.

Balancing the Math.   The PMS monitors its own mathematics, but a manual system relies on a mathematical check of additions and subtractions. *Cross footing*— horizontally adding the transcript columns—ensures the accuracy of all the values on the transcript, including the figures copied from the folios.

Copying folios onto the transcript is step 1 in its preparation. Step 2 is totaling the columns. Each column total is then verified, which proves the accuracy of the posting and the mathematics of the addition. As explained earlier, the totals are verified against other documents: chiefly vouchers and control sheets. The entire transcript is then checked with a mathematical proof.

The transcript replicates the folios. One by one, each folio, including all of the yet undiscovered errors, is copied onto the transcript. Among the errors will be transpositions and slides made by the cashier acting as the posting clerk, and errors made by the night auditor in preparing the folios. These include incorrect postings of room rates and taxes, and addition and subtraction errors in totaling the folios and carrying forward the balances.

If errors on the folios are copied onto the transcript, errors on the transcript will necessitate corrections to the folios, the original record. Since each line of the transcript represents a folio, an error on any line is an error from that folio. Each mistake must be traced to and corrected on the folio. That remains the major objective of the night audit. Incorrect folios make for very unhappy guests!

The *mathematical proof* of the transcript begins with the total charge (or total debit) column (Exhibit 13–4, column 16). The sum of this total charge column should agree with the sum obtained from cross-footing the totals of all the previous

EXHIBIT 13–8

Room attendants prepare floor status reports and forward them to the linen room for consolidation as the housekeeper's report.

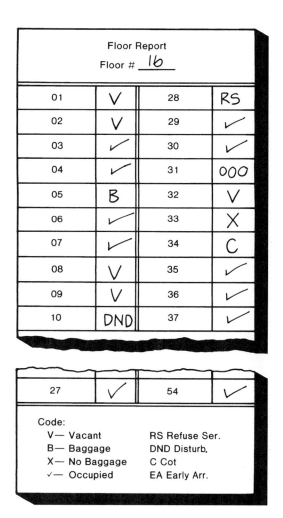

columns. In Exhibit 13–4, notice that the total of column 16 must be the sum of the opening balance total (column 4 minus column 5) plus the sum of all daily charges, the totals of columns 6 through 15.

This simply means that the amount that guests owed the hotel when the day started (column 4 minus column 5) is increased by the amount of purchases that guests made throughout the day (columns 6 through 15). Column 16 reflects that new total.

The accuracy of the totals of columns 6 through 15 has been verified against vouchers and control sheets. The opening balance columns (4 and 5) can also be proved because today's opening balance is the closing balance of yesterday. This opening balance–closing balance relationship is true whether the inventory being counted is liquor, food, linen, or accounts receivable on a transcript. The closing count of one day is the opening count of the next. The night auditor compares the closing balance of yesterday's transcript (columns 21 and 22)—which is returned to the front desk after the income auditor is finished—to today's opening balances (columns 4 and 5).

Proving the closing balances of today's transcript (Exhibit 13–4, columns 21 and 22) is similar to the cross-footing used to prove column 16. In fact, the auditor starts with column 16. Credits (cash receipts, column 17; allowances, 18; and transfers, 19) are subtracted from the total debits (16). The difference (column 16 minus the sum of columns 17, 18, and 19) is compared to the closing balance, which is itself composed of entries in two columns—21 minus 22.

This simply means that the amount that guests would have owed the hotel at the end of the day (column 16) is reduced by the amount that they paid during the day (columns 17, 18, and 19). The closing debt is the net balance still outstanding.

The closing balance has two columns: Column 21 is the debit and column 22 the credit. The transcript can have closing balances that are either debits or credits. The transcript is a copy of the folios and the folios have either debit or credit balances. Usually, they're debits, with credit balances representing unused advance deposits (Exhibit 13–1, column 2, October 6th).

Presented vertically in the traditional mathematical form, rather than the horizontal cross-footing of the transcript, the proof appears less confusing:

$$
\begin{array}{l}
\text{Opening balance (columns 4 and 5: debit} - \text{credit)} \\
+ \text{ Daily charges (columns 6 through 15: debits)} \\
\hline
= \text{Total charges (column 16: total debits)} \\
- \text{ Daily credits (columns 17 through 20)} \\
\hline
= \text{Closing balance (columns 21 and 22: debit} - \text{credit)}
\end{array}
$$

Some audits exclude the opening balance from the debit (column 16) verification. Total charges are then the total charges of that day only, not including the opening balance. The mathematical proof of the opening columns is delayed, then, until the computation for the closing columns.

$$
\begin{array}{l}
\text{Opening balance (columns 4 and 5: debit} - \text{credit)} \\
+ \text{ Total charges (column 16: debits for the day)} \\
- \text{ Daily credits (columns 17 through 20)} \\
\hline
= \text{Closing balance (columns 21 and 22: debit} - \text{credit)}
\end{array}
$$

The Property Management System

The night audit provides the most spectacular demonstration of the property management system in action. Only those who have machine-posted hundreds of folios or hand-copied pages of transcripts can appreciate the savings in time and annoyance. In less than one hour—10 to 15 minutes for a small hotel—the tedious tasks of posting room rates and taxes, balancing the folios, and totaling the charges are finished. That's a job that once took several persons an entire night to complete. Labor savings, the oft-touted but rarely delivered advantage of computer installations, is certainly evident in the night audit. Since a minimum crew is always needed, the greatest labor savings are in the largest hotels.

The computer has altered the mechanics of the audit, its purpose, and its scope. Traditionally, the night audit concentrated on finding and correcting errors—except the errors were caused by the system. Initial errors, transmittal errors, posting errors, and errors of addition are inherent in the hand audit.

The entire thrust of the hand audit is discovery and repair. The computer audit has no such problems. The information that is input with the departmental POS appears everywhere, and everywhere it appears the same. Of course, there are errors of input, and these shall be discussed shortly. There are also errors in the computer itself—in the computer program, a computer bug. That problem has grown so serious that the condition has been upgraded from bug to virus. Viruses or glitches, errors such as dropped letters or misplaced decimal points, are not errors of audit. Errors of this type increase dramatically as additional interfaces (linkage between equipment pieces and other systems) take place.

The Transcript's PMS Equivalent

The property management system is updated daily in a process akin to the manual night audit with its room postings and transcript spreadsheet. Although the PMS update could be done at any time—so could the transcript, for that matter—the quiet hours of the early morning are favored for both. Like the manual system, the PMS has a closeout hour. During this time, departmental point-of-sale terminals cannot interface with the PMS. They must wait until the conclusion of the audit.

Closing Routine.   Updating the PMS requires the night auditor to monitor what is happening rather than to make it happen. Room charges and room taxes are posted automatically. It is an internal function that the auditor doesn't see until the job is completed with a hard-copy printout. The printout is not intrinsic to the job, but it is desirable. With a PMS hard-copy equivalent of the transcript, the hotel is able to settle guest accounts in the event of a computer crash. At least the folio balances that started the day are available on hard copy.

Departmental reconciliations similar to the hand transcript's departmental control sheet balances are also made with a PMS. Rare discrepancies are corrected by comparing the PMS audit figures (essentially, the daily report data) to the receivable debits (register readings and vouchers) and credits (cash receipts and credit slips).

POS terminals are not used by every hotel. Even those that have them may operate some departments manually. If so, the manual system of vouchers, control sheets, and folios may be partially in place. Even if this is so, the night audit is simplified tremendously with the PMS. The property management system creates the folios and the spreadsheet electronically and ensures the accuracy of the mathematics.

The night auditor finishes the PMS audit with an end-of-the-day routine much like that of the hand audit. A trial balance of debits and credits is made. Debits are charges to the receivable folios; credits are earnings in the several departments. The day and date are closed and the next day opened. The POS terminals are put back on-line. Monthly and annual totals are accumulated as part of the reporting process that follows next. The sequence varies at each hotel. At some properties, the routine is preprogrammed; at others, the update proceeds by prompts from the system to which the auditor responds.

Folios of guests who are departing the following day may be printed as part of the audit procedure. Preprinting folios speeds the check-outs. Copies are filed by room number sequence in the cashier's well and produced without delay when the departing guest appears at the desk. If subsequent charges—breakfast, for example—alter the previous night's balance, the old folio is merely discarded and a new one printed.

A copy of the preprinted folio might be left under the guest-room door for use in express check-outs. This wouldn't be necessary if the hotel provides express check-out by means of the TV set.

Express Check-Out.   Express check-out is one of computerization's exciting stories because standing in departure lines is the bane of hotel guests. One of the first PMS innovations to focus on the problem was flexible terminals able to quickly shift from registration to departure status or vice versa. This increased the number of front-office stations when demand was greatest. Lines were shortened, but not enough.

Because early output printers were slow, many operations began printing the folios of expected departures during the previous night's audit. From printing them to delivering them to the room wasn't a large conceptual jump, but it created zip-out check-out, also called speedy check-out, no-wait check-out, or VIP check-out.

Zip-out check-out is only for guests using direct billing or credit cards—but that is almost everyone. At first, guests who wanted the service completed a request card. Later, every departure using a credit card had a folio under the door. If the folio was accurate, the guests left after completing one additional step: They either telephoned an extension to give notice, or they dropped a form with the key in a lobby box. The final folio was mailed to the guest within a day or two, and the charges were processed through the credit-card company.

Express check-out leaped ahead with the interface of Spectradyne's TV pay-movie system into the hotel's PMS. Delivering folios to the room was necessary no longer. The folio appeared on the television set any time the guest wanted it. From then on, the procedure was the same. With a click of the remote control, the guest signaled departure. As with zip-out check-out, the folio followed in the mail, and the credit-card charges were processed. An integrated PMS transfers the charges, which have been accumulated in the front-office folio, to the city ledger module.

Another great leap forward was taken when self-check-in/check-out terminals were interfaced with the ever-expanding PMS. At freestanding locations within the lobby, self-check-out terminals present guests with their folios and accept their credit cards to speed them on their way. This completes the PMS cycle, which was started when the guest registered at the same terminal (Exhibit 8–9). It is another step closer to the fully electronic hotel.

PMS Posting Errors.   The PMS does not guarantee error-free operations. Employees make mistakes whether the system is manual or electronic. Striking the wrong POS key means an overcharge—or undercharge—is posted. The PMS provides consistent figures throughout the system, but they will be the wrong value if the wrong key was struck. Charges are sometimes overlooked altogether—not posted at all. At other times, charges are posted twice. Human errors range all over the place—for example, cashiers may record credit-card charges as cash sales and cash payments as credit-card receipts. Property management systems do not create error-free environments, but they do minimize system-caused errors and facilitate error discovery.

The night auditor prints a detailed list of transactions as the first step in pinpointing errors. The hard copy itemizes transactions by register keys or by reference codes. Reference codes are illustrated on the folio figures throughout Chapter 10. Departmental cashiers need authority to post charges to someone's folio. A source document, such as a signed departmental voucher, provides that authority. Since most source documents are maintained in numerical sequence, the voucher number becomes the reference code. The POS program doesn't post until the cashier inputs that reference number or code.

A different code is used to validate the identity of the guest who is making the charge. The cashier inputs the guest's room number, which the guest provides, and on prompt, enters the first several letters of the guest's surname, which the guest also provides. The charge is processed, but not before the system matches the POS information with the registration data in the file of the PMS. Exhibit 13–2 illustrates the computer screen that a dining room cashier uses to post a charge.

Matching the guest-room keycard (with its magnetic strip) to the PMS's registration data file is another means of verifying the guest's identity. The guest inserts the keycard into a POS and the system verifies the identification. Implementation of this system has already begun, but it may be replaced before it even goes into general use. The smart cards of the next chapter suggest that one's own credit card may become the keycard for the next generation of electronic locks.

The POS reduces receivable losses by rejecting invalid postings. The guest may have checked out already; be a paid-in-advance customer with no charges permitted; or have exceeded the credit-card floor or other credit ceiling set by the hotel. Late charges are reduced dramatically when POS terminals are in place.

Reports from the Night Audit

Once information is captured by the computer, and it need be captured but once, an unlimited number of reports can be generated. The proper programs must be in place, of course, but they generally are with the turnkey systems that will be discussed very shortly. With programs in place, the same data can be arranged and reordered in a variety of ways. The single registration is a good example. The guest's geographic origin, source of reservation, membership in a convention, credit limits, and length of stay provide data for five different reports.

The ease of obtaining reports undoubtedly contributed to the vast numbers that were demanded when property management systems were first introduced. Much of that has shaken out. Management took control and pared the numbers by emphasizing exception reports. One no longer sees piles of reports prepared by the night auditor trashed, unread by the recipient the next day.

Still, the night audit produces a wide range of reports for all departments of the front office. Many of these are day-end summaries, since unit managers use (through display terminals or hard-copy print) the same data several times throughout the day. Some reports are traditional with the night audit: the balancing of accounts receivable, credit alerts, and statistical reports to the manager.

Turnkey Systems.   With rare exceptions, every hotel uses the same kinds of reports. Although the formats differ with each supplier, with some more user friendly than others, the purpose and content vary very little. It's difficult to say whether a uniform need caused the turnkey system, or whether mass production created similar needs property to property.

In a **turnkey** installation, the buyer merely "turns the key" to activate the system. Everything has been done in advance by the vendor. Nothing is ever quite that easy, but it is unlikely that the hotel industry would be so far along if the burden of development had remained with the individual hotel, which was the norm in the early stages of computer use by the lodging industry.

Prior to the turnkey concept, each hotel shopped among manufacturers for its own hardware. Then it developed its own software by employing computer specialists, who at that time knew nothing about the business of keeping a hotel. The large data processing departments, which appeared as a result of the in-house programming, disappeared quickly with the introduction of the turnkey package.

Management now purchases the system **off-the-shelf,** shopping among suppliers for a system that is close to what the hotel needs. And the systems *are* close to what is needed. Generic programs are much alike because hotels are much alike. Differences among the programs reflect the background of the vendors more than anything else. The differences diminish as second- and third-generation programs are developed. These later generations usually simplify the basic functions by improving flow and screening, and adding new or missing functions.

Turnkey companies now dominate the field. Single suppliers furnish both the hardware and the software. If the supplier specializes in one segment, other vendors supply the missing parts. Responsibility remains with the primary vendor, who puts together the package, gets it up and running, and trains the staff before turning over the key.

If necessary, vendors modify the off-the-shelf system to meet the hotel's special needs. Just as often, the hotel modifies its special needs to conform to the standard product. As a result, programs and reports are almost identical among hotels serviced by the same vendor, and very similar among hotels with different vendors.

Kinds of Reports.   Reports from the night audit fall into several categories: reservation reports; rooms management reports, including reports of room status; accounting reports; and reports to the manager.

Unless management remains selective, an excessive number of reports involving expensive machine time, labor, storage, and paper costs is spewed out nightly. Since a good deal of the information keeps changing, viewing it on screens is just as effective and far more economical. Reporting by exception is another approach to the issue.

Exception Reports.   Exception reports highlight situations that digress from the norm. Reporting everything that is as it should be serves no purpose. Reports by exception alert the reader to problem areas without requiring the time-consuming inspection of normal data. A report on credit limits is a good example. Listing the folio balance of every guest against the credit ceiling is unnecessary. It is unduly long and requires a tedious search to find the important information. An exception report lists only those folios that are at, above, or close to the hotel's limit. The size of the report is reduced and the important data is emphasized.

Some common exception reports are listed here:

Allowance Report: identifies who authorized each allowance, who received the allowance, the amount, and the reasons.

Cashier's Overage and Shortage Report: pinpoints by stations overages and shortages that exceed predetermined norms.

Comps Report: similar to an Allowance Report; identifies who authorized each comp, who received the comp, the amount, and the reasons.

No Luggage Report: lists occupied rooms in which there is no luggage (Exhibit 13–8); a credit report.

Room Rate Variance Report: compares actual rates to standard rate schedule and identifies the authority for granting the variance (not meaningful if the hotel is discounting frequently and deeply).

Skipper Report: provides room identification, dollar amount, and purported name and address.

Write-Off Report: lists daily write-offs, usually late charges, whose account balance is less than a specified amount.

Downtime Reports.   Downtime reports, for use when the computer crashes, provide insurance against disaster. Like a great deal of insurance, the reports usually go unused because emergencies rarely materialize. Downtime reports are dumped 24 hours later when the contingency has passed and the backup reports of the following day have been printed.

Basic downtime reports include the following:

Folio Balance Report: itemizes in room number sequence the balances due from receivables; comparable to columns 21 and 22 of a manual transcript (Exhibit 13–4).

Guest-List Report: alphabetizes registered guests with their room numbers; computer version of a manual information rack.

Room Status Report: identifies vacant, out-of-order, on change, and occupied rooms at the beginning of the new day; a computerized room count sheet (Exhibit 13–5).

Disk Backup: not a report, but part of the closing sequence of the auditor's shift; data is replicated onto another disk to be retrieved if a malfunction erases the working disk.

Credit Reports.   The night auditor is the credit manager's first line of defense. In that capacity, the night auditor handles both mundane matters and special credit alerts.

Mention has already been made of the auditor's responsibility to preprint the folios of expected check-outs. Although not so numerous, folios must also be prepared for guests who remain longer than one week. On the guest's seventh night, the auditor prints the folio (or prepares a new folio if the system is manual) for delivery to the guest the next day.

The night auditor also makes an analysis of guest account balances. With a manual system, the auditor scans the last column of the transcript (Exhibit 13–4, column 21) and itemizes those rooms with balances at or near the hotel's limit. The computer makes the same list.

If the audit team has time, additional credit duties may be assigned. There are occasional guests, especially walk-ins, that concern the credit manager. The night auditor might be asked to verify the guest's identity by getting a telephone number for that person or the person's business affiliation at the address given. Although the absence of a number is inconclusive, it is another bit of information for the credit department in making its evaluation.

All credit reports are sensitive and may be viewed as exception reports:

Credit Alert: a list of rooms whose folio charges exceed a given amount in a single day. That amount varies with the class of hotel.

Cumulative Charges Report: similar to the credit alert except a cumulative figure for the guest's entire stay.

Floor Report: a list of guests whose folio balances approach the maximum allowed the hotel by the credit-card company, or the maximum the credit-card allows on the guest's own card.

Three-Day Report: weekly statements that remain unpaid three days after billing.

Reservation Reports.   Computerizing the reservation function added a whole new dimension to the process. It introduced new reservation techniques, the 1–800-WATS number; it globalized the reservation network through the ultraswitch; and it facilitated instant confirmation for dates months away in hotels thousands of miles apart. No less important, computerized reservations produced reams of information.

Information is the power to decide. Reservation managers must know the number of rooms sold and the number available, by type, rate, and accommodations. They must know arrivals, departures, stayovers, cancellations, out of orders, and walk-ins, for a start. This information comes to the reservation department in a variety of reports.

Supplemental information flows from the same database. Which rooms are most popular and at which rates? Do no-show factors vary with the season and the day of the week? If so, by how much? How many rooms in which categories are turn-aways? How many reservations were walked? How many in-WATS calls were there? How many were initiated by travel agents? Questions of this type illustrate again the dual management–operations capability of the computer.

An alphabetical list of arrivals is an example of the computer in operations. It reduces the number of lost reservations and facilitates the recognition of VIPs. It helps the bellcaptain schedule a crew. It identifies group affiliation, which improves reservation and billing procedures.

Reservation data can be displayed on a monitor or preserved on hard copy for slower digestion and evaluation. A permanent copy turns the data into a report. Then it serves more as a management tool than an operational one. Although systems of different vendors format the reports differently, there is a common grouping for the reservation department, which includes the following:

Arrivals Report: an alphabetical list of the day's expected arrivals, individually and by groups.

Cancellation and Change Report: a list of reservation cancellations for the day or reservation changes and cancellations for a later date.

Central Reservations Report: an analysis of reservations made through the central reservations system, including numbers, kinds, rates, and fees paid.

Convention (Group) Delegates Report: a compilation of a group (and tour) room blocks; the number of rooms booked, and the number still available by rate category and name of group. Also called a Group Pick-up Report.

Daily Analysis Report: one or more reports on the number and percentage of reservations, arrivals, no-shows, walk-ins, and so on, by source (travel agent, housing bureau, etc.) and by type of guest (full rack, corporate rate, etc.).

Deposit Report: reservations by deposit status—deposits requested and received, deposits requested and not received, deposits not requested. Could be treated as an exception report.

Exhibit 13–9

Shown is a computer display of the room rack, including room type, rate, location, and status. The clerk's selection, lower left, must agree with previous input of room type requested. If satisfactory, the clerk exits with Y (yes), lower right.

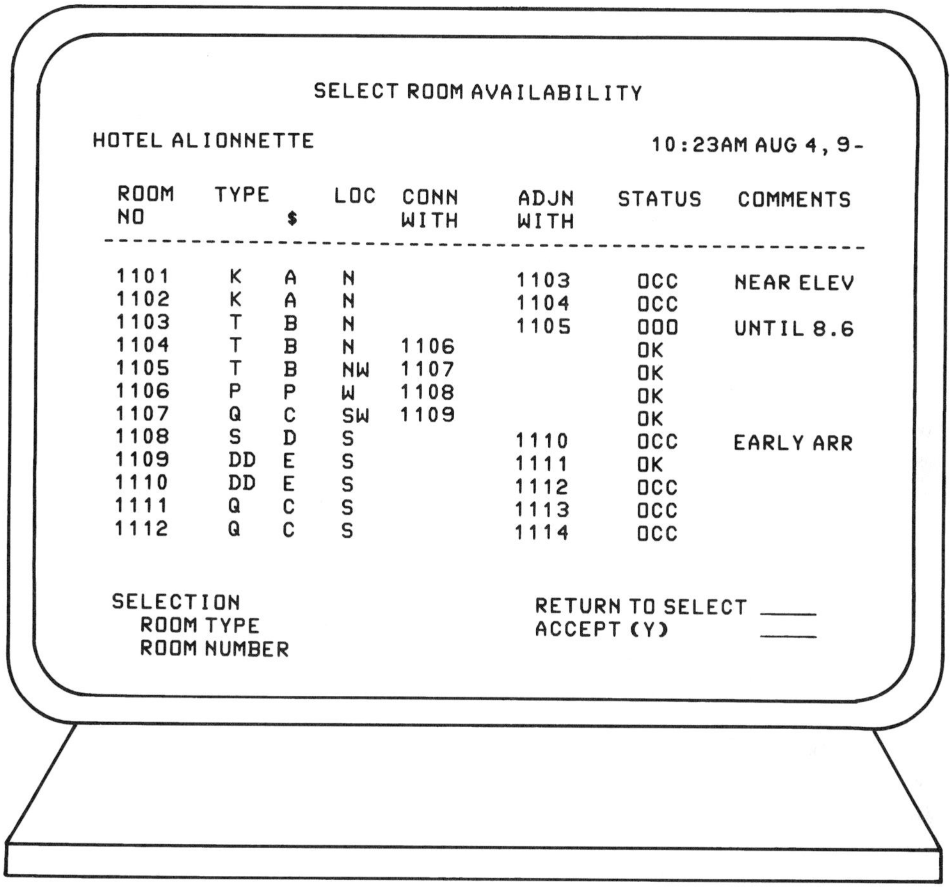

```
                    SELECT ROOM AVAILABILITY

    HOTEL ALIONNETTE                          10:23AM AUG 4, 9-

       ROOM    TYPE       LOC   CONN     ADJN    STATUS   COMMENTS
       NO        $              WITH     WITH
    -----------------------------------------------------------------
       1101    K    A      N             1103    OCC      NEAR ELEV
       1102    K    A      N             1104    OCC
       1103    T    B      N             1105    OOO      UNTIL 8.6
       1104    T    B      N    1106             OK
       1105    T    B      NW   1107             OK
       1106    P    P      W    1108             OK
       1107    Q    C      SW   1109             OK
       1108    S    D      S             1110    OCC      EARLY ARR
       1109    DD   E      S             1111    OK
       1110    DD   E      S             1112    OCC
       1111    Q    C      S             1113    OCC
       1112    Q    C      S             1114    OCC


    SELECTION                     RETURN TO SELECT _____
       ROOM TYPE                  ACCEPT (Y)
       ROOM NUMBER                                 _____
```

Forecast Report: one of a variety of names (extended arrival report, future availability report) for projecting reservation data forward over short or long durations (Exhibit 6–7).

Occupancy Report: a projection within the computer's horizon of expected occupancy by category of room.

Overbooking (or Walk) Report: a list of reservations walked, including their identification; the number of walk-ins denied; and the number farmed out to other properties.

Regrets Report: a report on the number of room requests denied.

Rooms Management Reports. Computerization has brought major procedural changes to the front office but not to the functions that need doing. Comparisons of the old and the new are best illustrated through the room rack. Unlike manual room racks, which one can see and physically manipulate, computerized racks are in computer memory, viewable only on the monitor screen (see Exhibit 13–9). Whether

Exhibit 13–10

This is a major menu display that is available to the room clerk. Each input number—6, for example—displays a second menu or mask (Exhibit 13–2) with which to complete the posting.

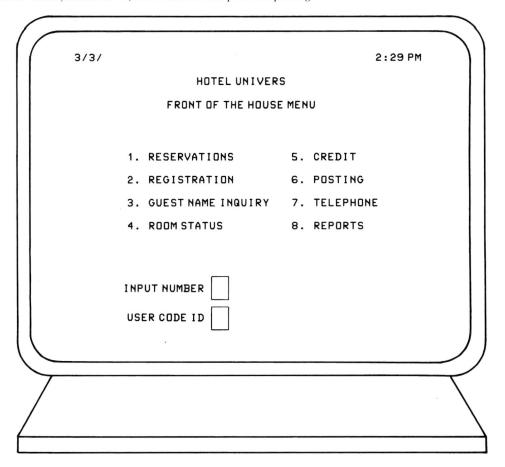

3/3/   2:29 PM

HOTEL UNIVERS

FRONT OF THE HOUSE MENU

1. RESERVATIONS   5. CREDIT

2. REGISTRATION   6. POSTING

3. GUEST NAME INQUIRY   7. TELEPHONE

4. ROOM STATUS   8. REPORTS

INPUT NUMBER [ ]
USER CODE ID [ ]

the clerk turns to one rack type or the other, the information is the same: room rates, location, connecting and adjoining rooms, bed types, and room status.

The computer restructures the data. It separates into different windows what is visible with one glance to the user of the manual rack. Separate menus (see Exhibit 13–10) are needed to view what the manual rack identifies as one class of information. With a glance at the manual rack, one sees the rooms vacant and occupied, the rooms out of order and on change, the names of the guests and their city of residence, the number in the party and their company or group affiliation, the rate on the room, and the anticipated check-out date. It doesn't work that way with an electronic system, where separate programs are needed for each function. Room identification (Exhibit 13–9) is different from guest identification (See Exhibit 13–11).

Far more information is available from the computer rack than from the manual rack, but the information has to be manipulated to provide the data. For example, the computerized rack can display all the vacant rooms on a given floor. All the king rooms in the tower or all the connecting rooms in the lanai building can be listed. Facts that would take many minutes to ascertain, if at all, from the manual rack are flashed onto the screen in seconds.

Exhibit 13–11

The computer monitor (or VDT—video display terminal) displays information about the individual guest (comparable to a manual room rack slip).

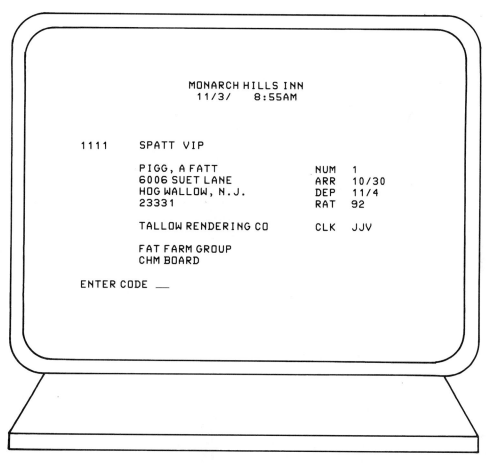

```
                    MONARCH HILLS INN
                    11/3/    8:55AM


        1111      SPATT VIP

                  PIGG, A FATT          NUM    1
                  6006 SUET LANE        ARR    10/30
                  HOG WALLOW, N.J.      DEP    11/4
                  23331                 RAT    92

                  TALLOW RENDERING CO   CLK    JJV

                  FAT FARM GROUP
                  CHM BOARD

        ENTER CODE __
```

Information is more complete and can be processed more rapidly with the computerized rack than with the manual one. This is true for the whole, although a greater amount of time may be required for the computer to process a single fact. In a contest to identify a guest whose name begins with either ''Mac'' or ''Mc,'' for example, the manual user may be able to beat out the computer user.

Computer reports for the rooms function include the following:

Change Report: identification of room changes, rate changes, and number in the party.

Convention Use Report: summary of the room use of conventions by group in order to justify the number of complimentary rooms.

Expected to Depart Report: list of anticipated departures. The converse would be a Stayover Report.

Flag Report: list of rooms flagged for special attention by the desk.

House Use Report: list of rooms occupied by hotel personnel.

Out-of-Order Report: list of rooms that are out of order and reasons.

Pick-Up Report: names and room numbers picked up by members of a specific group against its block.

Rate Analysis Report: display of distribution of rates by sources—reservations, walk-ins, travel-agency made, res system, hotel sales department, packages, company-made.

Room Productivity Report: evaluation of housekeeping's productivity in total and by individual room attendant.

VIP Report: list of distinguished guests and very important persons, including casino high rollers.

Room Status Reports.   Room status offers what is probably the best example of an old function with a new face. Whether the hotel uses a manual rack or a computer, room status (on change, vacant and ready, out-of-order, or occupied rooms) must be communicated between the desk and housekeeping. Clerks need to know which rooms are ready for sale, and housekeeping needs to know which rooms require attention. A room status display on the monitor is called up innumerable times throughout the day by both ends of the communication link.

The communication procedure hasn't changed with the computer. The cashier still puts the room on change as the guest checks out. (This is done electronically if the guest uses the speedy check-out option.) That's how the room clerk learns that a given room will be available soon. On change status tells housekeeping that the room needs attention. When the room is clean, the housekeeper updates the system, switching the on change room to ready. Immediately, the desk clerk has the information. The room is sold and the cycle begins anew. The faster the process goes around, the quicker the guest is settled and the room sale consummated.

Prior to the computer, the cashier–desk–housekeeping link was direct conversation person to person; by means of paper notations; by telephone calls; and, frequently, not at all. The chambermaid on the floor wasn't included in the communication loop. Although the critical link, she couldn't be reached at all. Today, the chambermaid communicates by telephone, not by conversation, but as an electronic input device to the computer. Either the chambermaid taps in through the telephone or by means of a terminal located in the linen closet on each floor. Personal PCs are being introduced into guest rooms to upgrade guest service, but they also provide the chambermaid with still another terminal.

With access to the computer, the housekeeper's office tracks room attendants as they dial in and out of the system (see Exhibit 13–12). Daily job assignments can also be computer designed. At the start of the shift, each employee gets a hard-copy list of rooms that each is to do. The printout also includes special assignments such as mirrors in the corridors, attention to sick guests, or messages from management to the staff.

In addition to the reports that housekeeping uses to manage the department, room status includes the following:

Out-of-Order Report: a special focus on out-of-order rooms containing dates the rooms went down, expected ready dates, and the causes of each OOO room.

Room Status List: a room-by-room identification of occupied and vacant rooms, made-up and not-ready rooms, out-of-order rooms, and on change rooms. (Also included among the downtime reports.)

EXHIBIT 13–12

A schedule of each room attendant is tracked by the PMS, allowing management to monitor productivity or to locate the room attendant for a special communication.

```
                    MAID-ROOM SCHEDULE              01:53 PM NOV 11

 NAME                              NUMBER  DUTY H    MESSAGE SIGNAL OFF
        NUMBER OF ROOMS ASSIGNED        0          BEGINNING ROOM NUMBER
 ROOM  U-R   IN      OUT    SL HK   CO  ROOM  U-R    IN      OUT    SL  HK  CO
 1200   A   9:35A   9:49A  SG OK   SO  1209   A                    SD   D   SO
 1201   A   9:50A  10:14A  SS OK   SO  1210   A   8:44A   9:02A   SD  OK   SO
 1202   A  11:50A  12:12P  SS OK   SO  1211   A   1:13P   1:48P   OK   I   OK
 1203   A   9:20A   9:35A  SS OK   SO  1212   A   9:03A   9:19A   SG  OK   SO
 1204   A  10:54A  11:17A  SM OK   SO  1213   A   1:48P            OK  57   DO
 1205   A  11:17A  11:50A  SD OK   SO  1214   A                    OK   D   DO
 1206   A  10:31A  10:54A  SS OK   SO  1215   A                    OK   D   DO
 1207   A  10:14A  10:31A  SS OK   SO
 1208   A  12:12P   1:13P  OK OK   OK

                                                            END DISPLAY
```

> **Permanent Guest Report:** list of permanent guests by room number and name.
>
> **Sick Guest Report:** list of sick guests by room number and name.

Accounts Receivable Reports. The computer electronically prepares the details of the many records that were discussed during the review of the manual audit. What is the very function of the manual night audit becomes a series of reports by the computerized night audit. Both the manual and the electronic audit deal with the day's accounts receivable. A cumulative inventory of accounts receivable is the essence of the audit. The opening balance of receivables, the amount owed to the hotel, is increased by new charges and decreased by payments made that day. The new balance is thus obtained; it becomes the opening balance of the following day's audit.

The computerized audit reflects this emphasis on receivables through a group of related reports:

> **Alpha List:** alphabetically lists the entire guest (account receivable) population. Other alpha lists include arrivals and departures.
>
> **City Ledger Transfers:** itemizes all the accounts transferred to city ledger that day.
>
> **Credit-Card Report:** reports amounts and identities of credit-card charges by both registered and nonregistered guests.
>
> **Daily Revenue Report:** analyzes revenue totals from all sources by outlet and means of payment. Comparable to the old machine audit D report (and sometimes called a D report).
>
> **Departmental Sales Journal:** shows the individual transactions of each department (comparable to the vertical columns of a hand transcript).
>
> **Guest Ledger Summary:** displays the daily activity for both the A and B folios of individual guest accounts—opening balance, charges and credits, and closing balance (comparable to the horizontal lines of a hand transcript).

Late Charge Report: identifies late charges that were transferred to city ledger that day.

Posting Report: displays posting activity by individual POS terminal (comparable to a departmental control sheet).

Room Revenue (Posting) Report: displays room, rate, and tax posted at the day's close. Room revenue can be obtained floor by floor (comparable to a room count sheet).

Reports to the Manager.   The final task of the income audit, or day audit, is a daily report to the manager. Difficulties in reconciling this income audit often delay its delivery until midday. To offset the wait, the night auditor leaves a preliminary report on the manager's desk. The night auditor's report to the manager is abbreviated because the night audit deals with accounts receivable sales and collections only, whereas the income audit reports cash flows as well.

Exhibit 13–13 illustrates an electronically prepared night auditor's report, which emphasizes two items: accounts receivable and room statistics. The receivables segment is familiar, of course, since it is just a replay (in another format) of the transcript formula presented earlier in the chapter (Exhibit 13–4):

Opening balance (columns 4 and 5: debit − credit)
+ Daily charges (columns 6 through 15: debits)

= Total charges (column 16: total debits)
− Daily credits (columns 17 through 20)

= Closing balance (columns 21 and 22: debit − credit).

Room Count, House Count, and Room Income.   Room count (number of rooms occupied), house count (number of guests), and room income (sales) are verified by the audit. Another computation, exactly the kind used with accounts receivable, structures the proof: opening inventory plus arrivals minus departures equals the closing inventory of room count, house count, and room income.

As with any running-balance computation—as with any inventory count—the closing balance of one day becomes the opening balance of the next. The other values in the computation are obtained from the corresponding reports: arrivals, departures, and changes. (Changes are registered guests making room and rate changes.)

	Room Count	House Count	Room Income
Opening balance	840	1,062	$174,200
+ Arrivals	316	391	80,100
= Total	1,156	1,453	$254,300
− Departures	88	122	16,400
= Total	1,068	1,331	$237,900
± Changes	+6	−2	+1,730
= Closing balance	1,074	1,329	$239,630

Statistics.   Room statistics are reported in another section of the night auditor's report to the manager. Statistics are merely special ways of grouping data in an

EXHIBIT 13–13

In an abbreviated night auditor's report to the manager, cumulative figures are not shown. This report is electronically prepared as part of the PMS audit. Basic elements include charge sales, a running balance of receivables, and room statistics.

```
THE CITY HOTEL,  ANYWHERE, U.S.A.                              Page 1
03/16   Night Auditor's Report
_____

        SALES                           ROOM STATISTICS

Rooms          $12,900.00       Total Rooms       320
Coffee Shop      1,524.80       House Use          -0-
Steak House        CLOSED       Out of Order       -0-
Cap'tn Bar         896.00       Complimentary      -0-
Telephone          990.76       Permanent            2
Laundry            100.51       Room Count         180
    Total Sales $16,412.07      Vacant             140
                                House Count        210

Other Charges:
  Cash Advances     987.76
  Taxes Payable     540.00
  Transfers         693.15
                 $18,632.98


    ACCOUNTS RECEIVABLE                 ROOM RATIOS

Opening Balance $44,651.07     % Occupancy            56.3
                               % Double Occupancy     16.7
Charges          18,632.98     Average Daily Rate   $71.67
    Total        $63,284.05     Rate/Room Avail.    $40.31

Credits            950.00

Closing Balance $62,334.05
```

orderly and usable manner. Statistics are the facts expressed in dollars, cents, or numbers. For example, instead of itemizing:

Guest A	Room 597	$50.25
Guest B	Room 643	$48.75
Guest C	Room 842	$59.25

and so on, one might say there are 220 guests in 189 rooms paying a total of $9,158. A great deal of information has been grouped, classified, and presented to become a statistic.

Taken the next step, these room figures are expressed in ratios, which are more meaningful than the simple statistic. So the 189 rooms sold is expressed in relation to the number of rooms available for sale, 270. The result is a percentage of occupancy, a mathematical expression of how many rooms were sold in relation to how many could have been sold. The occupancy percent is a widely quoted figure and one discussed as early as Chapter 1. Using the illustration, the percentage of occupancy is:

$$\frac{\text{Number of rooms sold (room count)}}{\text{Number of rooms available for sale}} = \frac{189}{270} = 70\%$$

A frequent companion to the percentage of occupancy computation is the Average Daily Rate (ADR). Both ratios appear in the night auditor's report to the manager. Sales per occupied room, as this figure is sometimes called, is the income from room sales divided by the number of rooms sold.

$$\frac{\text{Room income}}{\text{Number of rooms sold (room count)}} = \frac{\$9,158}{189} = \$48.46$$

A similar computation, sales per available room, is derived by dividing room income by the number of rooms available for sale rather than by the actual number of rooms sold.

$$\frac{\text{Room income}}{\text{Number of rooms available for sale}} = \frac{\$9,158}{270} = \$33.92$$

The fourth most frequently cited ratio in the manger's daily report is the percentage of double occupancy. Double occupancy is the relationship of rooms occupied by more than one guest to the total number of rooms occupied. That is what the following ratio expresses:

$$\frac{\text{Number of guests} - \text{Number of rooms sold}}{\text{Number of rooms sold}} = \frac{220 - 189}{189} = 16.4\%$$

Having finished the audit with the preparation of the night auditor's report to the manager, the night auditor lays aside the pencils and erasers—or more likely, rubs some stiff shoulders from working at the keyboard—and, at the end of the shift, goes home to bed.

Summary

Hotels balance their accounts receivable nightly. During this procedure, known as the night audit, the amounts owed by the individual accounts receivable are verified. Each receivable (folio) grows larger or smaller as the individual purchases services or pays down debt. These purchases and payments are the other side of each folio transaction. Therefore, as the audit proves the accuracy of the folio, it also verifies the transaction itself. Verifying sales transactions in outlets of the hotel and payments made with cash or credit card is part of proving the accounts receivable. Hence, the night audit audits both.

The night audit focuses on guest folios—on the accounts receivable. Since cash sales in the various outlets (food, beverage, etc.) do not have an impact on accounts receivable, cash sales are not part of the night audit. They are left, rather, to the income audit, which is completed each morning following the night audit.

The mechanics of the night audit have changed as hotel records have mutated from manual pencil-and-paper systems to computerized property management systems (PMS). The objectives have remained unchanged, however. In addition to an accurate folio and the verification of departmental sales, the night audit tabulates total accounts receivable. The amount that all accounts receivable owe the hotel changes almost by the minute. Each individual purchase of goods and services changes the amount due from total receivables. The audit determines that cumulative total each night. The figure is captured at a given moment, like a snapshot, after the closeout hour ends the day, and reported on the night auditor's report to the manager.

Tracking total accounts receivable is a simple computation. It is identical to the calculation used for any inventory count. The opening balance of receivables (the cumulative amount owed from the previous day) is increased by charges purchased by guests and decreased by payments made by guests. The closing balance thus derived becomes the opening balance of the following day. This calculation is very apparent when the audit is prepared on a manual spreadsheet called a transcript. Done by the computer, the result is visible but the process is not.

The PMS has simplified the work of the night audit, especially the posting of room rates and taxes. The PMS was introduced to the hotel industry to help manage information technology. It has done that job so well that additional services have been added to the PMS to improve the overall capability of the hotel. The next chapter enlarges on the PMS's capacity and hints of robotics yet to come.

Queries and Problems

1. Explain how the three backup reports discussed in the section "Downtime Reports" would be used in the event of a computer malfunction.

2. A guest checks in at 4:30 AM on Tuesday, January 8. Under hotel policy, the guest is to be charged for the room-night of Monday, January 7. The closeout hour of Monday, January 7, was 12:30 AM, January 8, and the room charge postings were handled automatically by the PMS at approximately 3:00 AM on that morning. The room rate is $72 and the tax is 5 percent; no other charges were incurred. Sketch a computer-prepared folio as it would appear when the guest departs on Wednesday, January 9, at 10:00 AM, and briefly explain who made which posting.

3.

Given

Rooms occupied	440
Rooms vacant	160
Total rooms sales	$32,330
House count	500

Required

The percentage of occupancy	_____
The percentage of double occupancy	_____
The average daily rate	_____
The average rate per available room	_____

4. Explain and then challenge the following statement: The night audit is nothing more than an inventory record.

5. The discussion on reservation reports cites a central reservation report that includes a statement about fees paid. Explain who pays what fees to whom and about how much those fees might be.

6. Is the transcript in balance? If not, what error or errors might account for the discrepancy? What percentage of sales tax is being charged in this community?

Allowances	$ 100.00
Telephone	670.70
Transfers to	395.05
Rooms	9,072.00
Cash advance	444.25
Debit transfer	395.50
Beverage	1,920.00
Credit-card charges	14,482.07
Cash	10,071.22
Closing balance	3,670.41
Opening balance	48,341.50
Rooms tax	725.76
Food	3,000.10
Closing balance	43,007.33
Opening balance	185.00
Total charges	$64,384.81

CHAPTER 14

Property Management
System Interfaces

Chapter Outline

The Call Accounting System

The telephone is the oldest of all property management system (PMS) interfaces. Telephones have been used in hotel rooms since the first ones were installed in New York City's Netherland Hotel in 1894.[1] Today's more sophisticated telephone systems are generally referred to as **call accounting systems (CAS).**

In addition to being the oldest property management system interface, telephone systems are also the most common PMS interface. Due to the number of telephone posting transactions and the front desk's need to activate in-room telephones as required by guest demands, the call accounting system is often interfaced to the PMS when no other system interfaces are present. Therefore, the CAS provides an excellent introduction to electronic interface technology.

Interface Technology

The Property Management System (PMS) in place at the front desk serves as more than just a mechanism to check guests in and out. It also serves as the electronic clearinghouse and interface center for a number of auxiliary electronic systems in the hotel. The energy management system (EMS), call accounting system (CAS), and electronic locking system (ELS) are three of the more common interfaces that operate in connection with the PMS. In-room movie or entertainment systems, self-check-in and self-check-out systems, in-room safes, and in-room minibar or beverage systems are additional examples of PMS interfaces.

In most cases, each of these interfaced systems stands alone with its own processing capabilities. The interface or connection between the stand-alone system (e.g., the EMS) and the PMS provides an uninterrupted flow of guest information. An energy management system interface, for example, allows the front-desk property management system to monitor room activity; shut-off heating systems, lighting, and nonessential electric outlets in unoccupied rooms; and adjust water temperatures as a function of occupancy. Although the EMS is a complete system with its own input, output, and processing, it functions better with a communication interface to the PMS.

Uniform Connectivity. The history of interface connectivity is one of hit and miss, trial and error. In the 1970s, there were close to 100 vendors of property management systems. Likewise, there were numerous manufacturers of point-of-sale systems (POS), call accounting systems, back-office accounting systems, and guest history databases.

An unsophisticated hotel operator could easily purchase a PMS, POS, and CAS from three separate vendors. Of course, each salesperson promised his or her system would interface with the other systems. Yet months later, the frustrated hotel operator could find no company willing to take responsibility for the interface. The POS vendor blamed the PMS vendor who blamed the CAS vendor, and so on.

There are plenty of horror stories about hotel operators who spent thousands of dollars on software programming to get one system to electronically interface with another. Many times, however, the hotel was left with a dysfunctional system. Downtime would be common, the interface would slow the processing speed of each system, and valuable data would be lost between the source system and the PMS. This last problem was the worst of all, because hotel revenue (say, from a CAS) was forever lost between systems!

The problem of incompatible interfaces has been essentially eradicated with today's state-of-the-art technologies. Practically every PMS has the capacity to interface with almost every auxiliary system. Indeed, if a property has a stand-alone system that has never been previously interfaced to any brand of PMS, the PMS vendor will often provide free interface software programming. This is a marketing approach many PMS vendors use to enable them to add another system to their list of compatible products. This has been so successful that there are few PMS system–auxiliary system incompatibilities anymore.

Standardization. In recent months, a consortium of hospitality computer vendors has begun establishing a standard platform against which all hardware, software, databases, and communication formats must conform. Although conformity will be voluntary, such standardization platforms have performed well in other industries.

By voluntarily following the standard requirements, vendors will be entitled to market their product as complying with the format. That's a powerful message, because hotel operators would be foolish to purchase noncomplying products. After all, purchasing a standardized product virtually guarantees smooth interfacing.

History of Hotel Telephone Services

In 1944, the Federal Communications Commission (FCC) approved a proposal that was to structure the economic relationship between the hotel industry and the telephone industry for almost four decades. The ruling required telephone companies to pay hotels a commission for all long-distance calls originating in hotel rooms. As expected, this rule expedited the general introduction of telephones into American hotels. Despite the success, the two industries battled about the size of the commission almost from the start. Hotels argued that the fee was too low to offset costs and earn a fair return. As evidence, they offered income and expense statements that showed profitless telephone departments. AT&T countered by arguing that the department shouldn't be a profit center. Most of the telephone usage, AT&T contended, was for the hotel's own business, a fair cost of operations.

Still, the hotel industry made a good argument. The 15 percent commission structure and labor-intensive nature of the system prevented hotels from making any profit at all. Hotels generally argued three common points:

1. Inaccurate room numbers of outward-calling guests cost hotels much of their commission. Immediately after dialing the number, guests were intercepted by telephone company operators and asked their room number. Since the operator had no way of verifying the room number, inaccurate room numbers (given either accidentally or purposely by the guest) were often charged. Later, when guests complained they were being charged for calls they did not make, the hotel credited the guests' accounts.

2. The 15 percent commission structure was insufficient to cover the costs of installation and maintenance of telephone equipment. As a result, hotels were scarcely able to break even when applying commissions against equipment charges.

3. And finally, late charges cost hotels their profit as well. In many cases, guest phone calls were not communicated to the hotel for several hours. During this time delay, it was possible for the guest to check out of the hotel without compensating the operation for the cost of the call.

The year 1981 was another critical date. Once again, the federal government acted to restructure the system. Within a short time, three traumas rocked the telephone industry. First, the large, integrated Bell system was dissolved, its long-line service separated from its local operations. Second, competition from other manufacturers and service companies was invited in, weakening the monopoly still further. And, third, hotels were permitted once again to levy their own fees on calls originating from their premises. The 1944 commission schedule had been rescinded.

The increased competition and the permissiveness of deregulation sent the hotels shopping for new telephone equipment and servicers. What they bought was the result of their previous technological and economic experience. Let's look briefly at this history before examining the current state of telephony.

Historical Pricing Distinctions.   As a quasi-utility, the telephone company was regulated by the FCC at the federal level and by 50 public service commissions (PSCs) at the state levels. Consequently, there were, and there still are, different rates for intrastate calls (those taking place within the state) and for interstate calls (those that pass from one state to another). Rates on intrastate calls vary from state to state, because each commission is free to act independently of its neighbor.

It wasn't all that bad for the telephone company. For nearly 40 years, hotels were prohibited by law from charging any fee on interstate calls and were severely limited by most states on intrastate calls.

Interstate Calls.   The Bell system paid a 15 percent commission on all interstate calls originating from the hotel. A smaller commission was paid for interstate calls charged to credit cards, charged to third parties, or charged collect. In turn, the telephone companies collected an equipment rental fee from the hotels. Hotels were not permitted to own telephones (neither were individual homeowners), so the lease fee was an ongoing cost. Less direct, but equally real, were the hotels' costs of billing the guests, collecting, and remitting to the telephone companies.

So when the telephone company quoted charges, the hotel added the federal tax and billed the guest for the total, but no more. The hotel collected from the guest, paid the telephone company on the basis of a monthly billing, and received a commission from the company on the same basis. The size of that 15 percent commission was one point of contention between the hotel industry and the telephone companies. But it is no longer.

On June 1, 1981, the FCC ruled that hotels could make their own surcharges on interstate calls, just as they had done prior to 1944. A stroke of the pen undid a 37-year experiment. Before the year was out, the Bell system had an announcement of its own: Commissions (estimated in 1981 at $230 million annually) would no longer be paid. Bell's decision was not mandated by the FCC. It was a business decision, and it was a gutsy one at that, since the new federal policy encouraged competition against the Bell system.

A series of court pronouncements destroyed once and for all the concept of the telephone as a utility. Competition was encouraged, and it appeared on the scene with some appealing deals. By an earlier court decision, the Carterfone Case allowed non-Bell equipment to be interconnected with Bell equipment.[2]

Motivated by a great deal of uncertainty and an equal lack of information, the AH&MA negotiated a year's delay with the Bell system. The 15 percent commission, which had caused such strident arguments earlier, looked awfully good in the face of uncertainty. Commissions were paid until December 31, 1982, while the hotel industry shopped for alternatives.

Intrastate Calls.   Although interstate calls are regulated by the FCC (the U.S. Constitution reserves the control of interstate commerce for the federal government), intrastate calls are not. Intrastate regulations are quite varied because the communications commissions of each state are free to act independently. Control varied from the very precise schedule put forth, until recently, by states like New York to practically no regulations at all, as in Virginia. Some states allowed a surcharge to be added to local or intrastate toll calls as the hotel's fee for telephone service. Some

EXHIBIT 14–1

Shown is the policy regarding notice of a telephone surcharge as required by the State of Florida. Other states are enacting similar legislation.

A public lodging establishment which imposes a surcharge for any telephone call must post notice of such surcharge in a conspicuous place located by each telephone from which a call which is subject to a surcharge may originate. Such notice must be plainly visible and no less than 3 inches by 5 inches in size and such notice shall include whether or not a surcharge applies, whether or not the telephone call has been attempted or completed.

telephone companies paid a commission on intrastate calls, usually with a maximum fee per call, just as they did with interstate calls. Some states allowed both the surcharge and the commission.

As telephoning became a market-oriented business, New York State and others began enacting consumer legislation. The legislation was a reaction to price gouging by the hotel industry. That was the industry's initial response to the removal of restrictions by the PSCs. Fees of 300 to 400 percent were added to local charges. Calls that could be made for 25¢ or 50¢ from lobby pay phones cost $1 or $2 when made from the room. New York and several of the other states now require the amount of the surcharge to be posted conspicuously by the telephone (see Exhibit 14–1). The charge is not regulated, only the posting of notice. The difficulties encountered with alternative operator services, discussed later, have accelerated the passage of such legislation.

Historical Billing Procedures.   Before automation, the guest's telephone request was completed by the hotel's operator, who dialed the local call. Long-distance numbers were passed on to the telephone company operator, who dialed that connection. The front office posted to the guest folio from a voucher forwarded by the hotel's telephone operator. Local calls were billed at a fixed amount per state regulations. Long-distance charges were called in by the telephone company after the call was completed.

Because of the telephone industry's sophisticated technology, automated billing came to the hotel's telephone department years before property management systems were installed. Each step that will now be reviewed might not seem significant today, but each one brought an incremental improvement in speed and accuracy to the billing cycle.

Long-Distance Billing.   Semiautomation came first to long-distance (LD) billing. The first development allowed guests to bypass the hotel operator and dial the telephone company's long-distance operator directly. This system also allowed the telephone company to send room charges directly to the hotel by way of teletype.

The next development allowed the guest to dial directly into the telephone company equipment (HOBIC—see next section). Except for billing, the guest now bypassed even the telephone company's operator. The equipment completed the call, and the charge was again teletyped to the front desk for posting. The posting was either made to the hand folio or was entered manually into the PMS. The next step, and we are there now, eliminated the teletypewriter. Instead, the telephone computer posts the charge to the property management system computer. The guest's bill is updated automatically. Moreover, if the guest challenges the charge, the telephone number called can be displayed on the CRT or printed on the folio.

HOBIC.   **HOBIC** (Hotel Outward Bound Information Center) is an acronym for the telephone company's long-distance network. Even today, HOBIC is the system that guests encounter when they use AT&T's traditional service. HOBIC, the workhorse of the precomputerized system, is still an option for certain hotels.

With HOBIC, the guest direct-dials long-distance calls from the room telephone. The first digit dialed, 8, tells the system that long distance is going through. Digit 1, or digit 0 to get the operator, follows; then comes the number to be called. Zero-digit operator intercepts are for person-to-person calls, third-party calls, credit-card calls, and collect calls. The distinction between digit 1 and digit 0 is critical. It dictated the strategy of AT&T following deregulation. The pursuit of that strategy accounted in large measure for the appearance of the alternative operator services (AOS).

Local Billing.   The billing of local calls is at the same degree of automation as long-distance billing. Call accounting, which will be discussed shortly, identifies the calling room and "posts" the charge through an interface with the property management system, just as the long-distance equipment does.

Eliminating local telephone charges has gained some hotel industry support, but it has not been sustained. It will not be a viable option until the operating incomes and the expenses of the telephone department are resolved. Increasing room rates would recapture the lost telephone income and probably be less irritating on an incident-by-incident basis. Motel 6 is one company that makes no charge for local calls and no surcharge for long-distance calls.

Overseas Billing.   FCC regulations govern surcharges on overseas calls originating in the United States. Yet the FCC has no authority on calls originating overseas in other nations, even if the United States is the destination of the call. Unlike the American hotels prior to deregulation, overseas properties have long considered the telephone department as a profit center—a big profit center. Surcharges of up to five times the cost of the call shocked American visitors who were accustomed to domestic rates.

A flood of complaints poured into AT&T as international business and tourism swelled, bringing an increase in the number of intercountry calls. AT&T's Long Lines estimate that 63 percent of vacationers and 83 percent of business travelers call to the United States while abroad. In 1975, the Bell system introduced Teleplan.

Teleplan is a voluntary agreement to cap the international surcharge fee on guest calls. Marketing pressure, and marketing pressure alone, brought about the change. AT&T agreed to advise international travelers of participating hotels if the hotels agreed to surcharge limits.

Logically enough, the first participants were the international U.S. chains, whose guests were primarily Americans calling back home. Hilton International was the first to join. Other American companies followed, building competitive pressure on non-U.S. chains, national tourist offices, and hotel associations.

Pressure from AT&T combined with the pressure from knowledgeable travelers produced results. Surcharge fees were reduced, maximum fees were established, and all fees were advertised.

Teleplan has been successful where it has been adopted. Unfortunately, it has not received enthusiastic approval. Less than 5 percent of the world's 300,000 hotels have Teleplan in place. AT&T had to try something else: USADirect.[3]

USADirect service is an appeal to the good pocketbook sense of the overseas traveler. Callers are encouraged to bypass hotels that have been reluctant to negotiate away their generous surcharges. But the call can originate anywhere. By dialing a special access code, the caller reaches an AT&T operator in the United States. The call is completed at international, operator-assisted rates, plus the cost of the local call, although it might be a toll-free number. This approach—dial a local or toll-free access number, enter the long-distance number you are calling, and punch in your account code—is common to literally all of today's long-distance carriers.

What Happened after Deregulation

Following deregulation of the telephone industry in 1981, hoteliers settled down to the task of choosing among several alternatives. That choice sums up the intent of the deregulation. Alternatives could be pursued, new telephone companies could be tried, special equipment could be tested, and profits could be made.

With AT&T out of the commission business, the scramble for a viable replacement began. The one-year delay negotiated with the telephone company passed quickly as one plan after the other was suggested. Three options faced the hotel industry.

First Option—Status Quo.   A very workable option, but one that was initially ignored, was to maintain the status quo. Keeping the HOBIC system of AT&T, which was in place and working very well, would cost nothing. No heavy investment in capital equipment, no new training for front-office personnel, and no change in guest habits would be required. The equipment and procedures were still Bell's, so the infrastructure and support of the telephone company were still there.

This plan required the hotel to levy its own commission. Guest telephone charges increased, because the hotel continued to pay the telephone company the operator-assisted rates, and the hotel's fee was added on. Some price resistance did appear among the guests. Compared to what happened elsewhere, and compared to what happened later on with alternative operator services, the price increases were moderate.

The do-nothing decision proved a wise one for the small hotel. It provided the luxury of time to examine what was happening elsewhere. After the fact, many larger hotels wished they, too, had waited. Some decisions proved disastrous.

Second Option—Install CAS Equipment.   The same technology that AT&T was using—HOBIC—was available for hotel use in the form of a microprocessor called **AIOD.** AIOD, *Automatic Identification of Outward Dialing,* enabled the hotel to identify the calling guest's room number without an operator intercept from the telephone company. Charges went through at direct-distance dialing (DDD) rates, rather than operator-assisted rates. AIOD was installed on hotel switchboards, but not without difficulty. That's when some hoteliers first learned about the smart switches.

Bell competitors began selling and installing switchboards (**private branch exchanges—PBXs**) after the Carterfone decision. The PBX connects the numerous internal lines—there are 7,500 such lines at the Las Vegas Hilton—to the outside telephone system. But all PBXs are not equal.

EXHIBIT 14–2

This is a graphical representation of a call accounting system. The automatic answer detection function offers two distinct possibilities. The time-out feature is for older systems that cannot detect when the call has been answered—it charges after, for example, a one-minute grace period (even if the telephone is still ringing). The ring-back mechanism only charges if the call was answered.

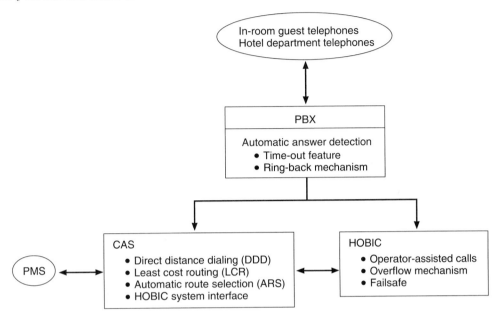

The potential of the new switchboards remained untapped until the need for identifying the room numbers arose. With smart switches in place, additional equipment like automatic identification of outward dialing (AIOD) or least cost routers (LCR) could be installed with little cost and difficulty (see Exhibit 14–2). Smart switches allowed the newest PBXs to function with AIOD and LCR as integral parts of the equipment. Additional property management capability could also be handled through the smart boards.

After committing to AIOD, many hoteliers learned, to their grief, that they had dumb switchboards. That opened a whole series of new decisions about which boards to acquire, from which company, with what options, and with whose money. It also opened the floodgates for unqualified third-party intermediaries to gain access to the unwary hotel industry.

One often-repeated story revolved around international calls. Most replacement carriers had no international capability. Nevertheless, hotels foolishly replaced all the HOBIC lines with their own. Even good call accounting systems leave some access to HOBIC. HOBIC serves as a failsafe mechanism, as an overflow mechanism, and as access to many places and services that other carriers do not provide (see Exhibit 14–2). Chief among these are the 0-digit services, including international calling.

Third Option—Shop the Competitors.   Other common carriers (OCC) were invited to compete with the Bell System and were assured *equal access* to residential and business users. Like third-party equipment purveyors, many companies appeared on the scene very early, yet only a few good ones remained after the shakeout.

EXHIBIT 14–3

Shown is a printout of long-distance charges generated by the call accounting system. The 555 exchange is used to mask actual telephone numbers; listen for its use in films and television.

	PLACE CALLED			NUMBER	TIME	MIN	TYP	CLASS	
A 2-22	LOS ANGELES	CA	213	555-7784	2245	6	1	S	1.51
A 2-22	HUNTITNBCH	CA	714	555-7711	1317	3	1	K	1.36
A 2-22	WICHITA	KS	316	555-5020	0747	2	1	B	.43
A 2-22	VAN NUYS	CA	213	555-7487	0916	2	1	K	.97
A 2-22	LEWISTON	ME	207	555-6141	1628	12	1	K	6.13
A 2-22	CHICAGO	IL	312	555-5134	1832	7	1	S	1.96
A 2-22	CANOGAPARK	CA	213	555-4815	1935	14	1	S	3.39
A 2-22	PHOENIX	AZ	602	555-4958	0810	2	1	K	.97
A 2-22	ROOPVILLE	GA	404	555-4422	0806	3	1	K	1.52
A 2-22	NO HOLLYWD	CA	213	555-9540	0908	1	1	K	.58
A 2-22	GREELEY	CO	303	555-5876	1750	38	1	S	9.91
A 2-22	STPETERSBG	FL	813	555-1411	1620	4	1	K	2.21
A 2-22	OCILLA	GA	912	555-7464	1238	1	1	K	.64
A 2-22	HUNTITNBCH	CA	714	555-7243	1801	5	1	S	1.28
A 2-22	CANOGAPARK	CA	213	555-4815	1114	8	1	K	3.31
A 2-22	CODY	WY	307	555-2245	1131	5	1	K	2.34
A 2-22	DRAPER	UT	801	555-5093	1745	3	1	S	.85
A 2-22	BOULDER	CO	303	555-1181	0902	7	1	K	3.20
A 2-22	LONG BEACH	CA	213	555-8832	1747	8	1	S	1.98
A 2-22	BAMMEL	TX	713	555-7580	0811	7	1	K	3.28
A 2-22	GREELEY	CO	303	555-7067	1723	10	1	S	2.69
A 2-22	FORD CITY	PA	412	555-9600	1656	12	1	K	4.56
A 2-22	LITTLETON	CO	303	555-9999	1331	2	1	K	1.05

* * * N24 * * *

Courtesy: Centel, Las Vegas, Nevada.

Among these are MCI, GTE (Sprint), and ITT. Many lesser-known names remain as resellers. They have no equipment of their own but buy AT&T WATS in bulk at discount and sell it to those hotels that have elected to go further into the telephone business.

Taking a quantum step, some hotels elected to move beyond call accounting by shopping among OCCs for the least expensive long-distance lines. To do this, more technology was needed—least cost routing (LCR) equipment. Here the emphasis is on the cost of the call, rather than the resale price. With reduced costs, small surcharges, which maintain the hotel's competitiveness, could produce substantial profit gains.

The smart switches of the LCR equipment working in tandem with the smart switches of the call accounting equipment evaluate each call and route it over the most economical trunk line. Eventually, the charge finds its way to the folio (see Exhibit 14–3). Cost of calls has come down, and gross income has gone up. The counterbalance has been the cost of the investment, of the consultants, and of the technology. Large commercial hotels, whose clients are heavy users of telephones, are able to amortize the costs more rapidly. They have a greater economic justification for their entry into the telephone business than do smaller hotels.

The role of the other players is equally clear. OCCs buck AT&T head-on, competing for customers and calling time (see Exhibit 14–4). Resellers buy large

Exhibit 14–4

Though still the leader, AT&T's market share has clearly eroded since deregulation in 1981.

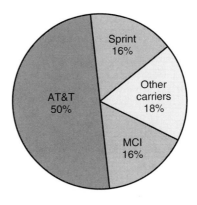

Exhibit 14–5

A baker's dozen of some clever seven-digit incoming 1–800 numbers found in the hospitality industry.

Company Name	Phone 1–800-
Clarion Hotels	Clarion
Club Med	Club Med
Colonial Williamsburg	History
Embassy Suites	Embassy
Harrah's (Atlantic City)	2 Harrah
Hilton Hotels	Hiltons
Marriott Hotels & Resorts	USA WKND
National Car Rental	Car Rent
Nikko Hotels International	Nikko US
Omni Hotels	The Omni
Ramada Hotels	2 Ramada
Southwest Airlines	I Fly SWA
Stouffer Renaissance Hotels	Hotels 1

quantities of discounted transmission capacity from AT&T or the OCCs and try to market it to the hotel as part of their least cost routing purchases.

WATS.   Like so much of the telecommunications field, **Wide Area Telephone Service** (sometimes called Wide Area Transmission Service), commonly called **WATS,** is putting on a new face. The original concept of one flat, monthly fee, for which the user could talk indefinitely at any time, has been modified. Charges are now based on increments of time. Rates vary according to the time of the day and the day of the week.

Hundreds of companies have gone into the resale of WATS lines. They buy long-distance lines from AT&T and other OCCs at quantity discounts and resell to customers at a lesser charge than the common carriers.

In-WATS (incoming toll-free 1–800 numbers) have a critical role in the development of central reservation offices, as Chapter 4 explained. It has become quite fashionable to substitute catchy phrases for traditional telephone numbers in an attempt to retain the number in the user's memory (see Exhibit 14–5).

Out-WATS have a critical role in call accounting system profitability. Hotels that route guest long-distance calls over WATS lines may save substantially over normal long-distance costs. These savings may be returned to the guest or are more likely converted into additional hotel profit.

Later Developments

The deregulation and divestiture of the telephone system is a lengthy affair. All of the problems are not behind us. Some new ones lie ahead. Some that lie ahead for the hotel business are the result of a long-lived strategy of AT&T, either planned or accidental. Alternative operator services is the most aggravating strategy of that group.

Alternative Operator Services.   Almost from the start, AT&T's attitude seems to have been antihotel. It dissolved the commission arrangement early on and lost the business of the hotel industry, which it probably could have had for the asking. Immediately afterward, AT&T began a campaign to convert hotel telephone users, mostly businesspersons, to credit cards and away from direct dialing in the guest rooms. It was not of AT&T's doing, but the price gouging by the hotels played into its hands. As guests grew angry about the unreasonable charges being levied by greedy hotels, they turned toward services for which the hotels did not charge—0-digit dialing. Many of the 0-digit charges required the credit card that AT&T was pushing.

Almost all hotels retained a HOBIC line regardless of whether they accepted another common carrier or installed call accounting. Some of the designated carriers did not operate 24 hours a day, did not reach every telephone in the United States, did not have international access, or did not provide 0-digit services. Hotels needed HOBIC lines.

Higher utilization of 0-digit calls meant less revenue for the hotel's call accounting system. Hotels weren't happy about that, especially in light of their significant investment (installation runs $1,000 to $1,500 per room) and monthly maintenance (monthly maintenance services cost around $20 per room) expenses. Therefore, the hotel industry was once again ripe for another round of third-party vendor promises.

The Good, Bad, and Ugly of AOS Services.   The positive side of alternative operator services (AOS) was money. AT&T had been very successful in its campaign. Direct dialing dropped from approximately 50 percent of the volume to about 20 percent. AT&T countered the industry's move toward AOS by resuming its commission on 0-digit dialing. To be eligible, the hotel must provide millions of call-minutes per month and pay a large monthly service fee. Effectively, only the large hotels were qualified. Besides, there was more money to the hotels from the higher commissions of the AOS.

High commissions from AOSs meant that the guests are paying high fees to get the service. That is the negative side of AOS. Although high rates can be explained, hotels didn't bother to do so. Guests were shocked when the charges arrived by way of their monthly business or residential bill. That sometimes took weeks, because the AOS had to run the charge through the local or regional telephone companies. And the fees were high—as much as 10 times the prevailing AT&T rate!

The hotel industry was back to the very same problem and to the very same, unsatisfactory, solution that it employed at the time of call accounting. Rates were exorbitant, third-party vendors were unreliable. AT&T was aloof, and the U.S. government was wondering whether it had done the right thing after all.

Ticking off the reasons for the high rates does little to appease guests. Here they are, anyway. Hotels want their commission, the bigger the better. AOS companies have their own expenses and profits. The cost of the call still has to be paid, even with discounted lines that may be greater than AT&T rates. The call needs to go to the operator center of the AOS. That's the first charge. The call is then forwarded to the AOS connection center, which might actually be in the direction opposite to the direction in which the call is headed, (''back-hauling''). Tack on another charge. When the call is completed through AT&T or the OCC, another cost is added. Finally, there is a 50¢ fee to get the local telephone companies to include the charge and collect the billing.

AOS Regulations.   The biggest and loudest complaints came from guests who were unaware of how the system worked and how much it cost. Hotels never told their guests things like: ''If there is no answer in 10 rings (or 45 seconds), you will be charged nevertheless''; ''If you use our convenient in-room AOS, the charge might be 10 times the AT&T operator-assisted rate''; ''If you prefer to 'splash off' the AOS and use AT&T, here's how to do it.''

Companies such as Stouffers heard the complaints and eliminated all 8–0 service charges. Others didn't hear and left the listening to the FCC and the state PSCs. On April 27, 1989, the FCC followed the lead of several states (Exhibit 14–1) and required that notice be posted. Moreover, it required that ''call blocking,'' which prevents a caller from reaching a competitive carrier, be halted.

Extreme problems beget extreme solutions. Several states—and Alabama has led the way—have disqualified AOS operations in their jurisdictions. Other states are controlling AOSs through price caps. Even federal legislation has redefined responsibilities and limitations. With the handwriting on the wall, the AOSs have combined to form a trade association, have implemented a code of ethics, and have started to repair the damage.

Other Telephone Considerations.   Aside from the preceding CAS discussion, there are numerous additional telephone-related issues for hotel management to consider. Among the most profitable may be the pay phone.

Profitable Pay Phones.   First it was call accounting, then AOS, and now pay phones. Of course, the scope is far greater than the hotel business. Whereas call accounting affected chiefly aggregators—hotels, hospitals, and dormitories—the deregulation of pay telephones touches the gas station, the convenience store, the shopping mall, the airport, and many, many more locations, restaurants included.

Anyone can own a telephone. That means anyone can own a pay phone. In the airport, the owner could be the airport authority. In the convenience store, it might be the 7-Eleven chain. And in the lobby, it is the hotel. Anyone who has done a modicum of travel has seen the variety of telephones in the national airports: phones for each company, one phone for all companies, phones that operate on credit-card magnetic strips, phones that operate with cash, phones in calling centers. The race is on.

Into the marketplace have come all of the players that we have seen before: the OCCs and the AOSs. And their roles and motivations are pretty much the same as they were with call accounting and 0+ calling: fees and commissions. It all came to a head on January 1, 1990, when pay phone locations (hotels, for example) were ordered to select a long-distance carrier. (Remember, interstate calls are controlled at the federal level.)

Hotels see profits as they did with call accounting. Instead of a paltry $30 per month from a 15 percent commission on an AT&T phone, they can get four times that much from a vending machine company partnership, and even more from out-right ownership. Furthermore, if they own their own instruments, nothing can stop them from running local calls through their own switchboard, long-distance calls through their call accounting system, and 0+ calls through their AOS. And the revenues are staggering. The typical gas station pay phone generates $350 to $400 per month. Hotel lobby pay phones often experience substantially higher revenues.

1–900 Premium-Priced Calls (PPCs).   Guests contact 1–900 numbers for a wide range of activities, including sports scores, horoscopes, trivia contests, opinion polls, stock quotes—and pornographic sex hotlines. Generally, PCCs charge guests for each minute they are on-line with the 1–900 number. Charges may range from under $1 per minute to as high as a $100 flat fee per call. However, no matter what the purpose or cost of the call, the hotel rarely shares in the revenue.

Here's how it works. The call accounting system only charges the guest's folio for the toll charge of the call. In some cases, this is a local call with maybe a $.50 charge attached. In other cases, it may post as a long-distance call generating, say, $.25 per minute. In any event, the guest is long gone when the 1–900 service charge shows up on the hotel's monthly telephone billing statement. Many hoteliers have been hit for thousands of dollars in uncollectible PPCs in a single month.

Although most telephone companies will forgo the charges for one month if the hotel complains, that is merely a short-term solution. More permanent solutions include the following:

1. Block all 1–900 telephone calls from the source. Sophisticated CASs can differentiate 1–900 prefix calls and prevent connection from occurring.

2. If the call accounting system cannot block the calls, possibly the local telephone company can. There may be a charge for this 1–900 prefix block, but it is probably money well spent.

3. If neither of the above-mentioned electronic solutions will work, good old-fashioned manual labor certainly will. During the night audit shift each day, have an employee search the printed CAS revenue report line by line. This report prints every single phone number dialed throughout the entire day from each hotel room. Check the report for phone numbers beginning with a 1–900 prefix. When found, charge the guest's folio some exorbitant fee—such as $100 for each call.

Feature Phones.   Today's in-room guest telephones have the capacity to perform a multitude of functions not generally associated with telephones. These "feature" phones have met with outstanding approval from hotel guests. Today, many hotels implement these phones as an added guest-room amenity for corporate travelers.

Feature phones are generally built with a data port to enable the guest to transmit or receive information via an attached personal computer. Indeed, many of these telephones have two lines—to permit the guest to talk on one line while receiving data on the second. Feature phones also offer one-button speed dialing to in-house departments or local merchants (who pay for the convenience of a captive audience). In addition, they usually offer a hold button and call-waiting function. Such phones are commonly found with a built-in speakerphone, alarm clock, and even an AM/FM radio.

Telephones of a higher (and more expensive) class are commonly referred to as *hard-wired multipurpose phones.* These phones may cost the property $500 or more per unit, but are easily justified from an energy-savings standpoint. Hard-wired telephones are available that can regulate temperature levels in the room; control as many as six remote lighting fixtures; turn the television set on, change the channels, and adjust the volume; open and close the curtains; and even change the room status to ''do not disturb.''

Many hard-wired telephones require the guest to activate the room by inserting a keycard in a specially designed slot. When the room is unoccupied, the system automatically disengages most lights, the television, the air conditioner, and some of the electrical outlets.

Guest-Room Locking Systems

All guests, corporate and vacationing travelers alike, demand safety and security in the guest room. Certain guest markets (e.g., corporate female travelers) place hotel security near the very top of their list when selecting a chain or independent hotel. And guests are not alone in their quest for enhanced security.

Hotel employees, managers, and owners are equally concerned with providing high levels of guest security. In the wake of numerous lawsuits charging hotels with inadequate standards of security, a heightened awareness has ensued. This awareness has not been lost on the insurance companies, either. Most insurers of lodging properties offer deep discounts for modern electronic security improvements such as electronic locking systems, property surveillance systems, and fire-system monitoring devices.

Major chains have also taken guest security to heart in recent years. A number of chains recommend (and some even require) that electronic security devices be installed in all new construction. Indeed, even AAA includes guest security protection as part of its property rating system!

Although security involves surveillance, intrusion detection, fire prevention, employee screening, and numerous other concerns, initial efforts have been directed toward lock and key security. It's here that some of the electronic smart switches hold the greatest promise.

Room Key Distribution

Even small lodging properties (100 to 200 rooms) find themselves inventorying and distributing hundreds if not thousands of keys per year. Keys are maintained for each of the guest rooms. In addition, keys are used to secure supplies, offices and sensitive areas, records, food and beverage centers, materials, dangerous locations, and cash. Each of these locked locations requires a number of keys because there may be several authorized key holders and the hotel maintains a copy of every outstanding key on the property. Indeed, the key cabinet, which maintains a copy of all keys on the property, is itself kept—you guessed it—under lock and key!!

With smart switches, there are no keys to track. The key is disposable or renewable, and each guest gets a new key and a new key combination. With traditional keys, the types that are still used in homes, key loss is staggering. Estimates put the number at one key per room each month. Many hotels have four or five lost keys per day. Before smart switches, lock replacement for Holiday Inns, for example, was pegged at $1 million annually.

There is a strong black market for hotel keys (up to $1,000 for a master key), and many hotel employees know about it. Forced entry into guest rooms is almost unknown, because access through stolen, duplicated, or master key blanks is so easy. One group of blitzers (6- to 10-person units) "did" nearly 200 rooms in Anaheim, California, in one morning. And *Los Angeles Magazine* reported the capture of one individual who had master keys for 17 hotels.

Those kinds of statistics, and the potential liability they represent, have made hoteliers quick converts to the smart switch electronic locking system (ELS).

Levels of Access.   Control of keys begins with an understanding of the kind and number of keys available. Most key systems are comprised of four or five levels of access. Although modern electronic locking systems have changed the format of that access, the terminology and the service performed by each level remain the same.

For the most part, each level of the hierarchy exceeds the level below. The guest-room key level (and the failsafe level) can access only one room. The next level, the maid or housekeeping level, can access an entire wing of rooms. The third level, the general manager or master level, can access the entire hotel property. And the final level, the emergency or E-key level, can access the entire property even when the guest-room deadbolt has been activated.

Although the levels of hierarchy are much the same with both ELS and standard hardware locking systems, electronic locking systems add a new dimension of security. The most recent electronic keycard being used can be designed to override and invalidate previous keycard combination codes.

For example, Daniel Adams checks into room 1111 on Monday evening. On Tuesday morning, Adams checks out of the hotel. Because the ELS keycard is disposable, he keeps the card as a souvenir for his daughter. Later in the morning, Adams realizes that he has left his wallet hidden in the room. Retrieving the keycard from his pocket, Adams is able to enter the room and find his wallet. That's because the hotel front desk has not yet rented room 1111 to a new guest.

Later in the morning, a maid inserts her housekeeping keycard and enters room 1111. Although she accessed the room after Adams, inserting a housekeeping card in the lock does not invalidate the guest's (Adams's) card. That's because the maid's card is on a separate level of the hierarchy. At this point, Adams could still access room 1111. Still later in the day, room 1111 is rented to Elizabeth Brown. Her insertion of the new guest level keycard into the lock electronically invalidates Adams's card. In fact, Brown's card is designed to invalidate all guest-level keycards with lower code sequences than her own. Likewise, Brown's card can only be overridden with a higher coded card inserted by the next new guest to check in to room 1111.

This scenario is true for most electronic locking systems in use today. However, some hotels have a more expensive hard-wired electronic locking system in place. A hard-wired ELS literally connects each room doorlock to the front-desk computer system. Therefore, with a hard-wired system, Adams's key would have been invalidated at the time he checked out (remember that in the Adam example, a new keycard must physically be inserted in the doorlock to invalidate the previous code).

The Guest-Room Key.   The single guest key, which fits either a standard bolt and deadlock (see Exhibit 14–6), an electronic lock (see Exhibit 14–7), or a nonelectronic lock (see Exhibit 14–8), gives the guest access to the room. It opens no other

EXHIBIT 14–6

Traditional key-in-knob locks are generally inadequate without an additional mortise, deadlock bolt. This lock is rekeyed by replacing the interchangeable core cylinder using a control key.

Courtesy: Schlage Lock Company, San Francisco, California.

room regardless of the size of the hotel. Two or three of the guest-room (sometimes called *change*) keys are available for guest use, with an equal number in reserve (see Exhibit 14–9). Rigid knobs on the corridor side of the guest room door prevent access to the room except by this key. And once the door is locked from within, all but emergency keys are shut out.

Locking the door from inside trips a signal that tells the room attendant that the room is occupied. This device is disappearing. Signal systems of all types—Do Not Disturb signs, lock signals, light systems, room service trays left in the corridor, signals on latches, and message notes on the door—tell the thief as well as the housekeeper whether the room is occupied.

Burglars have been known to enter a room marked by the guest to be made up, change the sign to Do Not Disturb, and finish their business in peace. Thieves will also enter when they hear the shower running. Knowing that the occupant is in the bath allows the intruder to work in the room without fear of being caught. For a similar reason, entries are often attempted while the guest is asleep. Burglars have an edge when they know where their victims are. Estimates suggest that one in every three guests fails to double-lock the door.

A guest might have several keys on the hotel key chain. In addition to the room key, an elevator key might be issued for access to the concierge floor. There might be a key for an in-room bar or a stocked refrigerator. In-room safes also have keys, as do special security closets within the room.

The Failsafe Key.   The second level in the key distribution hierarchy is only found with electronic locking systems. The failsafe level provides a preestablished option for use during computer downtime. Most hotels create at least two failsafe keys for each guest room. Once created, failsafe keys are secured by management until they are needed.

When the host ELS computer is down (inoperative), either due to a power outage or a hardware/software operations problem, the hotel resorts to the use of failsafe keys. Just like a new guest keycard, failsafe keys invalidate previous guest-level keycards. Yet failsafe keys do not alter the normal sequence of guest-level

EXHIBIT 14–7

Recodable electronic locks offer great versatility. The ELS keys themselves may look traditional (upper left illustration), or like plastic credit cards (upper right illustration). Any key format is possible as long as it provides a magnetic strip.

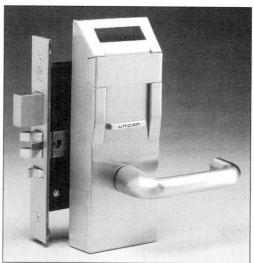

Courtesy: ILCO Unican, Inc., Montreal, Quebec.

key codes. They temporarily interrupt the stream of codes, but once the ELS computer is operational again, the new guest-level keycard will invalidate the failsafe key and everything will be back to normal.

Hotels create two failsafe keys to gain plenty of time. Two failsafe keys are good for two new check-ins. That's at least two days of failsafe operation. Once the ELS computer comes back on-line, front-office management will create new backup failsafe keys, always keeping at least two such keys in storage for another down period.

The Maid or Pass Key.   The next highest level in the key hierarchy is the maid level, also known as the housekeeping level, the pass key level, the submaster level,

EXHIBIT 14–8

A nonelectronic locking system utilizes mechanical hardware. As a result, there are no batteries, electrical connections, or host computers. Yet these nonelectronic locks are still able to change the lock code with each new guest key; they do so magnetically.

Courtesy: CORKEY Control Systems, Hayward, California.

the section level, or area key level. Each maid-level key controls the room attendant's section of the floor, usually 12 to 18 rooms. Since the pass key fits no other subset, both the hotel and the individual room attendant are protected. Well-trained employees of every department refuse guests' requests to be admitted to certain rooms. Pass keys are used for this purpose only after proper authorization is obtained from the desk.

Room attendants must not permit guests without identification—that is, a room key—to enter open rooms where they are working. Similarly, rooms must not be left unlocked if the room attendant is called away before the room is completed. Locked drop boxes welded to the housekeeping cart reduce a very common source of lost keys. Obviously, then, the room attendant's own keys should not be hung on the cart or left in the door or remain unattended in the floor linen closet. Employees must be trained to stay on the alert. For every pathetic-guest-in-a-wet-bathing-suit ruse that is uncovered, thieves will create another equally appealing stunt.

The Master Key.   The master or general manager level may be next in the key hierarchy. However, depending on the design of the hotel, there are a number of key hierarchy possibilities between the maid level and the master level. For example, some properties may wish to create an inspector- or floor-level key. This level would exceed the maid's key (which opens something like 12 to 18 rooms) by opening all rooms on a given floor or section (probably 60 to 100 rooms).

Another possibility is an executive housekeeping–level key that would probably open every room in the hotel. The difference between the executive housekeeping level and the general manager or master level is that the executive housekeeper is restricted from access to certain high-security areas. While the general manager level will access all locks in the hotel, the executive housekeeper may be denied access to such areas as the accounting office, the food and beverage department, and other administrative offices.

The Emergency Key. The highest level in the hierarchy is the emergency or E-key (sometimes called the grand master). Like the general manager-level key, the E-key can access every lock in the hotel. The difference is that the emergency key can access all rooms regardless of lock status. In other words, even when the guest has activated the deadbolt from inside the room, the E-key can still gain access. During periods of extreme emergency—for example, a guest has taken ill and cannot answer the door, or the fire department needs to enter a guest room—the E-key can literally be the difference between life or death!

Securing Keys and Locks. The loss of guests' personal belongings from their rooms can be traced to three causes: outsiders (intruders), insiders (employees), and the guests themselves. The smart-switch locks of modern technology have affected primarily the outsiders. However, there have been important spinoffs protecting the hotel from insiders and even from guests. Careless guests lose, misplace, forget, and accuse. Dishonest guests manipulate their hotel stays to bring claims against the property or against their own insurance companies.

The director of research and security for the AH&MA maintains that 30 percent of employees are honest; 30 percent are dishonest; and 40 percent must be protected from themselves—as opportunists, they will take advantage of weaknesses in the system.

The ELS Identification System. Electronic locking systems provide the best line of defense against unethical guests, employees, and even outsiders. That is because the ELS is a smart switch capable of communicating critical information to management.

Many a manager has dealt with an upset guest accusing a hotel employee of theft. In some cases, guests are correct about the employee who has wronged them; in other instances, guests are incorrect. Maybe the ''stolen'' wristwatch was merely misplaced, lost, or never packed in their luggage in the first place.

Answers to such questions and accusations are ready and waiting inside the microprocessor of the ELS. Hotel management need merely download the information to a handheld computer (or, in the case of a hard-wired ELS, the front-desk computer can access the information) to learn which keycards have accessed the guest's room during the period in question. Most systems hold at least the last dozen keycard entries—other systems hold substantially more. In many cases, the ELS keycard–access database provides enough information to solve the ''crime.''

Standard Key Identification Systems. Guests no longer return and retrieve the key several times during their stays. That's not true in certain foreign countries. Very heavy tags are still used on keys in Europe. Rarely does the guest carry such large keys away.

Encouraging guests to keep their keys means that they often take them home. Training cashiers and members of the uniformed services department (bellpersons, door attendants, and courtesy van drivers) to ask outgoing guests for the key is a simple idea that has never caught on. Most guests just need a reminder. Key drop boxes with printed reminders by exit doors, on courtesy buses, even at the airport (as a joint community effort) will trigger key returns. What about a sign that reads, ''You're not checked out until your key's checked in''?

Until as late as the 1980s, keys were completely identified as to room number, hotel, and address. A special arrangement was negotiated between the hotel association and the post office. Hotels would pay the postage on keys returned without an envelope through the mail. As security problems grew, the name and address were replaced by a post office box number. It was mere illusion. There was no difficulty in identifying the hotel when it was the only one in town, or when it had a distinct numbering system, or when the same box number appeared on the stationery.

Increased postage costs helped the decision, but it was security that ultimately forced hotels to drop all identification from the keys. Hotels that continue to use key identification place themselves in a precarious legal position. Even for internal use, room numbers no longer appear on keys.

Key identification grows less important as electronic locks, which use disposable keys, grow more popular. If anything, the trend might be accelerating. The hard, plastic, take-home key is a good means of advertising the hotel's In-WATS reservation number. The idea is valid enough to convince some sales departments to share the budget costs of key production with the rooms (or the engineering) department.

Personnel.   Security deals as much with people and procedures as with locks and keys. Security begins with the employment process. Good employment practices may be difficult to maintain as the labor pool shrinks during the nation's march toward the year 2000.

Control must be established over the numbers of employees who have legitimate access to keys. That includes all the front-office and uniformed service personnel, the housekeeping staff, and the maintenance crews—well over half of all the employees in the hotel. Control must be established on the distribution of keys to the vast number of guests who make legitimate demands for access to their rooms.

An earlier discussion pointed out what the room attendants and the housekeeping department must and must not do with keys on the guest-room floors. Good key security invariably focuses back on the front desk. Clerks must never issue keys without verifying the guest's identity, a procedure that takes but seconds with a rack or a computer. Still, in the pressure of the rush hours, many keys are issued with abandon. Almost anyone can request a key and get it.

Well-publicized lawsuits with huge settlements have pounded security into the minds of every hotel manager. Security is a serious matter. That's the attitude that must be instilled in the staff, who may otherwise treat the subject rather nonchalantly.

Physical alterations emphasize the personnel changes. Lobby designs now consider security. Garage elevators, for example, are no longer directly connected to the sleeping room core. Garage elevators return to the lobby so that front-office personnel can get a good look at the riders.

Hardware.   If the reported and unreported losses from guest rooms truly equal the $5,000 per room per year figure that is often quoted, there is strong economic incentive for buying the very best of locks.

Among the simple pieces of hardware being introduced are peepholes (observation ports), a code requirement in some jurisdictions, and chain latches. Latch guards are either of the chain-and-slide-variety or a simple cable chain looped from the door stud over the knob. Even though these devices (or others like Charlie bars on sliding doors) are provided, some guests opt not to use them. Reminders attached to the outside door, notices on the rooming slips, and bureau cards try to convince the guest to participate in his or her own security.

Doors, along with their frames, hinges, and pins, must be heavy and solid, especially those on motel units that open onto a parking lot. Space between the door frame (or door jamb) and the wall stud allows the frame to be spread, disengaging the lock.

All security devices should be cleared first with the fire marshall. Most fire codes, for example, require the deadbolt and the doorknob to be operated as one from inside the room. If the guest panics because of an emergency, the deadbolt is released with the turn of the knob.

Types of Locking Systems

There are three basic types of guest-room doorlocks available in the marketplace. The most basic of these locks is the standard mechanical keyed doorlock found in older lodging properties and personal residences. Next in line in terms of sophistication is the nonelectronic locking system doorlock. Nonelectronic locking systems offer many of the positive attributes found in ELS locks but cost substantially less. Electronic locking systems are the third type of doorlock available. ELSs come in both microfitted and hard-wired systems.

Standard Mechanical Doorlocks.   Although the handwriting is on the wall, even for mom-and-pop operations, mechanical locks are still widely used. They are more appropriate for the small property, which can track the history of the individual room lock. Rekeying mechanical locks can be done only by going from door to door and only by keeping good records. That's not feasible with large hotels, which favor the smart switches and their remote rekeying capability.

Changing Locks.   Changing locks originally meant just that: moving the entire lock from one room to another. Relocating locks is costly and time-consuming. Security for this type of system usually involves a total rekeying of the entire hotel once every 5 to 10 years. Individual rekeying is undertaken only in special circumstances. Special circumstances are generally ''after the fact,'' and fail to meet court definitions of reasonable care. With new technology, the method of rotating mechanical locks has changed.

One system uses a *removable lock core*. With a twist, a control key removes the whole pin-tumbler combination, allowing it to be used in some other housing. The key core is replaced with a different core using a different key. The lock housing remains intact. It is a rapid and effective means of rotating locks for either emergency situations or periodic replacements.

The other innovation, *changeable tumblers,* is even simpler. The change is made in the tumblers without removing the core. It is the key, not the tumbler, that is replaced (see Exhibit 14–10). Initially, a new cylinder is put into the current mortise hardware. Thereafter, rekeying is done at the door without removing the tumblers, the core, or the hardware.

Rekeying time is less than one minute for both the guest key and the master key, according to the manufacturer. Keys are not discarded; they are reused. A removable, colored room number disk snaps in and out of the key, which permits

EXHIBIT 14–10

Rekeying this deadbolt lock is done externally by changing the key, not the tumbler core, using two keyways for the master and the guest keys. The deadbolt portion of the lock should be no less than 5/8 inch square and should protrude into the frame more than 1/2 inch. Some jurisdictions are mandating 3/4 to 1 inch.

Courtesy: Winfield Locks, Inc., Costa Mesa, California.

the key to be used in other rooms. Changing disk colors distinguishes previously used keys from the combination currently in use.

Nonelectronic Locking Systems.   Access by nonelectronic keycard is a form of mechanical system. Because a card is used, there is often confusion between this mechanical system and electronic ones. Sometimes, even those managing the property don't know which system they have.

The mechanical lock uses a snap-off card with holes in the plastic (Exhibit 14–8). According to one manufacturer, 4 billion combinations are possible. Both sides of the card have the same configuration. The door opens when the configuration of holes on the guest card, inserted from the corridor, coincides with the configuration on the control card, which is inserted from the room side.

One variation employs a separate cylinder lock for access by employees and management. Changes can be made in the cylinder lock for the master, grandmaster, and E-keys without altering the guest card entry. In another variation, each change in the guest card is made without adjusting the cylinder access.

The recodeable cylinder is like the changeable tumblers just described. The whole system is like all the other mechanical systems. Someone needs to come to the door and change the card. The change could be done by the bellperson each and every time a new guest is roomed. The bellperson, who gains access through the cylinder lock, breaks off the card parts and completes the rekeying. Rekeying need not be done with each guest.

Benefits of a Nonelectronic System.   There are several reasons a hotel might select a nonelectronic locking system. First, when compared to standard mechanical locks, nonelectronic locking systems are far superior. Their rapid rekeying feature is foremost on the list of advantages over the traditional keyed lock.

In addition, nonelectronic locking systems offer many of the security advantages associated with electronic locking systems. Similar to an ELS, a new guest keycard inserted in the lock will invalidate the previous guest's card. Indeed, hotel managers who select nonelectronic locking systems can provide a strong defense in

court that their hotels are providing reasonable care and proper levels of guest security. However, the biggest reason newly constructed properties choose nonelectronic locking systems is cost—they are significantly less expensive than even the
cheapest of electronic locking systems.

Electronic Locking Systems.   Although electronic locking systems are the best of
all guest-room door-locking systems, they are expensive. Average costs range in
the neighborhood of $150 to $350 per door plus the cost of the dedicated computer
processor, one or more key-writing terminals, an audit trail interrogator, a printer,
software, and programming. Yet most newly constructed properties are installing
electronic locking systems. The price only seems high until you analyze the
alternatives.

Electronic locks save direct expenses in two ways—labor and key cost. They
also provide less direct monetary savings in terms of lower insurance premiums,
reduced liability risk, happier guests, and less property theft. In terms of direct
expenses, let's look at the experience of the San Diego Marriott Hotel and Marina.

This property was originally constructed with a standard mechanical locking
system in all 682 rooms. Today, this property has retrofitted an electronic locking
system in its original rooms, and here's why. Guests were constantly losing or
misplacing room keys. According to the property's chief engineer, it was not uncommon for the Marriott to rekey up to 40 rooms per day! Each lost room key
required the maintenance person to rekey the lock, make four copies of the key, and
log in each one. Key blanks cost $2 each (compared to electronic keycards, which
cost only about $.10 each). But the real expense was not key blanks; it was labor.
The maintenance department spent upwards of 30 hours per week rekeying doorlocks. Today, that same property spends less than three hours per week rekeying its
electronic locks.

Electric Power.   The system is energized either by a hard-wire hookup using utility
power or by a battery power pack on the door. The hard-wire installations have more
capability, but they are far more costly. Each door must be cabled to the console at
the front desk (there are also systems that use radio waves to communicate with the
front desk). This proves too expensive for retrofits, which tend toward the microfitted electronic systems.

Hard-wire installations need to provide for power failures, which make the locks
inoperative. One seldom-used option is a battery pack on each door. The batteries
have a life of one to three years. Small, portable computers with auxiliary power
packs can be carried door to door. However, that's not much of an option if the
entire system goes down. Large, centralized power packs are generally used, unless
the hotel has emergency generators that back up the entire hotel during power
failures.

The Control Center.   The control center is at the front desk, where the key is issued
as part of the registration process. What happens there depends on whether the
system is hard-wired or microfitted.

If the system is hard-wired, then the code in the card that is processed at the
time of registration is forwarded over the wires (or radio waves) to the lock in the
door. Hard-wiring makes the door code and the console code at the desk one and
the same. A self-correcting feature verifies the accuracy of the keycard, saving the
guest from a duplicate trip to the desk because the card doesn't work.

EXHIBIT 14–11

Combinations for individual room keycards are processed at the console in the front office. Each guest receives a disposable key, and the combination is changed between occupants.

Courtesy: ILCO Unican, Inc., Montreal, Quebec.

As previously discussed, microfitted electronic locking systems communicate with the desk by way of the keycard. Physically inserting the keycard in the lock updates the code sequence in the doorlock with the code sequence maintained at the front-desk control center (see Exhibit 14–11). If the two code sequences (the front-desk computer and the guest-room doorlock) become out of sync with each other, the doorlock may fail to accept the guest's keycard.

Assume that an arriving guest on the way to the room changes his mind. He returns to the desk, changes rooms, or leaves (DNS). The desk issued a key, which used the next sequence on the console. The key was not used, so the sequence in the lock was not advanced. Each time such an event occurs, the codes in the lock and the console become farther apart. Eventually, the door won't open. Several other causes account for a misplaced sequence, but the problem isn't frequent, so it isn't a serious one.

The Keycard.   A variety of codeable keys are in use, including some that look like conventional metal keys and others that resemble military dog tags (see Exhibit 14–7). In addition, there are "traditional" plastic cards and even some keypads in use. A keypad by the guest door eliminates even the semblance of a key. Access is gained by punching in a code (for example, a birthdate or an anniversary). Since the use of the plastic card has applications beyond mere entry to the room, the keypad is not likely to replace the card as standard equipment.

A small, green light, an audible beep, or sometimes both, indicates that the connection is made. That same signal alerts the room attendant to weak batteries that need replacing. As a security measure—no chance of leaving the key in the door—the lock will not operate until the key is removed. If the guest fails to act in time, the process needs to be repeated.

Other Common Interfaces

As hotels continue their trek and investment towards a fully automated and fully integrated property, a number of decisions face management. Depending on the size, type, age, and market of the property, certain applications and potential interfaces become more or less necessary. Whenever management seeks to enhance its current system, it must ask itself a series of questions.

Prior to the Interface

Although the questions below are designed around the concept of interfaced systems applications, they are probably appropriate for any hotel investment—management should ask the questions and analyze the answers before making any investment. The following is a partial list of considerations management should undertake prior to performing a system interface.

Degradation.   Management should first ask: *Will the interfaced system degrade my existing PMS?* Interfaced applications have a dedicated central processing unit and only "poll" or communicate with the host PMS. Still, interfaces act as "phantom" users, and there are limits to the numbers and types of interfaces appropriate for each property management system. When degradation occurs, the speed of the host PMS slows down. This slower operating time may affect service levels as well as guest and employee satisfaction.

It is critical to assess the degree of degradation that will occur prior to performing the interface. If the PMS is appreciably slowed, significant new hardware and software investment may be necessary. Clearly, then, management should apprise itself of this additional potential cost well in advance of performing the interface.

Synergy.   Another question management should ask itself is: *What is the synergistic value from the interface?* Most interfaces provide added value (synergy) to the existing property management system. For example, rather than manually turning on guest-room telephones and tracking, pricing, and posting calls, the electronic interface between the CAS and the PMS performs those functions automatically. However, if there is little or no synergy to be gained, management would be wise to forgo the interface.

Cost–Benefit.   Another question that must clearly be addressed asks: *Is there a positive cost–benefit relationship?* Management needs to clearly understand its purpose for the interface, the value added from this new application, and the cost of installing the system. If long-term employee and/or guest benefits are something less than the investment required for the hardware, software, training, and service, management might reconsider the venture.

There is currently a trend to automate everything in sight. Rather than analyzing the cost–benefit relationship, many properties merely follow the industry trend. Yet the reasons for interfacing applications are different for each property. If management cannot answer the cost–benefit question, it should not make the investment.

Has It Been Done Before?   Finally, management might ask: *Is this interface possible with my existing PMS?* Although less a problem with today's modern systems, some applications are simply not compatible (refer to the section earlier in this chapter on uniform connectivity). Management should be wary of interfacing two distinct vendors if no other property has successfully performed this feat. Unless the software companies are willing to perform the job with specific guarantees, stay away.

Although this is a legitimate list of questions a property must ask before acquiring a new interface, few properties go through this process. That is because most hotels follow the pack and install proven systems. There is very little first-time experimentation taking place in the hotel industry. Indeed, hotels have never had a pioneering spirit in terms of automation. Hoteliers exhibit a follow-the-leader mentality. They let other industries (e.g., the retail and airline sectors) perform the initial research and development, then let vendors tell them just exactly what they need, waiting patiently and watching a long while before making their own investments.

With this in mind, the remainder of this chapter examines several of the more popular—and proven—PMS interfaces.

Other PMS Interfaces

Aside from call accounting and electronic locking systems, there are several other common PMS interfaces. A sophisticated, fully integrated property might also boast a point-of-sale system (POS), an energy management system (EMS), and additional phone services.

Point-of-Sale.   Point-of-sale (POS) systems provide true synergy to the hotel operation in terms of labor savings, lower transcription error rates, and reduced late charges. That is because the POS communicates directly with the host PMS. No matter how distant from the front desk, a computer located at the point of sale (e.g., restaurants, lounges, gift shops, health club centers, etc.) is electronically linked to the front-office PMS.

A point-of-sale system removes the hotel from the labor-intensive, error-ridden, manually posted room charge process of yesteryear. The interface poses electronically the same questions the nonautomated system asked manually. Before accepting the room charge, the system polls the front-desk PMS and asks: Is the guest registered under that name and in that room? Is the amount of this charge acceptable to the guest's current credit status? If the PMS does not validate the transaction, the cashier needs to verify the guest's name, room number, and status. After the PMS validates the guest's ability to charge, the POS accepts the transaction and transmits the data directly to the guest folio. All the cashier must input at the POS is guest name, guest-room number, amount of transaction, and check voucher or reference code number.

There are no late charges from cashiers who forget to bring the check to the front desk. There are no errors of fact from posting the wrong amount to the wrong room. And labor is minimal because the POS interfaces directly with the PMS.

Energy Management. Energy management is another common interface to the property management system. By effectively controlling energy (e.g., heating, air conditioning, lights, and power to run equipment), the hotel can provide a full level of services and comfort to the guest while effectively minimizing utility-related costs. An energy management system (EMS) conserves electricity, gas, and water by electronically monitoring the property's mechanical equipment.

Generally, an energy management system saves money in three distinct ways, First, it conserves overall energy utilization by turning down or shutting off nonessential equipment. It also prevents premium charges on utility bills by shedding energy loads during otherwise peak demand periods. And it enhances the useful life of equipment by duty-cycling machines on and off.

Guest-Room Utilization. Because energy utilization in guest rooms represents as much as 80 percent (or more) of a property's total utility bill, a PMS interface offers substantial savings. Such interfaces often function around hard-wired electronic locking systems. That's because the hotel already has a physical (hard-wired) connection between every guest room and the front desk; the EMS simply adds a new dimension to electronic equipment already functioning.

As discussed earlier, a hard-wired ELS communicates directly with the front desk. Through the EMS, the property management system can reduce energy consumption in rooms currently unoccupied. Depending on the time of day and forecasted room demand, the EMS may decide to merely curtail normal heating and cooling by a few degrees, or it may substantially reduce energy consumption to reflect low occupancy.

Through the use of computer algorithms, the EMS may actually control the property management system by determining which rooms should be sold and which rooms should remain unoccupied. A guest checking into a 60 percent occupied house may be routed (through the room availability screen of the PMS) to a well-occupied floor. This would leave other floors or wings of the hotel totally empty of occupied rooms. In such cases, the computer could then shut down hallway ventilation systems, turn off every other ceiling light in the hallway, and reduce the temperature at the remote water heater site.

An EMS interface might also incorporate in-room occupancy sensors. Tied to the electronic locking system, these sensors use either infrared heat-sensing technology or ultrasonic motion detection equipment to register occupancy in the guest room. A door that has been opened from the inside (without using a keycard to gain access) probably indicates the occupant has left the guest room. This information is validated against the occupancy sensor technology, and if the room is truly unoccupied, the EMS reduces and turns off nonessential energy consumption.

Some less-sophisticated in-room occupancy sensors are not connected to the doorlock and merely sense body heat (infrared detection) or body movement (ultrasonic motion detection) without verification. Such equipment works fine except in those instances where a heavy sleeper pulls the blankets up over his head. In these situations, neither heat nor movement registers the room as occupied. The guest may be surprised to wake up and find the television turned off and the room temperature somewhat less than comfortable.

Supplemental Guest Services.   Some of the most exciting new innovations come in the form of supplemental guest services. Supplemental or *auxiliary* guest services are clearly designed with the guest in mind. They have a positive impact on the perception of quality service by providing the guest with some of the comforts of home or office. Examples of supplemental guest services—commonly viewed as additions to the call accounting system—include electronic voice messaging and automated wake-up systems.

Electronic Voice Messaging.   Guest telephone messages have historically been a cumbersome affair. Some callers wish to leave lengthy messages, operator-transcribed return telephone numbers are often incorrect, and the growing number of international travelers adds a non-English speaking component to many of the calls. Today's sophisticated hotels have answered most of these issues with the introduction of electronic voice messaging.

Electronic voice messaging or voice mailboxes are quite similar to the standard answering machine found in a person's home. However, rather than servicing one incoming telephone line, electronic mailbox systems may be capable of handling thousands of extensions. Mailboxes are usually designed to handle hotel executive office extensions as well as guest-room telephone lines.

Many systems allow newly arrived hotel guests a chance to record their own personalized messages. This is an especially powerful feature in an international market. Guests can leave customized messages in whatever language they speak, and the hotel does not need to translate their incoming messages.

Furthermore, these systems allow various hotel departments to prerecord messages into established voice mailboxes. An interested guest can call the main dining room mailbox and learn the special entrée of the night or the hours of operation. Another mailbox might be reserved for use by the concierge staff to promote certain activities in the hotel or across town. The possibilities from such a service are endless.

Automated Attendant Services.   Just as the electronic voice messaging system saves hotel labor by removing the PBX department from the job of taking guest messages, so, too, does the automated attendant system save PBX department labor. Automated attendant services actually remove the PBX department from answering the telephone at all. Instead, the caller is asked to select from a series of choices and to press the corresponding telephone digit accordingly.

Automated attendant systems are gaining popularity across the world. Most high-volume telephone centers sport some form of this service. In the hospitality industry, however, there are some guest-service purists who believe automated attendant systems are too impersonal and mechanical to find a home in such a customer-oriented business. Although they raise a good point as to when human contact can be replaced by automated services, they must realize that practically every national central reservation office currently operates some type of automated attendant system.

Automated Wake-Up Systems.   Automated wake-up systems are consistent with other auxiliary guest services because they both save labor and provide higher levels of customer service. Not only do automated wake-up systems remove the front-desk department from the repetitive task of phoning each guest room and waking the occupant, they also offer a number of unique features.

Although most automated wake-up systems require the front-desk employee to enter the room number and time of the wake-up call, some of the more sophisticated systems allow guests to directly input the wake-up time themselves. In addition, most systems produce reports identifying which rooms were called, the time of the calls, and the guest's wake-up status. Wake-up status—call was answered, call was not answered the first time but was eventually answered during one of the routine system callbacks, or phone was never answered—is an important tool for addressing potential guest complaints.

Automated wake-up systems also serve as a unique marketing medium because the groggy guest makes for a wonderful captive audience. In this regard, hotels not only inform guests about the day's weather conditions, they also describe the breakfast specials in the dining room. Some automated wake-up systems even provide an option for guests to self-design their own personalized wake-up calls!

Guest-Operated Interfaces

In addition to the property management system interfaces described in the preceding section, today's sophisticated lodging properties also provide a number of guest-operated interfaces. The idea of distinguishing interface functions as either property management system or guest-operated arises more as an organizational method than from any real difference in operation. Though customers can personally access the guest-operated interface but not the PMS interface, both function exactly alike.

The following section provides a brief overview of the more popular guest-operated interfaces. Included here are discussions involving in-room safes, in-room beverage or minibar systems, fire-safety systems, in-room entertainment systems, and smart cards.

In-Room Safes.   In-room safes (see Exhibit 14–12) may be either manual or electronic in nature. Both manual and electronic safes allow guests the opportunity to custom-design their own unique combination code. Few modern safes use the traditional lock and key—guests lose them too easily.

Electronic safes may be hard-wired to an interfaced central processing unit. If the PMS is interfaced, daily charges are posted automatically to the electronic folio. Otherwise, the room attendant records the use, just as he or she does with manual, in-room bars. Of course, the hotel can provide the safe without charge, as it does other amenities. Charging came about because purveyors developed quick payback schemes by which management could justify installing in-room safes.

Other than direct cost recovery, there are economic arguments for not charging. The safes reduce the number of thefts, and that should reduce the cost of insurance. Traffic at safe-deposit boxes falls dramatically, reducing front-office labor costs. Fewer claims means even larger savings in security and management time. Investigations, guest relations, reports, police inquiries, and correspondence may represent days of lost work. Legal fees, court costs, settlements, and more management time must be factored in if the case goes to trial. If there are no losses, there are no costs.

EXHIBIT 14–12

An in-room safe, a new amenity in many hotels, reduces guest losses and guest demands on front-desk personnel. Guests create their own code.

Courtesy: Elsafe of Nevada and Elsafe International, Vanvikan, Norway.

Evidence suggests that safes do reduce theft. Electronic door locks do battle with external theft and in-room safes with internal theft. Experts say that internal theft by employees is usually an impulsive act caused by temptation. The safe reduces employee opportunity. It also undermines guest moves to defraud the hotel or the insurance company.

In-Room Minibars. In-room beverage, minibar, or vending systems may be automatically interfaced to the property management system, semiautomatically interfaced (with a handheld microprocessor), or they may be fully manual in design (see Exhibit 14–13). Both the manual and the semiautomated minibars rely on a guest honor system. At the time of check-out, front-desk clerks ask departing guests if they had occasion to utilize the minibar in the last 24 hours. Although some departing guests will invariably cheat the hotel, minibar profits are significant enough to easily cover a sizable number of cheats.

Minibars are extremely convenient—that's their attraction. And guests are often willing to pay a premium for the convenience of having snacks and drinks available in the room. As a result, some hotels have realized rapid payback (sometimes in less than 12 months) from their in-room minibar systems.

With semiautomated minibars, changes in inventory are recorded on a handheld microprocessor by the room attendant or minibar employee. The microprocessor is capable of storing inventory information from several guest rooms before being downloaded via the telephone directly into the property management system interface (see Exhibit 14–14).

The delay in installing honor bars has been caused by jurisdictions such as New York State. Without control of consumption by minors, liquor was not permitted

EXHIBIT 14–13

Electronic in-room minibar systems can easily support 75–100 items for the guest. By design, the minibar allows some sections to remain at room temperature (such as those containing nuts and candy) while refrigerating other sections (such as those containing soda and champagne).

in the rooms. Automatically interfaced minibars have changed that: The system can be turned off at certain hours or whenever children are registered.

Electronic vending has brought additional benefits: eliminating the frequent late charge of the honor system, for one. Automatically interfaced minibars utilize fiberoptic sensors to identify when a product has been removed for consumption. These sensors are often programmed with a slight delay to allow for those guests who wish to handle, look at, and then possibly return the product to the refrigerator. Once the product has been removed for a period of time, the sensor alerts the interface, which then charges the guest folio for the minibar item. Not only does this minimize cheating and late charges, it also produces a restocking report that simplifies the job of the minibar employee. There is no longer any reason for the minibar employee to enter and check every guest room—only those from which an item was removed.

In-Room Entertainment Systems.   In-room movie or entertainment systems hold a great deal of promise for the years to come. However, the TV set remains an entertainment center above all else, at least for now. The availability of in-room movies, for which most hotels charge (using the electronic folio), is an upgrade from the standard set (see Exhibit 14–15). Videocassette viewing is another upgrade. Some hotels charge, and some don't; some rent films via electronic vending machines, and some supply them gratis on the concierge floors.

While not exactly entertainment, the proceedings taking place in the conference area of the hotel can be viewed on the TV screen in some hotels. Other TV channels offer airline schedules; news, sports and stock market reports; local restaurant

EXHIBIT 14–14

Sophisticated minibar systems like the Robobar schematic shown here allow the hotel to operate this amenity with maximum efficiency. Notable features of such systems are that room charges are automatically posted and the units can be remotely locked or unlocked to remain in compliance with local regulatory requirements. Also, the system uses fiberoptic technology on a real-time basis to prevent late charges, and it automatically produces stocking refill reports.

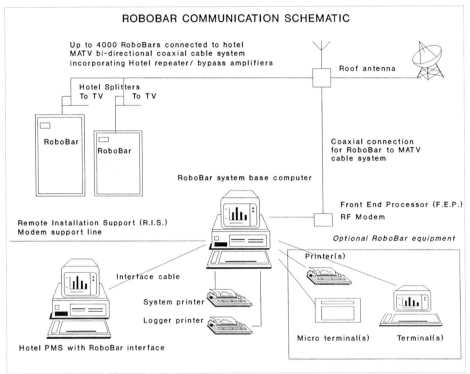

Courtesy: Minibar North America, Inc. Bethesda, MD.

guides; the guest folio; weather reports; advertising; and personal messages left for the guest.

When some of the capabilities of the telephone and personal computer are added in, the TV broadens its service offerings. Express check-out and room status are two common functions. A room-service menu can be viewed (changes are easier to make and less costly than printed menus) and orders placed. Other orders can also be placed: a morning wake-up call; a reservation in a dining room that hasn't opened; goods from shops in the hotel (or mall merchants, if the hotel is so located). Even airline tickets can be ordered. With a remote printer at the desk—eventually, perhaps, in the guest room—the tickets can also be picked up.

Fire-Safety Systems.   Although fire-safety systems are not truly guest-operated devices, they do monitor and detect activities occurring in the guest room. Like most interfaced functions, fire-safety systems began as stand-alone devices. An example is a single smoke detector in the corridor. Change came quickly after several widely publicized fires occurred. In quick response, many municipalities passed retrofit legislation. The emphasis was toward interfacing fire technology and the PMS, using the hard wires of the call accounting or locking systems, or through

EXHIBIT 14–15

Spectravision is the leader of in-room entertainment and technology. The top photo promotes many of the services available in a fully integrated system. The bottom photos show how simple it is for the guest to read messages, review the folio, and check out from the room.

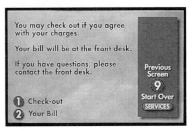

wireless broadcasting. Some jurisdictions mandated hard-wiring—integrating the control panels and the room communication systems.

Hard-wire systems tie each room sensor to a fire-control panel on the premises. In-room smoke detectors and sprinkler-head sensors can also be included to provide an early-warning network. An annunciator on the panel pinpoints the source of the smoke or fire. The interfaced system then does several things automatically:

- It releases the magnetic locks that hold open the fire doors.
- It adjusts the ventilation and air-handling (HVAC) systems to minimize the spread of fire and externally vent smoke as necessary.
- It automatically notifies guests in their rooms through the activation of horns or speakers, it may dial each guest-room telephone and play a prerecorded message, and it notifies the local fire department. On arrival at the scene, the fire department may be able to take control of the speakers and announce specific instructions.
- It automatically overrides all affected elevators and returns them to the ground floor.

Codes require evacuation routes in corridors and rooms to be clearly marked. In-room signage now identifies that route and the closest exit. Lighted, phosphorescent signs in the corridors at crawling height have gained popularity since their introduction in the Far East about a decade ago.

Instead of ignoring the reality of the danger, which had been the stance for a long time, hotel companies have begun communicating their concerns. Written booklets and evacuation instructions have been prepared. With electronic systems, audio instructions are also being offered. Other emergency systems use the music channels or the television speakers. The voice comes through even if the switch is off. Special hard-wired systems and in-room sprinklers are legislated in several places that have experienced especially deadly fires, such as Las Vegas and San Juan.

A message that is recorded tends to be more calming and informative than a live one made during the excitement of the emergency. Several hotels have gotten the local fire marshall to tape the message.

Smart Cards.   Like fire-safety systems, smart cards are not so much guest-operated devices as they are tools. Smart cards are tools that function inside and outside of the hotel. And if hotels follow their normal mode of operation with new technologies, smart cards will become staples of other industries long before they find functionality in the lodging arena.

Although smart cards are not especially popular in America, they are by no means a new form of technology. Introduced in France during the 1950s, smart cards have primarily found acceptance in Europe. However, the United States is following suit—both Visa and MasterCard have announced that all their credit cards will function as smart cards by the year 2000.

Smart cards are miniature computers scarcely different in size or appearance from a standard credit card. Unlike ''dumb'' credit cards, however, smart cards carry a sizable quantity of storage in their microchip databases. The average smart card contains about 8K of memory (roughly 15 pages of typed data). The memory can be accessed by a card-reader device that quickly scans and stores the card's information.

Retailers are utilizing smart cards as a means of tracking customer demographics and loyalties. Smart card technology provides marketers with names and addresses of customers, purchase patterns, income levels, hobbies, family size and type, and so on. By understanding certain habits and lifestyles of their customers, major retailers can better market their products and services. Likewise, customers benefit by receiving coupons and bonus points appropriate to their type of shopping.

Customer databases have been available in the hospitality industry for many years. Information about the customer's name, company, room preference, and frequency and length of stay is available to any hotel operating a property management system. However, this information has been poorly utilized.

Many hospitality industry executives agree the use of guest database information has been minimal at best. Although hotels have access to a wide range of guest data, few truly utilize it as a marketing tool. How pleased the guest would be to receive a greeting card in the mail from a favorite hotel, to receive a note of thanks for visiting a particular property five times in three months, or to find a bottle of his or her favorite wine waiting at check-in. In these days of intense competition, the delivery of customer service beyond the industry's standard level is necessary to ensure a hotel's profitable performance. A rise in the use of smart cards coupled with the renewed popularity of hotel credit cards will inevitably see new opportunities for the information imbedded in the guest database.

Summary

The lodging industry lagged behind most other businesses in terms of adopting computer automation in the 1970s. As a result, most hotel operations avoided the first generations of computer development, choosing instead to wait for the faster, cheaper, more perfected systems that were soon to follow. The waiting is over, and hospitality computer applications have gained acceptance at a dizzying rate. Today, technology prevails across all spectrums of the lodging industry.

Few properties operate without a computerized call accounting system (CAS). The CAS performs many tasks that historically belonged to the hotel telephone operator: It identifies when a guest call is made, the originating room, the duration, the destination, and the cost of the call. Once the long-distance carrier cost of the call is determined, most properties add a profit margin to help defray CAS equipment costs and to make a reasonable return on investment for the hotel. Some chains, however, choose to make no profit on either long-distance or local guest phone calls. Functioning in concert with the CAS are sophisticated guest-room telephones. These feature telephones are actually capable of serving as a remote control for a number of in-room services. Pressing a few buttons on the phone may close the drapes, dim the lights, adjust the temperature, or lower the television volume.

Another common technological interface found in hotels today is the electronic locking system (ELS). Few newly constructed hotels are built without some form of locking system technology. This technology may include nonelectronic locking systems that utilize specially encoded keys, but more often than not it will be an electronic locking system. The ELS may be microfitted (i.e., battery-operated) or hard-wired. Though more expensive, the hard-wired systems are capable of a number of sophisticated enhancements. Since each hard-wired lock is actually wired directly to the front desk, the hotel can integrate fire safety, occupancy sensors, and energy management components directly through the door lock.

In addition to the CAS and ELS, a number of guest-room or guest-service interfaces are also available in full-service, technologically sophisticated properties. Common guest-service interfaces include point-of-sale systems, energy management systems, and supplemental guest-service components such as electronic voice messaging, automated attendant, and wake-up services. In the guest room, there may be electronic-safe, minibar, entertainment, and fire-safety system interfaces.

Queries and Problems

1. The relationship of the telephone and hotel industries began to change in the late 1960s. List three major pieces of legislation, court rulings, findings by the FCC, or decisions by members of either industry that caused or contributed to the changes. How did each alter the way in which the hotel's telephone department operates?

2. As the hotel industry resolves the issue of uniform connectivity, some PMS vendors will comply with the new standards and others will not. What are the benefits to a hotel manager who purchases software from a vendor in compliance? Are there any disadvantages to purchasing products from a vendor in compliance with uniform connectivity standards?

3. Most hotel operations charge a premium for the convenience of placing long-distance phone calls directly from the room. This premium may be as little as 10 to 25 percent above the cost of the call. Other properties charge as much as 10 or more times the cost of the call. Assuming that the hotel announces its surcharge with a notice similar to the one shown in Exhibit 14–1, discuss the fairness of charging the guest such a premium. Is it ethical to charge a small premium (say, 10 to 25 percent)? Is it ethical to charge a large premium (say, 10 times the cost?) At what point does the hotel overstep the limits of ''fairness''?

4. Using professional terminology correctly is important to understanding and being understood. Identify the following acronyms and briefly discuss what they represent:

a. HOBIC	*f.* DDD
b. AOS	*g.* OCC
c. WATS	*h.* AT&T
d. PMS	*i.* PBX
e. FCC	*j.* AIOD

5. Identify by name the levels of keys that comprise the locking systems of most hotels. Explain who has access to which keys and what purpose is served by each level. How does the system work if the mechanical lock and key are replaced by the computer and the computer keycard?

6. Be creative and imagine the hotel room of the future. Describe several guest-operated interfaces or devices that might be available in your fictitious hotel room of tomorrow.

Notes

1. Donald E. Lundberg, *Inside Innkeeping* (Dubuque, IA: Wm. C. Brown, 1956), p. 91.
2. The magnitude of deregulation clouds an earlier landmark case. In 1968, at the instruction of the federal district court, the FCC ruled in favor of Carterfone, an interconnection between telephones and private two-way radios. The FCC overturned AT&T regulations, which prohibited the interconnection of privately owned devices. The immediate response was the sale of other, competitive, to-be-owned-not-leased telephones. More importantly, it opened a whole new interconnect industry.
3. Registered trademark.

Glossary

Words in italic in each definition are themselves defined elsewhere in the Glossary. (Words not listed might be found in the Index.)

A card   A form used with front-office posting machines to reconcile and report cash at the close of the first shift and alternate shifts thereafter; see *B card.*

account balance   The difference between the *debit* and *credit* values of the *guest bill.*

account (card)   See *guest bill.*

account receivable   A company, organization, or individual, *registered* or not, who has an outstanding bill with the hotel.

accounts receivable ledger   The aggregate of individual *account receivable* records.

adds   Last minute *reservations* added to the reservation list on the day of arrival.

adjoining rooms   Rooms that abut along the corridor but do not connect through private doors; cf. *connecting rooms.*

advance deposit   A deposit furnished by the guest on a room *reservation* that the hotel is holding.

advances   See *cash paid-outs.*

affiliated hotel   One of a chain, *franchise,* or *referral* system, the membership of which provides special advantages, particularly a national reservation system.

after departure (AD)   A *late charge.*

afternoon tea   A light snack comprising delicate sandwiches and small sweets served with tea, or even sherry.

agency ledger   A division of the *city ledger* dealing with *travel agency* accounts.

AIOD   Telephone equipment that provides *A*utomatic *I*dentification of *O*utward *D*ialing for billing purposes.

allowance   A reduction to the *folio,* as an adjustment either for unsatisfactory service or for a posting error. Also called a *rebate.*

amenities   Literally any extra product or service found in the hotel. A swimming pool, concierge desk, health spa, and so on are all technically known as *amenities.* However, this term has primarily come to be used for in-room guest products. Such complimentary in-room items as soap, shampoo, suntan lotion, mouthwash, body gel, and the like are most commonly considered amenities.

amenity creep   The proliferation of in-room guest products that results when hotels compete by offering better or more extensive amenity items.

Americans with Disabilities Act (ADA)   Established in 1990, the ADA prohibits discrimination against any guest or employee because of his or her disability.

American Hotel & Motel Association (AH&MA)   A federation of regional and state associations composed of individual hotel and motel properties throughout the Americas.

American plan (AP)   A method of quoting room *rates* where the charge includes room and three meals.

American Society of Association Executives (ASAE) An organization of the professional executives who head the nation's numerous associations.

American Society of Travel Agents (ASTA)   A professional association of retail *travel agents* and wholesale tour operators.

arrival, departure, and change sheet   A form on which all guest *check-ins, check-outs,* and *changes* are recorded; sometimes three separate forms.

arrival time That hour by which the guest specifies he or she will arrive to claim the *reservation.*

authorization code Response from a credit-card inquiry that approves the transaction and provides a number code for referral if problems arise; code for entry to a computer program.

available basis only Convention reservations that have no claim against the *block* of convention rooms because the requests arrived after the *cutoff date;* condition under which most special rates are allowed—no reservations permitted. See *blanket reservation.*

available rooms The number of guest rooms the hotel has for sale—either the total in the hotel or the number unoccupied on a given day.

Average Daily Rate (ADR) The average daily *rate* paid by guests; computed by dividing room revenue by the number of rooms occupied. More recently called *Sales per Room Occupied.*

back to back A sequence of consecutive *group* departures and arrivals usually arranged by tour operators so rooms are never vacant; a floor plan design that brings the piping of adjacent baths into a common shaft.

bank Coins and small bills given to the cashier for making change.

bank cards Credit cards issued by banks, usually for a smaller fee than that charged by *travel and entertainment cards.*

batch processing A computer procedure that collects and codes data, entering it into memory in batches; cf. *online computer.*

B card A form used with front-office posting machines to reconcile and report cash at the close of the second shift and alternate shifts thereafter; see *A card.*

bed and board Another term for the *American plan.*

bed and breakfast (B&B) Lodging and breakfast offered in a domestic setting by families in their own homes; less frequently, the *Continental plan.*

bed board A board placed under the mattress to provide a firmer sleeping surface.

bed-night See *guest-day.*

bed occupancy A ratio relating the number of bed spaces sold to the number available for sale.

bell captain The supervisor of the bellpersons and other uniformed service personnel; a proprietary in-room vending machine.

bell captain's log See *callbook.*

bellstand The bellperson's desk located in the lobby close to and visible from the front desk.

Bermuda plan A method of quoting room *rates,* where the charge includes a full breakfast as well as the room.

best available A *reservation* requesting (or a confirmation promising) the best room available or the best room to open prior to arrival.

B folio The second *folio* (the individual's folio) used with a *master account.*

blanket reservation A *block* of rooms held for a particular *group,* with individual members requesting assignments from that block.

block A restriction placed in a *pocket* of the *room rack* to limit the clerk's discretion in assigning the room; a number of rooms reserved for one *group.*

book To sell hotel space, either to an individual or to a *group* needing a *block* of rooms.

box Reservation term that allows no *reservations* from either side of the boxed dates to spill through; cf. *sell through.*

breakage The gain that accrues to the hotel or tour operator when meals or other services included in a *package* are not used by the guest.

brunch A meal served after breakfast but before lunch and taking the place of both.

bucket See *cashier's well.*

budget motel See *limited service.*

building cost rate formula A rule-of-thumb formula stating that the average room rate should equal $1 for every $1,000 of construction cost. See *rule-of-thumb rate.*

cabana A room on the beach (or by the pool) separated from the main *house* and sometimes furnished as a sleeping room.

café complet Coffee snack at midmorning or midafternoon.

California length An extra-long bed, about 80 inches to 82 inches instead of the usual 75 inches. Same as *hollywood length.*

call accounting system (CAS) Computerized program that prices and may record telephone calls on the guest's electronic *folio* through a *Property Management System (PMS)* interface.

callbook The bellperson's record of calls and activities.

call sheet The form used by the telephone operator to record the room and hour of the *morning call.*

cancellation A guest's request to the hotel to void a *reservation* previously made.

cancellation number Coded number provided by the *central reservations office* to a guest who cancels a *reservation.*

cash advance See *cash paid-outs.*

cash disbursement See *cash paid-outs.*

cashier's drop   A depository located in the front-desk area where others can witness cashiers depositing their *turn-ins.*

cashier's report   The cash *turn-in* form completed by a departmental cashier at the close of the *watch.*

cashier's well   The file that holds the guest *folios,* often recessed in the countertop; also known as *tub, bucket,* or *pit.*

cash paid-outs   Monies disbursed for guests, either advances or loans, and charged to their accounts like other departmental services.

cash sheet   The *departmental control sheet* maintained by the front-office cashier.

casualty factor   The number of *reservations* of a *group* (*cancellations* plus *no-shows*) that fail to appear.

cathode ray tube (CRT)   A television screen that displays information put out by the computer; also called a VDT, *video display terminal.*

central processing unit (CPU)   The *hardware/software* nucleus of the computer that performs and monitors the essential functions.

central reservations office (CRO)   A private or chain-operated office that accepts and processes reservations on behalf of its membership.

central reservations system (CRS)   The sophisticated hardware and software used by a central reservations office to accurately track and manage reservations requests for member properties.

change   Moving a party from one guest room to another; any change in room, *rate,* or number of occupants.

chargeback   Credit-card charges refused by the credit-card company for one reason or another.

check-in   All the procedures involved in receiving the guest and completing the *registration* sequence.

check-out   All the procedures involved in the departure of the guest and the settlement of the *account.*

check-out hour   That time by which guests must vacate rooms or be charged an additional day.

city ledger   An *accounts receivable ledger* of nonregistered guests.

city ledger journal   The form used to record transactions that affect the *city ledger.*

class   The quality of hotel, with *Average Daily Rate* the usual criterion.

closeout hour   Also called *close of the day.*

close of the day   An arbitrary hour that management designates to separate the records of one day from those of the next.

closet bed   See *Murphy bed.*

colored transparency   A colored celluloid strip placed in the *room rack pocket* as a *flag* or indicator of room status.

commercial hotel   A *transient hotel* catering to a business clientele.

commercial rate   A reduced room *rate* given to businesspersons to promote occupancy.

commissionable   An indication that the hotel will pay *travel agents* the standard fee for business placed.

comp   Short for "complimentary" accommodations—and occasionally food and beverage—furnished without charge.

company-made (reservation)   A *reservation* guaranteed by the arriving guest's company.

concession   A hotel tenant whose facilities and services are indistinguishable from those owned and operated by the hotel.

concierge   A European position, increasingly found in U.S. hotels, responsible for handling guests' needs, particularly those relating to out-of-hotel services; designation of the sleeping floor where these services are offered.

conference center   A property that caters to small business meetings, corporate retreats, and conferences. Generally considered smaller in size and more personable in nature than a convention property.

confirmed reservation   The hotel's agreement, usually in writing, to the guest's *reservation* request.

connecting (rooms)   *Adjoining rooms* with direct, private access, making use of the corridor unnecessary.

continental breakfast   A small meal including some combination of the following: bread, rolls, sweet rolls, juice, or coffee. Often set up in bulk by the innkeeper or host, continental breakfasts are usually self-service.

continental plan   A method of quoting room *rates* where the charge includes a *continental breakfast* as well as the room rate.

convention rate   See *run-of-the-house rate.*

convertible bed   See *sofa bed.*

corner (room)   An *outside room* on a corner of the building having two *exposures.*

correction sheet   A form used with front-office machines to record posting errors for later reconciliation by the *night auditor.*

cot   See *rollaway bed.*

coupon   A checklike form issued by *travel agencies* to their clients and used by the clients to settle their hotel accounts; a ticket issued by tour groups for the purchase of meals and other services to be charged against the master account. Also called a *voucher.*

credit   An accounting term that indicates a decrease in the *account receivable;* the opposite of *debit.*

cutoff date   That date on which the unsold *block* of reserved convention rooms is released for general sale.

cutoff hour   That time at which the day's unclaimed *reservations* are released for sale to the general public.

daily rooms report   See *room count sheet.*

day rate   A reduced charge for occupancy of less than overnight; used when the party arrives and departs the same day.

D card   The form on which the totals of the front-office posting machine are printed for use in the *night audit.*

dead room change   A physical change of rooms made by the hotel in the guest's absence so no tip is earned by the *last* bellperson.

debit   An accounting term that indicates an increase in the *account receivable;* the opposite of *credit.*

deluxe   A non-U.S. designation implying the best accommodations; unreliable unless part of an official rating system.

demi-pension (DP)   A non-U.S. method of quoting room *rates* similar to the *modified American plan (MAP)* but allowing the guest to select either luncheon or dinner along with breakfast and room; also called *half pension.*

density board (chart)   A *reservation* system where the number of rooms committed is controlled by type: *single, twin, queen,* etc.

departmental control sheet   A form maintained by each *operating department* for recording data from departmental *vouchers* before forwarding them to the front desk for *posting.*

deposit reservation   See *advance deposit.*

destination hotel   The objective of—and often the sole purpose for—the guest's trip; cf. *transient hotel.*

did not stay (DNS)   Means the guest left almost immediately after *registering.*

difference returnable   See *exchange.*

dine-around plan   A method of quoting *AP* or *MAP* room rates that allows guests to dine at any of several independent but cooperating hotels.

display room   See *sample room.*

double   A bed approximately 54 inches by 75 inches; the *rate* charged for two persons occupying one room; a room with a double bed.

double-double   See *twin-double.*

double occupancy   Room occupancy by two persons; a ratio relating the number of rooms double occupied to the number of rooms sold.

double occupancy rate   A *rate* used for tours where the per person charge is based on two to a room.

double-up   A designation of *double occupancy* by unrelated parties necessitating two *room rack slips.*

downgrade   Move a *reservation* or registered guest to a lesser accommodation or *class* of service; cf. *upgrade.*

downtime   That time span during which the computer is inoperative because of malfunction or preemptive operations.

ducat   See *stock card.*

due back   See *exchange.*

due bank   See *exchange.*

due bill   See *trade advertising contract.*

dump   To *checkout* early; another term for *understay.*

duplex   A two-story *suite* with a connecting stairwell.

early arrival   A guest who arrives a day or two earlier than the *reservation* calls for.

economy class   See *tourist class.*

efficiency   Accommodations that include kitchen facilities.

electronic data processing   A data handling system that relies on electronic (computer) equipment.

ell   A wing of a building usually at right angles to the main structure.

emergency key (E-key)   One key that opens all guest rooms, including those locked from within, even those with the room key still in the lock; also called the *grandmaster.*

en pension   See *full pension.*

European plan (EP)   A method of quoting room *rates* where the charge includes room accommodations only.

exchange   The excess of cash *turn-in* over net receipts; the difference is returnable (due back) to the front-office cashier; also called *due back, due bank,* or *difference returnable.*

executive floor   See *concierge* (floor).

executive room   See *studio.*

exposure   The direction (north, south, east, or west) or view (ocean, mountain) that the guest room faces.

express check-out   Mechanical or electronic methods of *check-out* that expedite the guest's departure and eliminate the need to stop at the desk; also called *zip-out.*

extra meals   An *American plan* charge made for dining room service over and above that to which the guest is entitled.

family plan   A special room *rate* that allows children to occupy their parent's room at no additional charge.

family room   See *twin-double.*

fam trip   Familiarization trip taken by *travel agents* at little or no cost to acquaint themselves with *properties* and destinations.

farm out   Assignment of guests to other *properties* when a full *house* precludes their accommodation.

fenced rates   A new addition to the list of reservations sales tools, these include specific instructions to or rules for the guest—for example, nonrefundable, advance purchase, and unalterable *reservations.*

first class   A non-U.S. designation for medium-priced accommodations with corresponding facilities and services.

F.I.T.   Foreign independent tour, but has come to mean free independent tour, a traveler who is not *group* affiliated.

flag   A device for calling the room clerk's attention to a particular room in the *room rack.*

flat rate   See *run-of-the-house rate.*

floor key   See *master key.*

floor (release) limit   The maximum amount of charges permitted a credit-card user at a given *property* without clearance; the limit is established for the property, not for the user.

folio   See *guest bill;* a folio is also called an *account card.*

forecast   A future projection of estimated business volume.

forecast scheduling   Work schedules established on the basis of sales projections.

forfeited deposit   A *reservation* deposit kept by the hotel when a *no-show* fails to cancel the reservation; also called a lost deposit.

franchise   An independently owned hotel or motel that appears to be part of a chain and pays a fee for this right of identity.

free sale   Occurs when a *travel agent,* airline, or other agency commits hotel space without specific prior confirmation with the *property.* See also *sell and report.*

from bill number . . . to bill number   A cross-reference of *account* numbers when the bill of a guest who remains beyond one week is transferred to a new *folio.*

front   The next bellperson eligible for a *rooming* assignment or other errand apt to produce a gratuity.

front office   A broad term that includes the physical front desk as well as the duties and functions involved in the sale and service of guest rooms.

full day   The measure of a chargeable day for accounting purposes; three meals for an *AP* hotel, overnight for an *EP.*

full house   Means 100 percent occupancy, all guest rooms sold.

full pension   A European term for the *American plan.* 00

full service   Means a complete line of services and departments are provided, in contrast to a *limited-service* hotel or motel.

futon   A Japanese sleeping arrangement made of many layers of cotton-quilted batting that is rolled up when not in use.

garni   A non-U.S. designation for hotels without restaurant service except for *continental breakfast.*

general cashier   The chief cashier with whom deposits are made and from whom *banks* are drawn.

general manager (GM)   The hotel's chief executive.

global distribution system (GDS)   The hardware, software, and computer lines over which travel agents, airlines, on-line subscription networks, and others access central reservations systems and individual property management systems.

grandmaster   One key that opens all guest rooms except those locked from within; see also *emergency key.*

graveyard   A work shift beginning about midnight.

greens fee   A charge for the use of the golf course.

group   A number of persons with whom the hotel deals (reservation, billing, etc.) as if they were one party.

guaranteed rate   The assurance of a fixed *rate* regardless of occupancy, often given in consideration of a large number of *room-nights* per year pledged by a company.

guaranteed reservation   Payment for the room is promised even if the occupant fails to arrive.

guest account   See *guest bill.*

guest bill   A special form used by hotels for keeping *transient account receivable* records; different forms used with hand-prepared and machine-prepared systems; also known as *folio* or *account card.*

guest check   The bill presented to patrons of the dining rooms and bars and often used as the department *voucher.*

guest-day (night)   The stay of one guest for one day (night); also known as a *room-night* or *bed-night.*

guest elevators   The front elevators for the exclusive use of the guests; employees are not permitted except for bellpersons when accompanying the guest to or from a room; cf. *service elevators.*

guest history (card)   A record of the guest's visits including rooms assigned, *rates,* special needs, and credit rating.

guest ledger   The accounts of registered guests as distinct from *city ledger* accounts; also known as the *rooms ledger* or *transient ledger.*

guest-night   See *guest-day.*

guest occupancy   See *bed occupancy.*

guest-service area   See *front office.*

half-board   See *modified American plan.*

half pension   See *demi-pension.*

handicap(ped) room   A guest room furnished with devices and built large enough to accommodate guests with physical handicaps.

hard copy   Computer term for material that has been printed rather than merely displayed.

hardware   The physical equipment (electronic and mechanical) of a computer installation and its peripheral components; cf. *software.*

hide-a-bed   See *sofa bed.*

high tea   A fairly substantial late afternoon or early evening meal.

HOBIC   An acronym for Hotel Outward Bound Information Center, the telephone company's long-distance hotel network.

holdover   See *overstay.*

hollywood bed   *Twin* beds joined by a common headboard.

hollywood length   An extra-long bed, about 80 inches to 82 inches instead of the usual 75 inches. Same as *California length.*

hospitality suite (room)   A facility used for entertaining, usually at conventions, trade shows, and similar meetings.

hostel   An inexpensive but supervised facility with limited services catering to young travelers on foot or bicycle.

hotelier   Innkeeper or hotelkeeper, originally from the French.

hotel manager   Hotel executive responsible for the front of the house, including *front office* housekeeping, and uniformed services; sometimes called hotel manager or house manager.

Hotel Sales and Marketing Association International (HSMAI)   An international association of hotel sales and marketing managers.

hot list   A list of lost or stolen credit cards furnished to hotels and other retailers by the credit-card companies.

house   A synonym for hotel, as in house bank, house count; see also *property.*

house bank   See *bank.*

house call   Telephone call made to the outside by a member of the staff for company business and not subject to charge.

house count   The number of registered guests.

housekeeper's report   A *linen room* summary of the status of guest rooms, used by the front desk to verify the accuracy of the *room rack.*

house laundry   A hotel-operated facility, in contrast to an *outside laundry* with which the hotel might contract.

house profit   The net profit before income taxes from all *operating departments* except store rentals and before provision for rent, taxes, interest, insurance, and depreciation;

renamed by the 1977 edition of the *USA,* ''total income before fixed charges.''

house rooms   Guest rooms set aside for hotel use and excluded, therefore, from *available rooms.*

housing bureau   A citywide reservation office, usually run by the convention bureau, for assigning *reservation* requests to participating hotels during a citywide convention.

Hubbart Room Rate Formula   A basis for determining room *rates* developed by Roy Hubbart and distributed by the *American Hotel & Motel Association.*

ideal average room rate   This formula assumes a hotel sells an equal number of rooms from both the least expensive upward and from the most expensive downward. The resulting average rate is a theoretical benchmark against which to compare actual operating results.

imprest petty cash   A technique for controlling petty cash disbursements by which a special, small cash fund is used for minor cash payments and periodically reimbursed.

incentive (group, guest, tour, or trip)   Persons who have won a hotel stay (usually with transportation included) as a reward for meeting and excelling their sales quotas or other company-established standards.

inclusive terms   Phrase that is sometimes used in Europe to designate the *American plan;* used to indicate that a price quoted includes tax and gratuity.

independent   A *property* with no chain or *franchise* affiliation, although one proprietor might own several such properties.

information rack   An alphabetic listing of registered guests with a room number cross-reference.

in-season rate   A *resort's* maximum rate, charged when the demand is heaviest, as it is during the middle of the summer or winter; cf. *off-season rate.*

inside call   A telephone call that enters the switchboard from inside the hotel; a telephone call that remains within the hotel; cf. *outside call.*

inside room   A guest room that faces an inner courtyard or light court enclosed by three or four sides of the building.

inspector   Supervisory position in the housekeeping department responsible for releasing *on change* rooms to ready status.

interface   Computer term designating the ability of one computer to communicate with another.

International Association of Travel Agents (IATA)   A professional affiliation which both lobbies on behalf of the travel industry and identifies/verifies legitimate travel agents to other vendors.

interstate call   A long-distance call that crosses state lines

intrastate call   A long-distance telephone call that originates and terminates within the same state.

in-WATS   See *Wide Area Telephone Service.*

IT number   The code assigned to an inclusive tour for identification and *booking.*

junior suite   One large room, sometimes with a half partition, furnished as both a *parlor* and a bedroom.

king   An extra-long, extra-wide *double* bed about 78 inches by 80 inches.

lanai   A Hawaiian term for ''veranda''; a room with a porch or balcony usually overlooking gardens or water.

last   The designation for the bellperson who most recently completed a *front.*

last room availability   A sophisticated reservations system that provides real-time access between the chain's central reservations system and the hotel's in-house property management system.

late arrival   A guest with a *reservation* who expects to arrive after the *cutoff* hour and so notifies the hotel.

late charge   A departmental charge that arrives at the front desk for billing after the guest has *checked out.*

late check-out   A departing guest who remains beyond the *check-out hour* with permission of the desk and thus without charge.

least cost router (LCR)   Telephone equipment that routes the call over the least expensive lines available. Also called automatic route selector (ARS).

light baggage   Insufficient luggage in quantity or quality on which to extend credit; the guest pays in advance.

limited service   A hotel or motel that provides little or no services other than the room; a *budget hotel (motel)*; cf. *full service.*

linen closet   A storage closet for linens and other housekeeping supplies usually located conveniently along the corridor for the use of the housekeeping staff.

linen room   The housekeeper's office and the center of operations for that department, including the storage of linens and uniforms.

lockout   Denying the guest access to the room, usually because of an unpaid bill; a key of that name.

log   A record of activities maintained by several *operating departments.*

lost and found   An area, usually under the housekeeper's jurisdiction, for the control and storage of lost-and-found items.

maid's report   A status-of-rooms report prepared by the room attendant and consolidated by the *linen room* to create a *housekeeper's report.*

mail and key rack   A piece of front-office equipment where both mail and keys are stored by room number.

maitre d'   The shortened form of maitire d'hotel, the headwaiter.

market mix   The variety and percentage distribution of hotel guests—conventioneer, tourist, businessperson, and so on.

master account   One *folio* prepared for a *group* (convention, company, tour) on which all group charges are accumulated.

master key   One key controlling several *pass keys* and opening all the guests rooms on one floor; also called a *floor key.*

menu   An array of function choices displayed to the computer user who selects the appropriate function.

message lamp   A light on or near the telephone, used to notify an occupant that the telephone operator has a message to relay.

minisuite   See *junior suite.*

minor departments   The less important *operating departments* (excluding room, food, and beverage) such as valet, laundry, and telephone.

miscellaneous charge order (MCO)   Airline *voucher* authorizing the sale of services to the guest named on the form, with payment due from the airline.

modified American plan (MAP)   A method of quoting room *rates* in which the charge includes breakfast and dinner as well as the room.

mom-and-pop   A small, family-owned business with limited capitalization in which the family, rather than paid employees, furnishes the bulk of the labor.

morning call   A *wake-up* telephone call made by the telephone operator at the guest's request.

Ms   An abbreviation used to indicate a female guest whose marital status is unknown.

Murphy bed   A standard bed that folds or swings into a wall or cabinet in a closetlike fashion.

NCR 2000   A front-office posting machine manufactured by the NCR Company; no longer in production.

NCR 4200   A front-office posting machine manufactured by the NCR Company and usually called a ''42''; no longer in production.

NCR paper   No carbon required; paper is specially treated to produce copies without carbon.

net rate   Room *rate* reduced by the commission charge.

net receipts   The difference between what the cashier took in and what was paid out.

night audit   A daily reconciliation of *accounts receivable* that is usually completed during the *graveyard* watch.

night auditor   The person or persons responsible for the *night audit.*

night clerk's report   An interim report prepared by the *night auditor* or night clerk and used until the day audit has been completed.

no reservation (NR)   See *walk-in.*

no-show   A *reservation* that fails to arrive.

occupancy, percentage of (occupancy percent)   A ratio relating the number of rooms sold to the number *available* for sale.

off line   See *batch processing.*

off-season rate   A reduced room rate charged by *resort* hotels when demand is lowest; cf. *in-season rate.*

off the shelf   Standardized, not customized, computer software.

off the street (OS)   See *walk-in.*

on change   The status of a room recently vacated but not yet available for new occupants.

one- (two-) pull dialing   One (two) digit telephone dialing (or Touch-Tone) that connects the caller to hotel services such as room service and bellstand.

on-line computer   Computer facilities hooked directly to input and output devices for instantaneous communication.

operating departments   Those divisions of the hotel directly involved with the service of the guest, in contrast to support divisions such as personnel and accounting.

out of inventory (OOI)   A significant problem has removed this room from availability. Although OOO rooms are usually available in only a matter of hours, OOI rooms may be unavailable for days or weeks.

out of order (OOO)   The room is not available for sale because of some planned or unexpected temporary shutdown of facilities.

outside call   A call that enters the switchboard from outside the hotel; a call that terminates outside the hotel; cf. *inside call.*

outside laundry (valet)   A nonhotel laundry or valet service contracted by the hotel in order to offer a full line of services; cf. *house laundry.*

outside room   A room on the perimeter of the building facing outward with an *exposure* more desirable than that of an *inside* room.

out-WATS   See *Wide Area Telephone Service.*

over or short   A discrepancy between the cash on hand and the amount that should be on hand.

overbooking   Committing more rooms to possible guest occupancy than are actually available.

override   Extra commission above standard percentage to encourage or reward quantity *bookings;* process by which the operator bypasses certain limits built into the computer program.

overstay   A guest who remains beyond the expiration of the anticipated stay.

package   A number of services (transportation, room, food, entertainment) normally purchased separately but put together and marketed at a reduced price made possible by volume and *breakage.*

paid in advance   A room charge that is collected prior to occupancy; it is the usual procedure when a guest has *light baggage;* with some motels, it is standard procedure for every guest.

paid-outs   See *cash paid-outs.*

parlor   The living room portion of a *suite.*

part-day rate (guest)   See *day rate.*

pass key   A submaster key limited to a single set of rooms (12 to 18) and allowing access to no other.

PBX   See *private branch exchange.*

penthouse   Accommodations, usually *suites,* located on the top floor(s) of the hotel.

percentage of occupancy   See *occupancy.*

permanent (guest)   A resident of long-term duration whose stay may or may not be formalized with a lease.

petite suite   See *junior suite.*

petty cash   See *imprest petty cash.*

pickup   The procedure used with front-office posting machines to accumulate the *folio* balance by entering the previous balance into the machine before posting the new charges; the figure so entered.

pit   See *cashier's well.*

plan   The basis on which room *rate* charges are made; see *American plan* and *European plan.*

plus, plus   Shorthand for the addition of tax and tip to the check or price per cover.

pocket   A portion of the *room rack* made to accept the *room rack slips* and provide a permanent record of accommodations and rates.

point-of-sale terminal (POS)   A computer term for input equipment immediately accessible at the place of sale for *on-line* input.

posting   Name for and the process of recording items in a record (e.g., a *folio*) or books of account.

preassign   *Reservations* are assigned and specific rooms *blocked* before the guest arrives.

preregistration   A procedure in which the hotel completes the registration prior to the guest's arrival; used with *groups* and tours to reduce congestion at the front desk, since individual guests do not then register.

private branch exchange (PBX)   A telephone switchboard.

projection   See *forecast.*

property   Refers to the hotel, including its personnel and physical facilities.

property management system (PMS)   The hotel's (*property's*) basic computer installation, designed for a variety of functions in both the back office and front office.

published rate Nondiscounted *rate* quoted or published by the hotel. See also *rack rate.*

quad Accommodations for four persons. See also *twin-double.*

quality assurance (QA) A managerial and operational approach that ensures a consistently high delivery level of service.

quality circles (QC) A technique used in a property's total quality management approach whereby representatives from related departments routinely join together for problem resolution and dialogue.

quality management (QM) See *quality assurance (QA)* and *total quality management (TQM).*

queen An extra-long, extra-wide *double bed* about 60 inches by 80 inches.

queuing theory A mathematical tool that management uses to obtain an optimum rate of customer flow. Also called *waiting-line theory.*

quote To state the room *rate* or other charges.

rack See *room rack.*

rack rate The standard *rate* established for and quoted from the *room rack.*

rate The charge made by the hotel for its room.

rate cutting A *rate* reduction that attracts business from competitors rather than creating new customers or markets.

rebate See *allowance.*

recap A summary (*recap*itulation) of the *transcript* sheets to obtain the day's grand totals.

referral A *reservation* system for *independently* owned properties developed to counter the reservation advantages of the chains and their *affiliates.*

registered, not assigned (RNA) A guest who has *registered* but is waiting for a specific room assignment until space becomes available.

register(ing) The procedure by which the arriving person signifies an intent to become a guest by completing and signing the *registration card;* the name for a book that served at one time as the registration card.

registration card (reg card) A form completed by the guest at the time of arrival giving name, address, and sometimes business affiliation.

reminder clock A special alarm clock that can be set at 5-minute intervals across a 24-hour day, used chiefly for *wake-up calls.*

reservation A mutual agreement between the guest and the hotel, the former to take accommodations at a given time for a given period and the latter to furnish the same.

reservation rack An alphabetical list of anticipated arrivals with a summary of their needs, filed chronologically by date of arrival.

residential hotel A hotel catering to long-term guests who have made the property their home and residence. See also *permanent guest.*

resident manager See *hotel manager.*

resort A hotel that caters to vacationing guests providing recreational and entertainment facilities; often a *destination hotel.*

rev-par Real estate shorthand for revenue per available room.

rollaway (bed) A portable utility bed approximately 30 inches by 72 inches; also called a *cot.*

room charge sheet See *room count sheet.*

room count The number of occupied rooms.

room count sheet A permanent record of the *room rack* prepared nightly and used to verify the accuracy of room statistics.

rooming (a guest) The entire procedure by which the desk greets and assigns new arrivals and the bell staff directs them to their rooms (rooms them).

rooming list The list of names furnished by a buying *group* in advance of arrival and used by the hotel to *preregister* and *preassign* the party.

rooming slip A form issued by the desk to the bellperson and left by the bellperson with the guest for verification of name, *rate,* and room.

room inspection report A checklist of the condition of the room prepared by the *inspector* when the room attendant has finished cleaning.

room-night See *guest-day.*

room rack A piece of front-office equipment representing the guest rooms in the form of metal *pockets* in which colors and symbols identify the accommodations.

room rack slip (card) A form prepared from the *registration card* identifying the occupant of each room and filed in the *pocket* of the *room rack* assigned to that guest.

rooms available See *available rooms.*

room service Food and beverage service provided in the privacy of the guest room by a designated (room service) waiter or waitress.

rooms ledger See *guest ledger.*

rule-of-thumb rate A guideline for setting room rates with the hotel charging $1 in rate for each $1,000 per room construction costs. See *building cost rate formula.*

run-of-the-house rate A special *group* rate generally the midpoint of the *rack rate* with a single, flat price applying to any room, *suites* excepted, on a *best available* basis.

ryokan A traditional Japanese inn. (Japanese pronunciation: Leo Gan)

safe-deposit boxes   Individual sections of the vault where guests store valuables and cashiers keep *house banks.*

Sales per Occupied Room   See *Average Daily Rate.*

sales rack   The front-office space for the storage and control of *stock cards* (*ducats* or *sales tickets*).

sales ticket   See *stock card.*

salon   The European designation for *parlor.*

sample room   A guest room used to merchandise and display goods, usually in combination with sleeping accommodations.

seamless connectivity   The next step beyond last room availability. Travel agents, airlines, on-line subscription networks, and others can access a property's room availability right down to the last room.

season rate   See *in-season rate.*

sell and report   Allows *wholesalers,* tour operators, hotel reps, and airline-reservation centers to ''free sell'' rooms, reporting back periodically; also called status control or *free sell.*

sell through   Denoting days for which no reservation arrivals are accepted; reservations for previous days will be accepted and allowed to stay through the date; cf. *box* date.

sell up   Convince the arriving guest to take a higher priced room than was planned or reserved.

service charge   A percentage (usually from 10 to 20 percent) added to the bill for distribution to service employees in lieu of direct tipping.

service elevators   Back elevators for use by employees (room service, housekeeping, maintenance, etc.) on hotel business and not readily visible to the guests; cf. *guest elevator.*

shoulder   Marketing term designating the period between peaks and valleys; the time on either side of the *in-season,* or the leveling off between two peaks.

Siberia   Jargon for a very undesirable room, one sold only after the *house* fills and then only after the guest has been alerted to its location or condition.

single   A bed approximately 36 inches by 75 inches; a room with accommodations for one; occupancy by one person; the *rate* charged for one person.

single supplement   An extra charge over the tour *package* price assessed for *single* occupancy when the total price was based on a *double-occupancy rate.*

sitting room   See *parlor.*

size   The capacity of the hotel as measured by the number of guest rooms.

skip   See *skipper.*

skipper   A guest who departs surreptitiously, leaving an unpaid bill.

sleeper   A departed guest whose *room rack slip* remains in the *rack* giving the appearance of an occupied room.

sleeper occupancy   See *bed occupancy.*

sleep out   A room that is taken, occupied, and paid for but not slept in.

slide   The transcription error caused by a misplaced decimal, as when 36.20 is written 3.62.

smart card   A credit card or other card containing a microprocessor capable of interfacing with the *PMS* or other computer configuration.

sofa bed   A sofa with fixed back and arms that unfolds into a standard *single* or *double bed;* also called a *hide-a-bed.*

software   The programs and routines that give instructions to the computer; cf. *hardware.*

special attention (SPATT)   A label assigned to important guests designated for special treatment.

split rate   Division of the total room *rate* charge among the room's several occupants.

split shift   A work pattern divided into two working periods with an unusually long period (more than a rest or mealtime) between.

spread rate   Assignment of group members or conventioneers using the standard rate distribution, although prices might be less than rack rates; cf. *run-of-the-house rate.*

star rating   An unreliable ranking (except for some well-known exceptions) of hotel facilities both in the United States and abroad.

star reservation   Indicates the arrival of an important guest—a *VIP.*

stay   Any guest who remains beyond a one-night stay, an anticipated check-out who fails to depart; *stayover.*

stayover   An anticipated check-out who remains beyond the stated date of departure; any guest who remains overnight; also called holdover or overstay.

stock card   A colored card of heavy paper with code designations representing the *room rack pocket* and used when the *room rack* is inaccessible to the room clerk; also called a *ducat.*

studio bed   A bed approximately 36 inches by 75 inches without headboard or footboard that serves as a sofa during the day; the room containing such a bed.

suite   A series of *connecting rooms* with one or more bedrooms and a *parlor;* suites occasionally include additional rooms such as a dining room. See *hospitality suite.*

summary transcript   See *recap.*

supper   A late-night meal; or the evening meal when the midday service is designated as dinner.

swing   The work shift between the day shift and the *graveyard* shift, usually starting between 3 PM and 4 PM.

take down   Cancel *reservations* without an *advance deposit* after the *cutoff hour.*

tally sheet   See *density board.*

TelAutograph   A proprietary piece of communication equipment that transcribes written messages.

time stamp   A clock mechanism that prints date and time when activated.

to-date   Designates a cumulative amount; the sum of all figures in the current period (usually monthly or annually) including the day or date in question.

total quality management (TQM)   A way to continuously improve performance at every level of operation, in every functional area of an organization, using all available human and capital resources. See also *quality assurance (QA).*

tour group   See *package.*

tourist class   A non-U.S. designation for *limited-service* hotels whose accommodations frequently lack private baths; also called *economy class.*

trade advertising contract   An agreement by which hotel accommodations are swapped for advertising space or broadcast time; also called a *due bill.*

traffic sheet   A *departmental control sheet* used by the telephone department.

transcript   A form used by the *night auditor* to accumulate and separate the day's charges by departments and guests.

transcript ruler   The headings of a transcript sheet attached to a straightedge and used as a column guide at the bottom of the long *transcript* sheet.

transfer   An accounting technique used to move a figure from one form to another, usually between *folios;* the movement of guests and/or luggage from one point to another (e.g., from the airline terminal to the hotel).

transfer folio   A special, unnumbered *folio* used to carry the guest's account beyond the first week when the original folio was numbered and cross referenced to the *registration card.*

transfer from   The *debit* portion of a *transfer* between accounts or ledgers.

transfer journal   A front-office form used to record *transfer* entries between different *accounts* or different ledgers.

transfer to   The *credit* portion of a *transfer* between accounts or ledgers.

transient guest   A short-term guest; see *transient hotel.*

transient hotel   A hotel catering to short-stay guests who stop en route to other destinations; cf. *destination hotel.*

transient ledger   See *guest ledger.*

transmittal form   The form provided by national credit-card companies for recording and remitting credit-card charges accumulated by the hotel.

transposition   A transcription error caused by reordering the sequence of digits, as when 389 is written as 398.

travel agent (TA)   An entrepreneur who *books* space and facilities for clients in hotels and public carriers and receives a commission for placing the business; hotels usually pay 10 percent.

travel and entertainment card (T&E)   A credit card issued by a proprietary company other than a hotel for which the user pays an annual fee; cf. *bank card.*

Travel Industry Association of America (TIA)   A non-profit association of many travel-related agencies and private businesses working to develop travel and tourism in the United States.

tray service   The fee charged *American plan* guests for *room service.*

tub   See *cashier's well.*

turn-away   To refuse *walk-in* business because rooms are unavailable; the guest so refused.

turn-downs   An evening service rendered by the housekeeping department, which replaces soiled bathroom linen and prepares the bed for use.

turn-in   The sum deposited with the *general cashier* by the departmental cashier at the close of each shift.

turnkey   A facility (computer, franchise, entire hotel) so complete that it is ready for use at the turn of a key.

twin   A bed approximately 39 inches by 75 inches to sleep one person; a room with two such beds.

twin-double   Two *double* beds; a room with two such beds capable of accommodating four persons.

twins   Two *twin* beds.

type   The market that a given hotel was historically designed to attract. The three traditional types include commercial, residential, and resort.

understay   A guest who *checks out* before the expiration of the anticipated stay.

A Uniform System of Accounts for Hotels (USA)   A manual of accounting terms, primarily incomes and expenses, to ensure industrywide uniformity in terminology and use.

United States Travel and Tourism Administration (USTTA)   A division of the Department of Commerce responsible for promoting travel to the United States. Successor to the U.S. Travel Service (USTS).

u-owe-me   See *exchange.*

upgrade   Move a *reservation* or registered guest to a better accommodation or class of service; cf. *downgrade.*

use rate   See *day rate*.

user friendly   Computer design, application, and implementation that minimizes the user's fears, encouraging purchase and use of the equipment.

vacancy   Occupancy of less than a *full house* so rooms are available for sale.

very important person (VIP)   A reservation or guest who warrants *special attention* and handling.

video display terminal (VDT)   See *cathode ray tube*.

voucher   The form used by the *operating departments* to notify the front desk of charges incurred by a particular guest; form furnished by a *travel agent* as a receipt for a client's advance *reservation* payment. See *coupon*.

waiting-line theory   See *queuing theory*.

wake-up call   See *morning call*.

walk (a guest)   To turn away guests holding confirmed *reservations* due to a lack of available rooms.

walk-in   A guest without a *reservation* who requests and receives accommodations.

walk-through   A thorough examination of the *property* by a hotel executive, *franchise* inspector, prospective buyer, and so on.

watch   Another term for the work shift.

WATS   See *Wide Area Telephone Service*.

who   An unidentified guest in a room that appears vacant in the *room rack*.

wholesaler   An entrepreneur who conceives, finances, and services *group* and *package* tours that he or she promotes (often through *travel agents*) to the general public.

Wide Area Telephone Service (WATS)   Long-distance telephone lines provided at special rates—even wholesaled—to large users; multiple lines may be purchased at multiple charges; separate charges are levied for incoming and outgoing WATS lines.

Worldwide Travel Vouchers (WTVs)   Form of payments drawn against a well-known financial institution (usually a major credit-card company.)

Xenodogheionology   The study of the history, lore, and stories associated with inns, hotels, and motels.

yield   The product of occupancy times *average daily rate*.

yield management   Controlling room *rates* and restricting occupancy in order to maximize gross revenue (*yield*) from all sources; a computerized program using artificial intelligence.

youth hostel   See *hostel*.

zero out   To balance the *account* as the guest *checks out* and makes settlement.

Zip-out   See *express checkout*.

Bibliography

Abbot, P. *Front Office: Procedures, Special Skills and Management.* Oxford: Butterworth-Heinemann, 1991.

The ABCs of Travel. New York: Public Transportation and Travel Division. Ziff-Davis Publishing Co., 1972.

Anolik, Alexander. *Travel, Tourism and Hospitality Law.* Elmsford, NY: National Publishers of the Black Hills, Inc., 1988.

Arthur, R., and D. Gladwell. *The Hotel Assistant Manager.* 3rd ed. London: Barrie & Rockliff, 1975.

Astroff, Milton, and James Abbey. *Convention Sales and Services.* 3rd ed. Cranbury, NJ: Waterbury Press, 1991.

Atlantic Institute, The. *Check & Credit Fraud Prevention Manual.* New York: Atcom Publishing, 1984.

Axler, Bruce. *Room Care for Hotels and Motels.* Indianapolis: ITT Educational Publications, 1974.

———. *Focus on . . . Security for Hotels, Motels, and Restaurants.* Indianapolis: ITT Educational Publications, 1974.

Baird, C., and L. Carla. *Front Office Assignments.* London: Pitman, 1988.

Baker, Sue. *Principles of Front Office Operations.* London: Cassell, 1992.

Barba, Stephen. ''Operating the Traditional American Plan Resort.'' In *The Practice of Hospitality Management,* ed. Pizam; Lewis; and Manning. Westport: Avi Publishing Co., Inc., 1982.

Bardi, James A. *Hotel Front Office Management.* New York: Van Nostrand Reinhold, 1990.

Beavis, J. R. S., and S. Medlik. *A Manual of Hotel Reception.* 3rd ed. London: William Heinemann Ltd., 1981.

Berman, Shelley. *A Hotel Is a Place . . .* Los Angeles: Price/ Stern/Sloan, Publishers Inc., 1972.

Boomer, Lucius. *Hotel Management.* New York: Harper & Row, 1938.

Braham, Bruce. *Computer Systems in the Hotel and Catering Industry.* London: Cassell Educational Ltd., 1988.

———. *Hotel Front Office.* 2nd ed. Gloucestershire, UK: Stanley Thornes, 1989.

Borsenik, Frank. *The Management of Maintenance and Engineering in the Hospitality Industry.* 3rd ed. New York: John Wiley & Sons, 1993.

Browning, Marjorie. *Night Audit Procedure.* Columbus: The Christopher Inn, March 1, 1969.

Bryson, McDowell, and Adele Ziminski. *The Concierge: Key to Hospitality.* NY: John Wiley & Sons, 1992.

Bucher, A. F. *101 Tips on Check Cashing.* New York: Ahrens Publishing Co., Inc., circa 1930.

Burstein, Harvey. *Hotel Security Management.* New York: Praeger Publishers, 1975.

Buzby, Walter J. *Hotel and Motel Security Management.* Los Angeles: Security World Publishing Co., 1976.

Chandler, Raymond. *Trouble Is My Business.* New York: Ballantine Books, 1972.

Collins, Galen. *Hospitality Information Technology: Learning How to Use It.* Dubuque, IA: Kendall/Hunt Publishing, 1992.

Coltman, Michael C. *Introduction to Travel and Tourism: An International Approach.* New York: Van Nostrand Reinhold, 1989.

Convention Liaison Council Manual. 4th ed. Convention Liaison Council, 1985.

Dahl, J. O. *Bellman and Elevator Operator.* Stamford: The Dahls, 1933. Revised by Crete Dahl.

———. *Room Clerk's Manual.* Stamford: The Dahls, 1933. Revised by Crete Dahl.

Deveau, Jack, and Jaap Penraat. *The Efficient Room Clerk.* New York: Learning Information Inc., 1968.

Dittmer, Paul R., and Gerald G. Griffin. *The Dimensions of the Hospitality Industry; An Introduction.* New York: Van Nostrand Reinhold, 1993.

Dix, Colin, and Chris Baird. *Front Office Operations,* 3rd ed. London: Pitman Publishing, 1988.

Drury, Tony, and Charles Ferrier. *Credit Cards.* London: Butterworths, 1984.

Dukas, Peter. *Hotel Front Office Management and Operations.* 3rd ed. Dubuque, IA: Wm. C. Brown, 1970.

Dunn, David. *Front Office Accounting Machines in Hotels.* Ithaca: Unpublished master's thesis, June 1965.

Dunseath, M., and J. Ransom. *The Hotel Bookkeeper Receptionist.* London: Barrie and Rockliff, 1967.

Expense and Payroll Dictionary. New York: Prepared for the American Hotel & Motel Association by Laventhol & Horwath, 1979.

Fidel, John. *Hotel Data Systems.* Rev. ed. Albuquerque, September 1972.

Foster, Dennis. *Rooms at the Inn: Front Office Operations and Administration.* Lake Forest, IL: Glencoe, 1992.

Front Office and Reservations. Burlingame, CA: Hyatt Corporation, 1978.

Front Office Courtesy Pays. Small Business Administration, Washington, D.C.: U.S. Government Printing Office, 1956.

Front Office Manual. New York: New Yorker Hotel, 1931.

Front Office Manual: Franchise Division. Sheraton Hotels & Inns, Worldwide [no date].

Front Office Operations Manual (of the) Hotel McCurdy, Evansville, Indiana. Research Bureau of the American Hotel Association, April 1923.

Front Office Procedures. East Lansing: Educational Institute of the American Hotel & Motel Association, 1976.

Front Office Selling. East Lansing: Educational Institute of the American Hotel & Motel Association [no date].

Front Office Selling ''Tips.'' New York: Hotel Sales Management Association, 1960.

Gee, Chuck Y.; James C. Makens; and Dexter J. L. Choy. *The Travel Industry.* 2nd ed. New York: Van Nostrand Reinhold, 1989.

Godowski, S. *Microcomputers in the Hotel and Catering Industry.* London: William Heinemann Ltd., 1988.

Gomes, Albert J. *Hospitality in Transition.* Houston: Pannell Kerr Forster, 1985.

Goodwin, John R., and Jolie R. Gaston. *Hotel Law, Principles and Cases.* 4th ed. Scottsdale, AR: Gorsuch Scarisbrick, Publishers, 1992.

Goodwin, John R., and James M. Rovelstad. *Travel and Lodging Law.* New York: John Wiley & Sons, 1980.

Gray, William S., and Salvatore C. Liguori. *Hotel & Motel Management & Operations.* Englewood Cliffs, NJ: Prentice Hall, 1980.

Guest Relations Training for Front Office Cashiers. Boston: Sheraton Corporation of America, 1961.

A Guide to Terminology in the Leisure Time Industries. Philadelphia: Laventhol & Horwath [no date].

Hall, Orrin. *Motel-Hotel Front Office Procedures.* Hollywood Beach, circa 1971.

Hamilton, Francis. *Hotel Front Office Management.* Miami, 1947.

Haszonics, Joseph. *Front Office Operation.* New York: ITT Educational Services, Inc., 1971.

Heldenbrand, H. V. *Front Office Psychology.* Evanston: John Wiley & Sons, 1944. Republished by American Hotel Register Company, Chicago, circa 1982.

Hilton, Conrad. *Be My Guest.* Englewood Cliffs, NJ: Prentice Hall, 1957.

Hitz, Ralph. *Standard Practice Manuals for Hotel Operation, I, Front Service Division.* 2nd ed. New York: Harper & Row, 1936.

The Hotelman Looks at the Business of Meetings. St. Paul: 3M Business Press, 1968.

Hubbart, Roy. *The Hubbart Formula for Evaluating Rate Structures of Hotel Rooms.* New York: American Hotel & Motel Association, 1952.

Hyatt Travel Futures Project Report on Business Travelers. New York: Prepared for Hyatt Hotels and Resorts by Research & Forecasts, Inc., December 1988.

Implications of Microcomputers in Small and Medium Hotel & Catering Firms. Prepared for the Hotel and Catering Industry Training Board by the Department of Hotel, Catering, and Tourism Management, University of Surrey, Guildford, Surrey, England, November 1980.

Iverson, Kathleen M. *Introduction to Hospitality Management.* New York: Van Nostrand Reinhold, 1989.

Jones, Christine, and Val Paul. *Accommodations Management.* London: Botsford Academic and Education, 1985.

Kasavana, Michael L. and Richard M. Brooks. *Managing Front Office Operations.* East Lansing: Educational Institute of the American Hotel & Motel Association, 1991.

Kasavana, Michael L., and John J. Cahill. *Managing Computers in the Hospitality Industry.* 2nd ed. East Lansing: Educational Institute of the American Hotel & Motel Association, 1992.

Lawrence, Janet. *Room Sales and Reception Management.* Boston: The Innkeeping Institute of America, 1970.

Lefler, Janet, and Salvatore Calanese. *The Correct Cashier.* New York: Ahrens Publishing Co., 1960.

Lewis, Robert C., and Richard E. Chambers. *Marketing Leadership in Hospitality: Foundations and Practices.* New York: Van Nostrand Reinhold, 1989.

Link Hospitality Consultants, Ltd. *Canadian Job Strategy Hotel Front Office Specialist.* Calgary: Southern Alberta Institute of Technology, 1986.

Lundberg, Donald. *The Hotel and Restaurant Business.* 5th ed. New York: Van Nostrand Reinhold, 1989.

———. *Front Office Human Relations.* Distributed by NU: PAK, P.O. Box 379, San Marcos, CA, 1979.

Martin, Robert J. *Professional Management of Housekeeping Operations.* 2nd ed. New York: John Wiley & Sons, 1991.

MasterCard International Frequent Business Traveler Study. Presented at the American Hotel & Motel Association Annual Meeting, November 14, 1983.

Medlik, S. *The Business of Hotels.* London: William Heinemann Ltd., 1980.

———. *Dictionary of Travel.* Oxford: Butterworth-Heinemann, 1993.

———. *Profile of the Hotel and Catering Industry.* 2nd ed. London: William Heinemann Ltd., 1978.

Meek, Howard B. *A Theory of Room Rates.* Ithaca: Cornell University, Department of Hotel Administration, June 1938.

A Meeting Planner's Guide to Master Account Billing. Developed by the Insurance Conference Planners, and published by The Educational Institute of the American Hotel & Motel Association, May 1980.

Metelka, Charles J. *The Dictionary of Hospitality, Travel and Tourism.* 3rd ed. Albany: Delmar Publishers Inc., 1989.

Ministry of Tourism. *The Front Desk Business.* Toronto: Ontario Ministry of Tourism, 1978.

Moreo, Patrick J. *Night Audit Workbook.* 3rd ed. Edina, MN: Bellwether Press, 1988.

Morrison, Alastair M. *Hospitality and Travel Marketing.* Albany, NY: Delmar Publishers, Inc., 1989.

Ogilvie, A. W. T. *Lecture Outline in Front Office.* American Hotel Association, 1923.

Paananen, Donna M. *Selling Out. A How-To Manual on Reservations Management.* East Lansing: Educational Institute of the American Hotel & Motel Association, 1985.

Paige, Grace, and Jane Paige. *The Hotel Receptionist.* 2nd ed. London: Holt, Rinehart and Winston, 1984.

———. *Hotel Front Desk Personnel.* Rev. ed. New York: Van Nostrand Reinhold, 1988.

Pfeiffer, W.; M. Voegele; and G. Wolley. *The Correct Service Department for Hotels, Motor Hotels, Motels, and Resorts.* New York: Ahrens Publishing Co., 1962.

Property Management and Point of Sale Systems: Guide to Selection. New York: American Hotel & Motel Association [date unknown].

Relieving Reservation Headaches. East Lansing: Educational Institute of the AH&MA, 1979.

Renner, Peter. *Basic Hotel Front Office Procedures.* 3rd ed. New York: Van Nostrand Reinhold, 1993.

Resale in the Lodging Industry: A Bell System Perspective. Nashville: AH&MA Mid-Year Meeting, April 1982.

Room Clerk, The Man Up Front. Temple, TX: Motel/Motor Inn Journal, 1977.

Rosenzweig, Stan. *Hotel/Motel Telephone Systems: Opportunities through Deregulation.* East Lansing: Educational Institute of the American Hotel & Motel Association, 1982.

Ross, Bruce. *Hotel Reservation Systems Present and Future.* Ithaca: Unpublished master's monograph, May 1977.

Rushmore, Stephen. *Hotel Investments: A Guide for Lenders and Owners.* Boston: Warren, Gorham & Lamont, 1990.

Rutherford, Denney G. *Hotel Management and Operations.* New York: Van Nostrand Reinhold, 1989.

Saunders, K. C. *Head Hall Porter.* London: Catering Education Research Institute, 1980.

———, and R. Pullen. *An Occupational Study of Room Maids in Hotels.* Middlesex: Middlesex Polytechnic, 1987.

Scatchard, Bill. *Upsetting the Applecart: A Common Sense Approach to Successful Hotel Operations for the '90s.* Tampa: Box 19156, 33686, 1994.

Schneider, Madelin, and Georgina Tucker. *The Professional Housekeeper.* New York: Van Nostrand Reinhold, 1989.

Self, Robert. *Long Distance for Less.* New York: Telecom Library, Inc., 1982.

Sherry, John. *How to Exclude and Eject Undesirable Guests.* Stamford: The Dahls, 1943.

Sicherman, Irving. *The Investment in the Lodging Business.* Scranton, PA: Sicherman, 1977.

Starting and Managing a Small Motel. Small Business Administration, Washington, D.C.: U.S. Government Printing Office, 1963.

The State of Technology in the Lodging Industry. New York: American Hotel & Motel Association, 1980.

Stiel, Holly. *Ultimate Service: The Complete Handbook to the World of the Concierge.* Englewood Cliffs, NJ: Prentice Hall, 1994.

Stutts, Alan, and Frank Borsenik. *Maintenance Handbook for Hotels, Motels, and Resorts.* New York: Van Nostrand Reinhold, 1990.

Successful Credit and Collection Techniques. East Lansing: Educational Institute of the American Hotel & Motel Association, 1981.

Tarbet, J. R. *A Handbook of Hotel Front Office Procedure.* Pullman: Student Book Corporation, circa 1955.

Taylor, Derek, and Richard Thomason. *Profitable Hotel Reception.* Elmsford, NY: Pergamon Press, 1982.

Trends in the Hotel-Motel Business. New York: Pannell Kerr Forster & Co., various years.

Uniformed-Service Training. Boston: Sheraton Corporation of America, 1960.

Uniform System of Accounts and Expense Dictionary for Small Hotels, Motels, and Motor Hotels. 4th ed. East Lansing: Educational Institute of the American Hotel & Motel Association, 1987.

A Uniform System of Accounts for Hotels. 8th ed. New York: Hotel Association of New York City, Inc., 1986.

Vallen, Jerome J., and James R. Abbey. *The Art and Science of Hospitality Management.* East Lansing: Educational Institute of the American Hotel & Motel Association, 1987.

Weissinger, Suzanne Stewart. *Hotel/Motel Operations.* Cincinnati: South-Western Publishing, 1989.

White, Paul, and Helen Beckley. *Hotel Reception.* 4th ed. London: Edward Arnold, 1982.

Wingenter, Tom, et al. *The Relationship of Lodging Prices to Occupancy: A Study of Accommodations in Northern Wisconsin.* Madison: University of Wisconsin Cooperative Extension Service, 1982–83.

Wittemann, Ad. *Hotel Room Clerk.* Las Vegas: Camelot Consultants, 1986.

Yellowstone Park Company Cashier Training Program. Yellowstone: Yellowstone Park Co., 1978.

Index